Oxford University Press, Ely House, London W. I

GLASGOW NEW YORK TORONTO MELBOURNE WELLINGTON
CAPE TOWN SALISBURY IBADAN NAIROBI LUSAKA ADDIS ABABA
DELHI BOMBAY CALCUTTA MADRAS KARACHI LAHORE DACCA
KUALA LUMPUR SINGAPORE HONG KONG TOKYO

THE WORLD'S CLASSICS

513

Poems of
ROBERT BROWNING

Oxford University Press, Ely House, London W. 1

GLASGOW NEW YORK TORONTO MELBOURNE WELLINGTON
CAPE TOWN IBADAN NAIROBI DAR ES SALAAM LUSAKA ADDIS ABABA
DELHI BOMBAY CALCUTTA MADRAS KARACHI LAHORE DACCA
KUALA LUMPUR SINGAPORE HONG KONG TOKYO

Poems of
ROBERT
BROWNING

A Selection made by
SIR HUMPHREY MILFORD

LONDON
OXFORD UNIVERSITY PRESS

ROBERT BROWNING

Born, London	.	.	.	7 May 1812
Died, Venice	.	.	.	12 December 1889

This selection from the whole of his work was first published in The World's Classics *in 1949 and reprinted in 1952, 1959, 1963, 1968, and 1972.*

ISBN 0 19 250513 0

PRINTED IN GREAT BRITAIN

CONTENTS

DRAMATIC LYRICS—*continued*

DRAMATIC ROMANCES—

CONTENTS

CONTENTS

AN INVOCATION

O Lyric Love, half angel and half bird
And all a wonder and a wild desire,—
Boldest of hearts that ever braved the sun,
Took sanctuary within the holier blue,
And sang a kindred soul out to his face,—
Yet human at the red-ripe of the heart—
When the first summons from the darkling earth
Reached thee amid thy chambers, blanched their blue,
And bared them of the glory—to drop down,
To toil for man, to suffer or to die,—
This is the same voice: can thy soul know change?
Hail then, and hearken from the realms of help!
Never may I commence my song, my due
To God who best taught song by gift of thee,
Except with bent head and beseeching hand—
That still, despite the distance and the dark,
What was, again may be; some interchange
Of grace, some splendour once thy very thought,
Some benediction anciently thy smile:
—Never conclude, but raising hand and head
Thither where eyes, that cannot reach, yet yearn
For all hope, all sustainment, all reward,
Their utmost up and on,—so blessing back
In those thy realms of help, that heaven thy home,
Some whiteness which, I judge, thy face makes proud,
Some wanness where, I think, thy foot may fall!

THE RING AND THE BOOK (1868)
Book I, concluding lines.

LYRICS FROM 'PARACELSUS'

I

[A voice from within.]

I HEAR a voice, perchance I heard
Long ago, but all too low,
So that scarce a care it stirred
If the voice were real or no:
I heard it in my youth when first
The waters of my life outburst:
But, now their stream ebbs faint, I hear
That voice, still low, but fatal-clear—
As if all poets, God ever meant
Should save the world, and therefore lent
Great gifts to, but who, proud, refused
To do his work, or lightly used
Those gifts, or failed through weak endeavour,
So, mourn cast off by him for ever,—
As if these leaned in airy ring
To take me; this the song they sing.

'Lost, lost! yet come,
With our wan troop make thy home.
Come, come! for we
Will not breathe, so much as breathe
Reproach to thee,
Knowing what thou sink'st beneath.
So sank we in those old years,
We who bid thee, come! thou last
Who, living yet, hast life o'erpast.
And altogether we, thy peers,
Will pardon crave for thee, the last
Whose trial is done, whose lot is cast
With those who watch but work no more,
Who gaze on life but live no more.
Yet we trusted thou shouldst speak
The message which our lips, too weak,
Refused to utter,—shouldst redeem

Our fault: such trust, and all a dream!
Yet we chose thee a birthplace
Where the richness ran to flowers:
Couldst not sing one song for grace?
Not make one blossom man's and ours?
Must one more recreant to his race
Die with unexerted powers,
And join us, leaving as he found
The world, he was to loosen, bound?
Anguish! ever and for ever;
Still beginning, ending never.
Yet, lost and last one, come!
How couldst understand, alas,
What our pale ghosts strove to say,
As their shades did glance and pass
Before thee night and day?
Thou wast blind as we were dumb:
Once more, therefore, come, O come!
How should we clothe, how arm the spirit
Shall next thy post of life inherit—
How guard him from thy speedy ruin?
Tell us of thy sad undoing
Here, where we sit, ever pursuing
Our weary task, ever renewing
Sharp sorrow, far from God who gave
Our powers, and man they could not save!'

II

Heap cassia, sandal-buds and stripes
   Of labdanum, and aloe-balls,
Smeared with dull nard an Indian wipes
   From out her hair: such balsam falls
   Down sea-side mountain pedestals,
From tree-tops where tired winds are fain,
Spent with the vast and howling main,
To treasure half their island-gain.

And strew faint sweetness from some old
   Egyptian's fine worm-eaten shroud

Which breaks to dust when once unrolled;
　Or shredded perfume, like a cloud
　From closet long to quiet vowed,
With mothed and dropping arras hung,
Mouldering her lute and books among,
As when a queen, long dead, was young.

III

　Over the sea our galleys went,
With cleaving prows in order brave
To a speeding wind and a bounding wave,
　A gallant armament:
Each bark built out of a forest-tree
　Left leafy and rough as first it grew,
And nailed all over the gaping sides,
Within and without, with black bull-hides,
Seethed in fat and suppled in flame,
To bear the playful billows' game:
So, each good ship was rude to see,
Rude and bare to the outward view,
　But each upbore a stately tent
Where cedar pales in scented row
Kept out the flakes of the dancing brine,
And an awning drooped the mast below,
In fold on fold of the purple fine,
That neither noontide nor starshine
Nor moonlight cold which maketh mad,
　Might pierce the regal tenement.
When the sun dawned, oh, gay and glad
We set the sail and plied the oar;
But when the night-wind blew like breath,
For joy of one day's voyage more,
We sang together on the wide sea,
Like men at peace on a peaceful shore;
Each sail was loosed to the wind so free,
Each helm made sure by the twilight star,
And in a sleep as calm as death,
We, the voyagers from afar,
　Lay stretched along, each weary crew

In a circle round its wondrous tent
Whence gleamed soft light and curled rich scent,
  And with light and perfume, music too:
So the stars wheeled round, and the darkness past,
And at morn we started beside the mast,
And still each ship was sailing fast.

Now, one morn, land appeared—a speck
Dim trembling betwixt sea and sky:
'Avoid it,' cried our pilot, 'check
  'The shout, restrain the eager eye!'
But the heaving sea was black behind
For many a night and many a day,
And land, though but a rock, drew nigh;
So, we broke the cedar pales away,
Let the purple awning flap in the wind,
  And a statue bright was on every deck!
We shouted, every man of us,
And steered right into the harbour thus,
With pomp and pæan glorious.

A hundred shapes of lucid stone!
  All day we built its shrine for each,
A shrine of rock for every one,
Nor paused till in the westering sun
  We sat together on the beach
To sing because our task was done.
When lo! what shouts and merry songs!
What laughter all the distance stirs!
A loaded raft with happy throngs
Of gentle islanders!
'Our isles are just at hand,' they cried,
  'Like cloudlets faint in even sleeping;
'Our temple-gates are opened wide,
  'Our olive-groves thick shade are keeping
'For these majestic forms'—they cried.
Oh, then we awoke with sudden start
From our deep dream, and knew, too late,
How bare the rock, how desolate,

Which had received our precious freight:
   Yet we called out—'Depart!
'Our gifts, once given, must here abide.
  'Our work is done; we have no heart
'To mar our work,'—we cried.

IV

Thus the Mayne glideth
Where my Love abideth.
Sleep's no softer: it proceeds
On through lawns, on through meads,
On and on, whate'er befall,
Meandering and musical,
Though the niggard pasturage
Bears not on its shaven ledge
Aught but weeds and waving grasses
To view the river as it passes,
Save here and there a scanty patch
Of primroses too faint to catch
A weary bee.   And scarce it pushes
Its gentle way through strangling rushes
Where the glossy kingfisher
Flutters when noon-heats are near,
Glad the shelving banks to shun,
Red and steaming in the sun,
Where the shrew-mouse with pale throat
Burrows, and the speckled stoat;
Where the quick sandpipers flit
In and out the marl and grit
That seems to breed them, brown as they:
Nought disturbs its quiet way,
Save some lazy stork that springs,
Trailing it with legs and wings,
Whom the shy fox from the hill
Rouses, creep he ne'er so still.

PIPPA PASSES

A DRAMA

I DEDICATE MY BEST INTENTIONS, IN THIS POEM,
ADMIRINGLY TO THE AUTHOR OF 'ION,'
AFFECTIONATELY TO MR. SERGEANT TALFOURD

R. B.

LONDON: 1841

PERSONS

PIPPA.	GOTTLIEB.	BLUPHOCKS.
OTTIMA.	SCHRAMM.	LUIGI *and his* MOTHER.
SEBALD.	JULES.	*Poor Girls.*
Foreign Students.	PHENE.	MONSIGNOR *and his Attendants.*

Austrian Police.

INTRODUCTION

NEW YEAR'S DAY AT ASOLO IN THE TREVISAN

SCENE. *A large mean airy chamber. A girl,* PIPPA, *from the Silk-mills, springing out of bed.*

DAY!
Faster and more fast,
O'er night's brim, day boils at last:
Boils, pure gold, o'er the cloud-cup's brim
Where spurting and suppressed it lay,
For not a froth-flake touched the rim
Of yonder gap in the solid gray
Of the eastern cloud, an hour away;
But forth one wavelet, then another, curled,
Till the whole sunrise, not to be suppressed,
Rose, reddened, and its seething breast
Flickered in bounds, grew gold, then overflowed the
world.
Oh, Day, if I squander a wavelet of thee,
A mite of my twelve hours' treasure,
The least of thy gazes or glances,
(Be they grants thou art bound to or gifts above measure)

One of thy choices or one of thy chances,
(Be they tasks God imposed thee or freaks at thy pleasure)
—My Day, if I squander such labour or leisure,
Then shame fall on Asolo, mischief on me!

Thy long blue solemn hours serenely flowing,
Whence earth, we feel, gets steady help and good—
Thy fitful sunshine-minutes, coming, going,
As if earth turned from work in gamesome mood—
All shall be mine! But thou must treat me not
As prosperous ones are treated, those who live
At hand here, and enjoy the higher lot,
In readiness to take what thou wilt give,
And free to let alone what thou refusest;
For, Day, my holiday, if thou ill-usest
Me, who am only Pippa,—old-year's sorrow,
Cast off last night, will come again to-morrow:
Whereas, if thou prove gentle, I shall borrow
Sufficient strength of thee for new-year's sorrow.
All other men and women that this earth
Belongs to, who all days alike possess,
Make general plenty cure particular dearth,
Get more joy one way, if another, less:
Thou art my single day, God lends to leaven
What were all earth else, with a feel of heaven,—
Sole light that helps me through the year, thy sun's!
Try now! Take Asolo's Four Happiest Ones—
And let thy morning rain on that superb
Great haughty Ottima; can rain disturb
Her Sebald's homage? All the while thy rain
Beats fiercest on her shrub-house window-pane,
He will but press the closer, breathe more warm
Against her cheek; how should she mind the storm?
And, morning past, if mid-day shed a gloom
O'er Jules and Phene,—what care bride and groom
Save for their dear selves? 'Tis their marriage-day;
And while they leave church and go home their way,
Hand clasping hand, within each breast would be
Sunbeams and pleasant weather spite of thee.

Then, for another trial, obscure thy eve
With mist,—will Luigi and his mother grieve—
The lady and her child, unmatched, forsooth,
She in her age, as Luigi in his youth,
For true content? The cheerful town, warm, close
And safe, the sooner that thou art morose,
Receives them. And yet once again, outbreak
In storm at night on Monsignor, they make
Such stir about,—whom they expect from Rome
To visit Asolo, his brother's home,
And say here masses proper to release
A soul from pain,—what storm dares hurt his peace?
Calm would he pray, with his own thoughts to ward
Thy thunder off, nor want the angels' guard.
But Pippa—just one such mischance would spoil
Her day that lightens the next twelve-month's toil
At wearisome silk-winding, coil on coil!
    And here I let time slip for nought!
Aha, you foolhardy sunbeam, caught
With a single splash from my ewer!
You that would mock the best pursuer,
Was my basin over-deep?
One splash of water ruins you asleep,
And up, up, fleet your brilliant bits
Wheeling and counterwheeling,
Reeling, broken beyond healing:
Now grow together on the ceiling!
That will task your wits.
Whoever it was quenched fire first, hoped to see
Morsel after morsel flee
As merrily, as giddily . . .
Meantime, what lights my sunbeam on,
Where settles by degrees the radiant cripple?
Oh, is it surely blown, my martagon?
New-blown and ruddy as St. Agnes' nipple,
Plump as the flesh-bunch on some Turk bird's poll!
Be sure if corals, branching 'neath the ripple
Of ocean, bud there,—fairies watch unroll
Such turban-flowers; I say, such lamps disperse

Thick red flame through that dusk green universe!
I am queen of thee, floweret!
And each fleshy blossom
Preserve I not—(safer
Than leaves that embower it,
Or shells that embosom)
—From weevil and chafer?
Laugh through my pane then; solicit the bee;
Gibe him, be sure; and, in midst of thy glee
Love thy queen, worship me!

—Worship whom else? For am I not, this day,
Whate'er I please? What shall I please to-day?
My morn, noon, eve and night—how spend my day?
To-morrow I must be Pippa who winds silk,
The whole year round, to earn just bread and milk:
But, this one day, I have leave to go,
And play out my fancy's fullest games;
I may fancy all day—and it shall be so—
That I taste of the pleasures, am called by the names
Of the Happiest Four in our Asolo!

See! Up the hill-side yonder, through the morning,
Some one shall love me, as the world calls love:
I am no less than Ottima, take warning!
The gardens, and the great stone house above,
And other house for shrubs, all glass in front,
Are mine; where Sebald steals, as he is wont,
To court me, while old Luca yet reposes:
And therefore, till the shrub-house door uncloses,
I . . . what now?—give abundant cause for prate
About me—Ottima, I mean—of late,
Too bold, too confident she'll still face down
The spitefullest of talkers in our town.
How we talk in the little town below!
   But love, love, love—there's better love, I know!
This foolish love was only day's first offer;
I choose my next love to defy the scoffer:
For do not our Bride and Bridegroom sally

Out of Possagno church at noon?
Their house looks over Orcana valley:
Why should not I be the bride as soon
As Ottima? For I saw, beside,
Arrive last night that little bride—
Saw, if you call it seeing her, one flash
Of the pale snow-pure cheek and black bright tresses,
Blacker than all except the black eyelash;
I wonder she contrives those lids no dresses!
—So strict was she, the veil
Should cover close her pale
Pure cheeks—a bride to look at and scarce touch,
Scarce touch, remember, Jules! For are not such
Used to be tended, flower-like, every feature,
As if one's breath would fray the lily of a creature?
A soft and easy life these ladies lead:
Whiteness in us were wonderful indeed.
Oh, save that brow its virgin dimness,
Keep that foot its lady primness,
Let those ankles never swerve
From their exquisite reserve,
Yet have to trip along the streets like me,
All but naked to the knee!
How will she ever grant her Jules a bliss
So startling as her real first infant kiss?
Oh, no—not envy, this!

—Not envy, sure!—for if you gave me
Leave to take or to refuse,
In earnest, do you think I'd choose
That sort of new love to enslave me?
Mine should have lapped me round from the beginning;
As little fear of losing it as winning:
Lovers grow cold, men learn to hate their wives,
And only parents' love can last our lives.
At eve the Son and Mother, gentle pair,
Commune inside our turret: what prevents
My being Luigi? While that mossy lair
Of lizards through the winter-time is stirred

With each to each imparting sweet intents
For this new-year, as brooding bird to bird—
(For I observe of late, the evening walk
Of Luigi and his mother, always ends
Inside our ruined turret, where they talk,
Calmer than lovers, yet more kind than friends)
—Let me be cared about, kept out of harm,
And schemed for, safe in love as with a charm;
Let me be Luigi! If I only knew
What was my mother's face—my father, too!
    Nay, if you come to that, best love of all
Is God's; then why not have God's love befall
Myself as, in the palace by the Dome,
Monsignor?—who to-night will bless the home
Of his dead brother; and God bless in turn
That heart which beats, those eyes which mildly burn
With love for all men! I, to-night at least,
Would be that holy and beloved priest.

Now wait!—even I already seem to share
In God's love: what does New-year's hymn declare?
What other meaning do these verses bear?

> All service ranks the same with **God**:
> If now, as formerly he trod
> Paradise, his presence fills
> Our earth, each only as God wills
> Can work—God's puppets, best and worst,
> Are we; there is no last nor first.

> Say not 'a small event!' Why 'small'?
> Costs it more pain that this, ye call
> A 'great event,' should come to pass,
> Than that? Untwine me from the mass
> Of deeds which make up life, one deed
> Power shall fall short in or exceed!

And more of it, and more of it!—oh yes—
I will pass each, and see their happiness,
And envy none—being just as great, no doubt,

Useful to men, and dear to God, as they!
A pretty thing to care about
So mightily, this single holiday!
But let the sun shine! Wherefore repine?
—With thee to lead me, O Day of mine,
Down the grass path grey with dew,
Under the pine-wood, blind with boughs,
Where the swallow never flew
Nor yet cicala dared carouse—
No, dared carouse!   [*She enters the street.*

I. MORNING

SCENE. *Up the Hill-side, inside the Shrub-house.* LUCA'S
   wife, OTTIMA, *and her paramour, the German* SEBALD.

Seb. [*sings*].

   Let the watching lids wink!
   Day's a-blaze with eyes, think!
   Deep into the night, drink!

Otti. Night? Such may be your Rhineland nights
   perhaps;
But this blood-red beam through the shutter's chink
—We call such light, the morning: let us see!
Mind how you grope your way, though! How these tall
Naked geraniums straggle! Push the lattice
Behind that frame!—Nay, do I bid you?—Sebald,
It shakes the dust down on me! Why, of course
The slide-bolt catches. Well, are you content,
Or must I find you something else to spoil?
Kiss and be friends, my Sebald! Is't full morning?
Oh, don't speak then!
         Seb.   Ay, thus it used to be.
Ever your house was, I remember, shut
Till mid-day; I observed that, as I strolled
On mornings through the vale here; country girls
Were noisy, washing garments in the brook,
Hinds drove the slow white oxen up the hills:
But no, your house was mute, would ope no eye.

And wisely: you were plotting one thing there,
Nature, another outside. I looked up—
Rough whitewood shutters, rusty iron bars,
Silent as death, blind in a flood of light.
Oh, I remember!—and the peasants laughed
And said, 'The old man sleeps with the young wife.'
This house was his, this chair, this window—his.

Otti. Ah, the clear morning! I can see St. Mark's;
That black streak is the belfry. Stop: Vicenza
Should lie . . . there's Padua, plain enough, that blue!
Look o'er my shoulder, follow my finger!

Seb.   Morning?
It seems to me a night with a sun added.
Where's dew, where's freshness? That bruised plant, I
     bruised
In getting through the lattice yestereve,
Droops as it did. See, here's my elbow's mark
I' the dust o' the sill.

Otti.   Oh, shut the lattice, pray!

Seb. Let me lean out. I cannot scent blood here,
Foul as the morn may be.

                    There, shut the world out!
How do you feel now, Ottima? There, curse
The world and all outside! Let us throw off
This mask: how do you bear yourself? Let's out
With all of it.

Otti.   Best never speak of it.

Seb. Best speak again and yet again of it.
Till words cease to be more than words. 'His blood,'
For instance—let those two words mean 'His blood'
And nothing more. Notice, I'll say them now,
'His blood.'

Otti.   Assuredly if I repented
The deed—

Seb. Repent? Who should repent, or why?
What puts that in your head? Did I once say
That I repented?

Otti.   No, I said the deed . . .

Seb. 'The deed' and 'the event'—just now it was

'Our passion's fruit'—the devil take such cant!
Say, once and always, Luca was a wittol,
I am his cut-throat, you are . . .

   Otti.   Here's the wine;
I brought it when we left the house above,
And glasses too—wine of both sorts. Black? White
    then?

   Seb. But am not I his cut-throat? What are you?

   Otti. There trudges on his business from the Duomo
Benet the Capuchin, with his brown hood
And bare feet; always in one place at church,
Close under the stone wall by the south entry,
I used to take him for a brown cold piece
Of the wall's self, as out of it he rose
To let me pass—at first, I say, I used:
Now, so has that dumb figure fastened on me,
I rather should account the plastered wall
A piece of him, so chilly does it strike.
This, Sebald?

   Seb.   No, the white wine—the white wine!
Well, Ottima, I promised no new year
Should rise on us the ancient shameful way;
Nor does it rise. Pour on! To your black eyes!
Do you remember last damned New Year's day?

   Otti. You brought those foreign prints. We looked at
    them
Over the wine and fruit. I had to scheme
To get him from the fire. Nothing but saying
His own set wants the proof-mark, roused him up
To hunt them out.

   Seb.   'Faith, he is not alive
To fondle you before my face.

   Otti.   Do you
Fondle me then! Who means to take your life
For that, my Sebald?

   Seb.   Hark you, Ottima!
One thing to guard against. We'll not make much
One of the other—that is, not make more
Parade of warmth, childish officious coil,

Than yesterday: as if, sweet, I supposed
Proof upon proof were needed now, now first,
To show I love you—yes, still love you—love you
In spite of Luca and what's come to him
—Sure sign we had him ever in our thoughts,
White sneering old reproachful face and all!
We'll even quarrel, love, at times, as if
We still could lose each other, were not tied
By this: conceive you?

 Otti.   Love!

 Seb.   Not tied so sure.
Because though I was wrought upon, have struck
His insolence back into him—am I
So surely yours?—therefore forever yours?

 Otti. Love, to be wise, (one counsel pays another)
Should we have—months ago, when first we loved,
For instance that May morning we two stole
Under the green ascent of sycamores—
If we had come upon a thing like that
Suddenly . . .

 Seb. 'A thing'—there again—'a thing!'

 Otti. Then, Venus' body, had we come upon
My husband Luca Gaddi's murdered corpse
Within there, at his couch-foot, covered close—
Would you have pored upon it? Why persist
In poring now upon it? For 'tis here
As much as there in the deserted house:
You cannot rid your eyes of it. For me,
Now he is dead I hate him worse: I hate . . .
Dare you stay here? I would go back and hold
His two dead hands, and say, 'I hate you worse,
'Luca, than . . .'

 Seb.   Off, off—take your hands off mine,
'Tis the hot evening—off! oh, morning is it?

 Otti. There's one thing must be done; you know what
   thing.
Come in and help to carry. We may sleep
Anywhere in the whole wide house to-night.

 Seb. What would come, think you, if we let him lie

Just as he is? Let him lie there until
The angels take him! He is turned by this
Off from his face beside, as you will see.

Otti. This dusty pane might serve for looking glass.
Three, four—four grey hairs! Is it so you said
A plait of hair should wave across my neck?
No—this way.

Seb.   Ottima, I would give your neck,
Each splendid shoulder, both those breasts of yours,
That this were undone! Killing! Kill the world
So Luca lives again!—ay, lives to sputter
His fulsome dotage on you—yes, and feign
Surprise that I return at eve to sup,
When all the morning I was loitering here—
Bid me despatch my business and begone.
I would . . .

Otti.   See!

Seb.   No, I'll finish. Do you think
I fear to speak the bare truth once for all?
All we have talked of, is, at bottom, fine
To suffer; there's a recompense in guilt;
One must be venturous and fortunate:
What is one young for, else? In age we'll sigh
O'er the wild reckless wicked days flown over;
Still, we have lived: the vice was in its place.
But to have eaten Luca's bread, have worn
His clothes, have felt his money swell my purse—
Do lovers in romances sin that way?
Why, I was starving when I used to call
And teach you music, starving while you plucked me
These flowers to smell!

Otti.   My poor lost friend!

Seb.   He gave me
Life, nothing less: what if he did reproach
My perfidy, and threaten, and do more—
Had he no right? What was to wonder at?
He sat by us at table quietly:
Why must you lean across till our cheeks touched?
Could he do less than make pretence to strike?

'Tis not the crime's sake—I'd commit ten crimes
Greater, to have this crime wiped out, undone!
And you—O how feel you? Feel you for me?

Otti. Well then, I love you better now than ever,
And best (look at me while I speak to you)—
Best for the crime; nor do I grieve, in truth,
This mask, this simulated ignorance,
This affectation of simplicity,
Falls off our crime; this naked crime of ours
May not now be looked over: look it down!
Great? let it be great; but the joys it brought,
Pay they or no its price? Come: they or it!
Speak not! The past, would you give up the past
Such as it is, pleasure and crime together?
Give up that noon I owned my love for you?
The garden's silence: even the single bee
Persisting in his toil, suddenly stopped,
And where he hid you only could surmise
By some campanula chalice set a-swing.
Who stammered—'Yes, I love you'?

Seb.   And I drew
Back; put far back your face with both my hands
Lest you should grow too full of me—your face
So seemed athirst for my whole soul and body!

Otti. And when I ventured to receive you here,
Made you steal hither in the mornings—

Seb.   When
I used to look up 'neath the shrub-house here,
Till the red fire on its glazed windows spread
To a yellow haze?

Otti.   Ah—my sign was, the sun
Inflamed the sere side of yon chestnut-tree
Nipped by the first frost.

Seb.   You would always laugh
At my wet boots: I had to stride thro' grass
Over my ankles.

Otti.   Then our crowning night!

Seb. The July night?

Otti.   The day of it too, Sebald!

When heaven's pillars seemed o'erbowed with heat,
Its black-blue canopy suffered descend
Close on us both, to weigh down each to each,
And smother up all life except our life.
So lay we till the storm came.

    Seb.   How it came!

    Otti. Buried in woods we lay, you recollect;
Swift ran the searching tempest overhead;
And ever and anon some bright white shaft
Burned thro' the pine-tree roof, here burned and there,
As if God's messenger thro' the close wood screen
Plunged and replunged his weapon at a venture,
Feeling for guilty thee and me: then broke
The thunder like a whole sea overhead—

    Seb. Yes!

    Otti.   —While I stretched myself upon you, hands
To hands, my mouth to your hot mouth, and shook
All my locks loose, and covered you with them—
You, Sebald, the same you!

    Seb.   Slower, Ottima!

    Otti. And as we lay—

    Seb.   Less vehemently! Love me!
Forgive me! Take not words, mere words, to heart!
Your breath is worse than wine! Breathe slow, speak slow!
Do not lean on me!

    Otti.   Sebald, as we lay,
Rising and falling only with our pants,
Who said, 'Let death come now! 'Tis right to die!
'Right to be punished! Nought completes such bliss
'But woe!' Who said that?

    Seb.   How did we ever rise?
Was't that we slept? Why did it end?

    Otti.   I felt you
Taper into a point the ruffled ends
Of my loose locks 'twixt both your humid lips.
My hair is fallen now: knot it again!

Seb. I kiss you now, dear Ottima, now and now!
This way? Will you forgive me—be once more
My great queen?

    Otti.   Bind it thrice about my brow;
Crown me your queen, your spirit's arbitress,
Magnificent in sin. Say that!

    Seb.   I crown you
My great white queen, my spirit's arbitress,
Magnificent . . .

    [*From without is heard the voice of* PIPPA, *singing*—

> The year 's at the spring
> And day 's at the morn;
> Morning 's at seven;
> The hill-side 's dew-pearled;
> The lark 's on the wing;
> The snail 's on the thorn:
> God 's in his heaven—
> All 's right with the world!

                             [PIPPA *passes.*

    Seb. God's in his heaven! Do you hear that? Who
  spoke?
You, you spoke!

    Otti.   Oh—that little ragged girl!
She must have rested on the step: we give them
But this one holiday the whole year round.
Did you ever see our silk-mills—their inside?
There are ten silk-mills now belong to you.
She stoops to pick my double heartsease . . . Sh!
She does not hear: call you out louder!

    Seb.   Leave me!
Go, get your clothes on—dress those shoulders!

    Otti.   Sebald?

    Seb. Wipe off that paint! I hate you.

    Otti.   Miserable!

    Seb. My God, and she is emptied of it now!
Outright now!—how miraculously gone
All of the grace—had she not strange grace once?
Why, the blank cheek hangs listless as it likes,

No purpose holds the features up together,
Only the cloven brow and puckered chin
Stay in their places: and the very hair,
That seemed to have a sort of life in it,
Drops, a dead web!

    Otti.   Speak to me—not of me!

    Seb. —That round great full-orbed face, where not an
        angle
Broke the delicious indolence—all broken!

    Otti. To me—not of me! Ungrateful, perjured cheat!
A coward too: but ingrate's worse than all.
Beggar—my slave—a fawning, cringing lie!
Leave me! Betray me! I can see your drift!
A lie that walks and eats and drinks!

    Seb.   My God!
Those morbid olive faultless shoulder-blades—
I should have known there was no blood beneath!

    Otti. You hate me then? You hate me then?

    Seb.   To think
She would succeed in her absurd attempt,
And fascinate by sinning, show herself
Superior—guilt from its excess superior
To innocence! That little peasant's voice
Has righted all again. Though I be lost,
I know which is the better, never fear,
Of vice or virtue, purity or lust,
Nature or trick! I see what I have done,
Entirely now! Oh I am proud to feel
Such torments—let the world take credit thence—
I, having done my deed, pay too its price!
I hate, hate—curse you! God's in his heaven!

    Otti.   —Me!
Me! no, no, Sebald, not yourself—kill me!
Mine is the whole crime. Do but kill me—then
Yourself—then—presently—first hear me speak!
I always meant to kill myself—wait, you!
Lean on my breast—not as a breast; don't love me
The more because you lean on me, my own
Heart's Sebald! There, there, both deaths presently!

Seb. My brain is drowned now—quite drowned: all
    I feel
Is . . . is, at swift-recurring intervals,
A hurry-down within me, as of waters
Loosened to smother up some ghastly pit:
There they go—whirls from a black fiery sea!
    Otti. Not me—to him, O God, be merciful!

Talk by the way, while PIPPA *is passing from the hill-
side to Orcana. Foreign* Students *of painting and
sculpture, from Venice, assembled opposite the house
of* JULES, *a young French statuary, at Possagno.*

1st Stud. Attention! My own post is beneath this
window, but the pomegranate clump yonder will hide
three or four of you with a little squeezing, and Schramm
and his pipe must lie flat in the balcony. Four, five—
who's a defaulter? We want everybody, for Jules must
not be suffered to hurt his bride when the jest's found
out.

2nd Stud. All here! Only our poet's away—never
having much meant to be present, moonstrike him! The
airs of that fellow, that Giovacchino! He was in violent
love with himself, and had a fair prospect of thriving in
his suit, so unmolested was it,—when suddenly a woman
falls in love with him, too; and out of pure jealousy he
takes himself off to Trieste, immortal poem and all:
whereto is this prophetical epitaph appended already, as
Bluphocks assures me,—'*Here a mammoth-poem lies,
Fouled to death by butterflies.*' His own fault, the simple-
ton! Instead of cramp couplets, each like a knife in your
entrails, he should write, says Bluphocks, both classically
and intelligibly.—*Æsculapius, an Epic. Catalogue of the
drugs: Hebe's plaister—One strip Cools your lip. Phœbus'
emulsion—One bottle Clears your throttle. Mercury's
bolus—One box Cures* . . .

3rd Stud. Subside, my fine fellow! If the marriage was
over by ten o'clock, Jules will certainly be here in a
minute with his bride.

2nd Stud. Good!—only, so should the poet's muse have

been universally acceptable, says Bluphocks, *et canibus nostris* ... and Delia not better known to our literary dogs than the boy Giovacchino!

1st Stud. To the point, now. Where's Gottlieb, the new-comer? Oh,—listen, Gottlieb, to what has called down this piece of friendly vengeance on Jules, of which we now assemble to witness the winding-up. We are all agreed, all in a tale, observe, when Jules shall burst out on us in a fury by and by: I am spokesman—the verses that are to undeceive Jules bear my name of Lutwyche— but each professes himself alike insulted by this strutting stone-squarer, who came alone from Paris to Munich, and thence with a crowd of us to Venice and Possagno here, but proceeds in a day or two alone again—oh, alone indubitably!—to Rome and Florence. He, forsooth, take up his portion with these dissolute, brutalized, heartless bunglers!—so he was heard to call us all: now, is Schramm brutalized, I should like to know? Am I heartless?

Gott. Why, somewhat heartless; for, suppose Jules a coxcomb as much as you choose, still, for this mere coxcombry, you will have brushed off—what do folks style it?—the bloom of his life. Is it too late to alter? These love-letters now, you call his—I can't laugh at them.

4th Stud. Because you never read the sham letters of our inditing which drew forth these.

Gott. His discovery of the truth will be frightful.

4th Stud. That's the joke. But you should have joined us at the beginning: there's no doubt he loves the girl— loves a model he might hire by the hour!

Gott. See here! 'He has been accustomed,' he writes, 'to have Canova's women about him, in stone, and the 'world's women beside him, in flesh; these being as much 'below, as those above, his soul's aspiration: but now he 'is to have the reality.' There you laugh again! I say, you wipe off the very dew of his youth.

1st Stud. Schramm! (Take the pipe out of his mouth, somebody!) Will Jules lose the bloom of his youth?

Schramm. Nothing worth keeping is ever lost in this world: look at a blossom—it drops presently, having done its service and lasted its time; but fruits succeed, and where would be the blossom's place could it continue? As well affirm that your eye is no longer in your body, because its earliest favourite, whatever it may have first loved to look on, is dead and done with—as that any affection is lost to the soul when its first object, whatever happened first to satisfy it, is superseded in due course. Keep but ever looking, whether with the body's eye or the mind's, and you will soon find something to look on! Has a man done wondering at women?—there follow men, dead and alive, to wonder at. Has he done wondering at men?— there's God to wonder at: and the faculty of wonder may be, at the same time, old and tired enough with respect to its first object, and yet young and fresh sufficiently, so far as concerns its novel one. Thus . . .

1st Stud. Put Schramm's pipe into his mouth again! There, you see! Well, this Jules . . . a wretched fribble— oh, I watched his disportings at Possagno, the other day! Canova's gallery—you know: there he marches first resolvedly past great works by the dozen without vouch-safing an eye: all at once he stops full at the *Psiche-fanciulla*—cannot pass that old acquaintance without a nod of encouragement—'In your new place, beauty? Then behave yourself as well here as at Munich—I see you!' Next he posts himself deliberately before the un-finished *Pietà* for half an hour without moving, till up he starts of a sudden, and thrusts his very nose into—I say, into—the group; by which gesture you are informed that precisely the sole point he had not fully mastered in Canova's practice was a certain method of using the drill in the articulation of the knee-joint—and that, likewise, has he mastered at length! Good-bye, therefore, to poor Canova—whose gallery no longer needs detain his suc-cessor Jules, the predestinated novel thinker in marble!

5th Stud. Tell him about the women: go on to the women!

1st Stud. Why, on that matter he could never be super-cilious enough. How should we be other (he said) than the poor devils you see, with those debasing habits we cherish? He was not to wallow in that mire, at least: he would wait, and love only at the proper time, and meanwhile put up with the *Psiche-fanciulla*. Now, I happened to hear of a young Greek—real Greek girl at Malamocco; a true Islander, do you see, with Alciphron's 'hair like sea-moss'—Schramm knows!—white and quiet as an apparition, and fourteen years old at farthest,—a daughter of Natalia, so she swears—that hag Natalia, who helps us to models at three *lire* an hour. We selected this girl for the heroine of our jest. So first, Jules received a scented letter—somebody had seen his Tydeus at the Academy, and my picture was nothing to it: a profound admirer bade him persevere—would make herself known to him ere long. (Paolina, my little friend of the *Fenice*, transcribes divinely.) And in due time, the mysterious correspondent gave certain hints of her peculiar charms— the pale cheeks, the black hair—whatever, in short, had struck us in our Malamocco model: we retained her name, too—Phene, which is, by interpretation, sea-eagle. Now, think of Jules finding himself distinguished from the herd of us by such a creature! In his very first answer he proposed marrying his monitress: and fancy us over these letters, two, three times a day, to receive and despatch! I concocted the main of it: relations were in the way— secrecy must be observed—in fine, would he wed her on trust, and only speak to her when they were indissolubly united? St—st—Here they come!

　6th Stud. Both of them! Heaven's love, speak softly, speak within yourselves!

　5th Stud. Look at the bridegroom! Half his hair in storm and half in calm,—patted down over the left temple, —like a frothy cup one blows on to cool it: and the same old blouse that he murders the marble in.

　2nd Stud. Not a rich vest like yours, Hannibal Scratchy! —rich, that your face may the better set it off.

　6th Stud. And the bride! Yes, sure enough, our Phene! Should you have known her in her clothes? How magnificently pale!

　Gott. She does not also take it for earnest, I hope?

1st Stud. Oh, Natalia's concern, that is! We settle with
Natalia.

6th Stud. She does not speak—has evidently let out no
word. The only thing is, will she equally remember the
rest of her lesson, and repeat correctly all those verses
which are to break the secret to Jules?

Gott. How he gazes on her! Pity—pity!

1st Stud. They go in: now, silence! You three,—not
nearer the window, mind, than that pomegranate: just
where the little girl, who a few minutes ago passed us
singing, is seated!

II. NOON

SCENE. *Over Orcana. The house of* JULES, *who crosses its*
    threshold with PHENE: *she is silent, on which* JULES
    begins—

Do not die, Phene! I am yours now, you
Are mine now; let fate reach me how she likes,
If you'll not die: so, never die! Sit here—
My work-room's single seat. I over-lean
This length of hair and lustrous front; they turn
Like an entire flower upward: eyes, lips, last
Your chin—no, last your throat turns: 'tis their scent
Pulls down my face upon you. Nay, look ever
This one way till I change, grow you—I could
Change into you, beloved!
                You by me,
And I by you; this is your hand in mine,
And side by side we sit: all's true. Thank God!
I have spoken: speak you!
               O my life to come!
My Tydeus must be carved that's there in clay;
Yet how be carved, with you about the room?
Where must I place you? When I think that once
This room-full of rough block-work seemed my heaven
Without you! Shall I ever work again,
Get fairly into my old ways again,
Bid each conception stand while, trait by trait,
My hand transfers its lineaments to stone?

Will my mere fancies live near you, their truth—
The live truth, passing and repassing me,
Sitting beside me?
          Now speak!
                    Only first,
See, all your letters! Was't not well contrived?
Their hiding-place is Psyche's robe; she keeps
Your letters next her skin: which drops out foremost?
Ah,—this that swam down like a first moonbeam
Into my world!
               Again those eyes complete
Their melancholy survey, sweet and slow,
Of all my room holds; to return and rest
On me, with pity, yet some wonder too:
As if God bade some spirit plague a world,
And this were the one moment of surprise
And sorrow while she took her station, pausing
O'er what she sees, finds good, and must destroy!
What gaze you at? Those? Books, I told you of;
Let your first word to me rejoice them, too:
This minion, a Coluthus, writ in red
Bistre and azure by Bessarion's scribe—
Read this line . . . no, shame—Homer's be the Greek
First breathed me from the lips of my Greek girl!
This Odyssey in coarse black, vivid type
With faded yellow blossoms 'twixt page and page,
To mark great places with due gratitude;
'*He said, and on Antinous directed*
'*A bitter shaft*' . . . a flower blots out the rest
Again upon your search? My statues, then!
—Ah, do not mind that—better that will look
When cast in bronze—an Almaign Kaiser, that,
Swart-green and gold, with truncheon based on hip.
This, rather, turn to! What, unrecognized?
I thought you would have seen that here you sit
As I imagined you,—Hippolyta,
Naked upon her bright Numidian horse.
Recall you this then? 'Carve in bold relief'—
So you commanded—'carve, against I come,

'A Greek, in Athens, as our fashion was,
'Feasting, bay-filleted and thunder-free,
'Who rises 'neath the lifted myrtle-branch.
' "Praise those who slew Hipparchus!" cry the guests,
' "While o'er thy head the singer's myrtle waves
' "As erst above our champion: stand up, all!" '
See, I have laboured to express your thought.
Quite round, a cluster of mere hands and arms,
(Thrust in all senses, all ways, from all sides,
Only consenting at the branch's end
They strain toward) serves for frame to a sole face,
The Praiser's, in the centre: who with eyes
Sightless, so bend they back to light inside
His brain where visionary forms throng up,
Sings, minding not that palpitating arch
Of hands and arms, nor the quick drip of wine
From the drenched leaves o'erhead, nor crowns cast off,
Violet and parsley crowns to trample on—
Sings, pausing as the patron-ghosts approve,
Devoutly their unconquerable hymn.
But you must say a 'well' to that—say 'well!'
Because you gaze—am I fantastic, sweet?
Gaze like my very life's-stuff, marble—marbly
Even to the silence! Why, before I found
The real flesh Phene, I inured myself
To see, throughout all nature, varied stuff
For better nature's birth by means of art:
With me, each substance tended to one form
Of beauty—to the human archetype.
On every side occurred suggestive germs
Of that—the tree, the flower—or take the fruit,—
Some rosy shape, continuing the peach,
Curved beewise o'er its bough; as rosy limbs,
Depending, nestled in the leaves; and just
From a cleft rose-peach the whole Dryad sprang.
But of the stuffs one can be master of,
How I divined their capabilities!
From the soft-rinded smoothening facile chalk
That yields your outline to the air's embrace,

Half-softened by a halo's pearly gloom;
Down to the crisp imperious steel, so sure
To cut its one confided thought clean out
Of all the world. But marble!—'neath my tools
More pliable than jelly—as it were
Some clear primordial creature dug from depths
In the earth's heart, where itself breeds itself,
And whence all baser substance may be worked;
Refine it off to air, you may,—condense it
Down to the diamond;—is not metal there,
When o'er the sudden speck my chisel trips?
—Not flesh, as flake off flake I scale, approach,
Lay bare those bluish veins of blood asleep?
Lurks flame in no strange windings where, surprised
By the swift implement sent home at once,
Flushes and glowings radiate and hover
About its track?
                    Phene? what—why is this?
That whitening cheek, those still dilating eyes!
Ah, you will die—I knew that you would die!

PHENE *begins, on his having long remained silent.*

Now the end's coming; to be sure, it must
Have ended sometime! Tush, why need I speak
Their foolish speech? I cannot bring to mind
One half of it, beside; and do not care
For old Natalia now, nor any of them.
Oh, you—what are you?—if I do not try
To say the words Natalia made me learn,
To please your friends,—it is to keep myself
Where your voice lifted me, by letting that
Proceed: but can it? Even you, perhaps,
Cannot take up, now you have once let fall,
The music's life, and me along with that—
No, or you would! We'll stay, then, as we are:
Above the world.
                    You creature with the eyes!
If I could look for ever up to them,
As now you let me,—I believe, all sin

All memory of wrong done, suffering borne,
Would drop down, low and lower, to the earth
Whence all that's low comes, and there touch and stay
—Never to overtake the rest of me,
All that, unspotted, reaches up to you,
Drawn by those eyes! What rises is myself,
Not me the shame and suffering; but they sink,
Are left, I rise above them. Keep me so,
Above the world!
                        But you sink, for your eyes
Are altering—altered! Stay—'I love you, love' . . .
I could prevent it if I understood:
More of your words to me: was't in the tone
Or the words, your power?
                                    Or stay—I will repeat
Their speech, if that contents you! Only change
No more, and I shall find it presently
Far back here, in the brain yourself filled up.
Natalia threatened me that harm should follow
Unless I spoke their lesson to the end,
But harm to me, I thought she meant, not you.
Your friends,—Natalia said they were your friends
And meant you well,—because, I doubted it,
Observing (what was very strange to see)
On every face, so different in all else,
The same smile girls like me are used to bear,
But never men, men cannot stoop so low;
Yet your friends, speaking of you, used that smile,
That hateful smirk of boundless self-conceit
Which seems to take possession of the world
And make of God a tame confederate,
Purveyor to their appetites . . . you know!
But still Natalia said they were your friends,
And they assented though they smiled the more,
And all came round me,—that thin Englishman
With light lank hair seemed leader of the rest;
He held a paper—'What we want,' said he,
Ending some explanation to his friends—
'Is something slow, involved and mystical,

'To hold Jules long in doubt, yet take his taste
'And lure him on until, at innermost
'Where he seeks sweetness' soul, he may find—this!
'—As in the apple's core, the noisome fly:
'For insects on the rind are seen at once,
'And brushed aside as soon, but this is found
'Only when on the lips or loathing tongue.'
And so he read what I have got by heart:
I'll speak it,—'Do not die, love! I am yours.'
No—is not that, or like that, part of words
Yourself began by speaking? Strange to lose
What cost such pains to learn! Is this more right?

I am a painter who cannot paint;
In my life, a devil rather than saint;
In my brain, as poor a creature too:
No end to all I cannot do!
Yet do one thing at least I can—
Love a man or hate a man
Supremely: thus my lore began.
Through the Valley of Love I went,
In the lovingest spot to abide,
And just on the verge where I pitched my tent,
I found Hate dwelling beside.
(Let the Bridegroom ask what the painter meant,
Of his Bride, of the peerless Bride!)
And further, I traversed Hate's grove,
In the hatefullest nook to dwell;
But lo, where I flung myself prone, couched Love
Where the shadow threefold fell.
(The meaning—those black bride's-eyes above,
Not a painter's lip should tell!)

'And here,' said he, 'Jules probably will ask,
'"You have black eyes, Love,—you are, sure enough,
'"My peerless bride,—then do you tell indeed
'"What needs some explanation! What means this?"'
—And I am to go on, without a word—

So, I grew wise in Love and Hate,
From simple that I was of late.

Once, when I loved, I would enlace
Breast, eyelids, hands, feet, form and face
Of her I loved, in one embrace—
As if by mere love I could love immensely!
Once, when I hated, I would plunge
My sword, and wipe with the first lunge
My foe's whole life out like a sponge—
As if by mere hate I could hate intensely!
But now I am wiser, know better the fashion
How passion seeks aid from its opposite passion:
And if I see cause to love more, hate more
Than ever man loved, ever hated before—
And seek in the Valley of Love,
The nest, or the nook in Hate's Grove,
Where my soul may surely reach
The essence, nought less, of each,
The Hate of all Hates, the Love
Of all Loves, in the Valley or Grove,—
I find them the very warders
Each of the other's borders.
When I love most, Love is disguised
In Hate; and when Hate is surprised
In Love, then I hate most: ask
How Love smiles through Hate's iron casque,
Hate grins through Love's rose-braided mask,—
And how, having hated thee,
I sought long and painfully
To reach thy heart, nor prick
The skin but pierce to the quick—
Ask this, my Jules, and be answered straight
By thy bride—how the painter Lutwyche can hate!

JULES *interposes.*

Lutwyche! Who else? But all of them, no doubt,
Hated me: they at Venice—presently
Their turn, however! You I shall not meet:
If I dreamed, saying this would wake me.

                            Keep
What's here, the gold—we cannot meet again,

Consider! and the money was but meant
For two years' travel, which is over now,
All chance or hope or care or need of it.
This—and what comes from selling these, my casts
And books and medals, except . . . let them go
Together, so the produce keeps you safe
Out of Natalia's clutches! If by chance
(For all's chance here) I should survive the gang
At Venice, root out all fifteen of them,
We might meet somewhere, since the world is wide.

> [*From without is heard the voice of* PIPPA, *singing—*
>
> *Give her but a least excuse to love me!*
> *When—where—*
> *How—can this arm establish her above me,*
> *If fortune fixed her as my lady there,*
> *There already, to eternally reprove me?*
>   ('*Hist!'—said Kate the Queen;*
>   *But 'Oh!'—cried the maiden, binding her tresses,*
>   ''*Tis only a page that carols unseen,*
>   '*Crumbling your hounds their messes!'*)
>
> *Is she wronged?—To the rescue of her honour,*
> *My heart!*
> *Is she poor?—What costs it to be styled a donor?*
> *Merely an earth to cleave, a sea to part.*
> *But that fortune should have thrust all this upon her!*
>   ('*Nay, list!'—bade Kate the Queen;*
>   *And still cried the maiden, binding her tresses,*
>   ''*Tis only a page that carols unseen,*
>   '*Fitting your hawks their jesses!'*)
>   [PIPPA *passes.*

JULES *resumes.*

What name was that the little girl sang forth?
Kate? The Cornaro, doubtless, who renounced
The crown of Cyprus to be lady here
At Asolo, where still her memory stays,
And peasants sing how once a certain page
Pined for the grace of her so far above
His power of doing good to, 'Kate the Queen—

'She never could be wronged, be poor,' he sighed,
'Need him to help her!'
                                        Yes, a bitter thing
To see our lady above all need of us;
Yet so we look ere we will love; not I,
But the world looks so. If whoever loves
Must be, in some sort, god or worshipper,
The blessing or the blest one, queen or page,
Why should we always choose the page's part?
Here is a woman with utter need of me,—
I find myself queen here, it seems!
                                        How strange!
Look at the woman here with the new soul,
Like my own Psyche,—fresh upon her lips
Alit, the visionary butterfly,
Waiting my word to enter and make bright,
Or flutter off and leave all blank as first.
This body had no soul before, but slept
Or stirred, was beauteous or ungainly, free
From taint or foul with stain, as outward things
Fastened their image on its passiveness:
Now, it will wake, feel, live—or die again!
Shall to produce form out of unshaped stuff
Be Art—and further, to evoke a soul
From form be nothing? This new soul is mine!

Now, to kill Lutwyche, what would that do?—save
A wretched dauber, men will hoot to death
Without me, from their hooting. Oh, to hear
God's voice plain as I heard it first, before
They broke in with their laughter! I heard them
Henceforth, not God.
                              To Ancona—Greece—some isle!
I wanted silence only; there is clay
Everywhere. One may do whate'er one likes
In Art: the only thing is, to make sure
That one does like it—which takes pains to know.
    Scatter all this, my Phene—this mad dream!
Who, what is Lutwyche, what Natalia's friends,

What the whole world except our love—my own,
Own Phene? But I told you, did I not,
Ere night we travel for your land—some isle
With the sea's silence on it? Stand aside—
I do but break these paltry models up
To begin Art afresh. Meet Lutwyche, I—
And save him from my statue meeting him?
Some unsuspected isle in the far seas!
Like a god going through his world, there stands
One mountain for a moment in the dusk,
Whole brotherhoods of cedars on its brow:
And you are ever by me while I gaze
—Are in my arms as now—as now—as now!
Some unsuspected isle in the far seas!
Some unsuspected isle in far-off seas!

Talk by the way, while PIPPA *is passing from Orcana to
the Turret. Two or three of the Austrian Police loitering with* BLUPHOCKS, *an English vagabond, just in view
of the Turret.*

Bluph.[1] So, that is your Pippa, the little girl who passed
us singing? Well, your Bishop's Intendant's money shall
be honestly earned:—now, don't make me that sour face
because I bring the Bishop's name into the business; we
know he can have nothing to do with such horrors: we
know that he is a saint and all that a bishop should be,
who is a great man beside. *Oh were but every worm a
maggot, Every fly a grig, Every bough a Christmas faggot,
Every tune a jig!* In fact, I have abjured all religions; but
the last I inclined to, was the Armenian: for I have
travelled, do you see, and at Koenigsberg, Prussia Improper (so styled because there's a sort of bleak hungry
sun there), you might remark over a venerable house-
porch, a certain Chaldee inscription; and brief as it is, a
mere glance at it used absolutely to change the mood of
every bearded passenger. In they turned, one and all;
the young and lightsome, with no irreverent pause, the

[1] 'He maketh his sun to rise on the evil and on the good, and
sendeth rain on the just and on the unjust.'

aged and decrepit, with a sensible alacrity: 'twas the
Grand Rabbi's abode, in short. Struck with curiosity, I
lost no time in learning Syriac—(these are vowels, you
dogs,—follow my stick's end in the mud—*Celarent, Darii,
Ferio!*) and one morning presented myself, spelling-book
in hand, a, b, c,—I picked it out letter by letter, and what
was the purport of this miraculous posy? Some cherished
legend of the past, you'll say—'*How Moses hocus-pocussed
Egypt's land with fly and locust,*'—or, '*How to Jonah
sounded harshish, Get thee up and go to Tarshish,*'—or,
'*How the angel meeting Balaam, Straight his ass returned
a salaam.*' In no wise! '*Shackabrack—Boach—somebody
or other—Isaach, Re-cei-ver, Pur-cha-ser and Ex-chan-ger
of—Stolen Goods!*' So, talk to me of the religion of
a bishop! I have renounced all bishops save Bishop
Beveridge—mean to live so—and die—*As some Greek
dog-sage, dead and merry, Hellward bound in Charon's
wherry, With food for both worlds, under and upper, Lupine-
seed and Hecate's supper, And never an obolus* . . .
(Though thanks to you, or this Intendant through you,
or this Bishop through his Intendant—I possess a burning
pocketful of *zwanzigers*) . . . *To pay the Stygian Ferry!*

1st Pol. There is the girl, then; go and deserve them the
moment you have pointed out to us Signor Luigi and his
mother. [*To the rest.*] I have been noticing a house
yonder, this long while: not a shutter unclosed since
morning!

2nd Pol. Old Luca Gaddi's, that owns the silk-mills
here: he dozes by the hour, wakes up, sighs deeply, says
he should like to be Prince Metternich, and then dozes
again, after having bidden young Sebald, the foreigner,
set his wife to playing draughts. Never molest such a
household, they mean well.

Bluph. Only, cannot you tell me something of this little
Pippa, I must have to do with? One could make something of that name. Pippa—that is, short for Felippa—
rhyming to *Panurge consults Hertrippa—Believest thou,
King Agrippa?* Something might be done with that
name.

2nd Pol. Put into rhyme that your head and a ripe musk-melon would not be dear at half a *zwanziger!* Leave this fooling, and look out; the afternoon's over or nearly so.

3rd Pol. Where in this passport of Signor Luigi does our Principal instruct you to watch him so narrowly? There? What's there beside a simple signature? (That English fool's busy watching.)

2nd Pol. Flourish all round—'Put all possible obstacles in his way;' oblong dot at the end—'Detain him till further advices reach you;' scratch at bottom—'Send him back on pretence of some informality in the above;' ink-spirt on right-hand side (which is the case here)— 'Arrest him at once.' Why and wherefore, I don't concern myself, but my instructions amount to this: if Signor Luigi leaves home to-night for Vienna—well and good, the passport deposed with us for our *visa* is really for his own use, they have misinformed the Office, and he means well; but let him stay over to-night—there has been the pretence we suspect, the accounts of his corresponding and holding intelligence with the Carbonari are correct, we arrest him at once, to-morrow comes Venice, and presently Spielberg. Bluphocks makes the signal, sure enough! That is he, entering the turret with his mother, no doubt.

III. EVENING

SCENE. *Inside the Turret on the Hill above Asolo.* LUIGI *and his* Mother *entering.*

Mother. If there blew wind, you'd hear a long sigh, easing
The utmost heaviness of music's heart.

Luigi. Here in the archway?

Mother   Oh no, no—in farther,
Where the echo is made, on the ridge.

Luigi.   Here surely, then.
How plain the tap of my heel as I leaped up!
Hark—'Lucius Junius!' The very ghost of a voice

Whose body is caught and kept by . . . what are those?
Mere withered wallflowers, waving overhead?
They seem an elvish group with thin bleached hair
That lean out of their topmost fortress—look
And listen, mountain men, to what we say,
Hand under chin of each grave earthy face.
Up and show faces all of you!—'All of you!'
That's the king dwarf with the scarlet comb; old Franz,
Come down and meet your fate? Hark—'Meet your
    fate!'
    Mother. Let him not meet it, my Luigi—do not
Go to his City! Putting crime aside,
Half of these ills of Italy are feigned:
Your Pellicos and writers for effect,
Write for effect.
    Luigi.   Hush! Say A. writes, and B.
    Mother. These A.s and B.s write for effect, I say.
Then, evil is in its nature loud, while good
Is silent; you hear each petty injury,
None of his virtues; he is old beside,
Quiet and kind, and densely stupid. Why
Do A. and B. not kill him themselves?
    Luigi.   They teach
Others to kill him—me—and, if I fail,
Others to succeed; now, if A. tried and failed,
I could not teach that: mine's the lesser task.
Mother, they visit night by night . . .
    Mother.   —You, Luigi?
Ah, will you let me tell you what you are?
    Luigi. Why not? Oh, the one thing you fear to hint,
You may assure yourself I say and say
Ever to myself! At times—nay, even as now
We sit—I think my mind is touched, suspect
All is not sound: but is not knowing that,
What constitutes one sane or otherwise?
I know I am thus—so, all is right again.
I laugh at myself as through the town I walk,
And see men merry as if no Italy
Were suffering; then I ponder—'I am rich,

'Young, healthy; why should this fact trouble me,
'More than it troubles these?' But it does trouble.
No, trouble's a bad word: for as I walk
There's springing and melody and giddiness,
And old quaint turns and passages of my youth,
Dreams long forgotten, little in themselves,
Return to me—whatever may amuse me:
And earth seems in a truce with me, and heaven
Accords with me, all things suspend their strife,
The very cicala laughs 'There goes he, and there!
'Feast him, the time is short; he is on his way
'For the world's sake: feast him this once, our friend!'
And in return for all this, I can trip
Cheerfully up the scaffold-steps. I go
This evening, mother!
    Mother.   But mistrust yourself—
Mistrust the judgment you pronounce on him!
    Luigi. Oh, there I feel!—am sure that I am right!
    Mother. Mistrust your judgment then, of the mere
        means
To this wild enterprise. Say, you are right,—
How should one in your state e'er bring to pass
What would require a cool head, a cold heart,
And a calm hand? You never will escape.
    Luigi. Escape? To even wish that, would spoil all.
The dying is best part of it. Too much
Have I enjoyed these fifteen years of mine,
To leave myself excuse for longer life:
Was not life pressed down, running o'er with joy,
That I might finish with it ere my fellows
Who, sparelier feasted, make a longer stay?
I was put at the board-head, helped to all
At first; I rise up happy and content.
God must be glad one loves his world so much.
I can give news of earth to all the dead
Who ask me:—last year's sunsets, and great stars
Which had a right to come first and see ebb
The crimson wave that drifts the sun away—
Those crescent moons with notched and burning rims

That strengthened into sharp fire, and there stood,
Impatient of the azure—and that day
In March, a double rainbow stopped the storm—
May's warm slow yellow moonlit summer nights—
Gone are they, but I have them in my soul!

   Mother. (He will not go!)

   Luigi.   You smile at me? 'Tis
     true,—
Voluptuousness, grotesqueness, ghastliness,
Environ my devotedness as quaintly
As round about some antique altar wreathe
The rose festoons, goats' horns, and oxen's skulls.

   Mother. See now: you reach the city, you must cross
His threshold—how?

   Luigi.   Oh, that's if we conspired!
Then would come pains in plenty, as you guess—
But guess not how the qualities most fit
For such an office, qualities I have,
Would little stead me, otherwise employed,
Yet prove of rarest merit only here.
Every one knows for what his excellence
Will serve, but no one ever will consider
For what his worst defect might serve: and yet
Have you not seen me range our coppice yonder
In search of a distorted ash?—I find
The wry spoilt branch a natural perfect bow.
Fancy the thrice-sage, thrice-precautioned man
Arriving at the palace on my errand!
No, no! I have a handsome dress packed up—
White satin here, to set off my black hair;
In I shall march—for you may watch your life out
Behind thick walls, make friends there to betray you;
More than one man spoils everything. March straight—
Only, no clumsy knife to fumble for.
Take the great gate and walk (not saunter) on
Thro' guards and guards——I have rehearsed it all
Inside the turret here a hundred times.
Don't ask the way of whom you meet, observe!
But where they cluster thickliest is the door

Of doors; they'll let you pass—they'll never blab
Each to the other, he knows not the favourite,
Whence he is bound and what's his business now.
Walk in—straight up to him; you have no knife:
Be prompt, how should he scream? Then, out with you!
Italy, Italy, my Italy!
You're free, you're free! Oh mother, I could dream
They got about me—Andrea from his exile,
Pier from his dungeon, Gualtier from his grave!
   Mother. Well, you shall go. Yet seems this patriotism
The easiest virtue for a selfish man
To acquire: he loves himself—and next, the world—
If he must love beyond,—but nought between:
As a short-sighted man sees nought midway
His body and the sun above. But you
Are my adored Luigi, ever obedient
To my least wish, and running o'er with love:
I could not call you cruel or unkind.
Once more, your ground for killing him!—then go!
   Luigi. Now do you try me, or make sport of me?
How first the Austrians got these provinces . . .
(If that is all, I'll satisfy you soon)
—Never by conquest but by cunning, for
That treaty whereby . . .
   Mother.   Well?
   Luigi.   (Sure, he's arrived,
The tell-tale cuckoo: spring's his confidant,
And he lets out her April purposes!)
Or . . . better go at once to modern time,
He has . . . they have . . . in fact, I understand
But can't restate the matter; that's my boast:
Others could reason it out to you, and prove
Things they have made me feel.
   Mother.   Why go to-night?
Morn's for adventure. Jupiter is now
A morning-star. I cannot hear you, Luigi!
   Luigi. 'I am the bright and morning-star,' saith God
And, 'to such an one I give the morning-star.'
The gift of the morning-star! Have I God's gift

Of the morning-star?

   Mother.   Chiara will love to see

That Jupiter an evening-star next June.

   Luigi. True, mother. Well for those who live through
June!

Great noontides, thunder-storms, all glaring pomps

That triumph at the heels of June the god

Leading his revel through our leafy world,

Yes, Chiara will be here.

   Mother.   In June: remember,

Yourself appointed that month for her coming.

   Luigi. Was that low noise the echo?

   Mother.   The night-wind.

She must be grown—with her blue eyes upturned

As if life were one long and sweet surprise:

In June she comes.

   Luigi.   We were to see together

The Titian at Treviso. There, again!

   [*From without is heard the voice of* PIPPA, *singing*—

> *A king lived long ago,*
> *In the morning of the world,*
> *When earth was nigher heaven than now:*
> *And the king's locks curled,*
> *Disparting o'er a forehead full*
> *As the milk-white space 'twixt horn and horn*
> *Of some sacrificial bull—*
> *Only calm as a babe new-born:*
> *For he was got to a sleepy mood,*
> *So safe from all decrepitude,*
> *Age with its bane, so sure gone by,*
> *(The gods so loved him while he dreamed)*
> *That, having lived thus long, there seemed*
> *No need the king should ever die.*

   Luigi. No need that sort of king should ever die!

> *Among the rocks his city was:*
> *Before his palace, in the sun,*
> *He sat to see his people pass,*

And judge them every one
From its threshold of smooth stone.
They haled him many a valley-thief
Caught in the sheep-pens, robber-chief
Swarthy and shameless, beggar-cheat,
Spy-prowler, or rough pirate found
On the sea-sand left aground;
And sometimes clung about his feet,
With bleeding lip and burning cheek,
A woman, bitterest wrong to speak
Of one with sullen thickset brows:
And sometimes from the prison-house
The angry priests a pale wretch brought,
Who through some chink had pushed and **pressed**
On knees and elbows, belly and breast,
Worm-like into the temple,—caught
He was by the very god,
Who ever in the darkness strode
Backward and forward, keeping watch
O'er his brazen bowls, such rogues to catch!
These, all and every one,
The king judged, sitting in the sun.

Luigi. That king should still judge sitting in the sun!

His councillors, on left and right,
Looked anxious up,—but no surprise
Disturbed the king's old smiling eyes
Where the very blue had turned to white.
'Tis said, a Python scared one day
The breathless city, till he came,
With forky tongue and eyes on flame,
Where the old king sat to judge alway;
But when he saw the sweepy hair
Girt with a crown of berries rare
Which the god will hardly give to wear
To the maiden who singeth, dancing bare
In the altar-smoke by the pine-torch lights,
At his wondrous forest rites,—
Seeing this, he did not dare

Approach that threshold in the sun,
Assault the old king smiling there.
Such grace had kings when the world begun!

                    [PIPPA *passes.*

Luigi. And such grace have they, now that the world
    ends!
The Python at the city, on the throne,
And brave men, God would crown for slaying him,
Lurk in bye-corners lest they fall his prey.
Are crowns yet to be won in this late time,
Which weakness makes me hesitate to reach?
'Tis God's voice calls: how could I stay? Farewell!

Talk by the way, while PIPPA *is passing from the Turret*
to the Bishop's Brother's House, close to the Duomo
S. Maria. Poor Girls *sitting on the steps.*

1st Girl. There goes a swallow to Venice—the stout
    seafarer!
Seeing those birds fly, makes one wish for wings.
Let us all wish; you wish first!

2nd Girl.   I? This sunset
To finish.

3rd Girl. That old—somebody I know,
Greyer and older than my grandfather,
To give me the same treat he gave last week—
Feeding me on his knee with fig-peckers,
Lampreys and red Breganze-wine, and mumbling
The while some folly about how well I fare,
Let sit and eat my supper quietly:
Since had he not himself been late this morning
Detained at—never mind where,—had he not . . .
'Eh, baggage, had I not!'—

2nd Girl.   How she can lie!

3rd Girl. Look there—by the nails!

2nd Girl.   What makes your fingers red!

3rd Girl. Dipping them into wine to write bad words
    with
On the bright table: how he laughed!

1st Girl.   My turn.
Spring's come and summer's coming. I would wear
A long loose gown, down to the feet and hands,
With plaits here, close about the throat, all day;
And all night lie, the cool long nights, in bed;
And have new milk to drink, apples to eat,
Deuzans and junetings, leather-coats . . . ah, I should say,
This is away in the fields—miles!
        3rd Girl.   Say at once
You'd be at home: she'd always be at home!
Now comes the story of the farm among
The cherry orchards, and how April snowed
White blossoms on her as she ran. Why, fool,
They've rubbed the chalk-mark out, how tall you were,
Twisted your starling's neck, broken his cage,
Made a dung-hill of your garden!
        1st Girl.   They, destroy
My garden since I left them? well—perhaps!
I would have done so: so I hope they have!
A fig-tree curled out of our cottage wall;
They called it mine, I have forgotten why,
It must have been there long ere I was born:
Cric—cric—I think I hear the wasps o'erhead
Pricking the papers strung to flutter there
And keep off birds in fruit-time—coarse long papers,
And the wasps eat them, prick them through and through.
        3rd Girl. How her mouth twitches! Where was I?—
                before
She broke in with her wishes and long gowns
And wasps—would I be such a fool!—Oh, here!
This is my way: I answer every one
Who asks me why I make so much of him—
(If you say, 'you love him'—straight 'he'll not be gulled!')
'He that seduced me when I was a girl
'Thus high—had eyes like yours, or hair like yours,
'Brown, red, white,'—as the case may be: that pleases!
See how that beetle burnishes in the path!
There sparkles he along the dust: and, there—
Your journey to that maize-tuft spoiled at least!

1st Girl. When I was young, they said if you killed
 one
Of those sunshiny beetles, that his friend
Up there, would shine no more that day nor next.

2nd Girl. When you were young? Nor are you young,
 that's true.
How your plump arms, that were, have dropped away!
Why, I can span them. Cecco beats you still?
No matter, so you keep your curious hair.
I wish they'd find a way to dye our hair
Your colour—any lighter tint, indeed,
Than black: the men say they are sick of black,
Black eyes, black hair!

4th Girl.   Sick of yours, like enough.
Do you pretend you ever tasted lampreys
And ortolans? Giovita, of the palace,
Engaged (but there's no trusting him) to slice me
Polenta with a knife that had cut up
An ortolan.

2nd Girl. Why, there! Is not that Pippa
We are to talk to, under the window,—quick,—
Where the lights are?

1st Girl.   That she? No, or she would sing,
For the Intendant said . . .

3rd Girl.   Oh, you sing first!
Then, if she listens and comes close . . . I'll tell you,—
Sing that song the young English noble made,
Who took you for the purest of the pure,
And meant to leave the world for you—what fun!

2nd Girl [*sings*].

> *You'll love me yet!—and I can tarry*
>   *Your love's protracted growing:*
> *June reared that bunch of flowers you carry,*
>   *From seeds of April's sowing.*
>
> *I plant a heartful now: some seed*
>   *At least is sure to strike,*
> *And yield—what you'll not pluck indeed,*
>   *Not love, but, may be, like.*

You'll look at least on love's remains,
A grave's one violet:
Your look?—that pays a thousand pains.
What's death? You'll love me yet!

3rd Girl [*to* PIPPA *who approaches*]. Oh, you may come closer—we shall not eat you! Why, you seem the very person that the great rich handsome Englishman has fallen so violently in love with. I'll tell you all about it.

IV. NIGHT

SCENE. *Inside the Palace by the Duomo.* MONSIGNOR, *dismissing his* Attendants.

Mon. Thanks, friends, many thanks! I chiefly desire life now, that I may recompense every one of you. Most I know something of already. What, a repast prepared? *Benedicto benedicatur* . . . ugh, ugh! Where was I? Oh, as you were remarking, Ugo, the weather is mild, very unlike winter-weather: but I am a Sicilian, you know, and shiver in your Julys here. To be sure, when 'twas full summer at Messina, as we priests used to cross in procession the great square on Assumption Day, you might see our thickest yellow tapers twist suddenly in two, each like a falling star, or sink down on themselves in a gore of wax. But go, my friends, but go! [*To the* Intendant.] Not you, Ugo! [*The others leave the apartment.*] I have long wanted to converse with you, Ugo.

Inten. Uguccio—

Mon. . . . 'guccio Stefani, man! of Ascoli, Fermo and Fossombruno;—what I do need instructing about, are these accounts of your administration of my poor brother's affairs. Ugh! I shall never get through a third part of your accounts: take some of these dainties before we attempt it, however. Are you bashful to that degree? For me, a crust and water suffice.

Inten. Do you choose this especial night to question me?

Mon. This night, Ugo. You have managed my late

brother's affairs since the death of our elder brother: fourteen years and a month, all but three days. On the Third of December, I find him . . .

Inten. If you have so intimate an acquaintance with your brother's affairs, you will be tender of turning so far back: they will hardly bear looking into, so far back.

Mon. Ay, ay, ugh, ugh,—nothing but disappointments here below! I remark a considerable payment made to yourself on this Third of December. Talk of disappointments! There was a young fellow here, Jules, a foreign sculptor I did my utmost to advance, that the Church might be a gainer by us both: he was going on hopefully enough, and of a sudden he notifies to me some marvellous change that has happened in his notions of Art. Here's his letter,—'He never had a clearly conceived Ideal within his brain till to-day. Yet since his hand could manage a chisel, he has practised expressing other men's Ideals; and, in the very perfection he has attained to, he foresees an ultimate failure: his unconscious hand will pursue its prescribed course of old years, and will reproduce with a fatal expertness the ancient types, let the novel one appear never so palpably to his spirit. There is but one method of escape: confiding the virgin type to as chaste a hand, he will turn painter instead of sculptor, and paint, not carve, its characteristics,'—strike out, I dare say, a school like Correggio: how think you, Ugo?

Inten. Is Correggio a painter?

Mon. Foolish Jules! and yet, after all, why foolish? He may—probably will—fail egregiously; but if there should arise a new painter, will it not be in some such way, by a poet now, or a musician (spirits who have conceived and perfected an Ideal through some other channel), transferring it to this, and escaping our conventional roads by pure ignorance of them; eh, Ugo? If you have no appetite, talk at least, Ugo!

Inten. Sir, I can submit no longer to this course of yours. First, you select the group of which I formed one,— next you thin it gradually,—always retaining me with your smile,—and so do you proceed till you have fairly got me

alone with you between four stone walls. And now then?
Let this farce, this chatter end now: what is it you want
with me?

Mon. Ugo!

Inten. From the instant you arrived, I felt your smile
on me as you questioned me about this and the other
article in those papers—why your brother should have
given me this villa, that *podere*,—and your nod at the end
meant,—what?

Mon. Possibly that I wished for no loud talk here. If
once you set me coughing, Ugo!—

Inten. I have your brother's hand and seal to all I
possess: now ask me what for! what service I did him—
ask me!

Mon. I would better not: I should rip up old disgraces,
let out my poor brother's weaknesses. By the way, Maffeo
of Forli (which, I forgot to observe, is your true name),
was the interdict ever taken off you, for robbing that
church at Cesena?

Inten. No, nor needs be: for when I murdered your
brother's friend, Pasquale, for him . . .

Mon. Ah, he employed you in that business, did he?
Well, I must let you keep, as you say, this villa and that
podere, for fear the world should find out my relations
were of so indifferent a stamp? Maffeo, my family is the
oldest in Messina, and century after century have my pro-
genitors gone on polluting themselves with every wickedness under heaven: my own father . . . rest his soul!—I
have, I know, a chapel to support that it may rest: my
dear two dead brothers were,—what you know tolerably
well; I, the youngest, might have rivalled them in vice,
if not in wealth: but from my boyhood I came out from
among them, and so am not partaker of their plagues.
My glory springs from another source; or if from this,
by contrast only,—for I, the bishop, am the brother of
your employers, Ugo. I hope to repair some of their
wrong, however; so far as my brother's ill-gotten treasure
reverts to me, I can stop the consequences of his crime:
and not one *soldo* shall escape me. Maffeo, the sword we

quiet men spurn away, you shrewd knaves pick up and commit murders with; what opportunities the virtuous forego, the villanous seize. Because, to pleasure myself apart from other considerations, my food would be millet-cake, my dress sackcloth, and my couch straw,—am I therefore to let you, the offscouring of the earth, seduce the poor and ignorant by appropriating a pomp these will be sure to think lessens the abominations so unaccountably and exclusively associated with it? Must I let villas and *poderi* go to you, a murderer and thief, that you may beget by means of them other murderers and thieves? No—if my cough would but allow me to speak!

Inten. What am I to expect? You are going to punish me?

Mon. —Must punish you, Maffeo. I cannot afford to cast away a chance. I have whole centuries of sin to redeem, and only a month or two of life to do it in. How should I dare to say . . .

Inten. 'Forgive us our trespasses'?

Mon. My friend, it is because I avow myself a very worm, sinful beyond measure, that I reject a line of conduct you would applaud perhaps. Shall I proceed, as it were, a-pardoning?—I?—who have no symptom of reason to assume that aught less than my strenuousest efforts will keep myself out of mortal sin, much less keep others out. No: I do trespass, but will not double that by allowing you to trespass.

Inten. And suppose the villas are not your brother's to give, nor yours to take? Oh, you are hasty enough just now!

Mon. 1, 2—No 3!—ay, can you read the substance of a letter, No 3, I have received from Rome? It is precisely on the ground there mentioned, of the suspicion I have that a certain child of my late elder brother, who would have succeeded to his estates, was murdered in infancy by you, Maffeo, at the instigation of my late younger brother—that the Pontiff enjoins on me not merely the bringing that Maffeo to condign punishment, but the taking all pains, as guardian of the infant's heritage for the Church, to recover it parcel by parcel, howsoever, whensoever, and wheresoever. While you are now gnawing those fingers, the police are engaged in sealing up your papers, Maffeo, and the mere raising my voice brings my people from the next room to dispose of yourself. But I want you to confess quietly, and save me raising my voice. Why, man, do I not know the old story? The heir between the succeeding heir, and this heir's ruffianly instrument, and their complot's effect, and the life of fear and bribes and ominous smiling silence? Did you throttle or stab my brother's infant? Come now!

Inten. So old a story, and tell it no better? When did such an instrument ever produce such an effect? Either the child smiles in his face; or, most likely, he is not fool enough to put himself in the employer's power so thoroughly: the child is always ready to produce—as you say—howsoever, wheresoever, and whensoever.

Mon. Liar!

Inten. Strike me? Ah, so might a father chastise! I shall sleep soundly to-night at least, though the gallows await me to-morrow; for what a life did I lead! Carlo of Cesena reminds me of his connivance, every time I pay his annuity; which happens commonly thrice a year. If I remonstrate, he will confess all to the good bishop—you!

Mon. I see through the trick, caitiff! I would you spoke truth for once. All shall be sifted, however—seven times sifted.

Inten. And how my absurd riches encumbered me! I dared not lay claim to above half my possessions. Let me but once unbosom myself, glorify Heaven, and die!

Sir, you are no brutal dastardly idiot like your brother I frightened to death: let us understand one another. Sir, I will make away with her for you—the girl—here close at hand; not the stupid obvious kind of killing; do not speak—know nothing of her nor of me! I see her every day—saw her this morning: of course there is to be no killing; but at Rome the courtesans perish off every three years, and I can entice her thither—have indeed begun operations already. There's a certain lusty blue-eyed florid-complexioned English knave, I and the Police employ occasionally. You assent, I perceive—no, that's not it—assent I do not say—but you will let me convert my present havings and holdings into cash, and give me time to cross the Alps? 'Tis but a little black-eyed pretty singing Felippa, gay silk-winding girl. I have kept her out of harm's way up to this present; for I always intended to make your life a plague to you with her. 'Tis as well settled once and for ever. Some women I have procured will pass Bluphocks, my handsome scoundrel, off for somebody; and once Pippa entangled!—you conceive? Through her singing? Is it a bargain?

[*From without is heard the voice of* PIPPA, *singing*—

> *Overhead the tree-tops meet,*
> *Flowers and grass spring 'neath one's feet;*
> *There was nought above me, nought below,*
> *My childhood had not learned to know:*
> *For, what are the voices of birds*
> *—Ay, and of beasts,—but words, our words,*
> *Only so much more sweet?*
> *The knowledge of that with my life begun.*
> *But I had so near made out the sun,*
> *And counted your stars, the seven and one,*
> *Like the fingers of my hand:*
> *Nay, I could all but understand*
> *Wherefore through heaven the white moon ranges;*
> *And just when out of her soft fifty changes*
> *No unfamiliar face might overlook me—*
> *Suddenly God took me.*

[PIPPA *passes.*

Mon. [*springing up*]. My people—one and all—all—within there! Gag this villain—tie him hand and foot! He dares ... I know not half he dares—but remove him—quick! *Miserere mei, Domine!* Quick, I say!

SCENE. PIPPA'S *chamber again. She enters it.*

The bee with his comb,
The mouse at her dray,
The grub in his tomb,

Wile winter away;
But the fire-fly and hedge-shrew and lob-worm, I pray,
How fare they?
Ha, ha, thanks for your counsel, my Zanze!
'Feast upon lampreys, quaff Breganze'—
The summer of life so easy to spend,
And care for to-morrow so soon put away!
But winter hastens at summer's end,
And fire-fly, hedge-shrew, lob-worm, pray,
How fare they?
No bidding me then to . . . what did Zanze say?
'Pare your nails pearlwise, get your small feet shoes
'More like' . . . (what said she?)—'and less like canoes!'
How pert that girl was!—would I be those pert
Impudent staring women! It had done me,
However, surely no such mighty hurt
To learn his name who passed that jest upon me:
No foreigner, that I can recollect,
Came, as she says, a month since, to inspect
Our silk-mills—none with blue eyes and thick rings
Of raw-silk-coloured hair, at all events.
Well, if old Luca keep his good intents,
We shall do better, see what next year brings.
I may buy shoes, my Zanze, not appear
More destitute than you perhaps next year!
Bluph . . . something! I had caught the uncouth name
But for Monsignor's people's sudden clatter
Above us—bound to spoil such idle chatter
As ours: it were indeed a serious matter
If silly talk like ours should put to shame
The pious man, the man devoid of blame.
The . . . ah but—ah but, all the same,
No mere mortal has a right
To carry that exalted air;
Best people are not angels quite:
While—not the worst of people's doings scare
The devil; so there's that proud look to spare!
    Which is mere counsel to myself, mind! for
I have just been the holy Monsignor:

And I was you too, Luigi's gentle mother,
And you too, Luigi!—how that Luigi started
Out of the turret—doubtlessly departed
On some good errand or another,
For he passed just now in a traveller's trim,
And the sullen company that prowled
About his path, I noticed, scowled
As if they had lost a prey in him.
And I was Jules the sculptor's bride,
And I was Ottima beside,
And now what am I?—tired of fooling.
Day for folly, night for schooling!
New Year's day is over and spent,
Ill or well, I must be content.
    Even my lily's asleep, I vow:
Wake up—here's a friend I've plucked you:
Call this flower a heart's-ease now!
Something rare, let me instruct you,
Is this, with petals triply swollen,
Three times spotted, thrice the pollen;
While the leaves and parts that witness
Old proportions and their fitness,
Here remain unchanged, unmoved now;
Call this pampered thing improved now!
Suppose there's a king of the flowers
And a girl-show held in his bowers—
'Look ye, buds, this growth of ours,'
Says he, 'Zanze from the Brenta,
'I have made her gorge polenta
'Till both cheeks are near as bouncing
'As her . . . name there's no pronouncing!
'See this heightened colour too,
'For she swilled Breganze wine
'Till her nose turned deep carmine;
''Twas but white when wild she grew.
'And only by this Zanze's eyes
'Of which we could not change the size,
'The magnitude of all achieved
'Otherwise, may be perceived.'

Oh what a drear dark close to my poor day!
How could that red sun drop in that black cloud?
Ah Pippa, morning's rule is moved away,
Dispensed with, never more to be allowed!
Day's turn is over, now arrives the night's.
Oh lark, be day's apostle
To mavis, merle and throstle,
Bid them their betters jostle
From day and its delights!
But at night, brother howlet, over the woods,
Toll the world to thy chantry;
Sing to the bats' sleek sisterhoods
Full complines with gallantry:
Then, owls and bats,
Cowls and twats,
Monks and nuns, in a cloister's moods,
Adjourn to the oak-stump pantry!

                    [*After she has begun to undress herself.*

Now, one thing I should like to really know:
How near I ever might approach all these
I only fancied being, this long day:
—Approach, I mean, so as to touch them, so
As to . . . in some way . . . move them—if you please,
Do good or evil to them some slight way.
For instance, if I wind
Silk to-morrow, my silk may bind

                              [*Sitting on the bedside.*

And border Ottima's cloak's hem.
Ah me, and my important part with them,
This morning's hymn half promised when I rose!
True in some sense or other, I suppose.

                              [*As she lies down.*

God bless me! I can pray no more to-night.
No doubt, some way or other, hymns say right.

> *All service ranks the same with God—*
> *With God, whose puppets, best and worst,*
> *Are we: there is no last nor first.*

                              [*She sleeps.*

DRAMATIC LYRICS

CAVALIER TUNES

I

MARCHING ALONG

I

KENTISH Sir Byng stood for his King,
Bidding the crop-headed Parliament swing:
And, pressing a troop unable to stoop
And see the rogues flourish and honest folk droop,
Marched them along, fifty-score strong,
Great-hearted gentlemen, singing this song.

II

God for King Charles! Pym and such carles
To the Devil that prompts 'em their treasonous parles!
Cavaliers, up! Lips from the cup,
Hands from the pasty, nor bite take nor sup
Till you're—

CHORUS. *Marching along, fifty-score strong,*
Great-hearted gentlemen, singing this song.

III

Hampden to hell, and his obsequies' knell
Serve Hazelrig, Fiennes, and young Harry as well!
England, good cheer! Rupert is near!
Kentish and loyalists, keep we not here

CHORUS. *Marching along, fifty-score strong,*
Great-hearted gentlemen, singing this song?

IV

Then, God for King Charles! Pym and his snarls
To the Devil that pricks on such pestilent carles!
Hold by the right, you double your might;
So, onward to Nottingham, fresh for the fight,

CHORUS. *March we along, fifty-score strong,*
Great-hearted gentlemen, singing this song!

II

GIVE A ROUSE

I

King Charles, and who'll do him right now?
King Charles, and who's ripe for fight now?
Give a rouse: here's, in hell's despite now,
King Charles!

II

Who gave me the goods that went since?
Who raised me the house that sank once?
Who helped me to gold I spent since?
Who found me in wine you drank once?

CHORUS. *King Charles, and who'll do him right now?*
King Charles, and who's ripe for fight now?
Give a rouse: here's, in hell's despite now,
King Charles!

III

To whom used my boy George quaff else,
By the old fool's side that begot him?
For whom did he cheer and laugh else,
While Noll's damned troopers shot him?

CHORUS. *King Charles, and who'll do him right now?*
King Charles, and who's ripe for fight now?
Give a rouse: here's, in hell's despite now,
King Charles!

III

BOOT AND SADDLE

I

Boot, saddle, to horse, and away!
Rescue my castle before the hot day
Brightens to blue from its silvery grey,

> CHORUS. *Boot, saddle, to horse, and away!*

II

Ride past the suburbs, asleep as you'd say;
Many's the friend there, will listen and pray
'God's luck to gallants that strike up the lay—

> CHORUS. *'Boot, saddle, to horse, and away!'*

III

Forty miles off, like a roebuck at bay,
Flouts Castle Brancepeth the Roundheads' array:
Who laughs, 'Good fellows ere this, by my fay,

> CHORUS. *'Boot, saddle, to horse, and away!'*

IV

Who? My wife Gertrude; that, honest and gay,
Laughs when you talk of surrendering, 'Nay!
'I've better counsellors; what counsel they?

> CHORUS. *'Boot, saddle, to horse, and away!'*

THE LOST LEADER

I

JUST for a handful of silver he left us,
    Just for a riband to stick in his coat—
Found the one gift of which fortune bereft us,
    Lost all the others she lets us devote;
They, with the gold to give, doled him out silver,
    So much was theirs who so little allowed:
How all our copper had gone for his service!
    Rags—were they purple, his heart had been proud!

We that had loved him so, followed him, honoured him,
     Lived in his mild and magnificent eye,
Learned his great language, caught his clear accents,
     Made him our pattern to live and to die!
Shakespeare was of us, Milton was for us,
     Burns, Shelley, were with us,—they watch from their
         graves!
He alone breaks from the van and the freemen,
     —He alone sinks to the rear and the slaves!

II

We shall march prospering,—not thro' his presence;
     Songs may inspirit us,—not from his lyre;
Deeds will be done,—while he boasts his quiescence,
     Still bidding crouch whom the rest bade aspire:
Blot out his name, then, record one lost soul more,
     One task more declined, one more foot-path untrod,
One more devils'-triumph and sorrow for angels,
     One wrong more to man, one more insult to God!
Life's night begins: let him never come back to us!
     There would be doubt, hesitation and pain,
Forced praise on our part—the glimmer of twilight,
     Never glad confident morning again!
Best fight on well, for we taught him—strike gallantly,
     Menace our heart ere we master his own;
Then let him receive the new knowledge and wait us,
     Pardoned in heaven, the first by the throne!

'HOW THEY BROUGHT THE GOOD NEWS FROM GHENT TO AIX'

[16—]

I

I sprang to the stirrup, and Joris, and he;
I galloped, Dirck galloped, we galloped all three;
'Good speed!' cried the watch, as the gate-bolts undrew;
'Speed!' echoed the wall to us galloping through;
Behind shut the postern, the lights sank to rest,
And into the midnight we galloped abreast.

II

Not a word to each other; we kept the great pace
Neck by neck, stride by stride, never changing our place;
I turned in my saddle and made its girths tight,
Then shortened each stirrup, and set the pique right,
Rebuckled the cheek-strap, chained slacker the bit,
Nor galloped less steadily Roland a whit.

III

'Twas moonset at starting; but while we drew near
Lokeren, the cocks crew and twilight dawned clear;
At Boom, a great yellow star came out to see;
At Düffeld, 'twas morning as plain as could be;
And from Mecheln church-steeple we heard the half-
chime,
So, Joris broke silence with, 'Yet there is time!'

IV

At Aershot, up leaped of a sudden the sun,
And against him the cattle stood black every one,
To stare thro' the mist at us galloping past,
And I saw my stout galloper Roland at last,
With resolute shoulders, each butting away
The haze, as some bluff river headland its spray:

V

And his low head and crest, just one sharp ear bent back
For my voice, and the other pricked out on his track;
And one eye's black intelligence,—ever that glance
O'er its white edge at me, his own master, askance!
And the thick heavy spume-flakes which aye and anon
His fierce lips shook upwards in galloping on.

VI

By Hasselt, Dirck groaned; and cried Joris, 'Stay spur!
'Your Roos galloped bravely, the fault's not in her,
'We'll remember at Aix'—for one heard the quick wheeze
Of her chest, saw the stretched neck and staggering knees,
And sunk tail, and horrible heave of the flank,
As down on her haunches she shuddered and sank.

VII

So, we were left galloping, Joris and I,
Past Looz and past Tongres, no cloud in the sky;
The broad sun above laughed a pitiless laugh,
'Neath our feet broke the brittle bright stubble like chaff;
Till over by Dalhem a dome-spire sprang white,
And 'Gallop,' gasped Joris, 'for Aix is in sight!'

VIII

'How they'll greet us!'—and all in a moment his roan
Rolled neck and croup over, lay dead as a stone;
And there was my Roland to bear the whole weight
Of the news which alone could save Aix from her fate,
With his nostrils like pits full of blood to the brim,
And with circles of red for his eye-sockets' rim.

IX

Then I cast loose my buffcoat, each holster let fall,
Shook off both my jack-boots, let go belt and all,
Stood up in the stirrup, leaned, patted his ear,
Called my Roland his pet-name, my horse without peer;
Clapped my hands, laughed and sang, any noise, bad or good,
Till at length into Aix Roland galloped and stood.

X

And all I remember is—friends flocking round
As I sat with his head 'twixt my knees on the ground;
And no voice but was praising this Roland of mine,
As I poured down his throat our last measure of wine,
Which (the burgesses voted by common consent)
Was no more than his due who brought good news from Ghent.

THROUGH THE METIDJA TO
ABD-EL-KADR

I

As I ride, as I ride,
With a full heart for my guide,
So its tide rocks my side,
As I ride, as I ride,
That, as I were double-eyed,
He, in whom our Tribes confide,
Is descried, ways untried
As I ride, as I ride.

II

As I ride, as I ride
To our Chief and his Allied,
Who dares chide my heart's pride
As I ride, as I ride?
Or are witnesses denied—
Through the desert waste and wide
Do I glide unespied
As I ride, as I ride?

III

As I ride, as I ride,
When an inner voice has cried,
The sands slide, nor abide
(As I ride, as I ride)
O'er each visioned homicide
That came vaunting (has he lied?)
To reside—where he died,
As I ride, as I ride.

IV

As I ride, as I ride,
Ne'er has spur my swift horse plied,
Yet his hide, streaked and pied,
As I ride, as I ride,

Shows where sweat has sprung and dried,
—Zebra-footed, ostrich-thighed—
How has vied stride with stride
As I ride, as I ride!

v

As I ride, as I ride,
Could I loose what Fate has tied,
Ere I pried, she should hide
(As I ride, as I ride)
All that's meant me—satisfied
When the Prophet and the Bride
Stops veins I'd have subside
As I ride, as I ride!

NATIONALITY IN DRINKS

I

My heart sank with our Claret-flask,
    Just now, beneath the heavy sedges
That serve this pond's black face for mask;
    And still at yonder broken edges
O' the hole, where up the bubbles glisten,
After my heart I look and listen.

II

Our laughing little flask, compelled
    Thro' depth to depth more bleak and shady;
As when, both arms beside her held,
    Feet straightened out, some gay French lady
Is caught up from life's light and motion,
And dropped into death's silent ocean!

———————

Up jumped Tokay on our table,
Like a pygmy castle-warder,
Dwarfish to see, but stout and able,
Arms and accoutrements all in order;
And fierce he looked North, then, wheeling South,
Blew with his bugle a challenge to Drouth,

Cocked his flap-hat with the tosspot-feather,
Twisted his thumb in his red moustache,
Jingled his huge brass spurs together,
Tightened his waist with its Buda sash,
And then, with an impudence nought could abash,
Shrugged his hump-shoulder, to tell the beholder,
For twenty such knaves he should laugh but the bolder:
And so, with his sword-hilt gallantly jutting,
And dexter-hand on his haunch abutting,
Went the little man, Sir Ausbruch, strutting!

Here's to Nelson's memory!
'Tis the second time that I, at sea,
Right off Cape Trafalgar here,
Have drunk it deep in British Beer.
Nelson for ever—any time
Am I his to command in prose or rhyme!
Give me of Nelson only a touch,
And I save it, be it little or much:
Here's one our Captain gives, and so
Down at the word, by George, shall it go!
He says that at Greenwich they point the beholder
To Nelson's coat, 'still with tar on the shoulder:
'For he used to lean with one shoulder digging,
'Jigging, as it were, and zig-zag-zigging
'Up against the mizen-rigging!'

GARDEN FANCIES

I

THE FLOWER'S NAME

I

HERE'S the garden she walked across,
    Arm in my arm, such a short while since:
Hark, now I push its wicket, the moss
    Hinders the hinges and makes them wince!

She must have reached this shrub ere she turned,
  As back with that murmur the wicket swung;
For she laid the poor snail, my chance foot spurned,
  To feed and forget it the leaves among.

II

Down this side of the gravel-walk
  She went while her robe's edge brushed the box:
And here she paused in her gracious talk
  To point me a moth on the milk-white phlox.
Roses, ranged in valiant row,
  I will never think that she passed you by!
She loves you noble roses, I know;
  But yonder, see, where the rock-plants lie!

III

This flower she stopped at, finger on lip,
  Stooped over, in doubt, as settling its claim;
Till she gave me, with pride to make no slip,
  Its soft meandering Spanish name:
What a name! Was it love or praise?
  Speech half-asleep or song half-awake?
I must learn Spanish, one of these days,
  Only for that slow sweet name's sake.

IV

Roses, if I live and do well,
  I may bring her, one of these days,
To fix you fast with as fine a spell,
  Fit you each with his Spanish phrase;
But do not detain me now; for she lingers
  There, like sunshine over the ground,
And ever I see her soft white fingers
  Searching after the bud she found.

V

Flower, you Spaniard, look that you grow not,
  Stay as you are and be loved for ever!
Bud, if I kiss you 'tis that you blow not:
  Mind, the shut pink mouth opens never!

VII

How did he like it when the live creatures
    Tickled and toused and browsed him all over,
And worm, slug, eft, with serious features,
    Came in, each one, for his right of trover?
—When the water-beetle with great blind deaf face
    Made of her eggs the stately deposit,
And the newt borrowed just so much of the preface
    As tiled in the top of his black wife's closet?

VIII

All that life and fun and romping,
    All that frisking and twisting and coupling,
While slowly our poor friend's leaves were swamping
    And clasps were cracking and covers suppling!
As if you had carried sour John Knox
    To the play-house at Paris, Vienna or Munich,
Fastened him into a front-row box,
    And danced off the ballet with trousers and tunic.

IX

Come, old martyr! What, torment enough is it?
    Back to my room shall you take your sweet self.
Good-bye, mother-beetle; husband-eft, *suffict!*
    See the snug niche I have made on my shelf!
A.'s book shall prop you up, B.'s shall cover you,
    Here's C. to be grave with, or D. to be gay,
And with E. on each side, and F. right over you,
    Dry-rot at ease till the Judgment-day!

SOLILOQUY OF THE SPANISH
CLOISTER

I

GR-R-R—there go, my heart's abhorrence!
    Water your damned flower-pots, do!
If hate killed men, Brother Lawrence,
    God's blood, would not mine kill you!

What? your myrtle-bush wants trimming?
  Oh, that rose has prior claims—
Needs its leaden vase filled brimming?
  Hell dry you up with its flames!

II

At the meal we sit together:
  Salve tibi! I must hear
Wise talk of the kind of weather,
  Sort of season, time of year:
Not a plenteous cork-crop: scarcely
  Dare we hope oak-galls, I doubt:
What's the Latin name for 'parsley'?
  What's the Greek name for Swine's Snout?

III

Whew! We'll have our platter burnished,
  Laid with care on our own shelf!
With a fire-new spoon we're furnished,
  And a goblet for ourself,
Rinsed like something sacrificial
  Ere 'tis fit to touch our chaps—
Marked with L. for our initial!
  (He-he! There his lily snaps!)

IV

Saint, forsooth! While brown Dolores
  Squats outside the Convent bank
With Sanchicha, telling stories,
  Steeping tresses in the tank,
Blue-black, lustrous, thick like horsehairs,
  —Can't I see his dead eye glow,
Bright as 'twere a Barbary corsair's?
  (That is, if he'd let it show!)

V

When he finishes refection,
  Knife and fork he never lays
Cross-wise, to my recollection,
  As do I, in Jesu's praise.

I the Trinity illustrate,
   Drinking watered orange-pulp—
In three sips the Arian frustrate;
   While he drains his at one gulp.

VI

Oh, those melons? If he's able
   We're to have a feast! so nice!
One goes to the Abbot's table,
   All of us get each a slice.
How go on your flowers? None double?
   Not one fruit-sort can you spy?
Strange!—And I, too, at such trouble,
   Keep them close-nipped on the sly!

VII

There's a great text in Galatians,
   Once you trip on it, entails
Twenty-nine distinct damnations,
   One sure, if another fails:
If I trip him just a-dying,
   Sure of heaven as sure can be,
Spin him round and send him flying
   Off to hell, a Manichee?

VIII

Or, my scrofulous French novel
   On grey paper with blunt type!
Simply glance at it, you grovel
   Hand and foot in Belial's gripe:
If I double down its pages
   At the woeful sixteenth print,
When he gathers his greengages,
   Ope a sieve and slip it in't?

IX

Or, there's Satan!—one might venture
   Pledge one's soul to him, yet leave
Such a flaw in the indenture
   As he'd miss till, past retrieve,

Blasted lay that rose-acacia
    We're so proud of! *Hy, Zy, Hine* . . .
'St, there's Vespers! *Plena gratiâ*
    Ave, Virgo! Gr-r-r—you swine!

THE LABORATORY

ANCIEN RÉGIME

I

Now that I, tying thy glass mask tightly,
May gaze thro' these faint smokes curling whitely,
As thou pliest thy trade in this devil's-smithy—
Which is the poison to poison her, prithee?

II

He is with her, and they know that I know
Where they are, what they do: they believe my tears flow
While they laugh, laugh at me, at me fled to the drear
Empty church, to pray God in, for them!—I am here.

III

Grind away, moisten and mash up thy paste,
Pound at thy powder,—I am not in haste!
Better sit thus, and observe thy strange things,
Than go where men wait me and dance at the King's.

IV

That in the mortar—you call it a gum?
Ah, the brave tree whence such gold oozings come!
And yonder soft phial, the exquisite blue,
Sure to taste sweetly,—is that poison too?

V

Had I but all of them, thee and thy treasures,
What a wild crowd of invisible pleasures!
To carry pure death in an earring, a casket,
A signet, a fan-mount, a filigree basket!

VI

Soon, at the King's, a mere lozenge to give,
And Pauline should have just thirty minutes to live!
But to light a pastile, and Elise, with her head
And her breast and her arms and her hands, should drop
    dead!

VII

Quick—is it finished? The colour's too grim!
Why not soft like the phial's, enticing and dim?
Let it brighten her drink, let her turn it and stir,
And try it and taste, ere she fix and prefer!

VIII

What a drop! She's not little, no minion like me!
That's why she ensnared him: this never will free
The soul from those masculine eyes,—say, 'no!'
To that pulse's magnificent come-and-go.

IX

For only last night, as they whispered, I brought
My own eyes to bear on her so, that I thought
Could I keep them one half minute fixed, she would fall
Shrivelled; she fell not; yet this does it all!

X

Not that I bid you spare her the pain;
Let death be felt and the proof remain:
Brand, burn up, bite into its grace—
He is sure to remember her dying face!

XI

Is it done? Take my mask off! Nay, be not morose;
It kills her, and this prevents seeing it close:
The delicate droplet, my whole fortune's fee!
If it hurts her, beside, can it ever hurt me?

XII

Now, take all my jewels, gorge gold to your fill,
You may kiss me, old man, on my mouth if you will!
But brush this dust off me, lest horror it brings
Ere I know it—next moment I dance at the King's!

THE CONFESSIONAL

[SPAIN]

I

It is a lie—their Priests, their Pope,
Their Saints, their . . . all they fear or hope
Are lies, and lies—there! through my door
And ceiling, there! and walls and floor,
There, lies, they lie—shall still be hurled
Till spite of them I reach the world!

II

You think Priests just and holy men!
Before they put me in this den
I was a human creature too,
With flesh and blood like one of you,
A girl that laughed in beauty's pride
Like lilies in your world outside.

III

I had a lover—shame avaunt!
This poor wrenched body, grim and gaunt,
Was kissed all over till it burned,
By lips the truest, love e'er turned
His heart's own tint: one night they kissed
My soul out in a burning mist.

IV

So, next day when the accustomed train
Of things grew round my sense again,
'That is a sin,' I said: and slow
With downcast eyes to church I go,
And pass to the confession-chair,
And tell the old mild father there.

V

But when I falter Beltran's name,
'Ha?' quoth the father; 'much I blame

'The sin; yet wherefore idly grieve?
'Despair not—strenuously retrieve!
'Nay, I will turn this love of thine
'To lawful love, almost divine;

VI

'For he is young, and led astray,
'This Beltran, and he schemes, men say,
'To change the laws of church and state,
'So, thine shall be an angel's fate,
'Who, ere the thunder breaks, should roll
'Its cloud away and save his soul.

VII

'For, when he lies upon thy breast,
'Thou mayst demand and be possessed
'Of all his plans, and next day steal
'To me, and all those plans reveal,
'That I and every priest, to purge
'His soul, may fast and use the scourge.'

VIII

That father's beard was long and white,
With love and truth his brow seemed bright;
I went back, all on fire with joy,
And, that same evening, bade the boy
Tell me, as lovers should, heart-free,
Something to prove his love of me.

IX

He told me what he would not tell
For hope of heaven or fear of hell;
And I lay listening in such pride!
And, soon as he had left my side,
Tripped to the church by morning-light
To save his soul in his despite.

X

I told the father all his schemes,
Who were his comrades, what their dreams;

'And now make haste,' I said, 'to pray
'The one spot from his soul away;
'To-night he comes, but not the same
'Will look!' At night he never came.

XI

Nor next night: on the after-morn,
I went forth with a strength new-born.
The church was empty; something drew
My steps into the street; I knew
It led me to the market-place:
Where, lo, on high, the father's face!

XII

That horrible black scaffold dressed,
That stapled block . . . God sink the rest!
That head strapped back, that blinding vest,
Those knotted hands and naked breast,
Till near one busy hangman pressed,
And, on the neck these arms caressed . . .

XIII

No part in aught they hope or fear!
No heaven with them, no hell!—and here,
No earth, not so much space as pens
My body in their worst of dens
But shall bear God and man my cry,
Lies—lies, again—and still, they lie!

CRISTINA

I

SHE should never have looked at me
    If she meant I should not love her!
There are plenty . . . men, you call such,
    I suppose . . . she may discover
All her soul to, if she pleases,
    And yet leave much as she found them:
But I'm not so, and she knew it
    When she fixed me, glancing round them.

II

What? To fix me thus meant nothing?
  But I can't tell (there's my weakness)
What her look said!—no vile cant, sure,
  About 'need to strew the bleakness
'Of some lone shore with its pearl-seed.
  'That the sea feels'—no 'strange yearning
'That such souls have, most to lavish
  'Where there's chance of least returning.'

III

Oh, we're sunk enough here, God knows!
  But not quite so sunk that moments,
Sure tho' seldom, are denied us,
  When the spirit's true endowments
Stand out plainly from its false ones,
  And apprise it if pursuing
Or the right way or the wrong way,
  To its triumph or undoing.

IV

There are flashes struck from midnights,
  There are fire-flames noondays kindle,
Whereby piled-up honours perish,
  Whereby swollen ambitions dwindle,
While just this or that poor impulse,
  Which for once had play unstifled,
Seems the sole work of a life-time
  That away the rest have trifled.

V

Doubt you if, in some such moment,
  As she fixed me, she felt clearly,
Ages past the soul existed,
  Here an age 'tis resting merely,
And hence fleets again for ages,
  While the true end, sole and single,
It stops here for is, this love-way,
  With some other soul to mingle?

VI

Else it loses what it lived for,
   And eternally must lose it;
Better ends may be in prospect,
   Deeper blisses (if you choose it),
But this life's end and this love-bliss
   Have been lost here. Doubt you whether
This she felt as, looking at me,
   Mine and her souls rushed together?

VII

Oh, observe! Of course, next moment,
   The world's honours, in derision,
Trampled out the light for ever:
   Never fear but there's provision
Of the devil's to quench knowledge
   Lest we walk the earth in rapture!
—Making those who catch God's secret
   Just so much more prize their capture!

VIII

Such am I: the secret's mine now!
   She has lost me, I have gained her;
Her soul's mine: and thus, grown perfect,
   I shall pass my life's remainder.
Life will just hold out the proving
   Both our powers, alone and blended:
And then, come next life quickly!
   This world's use will have been ended.

THE LOST MISTRESS

I

ALL's over, then: does truth sound bitter
   As one at first believes?
Hark, 'tis the sparrows' good-night twitter
   About your cottage eaves!

II

And the leaf-buds on the vine are woolly,
    I noticed that, to-day;
One day more bursts them open fully
    —You know the red turns grey.

III

To-morrow we meet the same then, dearest?
    May I take your hand in mine?
Mere friends are we,—well, friends the merest
    Keep much that I resign:

IV

For each glance of the eye so bright and black,
    Though I keep with heart's endeavour,—
Your voice, when you wish the snowdrops back,
    Though it stay in my soul for ever!—

V

Yet I will but say what mere friends say,
    Or only a thought stronger;
I will hold your hand but as long as all may,
    Or so very little longer!

EARTH'S IMMORTALITIES

FAME

SEE, as the prettiest graves will do in time,
Our poet's wants the freshness of its prime;
Spite of the sexton's browsing horse, the sods
Have struggled through its binding osier rods;
Headstone and half-sunk footstone lean awry,
Wanting the brick-work promised by-and-by;
How the minute grey lichens, plate o'er plate,
Have softened down the crisp-cut name and date!

LOVE

So, the year 's done with!
    (*Love me for ever!*)
All March begun with,
    April's endeavour;

May-wreaths that bound me
June needs must sever;
Now snows fall round me,
Quenching June's fever—
(*Love me for ever!*)

MEETING AT NIGHT

I

THE grey sea and the long black land;
And the yellow half-moon large and low;
And the startled little waves that leap
In fiery ringlets from their sleep,
As I gain the cove with pushing prow,
And quench its speed i' the slushy sand.

II

Then a mile of warm sea-scented beach;
Three fields to cross till a farm appears;
A tap at the pane, the quick sharp scratch
And blue spurt of a lighted match,
And a voice less loud, thro' its joys and fears,
Than the two hearts beating each to each!

PARTING AT MORNING

ROUND the cape of a sudden came the sea,
And the sun looked over the mountain's rim:
And straight was a path of gold for him,
And the need of a world of men for me.

SONG

I

NAY but you, who do not love her,
  Is she not pure gold, my mistress?
Holds earth aught—speak truth—above her?
  Aught like this tress, see, and this tress,
And this last fairest tress of all,
So fair, see, ere I let it fall?

II

Because, you spend your lives in praising;
   To praise, you search the wide world over:
Then why not witness, calmly gazing,
   If earth holds aught—speak truth—above her?
Above this tress, and this, I touch
But cannot praise, I love so much!

A WOMAN'S LAST WORD

I

LET's contend no more, Love,
   Strive nor weep:
All be as before, Love,
   —Only sleep!

II

What so wild as words are?
   I and thou
In debate, as birds are,
   Hawk on bough!

III

See the creature stalking
   While we speak!
Hush and hide the talking,
   Cheek on cheek!

IV

What so false as truth is,
   False to thee?
Where the serpent's tooth is
   Shun the tree—

V

Where the apple reddens
   Never pry—
Lest we lose our Edens,
   Eve and I.

VI

Be a god and hold me
   With a charm!
Be a man and fold me
   With thine arm!

VII

Teach me, only teach, Love!
   As I ought
I will speak thy speech, Love,
   Think thy thought—

VIII

Meet, if thou require it,
   Both demands,
Laying flesh and spirit
   In thy hands.

IX

That shall be to-morrow
   Not to-night:
I must bury sorrow
   Out of sight:

X

—Must a little weep, Love,
   (Foolish me!)
And so fall asleep, Love,
   Loved by thee.

EVELYN HOPE

I

BEAUTIFUL Evelyn Hope is dead!
   Sit and watch by her side an hour.
That is her book-shelf, this her bed;
   She plucked that piece of geranium-flower,
Beginning to die too, in the glass;
   Little has yet been changed, I think:
The shutters are shut, no light may pass
   Save two long rays thro' the hinge's chink.

II

Sixteen years old when she died!
   Perhaps she had scarcely heard my name;
It was not her time to love; beside,
   Her life had many a hope and aim,
Duties enough and little cares,
   And now was quiet, now astir,
Till God's hand beckoned unawares,—
   And the sweet white brow is all of her.

III

Is it too late then, Evelyn Hope?
   What, your soul was pure and true,
The good stars met in your horoscope,
   Made you of spirit, fire and dew—
And, just because I was thrice as old
   And our paths in the world diverged so wide,
Each was nought to each, must I be told?
   We were fellow mortals, nought beside?

IV

No, indeed! for God above
   Is great to grant, as mighty to make,
And creates the love to reward the love:
   I claim you still, for my own love's sake!
Delayed it may be for more lives yet,
   Through worlds I shall traverse, not a few:
Much is to learn, much to forget
   Ere the time be come for taking you.

V

But the time will come,—at last it will,
   When, Evelyn Hope, what meant (I shall say)
In the lower earth, in the years long still,
   That body and soul so pure and gay?
Why your hair was amber, I shall divine,
   And your mouth of your own geranium's red—
And what you would do with me, in fine,
   In the new life come in the old one's stead.

VI

I have lived (I shall say) so much since then,
   Given up myself so many times,
Gained me the gains of various men,
   Ransacked the ages, spoiled the climes;
Yet one thing, one, in my soul's full scope,
   Either I missed or itself missed me:
And I want and find you, Evelyn Hope!
   What is the issue? let us see!

VII

I loved you, Evelyn, all the while.
   My heart seemed full as it could hold?
There was place and to spare for the frank young smile,
   And the red young mouth, and the hair's young gold.
So, hush,—I will give you this leaf to keep:
   See, I shut it inside the sweet cold hand!
There, that is our secret: go to sleep!
   You will wake, and remember, and understand.

LOVE AMONG THE RUINS

I

WHERE the quiet-coloured end of evening smiles,
          Miles and miles
On the solitary pastures where our sheep
          Half-asleep
Tinkle homeward thro' the twilight, stray or stop
          As they crop—
Was the site of a city great and gay,
          (So they say)
Of our country's very capital, its prince
          Ages since
Held his court in, gathered councils, wielding far
          Peace or war.

II

Now,—the country does not even boast a tree,
  As you see,
To distinguish slopes of verdure, certain rills
  From the hills
Intersect and give a name to, (else they run
  Into one)
Where the domed and daring palace shot its spires
  Up like fires
O'er the hundred-gated circuit of a wall
  Bounding all,
Made of marble, men might march on nor be pressed,
  Twelve abreast.

III

And such plenty and perfection, see, of grass
  Never was!
Such a carpet as, this summer-time, o'erspreads
  And embeds
Every vestige of the city, guessed alone,
  Stock or stone—
Where a multitude of men breathed joy and woe
  Long ago;
Lust of glory pricked their hearts up, dread of shame
  Struck them tame;
And that glory and that shame alike, the gold
  Bought and sold.

IV

Now,—the single little turret that remains
  On the plains,
By the caper overrooted, by the gourd
  Overscored,
While the patching houseleek's head of blossom winks
  Through the chinks—
Marks the basement whence a tower in ancient time
  Sprang sublime,

And a burning ring, all round, the chariots traced
          As they raced,
And the monarch and his minions and his dames
          Viewed the games.

V

And I know, while thus the quiet-coloured eve
          Smiles to leave
To their folding, all our many-tinkling fleece
          In such peace,
And the slopes and rills in undistinguished grey
          Melt away—
That a girl with eager eyes and yellow hair
          Waits me there
In the turret whence the charioteers caught soul
          For the goal,
When the king looked, where she looks now, breathless,
          dumb
          Till I come.

VI

But he looked upon the city, every side,
          Far and wide,
All the mountains topped with temples, all the glades'
          Colonnades,
All the causeys, bridges, aqueducts,—and then,
          All the men!
When I do come, she will speak not, she will stand,
          Either hand
On my shoulder, give her eyes the first embrace
          Of my face,
Ere we rush, ere we extinguish sight and speech
          Each on each.

VII

In one year they sent a million fighters forth
          South and North,
And they built their gods a brazen pillar high
          As the sky,

Yet reserved a thousand chariots in full force—
      Gold, of course.
Oh heart! oh blood that freezes, blood that burns!
      Earth's returns
For whole centuries of folly, noise and sin!
      Shut them in,
With their triumphs and their glories and the rest!
      Love is best.

A LOVERS' QUARREL

I

Oh, what a dawn of day!
How the March sun feels like May!
    All is blue again
    After last night's rain,
And the South dries the hawthorn-spray.
    Only, my Love's away!
I'd as lief that the blue were grey!

II

Runnels, which rillets swell,
Must be dancing down the dell,
    With a foaming head
    On the beryl bed
Paven smooth as a hermit's cell;
    Each with a tale to tell,
Could my Love but attend as well.

III

Dearest, three months ago!
When we lived blocked-up with snow,
    When the wind would edge
    In and in his wedge,
In, as far as the point could go—
    Not to our ingle, though,
Where we loved each the other so!

IV

Laughs with so little cause!
We devised games out of straws.
　　　We would try and trace
　　　One another's face
In the ash, as an artist draws;
　　　Free on each other's flaws,
How we chattered like two church daws!

V

What's in the 'Times'?—a scold
At the Emperor deep and cold;
　　　He has taken a bride
　　　To his gruesome side,
That's as fair as himself is bold:
　　　There they sit ermine-stoled,
And she powders her hair with gold.

VI

Fancy the Pampas' sheen!
Miles and miles of gold and green
　　　Where the sunflowers blow
　　　In a solid glow,
And—to break now and then the screen—
　　　Black neck and eyeballs keen,
Up a wild horse leaps between!

VII

Try, will our table turn?
Lay your hands there light, and yearn
　　　Till the yearning slips
　　　Thro' the finger-tips
In a fire which a few discern,
　　　And a very few feel burn,
And the rest, they may live and learn!

VIII

Then we would up and pace,
For a change, about the place,
　　　Each with arm o'er neck:
　　　'Tis our quarter-deck,

We are seamen in woeful case.
    Help in the ocean-space!
Or, if no help, we'll embrace.

IX

See, how she looks now, dressed
In a sledging-cap and vest!
    'Tis a huge fur cloak—
    Like a reindeer's yoke
Falls the lappet along the breast:
    Sleeves for her arms to rest,
Or to hang, as my Love likes best.

X

Teach me to flirt a fan
As the Spanish ladies can,
    Or I tint your lip
    With a burnt stick's tip
And you turn into such a man!
    Just the two spots that span
Half the bill of the young male swan.

XI

Dearest, three months ago
When the mesmerizer Snow
    With his hand's first sweep
    Put the earth to sleep:
'Twas a time when the heart could show
    All—how was earth to know,
'Neath the mute hand's to-and-fro?

XII

Dearest, three months ago
When we loved each other so,
    Lived and loved the same
    Till an evening came
When a shaft from the devil's bow
    Pierced to our ingle-glow,
And the friends were friend and foe!

XIII

Not from the heart beneath—
'Twas a bubble born of breath,
    Neither sneer nor vaunt,
    Nor reproach nor taunt.
See a word, how it severeth!
    Oh, power of life and death
In the tongue, as the Preacher saith!

XIV

Woman, and will you cast
For a word, quite off at last
    Me, your own, your You,—
    Since, as truth is true,
I was You all the happy past—
    Me do you leave aghast
With the memories We amassed?

XV

Love, if you knew the light
That your soul casts in my sight,
    How I look to you
    For the pure and true
And the beauteous and the right,—
    Bear with a moment's spite
When a mere mote threats the white!

XVI

What of a hasty word?
Is the fleshly heart not stirred
    By a worm's pin-prick
    Where its roots are quick?
See the eye, by a fly's foot blurred—
    Ear, when a straw is heard
Scratch the brain's coat of curd!

XVII

Foul be the world or fair
More or less, how can I care?
    'Tis the world the same
    For my praise or blame,

And endurance is easy there.
    Wrong in the one thing rare—
Oh, it is hard to bear!

XVIII

Here's the spring back or close,
When the almond-blossom blows:
    We shall have the word
    In a minor third
There is none but the cuckoo knows:
    Heaps of the guelder-rose!
I must bear with it, I suppose.

XIX

Could but November come,
Were the noisy birds struck dumb
    At the warning slash
    Of his driver's-lash—
I would laugh like the valiant Thumb
    Facing the castle glum
And the giant's fee-faw-fum!

XX

Then, were the world well stripped
Of the gear wherein equipped
    We can stand apart,
    Heart dispense with heart
In the sun, with the flowers unnipped,—
    Oh, the world's hangings ripped,
We were both in a bare-walled crypt!

XXI

Each in the crypt would cry
'But one freezes here! and why?
    'When a heart, as chill,
    'At my own would thrill
'Back to life, and its fires out-fly?
    'Heart, shall we live or die?
'The rest, ... settle by-and-by!'

XXII

So, she'd efface the score,
And forgive me as before.
    It is twelve o'clock:
    I shall hear her knock
In the worst of a storm's uproar,
    I shall pull her through the door,
I shall have her for evermore!

UP AT A VILLA—DOWN IN THE CITY

(AS DISTINGUISHED BY AN ITALIAN PERSON OF QUALITY)

I

HAD I but plenty of money, money enough and to spare,
The house for me, no doubt, were a house in the city-
    square;
Ah, such a life, such a life, as one leads at the window
    there!

II

Something to see, by Bacchus, something to hear, at least!
There, the whole day long, one's life is a perfect feast;
While up at a villa one lives, I maintain it, no more than
    a beast.

III

Well now, look at our villa! stuck like the horn of a bull
Just on a mountain-edge as bare as the creature's skull,
Save a mere shag of a bush with hardly a leaf to pull!
—I scratch my own, sometimes, to see if the hair 's turned
    wool.

IV

But the city, oh the city—the square with the houses!
    Why?
They are stone-faced, white as a curd, there 's something
    to take the eye!
Houses in four straight lines, not a single front awry;

You watch who crosses and gossips, who saunters, who
hurries by;
Green blinds, as a matter of course, to draw when the sun
gets high;
And the shops with fanciful signs which are painted
properly.

V

What of a villa? Though winter be over in March by
rights,
'Tis May perhaps ere the snow shall have withered well
off the heights:
You've the brown ploughed land before, where the oxen
steam and wheeze,
And the hills over-smoked behind by the faint grey olive-
trees.

VI

Is it better in May, I ask you? You've summer all at
once;
In a day he leaps complete with a few strong April suns.
'Mid the sharp short emerald wheat, scarce risen three
fingers well,
The wild tulip, at end of its tube, blows out its great red
bell
Like a thin clear bubble of blood, for the children to pick
and sell.

VII

Is it ever hot in the square? There's a fountain to spout
and splash!
In the shade it sings and springs; in the shine such foam-
bows flash
On the horses with curling fish-tails, that prance and
paddle and pash
Round the lady atop in her conch—fifty gazers do not
abash,
Though all that she wears is some weeds round her waist
in a sort of sash.

VIII

All the year long at the villa, nothing to see though you
    linger,
Except yon cypress that points like death's lean lifted fore-
    finger.
Some think fireflies pretty, when they mix i' the corn and
    mingle,
Or thrid the stinking hemp till the stalks of it seem
    a-tingle.
Late August or early September, the stunning cicala is
    shrill,
And the bees keep their tiresome whine round the resinous
    firs on the hill.
Enough of the seasons,—I spare you the months of the
    fever and chill.

IX

Ere you open your eyes in the city, the blessed church-
    bells begin:
No sooner the bells leave off than the diligence rattles in:
You get the pick of the news, and it costs you never a pin.
By-and-by there's the travelling doctor gives pills, lets
    blood, draws teeth;
Or the Pulcinello-trumpet breaks up the market beneath.
At the post-office such a scene-picture—the new play,
    piping hot!
And a notice how, only this morning, three liberal thieves
    were shot.
Above it, behold the Archbishop's most fatherly of
    rebukes,
And beneath, with his crown and his lion, some little new
    law of the Duke's!
Or a sonnet with flowery marge, to the Reverend Don
    So-and-so
Who is Dante, Boccaccio, Petrarca, Saint Jerome and
    Cicero,
'And moreover,' (the sonnet goes rhyming,) 'the skirts of
    Saint Paul has reached,

'Having preached us those six Lent-lectures more unctu-
ous than ever he preached.'

Noon strikes,—here sweeps the procession! our Lady
borne smiling and smart

With a pink gauze gown all spangles, and seven swords
stuck in her heart!

Bang-whang-whang goes the drum, *tootle-te-tootle* the fife;

No keeping one's haunches still: it's the greatest pleasure
in life.

X

But bless you, it's dear—it's dear! fowls, wine, at double
the rate.

They have clapped a new tax upon salt, and what oil
pays passing the gate

It's a horror to think of. And so, the villa for me, not
the city!

Beggars can scarcely be choosers: but still—ah, the pity,
the pity!

Look, two and two go the priests, then the monks with
cowls and sandals,

And the penitents dressed in white shirts, a-holding the
yellow candles;

One, he carries a flag up straight, and another a cross
with handles,

And the Duke's guard brings up the rear, for the better
prevention of scandals:

Bang-whang-whang goes the drum, *tootle-te-tootle* the fife.

Oh, a day in the city-square, there is no such pleasure in
life!

A TOCCATA OF GALUPPI'S

I

OH Galuppi, Baldassaro, this is very sad to find!

I can hardly misconceive you; it would prove me deaf and
blind;

But although I take your meaning, 'tis with such a heavy
mind!

II

Here you come with your old music, and here's all the
    good it brings.
What, they lived once thus at Venice where the merchants
    were the kings,
Where Saint Mark's is, where the Doges used to wed the
    sea with rings?

III

Ay, because the sea's the street there; and 'tis arched by
    . . . what you call
. . . Shylock's bridge with houses on it, where they kept
    the carnival:
I was never out of England—it's as if I saw it all.

IV

Did young people take their pleasure when the sea was
    warm in May?
Balls and masks begun at midnight, burning ever to mid-
    day,
When they made up fresh adventures for the morrow, do
    you say?

V

Was a lady such a lady, cheeks so round and lips so red,—
On her neck the small face buoyant, like a bell-flower on
    its bed,
O'er the breast's superb abundance where a man might
    base his head?

VI

Well, and it was graceful of them—they'd break talk off
    and afford
—She, to bite her mask's black velvet—he, to finger on
    his sword,
While you sat and played Toccatas, stately at the clavi-
    chord?

VII

What? Those lesser thirds so plaintive, sixths diminished,
    sigh on sigh,
Told them something? Those suspensions, those solu-
    tions—'Must we die?'
Those commiserating sevenths—'Life might last! we can
    but try!'

VIII

'Were you happy?'—'Yes.'—'And are you still as
    happy?'—'Yes. And you?'
—'Then, more kisses!'—'Did *I* stop them, when a
    million seemed so few?'
Hark, the dominant's persistence till it must be answered
    to!

IX

So, an octave struck the answer. Oh, they praised you,
    I dare say!
'Brave Galuppi! that was music! good alike at grave and
    gay!
'I can always leave off talking when I hear a master play!'

X

Then they left you for their pleasure: till in due time, one
    by one,
Some with lives that came to nothing, some with deeds
    as well undone,
Death stepped tacitly and took them where they never
    see the sun.

XI

But when I sit down to reason, think to take my stand
    nor swerve,
While I triumph o'er a secret wrung from nature's close
    reserve,
In you come with your cold music till I creep thro' every
    nerve.

XII

Yes, you, like a ghostly cricket, creaking where a house
    was burned:
'Dust and ashes, dead and done with, Venice spent what
    Venice earned.
'The soul, doubtless, is immortal—where a soul can be
    discerned.

XIII

'Yours for instance: you know physics, something of
    geology,
'Mathematics are your pastime; souls shall rise in their
    degree;
'Butterflies may dread extinction,—you'll not die, it
    cannot be!

XIV

'As for Venice and her people, merely born to bloom and
    drop,
'Here on earth they bore their fruitage, mirth and folly
    were the crop:
'What of soul was left, I wonder, when the kissing had
    to stop?

XV

'Dust and ashes!' So you creak it, and I want the heart
    to scold.
Dear dead women, with such hair, too—what's become
    of all the gold
Used to hang and brush their bosoms? I feel chilly and
    grown old.

OLD PICTURES IN FLORENCE

I

THE morn when first it thunders in March,
    The eel in the pond gives a leap, they say:
As I leaned and looked over the aloed arch
    Of the villa-gate this warm March day,

No flash snapped, no dumb thunder rolled
 In the valley beneath where, white and wide
And washed by the morning water-gold,
 Florence lay out on the mountain-side.

II

River and bridge and street and square
 Lay mine, as much at my beck and call,
Through the live translucent bath of air,
 As the sights in a magic crystal ball.
And of all I saw and of all I praised,
 The most to praise and the best to see
Was the startling bell-tower Giotto raised:
 But why did it more than startle me?

III

Giotto, how, with that soul of yours,
 Could you play me false who loved you so?
Some slights if a certain heart endures
 Yet it feels, I would have your fellows know!
I' faith, I perceive not why I should care
 To break a silence that suits them best,
But the thing grows somewhat hard to bear
 When I find a Giotto join the rest.

IV

On the arch where olives overhead
 Print the blue sky with twig and leaf,
(That sharp-curled leaf which they never shed)
 'Twixt the aloes, I used to lean in chief,
And mark through the winter afternoons,
 By a gift God grants me now and then,
In the mild decline of those suns like moons,
 Who walked in Florence, besides her men.

V

They might chirp and chaffer, come and go
 For pleasure or profit, her men alive—
My business was hardly with them, I trow,
 But with empty cells of the human hive;

—With the chapter-room, the cloister-porch,
    The church's apsis, aisle or nave,
Its crypt, one fingers along with a torch,
    Its face set full for the sun to shave.

VI

Wherever a fresco peels and drops,
    Wherever an outline weakens and wanes
Till the latest life in the painting stops,
    Stands One whom each fainter pulse-tick pains:
One, wishful each scrap should clutch the brick,
    Each tinge not wholly escape the plaster,
—A lion who dies of an ass's kick,
    The wronged great soul of an ancient Master.

VII

For oh, this world and the wrong it does!
    They are safe in heaven with their backs to it,
The Michaels and Rafaels, you hum and buzz
    Round the works of, you of the little wit!
Do their eyes contract to the earth's old scope,
    Now that they see God face to face,
And have all attained to be poets, I hope?
    'Tis their holiday now, in any case.

VIII

Much they reck of your praise and you!
    But the wronged great souls—can they be quit
Of a world where their work is all to do,
    Where you style them, you of the little wit,
Old Master This and Early the Other,
    Not dreaming that Old and New are fellows:
A younger succeeds to an elder brother,
    Da Vincis derive in good time from Dellos.

IX

And here where your praise might yield returns,
    And a handsome word or two give help,
Here, after your kind, the mastiff girns
    And the puppy pack of poodles yelp.

What, not a word for Stefano there,
    Of brow once prominent and starry,
Called Nature's Ape and the world's despair
    For his peerless painting? (See Vasari.)

X

There stands the Master. Study, my friends,
    What a man's work comes to! So he plans it,
Performs it, perfects it, makes amends
    For the toiling and moiling, and then, *sic transit!*
Happier the thrifty blind-folk labour,
    With upturned eye while the hand is busy,
Not sidling a glance at the coin of their neighbour!
    'Tis looking downward that makes one dizzy.

XI

'If you knew their work you would deal your dole.'
    May I take upon me to instruct you?
When Greek Art ran and reached the goal,
    Thus much had the world to boast *in fructu*—
The Truth of Man, as by God first spoken,
    Which the actual generations garble,
Was re-uttered, and Soul (which Limbs betoken)
    And Limbs (Soul informs) made new in marble.

XII

So, you saw yourself as you wished you were,
    As you might have been, as you cannot be;
Earth here, rebuked by Olympus there:
    And grew content in your poor degree
With your little power, by those statues' godhead,
    And your little scope, by their eyes' full sway,
And your little grace, by their grace embodied,
    And your little date, by their forms that stay.

XIII

You would fain be kinglier, say, than I am?
    Even so, you will not sit like Theseus.
You would prove a model? The Son of Priam
    Has yet the advantage in arms' and knees' use.

You're wroth—can you slay your snake like Apollo?
  You're grieved—still Niobe's the grander!
You live—there's the Racers' frieze to follow:
  You die—there's the dying Alexander.

xiv

So, testing your weakness by their strength,
  Your meagre charms by their rounded beauty,
Measured by Art in your breadth and length,
  You learned—to submit is a mortal's duty.
—When I say 'you' 'tis the common soul,
  The collective, I mean: the race of Man
That receives life in parts to live in a whole,
  And grow here according to God's clear plan.

xv

Growth came when, looking your last on them all,
  You turned your eyes inwardly one fine day
And cried with a start—What if we so small
  Be greater and grander the while than they?
Are they perfect of lineament, perfect of stature?
  In both, of such lower types are we
Precisely because of our wider nature;
  For time, theirs—ours, for eternity.

xvi

To-day's brief passion limits their range;
  It seethes with the morrow for us and more.
They are perfect—how else? they shall never change:
  We are faulty—why not? we have time in store.
The Artificer's hand is not arrested
  With us; we are rough-hewn, nowise polished:
They stand for our copy, and, once invested
  With all they can teach, we shall see them abolished.

xvii

'Tis a life-long toil till our lump be leaven—
  The better! What's come to perfection perishes.
Things learned on earth, we shall practise in heaven:
  Works done least rapidly, Art most cherishes.

Thyself shalt afford the example, Giotto!
 Thy one work, not to decrease or diminish,
Done at a stroke, was just (was it not?) 'O!'
 Thy great Campanile is still to finish.

XVIII

Is it true that we are now, and shall be hereafter,
 But what and where depend on life's minute?
Hails heavenly cheer or infernal laughter
 Our first step out of the gulf or in it?
Shall Man, such step within his endeavour,
 Man's face, have no more play and action
Than joy which is crystallized for ever,
 Or grief, an eternal petrifaction?

XIX

On which I conclude, that the early painters,
 To cries of 'Greek Art and what more wish you?'—
Replied, 'To become now self-acquainters,
 'And paint man man, whatever the issue!
'Make new hopes shine through the flesh they fray,
 'New fears aggrandize the rags and tatters:
'To bring the invisible full into play!
 'Let the visible go to the dogs—what matters?'

XX

Give these, I exhort you, their guerdon and glory
 For daring so much, before they well did it.
The first of the new, in our race's story,
 Beats the last of the old; 'tis no idle quiddit.
The worthies began a revolution,
 Which if on earth you intend to acknowledge,
Why, honour them now! (ends my allocution)
 Nor confer your degree when the folk leave college.

XXI

There's a fancy some lean to and others hate—
 That, when this life is ended, begins
New work for the soul in another state,
 Where it strives and gets weary, loses and wins:

Where the strong and the weak, this world's congeries,
    Repeat in large what they practised in small,
Through life after life in unlimited series;
    Only the scale's to be changed, that's all.

XXII

Yet I hardly know. When a soul has seen
    By the means of Evil that Good is best,
And, through earth and its noise, what is heaven's
      serene,—
When our faith in the same has stood the test—
Why, the child grown man, you burn the rod,
    The uses of labour are surely done;
There remaineth a rest for the people of God:
    And I have had troubles enough, for one.

XXIII

But at any rate I have loved the season
    Of Art's spring-birth so dim and dewy;
My sculptor is Nicolo the Pisan,
    My painter—who but Cimabue?
Nor ever was man of them all indeed,
    From these to Ghiberti and Ghirlandajo,
Could say that he missed my critic-meed.
    So, now to my special grievance—heigh ho!

XXIV

Their ghosts still stand, as I said before,
    Watching each fresco flaked and rasped,
Blocked up, knocked out, or whitewashed o'er:
    —No getting again what the church has grasped!
The works on the wall must take their chance;
    'Works never conceded to England's thick clime!'
(I hope they prefer their inheritance
    Of a bucketful of Italian quick-lime.)

XXV

When they go at length, with such a shaking
    Of heads o'er the old delusion, sadly
Each master his way through the black streets taking,
    Where many a lost work breathes though badly—

Why don't they bethink them of who has merited?
    Why not reveal, while their pictures dree
Such doom, how a captive might be out-ferreted?
    Why is it they never remember me?

XXVI

Not that I expect the great Bigordi,
    Nor Sandro to hear me, chivalric, bellicose;
Nor the wronged Lippino; and not a word I
    Say of a scrap of Frà Angelico's:
But are you too fine, Taddeo Gaddi,
    To grant me a taste of your intonaco,
Some Jerome that seeks the heaven with a sad eye?
    Not a churlish saint, Lorenzo Monaco?

XXVII

Could not the ghost with the close red cap,
    My Pollajolo, the twice a craftsman,
Save me a sample, give me the hap
    Of a muscular Christ that shows the draughtsman?
No Virgin by him the somewhat petty,
    Of finical touch and tempera crumbly—
Could not Alesso Baldovinetti
    Contribute so much, I ask him humbly?

XXVIII

Margheritone of Arezzo,
    With the grave-clothes garb and swaddling barret
(Why purse up mouth and beak in a pet so,
    You bald old saturnine poll-clawed parrot?)
Not a poor glimmering Crucifixion,
    Where in the foreground kneels the donor?
If such remain, as is my conviction,
    The hoarding it does you but little honour.

XXIX

They pass; for them the panels may thrill,
    The tempera grow alive and tinglish;
Their pictures are left to the mercies still
    Of dealers and stealers, Jews and the English,

Who, seeing mere money's worth in their prize,
    Will sell it to somebody calm as Zeno
At naked High Art, and in ecstasies
    Before some clay-cold vile Carlino!

XXX

No matter for these! But Giotto, you,
    Have you allowed, as the town-tongues babble it,—
Oh, never! it shall not be counted true—
    That a certain precious little tablet
Which Buonarroti eyed like a lover,—
    Was buried so long in oblivion's womb
And, left for another than I to discover,
    Turns up at last! and to whom?—to whom?

XXXI

I, that have haunted the dim San Spirito,
    (Or was it rather the Ognissanti?)
Patient on altar-step planting a weary toe!
    Nay, I shall have it yet! *Detur amanti!*
My Koh-i-noor—or (if that's a platitude)
    Jewel of Giamschid, the Persian Sofi's eye;
So, in anticipative gratitude,
    What if I take up my hope and prophesy?

XXXII

When the hour grows ripe, and a certain dotard
    Is pitched, no parcel that needs invoicing,
To the worse side of the Mont Saint Gothard,
    We shall begin by way of rejoicing;
None of that shooting the sky (blank cartridge),
    Nor a civic guard, all plumes and lacquer,
Hunting Radetzky's soul like a partridge
    Over Morello with squib and cracker.

XXXIII

This time we'll shoot better game and bag 'em hot—
    No mere display at the stone of Dante,
But a kind of sober Witanagemot
    (Ex: 'Casa Guidi,' *quod videas ante*)

Shall ponder, once Freedom restored to Florence,
    How Art may return that departed with her.
Go, hated house, go each trace of the Loraine's,
    And bring us the days of Orgagna hither!

XXXIV

How we shall prologuize, how we shall perorate,
    Utter fit things upon art and history,
Feel truth at blood-heat and falsehood at zero rate,
    Make of the want of the age no mystery;
Contrast the fructuous and sterile eras,
    Show—monarchy ever its uncouth cub licks
Out of the bear's shape into Chimæra's,
    While Pure Art's birth is still the republic's.

XXXV

Then one shall propose in a speech (curt Tuscan,
    Expurgate and sober, with scarcely an 'issimo,')
To end now our half-told tale of Cambuscan,
    And turn the bell-tower's *alt* to *altissimo:*
And fine as the beak of a young beccaccia
    The Campanile, the Duomo's fit ally,
Shall soar up in gold full fifty braccia,
    Completing Florence, as Florence Italy.

XXXVI

Shall I be alive that morning the scaffold
    Is broken away, and the long-pent fire,
Like the golden hope of the world, unbaffled
    Springs from its sleep, and up goes the spire
While 'God and the People' plain for its motto,
    Thence the new tricolour flaps at the sky?
At least to foresee that glory of Giotto
    And Florence together, the first am I!

'DE GUSTIBUS——'

Your ghost will walk, you lover of trees,
 (If our loves remain)
  In an English lane,
By a cornfield-side a-flutter with poppies.
Hark, those two in the hazel coppice—
A boy and a girl, if the good fates please,
  Making love, say,—
  The happier they!
Draw yourself up from the light of the moon,
And let them pass, as they will too soon,
  With the bean-flowers' boon,
  And the blackbird's tune,
  And May, and June!

II

What I love best in all the world
Is a castle, precipice-encurled,
In a gash of the wind-grieved Apennine.
Or look for me, old fellow of mine,
(If I get my head from out the mouth
O' the grave, and loose my spirit's bands,
And come again to the land of lands)—
In a sea-side house to the farther South,
Where the baked cicala dies of drouth,
And one sharp tree—'tis a cypress—stands,
By the many hundred years red-rusted,
Rough iron-spiked, ripe fruit-o'ercrusted,
My sentinel to guard the sands
To the water's edge. For, what expands
Before the house, but the great opaque
Blue-breadth of sea without a break?
While, in the house, for ever crumbles
Some fragment of the frescoed walls,
From blisters where a scorpion sprawls.
A girl bare-footed brings, and tumbles
Down on the pavement, green-flesh melons,

And says there's news to-day—the king
Was shot at, touched in the liver-wing,
Goes with his Bourbon arm in a sling:
—She hopes they have not caught the felons.
Italy, my Italy!
Queen Mary's saying serves for me—
    (When fortune's malice
      Lost her—Calais)—
Open my heart and you will see
Graved inside of it, 'Italy.'
Such lovers old are I and she:
So it always was, so shall ever be!

HOME-THOUGHTS, FROM ABROAD

I

OH, to be in England
Now that April's there,
And whoever wakes in England
Sees, some morning, unaware,
That the lowest boughs and the brushwood sheaf
Round the elm-tree bole are in tiny leaf,
While the chaffinch sings on the orchard bough
In England—now!

II

And after April, when May follows,
And the whitethroat builds, and all the swallows!
Hark, where my blossomed pear-tree in the hedge
Leans to the field and scatters on the clover
Blossoms and dewdrops—at the bent spray's edge—
That's the wise thrush; he sings each song twice over,
Lest you should think he never could recapture
The first fine careless rapture!
And though the fields look rough with hoary dew,
All will be gay when noontide wakes anew
The buttercups, the little children's dower
—Far brighter than this gaudy melon-flower!

HOME-THOUGHTS, FROM THE SEA

NOBLY, nobly Cape Saint Vincent to the North-west died away;
Sunset ran, one glorious blood-red, reeking into Cadiz Bay;
Bluish 'mid the burning water, full in face Trafalgar lay;
In the dimmest North-east distance dawned Gibraltar grand and gray;
'Here and here did England help me: how can I help England?'—say,
Whoso turns as I, this evening, turn to God to praise and pray,
While Jove's planet rises yonder, silent over Africa.

SAUL

I

SAID Abner, 'At last thou art come! Ere I tell, ere thou speak,
'Kiss my cheek, wish me well!' Then I wished it, and did kiss his cheek.
And he, 'Since the King, O my friend, for thy countenance sent,
'Neither drunken nor eaten have we; nor until from his tent
'Thou return with the joyful assurance the King liveth yet,
'Shall our lip with the honey be bright, with the water be wet.
'For out of the black mid-tent's silence, a space of three days,
'Not a sound hath escaped to thy servants, of prayer nor of praise,
'To betoken that Saul and the Spirit have ended their strife,
'And that, faint in his triumph, the monarch sinks back upon life.

II

'Yet now my heart leaps, O beloved! God's child with
    his dew
'On thy gracious gold hair, and those lilies still living
    and blue
'Just broken to twine round thy harp-strings, as if no
    wild heat
'Were now raging to torture the desert!'

III

                Then I, as was meet,
Knelt down to the God of my fathers, and rose on my
    feet,
And ran o'er the sand burnt to powder. The tent was
    unlooped;
I pulled up the spear that obstructed, and under I
    stooped;
Hands and knees on the slippery grass-patch, all withered
    and gone,
That extends to the second enclosure, I groped my way
    on
Till I felt where the foldskirts fly open. Then once more
    I prayed,
And opened the foldskirts and entered, and was not
    afraid
But spoke, 'Here is David, thy servant!' And no voice
    replied.
At the first I saw nought but the blackness; but soon I
    descried
A something more black than the blackness—the vast,
    the upright
Main prop which sustains the pavilion: and slow into
    sight
Grew a figure against it, gigantic and blackest of
    all.
Then a sunbeam, that burst thro' the tent-roof, showed
    Saul.

IV

He stood as erect as that tent-prop, both arms stretched
    out wide
On the great cross-support in the centre, that goes to each
    side;
He relaxed not a muscle, but hung there as, caught in his
    pangs
And waiting his change, the king-serpent all heavily
    hangs,
Far away from his kind, in the pine, till deliverance come
With the spring-time,—so agonized Saul, drear and stark,
    blind and dumb.

V

Then I tuned my harp,—took off the lilies we twine
    round its chords
Lest they snap 'neath the stress of the noontide—those
    sunbeams like swords!
And I first played the tune all our sheep know, as, one
    after one,
So docile they come to the pen-door till folding be done.
They are white and untorn by the bushes, for lo, they
    have fed
Where the long grasses stifle the water within the stream's
    bed;
And now one after one seeks its lodging, as star follows
    star
Into eve and the blue far above us,—so blue and so far!

VI

—Then the tune, for which quails on the cornland will
    each leave his mate
To fly after the player; then, what makes the crickets
    elate
Till for boldness they fight one another: and then, what
    has weight
To set the quick jerboa a-musing outside his sand house—
There are none such as he for a wonder, half bird and
    half mouse!

God made all the creatures and gave them our love and
    our fear,
To give sign, we and they are his children, one family here.

VII

Then I played the help-tune of our reapers, their wine-
    song, when hand
Grasps at hand, eye lights eye in good friendship, and
    great hearts expand
And grow one in the sense of this world's life.—And then,
    the last song
When the dead man is praised on his journey—'Bear,
    bear him along
'With his few faults shut up like dead flowerets! Are
    balm-seeds not here
'To console us? The land has none left such as he on
    the bier.
'Oh, would we might keep thee, my brother!'—And then,
    the glad chaunt
Of the marriage,—first go the young maidens, next, she
    whom we vaunt
As the beauty, the pride of our dwelling.—And then, the
    great march
Wherein man runs to man to assist him and buttress an
    arch
Nought can break; who shall harm them, our friends?—
    Then, the chorus intoned
As the Levites go up to the altar in glory enthroned.
But I stopped here: for here in the darkness Saul groaned.

VIII

And I paused, held my breath in such silence, and listened
    apart;
And the tent shook, for mighty Saul shuddered: and
    sparkles 'gan dart
From the jewels that woke in his turban, at once with a
    start,
All its lordly male-sapphires, and rubies courageous at
    heart.

So the head: but the body still moved not, still hung there
    erect.

And I bent once again to my playing, pursued it un-
    checked,

As I sang,—

IX

'Oh, our manhood's prime vigour! No spirit feels
    waste,

'Not a muscle is stopped in its playing nor sinew un-
    braced.

'Oh, the wild joys of living! the leaping from rock up to
    rock,

'The strong rending of boughs from the fir-tree, the cool
    silver shock

'Of the plunge in a pool's living water, the hunt of the
    bear,

'And the sultriness showing the lion is couched in his lair.

'And the meal, the rich dates yellowed over with gold dust
    divine,

'And the locust-flesh steeped in the pitcher, the full
    draught of wine,

'And the sleep in the dried river-channel where bulrushes
    tell

'That the water was wont to go warbling so softly and well.

'How good is man's life, the mere living! how fit to employ

'All the heart and the soul and the senses for ever in joy!

'Hast thou loved the white locks of thy father, whose
    sword thou didst guard

'When he trusted thee forth with the armies, for glorious
    reward?

'Didst thou see the thin hands of thy mother, held up as
    men sung

'The low song of the nearly-departed, and hear her faint
    tongue

'Joining in while it could to the witness, "Let one more
    attest,

'"I have lived, seen God's hand thro' a lifetime, and all
    was for best"?

'Then they sung thro' their tears in strong triumph, not
    much, but the rest.
'And thy brothers, the help and the contest, the working
    whence grew
'Such result as, from seething grape-bundles, the spirit
    strained true:
'And the friends of thy boyhood—that boyhood of
    wonder and hope,
'Present promise and wealth of the future beyond the
    eye's scope,—
'Till lo, thou art grown to a monarch; a people is thine;
'And all gifts, which the world offers singly, on one head
    combine!
'On one head, all the beauty and strength, love and rage
    (like the throe
'That, a-work in the rock, helps its labour and lets the
    gold go)
'High ambition and deeds which surpass it, fame crown-
    ing them,—all
'Brought to blaze on the head of one creature—King
    Saul!'

                        x

And lo, with that leap of my spirit,—heart, hand, harp
    and voice,
Each lifting Saul's name out of sorrow, each bidding
    rejoice
Saul's fame in the light it was made for—as when, dare
    I say,
The Lord's army, in rapture of service, strains through its
    array,
And upsoareth the cherubim-chariot—'Saul!' cried I, and
    stopped,
And waited the thing that should follow. Then Saul, who
    hung propped
By the tent's cross-support in the centre, was struck by his
    name.
Have ye seen when Spring's arrowy summons goes right
    to the aim,

And some mountain, the last to withstand her, that held
(he alone,
While the vale laughed in freedom and flowers) on a broad
bust of stone
A year's snow bound about for a breastplate,—leaves
grasp of the sheet?
Fold on fold all at once it crowds thunderously down to
his feet,
And there fronts you, stark, black, but alive yet, your
mountain of old,
With his rents, the successive bequeathings of ages un-
told—
Yea, each harm got in fighting your battles, each furrow
and scar
Of his head thrust 'twixt you and the tempest—all hail,
there they are!
—Now again to be softened with verdure, again hold the
nest
Of the dove, tempt the goat and its young to the green on
his crest
For their food in the ardours of summer. One long
shudder thrilled
All the tent till the very air tingled, then sank and was
stilled
At the King's self left standing before me, released and
aware.
What was gone, what remained? All to traverse, 'twixt
hope and despair;
Death was past, life not come: so he waited. Awhile his
right hand
Held the brow, helped the eyes left too vacant forthwith
to remand
To their place what new objects should enter: 'twas Saul
as before.
I looked up and dared gaze at those eyes, nor was hurt
any more
Than by slow pallid sunsets in autumn, ye watch from the
shore,
At their sad level gaze o'er the ocean—a sun's slow decline

Over hills which, resolved in stern silence, o'erlap and
    entwine
Base with base to knit strength more intensely: so, arm
    folded arm
O'er the chest whose slow heavings subsided.

XI

                   What spell or what charm,
(For, awhile there was trouble within me) what next
    should I urge
To sustain him where song had restored him?—Song
    filled to the verge
His cup with the wine of this life, pressing all that it yields
Of mere fruitage, the strength and the beauty: beyond,
    on what fields,
Glean a vintage more potent and perfect to brighten the
    eye
And bring blood to the lip, and commend them the cup
    they put by?
He saith, 'It is good;' still he drinks not: he lets me praise
    life,
Gives assent, yet would die for his own part.

XII

                 Then fancies grew rife
Which had come long ago on the pasture, when round me
    the sheep
Fed in silence—above, the one eagle wheeled slow as in
    sleep;
And I lay in my hollow and mused on the world that
    might lie
'Neath his ken, though I saw but the strip 'twixt the hill
    and the sky:
And I laughed—'Since my days are ordained to be passed
    with my flocks,
'Let me people at least, with my fancies, the plains and
    the rocks,
'Dream the life I am never to mix with, and image the
    show

'Of mankind as they live in those fashions I hardly shall
        know!
'Schemes of life, its best rules and right uses, the courage
        that gains,
'And the prudence that keeps what men strive for.' And
        now these old trains
Of vague thought came again; I grew surer; so, once more
        the string
Of my harp made response to my spirit, as thus—

                         XIII

                                    'Yea, my King,'
I began—'thou dost well in rejecting mere comforts that
        spring
'From the mere mortal life held in common by man and
        by brute:
'In our flesh grows the branch of this life, in our soul it
        bears fruit.
'Thou hast marked the slow rise of the tree,—how its
        stem trembled first
'Till it passed the kid's lip, the stag's antler; then safely
        outburst
'The fan-branches all round; and thou mindest when
        these too, in turn
'Broke a-bloom and the palm-tree seemed perfect: yet
        more was to learn,
'E'en the good that comes in with the palm-fruit. Our
        dates shall we slight,
'When their juice brings a cure for all sorrow? or care for
        the plight
'Of the palm's self whose slow growth produced them?
        Not so! stem and branch
'Shall decay, nor be known in their place, while the palm-
        wine shall staunch
'Every wound of man's spirit in winter. I pour thee such
        wine.
'Leave the flesh to the fate it was fit for! the spirit be thine!
'By the spirit, when age shall o'ercome thee, thou still
        shalt enjoy

'More indeed, than at first when, inconscious, the life of a
  boy.

'Crush that life, and behold its wine running! Each deed
  thou hast done

'Dies, revives, goes to work in the world; until e'en as
  the sun

'Looking down on the earth, though clouds spoil him,
  though tempests efface,

'Can find nothing his own deed produced not, must everywhere trace

'The results of his past summer-prime,—so, each ray of
  thy will,

'Every flash of thy passion and prowess, long over, shall
  thrill

'Thy whole people, the countless, with ardour, till they
  too give forth

'A like cheer to their sons, who in turn, fill the South and
  the North

'With the radiance thy deed was the germ of. Carouse in
  the past!

'But the license of age has its limit; thou diest at last:

'As the lion when age dims his eyeball, the rose at her
  height,

'So with man—so his power and his beauty for ever take
  flight.

'No! Again a long draught of my soul-wine! Look forth
  o'er the years!

'Thou hast done now with eyes for the actual; begin with
  the seer's!

'Is Saul dead? In the depth of the vale make his tomb—
  bid arise

'A grey mountain of marble heaped four-square, till,
  built to the skies,

'Let it mark where the great First King slumbers: whose
  fame would ye know?

'Up above see the rock's naked face, where the record
  shall go

'In great characters cut by the scribe,—Such was Saul,
  so he did;

'With the sages directing the work, by the populace
    chid,—

'For not half, they'll affirm, is comprised there! Which
    fault to amend,

'In the grove with his kind grows the cedar, whereon they
    shall spend

'(See, in tablets 'tis level before them) their praise, and
    record

'With the gold of the graver, Saul's story,—the states-
    man's great word

'Side by side with the poet's sweet comment. The river's
    a-wave

'With smooth paper-reeds grazing each other when
    prophet-winds rave:

'So the pen gives unborn generations their due and their
    part

'In thy being! Then, first of the mighty, thank God that
    thou art!'

XIV

And behold while I sang ... but O Thou who didst grant
    me that day,

And before it not seldom hast granted thy help to essay,

Carry on and complete an adventure,—my shield and my
    sword

In that act where my soul was thy servant, thy word was
    my word,—

Still be with me, who then at the summit of human
    endeavour

And scaling the highest, man's thought could, gazed
    hopeless as ever

On the new stretch of heaven above me—till, mighty to
    save,

Just one lift of thy hand cleared that distance—God's
    throne from man's grave!

Let me tell out my tale to its ending—my voice to my
    heart

Which can scarce dare believe in what marvels last night
    I took part,

As this morning I gather the fragments, alone with my
    sheep,
And still fear lest the terrible glory evanish like sleep!
For I wake in the grey dewy covert, while Hebron up-
    heaves
The dawn struggling with night on his shoulder, and
    Kidron retrieves
Slow the damage of yesterday's sunshine.

XV

                        I say then,—my song
While I sang thus, assuring the monarch, and ever more
    strong
Made a proffer of good to console him—he slowly
    resumed
His old motions and habitudes kingly. The right-hand
    replumed
His black locks to their wonted composure, adjusted the
    swathes
Of his turban, and see—the huge sweat that his counte-
    nance bathes,
He wipes off with the robe; and he girds now his loins as
    of yore,
And feels slow for the armlets of price, with the clasp set
    before.
He is Saul, ye remember in glory,—ere error had bent
The broad brow from the daily communion; and still,
    though much spent
Be the life and the bearing that front you, the same, God
    did choose,
To receive what a man may waste, desecrate, never quite
    lose.
So sank he along by the tent-prop till, stayed by the pile
Of his armour and war-cloak and garments, he leaned
    there awhile,
And sat out my singing,—one arm round the tent-prop,
    to raise
His bent head, and the other hung slack—till I touched
    on the praise

I foresaw from all men in all time, to the man patient
    there;
And thus ended, the harp falling forward. Then first I
    was 'ware
That he sat, as I say, with my head just above his vast
    knees
Which were thrust out on each side around me, like oak-
    roots which please
To encircle a lamb when it slumbers. I looked up to
    know
If the best I could do had brought solace: he spoke not,
    but slow
Lifted up the hand slack at his side, till he laid it with care
Soft and grave, but in mild settled will, on my brow: thro'
    my hair
The large fingers were pushed, and he bent back my head,
    with kind power—
All my face back, intent to peruse it, as men do a flower.
Thus held he me there with his great eyes that scrutinized
    mine—
And oh, all my heart how it loved him! but where was the
    sign?
I yearned—'Could I help thee, my father, inventing a
    bliss,
'I would add, to that life of the past, both the future and
    this;
'I would give thee new life altogether, as good, ages hence,
'As this moment,—had love but the warrant, love's heart
    to dispense!'

XVI

Then the truth came upon me. No harp more—no song
    more! outbroke—

XVII

'I have gone the whole round of creation: I saw and I
    spoke:
'I, a work of God's hand for that purpose, received in my
    brain

'And pronounced on the rest of his handwork—returned
    him again
'His creation's approval or censure: I spoke as I saw:
'I report, as a man may of God's work—all's love, yet
    all's law.
'Now I lay down the judgeship he lent me. Each faculty
    tasked
'To perceive him, has gained an abyss, where a dewdrop
    was asked.
'Have I knowledge? confounded it shrivels at Wisdom
    laid bare.
'Have I forethought? how purblind, how blank, to the
    Infinite Care!
'Do I task any faculty highest, to image success?
'I but open my eyes,—and perfection, no more and no
    less,
'In the kind I imagined, full-fronts me, and God is seen
    God
'In the star, in the stone, in the flesh, in the soul and the
    clod.
'And thus looking within and around me, I ever renew
'(With that stoop of the soul which in bending upraises
    it too)
'The submission of man's nothing-perfect to God's all-
    complete,
'As by each new obeisance in spirit, I climb to his feet.
'Yet with all this abounding experience, this deity known,
'I shall dare to discover some province, some gift of my
    own.
'There's a faculty pleasant to exercise, hard to hoodwink,
'I am fain to keep still in abeyance, (I laugh as I think)
'Lest, insisting to claim and parade in it, wot ye, I worst
'E'en the Giver in one gift.—Behold, I could love if I
    durst!
'But I sink the pretension as fearing a man may o'ertake
'God's own speed in the one way of love: I abstain for
    love's sake.
'—What, my soul? see thus far and no farther? when
    doors great and small,

'Nine-and-ninety flew ope at our touch, should the
    hundredth appal?
'In the least things have faith, yet distrust in the greatest
    of all?
'Do I find love so full in my nature, God's ultimate gift,
'That I doubt his own love can compete with it? Here,
    the parts shift?
'Here, the creature surpass the Creator,—the end, what
    Began?
'Would I fain in my impotent yearning do all for this
    man,
'And dare doubt he alone shall not help him, who yet
    alone can?
'Would it ever have entered my mind, the bare will, much
    less power,
'To bestow on this Saul what I sang of, the marvellous
    dower
'Of the life he was gifted and filled with? to make such a
    soul,
'Such a body, and then such an earth for insphering the
    whole?
'And doth it not enter my mind (as my warm tears attest)
'These good things being given, to go on, and give one
    more, the best?
'Ay, to save and redeem and restore him, maintain at the
    height
'This perfection,—succeed with life's day-spring, death's
    minute of night?
'Interpose at the difficult minute, snatch Saul the mistake,
'Saul the failure, the ruin he seems now,—and bid him
    awake
'From the dream, the probation, the prelude, to find
    himself set
'Clear and safe in new light and new life,—a new harmony
    yet
'To be run, and continued, and ended—who knows?—
    or endure!
'The man taught enough, by life's dream, of the rest to
    make sure;

'By the pain-throb, triumphantly winning intensified bliss,
'And the next world's reward and repose, by the struggles in this.

'I believe it! 'Tis thou, God, that givest, 'tis I who receive:
'In the first is the last, in thy will is my power to believe.
'All's one gift: thou canst grant it moreover, as prompt to my prayer
'As I breathe out this breath, as I open these arms to the air.
'From thy will, stream the worlds, life and nature, thy dread Sabaoth:
'*I* will?—the mere atoms despise me! Why am I not loth
'To look that, even that in the face too? Why is it I dare
'Think but lightly of such impuissance? What stops my despair?
'This;—'tis not what man Does which exalts him, but what man Would do!
'See the King—I would help him but cannot, the wishes fall through.
'Could I wrestle to raise him from sorrow, grow poor to enrich,
'To fill up his life, starve my own out, I would—knowing which,
'I know that my service is perfect. Oh, speak through me now!
'Would I suffer for him that I love? So wouldst thou—so wilt thou!
'So shall crown thee the topmost, ineffablest, uttermost crown—
'And thy love fill infinitude wholly, nor leave up nor down
'One spot for the creature to stand in! It is by no breath,
'Turn of eye, wave of hand, that salvation joins issue with death!
'As thy Love is discovered almighty, almighty be proved
'Thy power, that exists with and for it, of being Beloved!

'He who did most, shall bear most; the strongest shall
        stand the most weak.
''Tis the weakness in strength, that I cry for! my flesh,
        that I seek
'In the Godhead! I seek and I find it. O Saul, it shall be
'A Face like my face that receives thee; a Man like to me,
'Thou shalt love and be loved by, for ever: a Hand like
        this hand
'Shall throw open the gates of new life to thee! See the
        Christ stand!'

XIX

I know not too well how I found my way home in the
        night.
There were witnesses, cohorts about me, to left and to
        right.
Angels, powers, the unuttered, unseen, the alive, the
        aware:
I repressed, I got through them as hardly, as strugglingly
        there,
As a runner beset by the populace famished for news—
Life or death. The whole earth was awakened, hell loosed
        with her crews;
And the stars of night beat with emotion, and tingled and
        shot
Out in fire the strong pain of pent knowledge: but I
        fainted not,
For the Hand still impelled me at once and supported,
        suppressed
All the tumult, and quenched it with quiet, and holy
        behest,
Till the rapture was shut in itself, and the earth sank to
        rest.
Anon at the dawn, all that trouble had withered from
        earth—
Not so much, but I saw it die out in the day's tender birth;
In the gathered intensity brought to the grey of the hills;
In the shuddering forests' held breath; in the sudden
        wind-thrills;

In the startled wild beasts that bore off, each with eye
  sidling still
Though averted with wonder and dread; in the birds stiff
  and chill
That rose heavily, as I approached them, made stupid
  with awe:
E'en the serpent that slid away silent,—he felt the new law.
The same stared in the white humid faces upturned by the
  flowers;
The same worked in the heart of the cedar and moved the
  vine-bowers:
And the little brooks witnessing murmured, persistent and
  low,
With their obstinate, all but hushed voices—'E'en so, it
  is so!'

MY STAR

ALL that I know
  Of a certain star
Is, it can throw
  (Like the angled spar)
Now a dart of red,
  Now a dart of blue;
Till my friends have said
  They would fain see, too,
My star that dartles the red and the blue!
Then it stops like a bird; like a flower, hangs furled:
  They must solace themselves with the Saturn above it.
What matter to me if their star is a world?
  Mine has opened its soul to me; therefore I love it.

BY THE FIRE-SIDE

I

How well I know what I mean to do
  When the long dark autumn-evenings come:
And where, my soul, is thy pleasant hue?
  With the music of all thy voices, dumb
In life's November too!

II

I shall be found by the fire, suppose,
    O'er a great wise book as beseemeth age,
While the shutters flap as the cross-wind blows
    And I turn the page, and I turn the page,
Not verse now, only prose!

III

Till the young ones whisper, finger on lip,
    'There he is at it, deep in Greek:
'Now then, or never, out we slip
    'To cut from the hazels by the creek
'A mainmast for our ship!'

IV

I shall be at it indeed, my friends:
    Greek puts already on either side
Such a branch-work forth as soon extends
    To a vista opening far and wide,
And I pass out where it ends.

V

The outside-frame, like your hazel-trees:
    But the inside-archway widens fast,
And a rarer sort succeeds to these,
    And we slope to Italy at last
And youth, by green degrees.

VI

I follow wherever I am led,
    Knowing so well the leader's hand:
Oh woman-country, wooed not wed,
    Loved all the more by earth's male-lands,
Laid to their hearts instead!

VII

Look at the ruined chapel again
    Half-way up in the Alpine gorge!
Is that a tower, I point you plain,
    Or is it a mill, or an iron-forge
Breaks solitude in vain?

VIII

A turn, and we stand in the heart of things;
    The woods are round us, heaped and dim;
From slab to slab how it slips and springs,
    The thread of water single and slim,
Through the ravage some torrent brings!

IX

Does it feed the little lake below?
    That speck of white just on its marge
Is Pella; see, in the evening-glow,
    How sharp the silver spear-heads charge
When Alp meets heaven in snow!

X

On our other side is the straight-up rock;
    And a path is kept 'twixt the gorge and it
By boulder-stones where lichens mock
    The marks on a moth, and small ferns fit
Their teeth to the polished block.

XI

Oh the sense of the yellow mountain-flowers,
    And thorny balls, each three in one,
The chestnuts throw on our path in showers!
    For the drop of the woodland fruit's begun,
These early November hours,

XII

That crimson the creeper's leaf across
    Like a splash of blood, intense, abrupt,
O'er a shield else gold from rim to boss,
    And lay it for show on the fairy-cupped
Elf-needled mat of moss,

XIII

By the rose-flesh mushrooms, undivulged
    Last evening—nay, in to-day's first dew
Yon sudden coral nipple bulged,
    Where a freaked fawn-coloured flaky crew
Of toadstools peep indulged.

XIV

And yonder, at foot of the fronting ridge
    That takes the turn to a range beyond,
Is the chapel reached by the one-arched bridge
    Where the water is stopped in a stagnant pond
Danced over by the midge.

XV

The chapel and bridge are of stone alike,
    Blackish-grey and mostly wet;
Cut hemp-stalks steep in the narrow dyke.
    See here again, how the lichens fret
And the roots of the ivy strike!

XVI

Poor little place, where its one priest comes
    On a festa-day, if he comes at all,
To the dozen folk from their scattered homes,
    Gathered within that precinct small
By the dozen ways one roams—

XVII

To drop from the charcoal-burners' huts,
    Or climb from the hemp-dressers' low shed,
Leave the grange where the woodman stores his nuts,
    Or the wattled cote where the fowlers spread
Their gear on the rock's bare juts.

XVIII

It has some pretension too, this front,
    With its bit of fresco half-moon-wise
Set over the porch, Art's early wont:
    'Tis John in the Desert, I surmise,
But has borne the weather's brunt—

XIX

Not from the fault of the builder, though,
    For a pent-house properly projects
Where three carved beams make a certain show,
    Dating—good thought of our architect's—
'Five, six, nine, he lets you know.

XX

And all day long a bird sings there,
  And a stray sheep drinks at the pond at times;
The place is silent and aware;
  It has had its scenes, its joys and crimes,
But that is its own affair.

XXI

My perfect wife, my Leonor,
  Oh heart, my own, oh eyes, mine too,
Whom else could I dare look backward for,
  With whom beside should I dare pursue
The path grey heads abhor?

XXII

For it leads to a crag's sheer edge with them;
  Youth, flowery all the way, there stops—
Not they; age threatens and they contemn,
  Till they reach the gulf wherein youth drops,
One inch from life's safe hem!

XXIII

With me, youth led ... I will speak now,
  No longer watch you as you sit
Reading by fire-light, that great brow
  And the spirit-small hand propping it,
Mutely, my heart knows how—

XXIV

When, if I think but deep enough,
  You are wont to answer, prompt as rhyme;
And you, too, find without rebuff
  Response your soul seeks many a time
Piercing its fine flesh-stuff.

XXV

My own, confirm me! If I tread
  This path back, is it not in pride
To think how little I dreamed it led
  To an age so blest that, by its side,
Youth seems the waste instead?

XXVI

My own, see where the years conduct!
   At first, 'twas something our two souls
Should mix as mists do; each is sucked
   In each now: on, the new stream rolls,
Whatever rocks obstruct.

XXVII

Think, when our one soul understands
   The great Word which makes all things new,
When earth breaks up and heaven expands,
   How will the change strike me and you
In the house not made with hands?

XXVIII

Oh I must feel your brain prompt mine,
   Your heart anticipate my heart,
You must be just before, in fine,
   See and make me see, for your part,
New depths of the divine!

XXIX

But who could have expected this
   When we two drew together first
Just for the obvious human bliss,
   To satisfy life's daily thirst
With a thing men seldom miss?

XXX

Come back with me to the first of all,
   Let us lean and love it over again,
Let us now forget and now recall,
   Break the rosary in a pearly rain,
And gather what we let fall!

XXXI

What did I say?—that a small bird sings
   All day long, save when a brown pair
Of hawks from the wood float with wide wings
   Strained to a bell: 'gainst noon-day glare
You count the streaks and rings.

XXXII

But at afternoon or almost eve
 'Tis better; then the silence grows
To that degree, you half believe
 It must get rid of what it knows,
Its bosom does so heave.

XXXIII

Hither we walked then, side by side,
 Arm in arm and cheek to cheek,
And still I questioned or replied,
 While my heart, convulsed to really speak,
Lay choking in its pride.

XXXIV

Silent the crumbling bridge we cross,
 And pity and praise the chapel sweet,
And care about the fresco's loss,
 And wish for our souls a like retreat,
And wonder at the moss.

XXXV

Stoop and kneel on the settle under,
 Look through the window's grated square:
Nothing to see! For fear of plunder,
 The cross is down and the altar bare,
As if thieves don't fear thunder.

XXXVI

We stoop and look in through the grate,
 See the little porch and rustic door,
Read duly the dead builder's date;
 Then cross the bridge that we crossed before,
Take the path again—but wait!

XXXVII

Oh moment, one and infinite!
 The water slips o'er stock and stone;
The West is tender, hardly bright:
 How grey at once is the evening grown—
One star, its chrysolite!

XXXVIII

We two stood there with never a third,
　　But each by each, as each knew well:
The sights we saw and the sounds we heard,
　　The lights and the shades made up a spell
Till the trouble grew and stirred.

XXXIX

Oh, the little more, and how much it is!
　　And the little less, and what worlds away!
How a sound shall quicken content to bliss,
　　Or a breath suspend the blood's best play,
And life be a proof of this!

XL

Had she willed it, still had stood the screen
　　So slight, so sure, 'twixt my love and her:
I could fix her face with a guard between,
　　And find her soul as when friends confer,
Friends—lovers that might have been.

XLI

For my heart had a touch of the woodland-time,
　　Wanting to sleep now over its best.
Shake the whole tree in the summer-prime,
　　But bring to the last leaf no such test!
'Hold the last fast!' runs the rhyme.

XLII

For a chance to make your little much,
　　To gain a lover and lose a friend,
Venture the tree and a myriad such,
　　When nothing you mar but the year can mend:
But a last leaf—fear to touch!

XLIII

Yet should it unfasten itself and fall
　　Eddying down till it find your face
At some slight wind—best chance of all!
　　Be your heart henceforth its dwelling-place
You trembled to forestall!

XLIV

Worth how well, those dark grey eyes,
  That hair so dark and dear, how worth
That a man should strive and agonize,
  And taste a veriest hell on earth
For the hope of such a prize!

XLV

You might have turned and tried a man,
  Set him a space to weary and wear,
And prove which suited more your plan,
  His best of hope or his worst despair,
Yet end as he began.

XLVI

But you spared me this, like the heart you are,
  And filled my empty heart at a word.
If two lives join, there is oft a scar,
  They are one and one, with a shadowy third;
One near one is too far.

XLVII

A moment after, and hands unseen
  Were hanging the night around us fast;
But we knew that a bar was broken between
  Life and life: we were mixed at last
In spite of the mortal screen.

XLVIII

The forests had done it; there they stood;
  We caught for a moment the powers at play:
They had mingled us so, for once and good,
  Their work was done—we might go or stay,
They relapsed to their ancient mood.

XLIX

How the world is made for each of us!
  How all we perceive and know in it
Tends to some moment's product thus,
  When a soul declares itself—to wit,
By its fruit, the thing it does!

L

Be hate that fruit or love that fruit,
   It forwards the general deed of man,
And each of the Many helps to recruit
   The life of the race by a general plan;
Each living his own, to boot.

LI

I am named and known by that moment's feat;
   There took my station and degree;
So grew my own small life complete,
   As nature obtained her best of me—
One born to love you, sweet!

LII

And to watch you sink by the fire-side now
   Back again, as you mutely sit
Musing by fire-light, that great brow
   And the spirit-small hand propping it,
Yonder, my heart knows how!

LIII

So, earth has gained by one man the more,
   And the gain of earth must be heaven's gain too;
And the whole is well worth thinking o'er
   When autumn comes: which I mean to do
One day, as I said before.

ANY WIFE TO ANY HUSBAND

I

My love, this is the bitterest, that thou
Who art all truth, and who dost love me now
   As thine eyes say, as thy voice breaks to say—
Shouldst love so truly, and couldst love me still
A whole long life through, had but love its will,
   Would death that leads me from thee brook delay.

II

I have but to be by thee, and thy hand
Will never let mine go, nor heart withstand
   The beating of my heart to reach its place.
When shall I look for thee and feel thee gone?
When cry for the old comfort and find none?
   Never, I know! Thy soul is in thy face.

III

Oh, I should fade—'tis willed so! Might I save,
Gladly I would, whatever beauty gave
   Joy to thy sense, for that was precious too.
It is not to be granted. But the soul
Whence the love comes, all ravage leaves that whole;
   Vainly the flesh fades; soul makes all things new.

IV

It would not be because my eye grew dim
Thou couldst not find the love there, thanks to Him
   Who never is dishonoured in the spark
He gave us from his fire of fires, and bade
Remember whence it sprang, nor be afraid
   While that burns on, though all the rest grow dark.

V

So, how thou wouldst be perfect, white and clean
Outside as inside, soul and soul's demesne
   Alike, this body given to show it by!
Oh, three-parts through the worst of life's abyss,
What plaudits from the next world after this,
   Couldst thou repeat a stroke and gain the sky!

VI

And is it not the bitterer to think
That, disengage our hands and thou wilt sink
   Although thy love was love in very deed?
I know that nature! Pass a festive day,
Thou dost not throw its relic-flower away
   Nor bid its music's loitering echo speed.

VII

Thou let'st the stranger's glove lie where it fell;
If old things remain old things all is well,
  For thou art grateful as becomes man best:
And hadst thou only heard me play one tune,
Or viewed me from a window, not so soon
  With thee would such things fade as with the rest.

VIII

I seem to see! We meet and part; 'tis brief;
The book I opened keeps a folded leaf,
  The very chair I sat on, breaks the rank;
That is a portrait of me on the wall—
Three lines, my face comes at so slight a call:
  And for all this, one little hour to thank!

IX

But now, because the hour through years was fixed,
Because our inmost beings met and mixed,
  Because thou once hast loved me—wilt thou dare
Say to thy soul and Who may list beside,
'Therefore she is immortally my bride;
  'Chance cannot change my love, nor time impair.

X

'So, what if in the dusk of life that's left,
'I, a tired traveller of my sun bereft,
  'Look from my path when, mimicking the same,
'The fire-fly glimpses past me, come and gone?
'—Where was it till the sunset? where anon
  'It will be at the sunrise! What's to blame?'

XI

Is it so helpful to thee? Canst thou take
The mimic up, nor, for the true thing's sake,
  Put gently by such efforts at a beam?
Is the remainder of the way so long,
Thou need'st the little solace, thou the strong?
  Watch out thy watch, let weak ones doze and dream!

XII

—Ah, but the fresher faces! 'Is it true,'
Thou'lt ask, 'some eyes are beautiful and new?
   'Some hair,—how can one choose but grasp such
      wealth?
'And if a man would press his lips to lips
'Fresh as the wilding hedge-rose-cup there slips
   'The dew-drop out of, must it be by stealth?

XIII

'It cannot change the love still kept for Her,
'More than if such a picture I prefer
   'Passing a day with, to a room's bare side:
The painted form takes nothing she possessed,
Yet, while the Titian's Venus lies at rest,
   A man looks. Once more, what is there to chide?'

XIV

So must I see, from where I sit and watch,
My own self sell myself, my hand attach
   Its warrant to the very thefts from me—
Thy singleness of soul that made me proud,
Thy purity of heart I loved aloud,
   Thy man's-truth I was bold to bid God see!

XV

Love so, then, if thou wilt! Give all thou canst
Away to the new faces—disentranced,
   (Say it and think it) obdurate no more:
Re-issue looks and words from the old mint,
Pass them afresh, no matter whose the print
   Image and superscription once they bore!

XVI

Re-coin thyself and give it them to spend,—
It all comes to the same thing at the end,
   Since mine thou wast, mine art and mine shalt be,
Faithful or faithless, sealing up the sum
Or lavish of my treasure, thou must come
   Back to the heart's place here I keep for thee!

XVII

Only, why should it be with stain at all?
Why must I, 'twixt the leaves of coronal,
  Put any kiss of pardon on thy brow?
Why need the other women know so much,
And talk together, 'Such the look and such
  'The smile he used to love with, then as now!'

XVIII

Might I die last and show thee! Should I find
Such hardship in the few years left behind,
  If free to take and light my lamp, and go
Into thy tomb, and shut the door and sit,
Seeing thy face on those four sides of it
  The better that they are so blank, I know!

XIX

Why, time was what I wanted, to turn o'er
Within my mind each look, get more and more
  By heart each word, too much to learn at first;
And join thee all the fitter for the pause
'Neath the low doorway's lintel. That were cause
  For lingering, though thou calledst, if I durst!

XX

And yet thou art the nobler of us two:
What dare I dream of, that thou canst not do,
  Outstripping my ten small steps with one stride?
I'll say then, here's a trial and a task—
Is it to bear?—if easy, I'll not ask:
  Though love fail, I can trust on in thy pride.

XXI

Pride?—when those eyes forestall the life behind
The death I have to go through!—when I find,
  Now that I want thy help most, all of thee!
What did I fear? Thy love shall hold me fast
Until the little minute's sleep is past
  And I wake saved.—And yet it will not be!

TWO IN THE CAMPAGNA

I

I WONDER do you feel to-day
  As I have felt since, hand in hand,
We sat down on the grass, to stray
  In spirit better through the land,
This morn of Rome and May?

II

For me, I touched a thought, I know,
  Has tantalized me many times,
(Like turns of thread the spiders throw
  Mocking across our path) for rhymes
To catch at and let go.

III

Help me to hold it! First it left
  The yellowing fennel, run to seed
There, branching from the brickwork's cleft,
  Some old tomb's ruin: yonder weed
Took up the floating weft,

IV

Where one small orange cup amassed
  Five beetles,—blind and green they grope
Among the honey-meal: and last,
  Everywhere on the grassy slope
I traced it. Hold it fast!

V

The champaign with its endless fleece
  Of feathery grasses everywhere!
Silence and passion, joy and peace,
  An everlasting wash of air—
Rome's ghost since her decease.

VI

Such life here, through such lengths of hours,
    Such miracles performed in play,
Such primal naked forms of flowers,
    Such letting nature have her way
While heaven looks from its towers!

VII

How say you? Let us, O my dove,
    Let us be unashamed of soul,
As earth lies bare to heaven above!
    How is it under our control
To love or not to love?

VIII

I would that you were all to me,
    You that are just so much, no more.
Nor yours nor mine, nor slave nor free!
    Where does the fault lie? What the core
O' the wound, since wound must be?

IX

I would I could adopt your will,
    See with your eyes, and set my heart
Beating by yours, and drink my fill
    At your soul's springs,—your part my part
In life, for good and ill.

X

No. I yearn upward, touch you close,
    Then stand away. I kiss your cheek,
Catch your soul's warmth,—I pluck the rose
    And love it more than tongue can speak—
Then the good minute goes.

XI

Already how am I so far
    Out of that minute? Must I go
Still like the thistle-ball, no bar,
    Onward, whenever light winds blow,
Fixed by no friendly star?

XII

Just when I seemed about to learn!
 Where is the thread now? Off again!
The old trick! Only I discern—
 Infinite passion, and the pain
Of finite hearts that yearn.

MISCONCEPTIONS

I

THIS is a spray the Bird clung to,
 Making it blossom with pleasure,
Ere the high tree-top she sprung to,
 Fit for her nest and her treasure.
Oh, what a hope beyond measure
Was the poor spray's, which the flying feet hung to,—
So to be singled out, built in, and sung to!

II

This is a heart the Queen leant on,
 Thrilled in a minute erratic,
Ere the true bosom she bent on,
 Meet for love's regal dalmatic.
Oh, what a fancy ecstatic
Was the poor heart's, ere the wanderer went on—
Love to be saved for it, proffered to, spent on!

A SERENADE AT THE VILLA

I

THAT was I, you heard last night,
 When there rose no moon at all,
Nor, to pierce the strained and tight
 Tent of heaven, a planet small:
Life was dead and so was light.

II

Not a twinkle from the fly,
　　Not a glimmer from the worm;
When the crickets stopped their cry,
　　When the owls forbore a term,
You heard music; that was I.

III

Earth turned in her sleep with pain,
　　Sultrily suspired for proof:
In at heaven and out again,
　　Lightning!—where it broke the roof,
Bloodlike, some few drops of rain.

IV

What they could my words expressed,
　　O my love, my all, my one!
Singing helped the verses best,
　　And when singing's best was done,
To my lute I left the rest.

V

So wore the night; the East was gray,
　　White the broad-faced hemlock-flowers:
There would be another day;
　　Ere its first of heavy hours
Found me, I had passed away.

VI

What became of all the hopes,
　　Words and song and lute as well?
Say, this struck you—'When life gropes
　　'Feebly for the path where fell
'Light last on the evening slopes,

VII

'One friend in that path shall be,
　　'To secure my step from wrong;
'One to count night day for me,
　　'Patient through the watches long,
'Serving most with none to see.'

VIII

Never say—as something bodes—
  'So, the worst has yet a worse!'
'When life halts 'neath double loads,
  'Better the taskmaster's curse
'Than such music on the roads!

IX

'When no moon succeeds the sun,
  'Nor can pierce the midnight's tent
'Any star, the smallest one,
  'While some drops, where lightning rent,
'Show the final storm begun—

X

'When the fire-fly hides its spot,
  'When the garden-voices fail
'In the darkness thick and hot,—
  'Shall another voice avail,
'That shape be where these are not?

XI

'Has some plague a longer lease,
  'Proffering its help uncouth?
'Can't one even die in peace?
  'As one shuts one's eyes on youth,
'Is that face the last one sees?'

XII

Oh how dark your villa was,
  Windows fast and obdurate!
How the garden grudged me grass
  Where I stood—the iron gate
Ground its teeth to let me pass!

ONE WAY OF LOVE

I

ALL June I bound the rose in sheaves.
Now, rose by rose, I strip the leaves
And strew them where Pauline may pass.
She will not turn aside? Alas!
Let them lie. Suppose they die?
The chance was they might take her eye.

II

How many a month I strove to suit
These stubborn fingers to the lute!
To-day I venture all I know.
She will not hear my music? So!
Break the string; fold music's wing:
Suppose Pauline had bade me sing!

III

My whole life long I learned to love.
This hour my utmost art I prove
And speak my passion—heaven or hell?
She will not give me heaven? 'Tis well!
Lose who may—I still can say,
Those who win heaven, blest are they!

ANOTHER WAY OF LOVE

I

JUNE was not over
    Though past the full,
And the best of her roses
    Had yet to blow,
When a man I know
(But shall not discover,
    Since ears are dull,
    And time discloses)
Turned him and said with a man's true air,
Half sighing a smile in a yawn, as 'twere,—
'If I tire of your June, will she greatly care?'

II

Well, dear, in-doors with you!
　　True! serene deadness
Tries a man's temper.
　　What's in the blossom
　　June wears on her bosom?
Can it clear scores with you?
　　Sweetness and redness.
　　Eadem semper!
Go, let me care for it greatly or slightly!
If June mend her bower now, your hand left unsightly
By plucking the roses,—my June will do rightly.

III

And after, for pastime,
　　If June be refulgent
With flowers in completeness,
　　All petals, no prickles,
　　Delicious as trickles
Of wine poured at mass-time,—
　　And choose One indulgent
To redness and sweetness:
Or if, with experience of man and of spider,
June use my June-lightning, the strong insect-ridder,
And stop the fresh film-work,—why, June will consider.

A PRETTY WOMAN

I

THAT fawn-skin-dappled hair of hers,
　　And the blue eye
　　Dear and dewy,
And that infantine fresh air of hers!

II

To think men cannot take you, Sweet,
　　And enfold you,
　　Ay, and hold you,
And so keep you what they make you, Sweet!

III

You like us for a glance, you know—
    For a word's sake
    Or a sword's sake,
All's the same, whate'er the chance, you know.

IV

And in turn we make you ours, we say—
    You and youth too,
    Eyes and mouth too,
All the face composed of flowers, we say.

V

All's our own, to make the most of, Sweet—
    Sing and say for,
    Watch and pray for,
Keep a secret or go boast of, Sweet!

VI

But for loving, why, you would not, Sweet,
    Though we prayed you,
    Paid you, brayed you
In a mortar—for you could not, Sweet!

VII

So, we leave the sweet face fondly there:
    Be its beauty
    Its sole duty!
Let all hope of grace beyond, lie there!

VIII

And while the face lies quiet there,
    Who shall wonder
    That I ponder
A conclusion? I will try it there.

IX

As,—why must one, for the love foregone,
    Scout mere liking?
    Thunder-striking
Earth,—the heaven, we looked above for, gone!

X

Why, with beauty, needs there money be,
    Love with liking?
    Crush the fly-king
In his gauze, because no honey-bee?

XI

May not liking be so simple-sweet,
    If love grew there
    'Twould undo there
All that breaks the cheek to dimples sweet?

XII

Is the creature too imperfect, say?
    Would you mend it
    And so end it?
Since not all addition perfects aye!

XIII

Or is it of its kind, perhaps,
    Just perfection—
    Whence, rejection
Of a grace not to its mind, perhaps?

XIV

Shall we burn up, tread that face at once
    Into tinder,
    And so hinder
Sparks from kindling all the place at once?

XV

Or else kiss away one's soul on her?
    Your love-fancies!
    —A sick man sees
Truer, when his hot eyes roll on her!

XVI

Thus the craftsman thinks to grace the rose,—
    Plucks a mould-flower
    For his gold flower,
Uses fine things that efface the rose:

XVII

Rosy rubies make its cup more rose,
    Precious metals
    Ape the petals,—
Last, some old king locks it up, morose!

XVIII

Then how grace a rose? I know a way!
    Leave it, rather.
    Must you gather?
Smell, kiss, wear it—at last, throw away!

RESPECTABILITY

I

DEAR, had the world in its caprice
    Deigned to proclaim 'I know you both,
    'Have recognized your plighted troth,
'Am sponsor for you: live in peace!'—
How many precious months and years
    Of youth had passed, that speed so fast,
    Before we found it out at last,
The world, and what it fears?

II

How much of priceless life were spent
    With men that every virtue decks,
    And women models of their sex,
Society's true ornament,—
Ere we dared wander, nights like this,
    Thro' wind and rain, and watch the Seine,
    And feel the Boulevart break again
To warmth and light and bliss?

III

I know! the world proscribes not love;
    Allows my finger to caress
    Your lips' contour and downiness,
Provided it supply a glove.

The world's good word!—the Institute!
Guizot receives Montalembert!
Eh? Down the court three lampions flare:
Put forward your best foot!

LOVE IN A LIFE

I

ROOM after room,
I hunt the house through
We inhabit together.
Heart, fear nothing, for, heart, thou shalt find her—
Next time, herself!—not the trouble behind her
Left in the curtain, the couch's perfume!
As she brushed it, the cornice-wreath blossomed anew:
Yon looking-glass gleamed at the wave of her feather.

II

Yet the day wears,
And door succeeds door;
I try the fresh fortune—
Range the wide house from the wing to the centre.
Still the same chance! she goes out as I enter.
Spend my whole day in the quest,—who cares?
But 'tis twilight, you see,—with such suites to explore,
Such closets to search, such alcoves to importune!

LIFE IN A LOVE

ESCAPE me?
Never—
Beloved!
While I am I, and you are you,
  So long as the world contains us **both**,
  Me the loving and you the loth,
While the one eludes, must the other pursue.

My life is a fault at last, I fear:
  It seems too much like a fate, indeed!
    Though I do my best I shall scarce succeed.
But what if I fail of my purpose here?
It is but to keep the nerves at strain,
  To dry one's eyes and laugh at a fall,
And, baffled, get up and begin again,—
  So the chace takes up one's life, that's all.
While, look but once from your farthest bound
  At me so deep in the dust and dark,
No sooner the old hope goes to ground
  Than a new one, straight to the self-same mark,
I shape me—
Ever
Removed!

IN THREE DAYS

I

So, I shall see her in three days
And just one night, but nights are short,
Then two long hours, and that is morn.
See how I come, unchanged, unworn!
Feel, where my life broke off from thine,
How fresh the splinters keep and fine,—
Only a touch and we combine!

II

Too long, this time of year, the days!
But nights, at least the nights are short.
As night shows where her one moon is,
A hand's-breadth of pure light and bliss,
So life's night gives my lady birth
And my eyes hold her! What is worth
The rest of heaven, the rest of earth?

III

O loaded curls, release your store
Of warmth and scent, as once before
The tingling hair did, lights and darks
Outbreaking into fairy sparks,
When under curl and curl I pried
After the warmth and scent inside,
Thro' lights and darks how manifold—
The dark inspired, the light controlled!
As early Art embrowns the gold.

IV

What great fear, should one say, 'Three days
'That change the world might change as well
'Your fortune; and if joy delays,
'Be happy that no worse befell!'
What small fear, if another says,
'Three days and one short night beside
'May throw no shadow on your ways;
'But years must teem with change untried,
'With chance not easily defied,
'With an end somewhere undescried.'
No fear!—or if a fear be born
This minute, it dies out in scorn.
Fear? I shall see her in three days
And one night, now the nights are short,
Then just two hours, and that is morn.

IN A YEAR

I

NEVER any more,
    While I live,
Need I hope to see his face
    As before.
Once his love grown chill,
    Mine may strive:
Bitterly we re-embrace,
    Single still.

II

Was it something said,
   Something done,
Vexed him? was it touch of hand,
   Turn of head?
Strange! that very way
   Love begun:
I as little understand
   Love's decay.

III

When I sewed or drew,
   I recall
How he looked as if I sung,
   —Sweetly too.
If I spoke a word,
   First of all
Up his cheek the colour sprung,
   Then he heard.

IV

Sitting by my side,
   At my feet,
So he breathed but air I breathed,
   Satisfied!
I, too, at love's brim
   Touched the sweet:
I would die if death bequeathed
   Sweet to him.

V

'Speak, I love thee best!'
   He exclaimed:
'Let thy love my own foretell!'
   I confessed:
'Clasp my heart on thine
   'Now unblamed,
'Since upon thy soul as well
   'Hangeth mine!'

VI

Was it wrong to own,
   Being truth?
Why should all the giving prove
   His alone?
I had wealth and ease,
   Beauty, youth:
Since my lover gave me love,
   I gave these.

VII

That was all I meant,
   —To be just,
And the passion I had raised
   To content.
Since he chose to change
   Gold for dust,
If I gave him what he praised
   Was it strange?

VIII

Would he loved me yet,
   On and on,
While I found some way undreamed
   —Paid my debt!
Gave more life and more,
   Till, all gone,
He should smile 'She never seemed
   'Mine before.

IX

'What, she felt the while,
   'Must I think?
'Love's so different with us men!'
   He should smile:
'Dying for my sake—
   'White and pink!
'Can't we touch these bubbles then
   'But they break?'

X

Dear, the pang is brief,
  Do thy part,
Have thy pleasure! How perplexed
  Grows belief!
Well, this cold clay clod
  Was man's heart:
Crumble it, and what comes next?
  Is it God?

WOMEN AND ROSES

I

I DREAM of a red-rose tree.
And which of its roses three
Is the dearest rose to me?

II

Round and round, like a dance of snow
In a dazzling drift, as its guardians, go
Floating the women faded for ages,
Sculptured in stone, on the poet's pages.
Then follow women fresh and gay,
Living and loving and loved to-day.
Last, in the rear, flee the multitude of maidens,
Beauties yet unborn. And all, to one cadence,
They circle their rose on my rose tree.

III

Dear rose, thy term is reached,
Thy leaf hangs loose and bleached:
Bees pass it unimpeached.

IV

Stay then, stoop, since I cannot climb,
You, great shapes of the antique time!
How shall I fix you, fire you, freeze you,
Break my heart at your feet to please you?

Oh, to possess and be possessed!
Hearts that beat 'neath each pallid breast!
Once but of love, the poesy, the passion,
Drink but once and die!—In vain, the same fashion,
They circle their rose on my rose tree.

V

Dear rose, thy joy's undimmed,
Thy cup is ruby-rimmed,
Thy cup's heart nectar-brimmed.

VI

Deep, as drops from a statue's plinth
The bee sucked in by the hyacinth,
So will I bury me while burning,
Quench like him at a plunge my yearning,
Eyes in your eyes, lips on your lips!
Fold me fast where the cincture slips,
Prison all my soul in eternities of pleasure,
Girdle me for once! But no—the old measure,
They circle their rose on my rose tree.

VII

Dear rose without a thorn,
Thy bud's the babe unborn:
First streak of a new morn.

VIII

Wings, lend wings for the cold, the clear!
What is far conquers what is near.
Roses will bloom nor want beholders,
Sprung from the dust where our flesh moulders.
What shall arrive with the cycle's change?
A novel grace and a beauty strange.
I will make an Eve, be the artist that began her,
Shaped her to his mind!—Alas! in like manner
They circle their rose on my rose tree.

BEFORE

I

Let them fight it out, friend! things have gone too far.
God must judge the couple: leave them as they are
—Whichever one's the guiltless, to his glory,
And whichever one the guilt's with, to my story!

II

Why, you would not bid men, sunk in such a slough,
Strike no arm out further, stick and stink as now,
Leaving right and wrong to settle the embroilment,
Heaven with snaky hell, in torture and entoilment?

III

Who's the culprit of them? How must he conceive
God—the queen he caps to, laughing in his sleeve,
''Tis but decent to profess oneself beneath her:
'Still, one must not be too much in earnest, either!'

IV

Better sin the whole sin, sure that God observes;
Then go live his life out! Life will try his nerves,
When the sky, which noticed all, makes no disclosure,
And the earth keeps up her terrible composure.

V

Let him pace at pleasure, past the walls of rose,
Pluck their fruits when grape-trees graze him as he goes!
For he 'gins to guess the purpose of the garden,
With the sly mute thing, beside there, for a warden.

VI

What's the leopard-dog-thing, constant at his side,
A leer and lie in every eye of its obsequious hide?
When will come an end to all the mock obeisance,
And the price appear that pays for the misfeasance?

VII

So much for the culprit. Who's the martyred man?
Let him bear one stroke more, for be sure he can!
He that strove thus evil's lump with good to leaven,
Let him give his blood at last and get his heaven!

VIII

All or nothing, stake it! Trusts he God or no?
Thus far and no farther? farther? be it so!
Now, enough of your chicane of prudent pauses,
Sage provisos, sub-intents and saving-clauses!

IX

Ah, 'forgive' you bid him? While God's champion lives,
Wrong shall be resisted: dead, why, he forgives.
But you must not end my friend ere you begin him;
Evil stands not crowned on earth, while breath is in him.

X

Once more—Will the wronger, at this last of all,
Dare to say, 'I did wrong,' rising in his fall?
No?—Let go, then! Both the fighters to their places!
While I count three, step you back as many paces!

AFTER

TAKE the cloak from his face, and at first
    Let the corpse do its worst!

How he lies in his rights of a man!
    Death has done all death can.
And, absorbed in the new life he leads,
    He recks not, he heeds
Nor his wrong nor my vengeance; both strike
    On his senses alike,
And are lost in the solemn and strange
    Surprise of the change.
Ha, what avails death to erase
    His offence, my disgrace?

I would we were boys as of old
  In the field, by the fold:
His outrage, God's patience, man's scorn
  Were so easily borne!

I stand here now, he lies in his place:
  Cover the face!

THE GUARDIAN-ANGEL

A PICTURE AT FANO

I

DEAR and great Angel, wouldst thou only leave
  That child, when thou hast done with him, for me!
Let me sit all the day here, that when eve
  Shall find performed thy special ministry,
And time come for departure, thou, suspending
Thy flight, mayst see another child for tending,
  Another still, to quiet and retrieve.

II

Then I shall feel thee step one step, no more,
From where thou standest now, to where I gaze,
—And suddenly my head is covered o'er
  With those wings, white above the child who prays
Now on that tomb—and I shall feel thee guarding
Me, out of all the world; for me, discarding
  Yon heaven thy home, that waits and opes its door.

III

I would not look up thither past thy head
  Because the door opes, like that child, I know,
For I should have thy gracious face instead,
  Thou bird of God! And wilt thou bend me low
Like him, and lay, like his, my hands together,
And lift them up to pray, and gently tether
  Me, as thy lamb there, with thy garment's spread?

IV

If this was ever granted, I would rest
   My head beneath thine, while thy healing hands
Close-covered both my eyes beside thy breast,
   Pressing the brain, which too much thought expands,
Back to its proper size again, and smoothing
Distortion down till every nerve had soothing,
   And all lay quiet, happy and suppressed.

V

How soon all worldly wrong would be repaired!
   I think how I should view the earth and skies
And sea, when once again my brow was bared
   After thy healing, with such different eyes.
O world, as God has made it! All is beauty:
And knowing this, is love, and love is duty.
   What further may be sought for or declared?

VI

Guercino drew this angel I saw teach
   (Alfred, dear friend!)—that little child to pray,
Holding the little hands up, each to each
   Pressed gently,—with his own head turned away
Over the earth where so much lay before him
Of work to do, though heaven was opening o'er him,
   And he was left at Fano by the beach.

VII

We were at Fano, and three times we went
   To sit and see him in his chapel there,
And drink his beauty to our soul's content
   —My angel with me too: and since I care
For dear Guercino's fame (to which in power
And glory comes this picture for a dower,
   Fraught with a pathos so magnificent)—

VIII

And since he did not work thus earnestly
    At all times, and has else endured some wrong—
I took one thought his picture struck from me,
    And spread it out, translating it to song.
My love is here. Where are you, dear old friend?
How rolls the Wairoa at your world's far end?
    This is Ancona, yonder is the sea.

MEMORABILIA

I

AH, did you once see Shelley plain,
    And did he stop and speak to you,
And did you speak to him again?
    How strange it seems and new!

II

But you were living before that,
    And also you are living after;
And the memory I started at—
    My starting moves your laughter.

III

I crossed a moor, with a name of its own
    And a certain use in the world no doubt,
Yet a hand's-breadth of it shines alone
    'Mid the blank miles round about:

IV

For there I picked up on the heather
    And there I put inside my breast
A moulted feather, an eagle-feather!
    Well, I forget the rest.

POPULARITY

I

STAND still, true poet that you are!
  I know you; let me try and draw you.
Some night you'll fail us: when afar
  You rise, remember one man saw you,
Knew you, and named a star!

II

My star, God's glow-worm! Why extend
  That loving hand of his which leads you,
Yet locks you safe from end to end
  Of this dark world, unless he needs you,
Just saves your light to spend?

III

His clenched hand shall unclose at last,
  I know, and let out all the beauty:
My poet holds the future fast,
  Accepts the coming ages' duty,
Their present for this past.

IV

That day, the earth's feast-master's brow
  Shall clear, to God the chalice raising;
'Others give best at first, but thou
  'Forever set'st our table praising,
'Keep'st the good wine till now!'

V

Meantime, I'll draw you as you stand,
  With few or none to watch and wonder:
I'll say—a fisher, on the sand
  By Tyre the old, with ocean-plunder,
A netful, brought to land.

VI

Who has not heard how Tyrian shells
   Enclosed the blue, that dye of dyes
Whereof one drop worked miracles,
   And coloured like Astarte's eyes
Raw silk the merchant sells?

VII

And each bystander of them all
   Could criticize, and quote tradition
How depths of blue sublimed some pall
   —To get which, pricked a king's ambition;
Worth sceptre, crown and ball.

VIII

Yet there's the dye, in that rough mesh,
   The sea has only just o'erwhispered!
Live whelks, each lip's beard dripping fresh,
   As if they still the water's lisp heard
Through foam the rock-weeds thresh.

IX

Enough to furnish Solomon
   Such hangings for his cedar-house,
That, when gold-robed he took the throne
   In that abyss of blue, the Spouse
Might swear his presence shone

X

Most like the centre-spike of gold
   Which burns deep in the blue-bell's womb,
What time, with ardours manifold,
   The bee goes singing to her groom,
Drunken and overbold.

XI

Mere conchs! not fit for warp or woof!
   Till cunning come to pound and squeeze
And clarify,—refine to proof
   The liquor filtered by degrees,
While the world stands aloof.

XII

And there's the extract, flasked and fine,
  And priced and saleable at last!
And Hobbs, Nobbs, Stokes and Nokes combine
  To paint the future from the past,
Put blue into their line.

XIII

Hobbs hints blue,—straight he turtle eats:
  Nobbs prints blue,—claret crowns his cup:
Nokes outdares Stokes in azure feats,—
  Both gorge. Who fished the murex up?
What porridge had John Keats?

MASTER HUGUES OF SAXE-GOTHA

I

Hist, but a word, fair and soft!
  Forth and be judged, Master Hugues!
Answer the question I've put you so oft:
  What do you mean by your mountainous fugues?
See, we're alone in the loft,—

II

I, the poor organist here,
  Hugues, the composer of note,
Dead though, and done with, this many a year:
  Let's have a colloquy, something to quote,
Make the world prick up its ear!

III

See, the church empties apace:
  Fast they extinguish the lights.
Hallo there, sacristan! Five minutes' grace!
  Here's a crank pedal wants setting to rights,
Baulks one of holding the base.

IV

See, our huge house of the sounds,
   Hushing its hundreds at once,
Bids the last loiterer back to his bounds!
   —O you may challenge them, not a response
Get the church-saints on their rounds!

V

(Saints go their rounds, who shall doubt?
   —March, with the moon to admire,
Up nave, down chancel, turn transept about,
   Supervise all betwixt pavement and spire,
Put rats and mice to the rout—

VI

Aloys and Jurien and Just—
   Order things back to their place,
Have a sharp eye lest the candlesticks rust,
   Rub the church-plate, darn the sacrament-lace,
Clear the desk-velvet of dust.)

VII

Here's your book, younger folks shelve!
   Played I not off-hand and runningly,
Just now, your masterpiece, hard number twelve?
   Here's what should strike, could one handle it cun-
     ningly:
Help the axe, give it a helve!

VIII

Page after page as I played,
   Every bar's rest, where one wipes
Sweat from one's brow, I looked up and surveyed,
   O'er my three claviers, yon forest of pipes
Whence you still peeped in the shade.

IX

Sure you were wishful to speak?
    You, with brow ruled like a score,
Yes, and eyes buried in pits on each cheek,
    Like two great breves, as they wrote them of yore,
Each side that bar, your straight beak!

X

Sure you said—'Good, the mere notes!
    'Still, couldst thou take my intent,
'Know what procured me our Company's votes—
    'A master were lauded and sciolists shent,
'Parted the sheep from the goats!'

XI

Well then, speak up, never flinch!
    Quick, ere my candle's a snuff
—Burnt, do you see? to its uttermost inch—
    I believe in you, but that's not enough:
Give my conviction a clinch!

XII

First you deliver your phrase
    —Nothing propound, that I see,
Fit in itself for much blame or much praise—
    Answered no less, where no answer needs be:
Off start the Two on their ways.

XIII

Straight must a Third interpose,
    Volunteer needlessly help;
In strikes a Fourth, a Fifth thrusts in his nose,
    So the cry's open, the kennel's a-yelp,
Argument's hot to the close.

XIV

One dissertates, he is candid;
    Two must discept,—has distinguished;
Three helps the couple, if ever yet man did;
    Four protests; Five makes a dart at the thing wished:
Back to One, goes the case bandied.

XV

One says his say with a difference;
   More of expounding, explaining!
All now is wrangle, abuse, and vociferance;
   Now there's a truce, all's subdued, self-restraining:
Five, though, stands out all the stiffer hence.

XVI

One is incisive, corrosive;
   Two retorts, nettled, curt, crepitant;
Three makes rejoinder, expansive, explosive;
   Four overbears them all, strident and strepitant:
Five . . . O Danaides, O Sieve!

XVII

Now, they ply axes and crowbars;
   Now, they prick pins at a tissue
Fine as a skein of the casuist Escobar's
   Worked on the bone of a lie. To what issue?
Where is our gain at the Two-bars?

XVIII

Est fuga, volvitur rota.
   On we drift: where looms the dim port?
One, Two, Three, Four, Five, contribute their quota;
   Something is gained, if one caught but the import—
Show it us, Hugues of Saxe-Gotha!

XIX

What with affirming, denying,
   Holding, risposting, subjoining,
All's like . . . it's like . . . for an instance I'm trying . . .
   There! See our roof, its gilt moulding and groining
Under those spider-webs lying!

XX

So your fugue broadens and thickens,
   Greatens and deepens and lengthens,
Till we exclaim—'But where's music, the dickens?
   'Blot ye the gold, while your spider-web strengthens
'—Blacked to the stoutest of tickens?'

XXI

I for man's effort am zealous:
    Prove me such censure unfounded!
Seems it surprising a lover grows jealous—
    Hopes 'twas for something, his organ-pipes sounded,
Tiring three boys at the bellows?

XXII

Is it your moral of Life?
    Such a web, simple and subtle,
Weave we on earth here in impotent strife,
    Backward and forward each throwing his shuttle,
Death ending all with a knife?

XXIII

Over our heads truth and nature—
    Still our life's zigzags and dodges,
Ins and outs, weaving a new legislature—
    God's gold just shining its last where that lodges,
Palled beneath man's usurpature.

XXIV

So we o'ershroud stars and roses,
    Cherub and trophy and garland;
Nothings grow something which quietly closes
    Heaven's earnest eye: not a glimpse of the far land
Gets through our comments and glozes.

XXV

Ah but traditions, inventions,
    (Say we and make up a visage)
So many men with such various intentions,
    Down the past ages, must know more than this age!
Leave we the web its dimensions!

XXVI

Who thinks Hugues wrote for the deaf,
    Proved a mere mountain in labour?
Better submit; try again; what's the clef?
    'Faith, 'tis no trifle for pipe and for tabor—
Four flats, the minor in F

XXVII

Friend, your fugue taxes the finger:
　Learning it once, who would lose it?
Yet all the while a misgiving will linger,
　Truth's golden o'er us although we refuse it—
Nature, thro' cobwebs we string her.

XXVIII

Hugues! I advise *meâ pænâ*
　(Counterpoint glares like a Gorgon)
Bid One, Two, Three, Four, Five, clear the arena!
　Say the word, straight I unstop the full-organ,
Blare out the *mode Palestrina*.

XXIX

While in the roof, if I'm right there,
　. . . Lo you, the wick in the socket!
Hallo, you sacristan, show us a light there!
　Down it dips, gone like a rocket.
What, you want, do you, to come unawares,
Sweeping the church up for first morning-prayers,
And find a poor devil has ended his cares
At the foot of your rotten-runged rat-riddled stairs?
　Do I carry the moon in my pocket?

DRAMATIC ROMANCES

INCIDENT OF THE FRENCH CAMP

I

You know, we French stormed Ratisbon:
    A mile or so away,
On a little mound, Napoleon
    Stood on our storming-day;
With neck out-thrust, you fancy how,
    Legs wide, arms locked behind,
As if to balance the prone brow
    Oppressive with its mind.

II

Just as perhaps he mused 'My plans
    'That soar, to earth may fall,
'Let once my army-leader Lannes
    'Waver at yonder wall,'—
Out 'twixt the battery-smokes there flew
    A rider, bound on bound
Full-galloping; nor bridle drew
    Until he reached the mound.

III

Then off there flung in smiling joy,
    And held himself erect
By just his horse's mane, a boy:
    You hardly could suspect—
(So tight he kept his lips compressed,
    Scarce any blood came through)
You looked twice ere you saw his breast
    Was all but shot in two.

IV

'Well,' cried he, 'Emperor, by God's grace
   'We've got you Ratisbon!
'The Marshal's in the market-place,
   'And you'll be there anon
'To see your flag-bird flap his vans
   'Where I, to heart's desire,
'Perched him!' The chief's eye flashed; his plans
   Soared up again like fire.

V

The chief's eye flashed; but presently
   Softened itself, as sheathes
A film the mother-eagle's eye
   When her bruised eaglet breathes;
'You're wounded!' 'Nay,' the soldier's pride
   Touched to the quick, he said:
'I'm killed, Sire!' And his chief beside
   Smiling the boy fell dead.

THE PATRIOT

AN OLD STORY

I

It was roses, roses, all the way,
   With myrtle mixed in my path like mad:
The house-roofs seemed to heave and sway,
   The church-spires flamed, such flags they had,
A year ago on this very day.

II

The air broke into a mist with bells,
   The old walls rocked with the crowd and cries.
Had I said, 'Good folk, mere noise repels—
   'But give me your sun from yonder skies!'
They had answered, 'And afterward, what else?'

III

Alack, it was I who leaped at the sun
  To give it my loving friends to keep!
Nought man could do, have I left undone:
  And you see my harvest, what I reap
This very day, now a year is run.

IV

There's nobody on the house-tops now—
  Just a palsied few at the windows set;
For the best of the sight is, all allow,
  At the Shambles' Gate—or, better yet,
By the very scaffold's foot, I trow.

V

I go in the rain, and, more than needs,
  A rope cuts both my wrists behind;
And I think, by the feel, my forehead bleeds,
  For they fling, whoever has a mind,
Stones at me for my year's misdeeds.

VI

Thus I entered, and thus I go!
  In triumphs, people have dropped down dead.
'Paid by the world, what dost thou owe
  'Me?'—God might question; now instead,
'Tis God shall repay: I am safer so.

MY LAST DUCHESS

FERRARA

THAT's my last Duchess painted on the wall,
Looking as if she were alive. I call
That piece a wonder, now: Frà Pandolf's hands
Worked busily a day, and there she stands.
Will't please you sit and look at her? I said
'Frà Pandolf' by design, for never read
Strangers like you that pictured countenance,
The depth and passion of its earnest glance,

But to myself they turned (since none puts by
The curtain I have drawn for you, but I)
And seemed as they would ask me, if they durst,
How such a glance came there; so, not the first
Are you to turn and ask thus. Sir, 'twas not
Her husband's presence only, called that spot
Of joy into the Duchess' cheek: perhaps
Frà Pandolf chanced to say 'Her mantle laps
'Over my lady's wrist too much,' or 'Paint
'Must never hope to reproduce the faint
'Half-flush that dies along her throat:' such stuff
Was courtesy, she thought, and cause enough
For calling up that spot of joy. She had
A heart—how shall I say?—too soon made glad,
Too easily impressed; she liked whate'er
She looked on, and her looks went everywhere.
Sir, 'twas all one! My favour at her breast,
The dropping of the daylight in the West,
The bough of cherries some officious fool
Broke in the orchard for her, the white mule
She rode with round the terrace—all and each
Would draw from her alike the approving speech,
Or blush, at least. She thanked men,—good! but thanked
Somehow—I know not how—as if she ranked
My gift of a nine-hundred-years-old name
With anybody's gift. Who'd stoop to blame
This sort of trifling? Even had you skill
In speech—(which I have not)—to make your will
Quite clear to such an one, and say, 'Just this
'Or that in you disgusts me; here you miss,
'Or there exceed the mark'—and if she let
Herself be lessoned so, nor plainly set
Her wits to yours, forsooth, and made excuse,
—E'en then would be some stooping; and I choose
Never to stoop. Oh sir, she smiled, no doubt,
Whene'er I passed her; but who passed without
Much the same smile? This grew; I gave commands;
Then all smiles stopped together. There she stands
As if alive. Will't please you rise? We'll meet

The company below, then. I repeat,
The Count your master's known munificence
Is ample warrant that no just pretence
Of mine for dowry will be disallowed;
Though his fair daughter's self, as I avowed
At starting, is my object. Nay, we'll go
Together down, sir. Notice Neptune, though,
Taming a sea-horse, thought a rarity,
Which Claus of Innsbruck cast in bronze for me!

COUNT GISMOND

AIX IN PROVENCE

I

CHRIST God who savest man, save most
  Of men Count Gismond who saved me!
Count Gauthier, when he chose his post,
  Chose time and place and company
To suit it; when he struck at length
My honour, 'twas with all his strength.

II

And doubtlessly ere he could draw
  All points to one, he must have schemed!
That miserable morning saw
  Few half so happy as I seemed,
While being dressed in queen's array
To give our tourney prize away.

III

I thought they loved me, did me grace
  To please themselves; 'twas all their deed;
God makes, or fair or foul, our face;
  If showing mine so caused to bleed
My cousins' hearts, they should have dropped
A word, and straight the play had stopped.

IV

They, too, so beauteous! Each a queen
By virtue of her brow and breast;
Not needing to be crowned, I mean,
As I do. E'en when I was dressed,
Had either of them spoke, instead
Of glancing sideways with still head!

V

But no; they let me laugh, and sing
My birthday song quite through, adjust
The last rose in my garland, fling
A last look on the mirror, trust
My arms to each an arm of theirs,
And so descend the castle-stairs—

VI

And come out on the morning-troop
Of merry friends who kissed my cheek,
And called me queen, and made me stoop
Under the canopy—(a streak
That pierced it, of the outside sun,
Powdered with gold its gloom's soft dun)—

VII

And they could let me take my state
And foolish throne amid applause
Of all come there to celebrate
My queen's-day—Oh I think the cause
Of much was, they forgot no crowd
Makes up for parents in their shroud!

VIII

However that be, all eyes were bent
Upon me, when my cousins cast
Theirs down; 'twas time I should present
The victor's crown, but . . . there, 'twill last
No long time . . . the old mist again
Blinds me as then it did. How vain!

IX

See! Gismond's at the gate, in talk
    With his two boys: I can proceed.
Well, at that moment, who should stalk
    Forth boldly—to my face, indeed—
But Gauthier, and he thundered 'Stay!'
And all stayed. 'Bring no crowns, I say!

X

'Bring torches! Wind the penance-sheet
    'About her! Let her shun the chaste,
'Or lay herself before their feet!
    'Shall she whose body I embraced
'A night long, queen it in the day?
'For honour's sake no crowns, I say!'

XI

I? What I answered? As I live,
    I never fancied such a thing
As answer possible to give.
    What says the body when they spring
Some monstrous torture-engine's whole
Strength on it? No more says the soul.

XII

Till out strode Gismond; then I knew
    That I was saved. I never met
His face before, but, at first view,
    I felt quite sure that God had set
Himself to Satan; who would spend
A minute's mistrust on the end?

XIII

He strode to Gauthier, in his throat
    Gave him the lie, then struck his mouth
With one back-handed blow that wrote
    In blood men's verdict there. North, South,
East, West, I looked. The lie was dead,
And damned, and truth stood up instead.

XIV

This glads me most, that I enjoyed
  The heart of the joy, with my content
In watching Gismond unalloyed
  By any doubt of the event:
God took that on him—I was bid
Watch Gismond for my part: I did.

XV

Did I not watch him while he let
  His armourer just brace his greaves,
Rivet his hauberk, on the fret
  The while! His foot . . . my memory leaves
No least stamp out, nor how anon
He pulled his ringing gauntlets on.

XVI

And e'en before the trumpet's sound
  Was finished, prone lay the false knight,
Prone as his lie, upon the ground:
  Gismond flew at him, used no sleight
O' the sword, but open-breasted drove,
Cleaving till out the truth he clove.

XVII

Which done, he dragged him to my feet
  And said 'Here die, but end thy breath
'In full confession, lest thou fleet
  'From my first, to God's second death!
'Say, hast thou lied?' And, 'I have lied
'To God and her,' he said, and died.

XVIII

Then Gismond, kneeling to me, asked
  —What safe my heart holds, though no word
Could I repeat now, if I tasked
  My powers for ever, to a third
Dear even as you are. Pass the rest
Until I sank upon his breast.

XIX

Over my head his arm he flung
  Against the world; and scarce I felt
His sword (that dripped by me and swung)
  A little shifted in its belt:
For he began to say the while
How South our home lay many a mile.

XX

So 'mid the shouting multitude
  We two walked forth to never more
Return. My cousins have pursued
  Their life, untroubled as before
I vexed them. Gauthier's dwelling-place
God lighten! May his soul find grace!

XXI

Our elder boy has got the clear
  Great brow; tho' when his brother's black
Full eye shows scorn, it . . . Gismond here?
  And have you brought my tercel back?
I just was telling Adela
How many birds it struck since May.

THE BOY AND THE ANGEL

MORNING, evening, noon and night,
'Praise God!' sang Theocrite.

Then to his poor trade he turned,
Whereby the daily meal was earned.

Hard he laboured, long and well;
O'er his work the boy's curls fell.

But ever, at each period,
He stopped and sang, 'Praise God!'

Then back again his curls he threw,
And cheerful turned to work anew.

Said Blaise, the listening monk, 'Well done;
'I doubt not thou art heard, my son:

'As well as if thy voice to-day
'Were praising God, the Pope's great way.

'This Easter Day, the Pope at Rome
'Praises God from Peter's dome.'

Said Theocrite, 'Would God that I
'Might praise him, that great way, and die!'

Night passed, day shone,
And Theocrite was gone.

With God a day endures alway,
A thousand years are but a day.

God said in heaven, 'Nor day nor night
'Now brings the voice of my delight.'

Then Gabriel, like a rainbow's birth,
Spread his wings and sank to earth;

Entered, in flesh, the empty cell,
Lived there, and played the craftsman well;

And morning, evening, noon and night,
Praised God in place of Theocrite.

And from a boy, to youth he grew:
The man put off the stripling's hue:

The man matured and fell away
Into the season of decay:

And ever o'er the trade he bent,
And ever lived on earth content.

(He did God's will; to him, all one
If on the earth or in the sun.)

God said, 'A praise is in mine ear;
'There is no doubt in it, no fear:

'So sing old worlds, and so
'New worlds that from my footstool go.

'Clearer loves sound other ways:
'I miss my little human praise.'

Then forth sprang Gabriel's wings, off fell
The flesh disguise, remained the cell.

'Twas Easter Day: he flew to Rome,
And paused above Saint Peter's dome.

In the tiring-room close by
The great outer gallery,

With his holy vestments dight,
Stood the new Pope, Theocrite:

And all his past career
Came back upon him clear,

Since when, a boy, he plied his trade,
Till on his life the sickness weighed;

And in his cell, when death drew near,
An angel in a dream brought cheer:

And rising from the sickness drear
He grew a priest, and now stood here.

To the East with praise he turned,
And on his sight the angel burned.

'I bore thee from thy craftsman's cell
'And set thee here; I did not well.

'Vainly I left my angel-sphere,
'Vain was thy dream of many a year.

'Thy voice's praise seemed weak; it dropped—
'Creation's chorus stopped!

'Go back and praise again
'The early way, while I remain.

'With that weak voice of our disdain,
'Take up creation's pausing strain.

'Back to the cell and poor employ:
'Resume the craftsman and the boy!'

Theocrite grew old at home;
A new Pope dwelt in Peter's dome.

One vanished as the other died:
They sought God side by side.

INSTANS TYRANNUS

I

Of the million or two, more or less,
I rule and possess,
One man, for some cause undefined,
Was least to my mind.

II

I struck him, he grovelled of course—
For, what was his force?
I pinned him to earth with my weight
And persistence of hate:
And he lay, would not moan, would not curse,
As his lot might be worse.

III

'Were the object less mean, would he stand
'At the swing of my hand!
'For obscurity helps him and blots
'The hole where he squats.'
So, I set my five wits on the stretch
To inveigle the wretch.
All in vain! Gold and jewels I threw,
Still he couched there perdue;
I tempted his blood and his flesh,
Hid in roses my mesh,
Choicest cates and the flagon's best spilth:
Still he kept to his filth.

IV

Had he kith now or kin, were access
To his heart, did I press:
Just a son or a mother to seize!
No such booty as these.
Were it simply a friend to pursue
'Mid my million or two,
Who could pay me in person or pelf
What he owes me himself!

No: I could not but smile through my chafe:
For the fellow lay safe
As his mates do, the midge and the nit,
—Through minuteness, to wit.

V

Then a humour more great took its place
At the thought of his face,
The droop, the low cares of the mouth,
The trouble uncouth
'Twixt the brows, all that air one is fain
To put out of its pain.
And, 'no!' I admonished myself,
'Is one mocked by an elf,
'Is one baffled by toad or by rat?
'The gravamen's in that!
'How the lion, who crouches to suit
'His back to my foot,
'Would admire that I stand in debate!
'But the small turns the great
'If it vexes you,—that is the thing!
'Toad or rat vex the king?
'Though I waste half my realm to unearth
'Toad or rat, 'tis well worth!'

VI

So, I soberly laid my last plan
To extinguish the man.
Round his creep-hole, with never a break
Ran my fires for his sake;
Over-head, did my thunder combine
With my underground mine:
Till I looked from my labour content
To enjoy the event.

VII

When sudden . . . how think ye, the end?
Did I say 'without friend'?
Say rather, from marge to blue marge
The whole sky grew his targe

With the sun's self for visible boss,
While an Arm ran across
Which the earth heaved beneath like a breast
Where the wretch was safe prest!
Do you see? Just my vengeance complete,
The man sprang to his feet,
Stood erect, caught at God's skirts, and prayed!
—So, *I* was afraid!

MESMERISM

I

ALL I believed is true!
   I am able yet
   All I want, to get
By a method as strange as new:
Dare I trust the same to you?

II

If at night, when doors are shut,
   And the wood-worm picks,
   And the death-watch ticks,
And the bar has a flag of smut,
And a cat's in the water-butt—

III

And the socket floats and flares,
   And the house-beams groan,
   And a foot unknown
Is surmised on the garret-stairs,
And the locks slip unawares—

IV

And the spider, to serve his ends,
   By a sudden thread,
   Arms and legs outspread,
On the table's midst descends,
Comes to find, God knows what friends!—

V

If since eve drew in, I say,
    I have sat and brought
    (So to speak) my thought
To bear on the woman away,
Till I felt my hair turn grey—

VI

Till I seemed to have and hold,
    In the vacancy
    'Twixt the wall and me,
From the hair-plait's chestnut gold
To the foot in its muslin fold—

VII

Have and hold, then and there,
    Her, from head to foot,
    Breathing and mute,
Passive and yet aware,
In the grasp of my steady stare—

VIII

Hold and have, there and then,
    All her body and soul
    That completes my whole,
All that women add to men,
In the clutch of my steady ken—

IX

Having and holding, till
    I imprint her fast
    On the void at last
As the sun does whom he will
By the calotypist's skill—

X

Then,—if my heart's strength serve,
    And through all and each
    Of the veils I reach
To her soul and never swerve,
Knitting an iron nerve—

XI

Command her soul to advance
    And inform the shape
    Which has made escape
And before my countenance
Answers me glance for glance—

XII

I, still with a gesture fit
    Of my hands that best
    Do my soul's behest,
Pointing the power from it,
While myself do steadfast sit—

XIII

Steadfast and still the same
    On my object bent,
    While the hands give vent
To my ardour and my aim
And break into very flame—

XIV

Then I reach, I must believe,
    Not her soul in vain,
    For to me again
It reaches, and past retrieve
Is wound in the toils I weave;

XV

And must follow as I require,
    As befits a thrall,
    Bringing flesh and all,
Essence and earth-attire,
To the source of the tractile fire:

XVI

Till the house called hers, not mine,
    With a growing weight
    Seems to suffocate
If she break not its leaden line
And escape from its close confine.

XVII

Out of doors into the night!
    On to the maze
    Of the wild wood-ways,
Not turning to left nor right
From the pathway, blind with sight—

XVIII

Making thro' rain and wind
    O'er the broken shrubs,
    'Twixt the stems and stubs,
With a still, composed, strong mind,
Nor a care for the world behind—

XIX

Swifter and still more swift,
    As the crowding peace
    Doth to joy increase
In the wide blind eyes uplift
Thro' the darkness and the drift!

XX

While I—to the shape, I too
    Feel my soul dilate
    Nor a whit abate,
And relax not a gesture due,
As I see my belief come true.

XXI

For, there! have I drawn or no
    Life to that lip?
    Do my fingers dip
In a flame which again they throw
On the cheek that breaks a-glow?

XXII

Ha! was the hair so first?
    What, unfilleted,
    Made alive, and spread
Through the void with a rich outburst,
Chestnut gold-interspersed?

XXIII

Like the doors of a casket-shrine,
　　See, on either side,
　　Her two arms divide
Till the heart betwixt makes sign,
Take me, for I am thine!

XXIV

'Now—now'—the door is heard!
　　Hark, the stairs! and near—
　　Nearer—and here—
'Now!' and at call the third
She enters without a word.

XXV

On doth she march and on
　　To the fancied shape;
　　It is, past escape,
Herself, now: the dream is done
And the shadow and she are one.

XXVI

First I will pray. Do Thou
　　That ownest the soul,
　　Yet wilt grant control
To another, nor disallow
For a time, restrain me now!

XXVII

I admonish me while I may,
　　Not to squander guilt,
　　Since require Thou wilt
At my hand its price one day!
What the price is, who can say?

THE GLOVE

(PETER RONSARD *loquitur*.)

'HEIGHO!' yawned one day King Francis,
'Distance all value enhances!
'When a man's busy, why, leisure
'Strikes him as wonderful pleasure:
' 'Faith, and at leisure once is he?
'Straightway he wants to be busy.
'Here we've got peace; and aghast I'm
'Caught thinking war the true pastime.
'Is there a reason in metre?
'Give us your speech, master Peter!'
I who, if mortal dare say so,
Ne'er am at loss with my Naso,
'Sire,' I replied, 'joys prove cloudlets:
'Men are the merest Ixions'—
Here the King whistled aloud, 'Let's
'—Heigho—go look at our lions!'
Such are the sorrowful chances
If you talk fine to King Francis.

And so, to the courtyard proceeding,
Our company, Francis was leading,
Increased by new followers tenfold
Before he arrived at the penfold;
Lords, ladies, like clouds which bedizen
At sunset the western horizon.
And Sir De Lorge pressed 'mid the foremost
With the dame he professed to adore most.
Oh, what a face! One by fits eyed
Her, and the horrible pitside;
For the penfold surrounded a hollow
Which led where the eye scarce dared follow,
And shelved to the chamber secluded
Where Bluebeard, the great lion, brooded.
The King hailed his keeper, an Arab
As glossy and black as a scarab,

And bade him make sport and at once stir
Up and out of his den the old monster.
They opened a hole in the wire-work
Across it, and dropped there a firework,
And fled; one's heart's beating redoubled;
A pause, while the pit's mouth was troubled,
The blackness and silence so utter,
By the firework's slow sparkling and sputter;
Then earth in a sudden contortion
Gave out to our gaze her abortion.
Such a brute! Were I friend Clement Marot
(Whose experience of nature's but narrow,
And whose faculties move in no small mist
When he versifies David the Psalmist)
I should study that brute to describe you
Illum Juda Leonem de Tribu.
One's whole blood grew curdling and creepy
To see the black mane, vast and heapy,
The tail in the air stiff and straining,
The wide eyes, nor waxing nor waning,
As over the barrier which bounded
His platform, and us who surrounded
The barrier, they reached and they rested
On space that might stand him in best stead:
For who knew, he thought, what the amazement,
The eruption of clatter and blaze meant,
And if, in this minute of wonder,
No outlet, 'mid lightning and thunder,
Lay broad, and, his shackles all shivered,
The lion at last was delivered?
Ay, that was the open sky o'erhead!
And you saw by the flash on his forehead,
By the hope in those eyes wide and steady,
He was leagues in the desert already,
Driving the flocks up the mountain,
Or catlike couched hard by the fountain
To waylay the date-gathering negress:
So guarded he entrance or egress.
'How he stands!' quoth the King: 'we may well swear,

('No novice, we've won our spurs elsewhere
'And so can afford the confession,)
'We exercise wholesome discretion
'In keeping aloof from his threshold;
'Once hold you, those jaws want no fresh hold,
'Their first would too pleasantly purloin
'The visitor's brisket or surloin:
'But who's he would prove so fool-hardy?
'Not the best man of Marignan, pardie!'

The sentence no sooner was uttered,
Than over the rails a glove fluttered,
Fell close to the lion, and rested:
The dame 'twas, who flung it and jested
With life so, De Lorge had been wooing
For months past; he sat there pursuing
His suit, weighing out with nonchalance
Fine speeches like gold from a balance.

Sound the trumpet, no true knight's a tarrier!
De Lorge made one leap at the barrier,
Walked straight to the glove,—while the lion
Ne'er moved, kept his far-reaching eye on
The palm-tree-edged desert-spring's sapphire,
And the musky oiled skin of the Kaffir,—
Picked it up, and as calmly retreated,
Leaped back where the lady was seated,
And full in the face of its owner
Flung the glove.

                    'Your heart's queen, you dethrone her?
'So should I!'—cried the King—''twas mere vanity,
'Not love, set that task to humanity!'
Lords and ladies alike turned with loathing
From such a proved wolf in sheep's clothing.

Not so, I; for I caught an expression
In her brow's undisturbed self-possession
Amid the Court's scoffing and merriment,—
As if from no pleasing experiment
She rose, yet of pain not much heedful

So long as the process was needful,—
As if she had tried in a crucible,
To what 'speeches like gold' were reducible,
And, finding the finest prove copper,
Felt the smoke in her face was but proper;
To know what she had *not* to trust to,
Was worth all the ashes and dust too.
She went out 'mid hooting and laughter;
Clement Marot stayed; I followed after,
And asked, as a grace, what it all meant?
If she wished not the rash deed's recalment?
'For I'—so I spoke—'am a poet:
'Human nature,—behoves that I know it!

She told me, 'Too long had I heard
'Of the deed proved alone by the word:
'For my love—what De Lorge would not dare!
'With my scorn—what De Lorge could compare!
'And the endless descriptions of death
'He would brave when my lip formed a breath,
'I must reckon as braved, or, of course,
'Doubt his word—and moreover, perforce,
'For such gifts as no lady could spurn,
'Must offer my love in return.
'When I looked on your lion, it brought
'All the dangers at once to my thought,
'Encountered by all sorts of men,
'Before he was lodged in his den,—
'From the poor slave whose club or bare hands
'Dug the trap, set the snare on the sands,
'With no King and no Court to applaud,
'By no shame, should he shrink, overawed,
'Yet to capture the creature made shift,
'That his rude boys might laugh at the gift,
'—To the page who last leaped o'er the fence
'Of the pit, on no greater pretence
'Than to get back the bonnet he dropped,
'Lest his pay for a week should be stopped.
'So, wiser I judged it to make

THE GLOVE

'One trial what "death for my sake"
'Really meant, while the power was yet mine,
'Than to wait until time should define
'Such a phrase not so simply as I,
'Who took it to mean just "to die."
'The blow a glove gives is but weak:
'Does the mark yet discolour my cheek?
'But when the heart suffers a blow,
'Will the pain pass so soon, do you know?'

I looked, as away she was sweeping,
And saw a youth eagerly keeping
As close as he dared to the doorway.
No doubt that a noble should more weigh
His life than befits a plebeian;
And yet, had our brute been Nemean—
(I judge by a certain calm fervour
The youth stepped with, forward to serve her)
—He'd have scarce thought you did him the worst turn
If you whispered 'Friend, what you'd get, first earn!'
And when, shortly after, she carried
Her shame from the Court, and they married,
To that marriage some happiness, maugre
The voice of the Court, I dared augur.

For De Lorge, he made women with men vie,
Those in wonder and praise, these in envy;
And in short stood so plain a head taller
That he wooed and won . . . how do you call her?
The beauty, that rose in the sequel
To the King's love, who loved her a week well.
And 'twas noticed he never would honour
De Lorge (who looked daggers upon her)
With the easy commission of stretching
His legs in the service, and fetching
His wife from her chamber, those straying
Sad gloves she was always mislaying,
While the King took the closet to chat in,—
But of course this adventure came pat in.

And never the King told the story,
How bringing a glove brought such glory,
But the wife smiled—'His nerves are grown firmer:
'Mine he brings now and utters no murmur.'

Venienti occurrite morbo!
With which moral I drop my theorbo.

TIME'S REVENGES

I'VE a Friend, over the sea;
I like him, but he loves me.
It all grew out of the books I write;
They find such favour in his sight
That he slaughters you with savage looks
Because you don't admire my books.
He does himself though,—and if some vein
Were to snap to-night in this heavy brain,
To-morrow month, if I lived to try,
Round should I just turn quietly,
Or out of the bedclothes stretch my hand
Till I found him, come from his foreign land
To be my nurse in this poor place,
And make my broth and wash my face
And light my fire and, all the while,
Bear with his old good-humoured smile
That I told him 'Better have kept away
'Than come and kill me, night and day,
'With, worse than fever throbs and shoots,
'The creaking of his clumsy boots.'
I am as sure that this he would do,
As that Saint Paul's is striking two.
And I think I rather . . . woe is me!
—Yes, rather would see him than not see,
If lifting a hand could seat him there
Before me in the empty chair
To-night, when my head aches indeed,
And I can neither think nor read
Nor make these purple fingers hold
The pen; this garret's freezing cold!

And I've a Lady—there he wakes,
The laughing fiend and prince of snakes
Within me, at her name, to pray
Fate send some creature in the way
Of my love for her, to be down-torn,
Upthrust and outward-borne,
So I might prove myself that sea
Of passion which I needs must be!
Call my thoughts false and my fancies quaint
And my style infirm and its figures faint,
All the critics say, and more blame yet,
And not one angry word you get.
But, please you, wonder I would put
My cheek beneath that lady's foot
Rather than trample under mine
The laurels of the Florentine,
And you shall see how the devil spends
A fire God gave for other ends!
I tell you, I stride up and down
This garret, crowned with love's best crown,
And feasted with love's perfect feast,
To think I kill for her, at least,
Body and soul and peace and fame,
Alike youth's end and manhood's aim,
—So is my spirit, as flesh with sin,
Filled full, eaten out and in
With the face of her, the eyes of her,
The lips, the little chin, the stir
Of shadow round her mouth; and she
—I'll tell you,—calmly would decree
That I should roast at a slow fire,
If that would compass her desire
And make her one whom they invite
To the famous ball to-morrow night.

There may be heaven; there must be hell;
Meantime, there is our earth here—well!

THE ITALIAN IN ENGLAND

THAT second time they hunted me
From hill to plain, from shore to sea,
And Austria, hounding far and wide
Her blood-hounds thro' the country-side,
Breathed hot and instant on my trace,—
I made six days a hiding-place
Of that dry green old aqueduct
Where I and Charles, when boys, have plucked
The fire-flies from the roof above,
Bright creeping thro' the moss they love:
—How long it seems since Charles was lost!
Six days the soldiers crossed and crossed
The country in my very sight;
And when that peril ceased at night,
The sky broke out in red dismay
With signal fires; well, there I lay
Close covered o'er in my recess,
Up to the neck in ferns and cress,
Thinking on Metternich our friend,
And Charles's miserable end,
And much beside, two days; the third,
Hunger o'ercame me when I heard
The peasants from the village go
To work among the maize; you know,
With us in Lombardy, they bring
Provisions packed on mules, a string
With little bells that cheer their task,
And casks, and boughs on every cask
To keep the sun's heat from the wine;
These I let pass in jingling line,
And, close on them, dear noisy crew,
The peasants from the village, too;
For at the very rear would troop
Their wives and sisters in a group
To help, I knew. When these had passed,
I threw my glove to strike the last,
Taking the chance: she did not start,

Much less cry out, but stooped apart,
One instant rapidly glanced round,
And saw me beckon from the ground.
A wild bush grows and hides my crypt;
She picked my glove up while she stripped
A branch off, then rejoined the rest
With that; my glove lay in her breast.
Then I drew breath; they disappeared:
It was for Italy I feared.

An hour, and she returned alone
Exactly where my glove was thrown.
Meanwhile came many thoughts: on me
Rested the hopes of Italy.
I had devised a certain tale
Which, when 'twas told her, could not fail
Persuade a peasant of its truth;
I meant to call a freak of youth
This hiding, and give hopes of pay,
And no temptation to betray.
But when I saw that woman's face,
Its calm simplicity of grace,
Our Italy's own attitude
In which she walked thus far, and stood,
Planting each naked foot so firm,
To crush the snake and spare the worm—
At first sight of her eyes, I said,
'I am that man upon whose head
'They fix the price, because I hate
'The Austrians over us: the State
'Will give you gold—oh, gold so much!—
'If you betray me to their clutch,
'And be your death, for aught I know,
'If once they find you saved their foe.
'Now, you must bring me food and drink,
'And also paper, pen and ink,
'And carry safe what I shall write
'To Padua, which you'll reach at night
'Before the duomo shuts; go in,

'And wait till Tenebræ begin;
'Walk to the third confessional,
'Between the pillar and the wall,
'And kneeling whisper, *Whence comes peace?*
'Say it a second time, then cease;
'And if the voice inside returns,
'*From Christ and Freedom; what concerns*
'*The cause of Peace?*—for answer, slip
'My letter where you placed your lip;
'Then come back happy we have done
'Our mother service—I, the son,
'As you the daughter of our land!'

Three mornings more, she took her stand
In the same place, with the same eyes:
I was no surer of sun-rise
Than of her coming. We conferred
Of her own prospects, and I heard
She had a lover—stout and tall,
She said—then let her eyelids fall,
'He could do much'—as if some doubt
Entered her heart,—then, passing out,
'She could not speak for others, who
'Had other thoughts; herself she knew:'
And so she brought me drink and food.
After four days, the scouts pursued
Another path; at last arrived
The help my Paduan friends contrived
To furnish me: she brought the news.
For the first time I could not choose
But kiss her hand, and lay my own
Upon her head—'This faith was shown
'To Italy, our mother; she
'Uses my hand and blesses thee.'
She followed down to the sea-shore;
I left and never saw her more.

How very long since I have thought
Concerning—much less wished for—aught

Beside the good of Italy,
For which I live and mean to die!
I never was in love; and since
Charles proved false, what shall now convince.
My inmost heart I have a friend?
However, if I pleased to spend
Real wishes on myself—say, three—
I know at least what one should be.
I would grasp Metternich until
I felt his red wet throat distil
In blood thro' these two hands. And next,
—Nor much for that am I perplexed—
Charles, perjured traitor, for his part,
Should die slow of a broken heart
Under his new employers. Last
—Ah, there, what should I wish? For fast
Do I grow old and out of strength.
If I resolved to seek at length
My father's house again, how scared
They all would look, and unprepared!
My brothers live in Austria's pay
—Disowned me long ago, men say;
And all my early mates who used
To praise me so—perhaps induced
More than one early step of mine—
Are turning wise: while some opine
'Freedom grows license,' some suspect
'Haste breeds delay,' and recollect
They always said, such premature
Beginnings never could endure!
So, with a sullen 'All's for best,'
The land seems settling to its rest.
I think then, I should wish to stand
This evening in that dear, lost land,
Over the sea the thousand miles,
And know if yet that woman smiles
With the calm smile; some little farm
She lives in there, no doubt: what harm
If I sat on the door-side bench,

And, while her spindle made a trench
    Fantastically in the dust,
Inquired of all her fortunes—just
    Her children's ages and their names,
And what may be the husband's aims
For each of them. I'd talk this out,
And sit there, for an hour about,
Then kiss her hand once more, and lay
Mine on her head, and go my way.

    So much for idle wishing—how
It steals the time! To business now.

THE ENGLISHMAN IN ITALY

PIANO DI SORRENTO

FORTÙ, Fortù, my beloved one,
    Sit here by my side,
On my knees put up both little feet!
    I was sure, if I tried,
I could make you laugh spite of Scirocco.
    Now, open your eyes,
Let me keep you amused till he vanish
    In black from the skies,
With telling my memories over
    As you tell your beads;
All the Plain saw me gather, I garland
    —The flowers or the weeds.

Time for rain! for your long hot dry Autumn
    Had net-worked with brown
The white skin of each grape on the bunches,
    Marked like a quail's crown,
Those creatures you make such account of,
    Whose heads,—speckled white
Over brown like a great spider's back,
    As I told you last night,—
Your mother bites off for her supper.
    Red-ripe as could be,

Pomegranates were chapping and splitting
    In halves on the tree:
And betwixt the loose walls of great flintstone,
    Or in the thick dust
On the path, or straight out of the rock-side,
    Wherever could thrust
Some burnt sprig of bold hardy rock-flower
    Its yellow face up,
For the prize were great butterflies fighting,
    Some five for one cup.
So, I guessed, ere I got up this morning,
    What change was in store,
By the quick rustle-down of the quail-nets
    Which woke me before
I could open my shutter, made fast
    With a bough and a stone,
And look thro' the twisted dead vine-twigs,
    Sole lattice that's known.
Quick and sharp rang the rings down the net-poles,
    While, busy beneath,
Your priest and his brother tugged at them,
    The rain in their teeth.
And out upon all the flat house-roofs
    Where split figs lay drying,
The girls took the frails under cover:
    Nor use seemed in trying
To get out the boats and go fishing,
    For, under the cliff,
Fierce the black water frothed o'er the blind-rock.
    No seeing our skiff
Arrive about noon from Amalfi,
    —Our fisher arrive,
And pitch down his basket before us,
    All trembling alive
With pink and grey jellies, your sea-fruit;
    You touch the strange lumps,
And mouths gape there, eyes open, all manner
    Of horns and of humps,
Which only the fisher looks grave at,

While round him like imps
Cling screaming the children as naked
    And brown as his shrimps;
Himself too as bare to the middle
    —You see round his neck
The string and its brass coin suspended,
    That saves him from wreck.
But to-day not a boat reached Salerno,
    So back, to a man,
Came our friends, with whose help in the vineyards
    Grape-harvest began.
In the vat, halfway up in our house-side,
    Like blood the juice spins,
While your brother all bare-legged is dancing
    Till breathless he grins
Dead-beaten in effort on effort
    To keep the grapes under,
Since still when he seems all but master,
    In pours the fresh plunder
From girls who keep coming and going
    With basket on shoulder,
And eyes shut against the rain's driving;
    Your girls that are older,—
For under the hedges of aloe,
    And where, on its bed
Of the orchard's black mould, the love-apple
    Lies pulpy and red,
All the young ones are kneeling and filling
    Their laps with the snails
Tempted out by this first rainy weather,—
    Your best of regales,
As to-night will be proved to my sorrow,
    When, supping in state,
We shall feast our grape-gleaners (two dozen,
    Three over one plate)
With lasagne so tempting to swallow
    In slippery ropes,
And gourds fried in great purple slices,
    That colour of popes.

Meantime, see the grape bunch they've brought you:
> The rain-water slips
O'er the heavy blue bloom on each globe
> Which the wasp to your lips
Still follows with fretful persistence:
> Nay, taste, while awake,
This half of a curd-white smooth cheese-ball
> That peels, flake by flake,
Like an onion, each smoother and whiter;
> Next, sip this weak wine
From the thin green glass flask, with its stopper,
> A leaf of the vine;
And end with the prickly-pear's red flesh
> That leaves thro' its juice
The stony black seeds on your pearl-teeth.
> Scirocco is loose!
Hark, the quick, whistling pelt of the olives
> Which, thick in one's track,
Tempt the stranger to pick up and bite them,
> Tho' not yet half black!
How the old twisted olive trunks shudder,
> The medlars let fall
Their hard fruit, and the brittle great fig-trees
> Snap off, figs and all,
For here comes the whole of the tempest!
> No refuge, but creep
Back again to my side and my shoulder,
> And listen or sleep.

O how will your country show next week,
> When all the vine-boughs
Have been stripped of their foliage to pasture
> The mules and the cows?
Last eve, I rode over the mountains;
> Your brother, my guide,
Soon left me, to feast on the myrtles
> That offered, each side,
Their fruit-balls, black, glossy and luscious,—
> Or strip from the sorbs

A treasure, or, rosy and wondrous,
    Those hairy gold orbs!
But my mule picked his sure sober path out,
    Just stopping to neigh
When he recognized down in the valley
    His mates on their way
With the faggots and barrels of water;
    And soon we emerged
From the plain, where the woods could scarce follow:
    And still as we urged
Our way, the woods wondered, and left us,
    As up still we trudged
Though the wild path grew wilder each instant,
    And place was e'en grudged
'Mid the rock-chasms and piles of loose stones
    Like the loose broken teeth
Of some monster which climbed there to die
    From the ocean beneath—
Place was grudged to the silver-grey fume-weed
    That clung to the path,
And dark rosemary ever a-dying
    That, 'spite the wind's wrath,
So loves the salt rock's face to seaward,
    And lentisks as staunch
To the stone where they root and bear berries,
    And ... what shows a branch
Coral-coloured, transparent, with circlets
    Of pale seagreen leaves;
Over all trod my mule with the caution
    Of gleaners o'er sheaves,
Still, foot after foot like a lady,
    Till, round after round,
He climbed to the top of Calvano,
    And God's own profound
Was above me, and round me the mountains,
    And under, the sea,
And within me my heart to bear witness
    What was and shall be.
Oh, heaven and the terrible crystal!

No rampart excludes
Your eye from the life to be lived
    In the blue solitudes.
Oh, those mountains, their infinite movement!
    Still moving with you;
For, ever some new head and breast of them
    Thrusts into view
To observe the intruder; you see it
    If quickly you turn
And, before they escape you surprise them.
    They grudge you should learn
How the soft plains they look on, lean over
    And love (they pretend)
—Cower beneath them, the flat sea-pine crouches,
    The wild fruit-trees bend,
E'en the myrtle-leaves curl, shrink and shut:
    All is silent and grave:
'Tis a sensual and timorous beauty,
    How fair! but a slave.
So, I turned to the sea; and there slumbered
    As greenly as ever
Those isles of the siren, your Galli;
    No ages can sever
The Three, nor enable their sister
    To join them,—halfway
On the voyage, she looked at Ulysses—
    No farther to-day,
Tho' the small one, just launched in the wave,
    Watches breast-high and steady
From under the rock, her bold sister
    Swum halfway already.
Fortù, shall we sail there together
    And see from the sides
Quite new rocks show their faces, new haunts
    Where the siren abides?
Shall we sail round and round them, close over
    The rocks, tho' unseen,
That ruffle the grey glassy water
    To glorious green?

Then scramble from splinter to splinter,
    Reach land and explore,
On the largest, the strange square black turret
    With never a door,
Just a loop to admit the quick lizards;
    Then, stand there and hear
The birds' quiet singing, that tells us
    What life is, so clear?
—The secret they sang to Ulysses
    When, ages ago,
He heard and he knew this life's secret,
    I hear and I know.

Ah, see! The sun breaks o'er Calvano;
    He strikes the great gloom
And flutters it o'er the mount's summit
    In airy gold fume.
All is over. Look out, see the gipsy,
    Our tinker and smith,
Has arrived, set up bellows and forge,
    And down-squatted forthwith
To his hammering, under the wall there;
    One eye keeps aloof
The urchins that itch to be putting
    His jews'-harps to proof,
While the other, thro' locks of curled wire,
    Is watching how sleek
Shines the hog, come to share in the windfall
    —Chew, abbot's own cheek!
All is over. Wake up and come out now,
    And down let us go,
And see the fine things got in order
    At church for the show
Of the Sacrament, set forth this evening.
    To-morrow's the Feast
Of the Rosary's Virgin, by no means
    Of Virgins the least,
As you'll hear in the off-hand discourse
    Which (all nature, no art)

The Dominican brother, these three weeks,
 Was getting by heart.
Not a pillar nor post but is dizened
 With red and blue papers;
All the roof waves with ribbons, each altar
 A-blaze with long tapers;
But the great masterpiece is the scaffold
 Rigged glorious to hold
All the fiddlers and fifers and drummers
 And trumpeters bold,
Not afraid of Bellini nor Auber,
 Who, when the priest 's hoarse,
Will strike us up something that 's brisk
 For the feast's second course.
And then will the flaxen-wigged Image
 Be carried in pomp
Thro' the plain, while in gallant procession
 The priests mean to stomp.
All round the glad church lie old bottles
 With gunpowder stopped,
Which will be, when the Image re-enters,
 Religiously popped;
And at night from the crest of Calvano
 Great bonfires will hang,
On the plain will the trumpets join chorus,
 And more poppers bang.
At all events, come—to the garden,
 As far as the wall;
See me tap with a hoe on the plaster
 Till out there shall fall
A scorpion with wide angry nippers!

 —'Such trifles!' you say?
Fortù, in my England at home,
 Men meet gravely to-day
And debate, if abolishing Corn-laws
 Be righteous and wise
—If 'twere proper, Scirocco should vanish
 In black from the skies!

IN A GONDOLA

He sings.

I SEND my heart up to thee, all my heart
  In this my singing.
For the stars help me, and the sea bears part;
  The very night is clinging
Closer to Venice' streets to leave one space
  Above me, whence thy face
May light my joyous heart to thee its dwelling-place.

She speaks.

Say after me, and try to say
My very words, as if each word
Came from you of your own accord,
In your own voice, in your own way:
'This woman's heart and soul and brain
'Are mine as much as this gold chain
'She bids me wear; which' (say again)
'I choose to make by cherishing
'A precious thing, or choose to fling
'Over the boat-side, ring by ring.'
And yet once more say . . . no word more
Since words are only words. Give o'er!

Unless you call me, all the same,
Familiarly by my pet name,
Which if the Three should hear you call,
And me reply to, would proclaim
At once our secret to them all.
Ask of me, too, command me, blame—
Do, break down the partition-wall
'Twixt us, the daylight world beholds
Curtained in dusk and splendid folds!
What's left but—all of me to take?
I am the Three's: prevent them, slake
Your thirst! 'Tis said, the Arab sage,
In practising with gems, can loose

Their subtle spirit in his cruce
And leave but ashes: so, sweet mage,
Leave them my ashes when thy use
Sucks out my soul, thy heritage!

He sings.

I

Past we glide, and past, and past!
    What's that poor Agnese doing
Where they make the shutters fast?
    Grey Zanobi's just a-wooing
To his couch the purchased bride:
    Past we glide!

II

Past we glide, and past, and past!
    Why's the Pucci Palace flaring
Like a beacon to the blast?
    Guests by hundreds, not one caring
If the dear host's neck were wried:
    Past we glide!

She sings.

I

The moth's kiss, first!
Kiss me as if you made believe
You were not sure, this eve,
How my face, your flower, had pursed
Its petals up; so, here and there
You brush it, till I grow aware
Who wants me, and wide ope I burst.

II

The bee's kiss, now!
Kiss me as if you entered gay
My heart at some noonday,
A bud that dares not disallow
The claim, so all is rendered up,
And passively its shattered cup
Over your head to sleep I bow.

He sings.

I

What are we two?
I am a Jew,
And carry thee, farther than friends can pursue,
To a feast of our tribe;
Where they need thee to bribe
The devil that blasts them unless he imbibe
Thy . . . Scatter the vision for ever! And now,
As of old, I am I, thou art thou!

II

Say again, what we are?
The sprite of a star,
I lure thee above where the destinies bar
My plumes their full play
Till a ruddier ray
Than my pale one announce there is withering away
Some . . . Scatter the vision for ever! And now,
As of old, I am I, thou art thou!

He muses.

Oh, which were best, to roam or rest?
The land's lap or the water's breast?
To sleep on yellow millet-sheaves,
Or swim in lucid shallows just
Eluding water-lily leaves,
An inch from Death's black fingers, thrust
To lock you, whom release he must;
Which life were best on Summer eves?

He speaks, musing.

Lie back; could thought of mine improve you?
From this shoulder let there spring
A wing; from this, another wing;
Wings, not legs and feet, shall move you!
Snow-white must they spring, to blend
With your flesh, but I intend
They shall deepen to the end,

Broader, into burning gold,
Till both wings crescent-wise enfold
Your perfect self, from 'neath your feet
To o'er your head, where, lo, they meet
As if a million sword-blades hurled
Defiance from you to the world!

Rescue me thou, the only real!
And scare away this mad ideal
That came, nor motions to depart!
Thanks! Now, stay ever as thou art!

Still he muses.

I

What if the Three should catch at last
Thy serenader? While there's cast
Paul's cloak about my head, and fast
Gian pinions me, Himself has past
His stylet thro' my back; I reel;
And . . . is it thou I feel?

II

They trail me, these three godless knaves,
Past every church that saints and saves,
Nor stop till, where the cold sea raves
By Lido's wet accursed graves,
They scoop mine, roll me to its brink,
And . . . on thy breast I sink!

She replies, musing.

Dip your arm o'er the boat-side, elbow-deep,
As I do: thus: were death so unlike sleep,
Caught this way? Death's to fear from flame or steel,
Or poison doubtless; but from water—feel!
Go find the bottom! Would you stay me? There!
Now pluck a great blade of that ribbon-grass
To plait in where the foolish jewel was,
I flung away: since you have praised my hair,
'Tis proper to be choice in what I wear.

He speaks.

Row home? must we row home? Too surely
Know I where its front's demurely
Over the Giudecca piled;
Window just with window mating,
Door on door exactly waiting,
All's the set face of a child:
But behind it, where's a trace
Of the staidness and reserve,
And formal lines without a curve,
In the same child's playing-face?
No two windows look one way
O'er the small sea-water thread
Below them. Ah, the autumn day
I, passing, saw you overhead!
First, out a cloud of curtain blew,
Then a sweet cry, and last came you—
To catch your lory that must needs
Escape just then, of all times then,
To peck a tall plant's fleecy seeds,
And make me happiest of men.
I scarce could breathe to see you reach
So far back o'er the balcony
To catch him ere he climbed too high
Above you in the Smyrna peach
That quick the round smooth cord of gold,
This coiled hair on your head, unrolled,
Fell down you like a gorgeous snake
The Roman girls were wont, of old,
When Rome there was, for coolness' sake
To let lie curling o'er their bosoms.
Dear lory, may his beak retain
Ever its delicate rose stain
As if the wounded lotus-blossoms
Had marked their thief to know again!

Stay longer yet, for other's sake
Than mine! What should your chamber do?
—With all its rarities that ache

In silence while day lasts, but wake
At night-time and their life renew,
Suspended just to pleasure you
Who brought against their will together
These objects, and, while day lasts, weave
Around them such a magic tether
That dumb they look; your harp, believe,
With all the sensitive tight strings
Which dare not speak, now to itself
Breathes slumberously, as if some elf
Went in and out the chords, his wings
Make murmur wheresoe'er they graze,
As an angel may, between the maze
Of midnight palace-pillars, on
And on, to sow God's plagues, have gone
Through guilty glorious Babylon.
And while such murmurs flow, the nymph
Bends o'er the harp-top from her shell
As the dry limpet for the lymph
Come with a tune he knows so well.
And how your statues' hearts must swell!
And how your pictures must descend
To see each other, friend with friend!
Oh, could you take them by surprise,
You'd find Schidone's eager Duke
Doing the quaintest courtesies
To that prim saint by Haste-thee-Luke
And, deeper into her rock den,
Bold Castelfranco's Magdalen
You'd find retreated from the ken
Of that robed counsel-keeping Ser—
As if the Tizian thinks of her,
And is not, rather, gravely bent
On seeing for himself what toys
Are these, his progeny invent,
What litter now the board employs
Whereon he signed a document
That got him murdered! Each enjoys
Its night so well, you cannot break

The sport up, so, indeed must make
More stay with me, for others' sake.

She speaks.

I

To-morrow, if a harp-string, say,
Is used to tie the jasmine back
That overfloods my room with sweets,
Contrive your Zorzi somehow meets
My Zanze! If the ribbon's black,
The Three are watching: keep away!

II

Your gondola—let Zorzi wreathe
A mesh of water-weeds about
Its prow, as if he unaware
Had struck some quay or bridge-foot stair!
That I may throw a paper out
As you and he go underneath.

There's Zanze's vigilant taper; safe are we.
Only one minute more to-night with me?
Resume your past self of a month ago!
Be you the bashful gallant, I will be
The lady with the colder breast than snow.
Now bow you, as becomes, nor touch my hand
More than I touch yours when I step to land,
And say, 'All thanks, Siora!'—

Heart to heart
And lips to lips! Yet once more, ere we part,
Clasp me and make me thine, as mine thou art!

He is surprised, and stabbed.

It was ordained to be so, sweet!—and best
Comes now, beneath thine eyes, upon thy breast.
Still kiss me! Care not for the cowards! Care
Only to put aside thy beauteous hair
My blood will hurt! The Three, I do not scorn
To death, because they never lived: but I
Have lived indeed, and so—(yet one more kiss)—can die!

WARING

I

1

WHAT's become of Waring
Since he gave us all the slip,
Chose land-travel or seafaring,
Boots and chest or staff and scrip,
Rather than pace up and down
Any longer London town?

II

Who'd have guessed it from his lip
Or his brow's accustomed bearing,
On the night he thus took ship
Or started landward?—little caring
For us, it seems, who supped together
(Friends of his too, I remember)
And walked home thro' the merry weather,
The snowiest in all December.
I left his arm that night myself
For what's-his-name's, the new prose-poet
Who wrote the book there, on the shelf—
How, forsooth, was I to know it
If Waring meant to glide away
Like a ghost at break of day?
Never looked he half so gay!

III

He was prouder than the devil:
How he must have cursed our revel!
Ay and many other meetings,
Indoor visits, outdoor greetings,
As up and down he paced this London,
With no work done, but great works undone,
Where scarce twenty knew his name.
Why not, then, have earlier spoken,
Written, bustled? Who's to blame
If your silence kept unbroken?

'True, but there were sundry jottings,
'Stray-leaves, fragments, blurrs and blottings,
'Certain first steps were achieved
'Already which'—(is that your meaning?)
'Had well borne out whoe'er believed
'In more to come!' But who goes gleaning
Hedge-side chance-blades, while full-sheaved
Stand cornfields by him? Pride, o'erweening
Pride alone, puts forth such claims
O'er the day's distinguished names.

IV

Meantime, how much I loved him,
I find out now I've lost him.
I who cared not if I moved him,
Who could so carelessly accost him,
Henceforth never shall get free
Of his ghostly company,
His eyes that just a little wink
As deep I go into the merit
Of this and that distinguished spirit—
His cheeks' raised colour, soon to sink,
As long I dwell on some stupendous
And tremendous (Heaven defend us!)
Monstr'-inform'-ingens-horrend-ous
Demoniaco-seraphic
Penman's latest piece of graphic.
Nay, my very wrist grows warm
With his dragging weight of arm.
E'en so, swimmingly appears,
Through one's after-supper musings,
Some lost lady of old years
With her beauteous vain endeavour
And goodness unrepaid as ever;
The face, accustomed to refusings,
We, puppies that we were . . . Oh never
Surely, nice of conscience, scrupled
Being aught like false, forsooth, to?
Telling aught but honest truth to?

What a sin, had we centupled
Its possessor's grace and sweetness!
No! she heard in its completeness
Truth, for truth's a weighty matter,
And truth, at issue, we can't flatter!
Well, 'tis done with; she's exempt
From damning us thro' such a sally;
And so she glides, as down a valley,
Taking up with her contempt,
Past our reach; and in, the flowers
Shut her unregarded hours.

V

Oh, could I have him back once more,
This Waring, but one half-day more!
Back, with the quiet face of yore,
So hungry for acknowledgment
Like mine! I'd fool him to his bent.
Feed, should not he, to heart's content?
I'd say, 'to only have conceived,
'Planned your great works, apart from progress,
'Surpasses little works achieved!'
I'd lie so, I should be believed.
I'd make such havoc of the claims
Of the day's distinguished names
To feast him with, as feasts an ogress
Her feverish sharp-toothed gold-crowned child!
Or as one feasts a creature rarely
Captured here, unreconciled
To capture; and completely gives
Its pettish humours license, barely
Requiring that it lives.

VI

Ichabod, Ichabod,
The glory is departed!
Travels Waring East away?
Who, of knowledge, by hearsay,
Reports a man upstarted
Somewhere as a god,

Hordes grown European-hearted,
Millions of the wild made tame
On a sudden at his fame?
In Vishnu-land what Avatar?
Or who in Moscow, toward the Czar,
With the demurest of footfalls
Over the Kremlin's pavement bright
With serpentine and syenite,
Steps, with five other Generals
That simultaneously take snuff,
For each to have pretext enough
And kerchiefwise unfold his sash
Which, softness' self, is yet the stuff
To hold fast where a steel chain snaps,
And leave the grand white neck no gash?
Waring in Moscow, to those rough
Cold northern natures borne perhaps,
Like the lambwhite maiden dear
From the circle of mute kings
Unable to repress the tear,
Each as his sceptre down he flings,
To Dian's fane at Taurica,
Where now a captive priestess, she alway
Mingles her tender grave Hellenic speech
With theirs, tuned to the hailstone-beaten beach:
As pours some pigeon, from the myrrhy lands
Rapt by the whirlblast to fierce Scythian strands
Where breed the swallows, her melodious cry
Amid their barbarous twitter!
In Russia? Never! Spain were fitter!
Ay, most likely 'tis in Spain
That we and Waring meet again
Now, while he turns down that cool narrow lane
Into the blackness, out of grave Madrid
All fire and shine, abrupt as when there's slid
Its stiff gold blazing pall
From some black coffin-lid.
Or, best of all,
I love to think

The leaving us was just a feint;
Back here to London did he slink,
And now works on without a wink
Of sleep, and we are on the brink
Of something great in fresco-paint:
Some garret's ceiling, walls and floor,
Up and down and o'er and o'er
He splashes, as none splashed before
Since great Caldara Polidore.
Or Music means this land of ours
Some favour yet, to pity won
By Purcell from his Rosy Bowers,—
'Give me my so-long promised son,
'Let Waring end what I begun!'
Then down he creeps and out he steals
Only when the night conceals
His face; in Kent 'tis cherry-time,
Or hops are picking: or at prime
Of March he wanders as, too happy,
Years ago when he was young,
Some mild eve when woods grew sappy
And the early moths had sprung
To life from many a trembling sheath
Woven the warm boughs beneath;
While small birds said to themselves
What should soon be actual song,
And young gnats, by tens and twelves
Made as if they were the throng
That crowd around and carry aloft
The sound they have nursed, so sweet and pure,
Out of a myriad noises soft,
Into a tone that can endure
Amid the noise of a July noon
When all God's creatures crave their boon,
All at once and all in tune,
And get it, happy as Waring then,
Having first within his ken
What a man might do with men:
And far too glad, in the even-glow,

To mix with the world he meant to take
Into his hand, he told you, so—
And out of it his world to make,
To contract and to expand
As he shut or oped his hand.
Oh Waring, what's to really be?
A clear stage and a crowd to see!
Some Garrick, say, out shall not he
The heart of Hamlet's mystery pluck?
Or, where most unclean beasts are rife,
Some Junius—am I right?—shall tuck
His sleeve, and forth with flaying-knife!
Some Chatterton shall have the luck
Of calling Rowley into life!
Some one shall somehow run a muck
With this old world, for want of strife
Sound asleep. Contrive, contrive
To rouse us, Waring! Who's alive?
Our men scarce seem in earnest now.
Distinguished names!—but 'tis, somehow,
As if they played at being names
Still more distinguished, like the games
Of children. Turn our sport to earnest
With a visage of the sternest!
Bring the real times back, confessed
Still better than our very best!

II

I

'WHEN I last saw Waring . . .'
(How all turned to him who spoke!
You saw Waring? Truth or joke?
In land-travel or sea-faring?)

II

'We were sailing by Triest
'Where a day or two we harboured:
'A sunset was in the West,

'When, looking over the vessel's side,
'One of our company espied
'A sudden speck to larboard.
'And as a sea-duck flies and swims
'At once, so came the light craft up,
'With its sole lateen sail that trims
'And turns (the water round its rims
'Dancing, as round a sinking cup)
'And by us like a fish it curled,
'And drew itself up close beside,
'Its great sail on the instant furled,
'And o'er its thwarts a shrill voice cried,
'(A neck as bronzed as a Lascar's)
' "Buy wine of us, you English Brig?
' "Or fruit, tobacco and cigars?
' "A pilot for you to Triest?
' "Without one, look you ne'er so big,
' "They'll never let you up the bay!
' "We natives should know best."
'I turned, and "just those fellows' way,"
'Our captain said, "The 'long-shore thieves
' "Are laughing at us in their sleeves."

III

'In truth, the boy leaned laughing back;
'And one, half-hidden by his side
'Under the furled sail, soon I spied,
'With great grass hat and kerchief black,
'Who looked up with his kingly throat,
'Said somewhat, while the other shook
'His hair back from his eyes to look
'Their longest at us; then the boat,
'I know not how, turned sharply round,
'Laying her whole side on the sea
'As a leaping fish does; from the lee
'Into the weather, cut somehow
'Her sparkling path beneath our bow
'And so went off, as with a bound,
'Into the rosy and golden half

'O' the sky, to overtake the sun
'And reach the shore, like the sea-calf
'Its singing cave; yet I caught one
'Glance ere away the boat quite passed,
'And neither time nor toil could mar
'Those features: so I saw the last
'Of Waring!'—You? Oh, never star
Was lost here but it rose afar!
Look East, where whole new thousands are!
In Vishnu-land what Avatar?

THE TWINS

'Give' and 'It-shall-be-given-unto-you.'

I

GRAND rough old Martin Luther
    Bloomed fables—flowers on furze,
The better the uncouther:
    Do roses stick like burrs?

II

A beggar asked an alms
    One day at an abbey-door,
Said Luther; but, seized with qualms,
    The abbot replied, 'We're poor!

III

'Poor, who had plenty once,
    'When gifts fell thick as rain:
'But they give us nought, for the nonce,
    'And how should we give again?'

IV

Then the beggar, 'See your sins!
    'Of old, unless I err,
'Ye had brothers for inmates, twins,
    'Date and Dabitur.

V

'While Date was in good case
'Dabitur flourished too:
'For Dabitur's lenten face
'No wonder if Date rue.

VI

'Would ye retrieve the one?
'Try and make plump the other!
'When Date's penance is done,
'Dabitur helps his brother.

VII

'Only, beware relapse!'
The Abbot hung his head.
This beggar might be perhaps
An angel, Luther said.

A LIGHT WOMAN

I

So far as our story approaches the end,
    Which do you pity the most of us three?—
My friend, or the mistress of my friend
    With her wanton eyes, or me?

II

My friend was already too good to lose,
    And seemed in the way of improvement yet,
When she crossed his path with her hunting-noose
    And over him drew her net.

III

When I saw him tangled in her toils,
    A shame, said I, if she adds just him
To her nine-and-ninety other spoils,
    The hundredth for a whim!

IV

And before my friend be wholly hers,
   How easy to prove to him, I said,
An eagle's the game her pride prefers,
   Though she snaps at a wren instead!

V

So, I gave her eyes my own eyes to take,
   My hand sought hers as in earnest need,
And round she turned for my noble sake,
   And gave me herself indeed.

VI

The eagle am I, with my fame in the world,
   The wren is he, with his maiden face.
—You look away and your lip is curled?
   Patience, a moment's space!

VII

For see, my friend goes shaking and white;
   He eyes me as the basilisk:
I have turned, it appears, his day to night,
   Eclipsing his sun's disk.

VIII

And I did it, he thinks, as a very thief:
   'Though I love her—that, he comprehends—
'One should master one's passions, (love, in chief)
   'And be loyal to one's friends!'

IX

And she,—she lies in my hand as tame
   As a pear late basking over a wall;
Just a touch to try and off it came;
   'Tis mine,—can I let it fall?

X

With no mind to eat it, that's the worst!
   Were it thrown in the road, would the case assist?
'Twas quenching a dozen blue-flies' thirst
   When I gave its stalk a twist.

XI

And I,—what I seem to my friend, you see:
　　What I soon shall seem to his love, you guess:
What I seem to myself, do you ask of me?
　　No hero, I confess.

XII

'Tis an awkward thing to play with souls,
　　And matter enough to save one's own:
Yet think of my friend, and the burning coals
　　He played with for bits of stone!

XIII

One likes to show the truth for the truth;
　　That the woman was light is very true:
But suppose she says,—Never mind that youth!
　　What wrong have I done to you?

XIV

Well, any how, here the story stays,
　　So far at least as I understand;
And, Robert Browning, you writer of plays,
　　Here's a subject made to your hand!

THE LAST RIDE TOGETHER

I

I SAID—Then, dearest, since 'tis so,
Since now at length my fate I know,
Since nothing all my love avails,
Since all, my life seemed meant for, fails,
　　Since this was written and needs must be—
My whole heart rises up to bless
Your name in pride and thankfulness!
Take back the hope you gave,—I claim
Only a memory of the same,
　　—And this beside, if you will not blame,
　　　Your leave for one more last ride with me.

II

My mistress bent that brow of hers;
Those deep dark eyes where pride demurs
When pity would be softening through,
Fixed me a breathing-while or two
    With life or death in the balance: right!
The blood replenished me again;
My last thought was at least not vain:
I and my mistress, side by side
Shall be together, breathe and ride,
So, one day more am I deified.
    Who knows but the world may end to-night?

III

Hush! if you saw some western cloud
All billowy-bosomed, over-bowed
By many benedictions—sun's
And moon's and evening-star's at once—
    And so, you, looking and loving best,
Conscious grew, your passion grew
Cloud, sunset, moonrise, star-shine too,
Down on you, near and yet more near,
Till flesh must fade for heaven was here!—
Thus leant she and lingered—joy and fear!
    Thus lay she a moment on my breast.

IV

Then we began to ride. My soul
Smoothed itself out, a long-cramped scroll
Freshening and fluttering in the wind.
Past hopes already lay behind.
    What need to strive with a life awry?
Had I said that, had I done this,
So might I gain, so might I miss.
Might she have loved me? just as well
She might have hated, who can tell!
Where had I been now if the worst befell?
    And here we are riding, she and I.

V

Fail I alone, in words and deeds?
Why, all men strive and who succeeds?
We rode; it seemed my spirit flew,
Saw other regions, cities new,
    As the world rushed by on either side.
I thought,—All labour, yet no less
Bear up beneath their unsuccess.
Look at the end of work, contrast
The petty done, the undone vast,
This present of theirs with the hopeful past!
    I hoped she would love me; here we ride.

VI

What hand and brain went ever paired?
What heart alike conceived and dared?
What act proved all its thought had been?
What will but felt the fleshly screen?
    We ride and I see her bosom heave.
There's many a crown for who can reach.
Ten lines, a statesman's life in each!
The flag stuck on a heap of bones,
A soldier's doing! what atones?
They scratch his name on the Abbey-stones.
    My riding is better, by their leave.

VII

What does it all mean, poet? Well,
Your brains beat into rhythm, you tell
What we felt only; you expressed
You hold things beautiful the best,
    And pace them in rhyme so, side by side.
'Tis something, nay 'tis much: but then,
Have you yourself what's best for men?
Are you—poor, sick, old ere your time—
Nearer one whit your own sublime
Than we who never have turned a rhyme?
    Sing, riding's a joy! For me, I ride.

VIII

And you, great sculptor—so, you gave
A score of years to Art, her slave,
And that's your Venus, whence we turn
To yonder girl that fords the burn!
    You acquiesce, and shall I repine?
What, man of music, you grown grey
With notes and nothing else to say,
Is this your sole praise from a friend,
'Greatly his opera's strains intend,
'But in music we know how fashions end!'
    I gave my youth; but we ride, in fine.

IX

Who knows what's fit for us? Had fate
Proposed bliss here should sublimate
My being—had I signed the bond—
Still one must lead some life beyond,
    Have a bliss to die with, dim-descried.
This foot once planted on the goal,
This glory-garland round my soul,
Could I descry such? Try and test!
I sink back shuddering from the quest.
Earth being so good, would heaven seem best?
    Now, heaven and she are beyond this ride.

X

And yet—she has not spoke so long!
What if heaven be that, fair and strong
At life's best, with our eyes upturned
Whither life's flower is first discerned,
    We, fixed so, ever should so abide?
What if we still ride on, we two
With life for ever old yet new,
Changed not in kind but in degree,
The instant made eternity,—
And heaven just prove that I and she
    Ride, ride together, for ever ride?

THE PIED PIPER OF HAMELIN

A CHILD'S STORY

(Written for, and inscribed to, W. M. the Younger)

I

HAMELIN Town's in Brunswick,
　By famous Hanover city;
The river Weser, deep and wide,
Washes its wall on the southern side;
A pleasanter spot you never spied;
　But, when begins my ditty,
Almost five hundred years ago,
To see the townsfolk suffer so
　From vermin, was a pity.

II

Rats!
They fought the dogs and killed the cats,
　And bit the babies in the cradles,
And ate the cheeses out of the vats,
　And licked the soup from the cooks' own ladles,
Split open the kegs of salted sprats,
Made nests inside men's Sunday hats,
And even spoiled the women's chats
　　By drowning their speaking
　　With shrieking and squeaking
In fifty different sharps and flats.

III

At last the people in a body
　　To the Town Hall came flocking:
''Tis clear,' cried they, 'our Mayor's a noddy;
　'And as for our Corporation—shocking
'To think we buy gowns lined with ermine
'For dolts that can't or won't determine
'What's best to rid us of our vermin!

'You hope, because you're old and obese,
'To find in the furry civic robe ease?
'Rouse up, sirs! Give your brains a racking
'To find the remedy we're lacking,
'Or, sure as fate, we'll send you packing!'
At this the Mayor and Corporation
Quaked with a mighty consternation.

IV

An hour they sat in council,
    At length the Mayor broke silence:
'For a guilder I'd my ermine gown sell,
    'I wish I were a mile hence!
'It's easy to bid one rack one's brain—
'I'm sure my poor head aches again,
'I've scratched it so, and all in vain.
'Oh for a trap, a trap, a trap!'
Just as he said this, what should hap
At the chamber door but a gentle tap?
'Bless us,' cried the Mayor, 'what's that?'
(With the Corporation as he sat,
Looking little though wondrous fat;
Nor brighter was his eye, nor moister
Than a too-long-opened oyster,
Save when at noon his paunch grew mutinous
For a plate of turtle green and glutinous)
'Only a scraping of shoes on the mat?
'Anything like the sound of a rat
'Makes my heart go pit-a-pat!'

V

'Come in!'—the Mayor cried, looking bigger:
And in did come the strangest figure!
His queer long coat from heel to head
Was half of yellow and half of red,
And he himself was tall and thin,
With sharp blue eyes, each like a pin,
And light loose hair, yet swarthy skin,

No tuft on cheek nor beard on chin,
But lips where smiles went out and in;
There was no guessing his kith and kin:
And nobody could enough admire
The tall man and his quaint attire.
Quoth one: 'It's as my great-grandsire,
'Starting up at the Trump of Doom's tone,
'Had walked this way from his painted tombstone!'

VI

He advanced to the council-table:
And, 'Please your honours,' said he, 'I'm able,
'By means of a secret charm, to draw
    'All creatures living beneath the sun,
    'That creep or swim or fly or run,
'After me so as you never saw!
'And I chiefly use my charm
'On creatures that do people harm,
'The mole and toad and newt and viper;
'And people call me the Pied Piper.'
(And here they noticed round his neck
    A scarf of red and yellow stripe,
To match with his coat of the self-same cheque;
    And at the scarf's end hung a pipe;
And his fingers, they noticed, were ever straying
As if impatient to be playing
Upon this pipe, as low it dangled
Over his vesture so old-fangled.)
'Yet,' said he, 'poor piper as I am,
'In Tartary I freed the Cham,
    'Last June, from his huge swarms of gnats
'I eased in Asia the Nizam
    'Of a monstrous brood of vampyre-bats:
'And as for what your brain bewilders,
    'If I can rid your town of rats
'Will you give me a thousand guilders?'
'One? fifty thousand!'—was the exclamation
Of the astonished Mayor and Corporation.

VII

Into the street the Piper stept,
  Smiling first a little smile,
As if he knew what magic slept
  In his quiet pipe the while;
Then, like a musical adept,
To blow the pipe his lips he wrinkled,
And green and blue his sharp eyes twinkled,
Like a candle-flame where salt is sprinkled;
And ere three shrill notes the pipe uttered,
You heard as if an army muttered;
And the muttering grew to a grumbling;
And the grumbling grew to a mighty rumbling;
And out of the houses the rats came tumbling.
Great rats, small rats, lean rats, brawny rats,
Brown rats, black rats, grey rats, tawny rats,
Grave old plodders, gay young friskers,
  Fathers, mothers, uncles, cousins,
Cocking tails and pricking whiskers,
  Families by tens and dozens,
Brothers, sisters, husbands, wives—
Followed the Piper for their lives.
From street to street he piped advancing,
And step for step they followed dancing,
Until they came to the river Weser,
  Wherein all plunged and perished!
  —Save one who, stout as Julius Cæsar,
Swam across and lived to carry
  (As he, the manuscript he cherished)
To Rat-land home his commentary:
Which was, 'At the first shrill notes of the pipe,
'I heard a sound as of scraping tripe,
'And putting apples, wondrous ripe,
'Into a cider-press's gripe:
'And a moving away of pickle-tub-boards,
'And a leaving ajar of conserve-cupboards,
'And a drawing the corks of train-oil-flasks,
'And a breaking the hoops of butter-casks:

'And it seemed as if a voice
  '(Sweeter far than by harp or by psaltery
'Is breathed) called out, "Oh rats, rejoice!
  ' "The world is grown to one vast drysaltery!
' "So munch on, crunch on, take your nuncheon,
' "Breakfast, supper, dinner, luncheon!"
'And just as a bulky sugar-puncheon,
'All ready staved, like a great sun shone
'Glorious scarce an inch before me,
'Just as methought it said, "Come, bore me!"
'—I found the Weser rolling o'er me.'

VIII

You should have heard the Hamelin people
Ringing the bells till they rocked the steeple.
'Go,' cried the Mayor, 'and get long poles,
'Poke out the nests and block up the holes!
'Consult with carpenters and builders,
'And leave in our town not even a trace
'Of the rats!'—when suddenly, up the face
Of the Piper perked in the market-place,
With a, 'First, if you please, my thousand guilders!'

IX

A thousand guilders! The Mayor looked blue;
So did the Corporation too.
For council dinners made rare havoc
With Claret, Moselle, Vin-de-Grave, Hock;
And half the money would replenish
Their cellar's biggest butt with Rhenish.
To pay this sum to a wandering fellow
With a gipsy coat of red and yellow!
'Beside,' quoth the Mayor with a knowing wink,
'Our business was done at the river's brink;
'We saw with our eyes the vermin sink,
'And what's dead can't come to life, I think.
'So, friend, we're not the folks to shrink
'From the duty of giving you something for drink,
'And a matter of money to put in your poke;

'But as for the guilders, what we spoke
'Of them, as you very well know, was in joke.
'Beside, our losses have made us thrifty.
'A thousand guilders! Come, take fifty!'

X

The Piper's face fell, and he cried
'No trifling! I can't wait, beside!
'I've promised to visit by dinner-time
'Bagdat, and accept the prime
'Of the Head-Cook's pottage, all he's rich in,
'For having left, in the Caliph's kitchen,
'Of a nest of scorpions no survivor:
'With him I proved no bargain-driver,
'With you, don't think I'll bate a stiver!
'And folks who put me in a passion
'May find me pipe after another fashion.'

XI

'How?' cried the Mayor, 'd'ye think I brook
'Being worse treated than a Cook?
'Insulted by a lazy ribald
'With idle pipe and vesture piebald?
'You threaten us, fellow? Do your worst,
'Blow your pipe there till you burst!'

XII

Once more he stept into the street
      And to his lips again
   Laid his long pipe of smooth straight cane;
And ere he blew three notes (such sweet
Soft notes as yet musician's cunning
      Never gave the enraptured air)
There was a rustling that seemed like a bustling
Of merry crowds justling at pitching and hustling,
Small feet were pattering, wooden shoes clattering,
Little hands clapping and little tongues chattering,
And, like fowls in a farm-yard when barley is scattering,
Out came the children running.

All the little boys and girls,
With rosy cheeks and flaxen curls,
And sparkling eyes and teeth like pearls,
Tripping and skipping, ran merrily after
The wonderful music with shouting and laughter.

XIII

The Mayor was dumb, and the Council stood
As if they were changed into blocks of wood,
Unable to move a step, or cry
To the children merrily skipping by,
—Could only follow with the eye
That joyous crowd at the Piper's back.
But how the Mayor was on the rack,
And the wretched Council's bosoms beat,
As the Piper turned from the High Street
To where the Weser rolled its waters
Right in the way of their sons and daughters!
However he turned from South to West,
And to Koppelberg Hill his steps addressed,
And after him the children pressed;
Great was the joy in every breast.
'He never can cross that mighty top!
'He's forced to let the piping drop,
'And we shall see our children stop!'
When, lo, as they reached the mountain-side,
A wondrous portal opened wide,
As if a cavern was suddenly hollowed;
And the Piper advanced and the children followed,
And when all were in to the very last,
The door in the mountain-side shut fast.
Did I say, all? No! One was lame,
    And could not dance the whole of the way;
And in after years, if you would blame
    His sadness, he was used to say,—
'It's dull in our town since my playmates left!
'I can't forget that I'm bereft
'Of all the pleasant sights they see,
'Which the Piper also promised me.

'For he led us, he said, to a joyous land,
'Joining the town and just at hand,
'Where waters gushed and fruit-trees grew
'And flowers put forth a fairer hue,
'And everything was strange and new;
'The sparrows were brighter than peacocks here,
'And their dogs outran our fallow deer,
'And honey-bees had lost their stings,
'And horses were born with eagles' wings:
'And just as I became assured
'My lame foot would be speedily cured,
'The music stopped and I stood still,
'And found myself outside the hill,
'Left alone against my will,
'To go now limping as before,
'And never hear of that country more!'

XIV

Alas, alas for Hamelin!
    There came into many a burgher's pate
    A text which says that heaven's gate
    Opes to the rich at as easy rate
As the needle's eye takes a camel in!
The mayor sent East, West, North and South,
To offer the Piper, by word of mouth,
    Wherever it was men's lot to find him,
Silver and gold to his heart's content,
If he'd only return the way he went,
    And bring the children behind him.
But when they saw 'twas a lost endeavour,
And Piper and dancers were gone for ever,
They made a decree that lawyers never
    Should think their records dated duly
If, after the day of the month and year,
These words did not as well appear,
'And so long after what happened here
    'On the Twenty-second of July,
'Thirteen hundred and seventy-six:'
And the better in memory to fix

The place of the children's last retreat,
They called it, the Pied Piper's Street—
Where any one playing on pipe or tabor
Was sure for the future to lose his labour.
Nor suffered they hostelry or tavern
　　To shock with mirth a street so solemn;
But opposite the place of the cavern
　　They wrote the story on a column,
And on the great church-window painted
The same, to make the world acquainted
How their children were stolen away,
And there it stands to this very day.
And I must not omit to say
That in Transylvania there's a tribe
Of alien people who ascribe
The outlandish ways and dress
On which their neighbours lay such stress,
To their fathers and mothers having risen
Out of some subterraneous prison
Into which they were trepanned
Long time ago in a mighty band
Out of Hamelin town in Brunswick land,
But how or why, they don't understand.

XV

So, Willy, let me and you be wipers
Of scores out with all men—especially pipers!
And, whether they pipe us free frόm rats or frόm mice,
If we've promised them aught, let us keep our promise!

THE FLIGHT OF THE DUCHESS

I

YOU'RE my friend:
　　I was the man the Duke spoke to;
　　I helped the Duchess to cast off his yoke, too;
So here's the tale from beginning to end,
　　My friend!

II

Ours is a great wild country:
    If you climb to our castle's top,
    I don't see where your eye can stop;
For when you've passed the cornfield country,
Where vineyards leave off, flocks are packed,
And sheep-range leads to cattle-tract,
And cattle-tract to open-chase,
And open-chase to the very base
Of the mountain where, at a funeral pace,
Round about, solemn and slow,
One by one, row after row,
Up and up the pine-trees go,
So, like black priests up, and so
Down the other side again
    To another greater, wilder country,
That's one vast red drear burnt-up plain,
Branched through and through with many a vein
Whence iron's dug, and copper's dealt;
    Look right, look left, look straight before,—
Beneath they mine, above they smelt,
    Copper-ore and iron-ore,
And forge and furnace mould and melt,
    And so on, more and ever more,
Till at the last, for a bounding belt,
    Comes the salt sand hoar of the great sea-shore,
—And the whole is our Duke's country.

III

I was born the day this present Duke was—
    (And O, says the song, ere I was old!)
In the castle where the other Duke was—
    (When I was happy and young, not old!)
I in the kennel, he in the bower:
We are of like age to an hour.
My father was huntsman in that day;
Who has not heard my father say
That, when a boar was brought to bay,

Three times, four times out of five,
With his huntspear he'd contrive
To get the killing-place transfixed,
And pin him true, both eyes betwixt?
And that's why the old Duke would rather
He lost a salt-pit than my father,
And loved to have him ever in call;
That's why my father stood in the hall
When the old Duke brought his infant out
   To show the people, and while they passed
The wondrous bantling round about,
   Was first to start at the outside blast
As the Kaiser's courier blew his horn
Just a month after the babe was born.
'And,' quoth the Kaiser's courier, 'since
   'The Duke has got an heir, our Prince
     'Needs the Duke's self at his side:'
The Duke looked down and seemed to wince,
   But he thought of wars o'er the world wide,
Castles a-fire, men on their march,
The toppling tower, the crashing arch;
   And up he looked, and awhile he eyed
The row of crests and shields and banners
Of all achievements after all manners,
   And 'ay,' said the Duke with a surly pride.
   The more was his comfort when he died
At next year's end, in a velvet suit,
With a gilt glove on his hand, his foot
In a silken shoe for a leather boot,
Petticoated like a herald,
   In a chamber next to an ante-room,
   Where he breathed the breath of page and groom,
   What he called stink, and they, perfume:
—They should have set him on red Berold
Mad with pride, like fire to manage!
They should have got his cheek fresh tannage
Such a day as to-day in the merry sunshine!
Had they stuck on his fist a rough-foot merlin!
(Hark, the wind's on the heath at its game!

Oh for a noble falcon-lanner
To flap each broad wing like a banner,
And turn in the wind, and dance like flame!)
Had they broached a white-beer cask from Berlin
—Or if you incline to prescribe mere wine
Put to his lips, when they saw him pine,
A cup of our own Moldavia fine,
Cotnar for instance, green as May sorrel
And ropy with sweet,—we shall not quarrel.

IV

So, at home, the sick tall yellow Duchess
Was left with the infant in her clutches,
She being the daughter of God knows who:
    And now was the time to revisit her tribe.
Abroad and afar they went, the two,
    And let our people rail and gibe
At the empty hall and extinguished fire,
    As loud as we liked, but ever in vain,
Till after long years we had our desire,
    And back came the Duke and his mother again.

V

And he came back the pertest little ape
That ever affronted human shape;
Full of his travel, struck at himself.
    You'd say, he despised our bluff old ways?
—Not he! For in Paris they told the elf
    Our rough North land was the Land of Lays,
The one good thing left in evil days;
Since the Mid-Age was the Heroic Time,
    And only in wild nooks like ours
Could you taste of it yet as in its prime,
    And see true castles, with proper towers.
Young-hearted women, old-minded men,
And manners now as manners were then.
So, all that the old Dukes had been, without knowing it,
    This Duke would fain know he was, without being it;

'Twas not for the joy's self, but the joy of his showing it,
　　Nor for the pride's self, but the pride of our seeing it,
He revived all usages thoroughly worn-out,
The souls of them fumed-forth, the hearts of them torn-
　　　　out:
And chief in the chase his neck he perilled
On a lathy horse, all legs and length,
With blood for bone, all speed, no strength;
—They should have set him on red Berold
With the red eye slow consuming in fire,
And the thin stiff ear like an abbey-spire!

VI

Well, such as he was, he must marry, we heard:
And out of a convent, at the word,
Came the lady, in time of spring.
—Oh, old thoughts they cling, they cling!
That day, I know, with a dozen oaths
I clad myself in thick hunting-clothes
Fit for the chase of urochs or buffle
In winter-time when you need to muffle.
But the Duke had a mind we should cut a figure,
　　And so we saw the lady arrive:
My friend, I have seen a white crane bigger!
　　She was the smallest lady alive,
Made in a piece of nature's madness,
Too small, almost, for the life and gladness
　　That over-filled her, as some hive
Out of the bears' reach on the high trees
Is crowded with its safe merry bees:
In truth, she was not hard to please!
Up she looked, down she looked, round at the mead,
Straight at the castle, that's best indeed
To look at from outside the walls:
As for us, styled the 'serfs and thralls,'
She as much thanked me as if she had said it,
　(With her eyes, do you understand?)
Because I patted her horse while I led it;
　And Max, who rode on her other hand,

Said, no bird flew past but she inquired
What its true name was, nor ever seemed tired—
If that was an eagle she saw hover,
And the green and grey bird on the field was the plover.
When suddenly appeared the Duke:
　　And as down she sprung, the small foot pointed
On to my hand,—as with a rebuke,
　　And as if his backbone were not jointed,
The Duke stepped rather aside than forward,
　　And welcomed her with his grandest smile;
　　And, mind you, his mother all the while
Chilled in the rear, like a wind to Nor'ward;
And up, like a weary yawn, with its pullies
Went, in a shriek, the rusty portcullis;
And, like a glad sky the north-wind sullies,
The lady's face stopped its play,
As if her first hair had grown grey;
For such things must begin some one day.

VII

In a day or two she was well again;
As who should say, 'You labour in vain!
'This is all a jest against God, who meant
'I should ever be, as I am, content
'And glad in his sight; therefore, glad I will be.'
So, smiling as at first went she.

VIII

She was active, stirring, all fire—
Could not rest, could not tire—
To a stone she might have given life!
　　(I myself loved once, in my day)
—For a shepherd's, miner's, huntsman's wife,
　　(I had a wife, I know what I say)
Never in all the world such an one!
And here was plenty to be done,
And she that could do it, great or small,
She was to do nothing at all.
There was already this man in his post,

This in his station, and that in his office,
And the Duke's plan admitted a wife, at most,
    To meet his eye, with the other trophies,
Now outside the hall, now in it,
    To sit thus, stand thus, see and be seen,
At the proper place in the proper minute,
    And die away the life between.
And it was amusing enough, each infraction
    Of rule—(but for after-sadness that came)
To hear the consummate self-satisfaction
    With which the young Duke and the old dame
Would let her advise, and criticise,
And, being a fool, instruct the wise,
    And, child-like, parcel out praise or blame:
They bore it all in complacent guise,
As though an artificer, after contriving
A wheel-work image as if it were living,
Should find with delight it could motion to strike him!
So found the Duke, and his mother like him:
The lady hardly got a rebuff—
That had not been contemptuous enough,
With his cursed smirk, as he nodded applause,
And kept off the old mother-cat's claws.

IX

So, the little lady grew silent and thin,
    Paling and ever paling,
As the way is with a hid chagrin;
    And the Duke perceived that she was ailing,
And said in his heart, ''Tis done to spite me,
'But I shall find in my power to right me!'
Don't swear, friend! The old one, many a year,
Is in hell, and the Duke's self . . . you shall hear.

X

Well, early in autumn, at first winter-warning,
When the stag had to break with his foot, of a morning,
A drinking-hole out of the fresh tender ice
That covered the pond till the sun, in a trice,

Loosening it, let out a ripple of gold,
  And another and another, and faster and faster,
Till, dimpling to blindness, the wide water rolled:
  Then it so chanced that the Duke our master
Asked himself what were the pleasures in season,
  And found, since the calendar bade him be hearty,
He should do the Middle Age no treason
  In resolving on a hunting-party.
Always provided, old books showed the way of it!
  What meant old poets by their strictures?
And when old poets had said their say of it,
  How taught old painters in their pictures?
We must revert to the proper channels,
Workings in tapestry, paintings on panels,
And gather up woodcraft's authentic traditions:
Here was food for our various ambitions,
As on each case, exactly stated—
  To encourage your dog, now, the properest chirrup,
  Or best prayer to Saint Hubert on mounting your
    stirrup—
We of the household took thought and debated.
Blessed was he whose back ached with the jerkin
His sire was wont to do forest-work in;
Blesseder he who nobly sunk 'ohs'
And 'ahs' while he tugged on his grandsire's trunk-hose;
What signified hats if they had no rims on,
  Each slouching before and behind like the scallop,
  And able to serve at sea for a shallop,
Loaded with lacquer and looped with crimson?
So that the deer now, to make a short rhyme on't,
  What with our Venerers, Prickers and Verderers,
  Might hope for real hunters at length and not murderers,
And oh the Duke's tailor, he had a hot time on't!

XI

Now you must know that when the first dizziness
  Of flap-hats and buff-coats and jack-boots subsided,
    The Duke put this question, 'The Duke's part provided,
'Had not the Duchess some share in the business?'

For out of the mouth of two or three witnesses
Did he establish all fit-or-unfitnesses:
And, after much laying of heads together,
Somebody's cap got a notable feather
By the announcement with proper unction
That he had discovered the lady's function;
Since ancient authors gave this tenet,
   'When horns wind a mort and the deer is at siege,
'Let the dame of the castle prick forth on her jennet,
   'And, with water to wash the hands of her liege
'In a clean ewer with a fair toweling,
'Let her preside at the disemboweling.'
Now, my friend, if you had so little religion
   As to catch a hawk, some falcon-lanner,
   And thrust her broad wings like a banner
Into a coop for a vulgar pigeon;
And if day by day and week by week
   You cut her claws, and sealed her eyes,
And clipped her wings, and tied her beak,
   Would it cause you any great surprise
If, when you decided to give her an airing,
You found she needed a little preparing?
—I say, should you be such a curmudgeon,
If she clung to the perch, as to take it in dudgeon?
Yet when the Duke to his lady signified,
Just a day before, as he judged most dignified,
In what a pleasure she was to participate,—
   And, instead of leaping wide in flashes,
   Her eyes just lifted their long lashes,
As if pressed by fatigue even he could not dissipate,
And duly acknowledged the Duke's forethought,
But spoke of her health, if her health were worth aught,
Of the weight by day and the watch by night,
And much wrong now that used to be right,
So, thanking him, declined the hunting,—
Was conduct ever more affronting?
With all the ceremony settled—
   With the towel ready, and the sewer
   Polishing up his oldest ewer,

And the jennet pitched upon, a piebald,
    Black-barred, cream-coated and pink eye-balled,—
No wonder if the Duke was nettled!
And when she persisted nevertheless,—
Well, I suppose here's the time to confess
That there ran half round our lady's chamber
A balcony none of the hardest to clamber;
And that Jacynth the tire-woman, ready in waiting,
Stayed in call outside, what need of relating?
And since Jacynth was like a June rose, why, a fervent
Adorer of Jacynth of course was your servant;
And if she had the habit to peep through the casement,
    How could I keep at any vast distance?
    And so, as I say, on the lady's persistence,
The Duke, dumb-stricken with amazement,
Stood for a while in a sultry smother,
    And then, with a smile that partook of the awful,
Turned her over to his yellow mother
    To learn what was held decorous and lawful;
And the mother smelt blood with a cat-like instinct,
As her cheek quick whitened thro' all its quince-tint.
Oh, but the lady heard the whole truth at once!
    What meant she?—Who was she?—Her duty and
        station,
The wisdom of age and the folly of youth, at once,
    Its decent regard and its fitting relation—
In brief, my friend, set all the devils in hell free
And turn them out to carouse in a belfry
And treat the priests to a fifty-part canon,
And then you may guess how that tongue of hers ran
    on!
Well, somehow or other it ended at last
And, licking her whiskers, out she passed;
And after her,—making (he hoped) a face
    Like Emperor Nero or Sultan Saladin,
Stalked the Duke's self with the austere grace
    Of ancient hero or modern paladin,
From door to staircase—oh such a solemn
Unbending of the vertebral column!

XII

However, at sunrise our company mustered;
  And here was the huntsman bidding unkennel,
And there 'neath his bonnet the pricker blustered,
  With feather dank as a bough of wet fennel;
For the court-yard walls were filled with fog
You might have cut as an axe chops a log—
Like so much wool for colour and bulkiness;
And out rode the Duke in a perfect sulkiness,
Since, before breakfast, a man feels but queasily,
  And a sinking at the lower abdomen
  Begins the day with indifferent omen.
And lo, as he looked around uneasily,
The sun ploughed the fog up and drove it asunder
This way and that from the valley under;
  And, looking through the court-yard arch,
Down in the valley, what should meet him
  But a troop of Gipsies on their march?
No doubt with the annual gifts to greet him.

XIII

Now, in your land, Gipsies reach you, only
  After reaching all lands beside;
North they go, South they go, trooping or lonely,
  And still, as they travel far and wide,
Catch they and keep now a trace here, a trace there,
That puts you in mind of a place here, a place there.
But with us, I believe they rise out of the ground,
And nowhere else, I take it, are found
With the earth-tint yet so freshly embrowned:
Born, no doubt, like insects which breed on
The very fruit they are meant to feed on.
For the earth—not a use to which they don't turn it,
  The ore that grows in the mountain's womb,
  Or the sand in the pits like a honeycomb,
They sift and soften it, bake it and burn it—
Whether they weld you, for instance, a snaffle
With side-bars never a brute can baffle;

Or a lock that's a puzzle of wards within wards;
Or, if your colt's fore-foot inclines to curve inwards,
Horseshoes they hammer which turn on a swivel
And won't allow the hoof to shrivel.
Then they cast bells like the shell of the winkle
That keep a stout heart in the ram with their tinkle;
But the sand—they pinch and pound it like otters;
Commend me to Gipsy glass-makers and potters!
Glasses they'll blow you, crystal-clear,
Where just a faint cloud of rose shall appear,
As if in pure water you dropped and let die
A bruised black-blooded mulberry;
And that other sort, their crowning pride,
With long white threads distinct inside,
Like the lake-flower's fibrous roots which dangle
Loose such a length and never tangle,
Where the bold sword-lily cuts the clear waters,
And the cup-lily couches with all the white daughters:
Such are the works they put their hand to,
The uses they turn and twist iron and sand to.
And these made the troop, which our Duke saw sally
Toward his castle from out of the valley,
Men and women, like new-hatched spiders,
Come out with the morning to greet our riders.
And up they wound till they reached the ditch,
Whereat all stopped save one, a witch
That I knew, as she hobbled from the group,
By her gait directly and her stoop,
I, whom Jacynth was used to importune
To let that same witch tell us our fortune.
The oldest Gipsy then above ground;
And, sure as the autumn season came round,
She paid us a visit for profit or pastime,
And every time, as she swore, for the last time.
And presently she was seen to sidle
Up to the Duke till she touched his bridle,
So that the horse of a sudden reared up
As under its nose the old witch peered up
With her worn-out eyes, or rather eye-holes

Of no use now but to gather brine,
  And began a kind of level whine
Such as they used to sing to their viols
When their ditties they go grinding
Up and down with nobody minding:
And then, as of old, at the end of the humming
Her usual presents were forthcoming
—A dog-whistle blowing the fiercest of trebles,
(Just a sea-shore stone holding a dozen fine pebbles,)
Or a porcelain mouth-piece to screw on a pipe-end,—
And so she awaited her annual stipend.
But this time, the Duke would scarcely vouchsafe
  A word in reply; and in vain she felt
  With twitching fingers at her belt
  For the purse of sleek pine-martin pelt,
Ready to put what he gave in her pouch safe,—
Till, either to quicken his apprehension,
Or possibly with an after-intention,
She was come, she said, to pay her duty
To the new Duchess, the youthful beauty.
No sooner had she named his lady,
Than a shine lit up the face so shady,
And its smirk returned with a novel meaning—
For it struck him, the babe just wanted weaning;
If one gave her a taste of what life was and sorrow,
She, foolish to-day, would be wiser to-morrow;
And who so fit a teacher of trouble
As this sordid crone bent well-nigh double?
So, glancing at her wolf-skin vesture,
  (If such it was, for they grow so hirsute
  That their own fleece serves for natural fur-suit)
He was contrasting, 'twas plain from his gesture,
The life of the lady so flower-like and delicate
With the loathsome squalor of this helicat.
I, in brief, was the man the Duke beckoned
  From out of the throng, and while I drew near
He told the crone—as I since have reckoned
  By the way he bent and spoke into her ear
With circumspection and mystery—

The main of the lady's history,
Her frowardness and ingratitude:
And for all the crone's submissive attitude
I could see round her mouth the loose plaits tightening,
And her brow with assenting intelligence brightening,
    As though she engaged with hearty goodwill
    Whatever he now might enjoin to fulfil,
And promised the lady a thorough frightening.
And so, just giving her a glimpse
Of a purse, with the air of a man who imps
The wing of the hawk that shall fetch the hernshaw,
    He bade me take the Gipsy mother
    And set her telling some story or other
Of hill or dale, oak-wood or fernshaw,
To wile away a weary hour
For the lady left alone in her bower,
Whose mind and body craved exertion
And yet shrank from all better diversion.

XIV

Then clapping heel to his horse, the mere curveter,
    Out rode the Duke, and after his hollo
Horses and hounds swept, huntsman and servitor,
    And back I turned and bade the crone follow.
And what makes me confident what's to be told you
    Had all along been of this crone's devising,
Is, that, on looking round sharply, behold you,
    There was a novelty quick as surprising:
For first, she had shot up a full head in stature,
    And her step kept pace with mine nor faltered,
As if age had foregone its usurpature,
    And the ignoble mien was wholly altered,
And the face looked quite of another nature,
And the change reached too, whatever the change meant.
Her shaggy wolf-skin cloak's arrangement:
For where its tatters hung loose like sedges,
Gold coins were glittering on the edges,
Like the band-roll strung with tomans
Which proves the veil a Persian woman's:

And under her brow, like a snail's horns newly
   Come out as after the rain he paces,
Two unmistakeable eye-points duly
   Live and aware looked out of their places.
So, we went and found Jacynth at the entry
Of the lady's chamber standing sentry;
I told the command and produced my companion,
And Jacynth rejoiced to admit any one,
For since last night, by the same token,
Not a single word had the lady spoken:
They went in both to the presence together,
While I in the balcony watched the weather.

XV

And now, what took place at the very first of all,
I cannot tell, as I never could learn it:
Jacynth constantly wished a curse to fall
On that little head of hers and burn it
If she knew how she came to drop so soundly
   Asleep of a sudden and there continue
The whole time sleeping as profoundly
   As one of the boars my father would pin you
'Twixt the eyes where life holds garrison,
—Jacynth forgive me the comparison!
But where I begin my own narration
Is a little after I took my station
To breathe the fresh air from the balcony,
And, having in those days a falcon eye,
To follow the hunt thro' the open country,
   From where the bushes thinlier crested
The hillocks, to a plain where's not one tree.
   When, in a moment, my ear was arrested
By—was it singing, or was it saying,
Or a strange musical instrument playing
In the chamber?—and to be certain
I pushed the lattice, pulled the curtain,
And there lay Jacynth asleep,
Yet as if a watch she tried to keep,
In a rosy sleep along the floor

With her head against the door;
While in the midst, on the seat of state,
Was a queen—the Gipsy woman late,
With head and face downbent
On the lady's head and face intent:
For, coiled at her feet like a child at ease,
The lady sat between her knees
And o'er them the lady's clasped hands met,
And on those hands her chin was set,
And her upturned face met the face of the crone
Wherein the eyes had grown and grown
As if she could double and quadruple
At pleasure the play of either pupil
    —Very like, by her hands' slow fanning,
As up and down like a gor-crow's flappers
They moved to measure, or bell-clappers.
    I said 'Is it blessing, is it banning,
'Do they applaud you or burlesque you—
    'Those hands and fingers with no flesh on?'
But, just as I thought to spring in to the rescue,
    At once I was stopped by the lady's expression:
For it was life her eyes were drinking
From the crone's wide pair above unwinking,
    —Life's pure fire received without shrinking,
Into the heart and breast whose heaving
Told you no single drop they were leaving,
    —Life, that filling her, passed redundant
    Into her very hair, back swerving
Over each shoulder, loose and abundant,
    As her head thrown back showed the white throat
        curving;
And the very tresses shared in the pleasure,
Moving to the mystic measure,
Bounding as the bosom bounded.
I stopped short, more and more confounded,
As still her cheeks burned and eyes glistened,
As she listened and she listened:
When all at once a hand detained me,
The selfsame contagion gained me,

And I kept time to the wondrous chime,
Making out words and prose and rhyme,
Till it seemed that the music furled
   Its wings like a task fulfilled, and dropped
   From under the words it first had propped,
And left them midway in the world:
Word took word as hand takes hand,
I could hear at last, and understand,
And when I held the unbroken thread,
The Gipsy said:—

'And so at last we find my tribe.
   'And so I set thee in the midst,
'And to one and all of them describe
   'What thou saidst and what thou didst,
'Our long and terrible journey through,
'And all thou art ready to say and do
'In the trials that remain:
'I trace them the vein and the other vein
'That meet on thy brow and part again,
'Making our rapid mystic mark;
   'And I bid my people prove and probe
   'Each eye's profound and glorious globe
'Till they detect the kindred spark
'In those depths so dear and dark,
'Like the spots that snap and burst and flee,
'Circling over the midnight sea.
'And on that round young cheek of thine
   'I make them recognize the tinge,
'As when of the costly scarlet wine
   'They drip so much as will impinge
'And spread in a thinnest scale afloat
'One thick gold drop from the olive's coat
'Over a silver plate whose sheen
'Still thro' the mixture shall be seen.
'For so I prove thee, to one and all,
   'Fit, when my people ope their breast,
'To see the sign, and hear the call,
   'And take the vow, and stand the test

'Which adds one more child to the rest—
'When the breast is bare and the arms are wide,
'And the world is left outside.
'For there is probation to decree,
'And many and long must the trials be
'Thou shalt victoriously endure,
'If that brow is true and those eyes are sure;
'Like a jewel-finder's fierce assay
   'Of the prize he dug from its mountain-tomb—
'Let once the vindicating ray
   'Leap out amid the anxious gloom,
'And steel and fire have done their part
'And the prize falls on its finder's heart;
'So, trial after trial past,
'Wilt thou fall at the very last
'Breathless, half in trance
'With the thrill of the great deliverance,
   'Into our arms for evermore;
'And thou shalt know, those arms once curled
   'About thee, what we knew before,
'How love is the only good in the world.
'Henceforth be loved as heart can love,
'Or brain devise, or hand approve!
'Stand up, look below,
'It is our life at thy feet we throw
'To step with into light and joy;
'Not a power of life but we employ
'To satisfy thy nature's want;
'Art thou the tree that props the plant,
'Or the climbing plant that seeks the tree—
'Canst thou help us, must we help thee?
'If any two creatures grew into one,
'They would do more than the world has done:
'Though each apart were never so weak,
'Ye vainly through the world should seek
'For the knowledge and the might
'Which in such union grew their right:
'So, to approach at least that end,
'And blend,—as much as may be, blend

'Thee with us or us with thee,—
'As climbing plant or propping tree,
'Shall some one deck thee, over and down,
    'Up and about, with blossoms and leaves?
'Fix his heart's fruit for thy garland-crown,
    'Cling with his soul as the gourd-vine cleaves,
'Die on thy boughs and disappear
'While not a leaf of thine is sere?
'Or is the other fate in store,
'And art thou fitted to adore,
'To give thy wondrous self away,
'And take a stronger nature's sway?
'I foresee and could foretell
'Thy future portion, sure and well:
'But those passionate eyes speak true, speak true,
'Let them say what thou shalt do!
'Only be sure thy daily life,
'In its peace or in its strife,
'Never shall be unobserved;
    'We pursue thy whole career,
        'And hope for it, or doubt, or fear,—
'Lo, hast thou kept thy path or swerved,
'We are beside thee in all thy ways,
'With our blame, with our praise,
'Our shame to feel, our pride to show,
'Glad, angry—but indifferent, no!
'Whether it be thy lot to go,
'For the good of us all, where the haters meet
'In the crowded city's horrible street;
'Or thou step alone through the morass
'Where never sound yet was
'Save the dry quick clap of the stork's bill,
'For the air is still, and the water still,
'When the blue breast of the dipping coot
'Dives under, and all is mute.
'So, at the last shall come old age,
'Decrepit as befits that stage;
'How else wouldst thou retire apart
'With the hoarded memories of thy heart,

'And gather all to the very least
'Of the fragments of life's earlier feast,
'Let fall through eagerness to find
'The crowning dainties yet behind?
'Ponder on the entire past
'Laid together thus at last,
'When the twilight helps to fuse
'The first fresh with the faded hues,
'And the outline of the whole,
'As round eve's shades their framework roll,
'Grandly fronts for once thy soul.
'And then as, 'mid the dark, a gleam
    'Of yet another morning breaks,
'And like the hand which ends a dream,
'Death, with the might of his sunbeam,
    'Touches the flesh and the soul awakes,
'Then——'
                    Ay, then indeed something would happen!
    But what? For here her voice changed like a bird's;
    There grew more of the music and less of the
        words;
Had Jacynth only been by me to clap pen
To paper and put you down every syllable
    With those clever clerkly fingers,
    All I've forgotten as well as what lingers
In this old brain of mine that's but ill able
To give you even this poor version
    Of the speech I spoil, as it were, with stammering
    —More fault of those who had the hammering
    Of prosody into me and syntax,
    And did it, not with hobnails but tintacks!
But to return from this excursion,—
Just, do you mark, when the song was sweetest,
The peace most deep and the charm completest,
There came, shall I say, a snap—
    And the charm vanished!
    And my sense returned, so strangely banished,
And, starting as from a nap,
I knew the crone was bewitching my lady,

With Jacynth asleep; and but one spring made I
Down from the casement, round to the portal,
    Another minute and I had entered,—
When the door opened, and more than mortal
    Stood, with a face where to my mind centred
All beauties I ever saw or shall see,
The Duchess: I stopped as if struck by palsy.
She was so different, happy and beautiful,
    I felt at once that all was best,
    And that I had nothing to do, for the rest,
But wait her commands, obey and be dutiful.
Not that, in fact, there was any commanding;
    I saw the glory of her eye,
And the brow's height and the breast's expanding,
    And I was hers to live or to die.
As for finding what she wanted,
You know God Almighty granted
Such little signs should serve wild creatures
    To tell one another all their desires,
    So that each knows what his friend requires,
And does its bidding without teachers.
I preceded her; the crone
Followed silent and alone;
I spoke to her, but she merely jabbered
    In the old style; both her eyes had slunk
    Back to their pits; her stature shrunk;
    In short, the soul in its body sunk
Like a blade sent home to its scabbard.
We descended, I preceding;
Crossed the court with nobody heeding;
All the world was at the chase,
The court-yard like a desert place,
The stable emptied of its small fry;
I saddled myself the very palfrey
I remember patting while it carried her,
The day she arrived and the Duke married her.
And, do you know, though it's easy deceiving
Oneself in such matters, I can't help believing
The lady had not forgotten it either,

And knew the poor devil so much beneath her
Would have been only too glad for her service
To dance on hot ploughshares like a Turk dervise,
But, unable to pay proper duty where owing it,
Was reduced to that pitiful method of showing it:
For though the moment I began setting
His saddle on my own nag of Berold's begetting,
(Not that I meant to be obtrusive)
 She stopped me, while his rug was shifting,
 By a single rapid finger's lifting,
And, with a gesture kind but conclusive,
And a little shake of the head, refused me,—
I say, although she never used me,
Yet when she was mounted, the Gipsy behind her,
And I ventured to remind her,
I suppose with a voice of less steadiness
 Than usual, for my feeling exceeded me,
—Something to the effect that I was in readiness
 Whenever God should please she needed me,—
Then, do you know, her face looked down on me
With a look that placed a crown on me,
And she felt in her bosom,—mark, her bosom—
And, as a flower-tree drops its blossom,
Dropped me . . . ah, had it been a purse
Of silver, my friend, or gold that's worse,
Why, you see, as soon as I found myself
 So understood,—that a true heart so may gain
 Such a reward,—I should have gone home again,
Kissed Jacynth, and soberly drowned myself!
It was a little plait of hair
 Such as friends in a convent make
 To wear, each for the other's sake,—
This, see, which at my breast I wear,
Ever did (rather to Jacynth's grudgment),
And ever shall, till the Day of Judgment.
And then,—and then,—to cut short,—this is idle,
 These are feelings it is not good to foster,—
I pushed the gate wide, she shook the bridle,
 And the palfrey bounded,—and so we lost her.

XVI

When the liquor's out why clink the cannikin?
I did think to describe you the panic in
The redoubtable breast of our master the mannikin,
And what was the pitch of his mother's yellowness,
  How she turned as a shark to snap the spare-rib
  Clean off, sailors say, from a pearl-diving Carib,
When she heard, what she called the flight of the feloness
—But it seems such child's play,
What they said and did with the lady away!
And to dance on, when we've lost the music,
Always made me—and no doubt makes you—sick.
Nay, to my mind, the world's face looked so stern
As that sweet form disappeared through the postern,
She that kept it in constant good humour,
It ought to have stopped; there seemed nothing to do
    more.
But the world thought otherwise and went on,
And my head's one that its spite was spent on:
Thirty years are fled since that morning,
And with them all my head's adorning.
Nor did the old Duchess die outright,
As you expect, of suppressed spite,
The natural end of every adder
Not suffered to empty its poison-bladder:
But she and her son agreed, I take it,
That no one should touch on the story to wake it,
For the wound in the Duke's pride rankled fiery,
So, they made no search and small inquiry—
And when fresh Gipsies have paid us a visit, I've
Noticed the couple were never inquisitive,
But told them they're folks the Duke don't want here,
And bade them make haste and cross the frontier.
Brief, the Duchess was gone and the Duke was glad of it,
  And the old one was in the young one's stead,
  And took, in her place, the household's head,
And a blessed time the household had of it!
And were I not, as a man may say, cautious

How I trench, more than needs, on the nauseous,
I could favour you with sundry touches
Of the paint-smutches with which the Duchess
Heightened the mellowness of her cheek's yellowness
(To get on faster) until at last her
Cheek grew to be one master-plaster
Of mucus and fucus from mere use of ceruse:
In short, she grew from scalp to udder
Just the object to make you shudder.

XVII

You're my friend—
What a thing friendship is, world without end!
How it gives the heart and soul a stir-up
    As if somebody broached you a glorious runlet,
    And poured out, all lovelily, sparklingly, sunlit,
Our green Moldavia, the streaky syrup,
Cotnar as old as the time of the Druids—
Friendship may match with that monarch of fluids;
Each supples a dry brain, fills you its ins-and-outs,
Gives your life's hour-glass a shake when the thin sand
        doubts
Whether to run on or stop short, and guarantees
Age is not all made of stark sloth and arrant ease.
I have seen my little lady once more,
    Jacynth, the Gipsy, Berold, and the rest of it,
For to me spoke the Duke, as I told you before;
    I always wanted to make a clean breast of it;
And now it is made—why, my heart's blood, that went
        trickle,
    Trickle, but anon, in such muddy driblets,
Is pumped up brisk now, through the main ventricle,
    And genially floats me about the giblets.
I'll tell you what I intend to do:
I must see this fellow his sad life through—
He is our Duke, after all,
And I, as he says, but a serf and thrall.
My father was born here, and I inherit
    His fame, a chain he bound his son with;

Could I pay in a lump I should prefer it,
  But there's no mine to blow up and get done with:
So, I must stay till the end of the chapter.
For, as to our middle-age-manners-adapter,
Be it a thing to be glad on or sorry on,
Some day or other, his head in a morion
And breast in a hauberk, his heels he'll kick up,
Slain by an onslaught fierce of hiccup.
And then, when red doth the sword of our Duke rust,
And its leathern sheath lie o'ergrown with a blue crust,
Then I shall scrape together my earnings;
  For, you see, in the churchyard Jacynth reposes,
  And our children all went the way of the roses:
It's a long lane that knows no turnings.
One needs but little tackle to travel in;
  So, just one stout cloak shall I indue:
And for a staff, what beats the javelin
  With which his boars my father pinned you?
And then, for a purpose you shall hear presently,
  Taking some Cotnar, a tight plump skinful,
I shall go journeying, who but I, pleasantly!
  Sorrow is vain and despondency sinful.
What's a man's age? He must hurry more, that's all;
  Cram in a day, what his youth took a year to hold:
When we mind labour, then only, we're too old—
What age had Methusalem when he begat Saul?
And at last, as its haven some buffeted ship sees,
  (Come all the way from the north-parts with sperm oil)
I hope to get safely out of the turmoil
And arrive one day at the land of the Gipsies,
And find my lady, or hear the last news of her
From some old thief and son of Lucifer,
His forehead chapleted green with wreathy hop,
Sunburned all over like an Æthiop.
And when my Cotnar begins to operate
And the tongue of the rogue to run at a proper rate,
And our wine-skin, tight once, shows each flaccid dent,
I shall drop in with—as if by accident—
'You never knew, then, how it all ended,

'What fortune good or bad attended
'The little lady your Queen befriended?'
—And when that's told me, what's remaining?
This world's too hard for my explaining.
The same wise judge of matters equine
   Who still preferred some slim four-year-old
   To the big-boned stock of mighty Berold,
And, for strong Cotnar, drank French weak wine,
He also must be such a lady's scorner!
   Smooth Jacob still robs homely Esau:
   Now up, now down, the world's one see-saw.
—So, I shall find out some snug corner
Under a hedge, like Orson the wood-knight,
Turn myself round and bid the world good night;
And sleep a sound sleep till the trumpet's blowing
   Wakes me (unless priests cheat us laymen)
To a world where will be no further throwing
   Pearls before swine that can't value them. Amen!

A GRAMMARIAN'S FUNERAL

SHORTLY AFTER THE REVIVAL OF LEARNING IN EUROPE

LET us begin and carry up this corpse,
      Singing together.
Leave we the common crofts, the vulgar thorpes
      Each in its tether
Sleeping safe on the bosom of the plain,
      Cared-for till cock-crow:
Look out if yonder be not day again
      Rimming the rock-row!
That's the appropriate country; there, man's thought,
      Rarer, intenser,
Self-gathered for an outbreak, as it ought,
      Chafes in the censer.
Leave we the unlettered plain its herd and crop;
      Seek we sepulture
On a tall mountain, citied to the top,
      Crowded with culture!

All the peaks soar, but one the rest excels;
    Clouds overcome it;
No! yonder sparkle is the citadel's
    Circling its summit.
Thither our path lies; wind we up the heights:
    Wait ye the warning?
Our low life was the level's and the night's;
    He's for the morning.
Step to a tune, square chests, erect each head,
    'Ware the beholders!
This is our master, famous calm and dead,
    Borne on our shoulders.

Sleep, crop and herd! sleep, darkling thorpe and croft,
    Safe from the weather!
He, whom we convoy to his grave aloft,
    Singing together,
He was a man born with thy face and throat,
    Lyric Apollo!
Long he lived nameless: how should spring take note
    Winter would follow?
Till lo, the little touch, and youth was gone!
    Cramped and diminished,
Moaned he, 'New measures, other feet anon!
    'My dance is finished'?
No, that's the world's way: (keep the mountain-side,
    Make for the city!)
He knew the signal, and stepped on with pride
    Over men's pity;
Left play for work, and grappled with the world
    Bent on escaping:
'What's in the scroll,' quoth he, 'thou keepest furled?
    'Show me their shaping,
'Theirs who most studied man, the bard and sage,—
    'Give!'—So, he gowned him,
Straight got by heart that book to its last page:
    Learned, we found him.
Yea, but we found him bald too, eyes like lead,
    Accents uncertain:

'Time to taste life,' another would have said,
    'Up with the curtain!'
This man said rather, 'Actual life comes next?
    'Patience a moment!
'Grant I have mastered learning's crabbed text,
    'Still there's the comment.
'Let me know all! Prate not of most or least,
    'Painful or easy!
'Even to the crumbs I'd fain eat up the feast,
    'Ay, nor feel queasy.'
Oh, such a life as he resolved to live,
    When he had learned it,
When he had gathered all books had to give!
    Sooner, he spurned it.
Image the whole, then execute the parts—
    Fancy the fabric
Quite, ere you build, ere steel strike fire from quartz,
    Ere mortar dab brick!

(Here's the town-gate reached: there's the market-place
    Gaping before us.)
Yea, this in him was the peculiar grace
    (Hearten our chorus!)
That before living he'd learn how to live—
    No end to learning:
Earn the means first—God surely will contrive
    Use for our earning.
Others mistrust and say, 'But time escapes:
    'Live now or never!'
He said, 'What's time? Leave Now for dogs and apes!
    'Man has Forever.'
Back to his book then: deeper drooped his head:
    Calculus racked him:
Leaden before, his eyes grew dross of lead:
    Tussis attacked him.
'Now, master, take a little rest!'—not he!
    (Caution redoubled,
Step two abreast, the way winds narrowly!)
    Not a whit troubled

Back to his studies, fresher than at first,
    Fierce as a dragon
He (soul-hydroptic with a sacred thirst)
    Sucked at the flagon.
Oh, if we draw a circle premature,
    Heedless of far gain,
Greedy for quick returns of profit, sure
    Bad is our bargain!
Was it not great? did not he throw on God,
    (He loves the burthen)—
God's task to make the heavenly period
    Perfect the earthen?
Did not he magnify the mind, show clear
    Just what it all meant?
He would not discount life, as fools do here,
    Paid by instalment.
He ventured neck or nothing—heaven's success
    Found, or earth's failure:
'Wilt thou trust death or not?' He answered 'Yes:
    'Hence with life's pale lure!'
That low man seeks a little thing to do,
    Sees it and does it:
This high man, with a great thing to pursue,
    Dies ere he knows it.
That low man goes on adding one to one,
    His hundred's soon hit:
This high man, aiming at a million,
    Misses an unit.
That, has the world here—should he need the next,
    Let the world mind him!
This, throws himself on God, and unperplexed
    Seeking shall find him.
So, with the throttling hands of death at strife,
    Ground he at grammar;
Still, thro' the rattle, parts of speech were rife:
    While he could stammer
He settled *Hoti's* business—let it be!—
    Properly based *Oun*—
Gave us the doctrine of the enclitic *De*,

Dead from the waist down.
Well, here's the platform, here's the proper place:
Hail to your purlieus,
All ye highfliers of the feathered race,
Swallows and curlews!
Here's the top-peak; the multitude below
Live, for they can, there:
This man decided not to Live but Know—
Bury this man there?
Here—here's his place, where meteors shoot, clouds form,
Lightnings are loosened,
Stars come and go! Let joy break with the storm,
Peace let the dew send!
Lofty designs must close in like effects:
Loftily lying,
Leave him—still loftier than the world suspects,
Living and dying.

THE HERETIC'S TRAGEDY

A MIDDLE-AGE INTERLUDE

ROSA MUNDI; SEU, FULCITE ME FLORIBUS. A CONCEIT OF
MASTER GYSBRECHT, CANON-REGULAR OF SAINT JODO-
CUS-BY-THE-BAR, YPRES CITY. CANTUQUE, *Virgilius*.
AND HATH OFTEN BEEN SUNG AT HOCK-TIDE AND
FESTIVALS. GAVISUS ERAM, *Jessides*.

(It would seem to be a glimpse from the burning of Jacques du
Bourg-Molay, at Paris, A.D. 1314; as distorted by the refraction from
Flemish brain to brain, during the course of a couple of centuries.)

[Molay was Grand Master of the Templars when that order was
suppressed in 1312.]

I

PREADMONISHETH THE ABBOT DEODAET

THE Lord, we look to once for all,
Is the Lord we should look at, all at once:
He knows not to vary, saith Saint Paul,
Nor the shadow of turning, for the nonce.

See him no other than as he is!
  Give both the infinitudes their due—
Infinite mercy, but, I wis,
  As infinite a justice too.

[Organ: plagal-cadence.

  As infinite a justice too.

II

ONE SINGETH

John, Master of the Temple of God,
  Falling to sin the Unknown Sin,
What he bought of Emperor Aldabrod,
  He sold it to Sultan Saladin:
Till, caught by Pope Clement, a-buzzing there,
  Hornet-prince of the mad wasps' hive,
And clipt of his wings in Paris square,
  They bring him now to be burned alive.
    [*And wanteth there grace of lute or clavicithern, ye
      shall say to confirm him who singeth—*
  We bring John now to be burned alive.

III

In the midst is a goodly gallows built;
  'Twixt fork and fork, a stake is stuck;
But first they set divers tumbrils a-tilt,
  Make a trench all round with the city muck;
Inside they pile log upon log, good store;
  Faggots no few, blocks great and small,
Reach a man's mid-thigh, no less, no more,—
  For they mean he should roast in the sight of all.

CHORUS

  We mean he should roast in the sight of all.

IV

Good sappy bavins that kindle forthwith;
  Billets that blaze substantial and slow;
Pine-stump split deftly, dry as pith;
  Larch-heart that chars to a chalk-white glow:

Then up they hoist me John in a chafe,
  Sling him fast like a hog to scorch,
Spit in his face, then leap back safe,
  Sing 'Laudes' and bid clap-to the torch.

CHORUS

Laus Deo—who bids clap-to the torch.

V

John of the Temple, whose fame so bragged,
  Is burning alive in Paris square!
How can he curse, if his mouth is gagged?
  Or wriggle his neck, with a collar there?
Or heave his chest, which a band goes round?
  Or threat with his fist, since his arms are spliced?
Or kick with his feet, now his legs are bound?
  —Thinks John, I will call upon Jesus Christ.
                              [*Here one crosseth himself.*

VI

Jesus Christ—John had bought and sold,
  Jesus Christ—John had eaten and drunk;
To him, the Flesh meant silver and gold.
  (*Salvâ reverentiâ.*)
Now it was, 'Saviour, bountiful lamb,
  'I have roasted thee Turks, though men roast me!
'See thy servant, the plight wherein I am!
  'Art thou a saviour? Save thou me!'

CHORUS

'Tis John the mocker cries, 'Save thou me!'

VII

Who maketh God's menace an idle word?
  —Saith, it no more means what it proclaims,
Than a damsel's threat to her wanton bird?—
  For she too prattles of ugly names.

—Saith, he knoweth but one thing,—what he knows?
 That God is good and the rest is breath;
Why else is the same styled Sharon's rose?
 Once a rose, ever a rose, he saith.

CHORUS

O, John shall yet find a rose, he saith!

VIII

Alack, there be roses and roses, John!
 Some, honied of taste like your leman's tongue:
Some, bitter; for why? (roast gaily on!)
 Their tree struck root in devil's-dung.
When Paul once reasoned of righteousness
 And of temperance and of judgment to come,
Good Felix trembled, he could no less:
 John, snickering, crook'd his wicked thumb.

CHORUS

What cometh to John of the wicked thumb?

IX

Ha, ha, John plucketh now at his rose
 To rid himself of a sorrow at heart!
Lo,—petal on petal, fierce rays unclose;
 Anther on anther, sharp spikes outstart;
And with blood for dew, the bosom boils;
 And a gust of sulphur is all its smell;
And lo, he is horribly in the toils
 Of a coal-black giant flower of hell!

CHORUS

What maketh heaven, That maketh hell.

X

So, as John called now, through the fire amain,
 On the Name, he had cursed with, all his life—
To the Person, he bought and sold again—
 For the Face, with his daily buffets rife—

Feature by feature It took its place:
And his voice, like a mad dog's choking bark,
At the steady whole of the Judge's face—
Died. Forth John's soul flared into the dark.

SUBJOINETH THE ABBOT DEODAET

God help all poor souls lost in the dark!

HOLY-CROSS DAY

ON WHICH THE JEWS WERE FORCED TO ATTEND AN ANNUAL CHRISTIAN SERMON IN ROME.

['Now was come about Holy-Cross Day, and now must my lord preach his first sermon to the Jews: as it was of old cared for in the merciful bowels of the Church, that, so to speak, a crumb at least from her conspicuous table here in Rome should be, though but once yearly, cast to the famishing dogs, under-trampled and bespitten-upon beneath the feet of the guests. And a moving sight in truth, this, of so many of the besotted blind restif and ready-to-perish Hebrews! now maternally brought—nay (for He saith, 'Compel them to come in') haled, as it were, by the head and hair, and against their obstinate hearts, to partake of the heavenly grace. What awakening, what striving with tears, what working of a yeasty conscience! Nor was my lord wanting to himself on so apt an occasion; witness the abundance of conversions which did incontinently reward him: though not to my lord be altogether the glory.'—*Diary by the Bishop's Secretary*, 1600.]

What the Jews really said, on thus being driven to church, was rather to this effect:—

I

FEE, faw, fum! bubble and squeak!
Blessedest Thursday 's the fat of the week.
Rumble and tumble, sleek and rough,
Stinking and savoury, smug and gruff,
Take the church-road, for the bell's due chime
Gives us the summons—'tis sermon-time!

II

Boh, here 's Barnabas! Job, that 's you?
Up stumps Solomon—bustling too?
Shame, man! greedy beyond your years
To handsel the bishop's shaving-shears?
Fair play 's a jewel! Leave friends in the lurch?
Stand on a line ere you start for the church!

III

Higgledy piggledy, packed we lie,
Rats in a hamper, swine in a stye,
Wasps in a bottle, frogs in a sieve,
Worms in a carcase, fleas in a sleeve.
Hist! square shoulders, settle your thumbs
And buzz for the bishop—here he comes.

IV

Bow, wow, wow—a bone for the dog!
I liken his Grace to an acorned hog.
What, a boy at his side, with the bloom of a lass,
To help and handle my lord's hour-glass!
Didst ever behold so lithe a chine?
His cheek hath laps like a fresh-singed swine.

V

Aaron's asleep—shove hip to haunch,
Or somebody deal him a dig in the paunch!
Look at the purse with the tassel and knob,
And the gown with the angel and thingumbob!
What's he at, quotha? reading his text!
Now you've his curtsey—and what comes next?

VI

See to our converts—you doomed black dozen—
No stealing away—nor cog nor cozen!
You five, that were thieves, deserve it fairly;
You seven, that were beggars, will live less sparely;
You took your turn and dipped in the hat,
Got fortune—and fortune gets you; mind that!

VII

Give your first groan—compunction's at work;
And soft! from a Jew you mount to a Turk.
Lo, Micah,—the selfsame beard on chin
He was four times already converted in!
Here's a knife, clip quick—it's a sign of grace—
Or he ruins us all with his hanging-face.

VIII

Whom now is the bishop a-leering at?
I know a point where his text falls pat.
I'll tell him to-morrow, a word just now
Went to my heart and made me vow
I meddle no more with the worst of trades—
Let somebody else pay his serenades.

IX

Groan all together now, whee—hee—hee!
It's a-work, it's a-work, ah, woe is me!
It began, when a herd of us, picked and placed,
Were spurred through the Corso, stripped to the waist;
Jew brutes, with sweat and blood well spent
To usher in worthily Christian Lent.

X

It grew, when the hangman entered our bounds:
Yelled, pricked us out to his church like hounds!
It got to a pitch, when the hand indeed
Which gutted my purse would throttle my creed:
And it overflows when, to even the odd,
Men I helped to their sins help me to their God.

XI

But now, while the scapegoats leave our flock,
And the rest sit silent and count the clock,
Since forced to muse the appointed time
On these precious facts and truths sublime,—
Let us fitly employ it, under our breath,
In saying Ben Ezra's Song of Death.

XII

For Rabbi Ben Ezra, the night he died,
Called sons and sons' sons to his side,
And spoke, 'This world has been harsh and strange;
'Something is wrong: there needeth a change.
'But what, or where? at the last or first?
'In one point only we sinned, at worst.

XIII

'The Lord will have mercy on Jacob yet,
'And again in his border see Israel set.
'When Judah beholds Jerusalem,
'The stranger-seed shall be joined to them:
'To Jacob's House shall the Gentiles cleave.
'So the Prophet saith and his sons believe.

XIV

'Ay, the children of the chosen race
'Shall carry and bring them to their place:
'In the land of the Lord shall lead the same,
'Bondsmen and handmaids. Who shall blame,
'When the slaves enslave, the oppressed ones o'er
'The oppressor triumph for evermore?

XV

'God spoke, and gave us the word to keep,
'Bade never fold the hands nor sleep
''Mid a faithless world,—at watch and ward,
'Till Christ at the end relieve our guard.
'By His servant Moses the watch was set;
'Though near upon cock-crow, we keep it yet.

XVI

'Thou! if thou wast He, who at mid-watch came,
'By the starlight, naming a dubious name!
'And if, too heavy with sleep—too rash
'With fear—O Thou, if that martyr-gash
'Fell on Thee coming to take thine own,
'And we gave the Cross, when we owed the Throne—

XVII

'Thou art the Judge. We are bruised thus.
'But, the Judgment over, join sides with us!
'Thine too is the cause! and not more thine
'Than ours, is the work of these dogs and swine,
'Whose life laughs through and spits at their creed!
'Who maintain Thee in word, and defy Thee in deed!

XVIII

'We withstood Christ then? Be mindful how
'At least we withstand Barabbas now!
'Was our outrage sore? But the worst we spared,
'To have called these—Christians, had we dared!
'Let defiance to them pay mistrust of Thee,
'And Rome make amends for Calvary!

XIX

'By the torture, prolonged from age to age,
'By the infamy, Israel's heritage,
'By the Ghetto's plague, by the garb's disgrace,
'By the badge of shame, by the felon's place,
'By the branding-tool, the bloody whip,
'And the summons to Christian fellowship,—

XX

'We boast our proof that at least the Jew
'Would wrest Christ's name from the Devil's crew.
'Thy face took never so deep a shade
'But we fought them in it, God our aid!
'A trophy to bear, as we march, thy band,
'South, East, and on to the Pleasant Land!

[*Pope Gregory XVI abolished this bad business of the
Sermon.*—R. B.]

PROTUS

AMONG these latter busts we count by scores,
Half-emperors and quarter-emperors,
Each with his bay-leaf fillet, loose-thonged vest,
Loric[1] and low-browed Gorgon on the breast,—
One loves a baby face, with violets there,
Violets instead of laurel in the hair,
As those were all the little locks could bear.

---

[1] Cuirass or corslet of leather.

Now read here. 'Protus ends a period
'Of empery beginning with a god;
'Born in the porphyry chamber at Byzant,
'Queens by his cradle, proud and ministrant:
'And if he quickened breath there, 'twould like fire
'Pantingly through the dim vast realm transpire.
'A fame that he was missing spread afar:
'The world from its four corners, rose in war,
'Till he was borne out on a balcony
'To pacify the world when it should see.
'The captains ranged before him, one, his hand
'Made baby points at, gained the chief command.
'And day by day more beautiful he grew
'In shape, all said, in feature and in hue,
'While young Greek sculptors, gazing on the child,
'Became with old Greek sculpture reconciled.
'Already sages laboured to condense
'In easy tomes a life's experience:
'And artists took grave counsel to impart
'In one breath and one hand-sweep, all their art—
'To make his graces prompt as blossoming
'Of plentifully-watered palms in spring:
'Since well beseems it, whoso mounts the throne,
'For beauty, knowledge, strength, should stand alone,
'And mortals love the letters of his name.'

—Stop! Have you turned two pages? Still the same.
New reign, same date. The scribe goes on to say
How that same year, on such a month and day,
'John the Pannonian, groundedly believed
'A blacksmith's bastard, whose hard hand reprieved
'The Empire from its fate the year before,—
'Came, had a mind to take the crown, and wore
'The same for six years (during which the Huns
'Kept off their fingers from us), till his sons
'Put something in his liquor'—and so forth.
Then a new reign. Stay—'Take at its just worth'
(Subjoins an annotator) 'what I give
'As hearsay. Some think, John let Protus live

'And slip away. 'Tis said, he reached man's age
'At some blind northern court; made, first a page,
'Then tutor to the children; last, of use
'About the hunting-stables. I deduce
'He wrote the little tract "On worming dogs,"
'Whereof the name in sundry catalogues
'Is extant yet. A Protus of the race
'Is rumoured to have died a monk in Thrace,—
'And if the same, he reached senility.'

Here's John the Smith's rough-hammered head. Great
      eye,
Gross jaw and griped lips do what granite can
To give you the crown-grasper. What a man!

THE STATUE AND THE BUST

THERE's a palace in Florence, the world knows well,
And a statue watches it from the square,
And this story of both do our townsmen tell.

Ages ago, a lady there,
At the farthest window facing the East
Asked, 'Who rides by with the royal air?

The bridesmaids' prattle around her ceased;
She leaned forth, one on either hand;
They saw how the blush of the bride increased—

They felt by its beats her heart expand—
As one at each ear and both in a breath
Whispered, 'The Great-Duke Ferdinand.'

That self-same instant, underneath,
The Duke rode past in his idle way,
Empty and fine like a swordless sheath.

Gay he rode, with a friend as gay,
Till he threw his head back—'Who is she?'
—'A bride the Riccardi brings home to-day.'

Hair in heaps lay heavily
Over a pale brow spirit-pure—
Carved like the heart of a coal-black tree,

Crisped like a war-steed's encolure
And vainly sought to dissemble her eyes
Of the blackest black our eyes endure.

And lo, a blade for a knight's emprise
Filled the fine empty sheath of a man,—
The Duke grew straightway brave and wise.

He looked at her, as a lover can;
She looked at him, as one who awakes:
The past was a sleep, and her life began.

Now, love so ordered for both their sakes,
A feast was held that selfsame night
In the pile which the mighty shadow makes.

(For Via Larga is three-parts light,
But the palace overshadows one,
Because of a crime which may God requite!

To Florence and God the wrong was done,
Through the first republic's murder there
By Cosimo and his cursed son.)

The Duke (with the statue's face in the square)
Turned in the midst of his multitude
At the bright approach of the bridal pair.

Face to face the lovers stood
A single minute and no more,
While the bridegroom bent as a man subdued—

Bowed till his bonnet brushed the floor—
For the Duke on the lady a kiss conferred,
As the courtly custom was of yore.

In a minute can lovers exchange a word?
If a word did pass, which I do not think,
Only one out of the thousand heard.

That was the bridegroom. At day's brink
He and his bride were alone at last
In a bedchamber by a taper's blink.

Calmly he said that her lot was cast,
That the door she had passed was shut on her
Till the final catafalk repassed.

The world meanwhile, its noise and stir,
Through a certain window facing the East,
She could watch like a convent's chronicler.

Since passing the door might lead to a feast,
And a feast might lead to so much beside,
He, of many evils, chose the least.

'Freely I choose too,' said the bride—
'Your window and its world suffice,'
Replied the tongue, while the heart replied—

'If I spend the night with that devil twice,
'May his window serve as my loop of hell
'Whence a damned soul looks on paradise!

'I fly to the Duke who loves me well,
'Sit by his side and laugh at sorrow
'Ere I count another ave-bell.

''Tis only the coat of a page to borrow,
'And tie my hair in a horse-boy's trim,
'And I save my soul—but not to-morrow'—

(She checked herself and her eye grew dim)
'My father tarries to bless my state:
'I must keep it one day more for him.

'Is one day more so long to wait?
'Moreover the Duke rides past, I know;
'We shall see each other, sure as fate.'

She turned on her side and slept. Just so!
So we resolve on a thing and sleep:
So did the lady, ages ago.

That night the Duke said, 'Dear or cheap
'As the cost of this cup of bliss may prove
'To body or soul, I will drain it deep.'

And on the morrow, bold with love,
He beckoned the bridegroom (close on call,
As his duty bade, by the Duke's alcove)

And smiled ''Twas a very funeral,
'Your lady will think, this feast of ours,—
'A shame to efface, whate'er befall!

'What if we break from the Arno bowers,
'And try if Petraja, cool and green,
'Cure last night's fault with this morning's flowers?'

The bridegroom, not a thought to be seen
On his steady brow and quiet mouth,
Said, 'Too much favour for me so mean!

'But, alas! my lady leaves the South;
'Each wind that comes from the Apennine
'Is a menace to her tender youth:

'Nor a way exists, the wise opine,
'If she quits her palace twice this year,
'To avert the flower of life's decline.'

Quoth the Duke, 'A sage and a kindly fear.
'Moreover Petraja is cold this spring:
'Be our feast to-night as usual here!'

And then to himself—'Which night shall bring
'Thy bride to her lover's embraces, fool—
'Or I am the fool, and thou art the king!

'Yet my passion must wait a night, nor cool—
'For to-night the Envoy arrives from France
'Whose heart I unlock with thyself, my tool.

'I need thee still and might miss perchance.
'To-day is not wholly lost, beside,
'With its hope of my lady's countenance:

'For I ride—what should I do but ride?
'And passing her palace, if I list,
'May glance at its window—well betide!'

So said, so done: nor the lady missed
One ray that broke from the ardent brow,
Nor a curl of the lips where the spirit kissed.

Be sure that each renewed the vow,
No morrow's sun should arise and set
And leave them then as it left them now.

But next day passed, and next day yet,
With still fresh cause to wait one day more
Ere each leaped over the parapet.

And still, as love's brief morning wore,
With a gentle start, half smile, half sigh,
They found love not as it seemed before.

They thought it would work infallibly,
But not in despite of heaven and earth:
The rose would blow when the storm passed by.

Meantime they could profit in winter's dearth
By store of fruits that supplant the rose:
The world and its ways have a certain worth:

And to press a point while these oppose
Were simple policy; better wait:
We lose no friends and we gain no foes.

Meantime, worse fates than a lover's fate,
Who daily may ride and pass and look
Where his lady watches behind the grate!

And she—she watched the square like a book
Holding one picture and only one,
Which daily to find she undertook:

When the picture was reached the book was done,
And she turned from the picture at night to scheme
Of tearing it out for herself next sun.

So weeks grew months, years; gleam by gleam
The glory dropped from their youth and love,
And both perceived they had dreamed a dream;

Which hovered as dreams do, still above:
But who can take a dream for a truth?
Oh, hide our eyes from the next remove!

One day as the lady saw her youth
Depart, and the silver thread that streaked
Her hair, and, worn by the serpent's tooth,

The brow so puckered, the chin so peaked,—
And wondered who the woman was,
Hollow-eyed and haggard-cheeked,

Fronting her silent in the glass—
'Summon here,' she suddenly said,
'Before the rest of my old self pass,

'Him, the Carver, a hand to aid,
'Who fashions the clay no love will change,
'And fixes a beauty never to fade.

'Let Robbia's craft so apt and strange
'Arrest the remains of young and fair,
'And rivet them while the seasons range.

'Make me a face on the window there,
'Waiting as ever, mute the while,
'My love to pass below in the square!

'And let me think that it may beguile
'Dreary days which the dead must spend
'Down in their darkness under the aisle,

'To say, "What matters it at the end?
'"I did no more while my heart was warm
'"Than does that image, my pale-faced friend."

'Where is the use of the lip's red charm,
'The heaven of hair, the pride of the brow,
'And the blood that blues the inside arm—

'Unless we turn, as the soul knows how,
'The earthly gift to an end divine?
'A lady of clay is as good, I trow.'

But long ere Robbia's cornice, fine,
With flowers and fruits which leaves enlace,
Was set where now is the empty shrine—

(And, leaning out of a bright blue space,
As a ghost might lean from a chink of sky,
The passionate pale lady's face—

Eyeing ever, with earnest eye
And quick-turned neck at its breathless stretch,
Some one who ever is passing by—)

The Duke had sighed like the simplest wretch
In Florence, 'Youth—my dream escapes!
'Will its record stay?' And he bade them fetch

Some subtle moulder of brazen shapes—
'Can the soul, the will, die out of a man
'Ere his body find the grave that gapes?

'John of Douay shall effect my plan,
'Set me on horseback here aloft,
'Alive, as the crafty sculptor can,

'In the very square I have crossed so oft:
'That men may admire, when future suns
'Shall touch the eyes to a purpose soft,

'While the mouth and the brow stay brave in bronze—
'Admire and say, "When he was alive
'"How he would take his pleasure once!"

'And it shall go hard but I contrive
'To listen the while, and laugh in my tomb
'At idleness which aspires to strive.'

So! While these wait the trump of doom,
How do their spirits pass, I wonder,
Nights and days in the narrow room?

Still, I suppose, they sit and ponder
What a gift life was, ages ago,
Six steps out of the chapel yonder.

Only they see not God, I know,
Nor all that chivalry of his,
The soldier-saints who, row on row,

Burn upward each to his point of bliss—
Since, the end of life being manifest,
He had burned his way thro' the world to this.

I hear you reproach, 'But delay was best,
'For their end was a crime.'—Oh, a crime will do
As well, I reply, to serve for a test,

As a virtue golden through and through,
Sufficient to vindicate itself
And prove its worth at a moment's view!

Must a game be played for the sake of pelf?
Where a button goes, 'twere an epigram
To offer the stamp of the very Guelph.

The true has no value beyond the sham:
As well the counter as coin, I submit,
When your table's a hat, and your prize a dram.

Stake your counter as boldly every whit,
Venture as warily, use the same skill,
Do your best, whether winning or losing it,

If you choose to play!—is my principle.
Let a man contend to the uttermost
For his life's set prize, be it what it will!

The counter our lovers staked was lost
As surely as if it were lawful coin:
And the sin I impute to each frustrate ghost

Is—the unlit lamp and the ungirt loin,
Though the end in sight was a vice, I say.
You of the virtue (we issue join)
How strive you? *De te, fabula!*

PORPHYRIA'S LOVER

THE rain set early in to-night,
  The sullen wind was soon awake,
It tore the elm-tops down for spite,
  And did its worst to vex the lake:
  I listened with heart fit to break.
When glided in Porphyria; straight
  She shut the cold out and the storm,
And kneeled and made the cheerless grate
  Blaze up, and all the cottage warm;
  Which done, she rose, and from her form
Withdrew the dripping cloak and shawl,
  And laid her soiled gloves by, untied
Her hat and let the damp hair fall,
  And, last, she sat down by my side
  And called me. When no voice replied,
She put my arm about her waist,
  And made her smooth white shoulder bare,
And all her yellow hair displaced,
  And, stooping, made my cheek lie there,
  And spread, o'er all, her yellow hair,
Murmuring how she loved me—she
  Too weak, for all her heart's endeavour,
To set its struggling passion free
  From pride, and vainer ties dissever,
  And give herself to me for ever.
But passion sometimes would prevail,
  Nor could to-night's gay feast restrain
A sudden thought of one so pale
  For love of her, and all in vain:
  So, she was come through wind and rain,
Be sure I looked up at her eyes
  Happy and proud; at last I knew
Porphyria worshipped me; surprise
  Made my heart swell, and still it grew
  While I debated what to do.

That moment she was mine, mine, fair,
  Perfectly pure and good: I found
A thing to do, and all her hair
  In one long yellow string I wound
Three times her little throat around,
And strangled her. No pain felt she;
  I am quite sure she felt no pain.
As a shut bud that holds a bee,
  I warily oped her lids: again
Laughed the blue eyes without a stain.
And I untightened next the tress
  About her neck; her cheek once more
Blushed bright beneath my burning kiss:
  I propped her head up as before,
  Only, this time my shoulder bore
Her head, which droops upon it still:
  The smiling rosy little head,
So glad it has its utmost will,
  That all it scorned at once is fled,
  And I, its love, am gained instead!
Porphyria's love: she guessed not how
  Her darling one wish would be heard.
And thus we sit together now,
  And all night long we have not stirred,
  And yet God has not said a word!

'CHILDE ROLAND TO THE DARK
        TOWER CAME'

(*See Edgar's song in* 'LEAR')

I

MY first thought was, he lied in every word,
  That hoary cripple, with malicious eye
  Askance to watch the working of his lie
On mine, and mouth scarce able to afford
Suppression of the glee, that pursed and scored
  Its edge, at one more victim gained thereby.

II

What else should he be set for, with his staff?
    What, save to waylay with his lies, ensnare
    All travellers who might find him posted there,
And ask the road? I guessed what skull-like laugh
Would break, what crutch 'gin write my epitaph
    For pastime in the dusty thoroughfare,

III

If at his counsel I should turn aside
    Into that ominous tract which, all agree,
    Hides the Dark Tower. Yet acquiescingly
I did turn as he pointed: neither pride
Nor hope rekindling at the end descried,
    So much as gladness that some end might be.

IV

For, what with my whole world-wide wandering,
    What with my search drawn out thro' years, my hope
    Dwindled into a ghost not fit to cope
With that obstreperous joy success would bring,
I hardly tried now to rebuke the spring
    My heart made, finding failure in its scope.

V

As when a sick man very near to death
    Seems dead indeed, and feels begin and end
    The tears and takes the farewell of each friend,
And hears one bid the other go, draw breath
Freelier outside, ('since all is o'er,' he saith,
    'And the blow fallen no grieving can amend;')

VI

While some discuss if near the other graves
    Be room enough for this, and when a day
    Suits best for carrying the corpse away,
With care about the banners, scarves and staves:
And still the man hears all, and only craves
    He may not shame such tender love and stay.

VII

Thus, I had so long suffered in this quest,
  Heard failure prophesied so oft, been writ
  So many times among 'The Band'—to wit,
The knights who to the Dark Tower's search addressed
Their steps—that just to fail as they, seemed best,
  And all the doubt was now—should I be fit?

VIII

So, quiet as despair, I turned from him,
  That hateful cripple, out of his highway
  Into the path he pointed. All the day
Had been a dreary one at best, and dim
Was settling to its close, yet shot one grim
  Red leer to see the plain catch its estray.

IX

For mark! no sooner was I fairly found
  Pledged to the plain, after a pace or two,
  Than, pausing to throw backward a last view
O'er the safe road, 'twas gone; grey plain all round:
Nothing but plain to the horizon's bound.
  I might go on; nought else remained to do.

X

So, on I went. I think I never saw
  Such starved ignoble nature; nothing throve:
  For flowers—as well expect a cedar grove!
But cockle, spurge, according to their law
Might propagate their kind, with none to awe,
  You'd think; a burr had been a treasure-trove.

XI

No! penury, inertness and grimace,
  In some strange sort, were the land's portion. 'See
  'Or shut your eyes,' said Nature peevishly,
'It nothing skills: I cannot help my case:
''Tis the Last Judgment's fire must cure this place,
  'Calcine its clods and set my prisoners free.'

XII

If there pushed any ragged thistle-stalk
　　Above its mates, the head was chopped; the bents
　　Were jealous else. What made those holes and rents
In the dock's harsh swarth leaves, bruised as to baulk
All hope of greenness? 'tis a brute must walk
　　Pashing their life out, with a brute's intents.

XIII

As for the grass, it grew as scant as hair
　　In leprosy; thin dry blades pricked the mud
　　Which underneath looked kneaded up with blood.
One stiff blind horse, his every bone a-stare,
Stood stupefied, however he came there:
　　Thrust out past service from the devil's stud!

XIV

Alive? he might be dead for aught I know,
　　With that red gaunt and colloped neck a-strain,
　　And shut eyes underneath the rusty mane;
Seldom went such grotesqueness with such woe;
I never saw a brute I hated so;
　　He must be wicked to deserve such pain.

XV

I shut my eyes and turned them on my heart.
　　As a man calls for wine before he fights,
　　I asked one draught of earlier, happier sights,
Ere fitly I could hope to play my part.
Think first, fight afterwards—the soldier's art:
　　One taste of the old time sets all to rights.

XVI

Not it! I fancied Cuthbert's reddening face
　　Beneath its garniture of curly gold,
　　Dear fellow, till I almost felt him fold
An arm in mine to fix me to the place,
That way he used. Alas, one night's disgrace!
　　Out went my heart's new fire and left it cold.

XVII

Giles then, the soul of honour—there he stands
  Frank as ten years ago when knighted first.
  What honest man should dare (he said) he durst.
Good—but the scene shifts—faugh! what hangman hands
Pin to his breast a parchment! His own bands
  Read it. Poor traitor, spit upon and curst!

XVIII

Better this present than a past like that;
  Back therefore to my darkening path again!
  No sound, no sight as far as eye could strain.
Will the night send a howlet or a bat?
I asked: when something on the dismal flat
  Came to arrest my thoughts and change their train.

XIX

A sudden little river crossed my path
  As unexpected as a serpent comes.
  No sluggish tide congenial to the glooms;
This, as it frothed by, might have been a bath
For the fiend's glowing hoof—to see the wrath
  Of its black eddy bespate with flakes and spumes.

XX

So petty yet so spiteful! All along,
  Low scrubby alders kneeled down over it;
  Drenched willows flung them headlong in a fit
Of mute despair, a suicidal throng:
The river which had done them all the wrong,
  Whate'er that was, rolled by, deterred no whit.

XXI

Which, while I forded,—good saints, how I feared
  To set my foot upon a dead man's cheek,
  Each step, or feel the spear I thrust to seek
For hollows, tangled in his hair or beard!
—It may have been a water-rat I speared,
  But, ugh! it sounded like a baby's shriek.

XXII

Glad was I when I reached the other bank.
　　Now for a better country. Vain presage!
　　Who were the strugglers, what war did they wage,
Whose savage trample thus could pad the dank
Soil to a plash? Toads in a poisoned tank,
　　Or wild cats in a red-hot iron cage—

XXIII

The fight must so have seemed in that fell cirque.
　　What penned them there, with all the plain to choose?
　　No foot-print leading to that horrid mews,
None out of it. Mad brewage set to work
Their brains, no doubt, like galley-slaves the Turk
　　Pits for his pastime, Christians against Jews.

XXIV

And more than that—a furlong on—why, there!
　　What bad use was that engine for, that wheel,
　　Or brake, not wheel—that harrow fit to reel
Men's bodies out like silk? with all the air
Of Tophet's tool, on earth left unaware,
　　Or brought to sharpen its rusty teeth of steel.

XXV

Then came a bit of stubbed ground, once a wood,
　　Next a marsh, it would seem, and now mere earth
　　Desperate and done with; (so a fool finds mirth,
Makes a thing and then mars it, till his mood
Changes and off he goes!) within a rood—
　　Bog, clay and rubble, sand and stark black dearth.

XXVI

Now blotches rankling, coloured gay and grim,
　　Now patches where some leanness of the soil's
　　Broke into moss or substances like boils;
Then came some palsied oak, a cleft in him
Like a distorted mouth that splits its rim
　　Gaping at death, and dies while it recoils.

XXVII

And just as far as ever from the end!
  Nought in the distance but the evening, nought
  To point my footstep further! At the thought,
A great black bird, Apollyon's bosom-friend,
Sailed past, nor beat his wide wing dragon-penned
  That brushed my cap—perchance the guide I sought.

XXVIII

For, looking up, aware I somehow grew,
  'Spite of the dusk, the plain had given place
  All round to mountains—with such name to grace
Mere ugly heights and heaps now stolen in view.
How, thus they had surprised me,—solve it, you!
  How to get from them was no clearer case.

XXIX

Yet half I seemed to recognize some trick
  Of mischief happened to me, God knows when—
  In a bad dream perhaps. Here ended, then,
Progress this way. When, in the very nick
Of giving up, one time more, came a click
  As when a trap shuts—you're inside the den!

XXX

Burningly it came on me all at once,
  This was the place! those two hills on the right,
  Crouched like two bulls locked horn in horn in fight;
While to the left, a tall scalped mountain . . . Dunce,
Dotard, a-dozing at the very nonce,
  After a life spent training for the sight!

XXXI

What in the midst lay but the Tower itself?
  The round squat turret, blind as the fool's heart,
  Built of brown stone, without a counterpart
In the whole world. The tempest's mocking elf
Points to the shipman thus the unseen shelf
  He strikes on, only when the timbers start.

XXXII

Not see? because of night perhaps?—why, day
    Came back again for that! before it left,
    The dying sunset kindled through a cleft:
The hills, like giants at a hunting, lay,
Chin upon hand, to see the game at bay,—
    'Now stab and end the creature—to the heft!'

XXXIII

Not hear? when noise was everywhere! it tolled
    Increasing like a bell. Names in my ears
    Of all the lost adventurers my peers,—
How such a one was strong, and such was bold,
And such was fortunate, yet each of old
    Lost, lost! one moment knelled the woe of years.

XXXIV

There they stood, ranged along the hill-sides, met
    To view the last of me, a living frame
    For one more picture! in a sheet of flame
I saw them and I knew them all. And yet
Dauntless the slug-horn to my lips I set,
    And blew. *Childe Roland to the Dark Tower came.*

CHRISTMAS-EVE AND
EASTER-DAY

1850

CHRISTMAS EVE

I

OUT of the little chapel I burst
  Into the fresh night-air again.
Five minutes full, I waited first
  In the doorway, to escape the rain
That drove in gusts down the common's centre
  At the edge of which the chapel stands,
Before I plucked up heart to enter.
  Heaven knows how many sorts of hands
Reached past me, groping for the latch
Of the inner door that hung on catch
More obstinate the more they fumbled,
  Till, giving way at last with a scold
Of the crazy hinge, in squeezed or tumbled
One sheep more to the rest in fold,
And left me irresolute, standing sentry
In the sheepfold's lath-and-plaster entry,
Six feet long by three feet wide,
Partitioned off from the vast inside—
  I blocked up half of it at least.
No remedy; the rain kept driving.
  They eyed me much as some wild beast,
That congregation, still arriving,
Some of them by the main road, white
A long way past me into the night,
Skirting the common, then diverging;
Not a few suddenly emerging
From the common's self thro' the paling-gaps,
—They house in the gravel-pits perhaps,
Where the road stops short with its safeguard border
Of lamps, as tired of such disorder;—

But the most turned in yet more abruptly
   From a certain squalid knot of alleys,
Where the town's bad blood once slept corruptly,
   Which now the little chapel rallies
And leads into day again,—its priestliness
Lending itself to hide their beastliness
So cleverly (thanks in part to the mason),
And putting so cheery a whitewashed face on
Those neophytes too much in lack of it,
   That, where you cross the common as I did,
   And meet the party thus presided,
'Mount Zion' with Love-lane at the back of it,
They front you as little disconcerted
As, bound for the hills, her fate averted,
And her wicked people made to mind him,
Lot might have marched with Gomorrah behind him.

II

Well, from the road, the lanes or the common,
In came the flock: the fat weary woman,
Panting and bewildered, down-clapping
   Her umbrella with a mighty report,
Grounded it by me, wry and flapping,
   A wreck of whalebones; then, with a snort,
Like a startled horse, at the interloper
(Who humbly knew himself improper,
But could not shrink up small enough)
—Round to the door, and in,—the gruff
Hinge's invariable scold
Making my very blood run cold.
Prompt in the wake of her, up-pattered
On broken clogs, the many-tattered
Little old-faced peaking sister-turned-mother
Of the sickly babe she tried to smother
Somehow up, with its spotted face,
From the cold, on her breast, the one warm place;
She too must stop, wring the poor ends dry
Of a draggled shawl, and add thereby
Her tribute to the door-mat, sopping

Already from my own clothes' dropping,
Which yet she seemed to grudge I should stand on:
   Then, stooping down to take off her pattens,
She bore them defiantly, in each hand one,
Planted together before her breast
And its babe, as good as a lance in rest.
   Close on her heels, the dingy satins
Of a female something, past me flitted,
   With lips as much too white, as a streak
   Lay far too red on each hollow cheek;
And it seemed the very door-hinge pitied
All that was left of a woman once,
Holding at least its tongue for the nonce.
Then a tall yellow man, like the Penitent Thief,
With his jaw bound up in a handkerchief,
And eyelids screwed together tight,
Led himself in by some inner light.
And, except from him, from each that entered,
   I got the same interrogation—
'What, you the alien, you have ventured
   'To take with us, the elect, your station?
'A carer for none of it, a Gallio!'—
   Thus, plain as print, I read the glance
At a common prey, in each countenance
   As of huntsman giving his hounds the tallyho.
And, when the door's cry drowned their wonder,
   The draught, it always sent in shutting,
Made the flame of the single tallow candle
In the cracked square lantern I stood under,
   Shoot its blue lip at me, rebutting
As it were, the luckless cause of scandal:
I verily fancied the zealous light
(In the chapel's secret, too!) for spite
Would shudder itself clean off the wick,
With the airs of a Saint John's Candlestick.[1]
There was no standing it much longer.
'Good folks,' thought I, as resolve grew stronger,
'This way you perform the Grand-Inquisitor

     [1] See Rev. i. 20.

'When the weather sends you a chance visitor?
'You are the men, and wisdom shall die with you,
'And none of the old Seven Churches vie with you!
'But still, despite the pretty perfection
  'To which you carry your trick of exclusiveness,
'And, taking God's word under wise protection,
  'Correct its tendency to diffusiveness,
'And bid one reach it over hot plough-shares,—
  'Still, as I say, though you've found salvation,
'If I should choose to cry, as now, "Shares!"—
  'See if the best of you bars me my ration!
'I prefer, if you please, for my expounder
'Of the laws of the feast, the feast's own Founder;
'Mine's the same right with your poorest and sickliest
  'Supposing I don the marriage vestiment:
  'So, shut your mouth and open your Testament,
'And carve me my portion at your quickliest!'
Accordingly, as a shoemaker's lad
  With wizened face in want of soap,
  And wet apron wound round his waist like a rope,
(After stopping outside, for his cough was bad,
To get the fit over, poor gentle creature,
And so avoid disturbing the preacher)
—Passed in, I sent my elbow spikewise
At the shutting door, and entered likewise,
Received the hinge's accustomed greeting,
  And crossed the threshold's magic pentacle,
  And found myself in full conventicle,
—To wit, in Zion Chapel Meeting,
On the Christmas-Eve of 'Forty-nine,
  Which, calling its flock to their special clover,
  Found all assembled and one sheep over,
Whose lot, as the weather pleased, was mine.

III

I very soon had enough of it.
  The hot smell and the human noises,
And my neighbour's coat, the greasy cuff of it,
  Were a pebble-stone that a child's hand poises,

Compared with the pig-of-lead-like pressure
   Of the preaching man's immense stupidity,
As he poured his doctrine forth, full measure,
   To meet his audience's avidity.
You needed not the wit of the Sibyl
   To guess the cause of it all, in a twinkling:
   No sooner our friend had got an inkling
Of treasure hid in the Holy Bible,
(Whene'er 'twas the thought first struck him,
How death, at unawares, might duck him
Deeper than the grave, and quench
The gin-shop's light in hell's grim drench)
Than he handled it so, in fine irreverence,
   As to hug the book of books to pieces:
And, a patchwork of chapters and texts in severance,
   Not improved by the private dog's-ears and creases,
Having clothed his own soul with, he'd fain see equipt
   yours,—
So tossed you again your Holy Scriptures.
And you picked them up, in a sense, no doubt:
   Nay, had but a single face of my neighbours
   Appeared to suspect that the preacher's labours
Were help which the world could be saved without,
'Tis odds but I might have borne in quiet
A qualm or two at my spiritual diet,
Or (who can tell?) perchance even mustered
   Somewhat to urge in behalf of the sermon:
But the flock sat on, divinely flustered,
   Sniffing, methought, its dew of Hermon
With such content in every snuffle,
As the devil inside us loves to ruffle.
My old fat woman purred with pleasure,
   And thumb round thumb went twirling faster,
While she, to his periods keeping measure,
   Maternally devoured the pastor.
The man with the handkerchief untied it,
Showed us a horrible wen inside it,
Gave his eyelids yet another screwing,
And rocked himself as the woman was doing.

The shoemaker's lad, discreetly choking,
Kept down his cough. 'Twas too provoking!
My gorge rose at the nonsense and stuff of it;
    So, saying like Eve when she plucked the apple,
    'I wanted a taste, and now there's enough of it,'
I flung out of the little chapel.

IV

There was a lull in the rain, a lull
    In the wind too; the moon was risen,
And would have shone out pure and full,
    But for the ramparted cloud-prison,
Block on block built up in the West,
For what purpose the wind knows best,
Who changes his mind continually.
And the empty other half of the sky
Seemed in its silence as if it knew
What, any moment, might look through
A chance gap in that fortress massy:—
    Through its fissures you got hints
    Of the flying moon, by the shifting tints,
Now, a dull lion-colour, now, brassy
Burning to yellow, and whitest yellow,
Like furnace-smoke just ere flames bellow,
All a-simmer with intense strain
To let her through,—then blank again,
At the hope of her appearance failing.
Just by the chapel, a break in the railing
Shows a narrow path directly across;
'Tis ever dry walking there, on the moss—
Besides, you go gently all the way uphill.
    I stooped under and soon felt better;
My head grew lighter, my limbs more supple,
    As I walked on, glad to have slipt the fetter.
My mind was full of the scene I had left,
    That placid flock, that pastor vociferant,
    —How this outside was pure and different!
The sermon, now—what a mingled weft
Of good and ill! Were either less,

Its fellow had coloured the whole distinctly;
But alas for the excellent earnestness,
    And the truths, quite true if stated succinctly,
But as surely false, in their quaint presentment,
However to pastor and flock's contentment!
Say rather, such truths looked false to your eyes,
    With his provings and parallels twisted and twined,
Till how could you know them, grown double their size
    In the natural fog of the good man's mind,
Like yonder spots of our roadside lamps,
Haloed about with the common's damps?
Truth remains true, the fault's in the prover;
    The zeal was good, and the aspiration;
And yet, and yet, yet, fifty times over,
    Pharaoh received no demonstration,
By his Baker's dream of Baskets Three,
Of the doctrine of the Trinity,—
Although, as our preacher thus embellished it,
Apparently his hearers relished it
With so unfeigned a gust—who knows if
They did not prefer our friend to Joseph?
But so it is everywhere, one way with all of them!
    These people have really felt, no doubt,
A something, the motion they style the Call of them;
    And this is their method of bringing about,
By a mechanism of words and tones,
(So many texts in so many groans)
A sort of reviving and reproducing,
    More or less perfectly, (who can tell?)
The mood itself, which strengthens by using;
    And how that happens, I understand well.
A tune was born in my head last week,
Out of the thump-thump and shriek-shriek
    Of the train, as I came by it, up from Manchester;
And when, next week, I take it back again,
My head will sing to the engine's clack again,
    While it only makes my neighbour's haunches stir,
—Finding no dormant musical sprout
In him, as in me, to be jolted out.

'Tis the taught already that profits by teaching;
He gets no more from the railway's preaching
   Than, from this preacher who does the rail's office, I:
Whom therefore the flock cast a jealous eye on.
Still, why paint over their door 'Mount Zion,'
   To which all flesh shall come, saith the prophecy?

V

But wherefore be harsh on a single case?
   After how many modes, this Christmas-Eve,
Does the self-same weary thing take place?
   The same endeavour to make you believe,
And with much the same effect, no more:
   Each method abundantly convincing,
As I say, to those convinced before,
   But scarce to be swallowed without wincing
By the not-as-yet-convinced. For me,
I have my own church equally:
And in this church my faith sprang first!
   (I said, as I reached the rising ground,
And the wind began again, with a burst
   Of rain in my face, and a glad rebound
From the heart beneath, as if, God speeding me,
I entered his church-door, nature leading me)
—In youth I looked to these very skies,
And probing their immensities,
I found God there, his visible power;
   Yet felt in my heart, amid all its sense
   Of the power, an equal evidence
That his love, there too, was the nobler dower.
For the loving worm within its clod,
Were diviner than a loveless god
Amid his worlds, I will dare to say.
   You know what I mean: God's all, man's nought:
   But also, God, whose pleasure brought
Man into being, stands away
   As it were a handbreadth off, to give
   Room for the newly-made to live,
And look at him from a place apart,

And use his gifts of brain and heart,
Given, indeed, but to keep for ever.
Who speaks of man, then, must not sever
Man's very elements from man,
Saying, 'But all is God's'—whose plan
Was to create man and then leave him
Able, his own word saith, to grieve him,
But able to glorify him too,
As a mere machine could never do,
That prayed or praised, all unaware
Of its fitness for aught but praise and prayer,
Made perfect as a thing of course.
Man, therefore, stands on his own stock
Of love and power as a pin-point rock:
And, looking to God who ordained divorce
Of the rock from his boundless continent,
Sees, in his power made evident,
Only excess by a million-fold
O'er the power God gave man in the mould.
For, note: man's hand, first formed to carry
A few pounds' weight, when taught to marry
Its strength with an engine's, lifts a mountain,
　—Advancing in power by one degree;
　And why count steps through eternity?
But love is the ever-springing fountain:
Man may enlarge or narrow his bed
For the water's play, but the water-head—
How can he multiply or reduce it?
　As easy create it, as cause it to cease;
He may profit by it, or abuse it,
　But 'tis not a thing to bear increase
As power does: be love less or more
　In the heart of man, he keeps it shut
　Or opes it wide, as he pleases, but
Love's sum remains what it was before.
So, gazing up, in my youth, at love
As seen through power, ever above
All modes which make it manifest,
My soul brought all to a single test—

That he, the Eternal First and Last,
Who, in his power, had so surpassed
All man conceives of what is might,—
Whose wisdom, too, showed infinite,
—Would prove as infinitely good;
Would never, (my soul understood,)
With power to work all love desires,
Bestow e'en less than man requires;
That he who endlessly was teaching,
Above my spirit's utmost reaching,
What love can do in the leaf or stone,
(So that to master this alone,
This done in the stone or leaf for me,
I must go on learning endlessly)
Would never need that I, in turn,
   Should point him out defect unheeded,
And show that God had yet to learn
   What the meanest human creature needed,
—Not life, to wit, for a few short years,
Tracking his way through doubts and fears,
While the stupid earth on which I stay
   Suffers no change, but passive adds
   Its myriad years to myriads,
Though I, he gave it to, decay,
Seeing death come and choose about me,
And my dearest ones depart without me.
No: love which, on earth, amid all the shows of it,
   Has ever been seen the sole good of life in it,
   The love, ever growing there, spite of the strife in it,
Shall arise, made perfect, from death's repose of it.
And I shall behold thee, face to face,
O God, and in thy light retrace
How in all I loved here, still wast thou!
Whom pressing to, then, as I fain would now,
I shall find as able to satiate
   The love, thy gift, as my spirit's wonder
Thou art able to quicken and sublimate,
   With this sky of thine, that I now walk under,
And glory in thee for, as I gaze

Thus, thus! Oh, let men keep their ways
Of seeking thee in a narrow shrine—
Be this my way! And this is mine!

VI

For lo, what think you? suddenly
The rain and the wind ceased, and the sky
Received at once the full fruition
Of the moon's consummate apparition.
The black cloud-barricade was riven,
Ruined beneath her feet, and driven
Deep in the West; while, bare and breathless,
   North and South and East lay ready
For a glorious thing that, dauntless, deathless,
   Sprang across them and stood steady.
'Twas a moon-rainbow, vast and perfect,
From heaven to heaven extending, perfect
As the mother-moon's self, full in face.
It rose, distinctly at the base
   With its seven proper colours chorded,
Which still, in the rising, were compressed,
Until at last they coalesced,
   And supreme the spectral creature lorded
In a triumph of whitest white,
Above which intervened the night.
But above night too, like only the next,
   The second of a wondrous sequence,
   Reaching in rare and rarer frequence,
Till the heaven of heavens were circumflexed,
Another rainbow rose, a mightier,
Fainter, flushier and flightier,—
Rapture dying along its verge.
Oh, whose foot shall I see emerge,
Whose, from the straining topmost dark,
On to the keystone of that arc?

VII

This sight was shown me, there and then,—
Me, one out of a world of men,

Singled forth, as the chance might hap
To another if, in a thunderclap
Where I heard noise and you saw flame,
Some one man knew God called his name.
For me, I think I said, 'Appear!
'Good were it to be ever here.
'If thou wilt, let me build to thee
'Service-tabernacles three,
'Where, forever in thy presence,
'In ecstatic acquiescence,
'Far alike from thriftless learning
'And ignorance's undiscerning,
'I may worship and remain!'
   Thus at the show above me, gazing
With upturned eyes, I felt my brain
   Glutted with the glory, blazing
Throughout its whole mass, over and under
Until at length it burst asunder
And out of it bodily there streamed,
The too-much glory, as it seemed,
Passing from out me to the ground,
Then palely serpentining round
Into the dark with mazy error.

VIII

All at once I looked up with terror.
He was there.
He himself with his human air.
On the narrow pathway, just before.
I saw the back of him, no more—
He had left the chapel, then, as I
I forgot all about the sky
No face: only the sight
Of a sweepy garment, vast and white,
With a hem that I could recognize.
I felt terror, no surprise;
My mind filled with the cataract,
At one bound of the mighty fact.

'I remember, he did say
  'Doubtless that, to this world's end,
'Where two or three should meet and pray,
  'He would be in the midst, their friend;
'Certainly he was there with them!'
  And my pulses leaped for joy
  Of the golden thought without alloy,
That I saw his very vesture's hem.
Then rushed the blood back, cold and clear,
With a fresh enhancing shiver of fear;
And I hastened, cried out while I pressed
To the salvation of the vest,
'But not so, Lord! It cannot be
'That thou, indeed, art leaving me—
'Me, that have despised thy friends!
'Did my heart make no amends?
'Thou art the love of God—above
'His power, didst hear me place his love,
'And that was leaving the world for thee.
'Therefore thou must not turn from me
'As I had chosen the other part!
'Folly and pride o'ercame my heart.
'Our best is bad, nor bears thy test;
'Still, it should be our very best.
'I thought it best that thou, the spirit,
  'Be worshipped in spirit and in truth,
'And in beauty, as even we require it—
  'Not in the forms burlesque, uncouth,
'I left but now, as scarcely fitted
'For thee: I knew not what I pitied.
'But, all I felt there, right or wrong,
  'What is it to thee, who curest sinning?
'Am I not weak as thou art strong?
  'I have looked to thee from the beginning,
'Straight up to thee through all the world
'Which, like an idle scroll, lay furled
'To nothingness on either side:
'And since the time thou wast descried,
'Spite of the weak heart, so have I

'Lived ever, and so fain would die,
'Living and dying, thee before!
'But if thou leavest me——'

IX

Less or more,
I suppose that I spoke thus.
When,—have mercy, Lord, on us!
The whole face turned upon me full.
   And I spread myself beneath it,
   As when the bleacher spreads, to seethe it
In the cleansing sun, his wool,—
Steeps in the flood of noontide whiteness
   Some defiled, discoloured web—
So lay I, saturate with brightness.
   And when the flood appeared to ebb,
Lo, I was walking, light and swift,
   With my senses settling fast and steadying,
But my body caught up in the whirl and drift
   Of the vesture's amplitude, still eddying
On, just before me, still to be followed,
   As it carried me after with its motion:
What shall I say?—as a path were hollowed
   And a man went weltering through the ocean,
Sucked along in the flying wake
Of the luminous water-snake.
Darkness and cold were cloven, as through
I passed, upborne yet walking too.
And I turned to myself at intervals,—
'So he said, so it befalls.
'God who registers the cup
   'Of mere cold water, for his sake
'To a disciple rendered up,
   'Disdains not his own thirst to slake
'At the poorest love was ever offered:
'And because my heart I proffered,
'With true love trembling at the brim,
'He suffers me to follow him
'For ever, my own way,—dispensed

'From seeking to be influenced
'By all the less immediate ways
  'That earth, in worships manifold,
'Adopts to reach, by prayer and praise,
  'The garment's hem, which, lo, I hold!'

X

And so we crossed the world and stopped.
  For where am I, in city or plain,
  Since I am 'ware of the world again?
And what is this that rises propped
With pillars of prodigious girth?
Is it really on the earth,
This miraculous Dome of God?
Has the angel's measuring-rod
Which numbered cubits, gem from gem,
'Twixt the gates of the New Jerusalem,
Meted it out,—and what he meted,
Have the sons of men completed?
—Binding, ever as he bade,
Columns in the colonnade
With arms wide open to embrace
The entry of the human race
To the breast of . . . what is it, yon building,
Ablaze in front, all paint and gilding,
With marble for brick, and stones of price
For garniture of the edifice?
Now I see; it is no dream;
It stands there and it does not seem;
For ever, in pictures, thus it looks,
And thus I have read of it in books
Often in England, leagues away,
And wondered how these fountains play,
Growing up eternally
Each to a musical water-tree,
Whose blossoms drop, a glittering boon,
Before my eyes, in the light of the moon,
To the granite lavers underneath.
Liar and dreamer in your teeth!

I, the sinner that speak to you,
Was in Rome this night, and stood, and knew
Both this and more. For see, for see,
The dark is rent, mine eye is free
To pierce the crust of the outer wall,
And I view inside, and all there, all,
As the swarming hollow of a hive,
The whole Basilica alive!
Men in the chancel, body and nave,
Men on the pillars' architrave,
Men on the statues, men on the tombs
With popes and kings in their porphyry wombs,
All famishing in expectation
Of the main-altar's consummation.
For see, for see, the rapturous moment
Approaches, and earth's best endowment
Blends with heaven's; the taper-fires
Pant up, the winding brazen spires
Heave loftier yet the baldachin;
The incense-gaspings, long kept in,
Suspire in clouds; the organ blatant
Holds his breath and grovels latent,
As if God's hushing finger grazed him,
(Like Behemoth when he praised him)
At the silver bell's shrill tinkling,
Quick cold drops of terror sprinkling
On the sudden pavement strewed
With faces of the multitude.
Earth breaks up, time drops away,
In flows heaven, with its new day
Of endless life, when He who trod,
Very man and very God,
This earth in weakness, shame and pain,
Dying the death whose signs remain
Up yonder on the accursed tree,—
Shall come again, no more to be
Of captivity the thrall,
But the one God, All in all,
King of kings, Lord of lords,

As His servant John received the words,
'I died, and live for evermore!'

XI

Yet I was left outside the door.
'Why sit I here on the threshold-stone
'Left till He return, alone
'Save for the garment's extreme fold
'Abandoned still to bless my hold?'
My reason, to my doubt, replied,
As if a book were opened wide,
And at a certain page I traced
Every record undefaced,
Added by successive years,—
The harvestings of truth's stray ears
Singly gleaned, and in one sheaf
Bound together for belief.
Yes, I said—that he will go
And sit with these in turn, I know.
Their faith's heart beats, though her head swims
Too giddily to guide her limbs,
Disabled by their palsy-stroke
From propping mine. Though Rome's gross yoke
Drops off, no more to be endured,
Her teaching is not so obscured
By errors and perversities,
That no truth shines athwart the lies:
And he, whose eye detects a spark
Even where, to man's, the whole seems dark,
May well see flame where each beholder
Acknowledges the embers smoulder.
But I, a mere man, fear to quit
The clue God gave me as most fit
To guide my footsteps through life's maze,
Because himself discerns all ways
Open to reach him: I, a man
Able to mark where faith began
To swerve aside, till from its summit
Judgment drops her damning plummet,

Pronouncing such a fatal space
Departed from the founder's base:
He will not bid me enter too,
But rather sit, as now I do,
Awaiting his return outside.
—'Twas thus my reason straight replied
And joyously I turned, and pressed
The garment's skirt upon my breast,
Until, afresh its light suffusing me,
My heart cried—What has been abusing me
That I should wait here lonely and coldly
Instead of rising, entering boldly,
Baring truth's face, and letting drift
Her veils of lies as they choose to shift?
Do these men praise him? I will raise
My voice up to their point of praise!
I see the error; but above
The scope of error, see the love.—
Oh, love of those first Christian days!
—Fanned so soon into a blaze,
From the spark preserved by the trampled sect,
That the antique sovereign Intellect
Which then sat ruling in the world,
Like a change in dreams, was hurled
From the throne he reigned upon:
You looked up and he was gone.
Gone, his glory of the pen!
—Love, with Greece and Rome in ken,
Bade her scribes abhor the trick
Of poetry and rhetoric,
And exult with hearts set free,
In blessed imbecility
Scrawled, perchance, on some torn sheet
Leaving Sallust incomplete.
Gone, his pride of sculptor, painter!
—Love, while able to acquaint her
With the thousand statues yet
Fresh from chisel, pictures wet
From brush, she saw on every side,

Chose rather with an infant's pride
To frame those portents which impart
Such unction to true Christian Art.
Gone, music too! The air was stirred
By happy wings: Terpander's bird
(That, when the cold came, fled away)
Would tarry not the wintry day,—
As more-enduring sculpture must,
Till filthy saints rebuked the gust
With which they chanced to get a sight
Of some dear naked Aphrodite
They glanced a thought above the toes of,
By breaking zealously her nose off.
Love, surely, from that music's lingering,
Might have filched her organ-fingering,
Nor chosen rather to set prayings
To hog-grunts, praises to horse-neighings.
Love was the startling thing, the new:
Love was the all-sufficient too;
And seeing that, you see the rest:
As a babe can find its mother's breast
As well in darkness as in light,
Love shut our eyes, and all seemed right.
True, the world's eyes are open now:
—Less need for me to disallow
Some few that keep Love's zone unbuckled,
Peevish as ever to be suckled,
Lulled by the same old baby-prattle
With intermixture of the rattle,
When she would have them creep, stand steady
Upon their feet, or walk already,
Not to speak of trying to climb.
I will be wise another time,
And not desire a wall between us,
    When next I see a church-roof cover
So many species of one genus,
    All with foreheads bearing *lover*
Written above the earnest eyes of them;
    All with breasts that beat for beauty,

Whether sublimed, to the surprise of them,
  In noble daring, steadfast duty,
The heroic in passion, or in action,—
Or, lowered for sense's satisfaction,
To the mere outside of human creatures,
Mere perfect form and faultless features.
What? with all Rome here, whence to levy
  Such contributions to their appetite,
With women and men in a gorgeous bevy,
  They take, as it were, a padlock, clap it tight
On their southern eyes, restrained from feeding
On the glories of their ancient reading,
On the beauties of their modern singing,
On the wonders of the builder's bringing,
On the majesties of Art around them,—
  And, all these loves, late struggling incessant,
When faith has at last united and bound them,
  They offer up to God for a present?
Why, I will, on the whole, be rather proud of it,—
  And, only taking the act in reference
To the other recipients who might have allowed it,
  I will rejoice that God had the preference.

XII

So I summed up my new resolves:
  Too much love there can never be.
And where the intellect devolves
  Its function on love exclusively,
I, a man who possesses both,
Will accept the provision, nothing loth,
—Will feast my love, then depart elsewhere,
That my intellect may find its share.
And ponder, O soul, the while thou departest,
And see thou applaud the great heart of the artist,
Who, examining the capabilities
  Of the block of marble he has to fashion
  Into a type of thought or passion,—
Not always, using obvious facilities,

Shapes it, as any artist can
Into a perfect symmetrical man,
Complete from head to foot of the life-size,
Such as old Adam stood in his wife's eyes,—
But, now and then, bravely aspires to consummate
A Colossus by no means so easy to come at,
And uses the whole of his block for the bust,
    Leaving the mind of the public to finish it,
Since cut it ruefully short he must:
On the face alone he expends his devotion,
    He rather would mar than resolve to diminish it,
    —Saying, 'Applaud me for this grand notion
'Of what a face may be! As for completing it
    'In breast and body and limbs, do that, you!'
All hail! I fancy how, happily meeting it,
    A trunk and legs would perfect the statue,
Could man carve so as to answer volition,
    And how much nobler than petty cavils,
    Were a hope to find, in my spirit-travels,
Some artist of another ambition,
Who having a block to carve, no bigger,
    Has spent his power on the opposite quest,
    And believed to begin at the feet was best—
For so may I see, ere I die, the whole figure!

XIII

No sooner said than out in the night!
My heart beat lighter and more light:
And still, as before, I was walking swift,
    With my senses settling fast and steadying,
But my body caught up in the whirl and drift
    Of the vesture's amplitude, still eddying
On just before me, still to be followed,
    As it carried me after with its motion,
—What shall I say?—as a path were hollowed,
    And a man went weltering through the ocean,
Sucked along in the flying wake
Of the luminous water-snake.

XIV

Alone! I am left alone once more—
  (Save for the garment's extreme fold
  Abandoned still to bless my hold)
Alone, beside the entrance-door
Of a sort of temple,—perhaps a college,
—Like nothing I ever saw before
At home in England, to my knowledge.
The tall old quaint irregular town!
  It may be . . . though which, I can't affirm . . . any
  Of the famous middle-age towns of Germany;
And this flight of stairs where I sit down,
Is it Halle, Weimar, Cassel, Frankfort
Or Göttingen, I have to thank for't?
It may be Göttingen,—most likely.
Through the open door I catch obliquely
Glimpses of a lecture-hall;
  And not a bad assembly neither,
Ranged decent and symmetrical
  On benches, waiting what's to see there;
Which, holding still by the vesture's hem,
I also resolve to see with them,
Cautious this time how I suffer to slip
The chance of joining in fellowship
With any that call themselves his friends;
  As these folk do, I have a notion.
  But hist—a buzzing and emotion!
All settle themselves, the while ascends
By the creaking rail to the lecture-desk,
  Step by step, deliberate
  Because of his cranium's over-freight,
Three parts sublime to one grotesque,
If I have proved an accurate guesser,
The hawk-nosed high-cheek-boned Professor.
I felt at once as if there ran
A shoot of love from my heart to the man—
That sallow virgin-minded studious
  Martyr to mild enthusiasm,

As he uttered a kind of cough-preludious
  That woke my sympathetic spasm,
(Beside some spitting that made me sorry)
And stood, surveying his auditory
With a wan pure look, well nigh celestial,—
  Those blue eyes had survived so much!
  While, under the foot they could not smutch,
Lay all the fleshly and the bestial,
Over he bowed, and arranged his notes,
Till the auditory's clearing of throats
Was done with, died into a silence;
  And, when each glance was upward sent,
  Each bearded mouth composed intent,
And a pin might be heard drop half a mile hence,—
He pushed back higher his spectacles,
Let the eyes stream out like lamps from cells,
And giving his head of hair—a hake
  Of undressed tow, for colour and quantity—
One rapid and impatient shake,
  (As our own Young England adjusts a jaunty tie
When about to impart, on mature digestion,
Some thrilling view of the surplice-question)
—The Professor's grave voice, sweet though hoarse,
Broke into his Christmas-Eve discourse.

XV

And he began it by observing
  How reason dictated that men
Should rectify the natural swerving,
  By a reversion, now and then,
To the well-heads of knowledge, few
And far away, whence rolling grew
The life-stream wide whereat we drink,
Commingled, as we needs must think,
With waters alien to the source;
To do which, aimed this eve's discourse;
Since, where could be a fitter time
For tracing backward to its prime
This Christianity, this lake,

This reservoir, whereat we slake,
From one or other bank, our thirst?
So, he proposed inquiring first
Into the various sources whence
   This Myth of Christ is derivable;
Demanding from the evidence,
   (Since plainly no such life was liveable)
How these phenomena should class?
Whether 'twere best opine Christ was,
Or never was at all, or whether
He was and was not, both together—
It matters little for the name,
So the idea be left the same.
Only, for practical purpose' sake,
'Twas obviously as well to take
The popular story,—understanding
   How the ineptitude of the time,
And the penman's prejudice, expanding
   Fact into fable fit for the clime,
Had, by slow and sure degrees, translated it
   Into this myth, this Individuum,—
Which, when reason had strained and abated it
   Of foreign matter, left, for residuum,
A Man!—a right true man, however,
Whose work was worthy a man's endeavour:
Work, that gave warrant almost sufficient
   To his disciples, for rather believing
He was just omnipotent and omniscient,
   As it gives to us, for as frankly receiving
His word, their tradition,—which, though it meant
Something entirely different
From all that those who only heard it,
In their simplicity thought and averred it,
Had yet a meaning quite as respectable:
For, among other doctrines delectable,
Was he not surely the first to insist on
   The natural sovereignty of our race?—
   Here the lecturer came to a pausing-place.
And while his cough, like a drouthy piston,

Tried to dislodge the husk that grew to him,
I seized the occasion of bidding adieu to him,
The vesture still within my hand.

XVI

I could interpret its command.
This time he would not bid me enter
The exhausted air-bell of the Critic.
Truth's atmosphere may grow mephitic
When Papist struggles with Dissenter,
Impregnating its pristine clarity,
—One, by his daily fare's vulgarity,
    Its gust of broken meat and garlic;
—One, by his soul's too-much presuming
To turn the frankincense's fuming
    And vapours of the candle starlike
Into the cloud her wings she buoys on.
    Each, that thus sets the pure air seething,
    May poison it for healthy breathing—
But the Critic leaves no air to poison;
Pumps out with ruthless ingenuity
Atom by atom, and leaves you—vacuity.
Thus much of Christ does he reject?
And what retain? His intellect?
What is it I must reverence duly?
Poor intellect for worship, truly,
Which tells me simply what was told
    (If mere morality, bereft
    Of the God in Christ, be all that's left)
Elsewhere by voices manifold;
With this advantage, that the stater
    Made nowise the important stumble
    Of adding, he, the sage and humble,
Was also one with the Creator.
You urge Christ's followers' simplicity:
    But how does shifting blame, evade it?
Have wisdom's words no more felicity?
    The stumbling-block, his speech—who laid it?

How comes it that for one found able
To sift the truth of it from fable,
Millions believe it to the letter?
Christ's goodness, then—does that fare better?
Strange goodness, which upon the score
　　Of being goodness, the mere due
Of man to fellow-man, much more
　　To God,—should take another view
Of its possessor's privilege,
And bid him rule his race! You pledge
Your fealty to such rule? What, all—
From heavenly John and Attic Paul,
And that brave weather-battered Peter,
Whose stout faith only stood completer
For buffets, sinning to be pardoned,
As, the more his hands hauled nets, they hardened,--
All, down to you, the man of men,
Professing here at Göttingen,
Compose Christ's flock! They, you and I,
Are sheep of a good man! And why?
The goodness,—how did he acquire it?
Was it self-gained, did God inspire it?
Choose which; then tell me, on what ground
Should its possessor dare propound
His claim to rise o'er us an inch?
　　Were goodness all some man's invention,
　　Who arbitrarily made mention
What we should follow, and whence flinch,—
What qualities might take the style
　　Of right and wrong,—and had such guessing
　　Met with as general acquiescing
As graced the alphabet erewhile,
When A got leave an Ox to be,
No Camel (quoth the Jews) like G,[1]—
For thus inventing thing and title
Worship were that man's fit requital.
But if the common conscience must
Be ultimately judge, adjust

[1] Gimel, the Hebrew G, means camel

Its apt name to each quality
Already known,—I would decree
Worship for such mere demonstration
   And simple work of nomenclature,
    Only the day I praised, not nature,
But Harvey, for the circulation.
I would praise such a Christ, with pride
And joy, that he, as none beside,
Had taught us how to keep the mind
God gave him, as God gave his kind,
Freer than they from fleshly taint:
I would call such a Christ our Saint,
As I declare our Poet, him
Whose insight makes all others dim:
A thousand poets pried at life,
And only one amid the strife
Rose to be Shakespeare: each shall take
His crown, I'd say, for the world's sake—
Though some objected—'Had we seen
'The heart and head of each, what screen
'Was broken there to give them light,
'While in ourselves it shuts the sight,
'We should no more admire, perchance,
'That these found truth out at a glance,
'Than marvel how the bat discerns
'Some pitch-dark cavern's fifty turns,
'Led by a finer tact, a gift
'He boasts, which other birds must shift
'Without, and grope as best they can.'
No, freely I would praise the man,—
Nor one whit more, if he contended
That gift of his, from God descended.
Ah friend, what gift of man's does not?
No nearer something, by a jot,
Rise an infinity of nothings
   Than one: take Euclid for your teacher:
Distinguish kinds: do crownings, clothings,
   Make that creator which was creature?
Multiply gifts upon man's head,

And what, when all's done, shall be said
But—the more gifted he, I ween!
   That one's made Christ, this other, Pilate,
And this might be all that has been,—
   So what is there to frown or smile at?
What is left for us, save, in growth
Of soul, to rise up, far past both,
From the gift looking to the giver,
And from the cistern to the river,
And from the finite to infinity,
And from man's dust to God's divinity?

XVII

Take all in a word: the truth in God's breast
Lies trace for trace upon ours impressed:
Though he is so bright and we so dim,
We are made in his image to witness him:
   And were no eye in us to tell,
   Instructed by no inner sense,
The light of heaven from the dark of hell,
   That light would want its evidence,—
Though justice, good and truth were still
Divine, if, by some demon's will,
Hatred and wrong had been proclaimed
Law through the worlds, and right misnamed.
No mere exposition of morality
Made or in part or in totality,
Should win you to give it worship, therefore:
And, if no better proof you will care for,
—Whom do you count the worst man upon earth?
   Be sure, he knows, in his conscience, more
Of what right is, than arrives at birth
   In the best man's acts that we bow before:
This last knows better—true, but my fact is,
'Tis one thing to know, and another to practise.
And thence I conclude that the real God-function
Is to furnish a motive and injunction
For practising what we know already.
And such an injunction and such a motive

As the God in Christ, do you waive, and 'heady,
'High-minded,' hang your tablet-votive
Outside the fane on a finger-post?
Morality to the uttermost,
Supreme in Christ as we all confess,
Why need we prove would avail no jot
To make him God, if God he were not?
What is the point where himself lays stress?
Does the precept run 'Believe in good,
'In justice, truth, now understood
'For the first time?'—or, 'Believe in me,
'Who lived and died, yet essentially
'Am Lord of Life?' Whoever can take
The same to his heart and for mere love's sake
Conceive of the love,—that man obtains
A new truth; no conviction gains
Of an old one only, made intense
By a fresh appeal to his faded sense.

XVIII

Can it be that he stays inside?
  Is the vesture left me to commune with?
  Could my soul find aught to sing in tune with
Even at this lecture, if she tried?
Oh, let me at lowest sympathize
With the lurking drop of blood that lies
In the desiccated brain's white roots
Without throb for Christ's attributes,
As the lecturer makes his special boast!
If love's dead there, it has left a ghost.
Admire we, how from heart to brain
  (Though to say so strike the doctors dumb)
One instinct rises and falls again,
  Restoring the equilibrium.
And how when the Critic had done his best,
And the pearl of price, at reason's test,
Lay dust and ashes levigable
On the Professor's lecture-table,—

When we looked for the inference and monition
That our faith, reduced to such condition,
Be swept forthwith to its natural dust-hole,—
   He bids us, when we least expect it,
Take back our faith,—if it be not just whole,
   Yet a pearl indeed, as his tests affect it,
Which fact pays damage done rewardingly,
So, prize we our dust and ashes accordingly!
'Go home and venerate the myth
'I thus have experimented with—
'This man, continue to adore him
'Rather than all who went before him,
'And all who ever followed after!'—
   Surely for this I may praise you, my brother!
Will you take the praise in tears or laughter?
   That's one point gained: can I compass another?
Unlearned love was safe from spurning—
Can't we respect your loveless learning?
Let us at least give learning honour!
What laurels had we showered upon her,
Girding her loins up to perturb
Our theory of the Middle Verb;
Or Turk-like brandishing a scimitar
O'er anapæsts in comic-trimeter;
Or curing the halt and maimed 'Iketides,'[1]
While we lounged on at our indebted ease:
Instead of which, a tricksy demon
Sets her at Titus or Philemon!
When ignorance wags his ears of leather
And hates God's word, 'tis altogether;
Nor leaves he his congenial thistles
To go and browse on Paul's Epistles.
—And you, the audience, who might ravage
The world wide, enviably savage,
Nor heed the cry of the retriever,
More than Herr Heine (before his fever),—
I do not tell a lie so arrant
   As say my passion's wings are furled up,

    [1] *The Suppliants*, a fragment of a play by Æschylus.

And, without plainest heavenly warrant,
 I were ready and glad to give the world up—
But still, when you rub brow meticulous,
 And ponder the profit of turning holy
 If not for God's, for your own sake solely,
—God forbid I should find you ridiculous!
Deduce from this lecture all that eases you,
Nay, call yourselves, if the calling pleases you,
'Christians,'—abhor the deist's pravity,—
Go on, you shall no more move my gravity
Than, when I see boys ride a-cockhorse,
I find it in my heart to embarrass them
By hinting that their stick's a mock horse,
And they really carry what they say carries them.

XIX

So sat I talking with my mind.
 I did not long to leave the door
 And find a new church, as before,
But rather was quiet and inclined
To prolong and enjoy the gentle resting
From further tracking and trying and testing.
'This tolerance is a genial mood!'
(Said I, and a little pause ensued.)
'One trims the bark 'twixt shoal and shelf,
 'And sees, each side, the good effects of it,
'A value for religion's self,
 'A carelessness about the sects of it.
'Let me enjoy my own conviction,
 'Not watch my neighbour's faith with fretfulness,
'Still spying there some dereliction
 'Of truth, perversity, forgetfulness!
'Better a mild indifferentism,
 'Teaching that both our faiths (though duller
'His shine through a dull spirit's prism)
 'Originally had one colour!
'Better pursue a pilgrimage
 'Through ancient and through modern times
 'To many peoples, various climes,

'Where I may see saint, savage, sage
'Fuse their respective creeds in one
'Before the general Father's throne!'

XX

—'Twas the horrible storm began afresh!
The black night caught me in his mesh,
Whirled me up, and flung me prone.
I was left on the college-step alone.
I looked, and far there, ever fleeting
Far, far away, the receding gesture,
And looming of the lessening vesture!—
Swept forward from my stupid hand,
While I watched my foolish heart expand
In the lazy glow of benevolence,
    O'er the various modes of man's belief.
I sprang up with fear's vehemence.

    Needs must there be one way, our chief
Best way of worship: let me strive
To find it, and when found, contrive
My fellows also take their share!
This constitutes my earthly care:
God's is above it and distinct.
For I, a man, with men am linked
And not a brute with brutes; no gain
That I experience, must remain
Unshared: but should my best endeavour
To share it, fail—subsisteth ever
God's care above, and I exult
That God, by God's own ways occult,
May—doth, I will believe—bring back
All wanderers to a single track.
Meantime, I can but testify
God's care for me—no more, can I—
It is but for myself I know;
    The world rolls witnessing around me
    Only to leave me as it found me;
Men cry there, but my ear is slow:

Their races flourish or decay
—What boots it, while yon lucid way
Loaded with stars divides the vault?
But soon my soul repairs its fault
When, sharpening sense's hebetude,
She turns on my own life! So viewed,
No mere mote's-breadth but teems immense
With witnessings of providence:
And woe to me if when I look
Upon that record, the sole book
Unsealed to me, I take no heed
Of any warning that I read!
Have I been sure, this Christmas-Eve,
God's own hand did the rainbow weave,
Whereby the truth from heaven slid
Into my soul?—I cannot bid
The world admit he stooped to heal
My soul, as if in a thunder-peal
Where one heard noise, and one saw flame,
I only knew he named my name:
But what is the world to me, for sorrow
Or joy in its censure, when to-morrow
It drops the remark, with just-turned head
Then, on again, 'That man is dead'?
Yes, but for me—my name called,—drawn
As a conscript's lot from the lap's black yawn,
He has dipt into on a battle-dawn:
Bid out of life by a nod, a glance,—
Stumbling, mute-mazed, at nature's chance,—
With a rapid finger circled round,
Fixed to the first poor inch of ground
To fight from, where his foot was found;
Whose ear but a minute since lay free
To the wide camp's buzz and gossipry—
Summoned, a solitary man
To end his life where his life began,
From the safe glad rear, to the dreadful van!
Soul of mine, hadst thou caught and held
By the hem of the vesture!—

XXI

And I caught
At the flying robe, and unrepelled
    Was lapped again in its folds full-fraught
With warmth and wonder and delight,
God's mercy being infinite.
For scarce had the words escaped my tongue,
When, at a passionate bound, I sprung,
Out of the wandering world of rain,
Into the little chapel again.

XXII

How else was I found there, bolt upright
    On my bench, as if I had never left it?
—Never flung out on the common at night,
    Nor met the storm and wedge-like cleft it,
Seen the raree-show of Peter's successor,
Or the laboratory of the Professor!
For the Vision, that was true, I wist,
True as that heaven and earth exist.
There sat my friend, the yellow and tall,
    With his neck and its wen in the selfsame place;
Yet my nearest neighbour's cheek showed gall.
    She had slid away a contemptuous space:
And the old fat woman, late so placable,
Eyed me with symptoms, hardly mistakable,
Of her milk of kindness turning rancid.
In short, a spectator might have fancied
    That I had nodded, betrayed by slumber,
Yet kept my seat, a warning ghastly,
    Through the heads of the sermon, nine in number,
And woke up now at the tenth and lastly.
But again, could such disgrace have happened?
    Each friend at my elbow had surely nudged it;
And, as for the sermon, where did my nap end?
    Unless I heard it, could I have judged it?
Could I report as I do at the close,
First, the preacher speaks through his nose:

Second, his gesture is too emphatic:
   Thirdly, to waive what's pedagogic,
   The subject-matter itself lacks logic:
Fourthly, the English is ungrammatic.
Great news! the preacher is found no Pascal,
Whom, if I pleased, I might to the task call
Of making square to a finite eye
The circle of infinity,
And find so all-but-just-succeeding!
Great news! the sermon proves no reading
Where bee-like in the flowers I bury me,
Like Taylor's, the immortal Jeremy!
And now that I know the very worst of him,
What was it I thought to obtain at first of him?
Ha! Is God mocked, as he asks?
Shall I take on me to change his tasks,
And dare, despatched to a river-head
   For a simple draught of the element,
   Neglect the thing for which he sent,
And return with another thing instead?—
Saying, 'Because the water found
'Welling up from underground,
'Is mingled with the taints of earth,
'While thou, I know, dost laugh at dearth,
'And couldst, at wink or word, convulse
'The world with the leap of a river-pulse,—
'Therefore I turned from the oozings muddy,
   'And bring thee a chalice I found, instead:
'See the brave veins in the breccia ruddy!
   'One would suppose that the marble bled.
'What matters the water? A hope I have nursed:
'The waterless cup will quench my thirst.'
—Better have knelt at the poorest stream
   That trickles in pain from the straitest rift!
   For the less or the more is all God's gift,
Who blocks up or breaks wide the granite-seam.
And here, is there water or not, to drink?
I then, in ignorance and weakness,
Taking God's help, have attained to think

My heart does best to receive in meekness
That mode of worship, as most to his mind,
Where earthly aids being cast behind,
His All in All appears serene
With the thinnest human veil between,
Letting the mystic lamps, the seven,
   The many motions of his spirit,
Pass, as they list, to earth from heaven.
   For the preacher's merit or demerit,
It were to be wished the flaws were fewer
   In the earthen vessel, holding treasure
Which lies as safe in a golden ewer;
   But the main thing is, does it hold good measure?
Heaven soon sets right all other matters!—
   Ask, else, these ruins of humanity,
This flesh worn out to rags and tatters,
   This soul at struggle with insanity,
Who thence take comfort—can I doubt?—
Which an empire gained, were a loss without.
May it be mine! And let us hope
That no worse blessing befall the Pope,
Turned sick at last of to-day's buffoonery.
   Of posturings and petticoatings,
   Beside his Bourbon bully's gloatings
In the bloody orgies of drunk poltroonery!
Nor may the Professor forego its peace
   At Göttingen presently, when, in the dusk
Of his life, if his cough, as I fear, should increase,
   Prophesied of by that horrible husk—
When thicker and thicker the darkness fills
The world through his misty spectacles,
And he gropes for something more substantial
   Than a fable, myth or personification,—
May Christ do for him what no mere man shall,
   And stand confessed as the God of salvation!
Meantime, in the still recurring fear
   Lest myself, at unawares, be found,
   While attacking the choice of my neighbours round,
With none of my own made—I choose here!

The giving out of the hymn reclaims me;
I have done: and if any blames me,
Thinking that merely to touch in brevity
    The topics I dwell on, were unlawful,—
Or worse, that I trench, with undue levity,
    On the bounds of the holy and the awful,—
I praise the heart, and pity the head of him,
And refer myself to THEE, instead of him,
Who head and heart alike discernest,
    Looking below light speech we utter,
    When frothy spume and frequent sputter
Prove that the soul's depths boil in earnest!
May truth shine out, stand ever before us!
I put up pencil and join chorus
To Hepzibah Tune, without further apology,
    The last five verses of the third section
    Of the seventeenth hymn of Whitfield's Collection,
To conclude with the doxology.

EASTER-DAY

I

How very hard it is to be
A Christian! Hard for you and me,
—Not the mere task of making real
That duty up to its ideal,
Effecting thus, complete and whole,
A purpose of the human soul—
For that is always hard to do;
But hard, I mean, for me and you
To realize it, more or less,
With even the moderate success
Which commonly repays our strife
To carry out the aims of life.
'This aim is greater,' you will say,
'And so more arduous every way.'
—But the importance of their fruits
Still proves to man, in all pursuits,

Proportional encouragement.
'Then, what if it be God's intent
'That labour to this one result
'Should seem unduly difficult?'
Ah, that's a question in the dark—
And the sole thing that I remark
Upon the difficulty, this;
We do not see it where it is,
At the beginning of the race:
As we proceed, it shifts its place,
And where we looked for crowns to fall,
We find the tug's to come,—that's all.

II

At first you say, 'The whole, or chief
'Of difficulties, is belief.
'Could I believe once thoroughly,
'The rest were simple. What? Am I
'An idiot, do you think,—a beast?
'Prove to me, only that the least
'Command of God is God's indeed,
'And what injunction shall I need
'To pay obedience? Death so nigh,
'When time must end, eternity
'Begin,—and cannot I compute,
'Weigh loss and gain together, suit
'My actions to the balance drawn,
'And give my body to be sawn
'Asunder, hacked in pieces, tied
'To horses, stoned, burned, crucified,
'Like any martyr of the list?
'How gladly!—if I make acquist,
'Through the brief minute's fierce annoy,
'Of God's eternity of joy.'

III

—And certainly you name the point
Whereon all turns: for could you joint
This flexile finite life once tight
Into the fixed and infinite,

You, safe inside, would spurn what's out,
With carelessness enough, no doubt—
Would spurn mere life: but when time brings
To their next stage your reasonings,
Your eyes, late wide, begin to wink
Nor see the path so well, I think.

IV

You say, 'Faith may be, one agrees,
'A touchstone for God's purposes,
'Even as ourselves conceive of them.
'Could he acquit us or condemn
'For holding what no hand can loose,
'Rejecting when we can't but choose?
'As well award the victor's wreath
'To whosoever should take breath
'Duly each minute while he lived—
'Grant heaven, because a man contrived
'To see its sunlight every day
'He walked forth on the public way.
'You must mix some uncertainty
'With faith, if you would have faith be.
'Why, what but faith, do we abhor
'And idolize each other for—
'Faith in our evil or our good,
'Which is or is not understood
'Aright by those we love or those
'We hate, thence called our friends or foes?
'Your mistress saw your spirit's grace,
'When, turning from the ugly face,
'I found belief in it too hard;
'And she and I have our reward.
'—Yet here a doubt peeps: well for us
'Weak beings, to go using thus
'A touchstone for our little ends,
'Trying with faith the foes and friends;
'—But God, bethink you! I would fain
'Conceive of the Creator's reign

'As based upon exacter laws
'Than creatures build by with applause.
'In all God's acts—(as Plato cries
'He doth)—he should geometrize.
'Whence, I desiderate . . .'

V

     I see!
You would grow as a natural tree,
Stand as a rock, soar up like fire.
The world's so perfect and entire,
Quite above faith, so right and fit!
Go there, walk up and down in it!
No. The creation travails, groans—
Contrive your music from its moans,
Without or let or hindrance, friend!
That's an old story, and its end
As old—you come back (be sincere)
With every question you put here
(Here where there once was, and is still,
We think, a living oracle,
Whose answers you stand carping at)
This time flung back unanswered flat,—
Beside, perhaps, as many more
As those that drove you out before,
Now added, where was little need.
Questions impossible, indeed,
To us who sat still, all and each
Persuaded that our earth had speech,
Of God's, writ down, no matter if
In cursive type or hieroglyph,—
Which one fact freed us from the yoke
Of guessing why He never spoke.
You come back in no better plight
Than when you left us,—am I right?

VI

So, the old process, I conclude,
Goes on, the reasoning's pursued
Further. You own, ''Tis well averred,

'A scientific faith's absurd,
'—Frustrates the very end 'twas meant
'To serve. So, I would rest content
'With a mere probability,
'But, probable; the chance must lie
'Clear on one side,—lie all in rough,
'So long as there be just enough
'To pin my faith to, though it hap
'Only at points: from gap to gap
'One hangs up a huge curtain so,
'Grandly, nor seeks to have it go
'Foldless and flat along the wall.
'What care I if some interval
'Of life less plainly may depend
'On God? I'd hang there to the end;
'And thus I should not find it hard
'To be a Christian and debarred
'From trailing on the earth, till furled
'Away by death.—Renounce the world!
'Were that a mighty hardship? Plan
'A pleasant life, and straight some man
'Beside you, with, if he thought fit,
'Abundant means to compass it,
'Shall turn deliberate aside
'To try and live as, if you tried
'You clearly might, yet most despise.
'One friend of mine wears out his eyes,
'Slighting the stupid joys of sense,
'In patient hope that, ten years hence,
'"Somewhat completer," he may say,
'"My list of *coleoptera!*"
'While just the other who most laughs
'At him, above all epitaphs
'Aspires to have his tomb describe
'Himself as sole among the tribe
'Of snuffbox-fanciers, who possessed
'A Grignon with the Regent's crest.
'So that, subduing, as you want,
'Whatever stands predominant

'Among my earthly appetites
'For tastes and smells and sounds and sights,
'I shall be doing that alone,
'To gain a palm-branch and a throne.
'Which fifty people undertake
'To do, and gladly, for the sake
'Of giving a Semitic guess,
'Or playing pawns at blindfold chess.'

VII

Good: and the next thing is,—look round
For evidence enough! 'Tis found,
No doubt: as is your sort of mind,
So is your sort of search: you'll find
What you desire, and that's to be
A Christian. What says history?
How comforting a point it were
To find some mummy-scrap declare
There lived a Moses! Better still,
Prove Jonah's whale translatable
Into some quicksand of the seas,
Isle, cavern, rock, or what you please,
That faith might flap her wings and crow
From such an eminence! Or, no—
The human heart's best; you prefer
Making that prove the minister
To truth; you probe its wants and needs,
And hopes and fears, then try what creeds
Meet these most aptly,—resolute
That faith plucks such substantial fruit
Wherever these two correspond,
She little needs to look beyond,
And puzzle out who Orpheus was,
Or Dionysius Zagrias.
You'll find sufficient, as I say,
To satisfy you either way;
You wanted to believe; your pains
Are crowned—you do: and what remains?
'Renounce the world!'—Ah, were it done

By merely cutting one by one
Your limbs off, with your wise head last,
How easy were it!—how soon past,
If once in the believing mood!
'Such is man's usual gratitude,
'Such thanks to God do we return,
'For not exacting that we spurn
'A single gift of life, forego
'One real gain,—only taste them so
'With gravity and temperance,
'That those mild virtues may enhance
'Such pleasures, rather than abstract—
'Last spice of which, will be the fact
'Of love discerned in every gift;
'While, when the scene of life shall shift,
'And the gay heart be taught to ache,
'As sorrows and privations take
'The place of joy,—the thing that seems
'Mere misery, under human schemes,
'Becomes, regarded by the light
'Of love, as very near, or quite
'As good a gift as joy before.
'So plain is it that, all the more
'A dispensation's merciful,
'More pettishly we try and cull
'Briars, thistles, from our private plot,
'To mar God's ground where thorns are not!'

VIII

Do you say this, or I?—Oh, you!
Then, what, my friend?—(thus I pursue
Our parley)—you indeed opine
That the Eternal and Divine
Did, eighteen centuries ago,
In very truth . . . Enough! you know
The all-stupendous tale,—that Birth,
That Life, that Death! And all, the earth
Shuddered at,—all, the heavens grew black
Rather than see; all, nature's rack

And throe at dissolution's brink
Attested,—all took place, you think,
Only to give our joys a zest,
And prove our sorrows for the best?
We differ, then! Where I, still pale
And heartstruck at the dreadful tale,
Waiting to hear God's voice declare
What horror followed for my share,
As implicated in the deed,
Apart from other sins,—concede
That if He blacked out in a blot
My brief life's pleasantness, 'twere not
So very disproportionate!
Or there might be another fate—
I certainly could understand
(If fancies were the thing in hand)
How God might save, at that day's price,
The impure in their impurities,
Give licence formal and complete
To choose the fair and pick the sweet.
But there be certain words, broad, plain,
Uttered again and yet again,
Hard to mistake or overgloss—
Announcing this world's gain for loss,
And bidding us reject the same:
The whole world lieth (they proclaim)
In wickedness,—come out of it!
Turn a deaf ear, if you think fit,
But I who thrill through every nerve
At thought of what deaf ears deserve—
How do you counsel in the case?

IX

'I'd take, by all means, in your place,
'The safe side, since it so appears:
'Deny myself, a few brief years,
'The natural pleasure, leave the fruit
'Or cut the plant up by the root.

'Remember what a martyr said
'On the rude tablet overhead!
'"I was born sickly, poor and mean,
'"A slave: no misery could screen
'"The holders of the pearl of price
'"From Cæsar's envy; therefore twice
'"I fought with beasts, and three times saw
'"My children suffer by his law;
'"At last my own release was earned:
'"I was some time in being burned,
'"But at the close a Hand came through
'"The fire above my head, and drew
'"My soul to Christ, whom now I see.
'"Sergius, a brother, writes for me
'"This testimony on the wall—
'"For me, I have forgot it all."
'You say right; this were not so hard!
'And since one nowise is debarred
'From this, why not escape some sins
'By such a method?'

X

              Then begins
To the old point revulsion new—
(For 'tis just this I bring you to)
If after all we should mistake,
And so renounce life for the sake
Of death and nothing else? You hear
Each friend we jeered at, send the jeer
Back to ourselves with good effect—
'There were my beetles to collect!
'My box—a trifle, I confess,
'But here I hold it, ne'ertheless!'
Poor idiots, (let us pluck up heart
And answer) we, the better part
Have chosen, though 'twere only hope,—
Nor envy moles like you that grope
Amid your veritable muck,
More than the grasshoppers would truck,

For yours, their passionate life away,
That spends itself in leaps all day
To reach the sun, you want the eyes
To see, as they the wings to rise
And match the noble hearts of them!
Thus the contemner we contemn,—
And, when doubt strikes us, thus we ward
Its stroke off, caught upon our guard,
—Not struck enough to overturn
Our faith, but shake it—make us learn
What I began with, and, I wis,
End, having proved,—how hard it is
To be a Christian!

XI

          'Proved, or not,
'Howe'er you wis, small thanks, I wot,
'You get of mine, for taking pains
'To make it hard to me. Who gains
'By that, I wonder? Here I live
'In trusting ease; and here you drive
'At causing me to lose what most
'Yourself would mourn for had you lost!'

XII

But, do you see, my friend, that thus
You leave Saint Paul for Æschylus?
—Who made his Titan's arch-device
The giving men *blind hopes* to spice
The meal of life with, else devoured
In bitter haste, while lo, death loured
Before them at the platter's edge!
If faith should be, as I allege,
Quite other than a condiment
To heighten flavours with, or meant
(Like that brave curry of his Grace)
To take at need the victuals' place?
If, having dined, you would digest
Besides, and turning to your rest
Should find instead . . .

XIII

Now, you shall see
And judge if a mere foppery
Pricks on my speaking! I resolve
To utter—yes, it shall devolve
On you to hear as solemn, strange
And dread a thing as in the range
Of facts,—or fancies, if God will!—
E'er happened to our kind! I still
Stand in the cloud and, while it wraps
My face, ought not to speak perhaps;
Seeing that if I carry through
My purpose, if my words in you
Find a live actual listener,
My story, reason must aver
False after all—the happy chance!
While, if each human countenance
I meet in London day by day,
Be what I fear,—my warnings fray
No one, and no one they convert,
And no one helps me to assert
How hard it is to really be
A Christian, and in vacancy
I pour this story!

XIV

I commence
By trying to inform you, whence
It comes that every Easter-night
As now, I sit up, watch, till light,
Upon those chimney-stacks and roofs,
Give, through my window-pane, grey proofs
That Easter-day is breaking slow.
On such a night three years ago,
It chanced that I had cause to cross
The common, where the chapel was,
Our friend spoke of, the other day—
You've not forgotten, I dare say.

I fell to musing of the time
So close, the blessed matin-prime
All hearts leap up at, in some guise—
One could not well do otherwise.
Insensibly my thoughts were bent
Toward the main point; I overwent
Much the same ground of reasoning
As you and I just now. One thing
Remained, however—one that tasked
My soul to answer; and I asked,
Fairly and frankly, what might be
That History, that Faith, to me
—Me there—not me in some domain
Built up and peopled by my brain,
Weighing its merits as one weighs
Mere theories for blame or praise,
—The kingcraft of the Lucumons,
Or Fourier's scheme, its pros and cons,—
But my faith there, or none at all.
'How were my case, now, did I fall
'Dead here, this minute—should I lie
'Faithful or faithless?' Note that I
Inclined thus ever!—little prone
For instance, when I lay alone
In childhood, to go calm to sleep
And leave a closet where might keep
His watch perdue some murderer
Waiting till twelve o'clock to stir,
As good authentic legends tell:
'He might: but how improbable!
'How little likely to deserve
'The pains and trial to the nerve
'Of thrusting head into the dark!'—
Urged my old nurse, and bade me mark
Beside, that, should the dreadful scout
Really lie hid there, and leap out
At first turn of the rusty key,
Mine were small gain that she could see,
Killed not in bed but on the floor,

And losing one night's sleep the more.
I tell you, I would always burst
The door ope, know my fate at first.
This time, indeed, the closet penned
No such assassin: but a friend
Rather, peeped out to guard me, fit
For counsel, Common Sense, to wit,
Who said a good deal that might pass,—
Heartening, impartial too, it was,
Judge else: 'For, soberly now,—who
'Should be a Christian if not you?'
(Hear how he smoothed me down.) 'One takes
'A whole life, sees what course it makes
'Mainly, and not by fits and starts—
'In spite of stoppage which imparts
'Fresh value to the general speed.
'A life, with none, would fly indeed:
'Your progressing is slower—right!
'We deal with progress and not flight.
'Through baffling senses passionate,
'Fancies as restless,—with a freight
'Of knowledge cumbersome enough
'To sink your ship when waves grow rough,
'Though meant for ballast in the hold,—
'I find, 'mid dangers manifold,
'The good bark answers to the helm
'Where faith sits, easier to o'erwhelm
'Than some stout peasant's heavenly guide,
'Whose hard head could not, if it tried,
'Conceive a doubt, nor understand
'How senses hornier than his hand
'Should 'tice the Christian off his guard.
'More happy! But shall we award
'Less honour to the hull which, dogged
'By storms, a mere wreck, waterlogged,
'Masts by the board, her bulwarks gone
'And stanchions going, yet bears on,—
'Than to mere life-boats, built to save,
'And triumph o'er the breaking wave?

M

'Make perfect your good ship as these,
'And what were her performances!'
I added—'Would the ship reach home!
'I wish indeed "God's kingdom come—"
'The day when I shall see appear
'His bidding, as my duty, clear
'From doubt! And it shall dawn, that day,
'Some future season; Easter may
'Prove, not impossibly, the time—
'Yes, that were striking—fates would chime
'So aptly! Easter-morn, to bring
'The Judgment!—deeper in the spring
'Than now, however, when there's snow
'Capping the hills; for earth must show
'All signs of meaning to pursue
'Her tasks as she was wont to do
'—The skylark, taken by surprise
'As we ourselves, shall recognize
'Sudden the end. For suddenly
'It comes; the dreadfulness must be
'In that; all warrants the belief—
'"At night it cometh like a thief."
'I fancy why the trumpet blows;
'—Plainly, to wake one. From repose
'We shall start up, at last awake
'From life, that insane dream we take
'For waking now, because it seems.
'And as, when now we wake from dreams,
'We laugh, while we recall them, "Fool,
'"To let the chance slip, linger cool
'"When such adventure offered! Just
'"A bridge to cross, a dwarf to thrust
'"Aside, a wicked mage to stab—
'"And, lo ye, I had kissed Queen Mab!"
'So shall we marvel why we grudged
'Our labour here, and idly judged
'Of heaven, we might have gained, but lose!
'Lose? Talk of loss, and I refuse
'To plead at all! You speak no worse

'Nor better than my ancient nurse
'When she would tell me in my youth
'I well deserved that shapes uncouth
'Frighted and teased me in my sleep:
'Why could I not in memory keep
'Her precept for the evil's cure?
'"Pinch your own arm, boy, and be sure
'"You'll wake forthwith!"'

XV

          And as I said
This nonsense, throwing back my head
With light complacent laugh, I found
Suddenly all the midnight round
One fire. The dome of heaven had stood
As made up of a multitude
Of handbreadth cloudlets, one vast rack
Of ripples infinite and black,
From sky to sky. Sudden there went,
Like horror and astonishment,
A fierce vindictive scribble of red
Quick flame across, as if one said
(The angry scribe of Judgment) 'There—
'Burn it!' And straight I was aware
That the whole ribwork round, minute
Cloud touching cloud beyond compute,
Was tinted, each with its own spot
Of burning at the core, till clot
Jammed against clot, and spilt its fire
Over all heaven, which 'gan suspire
As fanned to measure equable,—
Just so great conflagrations kill
Night overhead, and rise and sink,
Reflected. Now the fire would shrink
And wither off the blasted face
Of heaven, and I distinct might trace
The sharp black ridgy outlines left
Unburned like network—then, each cleft

The fire had been sucked back into,
Regorged, and out it surging flew
Furiously, and night writhed inflamed,
Till, tolerating to be tamed
No longer, certain rays world-wide
Shot downwardly. On every side
Caught past escape, the earth was lit;
As if a dragon's nostril split
And all his famished ire o'erflowed;
Then, as he winced at his lord's goad,
Back he inhaled: whereat I found
The clouds into vast pillars bound,
Based on the corners of the earth,
Propping the skies at top: a dearth
Of fire i' the violet intervals,
Leaving exposed the utmost walls
Of time, about to tumble in
And end the world.

XVI

         I felt begin
The Judgment-Day: to retrocede
Was too late now. 'In very deed,'
(I uttered to myself) 'that Day!'
The intuition burned away
All darkness from my spirit too:
There, stood I, found and fixed, I knew,
Choosing the world. The choice was made;
And naked and disguiseless stayed,
And unevadable, the fact.
My brain held all the same compact
Its senses, nor my heart declined
Its office; rather, both combined
To help me in this juncture. I
Lost not a second,—agony
Gave boldness: since my life had end
And my choice with it—best defend,
Applaud both! I resolved to say,
'So was I framed by thee, such way

'I put to use thy senses here!
'It was so beautiful, so near,
'Thy world,—what could I then but choose
'My part there? Nor did I refuse
'To look above the transient boon
'Of time; but it was hard so soon
'As in a short life, to give up
'Such beauty: I could put the cup
'Undrained of half its fulness, by;
'But, to renounce it utterly,
'—That was too hard! Nor did the cry
'Which bade renounce it, touch my brain
'Authentically deep and plain
'Enough to make my lips let go.
'But Thou, who knowest all, dost know
'Whether I was not, life's brief while,
'Endeavouring to reconcile
'Those lips (too tardily, alas!)
'To letting the dear remnant pass,
'One day,—some drops of earthly good
'Untasted! Is it for this mood,
'That Thou, whose earth delights so well,
'Hast made its complement a hell?'

XVII

A final belch of fire like blood,
Overbroke all heaven in one flood
Of doom. Then fire was sky, and sky
Fire, and both, one brief ecstasy,
Then ashes. But I heard no noise
(Whatever was) because a voice
Beside me spoke thus, 'Life is done,
'Time ends, Eternity's begun,
'And thou art judged for evermore.'

XVIII

I looked up; all seemed as before;
Of that cloud-Tophet overhead
No trace was left: I saw instead

The common round me, and the sky
Above, stretched drear and emptily
Of life. 'Twas the last watch of night,
Except what brings the morning quite;
When the armed angel, conscience-clear,
His task nigh done, leans o'er his spear
And gazes on the earth he guards,
Safe one night more through all its wards,
Till God relieve him at his post.
'A dream—a waking dream at most!'
(I spoke out quick, that I might shake
The horrid nightmare off, and wake.)
'The world gone, yet the world is here?
'Are not all things as they appear?
'Is Judgment past for me alone?
'—And where had place the great white throne?
'The rising of the quick and dead?
'Where stood they, small and great? Who read
'The sentence from the opened book?'
So, by degrees, the blood forsook
My heart, and let it beat afresh;
I knew I should break through the mesh
Of horror, and breathe presently:
When, lo, again, the voice by me!

XIX

I saw . . . Oh brother, 'mid far sands
The palm-tree-cinctured city stands,
Bright-white beneath, as heaven, bright-blue,
Leans o'er it, while the years pursue
Their course, unable to abate
Its paradisal laugh at fate!
One morn,—the Arab staggers blind
O'er a new tract of death, calcined
To ashes, silence, nothingness,—
And strives, with dizzy wits, to guess
Whence fell the blow. What if, 'twixt skies
And prostrate earth, he should surprise

The imaged vapour, head to foot,
Surveying, motionless and mute,
Its work, ere, in a whirlwind rapt
It vanish up again?—So hapt
My chance. HE stood there. Like the smoke
Pillared o'er Sodom, when day broke,—
I saw Him. One magnific pall
Mantled in massive fold and fall
His head, and coiled in snaky swathes
About His feet: night's black, that bathes
All else, broke, grizzled with despair,
Against the soul of blackness there.
A gesture told the mood within—
That wrapped right hand which based the chin,
That intense meditation fixed
On His procedure,—pity mixed
With the fulfilment of decree.
Motionless, thus, He spoke to me,
Who fell before His feet, a mass,
No man now.

XX

'All is come to pass.
'Such shows are over for each soul
'They had respect to. In the roll
'Of Judgment which convinced mankind
'Of sin, stood many, bold and blind,
'Terror must burn the truth into:
'Their fate for them!—thou hadst to do
'With absolute omnipotence,
'Able its judgments to dispense
'To the whole race, as every one
'Were its sole object. Judgment done,
'God is, thou art,—the rest is hurled
'To nothingness for thee. This world,
'This finite life, thou hast preferred,
'In disbelief of God's plain word,
'To heaven and to infinity.
'Here the probation was for thee,

'To show thy soul the earthly mixed
'With heavenly, it must choose betwixt.
'The earthly joys lay palpable,—
'A taint, in each, distinct as well;
'The heavenly flitted, faint and rare,
'Above them, but as truly were
'Taintless, so, in their nature, best.
'Thy choice was earth: thou didst attest
''Twas fitter spirit should subserve
'The flesh, than flesh refine to nerve
'Beneath the spirit's play. Advance
'No claim to their inheritance
'Who chose the spirit's fugitive
'Brief gleams, and yearned, "This were to live
'"Indeed, if rays, completely pure
'"From flesh that dulls them, could endure,—
'"Not shoot in meteor-light athwart
'"Our earth, to show how cold and swart
'"It lies beneath their fire, but stand
'"As stars do, destined to expand,
'"Prove veritable worlds, our home!"
'Thou saidst,—"Let spirit star the dome
'"Of sky, that flesh may miss no peak,
'"No nook of earth,—I shall not seek
'"Its service further!" Thou art shut
'Out of the heaven of spirit; glut
'Thy sense upon the world: 'tis thine
'For ever—take it!'

XXI

     'How? Is mine,
'The world?' (I cried, while my soul broke
Out in a transport.) 'Hast Thou spoke
'Plainly in that? Earth's exquisite
'Treasures of wonder and delight,
'For me?'

XXII

    The austere voice returned,—
'So soon made happy? Hadst thou learned

'What God accounteth happiness,
'Thou wouldst not find it hard to guess
'What hell may be his punishment
'For those who doubt if God invent
'Better than they. Let such men rest
'Content with what they judged the best.
'Let the unjust usurp at will:
'The filthy shall be filthy still:
'Miser, there waits the gold for thee!
'Hater, indulge thine enmity!
'And thou, whose heaven self-ordained
'Was, to enjoy earth unrestrained,
'Do it! Take all the ancient show!
'The woods shall wave, the rivers flow,
'And men apparently pursue
'Their works, as they were wont to do,
'While living in probation yet.
'I promise not thou shalt forget
'The past, now gone to its account;
'But leave thee with the old amount
'Of faculties, nor less nor more,
'Unvisited, as heretofore,
'By God's free spirit, that makes an end.
'So, once more, take thy world! Expend
'Eternity upon its shows,
'Flung thee as freely as one rose
'Out of a summer's opulence,
'Over the Eden-barrier whence
'Thou art excluded. Knock in vain!'

XXIII

I sat up. All was still again.
I breathed free: to my heart, back fled
The warmth. 'But, all the world!'—I said.
I stooped and picked a leaf of fern,
And recollected I might learn
From books, how many myriad sorts
Of fern exist, to trust reports,

Each as distinct and beautiful
As this, the very first I cull.
Think, from the first leaf to the last!
Conceive, then, earth's resources! Vast
Exhaustless beauty, endless change
Of wonder! And this foot shall range
Alps, Andes,—and this eye devour
The bee-bird and the aloe-flower?

XXIV

Then the voice, 'Welcome so to rate
'The arras-folds that variegate
'The earth, God's antechamber, well!
'The wise, who waited there, could tell
'By these, what royalties in store
'Lay one step past the entrance-door.
'For whom, was reckoned, not too much,
'This life's munificence? For such
'As thou,—a race, whereof scarce one
'Was able, in a million,
'To feel that any marvel lay
'In objects round his feet all day;
'Scarce one, in many millions more,
'Willing, if able, to explore
'The secreter, minuter charm!
'—Brave souls, a fern-leaf could disarm
'Of power to cope with God's intent,—
'Or scared if the south firmament
'With north-fire did its wings refledge!
'All partial beauty was a pledge
'Of beauty in its plenitude:
'But since the pledge sufficed thy mood,
'Retain it! plenitude be theirs
'Who looked above!'

XXV

Though sharp despairs
Shot through me, I held up, bore on.
'What matter though my trust were gone

'From natural things? Henceforth my part
'Be less with nature than with art!
'For art supplants, gives mainly worth
'To nature; 'tis man stamps the earth—
'And I will seek his impress, seek
'The statuary of the Greek,
'Italy's painting—there my choice
'Shall fix!'

XXVI

   'Obtain it!' said the voice,
'—The one form with its single act,
'Which sculptors laboured to abstract,
'The one face, painters tried to draw,
'With its one look, from throngs they saw.
'And that perfection in their soul,
'These only hinted at? The whole,
'They were but parts of? What each laid
'His claim to glory on?—afraid
'His fellow-men should give him rank
'By mere tentatives which he shrank
'Smitten at heart from, all the more,
'That gazers pressed in to adore!
'"Shall I be judged by only these?"
'If such his soul's capacities,
'Even while he trod the earth,—think, now,
'What pomp in Buonarroti's brow,
'With its new palace-brain where dwells
'Superb the soul, unvexed by cells
'That crumbled with the transient clay!
'What visions will his right hand's sway
'Still turn to forms, as still they burst
'Upon him? How will he quench thirst,
'Titanically infantine,
'Laid at the breast of the Divine?
'Does it confound thee,—this first page
'Emblazoning man's heritage?—
'Can this alone absorb thy sight,
'As pages were not infinite,—

'Like the omnipotence which tasks
'Itself to furnish all that asks
'The soul it means to satiate?
'What was the world, the starry state
'Of the broad skies,—what, all displays
'Of power and beauty intermixed,
'Which now thy soul is chained betwixt,—
'What else than needful furniture
'For life's first stage? God's work, be sure,
'No more spreads wasted, than falls scant!
'He filled, did not exceed, man's want
'Of beauty in this life. But through
'Life pierce,—and what has earth to do,
'Its utmost beauty's appanage,
'With the requirement of next stage?
'Did God pronounce earth "very good"?
'Needs must it be, while understood
'For man's preparatory state;
'Nought here to heighten nor abate;
'Transfer the same completeness here,
'To serve a new state's use,—and drear
'Deficiency gapes every side!
'The good, tried once, were bad, retried.
'See the enwrapping rocky niche,
'Sufficient for the sleep in which
'The lizard breathes for ages safe:
'Split the mould—and as light would chafe
'The creature's new world-widened sense,
'Dazzled to death at evidence
'Of all the sounds and sights that broke
'Innumerous at the chisel's stroke,—
'So, in God's eye, the earth's first stuff
'Was, neither more nor less, enough
'To house man's soul, man's need fulfil.
'Man reckoned it immeasurable?
'So thinks the lizard of his vault!
'Could God be taken in default,
'Short of contrivances, by you,—
'Or reached, ere ready to pursue

'His progress through eternity?
'That chambered rock, the lizard's world,
'Your easy mallet's blow has hurled
'To nothingness for ever; so,
'Has God abolished at a blow
'This world, wherein his saints were pent,—
'Who, though found grateful and content,
'With the provision there, as thou,
'Yet knew he would not disallow
'Their spirit's hunger, felt as well,—
'Unsated,—not unsatable,
'As paradise gives proof. Deride
'Their choice now, thou who sit'st outside!'

XXVII

I cried in anguish, 'Mind, the mind,
'So miserably cast behind,
'To gain what had been wisely lost!
'Oh, let me strive to make the most
'Of the poor stinted soul, I nipped
'Of budding wings, else now equipped
'For voyage from summer isle to isle!
'And though she needs must reconcile
'Ambition to the life on ground,
'Still, I can profit by late found
'But precious knowledge. Mind is best—
'I will seize mind, forego the rest,
'And try how far my tethered strength
'May crawl in this poor breadth and length.
'Let me, since I can fly no more,
'At least spin dervish-like about
'(Till giddy rapture almost doubt
'I fly) through circling sciences,
'Philosophies and histories!
'Should the whirl slacken there, then verse,
'Fining to music, shall asperse
'Fresh and fresh fire-dew, till I strain
'Intoxicate, half-break my chain!

'Not joyless, though more favoured feet
'Stand calm, where I want wings to beat
'The floor. At least earth's bond is broke!'

XXVIII

Then, (sickening even while I spoke)
'Let me alone! No answer, pray,
'To this! I know what Thou wilt say!
'All still is earth's,—to know, as much
'As feel its truths, which if we touch
'With sense, or apprehend in soul,
'What matter? I have reached the goal—
'"Whereto does knowledge serve!" will burn
'My eyes, too sure, at every turn!
'I cannot look back now, nor stake
'Bliss on the race, for running's sake.
'The goal's a ruin like the rest!'—
'And so much worse thy latter quest,'
(Added the voice) 'that even on earth—
'Whenever, in man's soul, had birth
'Those intuitions, grasps of guess,
'Which pull the more into the less,
'Making the finite comprehend
'Infinity,—the bard would spend
'Such praise alone, upon his craft,
'As, when wind-lyres obey the waft,
'Goes to the craftsman who arranged
'The seven strings, changed them and rechanged—
'Knowing it was the South that harped.
'He felt his song, in singing, warped;
'Distinguished his and God's part: whence
'A world of spirit as of sense
'Was plain to him, yet not too plain,
'Which he could traverse, not remain
'A guest in:—else were permanent
'Heaven on the earth its gleams were meant
'To sting with hunger for full light,—
'Made visible in verse, despite

'The veiling weakness,—truth by means
'Of fable, showing while it screens,—
'Since highest truth, man e'er supplied,
'Was ever fable on outside.
'Such gleams made bright the earth an age;
'Now the whole sun's his heritage!
'Take up thy world, it is allowed,
'Thou who hast entered in the cloud!'

XXIX

Then I—'Behold, my spirit bleeds,
'Catches no more at broken reeds,—
'But lilies flower those reeds above:
'I let the world go, and take love!
'Love survives in me, albeit those
'I love be henceforth masks and shows,
'Not living men and women: still
'I mind how love repaired all ill,
'Cured wrong, soothed grief, made earth amends
'With parents, brothers, children, friends!
'Some semblance of a woman yet
'With eyes to help me to forget,
'Shall look on me; and I will match
'Departed love with love, attach
'Old memories to new dreams, nor scorn
'The poorest of the grains of corn
'I save from shipwreck on this isle,
'Trusting its barrenness may smile
'With happy foodful green one day,
'More precious for the pains. I pray,—
'Leave to love, only!'

XXX

                    At the word,
The form, I looked to have been stirred
With pity and approval, rose
O'er me, as when the headsman throws
Axe over shoulder to make end—
I fell prone, letting Him expend

His wrath, while thus the inflicting voice
Smote me. 'Is this thy final choice?
'Love is the best? 'Tis somewhat late!
'And all thou dost enumerate
'Of power and beauty in the world,
'The mightiness of love was curled
'Inextricably round about.
'Love lay within it and without,
'To clasp thee,—but in vain! Thy soul
'Still shrunk from Him who made the whole,
'Still set deliberate aside
'His love!—Now take love! Well betide
'Thy tardy conscience! Haste to take
'The show of love for the name's sake,
'Remembering every moment Who,
'Beside creating thee unto
'These ends, and these for thee, was said
'To undergo death in thy stead
'In flesh like thine: so ran the tale.
'What doubt in thee could countervail
'Belief in it? Upon the ground
'"That in the story had been found
'"Too much love! How could God love so?"
'He who in all his works below
'Adapted to the needs of man,
'Made love the basis of the plan,—
'Did love, as was demonstrated:
'While man, who was so fit instead
'To hate, as every day gave proof,—
'Man thought man, for his kind's behoof,
'Both could and did invent that scheme
'Of perfect love: 'twould well beseem
'Cain's nature thou wast wont to praise,
'Not tally with God's usual ways!'

XXXI

And I cowered deprecatingly—
'Thou Love of God! Or let me die,
'Or grant what shall seem heaven almost!

'Let me not know that all is lost,
'Though lost it be—leave me not tied
'To this despair, this corpse-like bride!
'Let that old life seem mine—no more—
'With limitation as before,
'With darkness, hunger, toil, distress:
'Be all the earth a wilderness!
'Only let me go on, go on,
'Still hoping ever and anon
'To reach one eve the Better Land!'

XXXII

Then did the form expand, expand—
I knew Him through the dread disguise
As the whole God within His eyes
Embraced me.

XXXIII

When I lived again,
The day was breaking,—the grey plain
I rose from, silvered thick with dew.
Was this a vision? False or true?
Since then, three varied years are spent,
And commonly my mind is bent
To think it was a dream—be sure
A mere dream and distemperature—
The last day's watching: then the night,—
The shock of that strange Northern Light
Set my head swimming, bred in me
A dream. And so I live, you see,
Go through the world, try, prove, reject,
Prefer, still struggling to effect
My warfare; happy that I can
Be crossed and thwarted as a man,
Not left in God's contempt apart,
With ghastly smooth life, dead at heart,
Tame in earth's paddock as her prize.
Thank God, she still each method tries
To catch me, who may yet escape,

She knows,—the fiend in angel's shape!
Thank God, no paradise stands barred
To entry, and I find it hard
To be a Christian, as I said!
Still every now and then my head
Raised glad, sinks mournful—all grows drear
Spite of the sunshine, while I fear
And think, 'How dreadful to be grudged
'No ease henceforth, as one that's judged.
'Condemned to earth for ever, shut
'From heaven!'
        But Easter-Day breaks! But
Christ rises! Mercy every way
Is infinite,—and who can say?

IN A BALCONY
1855

PERSONS

NORBERT.   CONSTANCE.   THE QUEEN.

CONSTANCE *and* NORBERT.

Nor. Now!

Con.   Not now!

Nor.   Give me them again, those
hands:
Put them upon my forehead, how it throbs!
Press them before my eyes, the fire comes through!
You cruellest, you dearest in the world,
Let me! The Queen must grant whate'er I ask—
How can I gain you and not ask the Queen?
There she stays waiting for me, here stand you;
Some time or other this was to be asked;
Now is the one time—what I ask, I gain:
Let me ask now, Love!

Con.   Do, and ruin us.

Nor. Let it be now, Love! All my soul breaks forth.
How I do love you! Give my love its way!
A man can have but one life and one death,
One heaven, one hell. Let me fulfil my fate—
Grant me my heaven now! Let me know you mine,
Prove you mine, write my name upon your brow,
Hold you and have you, and then die away,
If God please, with completion in my soul!

Con. I am not yours then? How content this man!
I am not his—who change into himself,
Have passed into his heart and beat its beats,
Who give my hands to him, my eyes, my hair,
Give all that was of me away to him—
So well, that now, my spirit turned his own,
Takes part with him against the woman here,
Bids him not stumble at so mere a straw

As caring that the world be cognizant
How he loves her and how she worships him.
You have this woman, not as yet that world.
Go on, I bid, nor stop to care for me
By saving what I cease to care about,
The courtly name and pride of circumstance—
The name you'll pick up and be cumbered with
Just for the poor parade's sake, nothing more;
Just that the world may slip from under you—
Just that the world may cry 'So much for him—
'The man predestined to the heap of crowns:
'There goes his chance of winning one, at least!'

   Nor. The world!

   Con.   You love it. Love me quite as well,
And see if I shall pray for this in vain!
Why must you ponder what it knows or thinks?

   Nor. You pray for—what, in vain?

   Con.   Oh my heart's heart,
How I do love you, Norbert! That is right:
But listen, or I take my hands away!
You say, 'let it be now': you would go now
And tell the Queen, perhaps six steps from us,
You love me—so you do, thank God!

   Nor.   Thank God!

   Con. Yes, Norbert,—but you fain would tell your love,
And, what succeeds the telling, ask of her
My hand. Now take this rose and look at it,
Listening to me. You are the minister,
The Queen's first favourite, nor without a cause.
To-night completes your wonderful year's-work
(This palace-feast is held to celebrate)
Made memorable by her life's success,
The junction of two crowns, on her sole head,
Her house had only dreamed of anciently:
That this mere dream is grown a stable truth,
To-night's feast makes authentic. Whose the praise?
Whose genius, patience, energy, achieved
What turned the many heads and broke the hearts?
You are the fate, your minute's in the heaven.

Next comes the Queen's turn. 'Name your own reward!'
With leave to clench the past, chain the to-come,
Put out an arm and touch and take the sun
And fix it ever full-faced on your earth,
Possess yourself supremely of her life,—
You choose the single thing she will not grant;
Nay, very declaration of which choice
Will turn the scale and neutralize your work:
At best she will forgive you, if she can.
You think I'll let you choose—her cousin's hand?

   Nor. Wait. First, do you retain your old belief
The Queen is generous,—nay, is just?

   Con.   There, there!
So men make women love them, while they know
No more of women's hearts than . . . look you here,
You that are just and generous beside,
Make it your own case! For example now,
I'll say—I let you kiss me, hold my hands—
Why? do you know why? I'll instruct you, then—
The kiss, because you have a name at court;
This hand and this, that you may shut in each
A jewel, if you please to pick up such.
That's horrible? Apply it to the Queen—
Suppose I am the Queen to whom you speak:
'I was a nameless man; you needed me:
'Why did I proffer you my aid? there stood
'A certain pretty cousin at your side.
'Why did I make such common cause with you?
'Access to her had not been easy else.
'You give my labour here abundant praise?
''Faith, labour, which she overlooked, grew play.
'How shall your gratitude discharge itself?
'Give me her hand!'

   Nor.   And still I urge the same.
Is the Queen just? just—generous or no!

   Con. Yes, just. You love a rose; no harm in that:
But was it for the rose's sake or mine
You put it in your bosom? mine, you said—
Then. mine you still must say or else be false.

You told the Queen you served her for herself;
If so, to serve her was to serve yourself,
She thinks, for all your unbelieving face!
I know her. In the hall, six steps from us,
One sees the twenty pictures; there's a life
Better than life, and yet no life at all.
Conceive her born in such a magic dome,
Pictures all round her! why, she sees the world,
Can recognize its given things and facts,
The fight of giants or the feast of gods,
Sages in senate, beauties at the bath,
Chases and battles, the whole earth's display,
Landscape and sea-piece, down to flowers and fruit—
And who shall question that she knows them all,
In better semblance than the things outside?
Yet bring into the silent gallery
Some live thing to contrast in breath and blood,
Some lion, with the painted lion there—
You think she'll understand composedly?
—Say, 'that's his fellow in the hunting-piece
'Yonder, I've turned to praise a hundred times?'
Not so. Her knowledge of our actual earth,
Its hopes and fears, concerns and sympathies,
Must be too far, too mediate, too unreal.
The real exists for us outside, not her:
How should it, with that life in these four walls—
That father and that mother, first to last
No father and no mother—friends, a heap,
Lovers, no lack—a husband in due time,
And every one of them alike a lie!
Things painted by a Rubens out of nought
Into what kindness, friendship, love should be;
All better, all more grandiose than the life,
Only no life; mere cloth and surface-paint,
You feel, while you admire. How should she feel?
Yet now that she has stood thus fifty years
The sole spectator in that gallery,
You think to bring this warm real struggling love
In to her of a sudden, and suppose

She'll keep her state untroubled? Here's the truth—
She'll apprehend truth's value at a glance,
Prefer it to the pictured loyalty?
You only have to say, 'so men are made,
'For this they act; the thing has many names,
'But this the right one: and now, Queen, be just!'
Your life slips back; you lose her at the word:
You do not even for amends gain me.
He will not understand; oh, Norbert, Norbert,
Do you not understand?

    Nor.   The Queen's the Queen;
I am myself—no picture, but alive
In every nerve and every muscle, here
At the palace-window o'er the people's street,
As she in the gallery where the pictures glow:
The good of life is precious to us both.
She cannot love; what do I want with rule?
When first I saw your face a year ago
I knew my life's good, my soul heard one voice—
'The woman yonder, there's no use of life
'But just to obtain her! heap earth's woes in one
'And bear them—make a pile of all earth's joys
'And spurn them, as they help or help not this;
'Only, obtain her!' How was it to be?
I found you were the cousin of the Queen;
I must then serve the Queen to get to you.
No other way. Suppose there had been one,
And I, by saying prayers to some white star
With promise of my body and my soul,
Might gain you,—should I pray the star or no?
Instead, there was the Queen to serve! I served,
Helped, did what other servants failed to do.
Neither she sought nor I declared my end.
Her good is hers, my recompense be mine,—
I therefore name you as that recompense.
She dreamed that such a thing could never be?
Let her wake now. She thinks there was more cause
In love of power, high fame, pure loyalty?
Perhaps she fancies men wear out their lives

Chasing such shades. Then, I've a fancy too;
I worked because I want you with my soul:
I therefore ask your hand. Let it be now!

    Con. Had I not loved you from the very first,
Were I not yours, could we not steal out thus
So wickedly, so wildly, and so well,
You might become impatient. What's conceived
Of us without here, by the folk within?
Where are you now? immersed in cares of state—
Where am I now? intent on festal robes—
We two, embracing under death's spread hand!
What was this thought for, what that scruple of yours
Which broke the council up?—to bring about
One minute's meeting in the corridor!
And then the sudden sleights, strange secrecies,
Complots inscrutable, deep telegraphs,
Long-planned chance-meetings, hazards of a look,
'Does she know? does she not know? saved or lost?'
A year of this compression's ecstasy
All goes for nothing! you would give this up
For the old way, the open way, the world's,
His way who beats, and his who sells his wife!
What tempts you?—their notorious happiness
Makes you ashamed of ours? The best you'll gain
Will be—the Queen grants all that you require,
Concedes the cousin, rids herself of you
And me at once, and gives us ample leave
To live like our five hundred happy friends.
The world will show us with officious hand
Our chamber-entry, and stand sentinel
Where we so oft have stolen across its traps!
Get the world's warrant, ring the falcons' feet,
And make it duty to be bold and swift,
Which long ago was nature. Have it so!
We never hawked by rights till flung from fist?
Oh, the man's thought! no woman's such a fool.

    Nor. Yes, the man's thought and my thought, which
      is more—
One made to love you, let the world take note!

Have I done worthy work? be love's the praise,
Though hampered by restrictions, barred against
By set forms, blinded by forced secrecies!
Set free my love, and see what love can do
Shown in my life—what work will spring from that!
The world is used to have its business done
On other grounds, find great effects produced
For power's sake, fame's sake, motives in men's mouth.
So, good: but let my low ground shame their high!
Truth is the strong thing. Let man's life be true!
And love's the truth of mine. Time prove the rest!
I choose to wear you stamped all over me,
Your name upon my forehead and my breast,
You, from the sword's blade to the ribbon's edge,
That men may see, all over, you in me—
That pale loves may die out of their pretence
In face of mine, shames thrown on love fall off.
Permit this, Constance! Love has been so long
Subdued in me, eating me through and through,
That now 'tis all of me and must have way.
Think of my work, that chaos of intrigues,
Those hopes and fears, surprises and delays,
That long endeavour, earnest, patient, slow,
Trembling at last to its assured result:
Then think of this revulsion! I resume
Life after death, (it is no less than life,
After such long unlovely labouring days)
And liberate to beauty life's great need
O' the beautiful, which, while it prompted work,
Suppressed itself erewhile. This eve's the time,
This eve intense with yon first trembling star
We seem to pant and reach; scarce aught between
The earth that rises and the heaven that bends;
All nature self-abandoned, every tree
Flung as it will, pursuing its own thoughts
And fixed so, every flower and every weed,
No pride, no shame, no victory, no defeat;
All under God, each measured by itself.
These statues round us stand abrupt, distinct,

The strong in strength, the weak in weakness fixed,
The Muse for ever wedded to her lyre,
Nymph to her fawn, and Silence to her rose:
See God's approval on his universe!
Let us do so—aspire to live as these
In harmony with truth, ourselves being true!
Take the first way, and let the second come!
My first is to possess myself of you;
The music sets the march-step—forward, then!
And there's the Queen, I go to claim you of,
The world to witness, wonder and applaud.
Our flower of life breaks open. No delay!

    Con. And so shall we be ruined, both of us.
Norbert, I know her to the skin and bone:
You do not know her, were not born to it,
To feel what she can see or cannot see.
Love, she is generous,—ay, despite your smile,
Generous as you are: for, in that thin frame
Pain-twisted, punctured through and through with cares,
There lived a lavish soul until it starved,
Debarred of healthy food. Look to the soul—
Pity that, stoop to that, ere you begin
(The true man's-way) on justice and your rights,
Exactions and acquittance of the past!
Begin so—see what justice she will deal!
We women hate a debt as men a gift.
Suppose her some poor keeper of a school
Whose business is to sit thro' summer months
And dole out children leave to go and play,
Herself superior to such lightness—she
In the arm-chair's state and pædagogic pomp—
To the life, the laughter, sun and youth outside:
We wonder such a face looks black on us?
I do not bid you wake her tenderness,
(That were vain truly—none is left to wake)
But let her think her justice is engaged
To take the shape of tenderness, and mark
If she'll not coldly pay its warmest debt!
Does she love me, I ask you? not a whit:

Yet, thinking that her justice was engaged
To help a kinswoman, she took me up—
Did more on that bare ground than other loves
Would do on greater argument. For me,
I have no equivalent of such cold kind
To pay her with, but love alone to give
If I give anything. I give her love:
I feel I ought to help her, and I will.
So, for her sake, as yours, I tell you twice
That women hate a debt as men a gift.
If I were you, I could obtain this grace—
Could lay the whole I did to love's account,
Nor yet be very false as courtiers go—
Declaring my success was recompense;
It would be so, in fact: what were it else?
And then, once loose her generosity,—
Oh, how I see it!—then, were I but you,
To turn it, let it seem to move itself,
And make it offer what I really take,
Accepting just, in the poor cousin's hand,
Her value as the next thing to the Queen's—
Since none love Queens directly, none dare that,
And a thing's shadow or a name's mere echo
Suffices those who miss the name and thing!
You pick up just a ribbon she has worn,
To keep in proof how near her breath you came.
Say, I'm so near I seem a piece of her—
Ask for me that way—(oh, you understand)
You'd find the same gift yielded with a grace,
Which, if you make the least show to extort . . .
—You'll see! and when you have ruined both of us,
Dissertate on the Queen's ingratitude!

   Nor. Then, if I turn it that way, you consent?
'Tis not my way; I have more hope in truth:
Still, if you won't have truth—why, this indeed,
Were scarcely false, as I'd express the sense.
Will you remain here?

   Con.   O best heart of mine,
How I have loved you! then, you take my way?

Are mine as you have been her minister,
Work out my thought, give it effect for me,
Paint plain my poor conceit and make it serve?
I owe that withered woman everything—
Life, fortune, you, remember! Take my part—
Help me to pay her! Stand upon your rights?
You, with my rose, my hands, my heart on you?
Your rights are mine—you have no rights but mine.

    Nor. Remain here. How you know me!
    Con.   Ah, but still——
    [*He breaks from her: she remains. Dance-music from
      within.*

Enter the QUEEN.

    Queen. Constance? She is here as he said. Speak
    quick!
Is it so? Is it true or false? One word!
    Con. True.
    Queen.   Mercifullest Mother, thanks to thee!
    Con. Madam?
    Queen.   I love you, Constance, from my soul.
Now say once more, with any words you will,
'Tis true, all true, as true as that I speak.
    Con. Why should you doubt it?
    Queen.   Ah, why doubt? why
    doubt?
Dear, make me see it! Do you see it so?
None see themselves; another sees them best.
You say 'why doubt it?'—you see him and me.
It is because the Mother has such grace
That if we had but faith—wherein we fail—
Whate'er we yearn for would be granted us;
Yet still we let our whims prescribe despair,
Our fancies thwart and cramp our will and power,
And, while accepting life, abjure its use.
Constance, I had abjured the hope of love
And being loved, as truly as yon palm
The hope of seeing Egypt from that plot.
    Con. Heaven!

Queen.   But it was so, Constance, it was so!
Men say—or do men say it? fancies say—
'Stop here, your life is set, you are grown old.
'Too late—no love for you, too late for love—
'Leave love to girls. Be queen: let Constance love.'
One takes the hint—half meets it like a child,
Ashamed at any feelings that oppose.
'Oh love, true, never think of love again!
'I am a queen: I rule, not love forsooth.'
So it goes on; so a face grows like this,
Hair like this hair, poor arms as lean as these,
Till,—nay, it does not end so, I thank God!

 Con. I cannot understand—
 Queen.   The happier you!
Constance, I know not how it is with men:
For women (I am a woman now like you)
There is no good of life but love—but love!
What else looks good, is some shade flung from love;
Love gilds it, gives it worth. Be warned by me,
Never you cheat yourself one instant! Love,
Give love, ask only love, and leave the rest!
O Constance, how I love you!
 Con.   I love you.
 Queen. I do believe that all is come through you.
I took you to my heart to keep it warm
When the last chance of love seemed dead in me;
I thought your fresh youth warmed my withered heart.
Oh, I am very old now, am I not?
Not so! it is true and it shall be true!
 Con. Tell it me: let me judge if true or false.
 Queen. Ah, but I fear you! you will look at me
And say, 'she's old, she's grown unlovely quite
'Who ne'er was beauteous: men want beauty still.'
Well, so I feared—the curse! so I felt sure!
 Con. Be calm. And now you feel not sure, you say?
 Queen. Constance, he came,—the coming was not
  strange—
Do not I stand and see men come and go?
I turned a half-look from my pedestal

Where I grow marble—'one young man the more!
'He will love some one; that is nought to me:
'What would he with my marble stateliness?'
Yet this seemed somewhat worse than heretofore;
The man more gracious, youthful, like a god,
And I still older, with less flesh to change—
We two those dear extremes that long to touch.
It seemed still harder when he first began
To labour at those state-affairs, absorbed
The old way for the old end—interest.
Oh, to live with a thousand beating hearts
Around you, swift eyes, serviceable hands,
Professing they've no care but for your cause,
Thought but to help you, love but for yourself,—
And you the marble statue all the time
They praise and point at as preferred to life,
Yet leave for the first breathing woman's smile,
First dancer's, gipsy's or street baladine's!
Why, how I have ground my teeth to hear men's speech
Stifled for fear it should alarm my ear,
Their gait subdued lest step should startle me,
Their eyes declined, such queendom to respect,
Their hands alert, such treasure to preserve,
While not a man of them broke rank and spoke,
Wrote me a vulgar letter all of love,
Or caught my hand and pressed it like a hand!
There have been moments, if the sentinel
Lowering his halbert to salute the queen,
Had flung it brutally and clasped my knees,
I would have stooped and kissed him with my soul.
 Con. Who could have comprehended?
 Queen.   Ay, who—who?
Who, no one, Constance, but this one who did.
Not they, not you, not I. Even now perhaps
It comes too late—would you but tell the truth.
 Con. I wait to tell it.
 Queen.   Well, you see, he came,
Outfaced the others, did a work this year
Exceeds in value all was ever done,

You know—it is not I who say it—all
Say it. And so (a second pang and worse)
I grew aware not only of what he did,
But why so wondrously. Oh, never work
Like his was done for work's ignoble sake—
Souls need a finer aim to light and lure!
I felt, I saw, he loved—loved somebody.
And Constance, my dear Constance, do you know,
I did believe this while 'twas you he loved.

 Con. Me, madam?

 Queen.   It did seem to me, your face
Met him where'er he looked: and whom but you
Was such a man to love? It seemed to me,
You saw he loved you, and approved his love,
And both of you were in intelligence.
You could not loiter in that garden, step
Into this balcony, but I straight was stung
And forced to understand. It seemed so true,
So right, so beautiful, so like you both,
That all this work should have been done by him
Not for the vulgar hope of recompense,
But that at last—suppose, some night like this—
Borne on to claim his due reward of me,
He might say 'Give her hand and pay me so.'
And I (O Constance, you shall love me now!)
I thought, surmounting all the bitterness,
—'And he shall have it. I will make her blest,
'My flower of youth, my woman's self that was,
'My happiest woman's self that might have been!
'These two shall have their joy and leave me here.'
Yes—yes!

 Con. Thanks!

 Queen. And the word was on my lips
When he burst in upon me. I looked to hear
A mere calm statement of his just desire
For payment of his labour. When—O heaven,
How can I tell you? lightning on my eyes
And thunder in my ears proved that first word
Which told 'twas love of me, of me, did all—

He loved me—from the first step to the last,
Loved me!

Con.   You hardly saw, scarce heard him speak
Of love: what if you should mistake?

Queen.   No, no—
No mistake! Ha, there shall be no mistake!
He had not dared to hint the love he felt—
You were my reflex—(how I understood!)
He said you were the ribbon I had worn,
He kissed my hand, he looked into my eyes,
And love, love came at end of every phrase.
Love is begun; this much is come to pass:
The rest is easy. Constance, I am yours!
I will learn, I will place my life on you,
Teach me but how to keep what I have won!
Am I so old? This hair was early grey;
But joy ere now has brought hair brown again,
And joy will bring the cheek's red back, I feel.
I could sing once too; that was in my youth.
Still, when men paint me, they declare me . . . yes,
Beautiful—for the last French painter did!
I know they flatter somewhat; you are frank—
I trust you. How I loved you from the first!
Some queens would hardly seek a cousin out
And set her by their side to take the eye:
I must have felt that good would come from you.
I am not generous—like him—like you!
But he is not your lover after all:
It was not you he looked at. Saw you him?
You have not been mistaking words or looks?
He said you were the reflex of myself.
And yet he is not such a paragon
To you, to younger women who may choose
Among a thousand Norberts. Speak the truth!
You know you never named his name to me:
You know, I cannot give him up—ah God,
Not up now, even to you!

Con.   Then calm yourself.

Queen. See, I am old—look here, you happy girl!

I will not play the fool, deceive—ah, whom?
'Tis all gone: put your cheek beside my cheek
And what a contrast does the moon behold!
But then I set my life upon one chance,
The last chance and the best—am *I* not left,
My soul, myself? All women love great men
If young or old; it is in all the tales:
Young beauties love old poets who can love
Why should not he, the poems in my soul,
The passionate faith, the pride of sacrifice,
Life-long, death-long? I throw them at his feet.
Who cares to see the fountain's very shape,
Whether it be a Triton's or a Nymph's
That pours the foam, makes rainbows all around?
You could not praise indeed the empty conch;
But I'll pour floods of love and hide myself.
How I will love him! Cannot men love love?
Who was a queen and loved a poet once
Humpbacked, a dwarf? ah, women can do that!
Well, but men too; at least, they tell you so.
They love so many women in their youth,
And even in age they all love whom they please;
And yet the best of them confide to friends
That 'tis not beauty makes the lasting love—
They spend a day with such and tire the next:
They like soul,—well then, they like phantasy,
Novelty even. Let us confess the truth,
Horrible though it be, that prejudice,
Prescription . . . curses! they will love a queen.
They will, they do: and will not, does not—he?

 Con. How can he? You are wedded: 'tis a name
We know, but still a bond. Your rank remains,
His rank remains. How can he, nobly souled
As you believe and I incline to think,
Aspire to be your favourite, shame and all?

  Queen. Hear her! There, there now—could she love
   like me?
What did I say of smooth-cheeked youth and grace?
See all it does or could do! so youth loves!

Oh, tell him, Constance, you could never do
What I will—you, it was not born in! I
Will drive these difficulties far and fast
As yonder mists curdling before the moon.
I'll use my light too, gloriously retrieve
My youth from its enforced calamity,
Dissolve that hateful marriage, and be his,
His own in the eyes alike of God and man.

   Con. You will do—dare do . . . pause on what you
     say!

   Queen. Hear her! I thank you, sweet, for that surprise.
You have the fair face: for the soul, see mine!
I have the strong soul: let me teach you, here.
I think I have borne enough and long enough,
And patiently enough, the world remarks,
To have my own way now, unblamed by all.
It does so happen (I rejoice for it)
This most unhoped-for issue cuts the knot.
There's not a better way of settling claims
Than this; God sends the accident express:
And were it for my subjects' good, no more,
'Twere best thus ordered. I am thankful now,
Mute, passive, acquiescent. I receive,
And bless God simply, or should almost fear
To walk so smoothly to my ends at last.
Why, how I baffle obstacles, spurn fate!
How strong I am! Could Norbert see me now!

   Con. Let me consider. It is all too strange.

   Queen. You, Constance, learn of me; do you, like me!
You are young, beautiful: my own, best girl,
You will have many lovers, and love one—
Light hair, not hair like Norbert's, to suit yours:
Taller than he is, since yourself are tall.
Love him, like me! Give all away to him;
Think never of yourself; throw by your pride,
Hope, fear,—your own good as you saw it once,
And love him simply for his very self.
Remember, I (and what am I to you?)
Would give up all for one, leave throne, lose life,

Do all but just unlove him! He loves me.
  Con. He shall.
  Queen.   You, step inside my inmost heart!
Give me your own heart: let us have one heart!
I'll come to you for counsel; 'this he says,
'This he does; what should this amount to, pray?
'Beseech you, change it into current coin!
'Is that worth kisses? Shall I please him there?'
And then we'll speak in turn of you—what else?
Your love, according to your beauty's worth,
For you shall have some noble love, all gold:
Whom choose you? we will get him at your choice.
—Constance, I leave you. Just a minute since,
I felt as I must die or be alone
Breathing my soul into an ear like yours:
Now, I would face the world with my new life,
Wear my new crown. I'll walk around the rooms,
And then come back and tell you how it feels.
How soon a smile of God can change the world!
How we are made for happiness—how work
Grows play, adversity a winning fight!
True, I have lost so many years: what then!
Many remain: God has been very good.
You, stay here! 'Tis as different from dreams,
From the mind's cold calm estimate of bliss,
As these stone statues from the flesh and blood.
The comfort thou hast caused mankind, God's moon!

  [*She goes out, leaving* CONSTANCE. *Dance-music from
      within.*

NORBERT *enters.*

  Nor. Well? we have but one minute and one word!
  Con. I am yours, Norbert!
  Nor.   Yes, mine.
  Con.   Not till now!
You were mine. Now I give myself to you.
  Nor. Constance?
  Con.   Your own! I know the thriftier way
Of giving—haply, 'tis the wiser way.

Meaning to give a treasure, I might dole
Coin after coin out (each, as that were all,
With a new largess still at each despair)
And force you keep in sight the deed, preserve
Exhaustless till the end my part and yours,
My giving and your taking; both our joys
Dying together. Is it the wiser way?
I choose the simpler; I give all at once.
Know what you have to trust to, trade upon!
Use it, abuse it,—anything but think
Hereafter, 'Had I known she loved me so,
'And what my means, I might have thriven with it.'
This is your means. I give you all myself.

　　Nor. I take you and thank God.

　　Con.　　　　　　　　Look on through years!
We cannot kiss, a second day like this;
Else were this earth no earth.

　　Nor.　　　　　　　With this day's heat
We shall go on through years of cold.

　　Con.　　　　　　　　　　So, best!
—I try to see those years—I think I see.
You walk quick and new warmth comes; you look back
And lay all to the first glow—not sit down
For ever brooding on a day like this
While seeing embers whiten and love die.
Yes, love lives best in its effect; and mine,
Full in its own life, yearns to live in yours.

　　Nor. Just so. I take and know you all at once.
Your soul is disengaged so easily,
Your face is there, I know you; give me time,
Let me be proud and think you shall know me.
My soul is slower: in a life I roll
The minute out whereto you condense yours—
The whole slow circle round you I must move,
To be just you. I look to a long life
To decompose this minute, prove its worth.
'Tis the sparks' long succession one by one
Shall show you, in the end, what fire was crammed
In that mere stone you struck: how could you know,

If it lay ever unproved in your sight,
As now my heart lies? your own warmth would hide
Its coldness, were it cold.

    Con.   But how prove, how?

    Nor. Prove in my life, you ask?

    Con.   Quick, Norbert—how?

    Nor. That's easy told. I count life just a stuff
To try the soul's strength on, educe the man.
Who keeps one end in view makes all things serve.
As with the body—he who hurls a lance
Or heaps up stone on stone, shows strength alike:
So must I seize and task all means to prove
And show this soul of mine, you crown as yours,
And justify us both.

    Con.   Could you write books,
Paint pictures! One sits down in poverty
And writes or paints, with pity for the rich.

    Nor. And loves one's painting and one's writing, then,
And not one's mistress! All is best, believe,
And we best as no other than we are.
We live, and they experiment on life—
Those poets, painters, all who stand aloof
To overlook the farther. Let us be
The thing they look at! I might take your face
And write of it and paint it—to what end?
For whom? what pale dictatress in the air
Feeds, smiling sadly, her fine ghost-like form
With earth's real blood and breath, the beauteous life
She makes despised for ever? You are mine,
Made for me, not for others in the world,
Nor yet for that which I should call my art,
The cold calm power to see how fair you look.
I come to you; I leave you not, to write
Or paint. You are, I am: let Rubens there
Paint us!

    Con. So, best!

    Nor.   I understand your soul.
You live, and rightly sympathize with life,
With action, power, success. This way is straight;

And time were short beside, to let me change
The craft my childhood learnt: my craft shall serve.
Men set me here to subjugate, enclose,
Manure their barren lives, and force thence fruit
First for themselves, and afterward for me
In the due tithe; the task of some one soul,
Through ways of work appointed by the world.
I am not bid create—men see no star
Transfiguring my brow to warrant that—
But find and bind and bring to bear their wills.
So I began: to-night sees how I end.
What if it see, too, power's first outbreak here
Amid the warmth, surprise and sympathy,
And instincts of the heart that teach the head?
What if the people have discerned at length
The dawn of the next nature, novel brain
Whose will they venture in the place of theirs,
Whose work, they trust, shall find them as novel ways
To untried heights which yet he only sees?
I felt it when you kissed me. See this Queen,
This people—in our phrase, this mass of men—
See how the mass lies passive to my hand
Now that my hand is plastic, with you by
To make the muscles iron! Oh, an end
Shall crown this issue as this crowns the first!
My will be on this people! then, the strain,
The grappling of the potter with his clay,
The long uncertain struggle,—the success
And consummation of the spirit-work,
Some vase shaped to the curl of the god's lip,
While rounded fair for human sense to see
The Graces in a dance men recognize
With turbulent applause and laughs of heart!
So triumph ever shall renew itself;
Ever shall end in efforts higher yet,
Ever begin . . .

    Con.   I ever helping?
    Nor.   Thus!

                [*As he embraces her, the* QUEEN *enters.*

Con. Hist, madam! So have I performed my part.
You see your gratitude's true decency,
Norbert? A little slow in seeing it!
Begin, to end the sooner! What's a kiss?

Nor. Constance?

Con.   Why, must I teach it you again?
You want a witness to your dulness, sir?
What was I saying these ten minutes long?
Then I repeat—when some young handsome man
Like you has acted out a part like yours,
Is pleased to fall in love with one beyond,
So very far beyond him, as he says—
So hopelessly in love that but to speak
Would prove him mad,—he thinks judiciously,
And makes some insignificant good soul,
Like me, his friend, adviser, confidant,
And very stalking-horse to cover him
In following after what he dares not face.
When his end's gained—(sir, do you understand?)
When she, he dares not face, has loved him first,
—May I not say so, madam?—tops his hope,
And overpasses so his wildest dream,
With glad consent of all, and most of her
The confidant who brought the same about—
Why, in the moment when such joy explodes,
I do hold that the merest gentleman
Will not start rudely from the stalking-horse,
Dismiss it with a 'There, enough of you!'
Forget it, show his back unmannerly:
But like a liberal heart will rather turn
And say, 'A tingling time of hope was ours;
'Betwixt the fears and falterings, we two lived
'A chanceful time in waiting for the prize:
'The confidant, the Constance, served not ill.
'And though I shall forget her in due time,
'Her use being answered now, as reason bids,
'Nay as herself bids from her heart of hearts,—
'Still, she has rights, the first thanks go to her,
'The first good praise goes to the prosperous tool,

'And the first—which is the last—rewarding kiss.'

 Nor. Constance, it is a dream—ah, see, you smile!

 Con. So, now his part being properly performed,
Madam, I turn to you and finish mine
As duly; I do justice in my turn.
Yes, madam, he has loved you—long and well;
He could not hope to tell you so—'twas I
Who served to prove your soul accessible,
I led his thoughts on, drew them to their place
When they had wandered else into despair,
And kept love constant toward its natural aim.
Enough, my part is played; you stoop half-way
And meet us royally and spare our fears:
'Tis like yourself. He thanks you, so do I.
Take him—with my full heart! my work is praised
By what comes of it. Be you happy, both!
Yourself—the only one on earth who can—
Do all for him, much more than a mere heart
Which though warm is not useful in its warmth
As the silk vesture of a queen! fold that
Around him gently, tenderly. For him—
For him,—he knows his own part!

 Nor.   Have you done?
I take the jest at last. Should I speak now?
Was yours the wager, Constance, foolish child,
Or did you but accept it? Well—at least
You lose by it.

 Con.   Nay, madam, 'tis your turn!
Restrain him still from speech a little more,
And make him happier as more confident!
Pity him, madam, he is timid yet!
Mark, Norbert! Do not shrink now! Here I yield
My whole right in you to the Queen, observe!
With her go put in practice the great schemes
You teem with, follow the career else closed—
Be all you cannot be except by her!
Behold her!—Madam, say for pity's sake
Anything—frankly say you love him! Else
He'll not believe it: there's more earnest in

His fear than you conceive: I know the man!

Nor. I know the woman somewhat, and confess
I thought she had jested better: she begins
To overcharge her part. I gravely wait
Your pleasure, madam: where is my reward?

Queen. Norbert, this wild girl (whom I recognize
Scarce more than you do, in her fancy-fit,
Eccentric speech and variable mirth,
Not very wise perhaps and somewhat bold,
Yet suitable, the whole night's work being strange)
—May still be right: I may do well to speak
And make authentic what appears a dream
To even myself. For, what she says, is true:
Yes, Norbert—what you spoke just now of love,
Devotion, stirred no novel sense in me,
But justified a warmth felt long before.
Yes, from the first—I loved you, I shall say:
Strange! but I do grow stronger, now 'tis said.
Your courage helps mine: you did well to speak
To-night, the night that crowns your twelvemonths' toil:
But still I had not waited to discern
Your heart so long, believe me! From the first
The source of so much zeal was almost plain,
In absence even of your own words just now
Which hazarded the truth. 'Tis very strange,
But takes a happy ending—in your love
Which mine meets: be it so! as you chose me,
So I choose you.

Nor.   And worthily you choose.
I will not be unworthy your esteem,
No, madam. I do love you; I will meet
Your nature, now I know it. This was well.
I see,—you dare and you are justified:
But none had ventured such experiment,
Less versed than you in nobleness of heart,
Less confident of finding such in me.
I joy that thus you test me ere you grant
The dearest richest beauteousest and best
Of women to my arms: 'tis like yourself.

So—back again into my part's set words—
Devotion to the uttermost is yours,
But no, you cannot, madam, even you,
Create in me the love our Constance does.
Or—something truer to the tragic phrase—
Not yon magnolia-bell superb with scent
Invites a certain insect—that's myself—
But the small eye-flower nearer to the ground.
I take this lady.

    Con.   Stay—not hers, the trap—
Stay, Norbert—that mistake were worst of all!
He is too cunning, madam! It was I,
I, Norbert, who . . .

    Nor.   You, was it, Constance? Then,
But for the grace of this divinest hour
Which gives me you, I might not pardon here!
I am the Queen's; she only knows my brain:
She may experiment upon my heart
And I instruct her too by the result.
But you, sweet, you who know me, who so long
Have told my heart-beats over, held my life
In those white hands of yours,—it is not well!

    Con. Tush! I have said it, did I not say it all?
The life, for her—the heart-beats, for her sake!

    Nor. Enough! my cheek grows red, I think. Your
test?
There's not the meanest woman in the world,
Not she I least could love in all the world,
Whom, did she love me, had love proved itself,
I dare insult as you insult me now.
Constance, I could say, if it must be said,
'Take back the soul you offer, I keep mine!'
But—'Take the soul still quivering on your hand,
'The soul so offered, which I cannot use,
'And, please you, give it to some playful friend,
'For—what's the trifle he requites me with?'
I, tempt a woman, to amuse a man,
That two may mock her heart if it succumb?
No: fearing God and standing 'neath his heaven,

I would not dare insult a woman so,
Were she the meanest woman in the world,
And he, I cared to please, ten emperors!
   Con. Norbert!
   Nor.   I love once as I live but once.
What case is this to think or talk about?
I love you. Would it mend the case at all
If such a step as this killed love in me?
Your part were done: account to God for it!
But mine—could murdered love get up again,
And kneel to whom you please to designate,
And make you mirth? It is too horrible.
You did not know this, Constance? now you know
That body and soul have each one life, but one:
And here's my love, here, living, at your feet.
   Con. See the Queen! Norbert—this one more last
       word—
If thus you have taken jest for earnest—thus
Loved me in earnest . . .
   Nor.   Ah, no jest holds here!
Where is the laughter in which jests break up,
And what this horror that grows palpable?
Madam—why grasp you thus the balcony?
Have I done ill? Have I not spoken truth?
How could I other? Was it not your test,
To try me, what my love for Constance meant?
Madam, your royal soul itself approves,
The first, that I should choose thus! so one takes
A beggar,—asks him, what would buy his child?
And then approves the expected laugh of scorn
Returned as something noble from the rags.
Speak, Constance, I'm the beggar! Ha, what's this?
You two glare each at each like panthers now.
Constance, the world fades; only you stand there!
You did not, in to-night's wild whirl of things,
Sell me—your soul of souls, for any price?
No—no—'tis easy to believe in you!
Was it your love's mad trial to o'ertop
Mine by this vain self-sacrifice? well, still—

Though I might curse, I love you. I am love
And cannot change: love's self is at your feet!

                           [*The* QUEEN *goes out.*

    Con. Feel my heart; let it die against your own!

    Nor. Against my own. Explain not; let this be!
This is life's height.

    Con.   Yours, yours, yours!

    Nor.   You and I—
Why care by what meanders we are here
I' the centre of the labyrinth? Men have died
Trying to find this place, which we have found.

    Con. Found, found!

    Nor.   Sweet, never fear what she can do!
We are past harm now.

    Con.   On the breast of God.
I thought of men—as if you were a man.
Tempting him with a crown!

    Nor.   This must end here:
It is too perfect.

    Con.   There's the music stopped.
What measured heavy tread? It is one blaze
About me and within me.

    Nor.   Oh, some death
Will run its sudden finger round this spark
And sever us from the rest!

    Con.   And so do well.
Now the doors open.

    Nor.   'Tis the guard comes.

    Con.   Kiss!

MEN AND WOMEN

'TRANSCENDENTALISM: A POEM IN TWELVE BOOKS'

Stop playing, poet! May a brother speak?
'Tis you speak, that's your error. Song's our art:
Whereas you please to speak these naked thoughts
Instead of draping them in sights and sounds.
—True thoughts, good thoughts, thoughts fit to treasure
    up!
But why such long prolusion and display,
Such turning and adjustment of the harp,
And taking it upon your breast, at length,
Only to speak dry words across its strings?
Stark-naked thought is in request enough:
Speak prose and hollo it till Europe hears!
The six-foot Swiss tube, braced about with bark,
Which helps the hunter's voice from Alp to Alp—
Exchange our harp for that,—who hinders you?

    But here's your fault; grown men want thought, you
        think;
Thought's what they mean by verse, and seek in verse.
Boys seek for images and melody,
Men must have reason—so, you aim at men.
Quite otherwise! Objects throng our youth, 'tis true;
We see and hear and do not wonder much:
If you could tell us what they mean, indeed!
As German Boehme never cared for plants
Until it happed, a-walking in the fields,
He noticed all at once that plants could speak,
Nay, turned with loosened tongue to talk with him.
That day the daisy had an eye indeed—
Colloquized with the cowslip on such themes!
We find them extant yet in Jacob's prose.

But by the time youth slips a stage or two
While reading prose in that tough book he wrote
(Collating and emendating the same
And settling on the sense most to our mind),
We shut the clasps and find life's summer past.
Then, who helps more, pray, to repair our loss—
Another Boehme with a tougher book
And subtler meanings of what roses say,—
Or some stout Mage like him of Halberstadt,[1]
John, who made things Boehme wrote thoughts about?
He with a 'look you!' vents a brace of rhymes,
And in there breaks the sudden rose herself,
Over us, under, round us every side,
Nay, in and out the tables and the chairs
And musty volumes, Boehme's book and all,—
Buries us with a glory, young once more,
Pouring heaven into this shut house of life.

So come, the harp back to your heart again!
You are a poem, though your poem's naught.
The best of all you showed before, believe,
Was your own boy-face o'er the finer chords
Bent, following the cherub at the top
That points to God with his paired half-moon wings.

HOW IT STRIKES A CONTEMPORARY

I ONLY knew one poet in my life:
And this, or something like it, was his way.

You saw go up and down Valladolid,
A man of mark, to know next time you saw.
His very serviceable suit of black
Was courtly once and conscientious still,
And many might have worn it, though none did:
The cloak, that somewhat shone and showed the threads,
Had purpose, and the ruff, significance.
He walked and tapped the pavement with his cane,

---

[1] John of Halberstadt, a magician botanist and a chymist.

Scenting the world, looking it full in face,
An old dog, bald and blindish, at his heels.
They turned up, now, the alley by the church,
That leads nowhither; now, they breathed themselves
On the main promenade just at the wrong time:
You'd come upon his scrutinizing hat,
Making a peaked shade blacker than itself
Against the single window spared some house
Intact yet with its mouldered Moorish work,—
Or else surprise the ferrel of his stick
Trying the mortar's temper 'tween the chinks
Of some new shop a-building, French and fine.
He stood and watched the cobbler at his trade,
The man who slices lemons into drink,
The coffee-roaster's brazier, and the boys
That volunteer to help him turn its winch.
He glanced o'er books on stalls with half an eye,
And fly-leaf ballads on the vendor's string,
And broad-edge bold-print posters by the wall.
He took such cognizance of men and things,
If any beat a horse, you felt he saw;
If any cursed a woman, he took note;
Yet stared at nobody,—you stared at him,
And found, less to your pleasure than surprise,
He seemed to know you and expect as much.
So, next time that a neighbour's tongue was loosed,
It marked the shameful and notorious fact,
We had among us, not so much a spy,
As a recording chief-inquisitor,
The town's true master if the town but knew!
We merely kept a governor for form,
While this man walked about and took account
Of all thought, said and acted, then went home,
And wrote it fully to our Lord the King
Who has an itch to know things, he knows why,
And reads them in his bedroom of a night.
Oh, you might smile! there wanted not a touch,
A tang of . . . well, it was not wholly ease
As back into your mind the man's look came.

Stricken in years a little,—such a brow
His eyes had to live under!—clear as flint
On either side the formidable nose
Curved, cut and coloured like an eagle's claw.
Had he to do with A.'s surprising fate?
When altogether old B. disappeared
And young C. got his mistress,—was't our friend,
His letter to the King, that did it all?
What paid the bloodless man for so much pains?
Our Lord the King has favourites manifold,
And shifts his ministry some once a month;
Our city gets new governors at whiles,—
But never word or sign, that I could hear,
Notified to this man about the streets
The King's approval of those letters conned
The last thing duly at the dead of night.
Did the man love his office? Frowned our Lord,
Exhorting when none heard—'Beseech me not!
'Too far above my people,—beneath me!
'I set the watch,—how should the people know?
'Forget them, keep me all the more in mind!'
Was some such understanding 'twixt the two?

I found no truth in one report at least—
That if you tracked him to his home, down lanes
Beyond the Jewry, and as clean to pace,
You found he ate his supper in a room
Blazing with lights, four Titians on the wall,
And twenty naked girls to change his plate!
Poor man, he lived another kind of life
In that new stuccoed third house by the bridge,
Fresh-painted, rather smart than otherwise!
The whole street might o'erlook him as he sat,
Leg crossing leg, one foot on the dog's back,
Playing a decent cribbage with his maid
(Jacynth, you're sure her name was) o'er the cheese
And fruit, three red halves of starved winter-pears,
Or treat of radishes in April. Nine,
Ten, struck the church clock, straight to bed went he.

My father, like the man of sense he was,
Would point him out to me a dozen times;
''St—'St,' he'd whisper, 'the Corregidor!'
I had been used to think that personage
Was one with lacquered breeches, lustrous belt,
And feathers like a forest in his hat,
Who blew a trumpet and proclaimed the news,
Announced the bull-fights, gave each church its turn,
And memorized the miracle in vogue!
He had a great observance from us boys;
We were in error; that was not the man.

I'd like now, yet had haply been afraid,
To have just looked, when this man came to die,
And seen who lined the clean gay garret-sides
And stood about the neat low truckle-bed,
With the heavenly manner of relieving guard.
Here had been, mark, the general-in-chief,
Thro' a whole campaign of the world's life and death,
Doing the King's work all the dim day long,
In his old coat and up to knees in mud,
Smoked like a herring, dining on a crust,—
And, now the day was won, relieved at once!
No further show or need for that old coat,
You are sure, for one thing! Bless us, all the while
How sprucely we are dressed out, you and I!
A second, and the angels alter that.
Well, I could never write a verse,—could you?
Let's to the Prado and make the most of time.

ARTEMIS PROLOGIZES

I AM a goddess of the ambrosial courts,
And save by Here, Queen of Pride, surpassed
By none whose temples whiten this the world.
Through heaven I roll my lucid moon along;
I shed in hell o'er my pale people peace;
On earth I, caring for the creatures, guard
Each pregnant yellow wolf and fox-bitch sleek,

And every feathered mother's callow brood,
And all that love green haunts and loneliness.
Of men, the chaste adore me, hanging crowns
Of poppies red to blackness, bell and stem,
Upon my image at Athenai here;
And this dead Youth, Asclepios bends above,
Was dearest to me. He, my buskined step
To follow through the wild-wood leafy ways,
And chase the panting stag, or swift with darts
Stop the swift ounce, or lay the leopard low,
Neglected homage to another god:
Whence Aphrodite, by no midnight smoke
Of tapers lulled, in jealousy despatched
A noisome lust that, as the gadbee stings,
Possessed his stepdame Phaidra for himself
The son of Theseus her great absent spouse.
Hippolutos exclaiming in his rage
Against the fury of the Queen, she judged
Life insupportable; and, pricked at heart
An Amazonian stranger's race should dare
To scorn her, perished by the murderous cord:
Yet, ere she perished, blasted in a scroll
The fame of him her swerving made not swerve.
And Theseus, read, returning, and believed,
And exiled, in the blindness of his wrath,
The man without a crime who, last as first,
Loyal, divulged not to his sire the truth.
Now Theseus from Poseidon had obtained
That of his wishes should be granted three,
And one he imprecated straight—'Alive
'May ne'er Hippolutos reach other lands!'
Poseidon heard, ai ai! And scarce the prince
Had stepped into the fixed boots of the car
That give the feet a stay against the strength
Of the Henetian horses, and around
His body flung the rein, and urged their speed
Along the rocks and shingles of the shore,
When from the gaping wave a monster flung
His obscene body in the coursers' path.

These, mad with terror, as the sea-bull sprawled
Wallowing about their feet, lost care of him
That reared them; and the master-chariot-pole
Snapping beneath their plunges like a reed,
Hippolutos, whose feet were trammelled fast,
Was yet dragged forward by the circling rein
Which either hand directed; nor they quenched
The frenzy of their flight before each trace,
Wheel-spoke and splinter of the woeful car,
Each boulder-stone, sharp stub and spiny shell,
Huge fish-bone wrecked and wreathed amid the sands
On that detested beach, was bright with blood
And morsels of his flesh: then fell the steeds
Head foremost, crashing in their mooned fronts,
Shivering with sweat, each white eye horror-fixed.
His people, who had witnessed all afar,
Bore back the ruins of Hippolutos.
But when his sire, too swoln with pride, rejoiced
(Indomitable as a man foredoomed)
That vast Poseidon had fulfilled his prayer,
I, in a flood of glory visible,
Stood o'er my dying votary and, deed
By deed, revealed, as all took place, the truth.
Then Theseus lay the woefullest of men,
And worthily; but ere the death-veils hid
His face, the murdered prince full pardon breathed
To his rash sire. Whereat Athenai wails.

So I, who ne'er forsake my votaries,
Lest in the cross-way none the honey-cake
Should tender, nor pour out the dog's hot life;
Lest at my fane the priests disconsolate
Should dress my image with some faded poor
Few crowns, made favours of, nor dare object
Such slackness to my worshippers who turn
Elsewhere the trusting heart and loaded hand,
As they had climbed Olumpos to report
Of Artemis and nowhere found her throne—
I interposed: and, this eventful night,—

(While round the funeral pyre the populace
Stood with fierce light on their black robes which bound
Each sobbing head, while yet their hair they clipped
O'er the dead body of their withered prince,
And, in his palace, Theseus prostrated
On the cold hearth, his brow cold as the slab
'Twas bruised on, groaned away the heavy grief—
As the pyre fell, and down the cross logs crashed
Sending a crowd of sparkles through the night,
And the gay fire, elate with mastery,
Towered like a serpent o'er the clotted jars
Of wine, dissolving oils and frankincense,
And splendid gums like gold),—my potency
Conveyed the perished man to my retreat
In the thrice-venerable forest here.
And this white-bearded sage who squeezes now
The berried plant, is Phoibos' son of fame,
Asclepios, whom my radiant brother taught
The doctrine of each herb and flower and root,
To know their secret'st virtue and express
The saving soul of all: who so has soothed
With lavers the torn brow and murdered cheeks,
Composed the hair and brought its gloss again,
And called the red bloom to the pale skin back,
And laid the strips and jagged ends of flesh
Even once more, and slacked the sinew's knot
Of every tortured limb—that now he lies
As if mere sleep possessed him underneath
These interwoven oaks and pines. Oh cheer,
Divine presenter of the healing rod,
Thy snake, with ardent throat and lulling eye,
Twines his lithe spires around! I say, much cheer!
Proceed thou with thy wisest pharmacies!
And ye, white crowd of woodland sister-nymphs,
Ply, as the sage directs, these buds and leaves
That strew the turf around the twain! While I
Await, in fitting silence, the event.

AN EPISTLE

CONTAINING THE STRANGE MEDICAL EXPERIENCE OF
KARSHISH, THE ARAB PHYSICIAN.

KARSHISH, the picker-up of learning's crumbs,
The not-incurious in God's handiwork
(This man's-flesh he hath admirably made,
Blown like a bubble, kneaded like a paste,
To coop up and keep down on earth a space
That puff of vapour from its mouth, man's soul)
—To Abib, all-sagacious in our art,
Breeder in me of what poor skill I boast,
Like me inquisitive how pricks and cracks
Befall the flesh through too much stress and strain,
Whereby the wily vapour fain would slip
Back and rejoin its source before the term,—
And aptest in contrivance (under God)
To battle it by deftly stopping such:—
The vagrant Scholar to his Sage at home
Sends greeting (health and knowledge, fame with peace)
Three samples of true snakestone—rarer still,
One of the other sort, the melon-shaped,
(But fitter, pounded fine, for charms than drugs)
And writeth now the twenty-second time.

My journeyings were brought to Jericho:
Thus I resume. Who studious in our art
Shall count a little labour unrepaid?
I have shed sweat enough, left flesh and bone
On many a flinty furlong of this land.
Also, the country-side is all on fire
With rumours of a marching hitherward:
Some say Vespasian cometh, some, his son.
A black lynx snarled and pricked a tufted ear;
Lust of my blood inflamed his yellow balls:
I cried and threw my staff and he was gone.
Twice have the robbers stripped and beaten me,
And once a town declared me for a spy;

But at the end, I reach Jerusalem,
Since this poor covert where I pass the night,
This Bethany, lies scarce the distance thence
A man with plague-sores at the third degree
Runs till he drops down dead. Thou laughest here!
'Sooth, it elates me, thus reposed and safe,
To void the stuffing of my travel-scrip
And share with thee whatever Jewry yields.
A viscid choler is observable
In tertians, I was nearly bold to say;
And falling-sickness hath a happier cure
Than our school wots of: there's a spider here
Weaves no web, watches on the ledge of tombs,
Sprinkled with mottles on an ash-grey back;
Take five and drop them . . . but who knows his mind,
The Syrian runagate I trust this to?
His service payeth me a sublimate
Blown up his nose to help the ailing eye.
Best wait: I reach Jerusalem at morn,
There set in order my experiences,
Gather what most deserves, and give thee all—
Or I might add, Judæa's gum-tragacanth
Scales off in purer flakes, shines clearer-grained,
Cracks 'twixt the pestle and the porphyry,
In fine exceeds our produce. Scalp-disease
Confounds me, crossing so with leprosy—
Thou hadst admired one sort I gained at Zoar—
But zeal outruns discretion. Here I end.

　　Yet stay: my Syrian blinketh gratefully,
Protesteth his devotion is my price—
Suppose I write what harms not, though he steal?
I half resolve to tell thee, yet I blush,
What set me off a-writing first of all.
An itch I had, a sting to write, a tang!
For, be it this town's barrenness—or else
The Man had something in the look of him—
His case has struck me far more than 'tis worth.
So, pardon if—(lest presently I lose

In the great press of novelty at hand
The care and pains this somehow stole from me)
I bid thee take the thing while fresh in mind,
Almost in sight—for, wilt thou have the truth?
The very man is gone from me but now,
Whose ailment is the subject of discourse.
Thus then, and let thy better wit help all!

'Tis but a case of mania—subinduced
By epilepsy, at the turning-point
Of trance prolonged unduly some three days:
When, by the exhibition of some drug
Or spell, exorcization, stroke of art
Unknown to me and which 'twere well to know,
The evil thing out-breaking all at once
Left the man whole and sound of body indeed,—
But, flinging (so to speak) life's gates too wide,
Making a clear house of it too suddenly,
The first conceit that entered might inscribe
Whatever it was minded on the wall
So plainly at that vantage, as it were,
(First come, first served) that nothing subsequent
Attaineth to erase those fancy-scrawls
The just-returned and new-established soul
Hath gotten now so thoroughly by heart
That henceforth she will read or these or none.
And first—the man's own firm conviction rests
That he was dead (in fact they buried him)
—That he was dead and then restored to life
By a Nazarene physician of his tribe:
—'Sayeth, the same bade 'Rise,' and he did rise.
'Such cases are diurnal,' thou wilt cry.
Not so this figment!—not, that such a fume,
Instead of giving way to time and health,
Should eat itself into the life of life,
As saffron tingeth flesh, blood, bones and all!
For see, how he takes up the after-life.
The man—it is one Lazarus a Jew,
Sanguine, proportioned, fifty years of age,

The body's habit wholly laudable,
As much, indeed, beyond the common health
As he were made and put aside to show.
Think, could we penetrate by any drug
And bathe the wearied soul and worried flesh,
And bring it clear and fair, by three days' sleep!
Whence has the man the balm that brightens all?
This grown man eyes the world now like a child.
Some elders of his tribe, I should premise,
Led in their friend, obedient as a sheep,
To bear my inquisition. While they spoke,
Now sharply, now with sorrow,—told the case,—
He listened not except I spoke to him,
But folded his two hands and let them talk.
Watching the flies that buzzed: and yet no fool.
And that's a sample how his years must go.
Look, if a beggar, in fixed middle-life,
Should find a treasure,—can he use the same
With straitened habits and with tastes starved small,
And take at once to his impoverished brain
The sudden element that changes things,
That sets the undreamed-of rapture at his hand
And puts the cheap old joy in the scorned dust?
Is he not such an one as moves to mirth—
Warily parsimonious, when no need,
Wasteful as drunkenness at undue times?
All prudent counsel as to what befits
The golden mean, is lost on such an one:
The man's fantastic will is the man's law.
So here—we call the treasure knowledge, say,
Increased beyond the fleshly faculty—
Heaven opened to a soul while yet on earth,
Earth forced on a soul's use while seeing heaven:
The man is witless of the size, the sum,
The value in proportion of all things,
Or whether it be little or be much.
Discourse to him of prodigious armaments
Assembled to besiege his city now,
And of the passing of a mule with gourds—

'Tis one! Then take it on the other side,
Speak of some trifling fact,—he will gaze rapt
With stupor at its very littleness,
(Far as I see) as if in that indeed
He caught prodigious import, whole results;
And so will turn to us the bystanders
In ever the same stupor (note this point)
That we too see not with his opened eyes.
Wonder and doubt come wrongly into play,
Preposterously, at cross purposes.
Should his child sicken unto death,—why, look
For scarce abatement of his cheerfulness,
Or pretermission of the daily craft!
While a word, gesture, glance from that same child
At play or in the school or laid asleep,
Will startle him to an agony of fear,
Exasperation, just as like. Demand
The reason why—''tis but a word,' object—
'A gesture'—he regards thee as our lord
Who lived there in the pyramid alone,
Looked at us (dost thou mind?) when, being young,
We both would unadvisedly recite
Some charm's beginning, from that book of his,
Able to bid the sun throb wide and burst
All into stars, as suns grown old are wont.
Thou and the child have each a veil alike
Thrown o'er your heads, from under which ye both
Stretch your blind hands and trifle with a match
Over a mine of Greek fire, did ye know!
He holds on firmly to some thread of life—
(It is the life to lead perforcedly)
Which runs across some vast distracting orb
Of glory on either side that meagre thread,
Which, conscious of, he must not enter yet—
The spiritual life around the earthly life:
The law of that is known to him as this,
His heart and brain move there, his feet stay here.
So is the man perplext with impulses
Sudden to start off crosswise, not straight on,

Proclaiming what is right and wrong across,
And not along, this black thread through the blaze—
'It should be' baulked by 'here it cannot be.'
And oft the man's soul springs into his face
As if he saw again and heard again
His sage that bade him 'Rise' and he did rise.
Something, a word, a tick o' the blood within
Admonishes: then back he sinks at once
To ashes, who was very fire before,
In sedulous recurrence to his trade
Whereby he earneth him the daily bread;
And studiously the humbler for that pride,
Professedly the faultier that he knows
God's secret, while he holds the thread of life.
Indeed the especial marking of the man
Is prone submission to the heavenly will—
Seeing it, what it is, and why it is.
'Sayeth, he will wait patient to the last
For that same death which must restore his being
To equilibrium, body loosening soul
Divorced even now by premature full growth:
He will live, nay, it pleaseth him to live
So long as God please, and just how God please.
He even seeketh not to please God more
(Which meaneth, otherwise) than as God please.
Hence, I perceive not he affects to preach
The doctrine of his sect whate'er it be,
Make proselytes as madmen thirst to do:
How can he give his neighbour the real ground,
His own conviction? Ardent as he is—
Call his great truth a lie, why, still the old
'Be it as God please' reassureth him.
I probed the sore as thy disciple should:
'How, beast,' said I, 'this stolid carelessness
'Sufficeth thee, when Rome is on her march
'To stamp out like a little spark thy town,
'Thy tribe, thy crazy tale and thee at once?'
He merely looked with his large eyes on me.
The man is apathetic, you deduce?

Contrariwise, he loves both old and young,
Able and weak, affects the very brutes
And birds—how say I? flowers of the field—
As a wise workman recognizes tools
In a master's workshop, loving what they make.
Thus is the man as harmless as a lamb:
Only impatient, let him do his best,
At ignorance and carelessness and sin—
An indignation which is promptly curbed:
As when in certain travel I have feigned
To be an ignoramus in our art
According to some preconceived design,
And happed to hear the land's practitioners
Steeped in conceit sublimed by ignorance,
Prattle fantastically on disease,
Its cause and cure—and I must hold my peace!

Thou wilt object—Why have I not ere this
Sought out the sage himself, the Nazarene
Who wrought this cure, inquiring at the source,
Conferring with the frankness that befits?
Alas! it grieveth me, the learned leech
Perished in a tumult many years ago,
Accused,—our learning's fate,—of wizardry,
Rebellion, to the setting up a rule
And creed prodigious as described to me.
His death, which happened when the earthquake fell
(Prefiguring, as soon appeared, the loss
To occult learning in our lord the sage
Who lived there in the pyramid alone)
Was wrought by the mad people—that's their wont!
On vain recourse, as I conjecture it,
To his tried virtue, for miraculous help—
How could he stop the earthquake? That's their
          way!
The other imputations must be lies:
But take one, though I loathe to give it thee,
In mere respect for any good man's fame.
(And after all, our patient Lazarus

Is stark mad; should we count on what he says?
Perhaps not: though in writing to a leech
'Tis well to keep back nothing of a case.)
This man so cured regards the curer, then,
As—God forgive me! who but God himself,
Creator and sustainer of the world,
That came and dwelt in flesh on it awhile!
—'Sayeth that such an one was born and lived,
Taught, healed the sick, broke bread at his own house,
Then died, with Lazarus by, for aught I know,
And yet was . . . what I said nor choose repeat,
And must have so avouched himself, in fact,
In hearing of this very Lazarus
Who saith—but why all this of what he saith?
Why write of trivial matters, things of price
Calling at every moment for remark?
I noticed on the margin of a pool
Blue-flowering borage, the Aleppo sort,
Aboundeth, very nitrous. It is strange!

Thy pardon for this long and tedious case,
Which, now that I review it, needs must seem
Unduly dwelt on, prolixly set forth!
Nor I myself discern in what is writ
Good cause for the peculiar interest
And awe indeed this man has touched me with.
Perhaps the journey's end, the weariness
Had wrought upon me first. I met him thus:
I crossed a ridge of short sharp broken hills
Like an old lion's cheek-teeth. Out there came
A moon made like a face with certain spots
Multiform, manifold and menacing:
Then a wind rose behind me. So we met
In this old sleepy town at unaware,
The man and I. I send thee what is writ.
Regard it as a chance, a matter risked
To this ambiguous Syrian—he may lose,
Or steal, or give it thee with equal good.
Jerusalem's repose shall make amends

For time this letter wastes, thy time and mine;
Till when, once more thy pardon and farewell!

The very God! think, Abib; dost thou think?
So, the All-Great, were the All-Loving too—
So, through the thunder comes a human voice
Saying, 'O heart I made, a heart beats here!
'Face, my hands fashioned, see it in myself!
'Thou hast no power nor mayst conceive of mine,
'But love I gave thee, with myself to love,
'And thou must love me who have died for thee!'
The madman saith He said so: it is strange.

JOHANNES AGRICOLA IN MEDITATION

THERE's heaven above, and night by night
    I look right through its gorgeous roof;
No suns and moons though e'er so bright
    Avail to stop me; splendour-proof
    I keep the broods of stars aloof:
For I intend to get to God,
    For 'tis to God I speed so fast,
For in God's breast, my own abode,
    Those shoals of dazzling glory, passed,
    I lay my spirit down at last.
I lie where I have always lain,
    God smiles as he has always smiled;
Ere suns and moons could wax and wane,
    Ere stars were thundergirt, or piled
    The heavens, God thought on me his child;
Ordained a life for me, arrayed
    Its circumstances every one
To the minutest; ay, God said
    This head this hand should rest upon
    Thus, ere he fashioned star or sun.
And having thus created me,
    Thus rooted me, he bade me grow,
Guiltless for ever, like a tree
    That buds and blooms, nor seeks to know

The law by which it prospers so:
But sure that thought and word and deed
  All go to swell his love for me,
Me, made because that love had need
  Of something irreversibly
  Pledged solely its content to be.
Yes, yes, a tree which must ascend,
  No poison-gourd foredoomed to stoop!
I have God's warrant, could I blend
  All hideous sins, as in a cup,
  To drink the mingled venoms up;
Secure my nature will convert
  The draught to blossoming gladness fast:
While sweet dews turn to the gourd's hurt,
  And bloat, and while they bloat it, blast,
  As from the first its lot was cast.
For as I lie, smiled on, full-fed
  By unexhausted power to bless,
I gaze below on hell's fierce bed,
  And those its waves of flame oppress,
  Swarming in ghastly wretchedness;
Whose life on earth aspired to be
  One altar-smoke, so pure!—to win
If not love like God's love for me,
  At least to keep his anger in;
  And all their striving turned to sin.
Priest, doctor, hermit, monk grown white
  With prayer, the broken-hearted nun,
The martyr, the wan acolyte,
  The incense-swinging child,—undone
  Before God fashioned star or sun!
God, whom I praise; how could I praise,
  If such as I might understand,
Make out and reckon on his ways,
  And bargain for his love, and stand,
  Paying a price, at his right hand?

PICTOR IGNOTUS

FLORENCE, 15—

I COULD have painted pictures like that youth's
  Ye praise so. How my soul springs up! No bar
Stayed me—ah, thought which saddens while it soothes!
  —Never did fate forbid me, star by star,
To outburst on your night with all my gift
  Of fires from God: nor would my flesh have shrunk
From seconding my soul, with eyes uplift
  And wide to heaven, or, straight like thunder, sunk
To the centre, of an instant; or around
  Turned calmly and inquisitive, to scan
The licence and the limit, space and bound,
  Allowed to truth made visible in man.
And, like that youth ye praise so, all I saw,
  Over the canvas could my hand have flung,
Each face obedient to its passion's law,
  Each passion clear proclaimed without a tongue;
Whether Hope rose at once in all the blood,
  A-tiptoe for the blessing of embrace,
Or Rapture drooped the eyes, as when her brood
  Pull down the nesting dove's heart to its place;
Or Confidence lit swift the forehead up,
  And locked the mouth fast, like a castle braved,—
O human faces, hath it spilt, my cup?
  What did ye give me that I have not saved?
Nor will I say I have not dreamed (how well!)
  Of going—I, in each new picture,—forth,
As, making new hearts beat and bosoms swell,
  To Pope or Kaiser, East, West, South, or North,
Bound for the calmly-satisfied great State,
  Or glad aspiring little burgh, it went,
Flowers cast upon the car which bore the freight,
  Through old streets named afresh from the event,
Till it reached home, where learned age should greet
  My face, and youth, the star not yet distinct
Above his hair, lie learning at my feet!—
  Oh, thus to live, I and my picture, linked

With love about, and praise, till life should end,
   And then not go to heaven, but linger here,
Here on my earth, earth's every man my friend,—
   The thought grew frightful, 'twas so wildly dear!
But a voice changed it. Glimpses of such sights
   Have scared me, like the revels through a door
Of some strange house of idols at its rites!
   This world seemed not the world it was before:
Mixed with my loving trusting ones, there trooped
   . . . Who summoned those cold faces that begun
To press on me and judge me? Though I stooped
   Shrinking, as from the soldiery a nun,
They drew me forth, and spite of me . . . enough!
   These buy and sell our pictures, take and give,
Count them for garniture and household-stuff,
   And where they live needs must our pictures live
And see their faces, listen to their prate,
   Partakers of their daily pettiness,
Discussed of,—'This I love, or this I hate,
   'This likes me more, and this affects me less!'
Wherefore I chose my portion. If at whiles
   My heart sinks, as monotonous I paint
These endless cloisters and eternal aisles
   With the same series, Virgin, Babe and Saint,
With the same cold calm beautiful regard,—
   At least no merchant traffics in my heart;
The sanctuary's gloom at least shall ward
   Vain tongues from where my pictures stand apart:
Only prayer breaks the silence of the shrine
   While, blackening in the daily candle-smoke,
They moulder on the damp wall's travertine,
   'Mid echoes the light footstep never woke.
So, die my pictures! surely, gently die!
   O youth, men praise so,—holds their praise its worth?
Blown harshly, keeps the trump its golden cry?
   Tastes sweet the water with such specks of earth?

FRA LIPPO LIPPI

I AM poor brother Lippo, by your leave!
You need not clap your torches to my face.
Zooks, what's to blame? you think you see a monk!
What, 'tis past midnight, and you go the rounds,
And here you catch me at an alley's end
Where sportive ladies leave their doors ajar?
The Carmine's my cloister: hunt it up,
Do,—harry out, if you must show your zeal,
Whatever rat, there, haps on his wrong hole,
And nip each softling of a wee white mouse,
Weke, weke, that's crept to keep him company!
Aha, you know your betters! Then, you'll take
Your hand away that's fiddling on my throat,
And please to know me likewise. Who am I?
Why, one, sir, who is lodging with a friend
Three streets off—he's a certain . . . how d'ye call?
Master—a . . . Cosimo of the Medici,
I' the house that caps the corner. Boh! you were best!
Remember and tell me, the day you're hanged,
How you affected such a gullet's-gripe!
But you, sir, it concerns you that your knaves
Pick up a manner nor discredit you:
Zooks, are we pilchards, that they sweep the streets
And count fair prize what comes into their net?
He's Judas to a tittle, that man is!
Just such a face! Why, sir, you make amends.
Lord, I'm not angry! Bid your hangdogs go
Drink out this quarter-florin to the health
Of the munificent House that harbours me
(And many more beside, lads! more beside!)
And all's come square again. I'd like his face—
His, elbowing on his comrade in the door
With the pike and lantern,—for the slave that holds
John Baptist's head a-dangle by the hair
With one hand ('Look you, now,' as who should say)
And his weapon in the other, yet unwiped!
It's not your chance to have a bit of chalk,

A wood-coal or the like? or you should see!
Yes, I'm the painter, since you style me so.
What, brother Lippo's doings, up and down,
You know them and they take you? like enough!
I saw the proper twinkle in your eye—
'Tell you, I liked your looks at very first.
Let's sit and set things straight now, hip to haunch.
Here's spring come, and the nights one makes up bands
To roam the town and sing out carnival,
And I've been three weeks shut within my mew,
A-painting for the great man, saints and saints
And saints again. I could not paint all night—
Ouf! I leaned out of window for fresh air.
There came a hurry of feet and little feet,
A sweep of lute-strings, laughs, and whifts of song,—
Flower o' the broom,
Take away love, and our earth is a tomb!
Flower o' the quince,
I let Lisa go, and what good in life since?
Flower o' the thyme—and so on. Round they went.
Scarce had they turned the corner when a titter
Like the skipping of rabbits by moonlight,—three slim
    shapes,
And a face that looked up . . . zooks, sir, flesh and blood,
That's all I'm made of! Into shreds it went,
Curtain and counterpane and coverlet,
All the bed-furniture—a dozen knots,
There was a ladder! Down I let myself,
Hands and feet, scrambling somehow, and so dropped,
And after them. I came up with the fun
Hard by Saint Laurence, hail fellow, well met,—
Flower o' the rose,
If I've been merry, what matter who knows?
And so as I was stealing back again
To get to bed and have a bit of sleep
Ere I rise up to-morrow and go work
On Jerome knocking at his poor old breast
With his great round stone to subdue the flesh,
You snap me of the sudden. Ah, I see!

Though your eye twinkles still, you shake your head—
Mine's shaved—a monk, you say—the sting's in that!
If Master Cosimo announced himself,
Mum's the word naturally; but a monk!
Come, what am I a beast for? tell us, now!
I was a baby when my mother died
And father died and left me in the street.
I starved there, God knows how, a year or two
On fig-skins, melon-parings, rinds and shucks,
Refuse and rubbish. One fine frosty day,
My stomach being empty as your hat,
The wind doubled me up and down I went.
Old Aunt Lapaccia trussed me with one hand,
(Its fellow was a stinger as I knew)
And so along the wall, over the bridge,
By the straight cut to the convent. Six words there,
While I stood munching my first bread that month:
'So, boy, you're minded,' quoth the good fat father
Wiping his own mouth, 'twas refection-time,—
'To quit this very miserable world?
'Will you renounce' ... 'the mouthful of bread?' thought I;
By no means! Brief, they made a monk of me;
I did renounce the world, its pride and greed,
Palace, farm, villa, shop and banking-house,
Trash, such as these poor devils of Medici
Have given their hearts to—all at eight years old.
Well, sir, I found in time, you may be sure,
'Twas not for nothing—the good bellyful,
The warm serge and the rope that goes all round,
And day-long blessed idleness beside!
'Let's see what the urchin's fit for'—that came next.
Not overmuch their way, I must confess.
Such a to-do! They tried me with their books:
Lord, they'd have taught me Latin in pure waste!
Flower o' the clove,
All the Latin I construe is, 'amo' I love!
But, mind you, when a boy starves in the streets
Eight years together, as my fortune was,
Watching folk's faces to know who will fling

The bit of half-stripped grape-bunch he desires,
And who will curse or kick him for his pains,—
Which gentleman processional and fine,
Holding a candle to the Sacrament,
Will wink and let him lift a plate and catch
The droppings of the wax to sell again,
Or holla for the Eight and have him whipped,—
How say I?—nay, which dog bites, which lets drop
His bone from the heap of offal in the street,—
Why, soul and sense of him grow sharp alike,
He learns the look of things, and none the less
For admonition from the hunger-pinch.
I had a store of such remarks, be sure,
Which, after I found leisure, turned to use.
I drew men's faces on my copy-books,
Scrawled them within the antiphonary's marge,
Joined legs and arms to the long music-notes,
Found eyes and nose and chin for A's and B's,
And made a string of pictures of the world
Betwixt the ins and outs of verb and noun,
On the wall, the bench, the door. The monks looked black.
'Nay,' quoth the Prior, 'turn him out, d'ye say?
'In no wise. Lose a crow and catch a lark.
'What if at last we get our man of parts,
'We Carmelites, like those Camaldolese
'And Preaching Friars, to do our church up fine
'And put the front on it that ought to be!'
And hereupon he bade me daub away.
Thank you! my head being crammed, the walls a blank,
Never was such prompt disemburdening.
First, every sort of monk, the black and white,
I drew them, fat and lean: then, folk at church,
From good old gossips waiting to confess
Their cribs of barrel-droppings, candle-ends,—
To the breathless fellow at the altar-foot,
Fresh from his murder, safe and sitting there
With the little children round him in a row
Of admiration, half for his beard and half
For that white anger of his victim's son

Shaking a fist at him with one fierce arm,
Signing himself with the other because of Christ
(Whose sad face on the cross sees only this
After the passion of a thousand years)
Till some poor girl, her apron o'er her head,
(Which the intense eyes looked through) came at eve
On tiptoe, said a word, dropped in a loaf,
Her pair of earrings and a bunch of flowers
(The brute took growling), prayed, and so was gone.
I painted all, then cried "'Tis ask and have;
'Choose, for more's ready!'—laid the ladder flat,
And showed my covered bit of cloister-wall.
The monks closed in a circle and praised loud
Till checked, taught what to see and not to see,
Being simple bodies,—'That's the very man!
'Look at the boy who stoops to pat the dog!
'That woman's like the Prior's niece who comes
'To care about his asthma: it's the life!'
But there my triumph's straw-fire flared and funked;
Their betters took their turn to see and say:
The Prior and the learned pulled a face
And stopped all that in no time. 'How? what's here?
'Quite from the mark of painting, bless us all!
'Faces, arms, legs and bodies like the true
'As much as pea and pea! it's devil's-game!
'Your business is not to catch men with show,
'With homage to the perishable clay,
'But lift them over it, ignore it all,
'Make them forget there's such a thing as flesh.
'Your business is to paint the souls of men—
'Man's soul, and it's a fire, smoke . . . no, it's not . . .
'It's vapour done up like a new-born babe—
'(In that shape when you die it leaves your mouth)
'It's . . . well, what matters talking, it's the soul!
'Give us no more of body than shows soul!
'Here's Giotto, with his Saint a-praising God,
'That sets us praising,—why not stop with him?
'Why put all thoughts of praise out of our head
'With wonder at lines, colours, and what not?

'Paint the soul, never mind the legs and arms!
'Rub all out, try at it a second time.
'Oh, that white smallish female with the breasts,
'She's just my niece . . . Herodias, I would say,—
'Who went and danced and got men's heads cut off!
'Have it all out!' Now, is this sense, I ask?
A fine way to paint soul, by painting body
So ill, the eye can't stop there, must go further
And can't fare worse! Thus, yellow does for white
When what you put for yellow's simply black,
And any sort of meaning looks intense
When all beside itself means and looks nought.
Why can't a painter lift each foot in turn,
Left foot and right foot, go a double step,
Make his flesh liker and his soul more like,
Both in their order? Take the prettiest face,
The Prior's niece . . . patron-saint—is it so pretty
You can't discover if it means hope, fear,
Sorrow or joy? won't beauty go with these?
Suppose I've made her eyes all right and blue,
Can't I take breath and try to add life's flash,
And then add soul and heighten them threefold?
Or say there's beauty with no soul at all—
(I never saw it—put the case the same—)
If you get simple beauty and nought else,
You get about the best thing God invents:
That's somewhat: and you'll find the soul you have
    missed,
Within yourself, when you return him thanks.
'Rub all out!' Well, well, there's my life, in short.
And so the thing has gone on ever since.
I'm grown a man no doubt, I've broken bounds:
You should not take a fellow eight years old
And make him swear to never kiss the girls.
I'm my own master, paint now as I please—
Having a friend, you see, in the Corner-house!
Lord, it's fast holding by the rings in front—
Those great rings serve more purposes than just
To plant a flag in, or tie up a horse!

And yet the old schooling sticks, the old grave eyes
Are peeping o'er my shoulder as I work,
The heads shake still—'It 's art's decline, my son!
'You're not of the true painters, great and old;
'Brother Angelico's the man, you'll find;
'Brother Lorenzo stands his single peer:
'Fag on at flesh, you'll never make the third!'
Flower o' the pine,
You keep your mistr . . . manners, and I'll stick to mine!
I'm not the third, then: bless us, they must know!
Don't you think they're the likeliest to know,
They with their Latin? So, I swallow my rage,
Clench my teeth, suck my lips in tight, and paint
To please them—sometimes do and sometimes don't;
For, doing most, there's pretty sure to come
A turn, some warm eve finds me at my saints—
A laugh, a cry, the business of the world—
(*Flower o' the peach,*
Death for us all, and his own life for each!)
And my whole soul revolves, the cup runs over,
The world and life's too big to pass for a dream,
And I do these wild things in sheer despite,
And play the fooleries you catch me at,
In pure rage! The old mill-horse, out at grass
After hard years, throws up his stiff heels so,
Although the miller does not preach to him
The only good of grass is to make chaff.
What would men have? Do they like grass or no—
May they or mayn't they? all I want's the thing
Settled for ever one way. As it is,
You tell too many lies and hurt yourself:
You don't like what you only like too much,
You do like what, if given you at your word,
You find abundantly detestable.
For me, I think I speak as I was taught;
I always see the garden and God there
A-making man's wife: and, my lesson learned,
The value and significance of flesh,
I can't unlearn ten minutes afterwards.

You understand me: I'm a beast, I know.
But see, now—why, I see as certainly
As that the morning-star's about to shine,
What will hap some day. We've a youngster here
Comes to our convent, studies what I do,
Slouches and stares and lets no atom drop:
His name is Guidi—he'll not mind the monks—
They call him Hulking Tom, he lets them talk—
He picks my practice up—he'll paint apace,
I hope so—though I never live so long,
I know what's sure to follow. You be judge!
You speak no Latin more than I, belike;
However, you're my man, you've seen the world
—The beauty and the wonder and the power,
The shapes of things, their colours, lights and shades,
Changes, surprises,—and God made it all!
—For what? Do you feel thankful, ay or no,
For this fair town's face, yonder river's line,
The mountain round it and the sky above,
Much more the figures of man, woman, child,
These are the frame to? What's it all about?
To be passed over, despised? or dwelt upon,
Wondered at? oh, this last of course!—you say.
But why not do as well as say,—paint these
Just as they are, careless what comes of it?
God's works—paint any one, and count it crime
To let a truth slip. Don't object, 'His works
'Are here already; nature is complete:
'Suppose you reproduce her—(which you can't)
'There's no advantage! you must beat her, then.'
For, don't you mark? we're made so that we love
First when we see them painted, things we have passed
Perhaps a hundred times nor cared to see;
And so they are better, painted—better to us,
Which is the same thing. Art was given for that;
God uses us to help each other so,
Lending our minds out. Have you noticed, now,
Your cullion's hanging face? A bit of chalk,
And trust me but you should, though! How much more,

If I drew higher things with the same truth!
That were to take the Prior's pulpit-place,
Interpret God to all of you! Oh, oh,
It makes me mad to see what men shall do
And we in our graves! This world's no blot for us,
Nor blank; it means intensely, and means good:
To find its meaning is my meat and drink.
'Ay, but you don't so instigate to prayer!'
Strikes in the Prior: 'when your meaning's plain
'It does not say to folk—remember matins,
'Or, mind you fast next Friday!' Why, for this
What need of art at all? A skull and bones,
Two bits of stick nailed crosswise, or, what's best,
A bell to chime the hour with, does as well.
I painted a Saint Laurence six months since
At Prato, splashed the fresco in fine style:
'How looks my painting, now the scaffold's down?'
I ask a brother: 'Hugely,' he returns—
'Already not one phiz of your three slaves
'Who turn the Deacon off his toasted side,
'But's scratched and prodded to our heart's content,
'The pious people have so eased their own
'With coming to say prayers there in a rage:
'We get on fast to see the bricks beneath.
'Expect another job this time next year,
'For pity and religion grow i' the crowd—
'Your painting serves its purpose!' Hang the fools!

—That is—you'll not mistake an idle word
Spoke in a huff by a poor monk, God wot,
Tasting the air this spicy night which turns
The unaccustomed head like Chianti wine!
Oh, the church knows! don't misreport me, now!
It's natural a poor monk out of bounds
Should have his apt word to excuse himself:
And hearken how I plot to make amends.
I have bethought me: I shall paint a piece
. . . There's for you! Give me six months, then go, see
Something in Sant' Ambrogio's! Bless the nuns!

They want a cast o' my office. I shall paint
God in the midst, Madonna and her babe,
Ringed by a bowery flowery angel-brood,
Lilies and vestments and white faces, sweet
As puff on puff of grated orris-root
When ladies crowd to church at midsummer.
And then i' the front, of course a saint or two—
Saint John, because he saves the Florentines,
Saint Ambrose, who puts down in black and white
The convent's friends and gives them a long day,
And Job, I must have him there past mistake,
The man of Uz (and Us without the z,
Painters who need his patience). Well, all these
Secured at their devotion, up shall come
Out of a corner when you least expect,
As one by a dark stair into a great light,
Music and talking, who but Lippo! I!—
Mazed, motionless and moonstruck—I'm the man!
Back I shrink—what is this I see and hear?
I, caught up with my monk's-things by mistake,
My old serge gown and rope that goes all round,
I, in this presence, this pure company!
Where's a hole, where's a corner for escape?
Then steps a sweet angelic slip of a thing
Forward, puts out a soft palm—'Not so fast!'
—Addresses the celestial presence, 'nay—
'He made you and devised you, after all,
'Though he's none of you! Could Saint John there
     draw—
'His camel-hair make up a painting-brush?
'We come to brother Lippo for all that,
'*Iste perfecit opus!*' So, all smile—
I shuffle sideways with my blushing face
Under the cover of a hundred wings
Thrown like a spread of kirtles when you're gay
And play hot cockles, all the doors being shut,
Till, wholly unexpected, in there pops
The hothead husband! Thus I scuttle off
To some safe bench behind, not letting go

The palm of her, the little lily thing
That spoke the good word for me in the nick,
Like the Prior's niece . . . Saint Lucy, I would say.
And so all's saved for me, and for the church
A pretty picture gained. Go, six months hence!
Your hand, sir, and good-bye: no lights, no lights!
The street's hushed, and I know my own way back,
Don't fear me! There's the grey beginning. Zooks!

ANDREA DEL SARTO

(CALLED 'THE FAULTLESS PAINTER')

But do not let us quarrel any more,
No, my Lucrezia; bear with me for once:
Sit down and all shall happen as you wish.
You turn your face, but does it bring your heart?
I'll work then for your friend's friend, never fear,
Treat his own subject after his own way,
Fix his own time, accept too his own price,
And shut the money into this small hand
When next it takes mine. Will it? tenderly?
Oh, I'll content him,—but to-morrow, Love!
I often am much wearier than you think,
This evening more than usual, and it seems
As if—forgive now—should you let me sit
Here by the window with your hand in mine
And look a half-hour forth on Fiesole,
Both of one mind, as married people use,
Quietly, quietly the evening through,
I might get up to-morrow to my work
Cheerful and fresh as ever. Let us try.
To-morrow, how you shall be glad for this!
Your soft hand is a woman of itself,
And mine the man's bared breast she curls inside.
Don't count the time lost, neither; you must serve
For each of the five pictures we require:
It saves a model. So! keep looking so—
My serpentining beauty, rounds on rounds!

—How could you ever prick those perfect ears,
Even to put the pearl there! oh, so sweet—
My face, my moon, my everybody's moon,
Which everybody looks on and calls his,
And, I suppose, is looked on by in turn,
While she looks—no one's: very dear, no less.
You smile? why, there's my picture ready made,
There's what we painters call our harmony!
A common greyness silvers everything,—
All in a twilight, you and I alike
—You, at the point of your first pride in me
(That's gone, you know),—but I, at every point;
My youth, my hope, my art, being all toned down
To yonder sober pleasant Fiesole.
There's the bell clinking from the chapel-top;
That length of convent-wall across the way
Holds the trees safer, huddled more inside;
The last monk leaves the garden; days decrease,
And autumn grows, autumn in everything.
Eh? the whole seems to fall into a shape
As if I saw alike my work and self
And all that I was born to be and do,
A twilight-piece. Love, we are in God's hand.
How strange now, looks the life he makes us lead;
So free we seem, so fettered fast we are!
I feel he laid the fetter: let it lie!
This chamber for example—turn your head—
All that's behind us! You don't understand
Nor care to understand about my art,
But you can hear at least when people speak:
And that cartoon, the second from the door
—It is the thing, Love! so such things should be—
Behold Madonna!—I am bold to say.
I can do with my pencil what I know,
What I see, what at bottom of my heart
I wish for, if I ever wish so deep—
Do easily, too—when I say, perfectly,
I do not boast, perhaps: yourself are judge,
Who listened to the Legate's talk last week,

And just as much they used to say in France.
At any rate 'tis easy, all of it!
No sketches first, no studies, that's long past:
I do what many dream of, all their lives,
—Dream? strive to do, and agonize to do,
And fail in doing. I could count twenty such
On twice your fingers, and not leave this town,
Who strive—you don't know how the others strive
To paint a little thing like that you smeared
Carelessly passing with your robes afloat,—
Yet do much less, so much less, Someone says,
(I know his name, no matter)—so much less!
Well, less is more, Lucrezia: I am judged.
There burns a truer light of God in them,
In their vexed beating stuffed and stopped-up brain,
Heart, or whate'er else, than goes on to prompt
This low-pulsed forthright craftsman's hand of mine.
Their works drop groundward, but themselves, I know,
Reach many a time a heaven that's shut to me,
Enter and take their place there sure enough,
Though they come back and cannot tell the world.
My works are nearer heaven, but I sit here.
The sudden blood of these men! at a word—
Praise them, it boils, or blame them, it boils too.
I, painting from myself and to myself,
Know what I do, am unmoved by men's blame
Or their praise either. Somebody remarks
Morello's outline there is wrongly traced,
His hue mistaken; what of that? or else,
Rightly traced and well ordered; what of that?
Speak as they please, what does the mountain care?
Ah, but a man's reach should exceed his grasp,
Or what's a heaven for? All is silver-grey,
Placid and perfect with my art: the worse!
I know both what I want and what might gain,
And yet how profitless to know, to sigh
'Had I been two, another and myself,
'Our head would have o'erlooked the world!' No doubt
Yonder's a work now, of that famous youth

The Urbinate who died five years ago.
('Tis copied, George Vasari sent it me.)
Well, I can fancy how he did it all,
Pouring his soul, with kings and popes to see,
Reaching, that heaven might so replenish him,
Above and through his art—for it gives way;
That arm is wrongly put—and there again—
A fault to pardon in the drawing's lines,
Its body, so to speak: its soul is right,
He means right—that, a child may understand.
Still, what an arm! and I could alter it:
But all the play, the insight and the stretch—
Out of me, out of me! And wherefore out?
Had you enjoined them on me, given me soul,
We might have risen to Rafael, I and you!
Nay, Love, you did give all I asked, I think—
More than I merit, yes, by many times.
But had you—oh, with the same perfect brow,
And perfect eyes, and more than perfect mouth,
And the low voice my soul hears, as a bird
The fowler's pipe, and follows to the snare—
Had you, with these the same, but brought a mind!
Some women do so. Had the mouth there urged
'God and the glory! never care for gain.
'The present by the future, what is that?
'Live for fame, side by side with Agnolo!
'Rafael is waiting: up to God, all three!'
I might have done it for you. So it seems:
Perhaps not. All is as God over-rules.
Beside, incentives come from the soul's self;
The rest avail not. Why do I need you?
What wife had Rafael, or has Agnolo?
In this world, who can do a thing, will not;
And who would do it, cannot, I perceive:
Yet the will's somewhat—somewhat, too, the power—
And thus we half-men struggle. At the end,
God, I conclude, compensates, punishes.
'Tis safer for me, if the award be strict,
That I am something underrated here,

Poor this long while, despised, to speak the truth.
I dared not, do you know, leave home all day,
For fear of chancing on the Paris lords.
The best is when they pass and look aside;
But they speak sometimes; I must bear it all.
Well may they speak! That Francis, that first time,
And that long festal year at Fontainebleau!
I surely then could sometimes leave the ground,
Put on the glory, Rafael's daily wear,
In that humane great monarch's golden look,—
One finger in his beard or twisted curl
Over his mouth's good mark that made the smile,
One arm about my shoulder, round my neck,
The jingle of his gold chain in my ear,
I painting proudly with his breath on me,
All his court round him, seeing with his eyes,
Such frank French eyes, and such a fire of souls
Profuse, my hand kept plying by those hearts,—
And, best of all, this, this, this face beyond,
This in the background, waiting on my work,
To crown the issue with a last reward!
A good time, was it not, my kingly days?
And had you not grown restless . . . but I know—
'Tis done and past; 'twas right, my instinct said;
Too live the life grew, golden and not grey,
And I'm the weak-eyed bat no sun should tempt
Out of the grange whose four walls make his world.
How could it end in any other way?
You called me, and I came home to your heart.
The triumph was—to reach and stay there; since
I reached it ere the triumph, what is lost?
Let my hands frame your face in your hair's gold,
You beautiful Lucrezia that are mine!
'Rafael did this, Andrea painted that;
'The Roman's is the better when you pray,
'But still the other's Virgin was his wife—'
Men will excuse me. I am glad to judge
Both pictures in your presence; clearer grows
My better fortune, I resolve to think.

For, do you know, Lucrezia, as God lives,
Said one day Agnolo, his very self,
To Rafael . . . I have known it all these years . . .
(When the young man was flaming out his thoughts
Upon a palace-wall for Rome to see,
Too lifted up in heart because of it)
'Friend, there's a certain sorry little scrub
'Goes up and down our Florence, none cares how,
'Who, were he set to plan and execute
'As you are, pricked on by your popes and kings,
'Would bring the sweat into that brow of yours!'
To Rafael's!—And indeed the arm is wrong.
I hardly dare . . . yet, only you to see,
Give the chalk here—quick, thus the line should go!
Ay, but the soul! he's Rafael! rub it out!
Still, all I care for, if he spoke the truth,
(What he? why, who but Michel Agnolo?
Do you forget already words like those?)
If really there was such a chance, so lost,—
Is, whether you're—not grateful—but more pleased.
Well, let me think so. And you smile indeed!
This hour has been an hour! Another smile?
If you would sit thus by me every night
I should work better, do you comprehend?
I mean that I should earn more, give you more.
See, it is settled dusk now; there's a star;
Morello's gone, the watch-lights show the wall,
The cue-owls speak the name we call them by.
Come from the window, love,—come in, at last,
Inside the melancholy little house
We built to be so gay with. God is just.
King Francis may forgive me: oft at nights
When I look up from painting, eyes tired out,
The walls become illumined, brick from brick
Distinct, instead of mortar, fierce bright gold,
That gold of his I did cement them with!
Let us but love each other. Must you go?
That Cousin here again? he waits outside?
Must see you—you, and not with me? Those loans?

More gaming debts to pay? you smiled for that?
Well, let smiles buy me! have you more to spend?
While hand and eye and something of a heart
Are left me, work's my ware, and what's it worth?
I'll pay my fancy. Only let me sit
The grey remainder of the evening out,
Idle, you call it, and muse perfectly
How I could paint, were I but back in France,
One picture, just one more—the Virgin's face,
Not yours this time! I want you at my side
To hear them—that is, Michel Agnolo—
Judge all I do and tell you of its worth.
Will you? To-morrow, satisfy your friend.
I take the subjects for his corridor,
Finish the portrait out of hand—there, there,
And throw him in another thing or two
If he demurs; the whole should prove enough
To pay for this same Cousin's freak. Beside,
What's better and what's all I care about,
Get you the thirteen scudi for the ruff!
Love, does that please you? Ah, but what does he,
The Cousin! what does he to please you more?

I am grown peaceful as old age to-night.
I regret little, I would change still less.
Since there my past life lies, why alter it?
The very wrong to Francis!—it is true
I took his coin, was tempted and complied,
And built this house and sinned, and all is said.
My father and my mother died of want.
Well, had I riches of my own? you see
How one gets rich! Let each one bear his lot.
They were born poor, lived poor, and poor they died:
And I have laboured somewhat in my time
And not been paid profusely. Some good son
Paint my two hundred pictures—let him try!
No doubt, there's something strikes a balance. Yes,
You loved me quite enough, it seems to-night.
This must suffice me here. What would one have?

In heaven, perhaps, new chances, one more chance—
Four great walls in the New Jerusalem,
Meted on each side by the angel's reed,
For Leonard, Rafael, Agnolo and me
To cover—the three first without a wife,
While I have mine! So—still they overcome
Because there's still Lucrezia,—as I choose.

Again the Cousin's whistle! Go, my Love.

THE BISHOP ORDERS HIS TOMB AT SAINT PRAXED'S CHURCH

ROME, 15—

VANITY, saith the preacher, vanity!
Draw round my bed: is Anselm keeping back?
Nephews—sons mine . . . ah God, I know not! Well—
She, men would have to be your mother once,
Old Gandolf envied me, so fair she was!
What's done is done, and she is dead beside,
Dead long ago, and I am Bishop since,
And as she died so must we die ourselves,
And thence ye may perceive the world's a dream.
Life, how and what is it? As here I lie
In this state-chamber, dying by degrees,
Hours and long hours in the dead night, I ask
'Do I live, am I dead?' Peace, peace seems all.
Saint Praxed's ever was the church for peace;
And so, about this tomb of mine. I fought
With tooth and nail to save my niche, ye know:
—Old Gandolf cozened me, despite my care;
Shrewd was that snatch from out the corner South
He graced his carrion with, God curse the same!
Yet still my niche is not so cramped but thence
One sees the pulpit o' the epistle-side,
And somewhat of the choir, those silent seats,
And up into the aery dome where live
The angels, and a sunbeam's sure to lurk:
And I shall fill my slab of basalt there,

And 'neath my tabernacle take my rest,
With those nine columns round me, two and two,
The odd one at my feet where Anselm stands:
Peach-blossom marble all, the rare, the ripe
As fresh-poured red wine of a mighty pulse.
—Old Gandolf with his paltry onion-stone,
Put me where I may look at him! True peach,
Rosy and flawless: how I earned the prize!
Draw close: that conflagration of my church
—What then? So much was saved if aught were missed!
My sons, ye would not be my death? Go dig
The white-grape vineyard where the oil-press stood,
Drop water gently till the surface sink,
And if ye find . . . Ah God, I know not, I! . . .
Bedded in store of rotten fig-leaves soft,
And corded up in a tight olive-frail,
Some lump, ah God, of *lapis lazuli*,
Big as a Jew's head cut off at the nape,
Blue as a vein o'er the Madonna's breast . . .
Sons, all have I bequeathed you, villas, all,
That brave Frascati villa with its bath,
So, let the blue lump poise between my knees,
Like God the Father's globe on both his hands
Ye worship in the Jesu Church so gay,
For Gandolf shall not choose but see and burst!
Swift as a weaver's shuttle fleet our years:
Man goeth to the grave, and where is he?
Did I say basalt for my slab, sons? Black—
'Twas ever antique-black I meant! How else
Shall ye contrast my frieze to come beneath?
The bas-relief in bronze ye promised me,
Those Pans and Nymphs ye wot of, and perchance
Some tripod, thyrsus, with a vase or so,
The Saviour at his sermon on the mount,
Saint Praxed in a glory, and one Pan
Ready to twitch the Nymph's last garment off,
And Moses with the tables . . . but I know
Ye mark me not! What do they whisper thee,
Child of my bowels, Anselm? Ah, ye hope

To revel down my villas while I gasp
Bricked o'er with beggar's mouldy travertine
Which Gandolf from his tomb-top chuckles at!
Nay, boys, ye love me—all of jasper, then!
'Tis jasper ye stand pledged to, lest I grieve.
My bath must needs be left behind, alas!
One block, pure green as a pistachio-nut,
There's plenty jasper somewhere in the world—
And have I not Saint Praxed's ear to pray
Horses for ye, and brown Greek manuscripts,
And mistresses with great smooth marbly limbs?
—That's if ye carve my epitaph aright,
Choice Latin, picked phrase, Tully's every word,
No gaudy ware like Gandolf's second line—
Tully, my masters? Ulpian serves his need!
And then how I shall lie through centuries,
And hear the blessed mutter of the mass,
And see God made and eaten all day long,
And feel the steady candle-flame, and taste
Good strong thick stupefying incense-smoke!
For as I lie here, hours of the dead night,
Dying in state and by such slow degrees,
I fold my arms as if they clasped a crook,
And stretch my feet forth straight as stone can point,
And let the bedclothes, for a mortcloth, drop
Into great laps and folds of sculptor's-work:
And as yon tapers dwindle, and strange thoughts
Grow, with a certain humming in my ears,
About the life before I lived this life,
And this life too, popes, cardinals and priests,
Saint Praxed at his sermon on the mount,
Your tall pale mother with her talking eyes,
And new-found agate urns as fresh as day,
And marble's language, Latin pure, discreet,
—Aha, ELUCESCEBAT quoth our friend?
No Tully, said I, Ulpian at the best!
Evil and brief hath been my pilgrimage.
All *lapis*, all, sons! Else I give the Pope
My villas! Will ye ever eat my heart?

Ever your eyes were as a lizard's quick,
The glitter like your mother's for my soul,
Or ye would heighten my impoverished frieze,
Piece out its starved design, and fill my vase
With grapes, and add a vizor and a Term,
And to the tripod ye would tie a lynx
That in his struggle throws the thyrsus down,
To comfort me on my entablature
Whereon I am to lie till I must ask
'Do I live, am I dead?' There, leave me, there!
For ye have stabbed me with ingratitude
To death—ye wish it—God, ye wish it! Stone—
Gritstone, a-crumble! Clammy squares which sweat
As if the corpse they keep were oozing through—
And no more *lapis* to delight the world!
Well go! I bless ye. Fewer tapers there,
But in a row: and, going, turn your backs
—Ay, like departing altar-ministrants,
And leave me in my church, the church for peace,
That I may watch at leisure if he leers—
Old Gandolf, at me, from his onion-stone,
As still he envied me, so fair she was!

BISHOP BLOUGRAM'S APOLOGY

No more wine? then we'll push back chairs and talk.
A final glass for me, though: cool, i' faith!
We ought to have our Abbey back, you see.
It's different, preaching in basilicas,
And doing duty in some masterpiece
Like this of brother Pugin's, bless his heart!
I doubt if they're half baked, those chalk rosettes,
Ciphers and stucco-twiddlings everywhere;
It's just like breathing in a lime-kiln: eh?
These hot long ceremonies of our church
Cost us a little—oh, they pay the price,
You take me—amply pay it! Now, we'll talk.

So, you despise me, Mr. Gigadibs.
No deprecation,—nay, I beg you, sir!
Beside 'tis our engagement: don't you know,
I promised, if you'd watch a dinner out,
We'd see truth dawn together?—truth that peeps
Over the glasses' edge when dinner's done,
And body gets its sop and holds its noise
And leaves soul free a little. Now 's the time:
Truth's break of day! You do despise me then.
And if I say, 'despise me,'—never fear!
I know you do not in a certain sense—
Not in my arm-chair, for example: here,
I well imagine you respect my place
(*Status, entourage*, worldly circumstance)
Quite to its value—very much indeed:
—Are up to the protesting eyes of you
In pride at being seated here for once—
You'll turn it to such capital account!
When somebody, through years and years to come,
Hints of the bishop,—names me—that's enough:
'Blougram? I knew him'—(into it you slide)
'Dined with him once, a Corpus Christi Day,
'All alone, we two; he's a clever man:
'And after dinner,—why, the wine you know,—
'Oh, there was wine, and good!—what with the wine . . .
''Faith, we began upon all sorts of talk!
'He's no bad fellow, Blougram; he had seen
'Something of mine he relished, some review:
'He's quite above their humbug in his heart,
'Half-said as much, indeed—the thing's his trade.
'I warrant, Blougram's sceptical at times:
'How otherwise? I liked him, I confess!'
Che che, my dear sir, as we say at Rome,
Don't you protest now! It's fair give and take;
You have had your turn and spoken your home-truths:
The hand's mine now, and here you follow suit.

Thus much conceded, still the first fact stays—
You do despise me; your ideal of life

Is not the bishop's: you would not be I.
You would like better to be Goethe, now,
Or Buonaparte, or, bless me, lower still,
Count D'Orsay,—so you did what you preferred,
Spoke as you thought, and, as you cannot help,
Believed or disbelieved, no matter what,
So long as on that point, whate'er it was,
You loosed your mind, were whole and sole yourself.
—That, my ideal never can include,
Upon that element of truth and worth
Never be based! for say they make me Pope—
(They can't—suppose it for our argument!)
Why, there I'm at my tether's end, I've reached
My height, and not a height which pleases you:
An unbelieving Pope won't do, you say.
It's like those eerie stories nurses tell,
Of how some actor on a stage played Death,
With pasteboard crown, sham orb and tinselled dart,
And called himself the monarch of the world;
Then, going in the tire-room afterward,
Because the play was done, to shift himself,
Got touched upon the sleeve familiarly,
The moment he had shut the closet door,
By Death himself. Thus God might touch a Pope
At unawares, ask what his baubles mean,
And whose part he presumed to play just now.
Best be yourself, imperial, plain and true!

So, drawing comfortable breath again,
You weigh and find, whatever more or less
I boast of my ideal realized
Is nothing in the balance when opposed
To your ideal, your grand simple life,
Of which you will not realize one jot.
I am much, you are nothing; you would be all,
I would be merely much: you beat me there.
No, friend, you do not beat me: hearken why!
The common problem, yours, mine, every one's,
Is—not to fancy what were fair in life

Provided it could be,—but, finding first
What may be, then find how to make it fair
Up to our means: a very different thing!
No abstract intellectual plan of life
Quite irrespective of life's plainest laws,
But one, a man, who is man and nothing more,
May lead within a world which (by your leave)
Is Rome or London, not Fool's-paradise.
Embellish Rome, idealize away,
Make paradise of London if you can,
You're welcome, nay, you're wise.

                                        A simile!
We mortals cross the ocean of this world
Each in his average cabin of a life;
The best's not big, the worst yields elbow-room.
Now for our six months' voyage—how prepare?
You come on shipboard with a landsman's list
Of things he calls convenient: so they are!
An India screen is pretty furniture,
A piano-forte is a fine resource,
All Balzac's novels occupy one shelf,
The new edition fifty volumes long;
And little Greek books, with the funny type
They get up well at Leipsic, fill the next:
Go on! slabbed marble, what a bath it makes!
And Parma's pride, the Jerome, let us add!
'Twere pleasant could Correggio's fleeting glow
Hang full in face of one where'er one roams,
Since he more than the others brings with him
Italy's self,—the marvellous Modenese!—
Yet was not on your list before, perhaps.
—Alas, friend, here's the agent . . . is't the name?
The captain, or whoever's master here—
You see him screw his face up; what's his cry
Ere you set foot on shipboard? 'Six feet square!'
If you won't understand what six feet mean,
Compute and purchase stores accordingly—
And if, in pique because he overhauls

Your Jerome, piano, bath, you come on board
Bare—why, you cut a figure at the first
While sympathetic landsmen see you off;
Not afterward, when long ere half seas over,
You peep up from your utterly naked boards
Into some snug and well-appointed berth,
Like mine for instance (try the cooler jug—
Put back the other, but don't jog the ice!)
And mortified you mutter 'Well and good;
'He sits enjoying his sea-furniture;
''Tis stout and proper, and there's store of it:
'Though I've the better notion, all agree,
'Of fitting rooms up. Hang the carpenter,
'Neat ship-shape fixings and contrivances—
'I would have brought my Jerome, frame and all!'
And meantime you bring nothing: never mind—
You've proved your artist-nature: what you don't
You might bring, so despise me, as I say.

Now come, let's backward to the starting-place.
See my way: we're two college friends, suppose.
Prepare together for our voyage, then;
Each note and check the other in his work,—
Here's mine, a bishop's outfit: criticize!
What's wrong? why won't you be a bishop too?

Why first, you don't believe, you don't and can't,
(Not statedly, that is, and fixedly
And absolutely and exclusively)
In any revelation called divine.
No dogmas nail your faith; and what remains
But say so, like the honest man you are?
First, therefore, overhaul theology!
Nay, I too, not a fool, you please to think,
Must find believing every whit as hard:
And if I do not frankly say as much,
The ugly consequence is clear enough.

Now wait, my friend: well, I do not believe—
If you'll accept no faith that is not fixed,

Absolute and exclusive, as you say.
You're wrong—I mean to prove it in due time.
Meanwhile, I know where difficulties lie
I could not, cannot solve, nor ever shall,
So give up hope accordingly to solve—
(To you, and over the wine). Our dogmas then
With both of us, though in unlike degree,
Missing full credence—overboard with them!
I mean to meet you on your own premise:
Good, there go mine in company with yours!

And now what are we? unbelievers both,
Calm and complete, determinately fixed
To-day, to-morrow and for ever, pray?
You'll guarantee me that? Not so, I think!
In no wise! all we've gained is, that belief,
As unbelief before, shakes us by fits,
Confounds us like its predecessor. Where's
The gain? how can we guard our unbelief,
Make it bear fruit to us?—the problem here.
Just when we are safest, there's a sunset-touch,
A fancy from a flower-bell, some one's death,
A chorus-ending from Euripides,—
And that's enough for fifty hopes and fears
As old and new at once as nature's self,
To rap and knock and enter in our soul,
Take hands and dance there, a fantastic ring,
Round the ancient idol, on his base again,—
The grand Perhaps! We look on helplessly.
There the old misgivings, crooked questions are—
This good God,—what he could do, if he would,
Would, if he could—then must have done long since:
If so, when, where and how? some way must be,—
Once feel about, and soon or late you hit
Some sense, in which it might be, after all.
Why not, 'The Way, the Truth, the Life'?

                                        —That way
Over the mountain, which who stands upon
Is apt to doubt if it be meant for a road;

While, if he views it from the waste itself,
Up goes the line there, plain from base to brow,
Not vague, mistakeable! what's a break or two
Seen from the unbroken desert either side?
And then (to bring in fresh philosophy)
What if the breaks themselves should prove at last
The most consummate of contrivances
To train a man's eye, teach him what is faith?
And so we stumble at truth's very test!
All we have gained then by our unbelief
Is a life of doubt diversified by faith,
For one of faith diversified by doubt:
We called the chess-board white,—we call it black.

'Well,' you rejoin, 'the end's no worse, at least
'We've reason for both colours on the board:
'Why not confess then, where I drop the faith
'And you the doubt, that I'm as right as you?'

Because, friend, in the next place, this being so,
And both things even,—faith and unbelief
Left to a man's choice,—we'll proceed a step,
Returning to our image, which I like.

A man's choice, yes—but a cabin-passenger's—
The man made for the special life o' the world—
Do you forget him? I remember though!
Consult our ship's conditions and you find
One and but one choice suitable to all,
The choice, that you unluckily prefer,
Turning things topsy-turvy—they or it
Going to the ground. Belief or unbelief
Bears upon life, determines its whole course,
Begins at its beginning. See the world
Such as it is,—you made it not, nor I;
I mean to take it as it is,—and you,
Not so you'll take it,—though you get nought else.
I know the special kind of life I like,
What suits the most my idiosyncrasy.

Brings out the best of me and bears me fruit
In power, peace, pleasantness and length of days.
I find that positive belief does this
For me, and unbelief, no whit of this.
—For you, it does, however?—that, we'll try!
'Tis clear, I cannot lead my life, at least,
Induce the world to let me peaceably,
Without declaring at the outset, 'Friends,
'I absolutely and peremptorily
'Believe!'—I say, faith is my waking life:
One sleeps, indeed, and dreams at intervals,
We know, but waking's the main point with us,
And my provision's for life's waking part.
Accordingly, I use heart, head and hand
All day, I build, scheme, study, and make friends;
And when night overtakes me, down I lie,
Sleep, dream a little, and get done with it,
The sooner the better, to begin afresh.
What's midnight doubt before the dayspring's faith?
You, the philosopher, that disbelieve,
That recognize the night, give dreams their weight—
To be consistent you should keep your bed,
Abstain from healthy acts that prove you man,
For fear you drowse perhaps at unawares!
And certainly at night you'll sleep and dream,
Live through the day and bustle as you please.
And so you live to sleep as I to wake,
To unbelieve as I to still believe?
Well, and the common sense o' the world calls you
Bed-ridden,—and its good things come to me.
Its estimation, which is half the fight,
That's the first-cabin comfort I secure:
The next . . . but you perceive with half an eye!
Come, come, it's best believing, if we may;
You can't but own that!

                        Next, concede again,
If once we choose belief, on all accounts
We can't be too decisive in our faith,

Conclusive and exclusive in its terms,
To suit the world which gives us the good things.
In every man's career are certain points
Whereon he dares not be indifferent;
The world detects him clearly, if he dare,
As baffled at the game, and losing life.
He may care little or he may care much
For riches, honour, pleasure, work, repose,
Since various theories of life and life's
Success are extant which might easily
Comport with either estimate of these;
And whoso chooses wealth or poverty,
Labour or quiet, is not judged a fool
Because his fellow would choose otherwise:
We let him choose upon his own account
So long as he's consistent with his choice.
But certain points, left wholly to himself,
When once a man has arbitrated on,
We say he must succeed there or go hang.
Thus, he should wed the woman he loves most
Or needs most, whatsoe'er the love or need—
For he can't wed twice. Then, he must avouch,
Or follow, at the least, sufficiently,
The form of faith his conscience holds the best,
Whate'er the process of conviction was:
For nothing can compensate his mistake
On such a point, the man himself being judge:
He cannot wed twice, nor twice lose his soul.

    Well now, there's one great form of Christian faith
I happened to be born in—which to teach
Was given me as I grew up, on all hands,
As best and readiest means of living by;
The same on examination being proved
The most pronounced moreover, fixed, precise
And absolute form of faith in the whole world—
Accordingly, most potent of all forms
For working on the world. Observe, my friend!
Such as you know me, I am free to say,

In these hard latter days which hamper one,
Myself—by no immoderate exercise
Of intellect and learning, but the tact
To let external forces work for me,
—Bid the street's stones be bread and they are bread;
Bid Peter's creed, or rather, Hildebrand's,
Exalt me o'er my fellows in the world
And make my life an ease and joy and pride;
It does so,—which for me's a great point gained,
Who have a soul and body that exact
A comfortable care in many ways.
There's power in me and will to dominate
Which I must exercise, they hurt me else:
In many ways I need mankind's respect,
Obedience, and the love that's born of fear:
While at the same time, there's a taste I have,
A toy of soul, a titillating thing,
Refuses to digest these dainties crude.
The naked life is gross till clothed upon:
I must take what men offer, with a grace
As though I would not, could I help it, take!
An uniform I wear though over-rich—
Something imposed on me, no choice of mine;
No fancy-dress worn for pure fancy's sake
And despicable therefore! now folk kneel
And kiss my hand—of course the Church's hand.
Thus I am made, thus life is best for me,
And thus that it should be I have procured;
And thus it could not be another way,
I venture to imagine.

                    You'll reply,
So far my choice, no doubt, is a success;
But were I made of better elements,
With nobler instincts, purer tastes, like you,
I hardly would account the thing success
Though it did all for me I say.

                    But, friend,
We speak of what is; not of what might be,

And how 'twere better if 'twere otherwise.
I am the man you see here plain enough:
Grant I'm a beast, why, beasts must lead beasts' lives!
Suppose I own at once to tail and claws;
The tailless man exceeds me: but being tailed
I'll lash out lion-fashion, and leave apes
To dock their stump and dress their haunches up.
My business is not to remake myself,
But make the absolute best of what God made.
Or—our first simile—though you prove me doomed
To a viler berth still, to the steerage-hole,
The sheep-pen or the pig-stye, I should strive
To make what use of each were possible;
And as this cabin gets upholstery,
That hutch should rustle with sufficient straw.

But, friend, I don't acknowledge quite so fast
I fail of all your manhood's lofty tastes
Enumerated so complacently,
On the mere ground that you forsooth can find
In this particular life I choose to lead
No fit provision for them. Can you not?
Say you, my fault is I address myself
To grosser estimators than should judge?
And that's no way of holding up the soul,
Which, nobler, needs men's praise perhaps, yet knows
One wise man's verdict outweighs all the fools'—
Would like the two, but, forced to choose, takes that.
I pine among my million imbeciles
(You think) aware some dozen men of sense
Eye me and know me, whether I believe
In the last winking Virgin, as I vow,
And am a fool, or disbelieve in her
And am a knave,—approve in neither case,
Withhold their voices though I look their way:
Like Verdi when, at his worst opera's end
(The thing they gave at Florence,—what's its name?)
While the mad houseful's plaudits near outbang
His orchestra of salt-box, tongs and bones,

He looks through all the roaring and the wreaths
Where sits Rossini patient in his stall.

Nay, friend, I meet you with an answer here—
That even your prime men who appraise their kind
Are men still, catch a wheel within a wheel,
See more in a truth than the truth's simple self,
Confuse themselves. You see lads walk the street
Sixty the minute; what's to note in that?
You see one lad o'erstride a chimney-stack;
Him you must watch—he's sure to fall, yet stands!
Our interest's on the dangerous edge of things.
The honest thief, the tender murderer,
The superstitious atheist, demirep
That loves and saves her soul in new French books—
We watch while these in equilibrium keep
The giddy line midway: one step aside,
They're classed and done with. I, then, keep the line
Before your sages,—just the men to shrink
From the gross weights, coarse scales and labels broad
You offer their refinement. Fool or knave?
Why needs a bishop be a fool or knave
When there's a thousand diamond weights between?
So, I enlist them. Your picked twelve, you'll find,
Profess themselves indignant, scandalized
At thus being held unable to explain
How a superior man who disbelieves
May not believe as well: that's Schelling's way!
It's through my coming in the tail of time,
Nicking the minute with a happy tact.
Had I been born three hundred years ago
They'd say, 'What's strange? Blougram of course
    believes;'
And, seventy years since, 'disbelieves of course.'
But now, 'He may believe; and yet, and yet
'How can he?' All eyes turn with interest.
Whereas, step off the line on either side—
You, for example, clever to a fault,
The rough and ready man who write apace,

Read somewhat seldomer, think perhaps even less—
You disbelieve! Who wonders and who cares?
Lord So-and-so—his coat bedropped with wax,
All Peter's chains about his waist, his back
Brave with the needlework of Noodledom—
Believes! Again, who wonders and who cares?
But I, the man of sense and learning too,
The able to think yet act, the this, the that,
I, to believe at this late time of day!
Enough; you see, I need not fear contempt.

　　—Except it's yours! Admire me as these may,
You don't. But whom at least do you admire?
Present your own perfection, your ideal,
Your pattern man for a minute—oh, make haste!
Is it Napoleon you would have us grow?
Concede the means; allow his head and hand,
(A large concession, clever as you are)
Good! In our common primal element
Of unbelief (we can't believe, you know—
We're still at that admission, recollect!)
Where do you find—apart from, towering o'er
The secondary temporary aims
Which satisfy the gross taste you despise—
Where do you find his star?—his crazy trust
God knows through what or in what? it's alive
And shines and leads him, and that's all we want.
Have we aught in our sober night shall point
Such ends as his were, and direct the means
Of working out our purpose straight as his,
Nor bring a moment's trouble on success
With after-care to justify the same?
—Be a Napoleon, and yet disbelieve—
Why, the man's mad, friend, take his light away!
What's the vague good o' the world, for which you
　　dare
With comfort to yourself blow millions up?
We neither of us see it! we do see
The blown-up millions—spatter of their brains

And writing of their bowels and so forth,
In that bewildering entanglement
Of horrible eventualities
Past calculation to the end of time!
Can I mistake for some clear word of God
(Which were my ample warrant for it all)
His puff of hazy instinct, idle talk,
'The State, that's I,' quack-nonsense about crowns,
And (when one beats the man to his last hold)
A vague idea of setting things to rights,
Policing people efficaciously,
More to their profit, most of all to his own;
The whole to end that dismallest of ends
By an Austrian marriage, cant to us the Church,
And resurrection of the old *régime*?
Would I, who hope to live a dozen years,
Fight Austerlitz for reasons such and such?
No: for, concede me but the merest chance
Doubt may be wrong—there's judgment, life to come!
With just that chance, I dare not. Doubt proves right?
This present life is all?—you offer me
Its dozen noisy years, without a chance
That wedding an archduchess, wearing lace,
And getting called by divers new-coined names,
Will drive off ugly thoughts and let me dine,
Sleep, read and chat in quiet as I like!
Therefore I will not.

                    Take another case
Fit up the cabin yet another way.
What say you to the poets? shall we write
Hamlet, Othello—make the world our own,
Without a risk to run of either sort?
I can't!—to put the strongest reason first.
'But try,' you urge, 'the trying shall suffice;
'The aim, if reached or not, makes great the life:
'Try to be Shakespeare, leave the rest to fate!'
Spare my self-knowledge—there's no fooling me!
If I prefer remaining my poor self,

I say so not in self-dispraise but praise.
If I'm a Shakespeare, let the well alone;
Why should I try to be what now I am?
If I'm no Shakespeare, as too probable,—
His power and consciousness and self-delight
And all we want in common, shall I find—
Trying for ever? while on points of taste
Wherewith, to speak it humbly, he and I
Are dowered alike—I'll ask you, I or he,
Which in our two lives realizes most?
Much, he imagined—somewhat, I possess.
He had the imagination; stick to that!
Let him say, 'In the face of my soul's works
'Your world is worthless and I touch it not
'Lest I should wrong them'—I'll withdraw my plea.
But does he say so? look upon his life!
Himself, who only can, gives judgment there.
He leaves his towers and gorgeous palaces
To build the trimmest house in Stratford town;
Saves money, spends it, owns the worth of things,
Giulio Romano's pictures, Dowland's lute;
Enjoys a show, respects the puppets, too,
And none more, had he seen its entry once,
Than 'Pandulph, of fair Milan cardinal.'
Why then should I who play that personage,
The very Pandulph Shakespeare's fancy made,
Be told that had the poet chanced to start
From where I stand now (some degree like mine
Being just the goal he ran his race to reach)
He would have run the whole race back, forsooth,
And left being Pandulph, to begin write plays?
Ah, the earth's best can be but the earth's best!
Did Shakespeare live, he could but sit at home
And get himself in dreams the Vatican,
Greek busts, Venetian paintings, Roman walls,
And English books, none equal to his own,
Which I read, bound in gold (he never did).
—Terni's fall, Naples' bay and Gothard's top—
Eh, friend? I could not fancy one of these;

But, as I pour this claret, there they are:
I've gained them—crossed St. Gothard last July
With ten mules to the carriage and a bed
Slung inside; is my hap the worse for that?
We want the same things, Shakespeare and myself,
And what I want, I have: he, gifted more,
Could fancy he too had them when he liked,
But not so thoroughly that, if fate allowed,
He would not have them also in my sense.
We play one game; I send the ball aloft
No less adroitly that of fifty strokes
Scarce five go o'er the wall so wide and high
Which sends them back to me: I wish and get.
He struck balls higher and with better skill,
But at a poor fence level with his head,
And hit—his Stratford house, a coat of arms,
Successful dealings in his grain and wool,—
While I receive heaven's incense in my nose
And style myself the cousin of Queen Bess.
Ask him, if this life's all, who wins the game?

Believe—and our whole argument breaks up.
Enthusiasm's the best thing, I repeat;
Only, we can't command it; fire and life
Are all, dead matter's nothing, we agree:
And be it a mad dream or God's very breath,
The fact's the same,—belief's fire, once in us,
Makes of all else mere stuff to show itself:
We penetrate our life with such a glow
As fire lends wood and iron—this turns steel,
That burns to ash—all's one, fire proves its power
For good or ill, since men call flare success.
But paint a fire, it will not therefore burn.
Light one in me, I'll find it food enough!
Why, to be Luther—that's a life to lead,
Incomparably better than my own.
He comes, reclaims God's earth for God, he says,
Sets up God's rule again by simple means,
Re-opens a shut book, and all is done.

He flared out in the flaring of mankind;
Such Luther's luck was: how shall such be mine?
If he succeeded, nothing's left to do:
And if he did not altogether—well,
Strauss is the next advance. All Strauss should be
I might be also. But to what result?
He looks upon no future: Luther did.
What can I gain on the denying side?
Ice makes no conflagration. State the facts,
Read the text right, emancipate the world—
The emancipated world enjoys itself
With scarce a thank-you: Blougram told it first
It could not owe a farthing,—not to him
More than Saint Paul! 'twould press its pay, you
        think?
Then add there's still that plaguy hundredth chance
Strauss may be wrong. And so a risk is run—
For what gain? not for Luther's, who secured
A real heaven in his heart throughout his life,
Supposing death a little altered things.

  'Ay, but since really you lack faith,' you cry,
'You run the same risk really on all sides,
'In cool indifference as bold unbelief.
'As well be Strauss as swing 'twixt Paul and him.
'It's not worth having, such imperfect faith,
'No more available to do faith's work
'Than unbelief like mine. Whole faith, or none!'

  Softly, my friend! I must dispute that point.
Once own the use of faith, I'll find you faith.
We're back on Christian ground. You call for faith:
I show you doubt, to prove that faith exists.
The more of doubt, the stronger faith, I say,
If faith o'ercomes doubt. How I know it does?
By life and man's free will, God gave for that!
To mould life as we choose it, shows our choice:
That's our one act, the previous work's his own.
You criticize the soul? it reared this tree—

This broad life and whatever fruit it bears!
What matter though I doubt at every pore,
Head-doubts, doubts at my fingers' ends,
Doubts in the trivial work of every day,
Doubts at the very bases of my soul
In the grand moments when she probes herself—
If finally I have a life to show,
The thing I did, brought out in evidence
Against the thing done to me underground
By hell and all its brood, for aught I know?
I say, whence sprang this? shows it faith or doubt?
All's doubt in me; where's break of faith in this?
It is the idea, the feeling and the love,
God means mankind should strive for and show forth
Whatever be the process to that end,—
And not historic knowledge, logic sound,
And metaphysical acumen, sure!
'What think ye of Christ,' friend? when all's done and
    said,
Like you this Christianity or not?
It may be false, but will you wish it true?
Has it your vote to be so if it can?
Trust you an instinct silenced long ago
That will break silence and enjoin you love
What mortified philosophy is hoarse,
And all in vain, with bidding you despise?
If you desire faith—then you've faith enough:
What else seeks God—nay, what else seek ourselves?
You form a notion of me, we'll suppose,
On hearsay; it's a favourable one:
'But still' (you add), 'there was no such good man,
'Because of contradiction in the facts.
'One proves, for instance, he was born in Rome,
'This Blougram; yet throughout the tales of him
'I see he figures as an Englishman.'
Well, the two things are reconcileable.
But would I rather you discovered that,
Subjoining—'Still, what matter though they be?
'Blougram concerns me nought, born here or there.'

Pure faith indeed—you know not what you ask!
Naked belief in God the Omnipotent,
Omniscient, Omnipresent, sears too much
The sense of conscious creatures to be borne.
It were the seeing him, no flesh shall dare.
Some think, Creation's meant to show him forth:
I say it's meant to hide him all it can,
And that's what all the blessed evil's for.
Its use in Time is to environ us,
Our breath, our drop of dew, with shield enough
Against that sight till we can bear its stress.
Under a vertical sun, the exposed brain
And lidless eye and disemprisoned heart
Less certainly would wither up at once
Than mind, confronted with the truth of him.
But time and earth case-harden us to live;
The feeblest sense is trusted most, the child
Feels God a moment, ichors o'er the place,
Plays on and grows to be a man like us.
With me, faith means perpetual unbelief
Kept quiet like the snake 'neath Michael's foot
Who stands calm just because he feels it writhe.
Or, if that's too ambitious,—here's my box—
I need the excitation of a pinch
Threatening the torpor of the inside-nose
Nigh on the imminent sneeze that never comes.
'Leave it in peace' advise the simple folk:
Make it aware of peace by itching-fits,
Say I—let doubt occasion still more faith!

You'll say, once all believed, man, woman, child,
In that dear middle-age these noodles praise.
How you'd exult if I could put you back
Six hundred years, blot out cosmogony,
Geology, ethnology, what not,
(Greek endings, each the little passing-bell
That signifies some faith's about to die),
And set you square with Genesis again,—
When such a traveller told you his last news,

He saw the ark a-top of Ararat
But did not climb there since 'twas getting dusk
And robber-bands infest the mountain's foot!
How should you feel, I ask, in such an age,
How act? As other people felt and did;
With soul more blank than this decanter's knob,
Believe—and yet lie, kill, rob, fornicate
Full in belief's face, like the beast you'd be!

No, when the fight begins within himself,
A man's worth something. God stoops o'er his head,
Satan looks up between his feet—both tug—
He's left, himself, i' the middle: the soul wakes
And grows. Prolong that battle through his life!
Never leave growing till the life to come!
Here, we've got callous to the Virgin's winks
That used to puzzle people wholesomely:
Men have outgrown the shame of being fools.
What are the laws of nature, not to bend
If the Church bid them?—brother Newman asks.
Up with the Immaculate Conception, then—
On to the rack with faith!—is my advice.
Will not that hurry us upon our knees,
Knocking our breasts, 'It can't be—yet it shall!
'Who am I, the worm, to argue with my Pope?
'Low things confound the high things!' and so forth.
That's better than acquitting God with grace
As some folk do. He's tried—no case is proved,
Philosophy is lenient—he may go!

You'll say, the old system's not so obsolete
But men believe still: ay, but who and where?
King Bomba's lazzaroni foster yet
The sacred flame, so Antonelli writes;
But even of these, what ragamuffin-saint
Believes God watches him continually,
As he believes in fire that it will burn,
Or rain that it will drench him? Break fire's law,
Sin against rain, although the penalty

Be just a singe or soaking? 'No,' he smiles;
'Those laws are laws that can enforce themselves.'

The sum of all is—yes, my doubt is great,
My faith's still greater, then my faith's enough.
I have read much, thought much, experienced much,
Yet would die rather than avow my fear
The Naples' liquefaction may be false,
When set to happen by the palace-clock
According to the clouds or dinner-time.
I hear you recommend, I might at least
Eliminate, decrassify my faith
Since I adopt it; keeping what I must
And leaving what I can—such points as this.
I won't—that is, I can't throw one away.
Supposing there's no truth in what I hold
About the need of trial to man's faith,
Still, when you bid me purify the same,
To such a process I discern no end.
Clearing off one excrescence to see two,
There's ever a next in size, now grown as big,
That meets the knife: I cut and cut again!
First cut the Liquefaction, what comes last
But Fichte's clever cut at God himself?
Experimentalize on sacred things!
I trust nor hand nor eye nor heart nor brain
To stop betimes: they all get drunk alike.
The first step, I am master not to take.

You'd find the cutting-process to your taste
As much as leaving growths of lies unpruned,
Nor see more danger in it,—you retort.
Your taste's worth mine; but my taste proves more wise
When we consider that the steadfast hold
On the extreme end of the chain of faith
Gives the advantage, makes the difference
With the rough purblind mass we seek to rule:
We are their lords, or they are free of us,
Just as we tighten or relax our hold.

So, other matters equal, we'll revert
To the first problem—which, if solved my way
And thrown into the balance, turns the scale—
How we may lead a comfortable life,
How suit our luggage to the cabin's size.

Of course you are remarking all this time
How narrowly and grossly I view life,
Respect the creature-comforts, care to rule
The masses, and regard complacently
'The cabin,' in our old phrase. Well, I do.
I act for, talk for, live for this world now,
As this world prizes action, life and talk:
No prejudice to what next world may prove,
Whose new laws and requirements, my best pledge
To observe then, is that I observe these now,
Shall do hereafter what I do meanwhile.
Let us concede (gratuitously though)
Next life relieves the soul of body, yields
Pure spiritual enjoyment: well, my friend,
Why lose this life i' the meantime, since its use
May be to make the next life more intense?

Do you know, I have often had a dream
(Work it up in your next month's article)
Of man's poor spirit in its progress, still
Losing true life for ever and a day
Through ever trying to be and ever being—
In the evolution of successive spheres—
Before its actual sphere and place of life,
Halfway into the next, which having reached,
It shoots with corresponding foolery
Halfway into the next still, on and off!
As when a traveller, bound from North to South,
Scouts fur in Russia: what's its use in France?
In France spurns flannel: where's its need in Spain?
In Spain drops cloth, too cumbrous for Algiers!
Linen goes next, and last the skin itself,
A superfluity at Timbuctoo.
When, through his journey, was the fool at ease?

I'm at ease now, friend; worldly in this world,
I take and like its way of life; I think
My brothers, who administer the means,
Live better for my comfort—that's good too;
And God, if he pronounce upon such life,
Approves my service, which is better still.
If he keep silence,—why, for you or me
Or that brute beast pulled-up in to-day's 'Times,'
What odds is't, save to ourselves, what life we lead?

    You meet me at this issue: you declare,—
All special-pleading done with—truth is truth,
And justifies itself by undreamed ways.
You don't fear but it's better, if we doubt,
To say so, act up to our truth perceived
However feebly. Do then,—act away!
'Tis there I'm on the watch for you. How one acts
Is, both of us agree, our chief concern:
And how you'll act is what I fain would see
If, like the candid person you appear,
You dare to make the most of your life's scheme
As I of mine, live up to its full law
Since there's no higher law that counter-checks.
Put natural religion to the test
You've just demolished the revealed with—quick,
Down to the root of all that checks your will,
All prohibition to lie, kill and thieve,
Or even to be an atheistic priest!
Suppose a pricking to incontinence—
Philosophers deduce you chastity
Or shame, from just the fact that at the first
Whoso embraced a woman in the field,
Threw club down and forewent his brains beside,
So, stood a ready victim in the reach
Of any brother savage, club in hand;
Hence saw the use of going out of sight
In wood or cave to prosecute his loves:
I read this in a French book t'other day.
Does law so analysed coerce you much?

Oh, men spin clouds of fuzz where matters end,
But you who reach where the first thread begins,
You'll soon cut that!—which means you can, but won't,
Through certain instincts, blind, unreasoned out,
You dare not set aside, you can't tell why,
But there they are, and so you let them rule.
Then, friend, you seem as much a slave as I,
A liar, conscious coward and hypocrite,
Without the good the slave expects to get,
In case he·has a master after all!
You own your instincts? why, what else do I,
Who want, am made for, and must have a God
Ere I can be aught, do aught?—no mere name
Want, but the true thing with what proves its truth,
To wit, a relation from that thing to me,
Touching from head to foot—which touch I feel,
And with it take the rest, this life of ours!
I live my life here; yours you dare not live.

—Not as I state it, who (you please subjoin)
Disfigure such a life and call it names.
While, to your mind, remains another way
For simple men: knowledge and power have rights,
But ignorance and weakness have rights too.
There needs no crucial effort to find truth
If here or there or anywhere about:
We ought to turn each side, try hard and see,
And if we can't, be glad we've earned at least
The right, by one laborious proof the more,
To graze in peace earth's pleasant pasturage.
Men are not angels, neither are they brutes:
Something we may see, all we cannot see.
What need of lying? I say, I see all,
And swear to each detail the most minute
In what I think a Pan's face—you, mere cloud:
I swear I hear him speak and see him wink,
For fear, if once I drop the emphasis,
Mankind may doubt there's any cloud at all.
You take the simple life—ready to see,

Willing to see (for no cloud's worth a face)—
And leaving quiet what no strength can move,
And which, who bids you move? who has the right?
I bid you; but you are God's sheep, not mine:
'*Pastor est tui Dominus.*' You find
In this the pleasant pasture of our life
Much you may eat without the least offence,
Much you don't eat because your maw objects,
Much you would eat but that your fellow-flock
Open great eyes at you and even butt,
And thereupon you like your mates so well
You cannot please yourself, offending them;
Though when they seem exorbitantly sheep,
You weigh your pleasure with their butts and bleats
And strike the balance. Sometimes certain fears
Restrain you, real checks since you find them so;
Sometimes you please yourself and nothing checks:
And thus you graze through life with not one lie,
And like it best.

           But do you, in truth's name?
If so, you beat—which means you are not I—
Who needs must make earth mine and feed my fill
Not simply unbutted at, unbickered with,
But motioned to the velvet of the sward
By those obsequious wethers' very selves.
Look at me, sir; my age is double yours:
At yours, I knew beforehand, so enjoyed,
What now I should be—as, permit the word,
I pretty well imagine your whole range
And stretch of tether twenty years to come.
We both have minds and bodies much alike:
In truth's name, don't you want my bishopric,
My daily bread, my influence and my state?
You're young. I'm old; you must be old one day;
Will you find then, as I do hour by hour,
Women their lovers kneel to, who cut curls
From your fat lap-dog's ear to grace a brooch—
Dukes, who petition just to kiss your ring—

With much beside you know or may conceive?
Suppose we die to-night: well, here am I,
Such were my gains, life bore this fruit to me,
While writing all the same my articles
On music, poetry, the fictile vase
Found at Albano, chess, Anacreon's Greek.
But you—the highest honour in your life,
The thing you'll crown yourself with, all your days, ·
Is—dining here and drinking this last glass
I pour you out in sign of amity
Before we part for ever. Of your power
And social influence, worldly worth in short,
Judge what's my estimation by the fact,
I do not condescend to enjoin, beseech,
Hint secrecy on one of all these words!
You're shrewd and know that should you publish one
The world would brand the lie—my enemies first,
Who'd sneer—'the bishop's an arch-hypocrite
'And knave perhaps, but not so frank a fool.'
Whereas I should not dare for both my ears
Breathe one such syllable, smile one such smile,
Before the chaplain who reflects myself—
My shade's so much more potent than your flesh.
What's your reward, self-abnegating friend?
Stood you confessed of those exceptional
And privileged great natures that dwarf mine—
A zealot with a mad ideal in reach,
A poet just about to print his ode,
A statesman with a scheme to stop this war,
An artist whose religion is his art—
I should have nothing to object: such men
Carry the fire, all things grow warm to them,
Their drugget's worth my purple, they beat me.
But you,—you're just as little those as I—
You, Gigadibs, who, thirty years of age,
Write stately for Blackwood's Magazine,
Believe you see two points in Hamlet's soul
Unseized by the Germans yet—which view you'll print—
Meantime the best you have to show being still

That lively lightsome article we took
Almost for the true Dickens,—what's its name?
'The Slum and Cellar, or Whitechapel life
'Limned after dark!' it made me laugh, I know,
And pleased a month, and brought you in ten pounds.
—Success I recognize and compliment,
And therefore give you, if you choose, three words
(The card and pencil-scratch is quite enough)
Which whether here, in Dublin or New York,
Will get you, prompt as at my eyebrow's wink,
Such terms as never you aspired to get
In all our own reviews and some not ours.
Go write your lively sketches! be the first
'Blougram, or The Eccentric Confidence'—
Or better simply say, 'The Outward-bound.'
Why, men as soon would throw it in my teeth
As copy and quote the infamy chalked broad
About me on the church-door opposite.
You will not wait for that experience though,
I fancy, howsoever you decide,
To discontinue—not detesting, not
Defaming, but at least—despising me!

Over his wine so smiled and talked his hour
Sylvester Blougram, styled *in partibus*
Episcopus, nec non—(the deuce knows what
It's changed to by our novel hierarchy)
With Gigadibs the literary man,
Who played with spoons, explored his plate's design,
And ranged the olive-stones about its edge,
While the great bishop rolled him out a mind
Long crumpled, till creased consciousness lay smooth.

For Blougram, he believed, say, half he spoke.
The other portion, as he shaped it thus
For argumentatory purposes,
He felt his foe was foolish to dispute.
Some arbitrary accidental thoughts
That crossed his mind, amusing because new,

He chose to represent as fixtures there,
Invariable convictions (such they seemed
Beside his interlocutor's loose cards
Flung daily down, and not the same way twice)
While certain hell-deep instincts, man's weak tongue
Is never bold to utter in their truth
Because styled hell-deep ('tis an old mistake
To place hell at the bottom of the earth)
He ignored these,—not having in readiness
Their nomenclature and philosophy:
He said true things, but called them by wrong names.
'On the whole,' he thought, 'I justify myself
'On every point where cavillers like this
'Oppugn my life: he tries one kind of fence,
'I close, he's worsted, that's enough for him.
'He's on the ground: if ground should break away
'I take my stand on, there's a firmer yet
'Beneath it, both of us may sink and reach.
'His ground was over mine and broke the first:
'So, let him sit with me this many a year!'

He did not sit five minutes. Just a week
Sufficed his sudden healthy vehemence.
Something had struck him in the 'Outward-bound'
Another way than Blougram's purpose was:
And having bought, not cabin-furniture
But settler's-implements (enough for three)
And started for Australia—there, I hope,
By this time he has tested his first plough,
And studied his last chapter of St. John.

CLEON

'As certain also of your own poets have said'—

[An imaginary person. The poet quoted by St. Paul was Aratus, a native of Tarsus.]

CLEON the poet (from the sprinkled isles,
Lily on lily, that o'erlace the sea,
And laugh their pride when the light wave lisps 'Greece')—
To Protus in his Tyranny: much health!

They give thy letter to me, even now:
I read and seem as if I heard thee speak.
The master of thy galley still unlades
Gift after gift; they block my court at last
And pile themselves along its portico
Royal with sunset, like a thought of thee:
And one white she-slave from the group dispersed
Of black and white slaves (like the chequer-work
Pavement, at once my nation's work and gift,
Now covered with this settle-down of doves),
One lyric woman, in her crocus vest
Woven of sea-wools, with her two white hands
Commends to me the strainer and the cup
Thy lip hath bettered ere it blesses mine.

Well-counselled, king, in thy munificence!
For so shall men remark, in such an act
Of love for him whose song gives life its joy,
Thy recognition of the use of life;
Nor call thy spirit barely adequate
To help on life in straight ways, broad enough
For vulgar souls, by ruling and the rest.
Thou, in the daily building of thy tower,—
Whether in fierce and sudden spasms of toil,
Or through dim lulls of unapparent growth,
Or when the general work 'mid good acclaim
Climbed with the eye to cheer the architect,—
Didst ne'er engage in work for mere work's sake—
Hadst ever in thy heart the luring hope
Of some eventual rest a-top of it,
Whence, all the tumult of the building hushed,
Thou first of men mightst look out to the East:
The vulgar saw thy tower, thou sawest the sun.
For this, I promise on thy festival
To pour libation, looking o'er the sea,
Making this slave narrate thy fortunes, speak
Thy great words, and describe thy royal face—
Wishing thee wholly where Zeus lives the most,
Within the eventual element of calm.

Thy letter's first requirement meets me here.
It is as thou hast heard: in one short life
I, Cleon, have effected all those things
Thou wonderingly dost enumerate.
That epos on thy hundred plates of gold
Is mine,—and also mine the little chant,
So sure to rise from every fishing-bark
When, lights at prow, the seamen haul their net.
The image of the sun-god on the phare,
Men turn from the sun's self to see, is mine;
The Pœcile,[1] o'er-storied its whole length,
As thou didst hear, with painting, is mine too.
I know the true proportions of a man
And woman also, not observed before;
And I have written three books on the soul,
Proving absurd all written hitherto,
And putting us to ignorance again.
For music,—why, I have combined the moods,
Inventing one. In brief, all arts are mine;
Thus much the people know and recognize,
Throughout our seventeen islands. Marvel not.
We of these latter days, with greater mind
Than our forerunners, since more composite,
Look not so great, beside their simple way,
To a judge who only sees one way at once,
One mind-point and no other at a time,—
Compares the small part of a man of us
With some whole man of the heroic age,
Great in his way—not ours, nor meant for ours.
And ours is greater, had we skill to know:
For, what we call this life of men on earth,
This sequence of the soul's achievements here
Being, as I find much reason to conceive,
Intended to be viewed eventually
As a great whole, not analysed to parts,
But each part having reference to all,—
How shall a certain part, pronounced complete,
Endure effacement by another part?

[1] The famous painted Porch on the Agora in Athens.

Was the thing done?—then, what's to do again?
See, in the chequered pavement opposite,
Suppose the artist made a perfect rhomb,
And next a lozenge, then a trapezoid—
He did not overlay them, superimpose
The new upon the old and blot it out,
But laid them on a level in his work,
Making at last a picture; there it lies.
So, first the perfect separate forms were made,
The portions of mankind; and after, so,
Occurred the combination of the same.
For where had been a progress, otherwise?
Mankind, made up of all the single men,—
In such a synthesis the labour ends.
Now mark me! those divine men of old time
Have reached, thou sayest well, each at one point
The outside verge that rounds our faculty;
And where they reached, who can do more than
         reach?
It takes but little water just to touch
At some one point the inside of a sphere,
And, as we turn the sphere, touch all the rest
In due succession: but the finer air
Which not so palpably nor obviously,
Though no less universally, can touch
The whole circumference of that emptied sphere,
Fills it more fully than the water did;
Holds thrice the weight of water in itself
Resolved into a subtler element.
And yet the vulgar call the sphere first full
Up to the visible height—and after, void;
Not knowing air's more hidden properties.
And thus our soul, misknown, cries out to Zeus
To vindicate his purpose in our life:
Why stay we on the earth unless to grow?
Long since, I imaged, wrote the fiction out,
That he or other god descended here
And, once for all, showed simultaneously
What, in its nature, never can be shown,

Piecemeal or in succession;—showed, I say,
The worth both absolute and relative
Of all his children from the birth of time,
His instruments for all appointed work.
I now go on to image,—might we hear
The judgment which should give the due to each,
Show where the labour lay and where the ease,
And prove Zeus' self, the latent everywhere!
This is a dream:—but no dream, let us hope,
That years and days, the summers and the springs,
Follow each other with unwaning powers.
The grapes which dye thy wine are richer far,
Through culture, than the wild wealth of the rock;
The suave plum than the savage-tasted drupe;
The pastured honey-bee drops choicer sweet;
The flowers turn double, and the leaves turn flowers;
That young and tender crescent-moon, thy slave,
Sleeping above her robe as buoyed by clouds,
Refines upon the women of my youth.
What, and the soul alone deteriorates?
I have not chanted verse like Homer, no—
Nor swept string like Terpander, no—nor carved
And painted men like Phidias and his friend:
I am not great as they are, point by point.
But I have entered into sympathy
With these four, running these into one soul,
Who, separate, ignored each other's art.
Say, is it nothing that I know them all?
The wild flower was the larger; I have dashed
Rose-blood upon its petals, pricked its cup's
Honey with wine, and driven its seed to fruit,
And show a better flower if not so large:
I stand myself. Refer this to the gods
Whose gift alone it is! which, shall I dare
(All pride apart) upon the absurd pretext
That such a gift by chance lay in my hand,
Discourse of lightly or depreciate?
It might have fallen to another's hand: what then?
I pass too surely: let at least truth stay!

And next, of what thou followest on to ask.
This being with me as I declare, O king,
My works, in all these varicoloured kinds,
So done by me, accepted so by men—
Thou askest, if (my soul thus in men's hearts)
I must not be accounted to attain
The very crown and proper end of life?
Inquiring thence how, now life closeth up,
I face death with success in my right hand:
Whether I fear death less than dost thyself
The fortunate of men? 'For' (writest thou)
'Thou leavest much behind, while I leave nought.
'Thy life stays in the poems men shall sing,
'The pictures men shall study; while my life,
'Complete and whole now in its power and joy,
'Dies altogether with my brain and arm,
'Is lost indeed; since, what survives myself?
'The brazen statue to o'erlook my grave,
'Set on the promontory which I named.
'And that—some supple courtier of my heir
'Shall use its robed and sceptred arm, perhaps,
'To fix the rope to, which best drags it down.
'I go then: triumph thou, who dost not go!'

Nay, thou art worthy of hearing my whole mind.
Is this apparent, when thou turn'st to muse
Upon the scheme of earth and man in chief,
That admiration grows as knowledge grows?
That imperfection means perfection hid,
Reserved in part, to grace the after-time?
If, in the morning of philosophy,
Ere aught had been recorded, nay perceived,
Thou, with the light now in thee, couldst have looked
On all earth's tenantry, from worm to bird,
Ere man, her last, appeared upon the stage—
Thou wouldst have seen them perfect, and deduced
The perfectness of others yet unseen.
Conceding which,—had Zeus then questioned thee
'Shall I go on a step, improve on this,

'Do more for visible creatures than is done?'
Thou wouldst have answered, 'Ay, by making each
'Grow conscious in himself—by that alone.
'All's perfect else: the shell sucks fast the rock,
'The fish strikes through the sea, the snake both swims
'And slides, forth range the beasts, the birds take flight,
'Till life's mechanics can no further go—
'And all this joy in natural life is put
'Like fire from off thy finger into each,
'So exquisitely perfect is the same.
'But 'tis pure fire, and they mere matter are;
'It has them, not they it: and so I choose
'For man, thy last premeditated work
'(If I might add a glory to the scheme)
'That a third thing should stand apart from both,
'A quality arise within his soul,
'Which, intro-active, made to supervise
'And feel the force it has, may view itself,
'And so be happy.' Man might live at first
The animal life: but is there nothing more?
In due time, let him critically learn
How he lives; and, the more he gets to know
Of his own life's adaptabilities,
The more joy-giving will his life become.
Thus man, who hath this quality, is best.

But thou, king, hadst more reasonably said:
'Let progress end at once,—man make no step
'Beyond the natural man, the better beast,
'Using his senses, not the sense of sense.'
In man there's failure, only since he left
The lower and inconscious forms of life.
We called it an advance, the rendering plain
Man's spirit might grow conscious of man's life,
And, by new lore so added to the old,
Take each step higher over the brute's head.
This grew the only life, the pleasure-house,
Watch-tower and treasure-fortress of the soul,
Which whole surrounding flats of natural life

Seemed only fit to yield subsistence to;
A tower that crowns a country. But alas,
The soul now climbs it just to perish there!
For thence we have discovered ('tis no dream—
We know this, which we had not else perceived)
That there's a world of capability
For joy, spread round about us, meant for us,
Inviting us; and still the soul craves all,
And still the flesh replies, 'Take no jot more
'Than ere thou clombst the tower to look abroad!
'Nay, so much less as that fatigue has brought
'Deduction to it.' We struggle, fain to enlarge
Our bounded physical recipiency,
Increase our power, supply fresh oil to life,
Repair the waste of age and sickness: no,
It skills not! life's inadequate to joy,
As the soul sees joy, tempting life to take.
They praise a fountain in my garden here
Wherein a Naiad sends the water-bow
Thin from her tube; she smiles to see it rise.
What if I told her, it is just a thread
From that great river which the hills shut up,
And mock her with my leave to take the same?
The artificer has given her one small tube
Past power to widen or exchange—what boots
To know she might spout oceans if she could?
She cannot lift beyond her first thin thread:
And so a man can use but a man's joy
While he sees God's. Is it for Zeus to boast,
'See, man, how happy I live, and despair—
'That I may be still happier—for thy use!'
If this were so, we could not thank our lord,
As hearts beat on to doing; 'tis not so—
Malice it is not. Is it carelessness?
Still, no. If care—where is the sign? I ask,
And get no answer, and agree in sum,
O king, with thy profound discouragement,
Who seest the wider but to sigh the more.
Most progress is most failure: thou sayest well.

    The last point now:—thou dost except a case—
Holding joy not impossible to one
With artist-gifts—to such a man as I
Who leave behind me living works indeed;
For, such a poem, such a painting lives.
What? dost thou verily trip upon a word,
Confound the accurate view of what joy is
(Caught somewhat clearer by my eyes than thine)
With feeling joy? confound the knowing how
And showing how to live (my faculty)
With actually living?—Otherwise
Where is the artist's vantage o'er the king?
Because in my great epos I display
How divers men young, strong, fair, wise, can act—
Is this as though I acted? if I paint,
Carve the young Phœbus, am I therefore young?
Methinks I'm older that I bowed myself
The many years of pain that taught me art!
Indeed, to know is something, and to prove
How all this beauty might be enjoyed, is more:
But, knowing nought, to enjoy is something too.
Yon rower, with the moulded muscles there,
Lowering the sail, is nearer it than I.
I can write love-odes: thy fair slave's an ode.
I get to sing of love, when grown too grey
For being beloved: she turns to that young man,
The muscles all a-ripple on his back.
I know the joy of kingship: well, thou art king.

    'But,' sayest thou—(and I marvel, I repeat,
To find thee trip on such a mere word) 'what
'Thou writest, paintest, stays; that does not die:
'Sappho survives, because we sing her songs,
'And Æschylus, because we read his plays!'
Why, if they live still, let them come and take
Thy slave in my despite, drink from thy cup,
Speak in my place. Thou diest while I survive?
Say rather that my fate is deadlier still,
In this, that every day my sense of joy

Grows more acute, my soul (intensified
By power and insight) more enlarged, more keen;
While every day my hairs fall more and more,
My hand shakes, and the heavy years increase—
The horror quickening still from year to year,
The consummation coming past escape
When I shall know most, and yet least enjoy—
When all my works wherein I prove my worth,
Being present still to mock me in men's mouths,
Alive still, in the praise of such as thou,
I, I the feeling, thinking, acting man,
The man who loved his life so over-much,
Sleep in my urn. It is so horrible,
I dare at times imagine to my need
Some future state revealed to us by Zeus,
Unlimited in capability
For joy, as this is in desire for joy,
—To seek which, the joy-hunger forces us:
That, stung by straitness of our life, made strait
On purpose to make prized the life at large—
Freed by the throbbing impulse we call death,
We burst there as the worm into the fly,
Who, while a worm still, wants his wings. But no!
Zeus has not yet revealed it; and alas,
He must have done so, were it possible!

　　Live long and happy, and in that thought die:
Glad for what was! Farewell. And for the rest,
I cannot tell thy messenger aright
Where to deliver what he bears of thine
To one called Paulus; we have heard his fame
Indeed, if Christus be not one with him—
I know not, nor am troubled much to know.
Thou canst not think a mere barbarian Jew,
As Paulus proves to be, one circumcized,
Hath access to a secret shut from us?
Thou wrongest our philosophy, O king,
In stooping to inquire of such an one,
As if his answer could impose at all!

He writeth, doth he? well, and he may write.
Oh, the Jew findeth scholars! certain slaves
Who touched on this same isle, preached him and Christ;
And (as I gathered from a bystander)
Their doctrine could be held by no sane man.

RUDEL TO THE LADY OF TRIPOLI

I

I KNOW a Mount, the gracious Sun perceives
First, when he visits, last, too, when he leaves
The world; and, vainly favoured, it repays
The day-long glory of his steadfast gaze
By no change of its large calm front of snow.
And underneath the Mount, a Flower I know,
He cannot have perceived, that changes ever
At his approach; and, in the lost endeavour
To live his life, has parted, one by one,
With all a flower's true graces, for the grace
Of being but a foolish mimic sun,
With ray-like florets round a disk-like face.
Men nobly call by many a name the Mount
As over many a land of theirs its large
Calm front of snow like a triumphal targe
Is reared, and still with old names, fresh names vie,
Each to its proper praise and own account:
Men call the Flower, the Sunflower, sportively.

II

Oh, Angel of the East, one, one gold look
Across the waters to this twilight nook,
—The far sad waters, Angel, to this nook!

III

Dear Pilgrim, art thou for the East indeed?
Go!—saying ever as thou dost proceed,
That I, French Rudel, choose for my device
A sunflower outspread like a sacrifice

Before its idol. See! These inexpert
And hurried fingers could not fail to hurt
The woven picture; 'tis a woman's skill
Indeed; but nothing baffled me, so, ill
Or well, the work is finished. Say, men feed
On songs I sing, and therefore bask the bees
On my flower's breast as on a platform broad:
But, as the flower's concern is not for these
But solely for the sun, so men applaud
In vain this Rudel, he not looking here
But to the East—the East! Go, say this, Pilgrim dear!

ONE WORD MORE[1]

TO E. B. B.

1855

I

THERE they are, my fifty men and women
Naming me the fifty poems finished!
Take them, Love, the book and me together:
Where the heart lies, let the brain lie also.

II

Rafael made a century of sonnets,
Made and wrote them in a certain volume
Dinted with the silver-pointed pencil
Else he only used to draw Madonnas:
These, the world might view—but one, the volume.
Who that one, you ask? Your heart instructs you.
Did she live and love it all her lifetime?
Did she drop, his lady of the sonnets,
Die, and let it drop beside her pillow
Where it lay in place of Rafael's glory,
Rafael's cheek so duteous and so loving—
Cheek, the world was wont to hail a painter's,
Rafael's cheek, her love had turned a poet's?

---

[1] [Originally appended to the collection of Poems called 'Men and Women', the greater portion of which has now been, more correctly, distributed under the other titles of this edition.—R. B. 1868.]

III

You and I would rather read that volume,
(Taken to his beating bosom by it)
Lean and list the bosom-beats of Rafael,
Would we not? than wonder at Madonnas—
Her, San Sisto names, and Her, Foligno,
Her, that visits Florence in a vision,
Her, that's left with lilies in the Louvre—
Seen by us and all the world in circle.

IV

You and I will never read that volume.
Guido Reni, like his own eye's apple
Guarded long the treasure-book and loved it.
Guido Reni dying, all Bologna
Cried, and the world cried too, 'Ours, the treasure!'
Suddenly, as rare things will, it vanished.

V

Dante once prepared to paint an angel:
Whom to please? You whisper 'Beatrice.'
While he mused and traced it and retraced it,
(Peradventure with a pen corroded
Still by drops of that hot ink he dipped for,
When, his left-hand i' the hair o' the wicked,
Back he held the brow and pricked its stigma,
Bit into the live man's flesh for parchment,
Loosed him, laughed to see the writing rankle,
Let the wretch go festering through Florence)—
Dante, who loved well because he hated,
Hated wickedness that hinders loving,
Dante standing, studying his angel,—
In there broke the folk of his Inferno.
Says he—'Certain people of importance'
(Such he gave his daily dreadful line to)
'Entered and would seize, forsooth, the poet.'
Says the poet—'Then I stopped my painting.'

VI

You and I would rather see that angel,
Painted by the tenderness of Dante,
Would we not?—than read a fresh Inferno.

VII

You and I will never see that picture.
While he mused on love and Beatrice,
While he softened o'er his outlined angel,
In they broke, those 'people of importance:'
We and Bice bear the loss for ever.

VIII

What of Rafael's sonnets, Dante's picture?
This: no artist lives and loves, that longs not
Once, and only once, and for one only,
(Ah, the prize!) to find his love a language
Fit and fair and simple and sufficient—
Using nature that's an art to others,
Not, this one time, art that's turned his nature.
Ay, of all the artists living, loving,
None but would forego his proper dowry,—
Does he paint? he fain would write a poem,—
Does he write? he fain would paint a picture,
Put to proof art alien to the artist's,
Once, and only once, and for one only,
So to be the man and leave the artist,
Gain the man's joy, miss the artist's sorrow.

IX

Wherefore? Heaven's gift takes earth's abatement!
He who smites the rock and spreads the water,
Bidding drink and live a crowd beneath him,
Even he, the minute makes immortal,
Proves, perchance, but mortal in the minute,
Desecrates, belike, the deed in doing.
While he smites, how can he but remember,
So he smote before, in such a peril,

When they stood and mocked—'Shall smiting help us?'
When they drank and sneered—'A stroke is easy!'
When they wiped their mouths and went their journey,
Throwing him for thanks—'But drought was pleasant.'
Thus old memories mar the actual triumph;
Thus the doing savours of disrelish;
Thus achievement lacks a gracious somewhat;
O'er-importuned brows becloud the mandate,
Carelessness or consciousness—the gesture.
For he bears an ancient wrong about him,
Sees and knows again those phalanxed faces,
Hears, yet one time more, the 'customed prelude—
'How shouldst thou, of all men, smite, and save us?'
Guesses what is like to prove the sequel—
'Egypt's flesh-pots—nay, the drought was better.'

X

Oh, the crowd must have emphatic warrant!
Theirs, the Sinai-forehead's cloven brilliance,
Right-arm's rod-sweep, tongue's imperial fiat.
Never dares the man put off the prophet.

XI

Did he love one face from out the thousands,
(Were she Jethro's daughter, white and wifely,
Were she but the Æthiopian bondslave,)
He would envy yon dumb patient camel,
Keeping a reserve of scanty water
Meant to save his own life in the desert;
Ready in the desert to deliver
(Kneeling down to let his breast be opened)
Hoard and life together for his mistress.

XII

I shall never, in the years remaining,
Paint you pictures, no, nor carve you statues,
Make you music that should all-express me;
So it seems: I stand on my attainment.
This of verse alone, one life allows me:

Verse and nothing else have I to give you.
Other heights in other lives, God willing:
All the gifts from all the heights, your own, Love!

XIII

Yet a semblance of resource avails us—
Shade so finely touched, love's sense must seize it.
Take these lines, look lovingly and nearly,
Lines I write the first time and the last time.
He who works in fresco, steals a hair-brush,
Curbs the liberal hand, subservient proudly,
Cramps his spirit, crowds its all in little,
Makes a strange art of an art familiar,
Fills his lady's missal-marge with flowerets.
He who blows thro' bronze, may breathe thro' silver,
Fitly serenade a slumbrous princess.
He who writes, may write for once as I do.

XIV

Love, you saw me gather men and women,
Live or dead or fashioned by my fancy,
Enter each and all, and use their service,
Speak from every mouth,—the speech, a poem.
Hardly shall I tell my joys and sorrows,
Hopes and fears, belief and disbelieving:
I am mine and yours—the rest be all men's,
Karshish, Cleon, Norbert and the fifty.
Let me speak this once in my true person,
Not as Lippo, Roland or Andrea,
Though the fruit of speech be just this sentence:
Pray you, look on these my men and women,
Take and keep my fifty poems finished;
Where my heart lies, let my brain lie also!
Poor the speech; be how I speak, for all things.

XV

Not but that you know me! Lo, the moon's self!
Here in London, yonder late in Florence,
Still we find her face, the thrice-transfigured.
Curving on a sky imbrued with colour,

Drifted over Fiesole by twilight,
Came she, our new crescent of a hair's-breadth.
Full she flared it, lamping Samminiato,
Rounder 'twixt the cypresses and rounder,
Perfect till the nightingales applauded.
Now, a piece of her old self, impoverished,
Hard to greet, she traverses the house-roofs,
Hurries with unhandsome thrift of silver,
Goes dispiritedly, glad to finish.

XVI

What, there's nothing in the moon noteworthy?
Nay: for if that moon could love a mortal,
Use, to charm him (so to fit a fancy),
All her magic ('tis the old sweet mythos),
She would turn a new side to her mortal,
Side unseen of herdsman, huntsman, steersman—
Blank to Zoroaster on his terrace,
Blind to Galileo on his turret,
Dumb to Homer, dumb to Keats—him, even!
Think, the wonder of the moonstruck mortal—
When she turns round, comes again in heaven,
Opens out anew for worse or better!
Proves she like some portent of an iceberg
Swimming full upon the ship it founders,
Hungry with huge teeth of splintered crystals?
Proves she as the paved work of a sapphire
Seen by Moses when he climbed the mountain?
Moses, Aaron, Nadab and Abihu
Climbed and saw the very God, the Highest,
Stand upon the paved work of a sapphire.
Like the bodied heaven in his clearness
Shone the stone, the sapphire of that paved work,
When they ate and drank and saw God also!

XVII

What were seen? None knows, none ever shall know.
Only this is sure—the sight were other,
Not the moon's same side, born late in Florence,

Dying now impoverished here in London.
God be thanked, the meanest of his creatures
Boasts two soul-sides, one to face the world with,
One to show a woman when he loves her!

XVIII

This I say of me, but think of you, Love!
This to you—yourself my moon of poets!
Ah, but that's the world's side, there's the wonder,
Thus they see you, praise you, think they know you!
There, in turn I stand with them and praise you—
Out of my own self, I dare to phrase it.
But the best is when I glide from out them,
Cross a step or two of dubious twilight,
Come out on the other side, the novel
Silent silver lights and darks undreamed of,
Where I hush and bless myself with silence.

XIX

Oh, their Rafael of the dear Madonnas,
Oh, their Dante of the dread Inferno,
Wrote one song—and in my brain I sing it,
Drew one angel—borne, see, on my bosom!

DRAMATIS PERSONÆ

1864

From 'JAMES LEE'S WIFE'

IN THE DOORWAY

I

THE swallow has set her six young on the rail,
    And looks sea-ward:
The water's in stripes like a snake, olive-pale
    To the leeward,—
On the weather-side, black, spotted white with the wind.
'Good fortune departs, and disaster's behind,'—
Hark, the wind with its wants and its infinite wail!

II

Our fig-tree, that leaned for the saltness, has furled
    Her five fingers,
Each leaf like a hand opened wide to the world
    Where there lingers
No glint of the gold, Summer sent for her sake:
How the vines writhe in rows, each impaled on its stake!
My heart shrivels up and my spirit shrinks curled.

III

Yet here are we two; we have love, house enough,
    With the field there,
This house of four rooms, that field red and rough,
    Though it yield there,
For the rabbit that robs, scarce a blade or a bent;
If a magpie alight now, it seems an event;
And they both will be gone at November's rebuff.

IV

But why must cold spread? but wherefore bring change
    To the spirit,
God meant should mate his with an infinite range,
    And inherit
His power to put life in the darkness and cold?
Oh, live and love worthily, bear and be bold!
Whom Summer made friends of, let Winter estrange!

AMONG THE ROCKS

I

Oh, good gigantic smile o' the brown old earth,
  This autumn morning! How he sets his bones
To bask i' the sun, and thrusts out knees and feet
For the ripple to run over in its mirth;
  Listening the while, where on the heap of stones
The white breast of the sea-lark twitters sweet.

II

That is the doctrine, simple, ancient, true;
  Such is life's trial, as old earth smiles and knows.
If you loved only what were worth your love,
Love were clear gain, and wholly well for you:
  Make the low nature better by your throes!
Give earth yourself, go up for gain above!

GOLD HAIR

A STORY OF PORNIC

I

Oh, the beautiful girl, too white,
  Who lived at Pornic, down by the sea,
Just where the sea and the Loire unite!
  And a boasted name in Brittany
She bore, which I will not write.

II

Too white, for the flower of life is red;
  Her flesh was the soft seraphic screen
Of a soul that is meant (her parents said)
  To just see earth, and hardly be seen,
And blossom in heaven instead.

III

Yet earth saw one thing, one how fair!
  One grace that grew to its full on earth:
Smiles might be sparse on her cheek so spare,
  And her waist want half a girdle's girth,
But she had her great gold hair.

IV

Hair, such a wonder of flix and floss,
  Freshness and fragrance—floods of it, too!
Gold, did I say? Nay, gold's mere dross:
  Here, Life smiled, 'Think what I meant to do!'
And Love sighed, 'Fancy my loss!'

V

So, when she died, it was scarce more strange
  Than that, when delicate evening dies,
And you follow its spent sun's pallid range,
  There's a shoot of colour startles the skies
With sudden, violent change,—

VI

That, while the breath was nearly to seek,
  As they put the little cross to her lips,
She changed; a spot came out on her cheek,
  A spark from her eye in mid-eclipse,
And she broke forth, 'I must speak!'

VII

'Not my hair!' made the girl her moan—
  'All the rest is gone or to go;
'But the last, last grace, my all, my own,
  'Let it stay in the grave, that the ghosts may know!
'Leave my poor gold hair alone!'

VIII

The passion thus vented, dead lay she;
    Her parents sobbed their worst on that;
All friends joined in, nor observed degree:
    For indeed the hair was to wonder at,
As it spread—not flowing free,

IX

But curled around her brow, like a crown,
    And coiled beside her cheeks, like a cap,
And calmed about her neck—ay, down
    To her breast, pressed flat, without a gap
I' the gold, it reached her gown.

X

All kissed that face, like a silver wedge
    'Mid the yellow wealth, nor disturbed its hair:
E'en the priest allowed death's privilege,
    As he planted the crucifix with care
On her breast, 'twixt edge and edge.

XI

And thus was she buried, inviolate
    Of body and soul, in the very space
By the altar; keeping saintly state
    In Pornic church, for her pride of race,
Pure life and piteous fate.

XII

And in after-time would your fresh tear fall,
    Though your mouth might twitch with a dubious smile,
As they told you of gold, both robe and pall,
    How she prayed them leave it alone awhile,
So it never was touched at all.

XIII

Years flew; this legend grew at last
    The life of the lady; all she had done,
All been, in the memories fading fast
    Of lover and friend, was summed in one
Sentence survivors passed:

XIV

To wit, she was meant for heaven, not earth;
　　Had turned an angel before the time:
Yet, since she was mortal, in such dearth
　　Of frailty, all you could count a crime
Was—she knew her gold hair's worth.

XV

At little pleasant Pornic church,
　　It chanced, the pavement wanted repair,
Was taken to pieces: left in the lurch,
　　A certain sacred space lay bare,
And the boys began research.

XVI

'Twas the space where our sires would lay a saint,
　　A benefactor,—a bishop, suppose,
A baron with armour-adornments quaint,
　　Dame with chased ring and jewelled rose,
Things sanctity saves from taint;

XVII

So we come to find them in after-days
　　When the corpse is presumed to have done with gauds
Of use to the living, in many ways:
　　For the boys get pelf, and the town applauds,
And the church deserves the praise.

XVIII

They grubbed with a will: and at length—*O cor
　　Humanum, pectora cæca*, and the rest!—
They found—no gaud they were prying for,
　　No ring, no rose, but—who would have guessed?—
A double Louis-d'or!

XIX

Here was a case for the priest: he heard,
　　Marked, inwardly digested, laid
Finger on nose, smiled, 'There's a bird
　　'Chirps in my ear': then, 'Bring a spade,
'Dig deeper!'—he gave the word.

XX

And lo, when they came to the coffin-lid,
   Or rotten planks which composed it once,
Why, there lay the girl's skull wedged amid
   A mint of money, it served for the nonce
To hold in its hair-heaps hid!

XXI

Hid there? Why? Could the girl be wont
   (She the stainless soul) to treasure up
Money, earth's trash and heaven's affront?
   Had a spider found out the communion-cup,
Was a toad in the christening-font?

XXII

Truth is truth: too true it was.
   Gold! She hoarded and hugged it first,
Longed for it, leaned o'er it, loved it—alas—
   Till the humour grew to a head and burst,
And she cried, at the final pass,—

XXIII

'Talk not of God, my heart is stone!
   'Nor lover nor friend—be gold for both!
'Gold I lack; and, my all, my own,
   'It shall hide in my hair. I scarce die loth
'If they let my hair alone!'

XXIV

Louis-d'or, some six times five,
   And duly double, every piece.
Now do you see? With the priest to shrive,
   With parents preventing her soul's release
By kisses that kept alive,—

XXV

With heaven's gold gates about to ope,
   With friends' praise, gold-like, lingering still,
An instinct had bidden the girl's hand grope
   For gold, the true sort—'Gold in heaven, if you will;
'But I keep earth's too, I hope.'

XXVI

Enough! The priest took the grave's grim yield:
  The parents, they eyed that price of sin
As if *thirty pieces* lay revealed
  On the place *to bury strangers in,*
The hideous Potter's Field.

XXVII

But the priest bethought him: ' "Milk that's spilt"
  '—You know the adage! Watch and pray!
'Saints tumble to earth with so slight a tilt!
  'It would build a new altar; that, we may!'
And the altar therewith was built.

XXVIII

Why I deliver this horrible verse?
  As the text of the sermon, which now I preach:
Evil or good may be better or worse
  In the human heart, but the mixture of each
Is a marvel and a curse.

XXIX

The candid incline to surmise of late
  That the Christian faith proves false, I find;
For our Essays-and-Reviews' debate
  Begins to tell on the public mind,
And Colenso's words have weight:

XXX

I still, to suppose it true, for my part,
  See reasons and reasons; this, to begin:
'Tis the faith that launched point-blank her dart
  At the head of a lie—taught Original Sin,
The Corruption of Man's Heart.

THE WORST OF IT

I

Would it were I had been false, not you!
  I that am nothing, not you that are all:
I, never the worse for a touch or two
  On my speckled hide; not you, the pride
Of the day, my swan, that a first fleck's fall
  On her wonder of white must unswan, undo!

II

I had dipped in life's struggle and, out again,
  Bore specks of it here, there, easy to see,
When I found my swan and the cure was plain;
  The dull turned bright as I caught your white
On my bosom: you saved me—saved in vain
  If you ruined yourself, and all through me!

III

Yes, all through the speckled beast that I am,
  Who taught you to stoop; you gave me yourself,
And bound your soul by the vows that damn:
  Since on better thought you break, as you ought,
Vows—words, no angel set down, some elf
  Mistook,—for an oath, an epigram!

IV

Yes, might I judge you, here were my heart,
  And a hundred its like, to treat as you pleased!
I choose to be yours, for my proper part,
  Yours, leave or take, or mar me or make;
If I acquiesce, why should you be teased
  With the conscience-prick and the memory-smart?

V

But what will God say? Oh, my sweet,
  Think, and be sorry you did this thing
Though earth were unworthy to feel your feet,
  There's a heaven above may deserve your love:
Should you forfeit heaven for a snapt gold ring
  And a promise broke, were it just or meet?

VI

And I to have tempted you! I, who tired
  Your soul, no doubt, till it sank! Unwise,
I loved and was lowly, loved and aspired,
  Loved, grieving or glad, till I made you mad,
And you meant to have hated and despised—
  Whereas, you deceived me nor inquired!

VII

She, ruined? How? No heaven for her?
  Crowns to give, and none for the brow
That looked like marble and smelt like myrrh?
  Shall the robe be worn, and the palm-branch borne,
And she go graceless, she graced now
  Beyond all saints, as themselves aver?

VIII

Hardly! That must be understood!
  The earth is your place of penance, then;
And what will it prove? I desire your good,
  But, plot as I may, I can find no way
How a blow should fall, such as falls on men,
  Nor prove too much for your womanhood.

IX

It will come, I suspect, at the end of life,
  When you walk alone, and review the past;
And I, who so long shall have done with strife,
  And journeyed my stage and earned my wage
And retired as was right,—I am called at last
  When the devil stabs you, to lend the knife.

X

He stabs for the minute of trivial wrong,
  Nor the other hours are able to save,
The happy, that lasted my whole life long:
  For a promise broke, not for first words spoke,
The true, the only, that turn my grave
  To a blaze of joy and a crash of song.

XI

Witness beforehand! Off I trip
  On a safe path gay through the flowers you flung:
My very name made great by your lip,
  And my heart a-glow with the good I know
Of a perfect year when we both were young,
  And I tasted the angels' fellowship.

XII

And witness, moreover . . . Ah, but wait!
  I spy the loop whence an arrow shoots!
It may be for yourself, when you meditate,
  That you grieve—for slain ruth, murdered truth.
'Though falsehood escape in the end, what boots?
  'How truth would have triumphed!'—you sigh too late.

XIII

Ay, who would have triumphed like you, I say!
  Well, it is lost now; well, you must bear,
Abide and grow fit for a better day:
  You should hardly grudge, could I be your judge!
But hush! For you, can be no despair:
  There's amends: 'tis a secret: hope and pray!

XIV

For I was true at least—oh, true enough!
  And, Dear, truth is not as good as it seems!
Commend me to conscience! Idle stuff!
  Much help is in mine, as I mope and pine,
And skulk through day, and scowl in my dreams
  At my swan's obtaining the crow's rebuff.

XV

Men tell me of truth now—'False!' I cry:
  Of beauty—'A mask, friend! Look beneath!'
We take our own method, the devil and I,
  With pleasant and fair and wise and rare:
And the best we wish to what lives, is—death;
  Which even in wishing, perhaps we lie!

XVI

Far better commit a fault and have done—
　　As you, Dear!—for ever; and choose the pure,
And look where the healing waters run,
　　And strive and strain to be good again,
And a place in the other world ensure,
　　All glass and gold, with God for its sun.

XVII

Misery! What shall I say or do?
　　I cannot advise, or, at least, persuade:
Most like, you are glad you deceived me—rue
　　No whit of the wrong: you endured too long,
Have done no evil and want no aid,
　　Will live the old life out and chance the new.

XVIII

And your sentence is written all the same,
　　And I can do nothing,—pray, perhaps:
But somehow the world pursues its game,—
　　If I pray, if I curse,—for better or worse:
And my faith is torn to a thousand scraps,
　　And my heart feels ice while my words breathe flame

XIX

Dear, I look from my hiding-place.
　　Are you still so fair? Have you still the eyes?
Be happy! Add but the other grace,
　　Be good! Why want what the angels vaunt?
I knew you once: but in Paradise,
　　If we meet, I will pass nor turn my face.

DÎS ALITER VISUM; OR, LE BYRON DE NOS JOURS

I

Stop, let me have the truth of that!
　　Is that all true? I say, the day
Ten years ago when both of us
　　Met on a morning, friends—as thus
We meet this evening, friends or what?—

II

Did you—because I took your arm
  And sillily smiled, 'A mass of brass
'That sea looks, blazing underneath!'
  While up the cliff-road edged with heath,
We took the turns nor came to harm—

III

Did you consider 'Now makes twice
  'That I have seen her, walked and talked
'With this poor pretty thoughtful thing,
  'Whose worth I weigh: she tries to sing;
'Draws, hopes in time the eye grows nice;

IV

'Reads verse and thinks she understands;
  'Loves all, at any rate, that's great,
'Good, beautiful; but much as we
  'Down at the bath-house love the sea,
'Who breathe its salt and bruise its sands:

V

'While . . . do but follow the fishing-gull
  'That flaps and floats from wave to cave!
'There's the sea-lover, fair my friend!
  'What then? Be patient, mark and mend!
'Had you the making of your skull?'

VI

And did you, when we faced the church
  With spire and sad slate roof, aloof
From human fellowship so far,
  Where a few graveyard crosses are,
And garlands for the swallows' perch,—

VII

Did you determine, as we stepped
  O'er the lone stone fence, 'Let me get
'Her for myself, and what's the earth
  'With all its art, verse, music, worth—
'Compared with love, found, gained, and kept?

VIII

'Schumann's our music-maker now;
 'Has his march-movement youth and mouth?
'Ingres's the modern man that paints;
 'Which will lean on me, of his saints?
'Heine for songs; for kisses, how?'

IX

And did you, when we entered, reached
 The votive frigate, soft aloft
Riding on air this hundred years,
 Safe-smiling at old hopes and fears,—
Did you draw profit while she preached?

X

Resolving, 'Fools we wise men grow!
 'Yes, I could easily blurt out curt
'Some question that might find reply
 'As prompt in her stopped lips, dropped eye,
'And rush of red to cheek and brow:

XI

'Thus were a match made, sure and fast,
 ''Mid the blue weed-flowers round the mound
'Where, issuing, we shall stand and stay
 'For one more look at baths and bay,
'Sands, sea-gulls, and the old church last—

XII

'A match 'twixt me, bent, wigged and lamed,
 'Famous, however, for verse and worse,
'Sure of the Fortieth spare Arm-chair
 'When gout and glory seat me there,
'So, one whose love-freaks pass unblamed,—

XIII

'And this young beauty, round and sound
 'As a mountain-apple, youth and truth
'With loves and doves, at all events
 'With money in the Three per Cents;
'Whose choice of me would seem profound:—

XIV

'She might take me as I take her.
  'Perfect the hour would pass, alas!
'Climb high, love high, what matter? Still,
  'Feet, feelings, must descend the hill:
'An hour's perfection can't recur.

XV

'Then follows Paris and full time
  'For both to reason: "Thus with us!"
'She'll sigh, "Thus girls give body and soul
  '"At first word, think they gain the goal,
'"When 'tis the starting-place they climb!

XVI

'"My friend makes verse and gets renown;
  '"Have they all fifty years, his peers?
'"He knows the world, firm, quiet and gay;
  '"Boys will become as much one day:
'"They're fools; he cheats, with beard less brown.

XVII

'"For boys say, *Love me or I die!*
  '"He did not say, *The truth is, youth*
'"*I want, who am old and know too much;*
  '"*I'd catch youth: lend me sight and touch!*
'"*Drop heart's blood where life's wheels grate dry!*"

XVIII

'While I should make rejoinder'—(then
  It was, no doubt, you ceased that least
Light pressure of my arm in yours)
  '"I can conceive of cheaper cures
'"For a yawning-fit o'er books and men.

XIX

'"What? All I am, was, and might be,
  '"All, books taught, art brought, life's whole strife,
'"Painful results since precious, just
  '"Were fitly exchanged, in wise disgust,
'"For two cheeks freshened by youth and sea?

XX

'"All for a nosegay!—what came first;
'"With fields on flower, untried each side:
'"I rally, need my books and men,
'"And find a nosegay": drop it, then,
'No match yet made for best or worst!'

XXI

That ended me. You judged the porch
    We left by, Norman; took our look
At sea and sky; wondered so few
    Find out the place for air and view;
Remarked the sun began to scorch;

XXII

Descended, soon regained the baths,
    And then, good-bye! Years ten since then:
Ten years! We meet: you tell me, now,
    By a window-seat for that cliff-brow,
On carpet-stripes for those sand-paths.

XXIII

Now I may speak: you fool, for all
    Your lore! WHO made things plain in vain?
What was the sea for? What, the grey
    Sad church, that solitary day,
Crosses and graves and swallows' call?

XXIV

Was there nought better than to enjoy?
    No feat which, done, would make time break,
And let us pent-up creatures through
    Into eternity, our due?
No forcing earth teach heaven's employ?

XXV

No wise beginning, here and now,
    What cannot grow complete (earth's feat)
And heaven must finish, there and then?
    No tasting earth's true food for men,
Its sweet in sad, its sad in sweet?

XXVI

No grasping at love, gaining a share
  O' the sole spark from God's life at strife
With death, so, sure of range above
  The limits here? For us and love,
Failure; but, when God fails, despair.

XXVII

This you call wisdom? Thus you add
  Good unto good again, in vain?
You loved, with body worn and weak;
  I loved, with faculties to seek:
Were both loves worthless since ill-clad?

XXVIII

Let the mere star-fish in his vault
  Crawl in a wash of weed, indeed,
Rose-jacynth to the finger-tips:
  He, whole in body and soul, outstrips
Man, found with either in default.

XXIX

But what's whole, can increase no more,
  Is dwarfed and dies, since here's its sphere.
The devil laughed at you in his sleeve!
  You knew not? That I well believe;
Or you had saved two souls: nay, four.

XXX

For Stephanie sprained last night her wrist,
  Ankle or something. 'Pooh,' cry you?
At any rate she danced, all say,
  Vilely; her vogue has had its day.
Here comes my husband from his whist.

TOO LATE

I

HERE was I with my arm and heart
  And brain, all yours for a word, a want
Put into a look—just a look, your part,—
  While mine, to repay it . . . vainest vaunt,
Were the woman, that's dead, alive to hear,
  Had her lover, that's lost, love's proof to show!
But I cannot show it; you cannot speak
  From the churchyard neither, miles removed,
Though I feel by a pulse within my cheek,
  Which stabs and stops, that the woman I loved
Needs help in her grave and finds none near,
  Wants warmth from the heart which sends it—so!

II

Did I speak once angrily, all the drear days
  You lived, you woman I loved so well,
Who married the other? Blame or praise,
  Where was the use then? Time would tell,
And the end declare what man for you,
  What woman for me, was the choice of God.
But, Edith dead! no doubting more!
  I used to sit and look at my life
As it rippled and ran till, right before,
  A great stone stopped it: oh, the strife
Of waves at the stone some devil threw
  In my life's midcurrent, thwarting God!

III

But either I thought, 'They may churn and chide
  'Awhile, my waves which came for their joy
'And found this horrible stone full-tide:
  'Yet I see just a thread escape, deploy
'Through the evening-country, silent and safe,
  'And it suffers no more till it finds the sea.'

Or else I would think, 'Perhaps some night
  'When new things happen, a meteor-ball
'May slip through the sky in a line of light,
  'And earth breathe hard, and landmarks fall,
'And my waves no longer champ nor chafe,
  'Since a stone will have rolled from its place: let be!'

IV

But, dead! All's done with: wait who may,
  Watch and wear and wonder who will.
Oh, my whole life that ends to-day!
  Oh, my soul's sentence, sounding still,
'The woman is dead that was none of his;
  'And the man that was none of hers may go!'
There's only the past left: worry that!
  Wreak, like a bull, on the empty coat,
Rage, its late wearer is laughing at!
  Tear the collar to rags, having missed his throat;
Strike stupidly on—'This, this and this,
  'Where I would that a bosom received the blow!'

V

I ought to have done more: once my speech,
  And once your answer, and there, the end,
And Edith was henceforth out of reach!
  Why, men do more to deserve a friend,
Be rid of a foe, get rich, grow wise,
  Nor, folding their arms, stare fate in the face.
Why, better even have burst like a thief
  And borne you away to a rock for us two,
In a moment's horror, bright, bloody and brief:
  Then changed to myself again—'I slew
'Myself in that moment; a ruffian lies
  'Somewhere: your slave, see, born in his place!'

VI

What did the other do? You be judge!
  Look at us, Edith! Here are we both!
Give him his six whole years: I grudge
  None of the life with you, nay, loathe

Myself that I grudged his start in advance
　Of me who could overtake and pass.
But, as if he loved you! No, not he,
　Nor anyone else in the world, 'tis plain:
Who ever heard that another, free
　As I, young, prosperous, sound and sane,
Poured life out, proffered it—'Half a glance
　'Of those eyes of yours and I drop the glass!'

VII

Handsome, were you? 'Tis more than they held,
　More than they said; I was 'ware and watched:
I was the 'scapegrace, this rat belled
　The cat, this fool got his whiskers scratched:
The others? No head that was turned, no heart
　Broken, my lady, assure yourself!
Each soon made his mind up; so and so
　Married a dancer, such and such
Stole his friend's wife, stagnated slow,
　Or maundered, unable to do as much,
And muttered of peace where he had no part:
　While, hid in the closet, laid on the shelf,—

VIII

On the whole, you were let alone, I think!
　So, you looked to the other, who acquiesced;
My rival, the proud man,—prize your pink
　Of poets! A poet he was! I've guessed:
He rhymed you his rubbish nobody read,
　Loved you and doved you—did not I laugh!
There was a prize! But we both were tried.
　Oh, heart of mine, marked broad with her mark,
Tekel, found wanting, set aside,
　Scorned! See, I bleed these tears in the dark
Till comfort come and the last be bled:
　He? He is tagging your epitaph.

IX

If it would only come over again!
    —Time to be patient with me, and probe
This heart till you punctured the proper vein,
    Just to learn what blood is: twitch the robe
From that blank lay-figure your fancy draped,
    Prick the leathern heart till the—verses spirt!
And late it was easy; late, you walked
    Where a friend might meet you; Edith's name
Arose to one's lip if one laughed or talked;
    If I heard good news, you heard the same;
When I woke, I knew that your breath escaped;
    I could bide my time, keep alive, alert.

X

And alive I shall keep and long, you will see!
    I knew a man, was kicked like a dog
From gutter to cesspool; what cared he
    So long as he picked from the filth his prog?
He saw youth, beauty and genius die,
    And jollily lived to his hundredth year.
But I will live otherwise: none of such life!
    At once I begin as I mean to end.
Go on with the world, get gold in its strife,
    Give your spouse the slip and betray your friend!
There are two who decline, a woman and I,
    And enjoy our death in the darkness here.

XI

I liked that way you had with your curls
    Wound to a ball in a net behind:
Your cheek was chaste as a quaker-girl's,
    And your mouth—there was never, to my mind,
Such a funny mouth, for it would not shut;
    And the dented chin too—what a chin!

There were certain ways when you spoke, some words
    That you know you never could pronounce:
You were thin, however; like a bird's
    Your hand seemed—some would say, the pounce
Of a scaly-footed hawk—all but!
    The world was right when it called you thin.

XII

But I turn my back on the world: I take
    Your hand, and kneel, and lay to my lips.
Bid me live, Edith! Let me slake
    Thirst at your presence! Fear no slips:
'Tis your slave shall pay, while his soul endures,
    Full due, love's whole debt, *summum jus.*
My queen shall have high observance, planned
    Courtship made perfect, no least line
Crossed without warrant. There you stand,
    Warm too, and white too: would this wine
Had washed all over that body of yours,
    Ere I drank it, and you down with it, thus!

ABT VOGLER

(AFTER HE HAS BEEN EXTEMPORIZING UPON THE MUSICAL
INSTRUMENT OF HIS INVENTION.)

I

WOULD that the structure brave, the manifold music I
    build,
    Bidding my organ obey, calling its keys to their work,
Claiming each slave of the sound, at a touch, as when
    Solomon willed
    Armies of angels that soar, legions of demons that lurk,
Man, brute, reptile, fly,—alien of end and of aim,
    Adverse, each from the other heaven-high, hell-deep
    removed,—
Should rush into sight at once as he named the ineffable
    Name,
    And pile him a palace straight, to pleasure the prin-
    cess he loved!

II

Would it might tarry like his, the beautiful building of
 mine,
   This which my keys in a crowd pressed and importuned
    to raise!
Ah, one and all, how they helped, would dispart now and
 now combine,
   Zealous to hasten the work, heighten their master his
    praise!
And one would bury his brow with a blind plunge down
 to hell,
   Burrow awhile and build, broad on the roots of things,
Then up again swim into sight, having based me my
 palace well,
   Founded it, fearless of flame, flat on the nether springs.

III

And another would mount and march, like the excellent
 minion he was,
   Ay, another and yet another, one crowd but with
    many a crest,
Raising my rampired walls of gold as transparent as glass,
   Eager to do and die, yield each his place to the rest:
For higher still and higher (as a runner tips with fire,
   When a great illumination surprises a festal night—
Outlining round and round Rome's dome from space to
 spire)
   Up, the pinnacled glory reached, and the pride of my
    soul was in sight.

IV

In sight? Not half! for it seemed, it was certain, to match
 man's birth,
   Nature in turn conceived, obeying an impulse as I;
And the emulous heaven yearned down, made effort to
 reach the earth,
   As the earth had done her best, in my passion, to scale
    the sky:

Novel splendours burst forth, grew familiar and dwelt
　　with mine,
　　Not a point nor peak but found and fixed its wander-
　　　　ing star;
Meteor-moons, balls of blaze: and they did not pale nor
　　pine,
　　For earth had attained to heaven, there was no more
　　　　near nor far.

V

Nay more; for there wanted not who walked in the glare
　　and glow,
　　Presences plain in the place; or, fresh from the Proto-
　　　　plast,
Furnished for ages to come, when a kindlier wind should
　　blow,
　　Lured now to begin and live, in a house to their liking
　　　　at last;
Or else the wonderful Dead who have passed through the
　　body and gone,
　　But were back once more to breathe in an old world
　　　　worth their new:
What never had been, was now; what was, as it shall be
　　anon;
　　And what is,—shall I say, matched both? for I was
　　　　made perfect too.

VI

All through my keys that gave their sounds to a wish of
　　my soul,
　　All through my soul that praised as its wish flowed
　　　　visibly forth,
All through music and me! For think, had I painted the
　　whole,
　　Why, there it had stood, to see, nor the process so
　　　　wonder-worth:

Had I written the same, made verse—still, effect proceeds
    from cause,
    Ye know why the forms are fair, ye hear how the tale
        is told;
It is all triumphant art, but art in obedience to laws,
    Painter and poet are proud in the artist-list enrolled:—

VII

But here is the finger of God, a flash of the will that
    can,
    Existent behind all laws, that made them and, lo, they
        are!
And I know not if, save in this, such gift be allowed to
    man,
    That out of three sounds he frame, not a fourth sound,
        but a star.
Consider it well: each tone of our scale in itself is nought;
    It is everywhere in the world—loud, soft, and all is
        said:
Give it to me to use! I mix it with two in my thought:
    And, there! Ye have heard and seen: consider and bow
        the head!

VIII

Well, it is gone at last, the palace of music I reared;
    Gone! and the good tears start, the praises that come
        too slow;
For one is assured at first, one scarce can say that he
    feared,
    That he even gave it a thought, the gone thing was to
        go
Never to be again! But many more of the kind
    As good, nay, better perchance: is this your comfort
        to me?
To me, who must be saved because I cling with my
    mind
    To the same, same self, same love, same God: ay, what
        was, shall be.

IX

Therefore to whom turn I but to thee, the ineffable Name?
  Builder and maker, thou, of houses not made with
    hands!
What, have fear of change from thee who art ever the
    same?
  Doubt that thy power can fill the heart that thy power
    expands?
There shall never be one lost good! What was, shall live
    as before;
  The evil is null, is nought, is silence implying sound;
What was good shall be good, with, for evil, so much
    good more;
  On the earth the broken arcs; in the heaven, a perfect
    round.

X

All we have willed or hoped or dreamed of good shall
    exist;
  Not its semblance, but itself; no beauty, nor good, nor
    power
Whose voice has gone forth, but each survives for the
    melodist
When eternity affirms the conception of an hour.
The high that proved too high, the heroic for earth too
    hard,
  The passion that left the ground to lose itself in the sky,
Are music sent up to God by the lover and the bard;
  Enough that he heard it once: we shall hear it by-and-
    by.

XI

And what is our failure here but a triumph's evidence
  For the fulness of the days? Have we withered or
    agonized?
Why else was the pause prolonged but that singing might
    issue thence?
  Why rushed the discords in but that harmony should
    be prized?

Sorrow is hard to bear, and doubt is slow to clear,
  Each sufferer says his say, his scheme of the weal and
    woe:
But God has a few of us whom he whispers in the ear;
  The rest may reason and welcome: 'tis we musicians
    know.

XII

Well, it is earth with me; silence resumes her reign:
  I will be patient and proud, and soberly acquiesce.
Give me the keys. I feel for the common chord again,
  Sliding by semitones, till I sink to the minor,—yes,
And I blunt it into a ninth, and I stand on alien ground,
  Surveying awhile the heights I rolled from into the
    deep;
Which, hark, I have dared and done, for my resting-place
  is found,
  The C Major of this life: so, now I will try to sleep.

RABBI BEN EZRA

I

      Grow old along with me!
      The best is yet to be,
The last of life, for which the first was made:
      Our times are in His hand
      Who saith 'A whole I planned,
'Youth shows but half; trust God: see all nor be afraid!'

II

      Not that, amassing flowers,
      Youth sighed 'Which rose make ours,
'Which lily leave and then as best recall?'
      Not that, admiring stars,
      It yearned 'Nor Jove, nor Mars;
'Mine be some figured flame which blends, transcends
    them all!'

III

Not for such hopes and fears
    Annulling youth's brief years,
Do I remonstrate: folly wide the mark!
    Rather I prize the doubt
    Low kinds exist without,
Finished and finite clods, untroubled by a spark.

IV

Poor vaunt of life indeed,
    Were man but formed to feed
On joy, to solely seek and find and feast:
    Such feasting ended, then
    As sure an end to men;
Irks care the crop-full bird? Frets doubt the maw-
    crammed beast?

V

Rejoice we are allied
    To That which doth provide
And not partake, effect and not receive!
    A spark disturbs our clod;
    Nearer we hold of God
Who gives, than of His tribes that take, I must believe.

VI

Then, welcome each rebuff
    That turns earth's smoothness rough,
Each sting that bids nor sit nor stand but go!
    Be our joys three-parts pain!
    Strive, and hold cheap the strain;
Learn, nor account the pang; dare, never grudge the
    throe!

VII

For thence,—a paradox
    Which comforts while it mocks,—
Shall life succeed in that it seems to fail:
    What I aspired to be,
    And was not, comforts me:
A brute I might have been, but would not sink i' the scale.

What is he but a brute
Whose flesh has soul to suit,
Whose spirit works lest arms and legs want play?
To man, propose this test—
Thy body at its best,
How far can that project thy soul on its lone way?

IX

Yet gifts should prove their use:
I own the Past profuse
Of power each side, perfection every turn:
Eyes, ears took in their dole,
Brain treasured up the whole;
Should not the heart beat once 'How good to live and learn?'

X

Not once beat 'Praise be Thine!
'I see the whole design,
'I, who saw power, see now love perfect too:
'Perfect I call Thy plan:
'Thanks that I was a man!
'Maker, remake, complete,—I trust what Thou shalt do!'

XI

For pleasant is this flesh;
Our soul, in its rose-mesh
Pulled ever to the earth, still yearns for rest;
Would we some prize might hold
To match those manifold
Possessions of the brute,—gain most, as we did best!

XII

Let us not always say
'Spite of this flesh to-day
'I strove, made head, gained ground upon the whole!'
As the bird wings and sings,
Let us cry 'All good things
Are ours, nor soul helps flesh more, now, than flesh helps soul!'

Therefore I summon age
To grant youth's heritage,
Life's struggle having so far reached its term:
    Thence shall I pass, approved
    A man, for aye removed
From the developed brute; a god though in the germ.

XIV

And I shall thereupon
Take rest, ere I be gone
Once more on my adventure brave and new:
    Fearless and unperplexed,
    When I wage battle next,
What weapons to select, what armour to indue.

XV

Youth ended, I shall try
My gain or loss thereby;
Leave the fire ashes, what survives is gold:
    And I shall weigh the same,
    Give life its praise or blame:
Young, all lay in dispute; I shall know, being old.

XVI

For note, when evening shuts,
A certain moment cuts
The deed off, calls the glory from the grey:
    A whisper from the west
    Shoots—'Add this to the rest,
'Take it and try its worth: here dies another day.'

XVII

So, still within this life,
Though lifted o'er its strife,
Let me discern, compare, pronounce at last,
    'This rage was right i' the main,
    'That acquiescence vain:
'The Future I may face now I have proved the Past.'

XVIII

For more is not reserved
To man, with soul just nerved
To act to-morrow what he learns to-day:
Here, work enough to watch
The Master work, and catch
Hints of the proper craft, tricks of the tool's true play.

XIX

As it was better, youth
Should strive, through acts uncouth,
Toward making, than repose on aught found made:
So, better, age, exempt
From strife, should know, than tempt
Further. Thou waitedest age: wait death nor be afraid!

XX

Enough now, if the Right
And Good and Infinite
Be named here, as thou callest thy hand thine own,
With knowledge absolute,
Subject to no dispute
From fools that crowded youth, nor let thee feel alone.

XXI

Be there, for once and all,
Severed great minds from small,
Announced to each his station in the Past!
Was I, the world arraigned,
Were they, my soul disdained,
Right? Let age speak the truth and give us peace at last!

XXII

Now, who shall arbitrate?
Ten men love what I hate,
Shun what I follow, slight what I receive;
Ten, who in ears and eyes
Match me: we all surmise,
They this thing, and I that: whom shall my soul believe?

XXIII

Not on the vulgar mass
Called 'work,' must sentence pass,
Things done, that took the eye and had the price;
O'er which, from level stand,
The low world laid its hand,
Found straightway to its mind, could value in a trice:

XXIV

But all, the world's coarse thumb
And finger failed to plumb,
So passed in making up the main account;
All instincts immature,
All purposes unsure,
That weighed not as his work, yet swelled the man's
amount:

XXV

Thoughts hardly to be packed
Into a narrow act,
Fancies that broke through language and escaped;
All I could never be,
All, men ignored in me,
This, I was worth to God, whose wheel the pitcher shaped.

XXVI

Ay, note that Potter's wheel,
That metaphor! and feel
Why time spins fast, why passive lies our clay,—
Thou, to whom fools propound,
When the wine makes its round,
Since life fleets, all is change; the Past gone, seize to-day!'

XXVII

Fool! All that is, at all,
Lasts ever, past recall;
Earth changes, but thy soul and God stand sure:
What entered into thee.
That was, is, and shall be:
Time's wheel runs back or stops: Potter and clay endure.

XXVIII

He fixed thee mid this dance
Of plastic circumstance,
This Present, thou, forsooth, wouldst fain arrest:
　　Machinery just meant
　　To give thy soul its bent,
Try thee and turn thee forth, sufficiently impressed.

XXIX

What though the earlier grooves
Which ran the laughing loves
Around thy base, no longer pause and press?
　　What though, about thy rim,
　　Skull-things in order grim
Grow out, in graver mood, obey the sterner stress?

XXX

Look not thou down but up!
To uses of a cup,
The festal board, lamp's flash and trumpet's peal,
　　The new wine's foaming flow,
　　The Master's lips a-glow!
Thou, heaven's consummate cup, what need'st thou with
　　earth's wheel?

XXXI

But I need, now as then,
Thee, God, who mouldest men;
And since, not even while the whirl was worst,
　　Did I,—to the wheel of life
　　With shapes and colours rife,
Bound dizzily,—mistake my end, to slake Thy thirst:

XXXII

So, take and use Thy work:
Amend what flaws may lurk,
What strain o' the stuff, what warpings past the aim!
　　My times be in Thy hand!
　　Perfect the cup as planned!
Let age approve of youth, and death complete the same!

From 'A DEATH IN THE DESERT'

[SUPPOSED of Pamphylax the Antiochene:
It is a parchment, of my rolls the fifth,
Hath three skins glued together, is all Greek
And goeth from *Epsilon* down to *Mu:*
Lies second in the surnamed Chosen Chest,
Stained and conserved with juice of terebinth,
Covered with cloth of hair, and lettered *Xi,*
From Xanthus, my wife's uncle, now at peace:
Mu and *Epsilon* stand for my own name.
I may not write it, but I make a cross
To show I wait His coming, with the rest.
And leave off here: beginneth Pamphylax.]

I said, 'If one should wet his lips with wine,
'And slip the broadest plantain-leaf we find,
'Or else the lappet of a linen robe,
'Into the water-vessel, lay it right,
'And cool his forehead just above the eyes,
'The while a brother, kneeling either side,
'Should chafe each hand and try to make it warm,—
'He is not so far gone but he might speak.'

This did not happen in the outer cave,
Nor in the secret chamber of the rock
Where, sixty days since the decree was out,
We had him, bedded on a camel-skin,
And waited for his dying all the while;
But in the midmost grotto: since noon's light
Reached there a little, and we would not lose
The last of what might happen on his face.

I at the head, and Xanthus at the feet,
With Valens and the Boy, had lifted him,
And brought him from the chamber in the depths,
And laid him in the light where we might see:
For certain smiles began about his mouth,
And his lids moved, presageful of the end.

Beyond and half way up the mouth o' the cave,
The Bactrian convert, having his desire,
Kept watch, and made pretence to graze a goat
That gave us milk, on rags of various herb,
Plantain and quitch, the rocks' shade keeps alive:
So that if any thief or soldier passed,
(Because the persecution was aware)
Yielding the goat up promptly with his life,
Such man might pass on, joyful at a prize,
Nor care to pry into the cool o' the cave.
Outside was all noon and the burning blue.

'Here is wine,' answered Xanthus,—dropped a drop;
I stooped and placed the lap of cloth aright,
Then chafed his right hand, and the Boy his left:
But Valens had bethought him, and produced
And broke a ball of nard, and made perfume.
Only, he did—not so much wake, as—turn
And smile a little, as a sleeper does
If any dear one call him, touch his face—
And smiles and loves, but will not be disturbed.

Then Xanthus said a prayer, but still he slept:
It is the Xanthus that escaped to Rome,
Was burned, and could not write the chronicle.

Then the Boy sprang up from his knees, and ran,
Stung by the splendour of a sudden thought,
And fetched the seventh plate of graven lead
Out of the secret chamber, found a place,
Pressing with finger on the deeper dints,
And spoke, as 'twere his mouth proclaiming first,
'I am the Resurrection and the Life.'

Whereat he opened his eyes wide at once,
And sat up of himself, and looked at us;
And thenceforth nobody pronounced a word:
Only, outside, the Bactrian cried his cry
Like the lone desert-bird that wears the ruff,
As signal we were safe, from time to time.

* * * * * *

CALIBAN UPON SETEBOS; OR, NATURAL THEOLOGY IN THE ISLAND

'Thou thoughtest that I was altogether such a one as thyself.'

['WILL sprawl, now that the heat of day is best,
Flat on his belly in the pit's much mire,
With elbows wide, fists clenched to prop his chin.
And, while he kicks both feet in the cool slush,
And feels about his spine small eft-things course,
Run in and out each arm, and make him laugh:
And while above his head a pompion-plant,
Coating the cave-top as a brow its eye,
Creeps down to touch and tickle hair and beard,
And now a flower drops with a bee inside,
And now a fruit to snap at, catch and crunch,—
He looks out o'er yon sea which sunbeams cross
And recross till they weave a spider-web
(Meshes of fire, some great fish breaks at times)
And talks to his own self, howe'er he please,
Touching that other, whom his dam called God.
Because to talk about Him, vexes—ha,
Could He but know! and time to vex is now,
When talk is safer than in winter-time.
Moreover Prosper and Miranda sleep
In confidence he drudges at their task,
And it is good to cheat the pair, and gibe,
Letting the rank tongue blossom into speech.]

Setebos, Setebos, and Setebos!
'Thinketh, He dwelleth i' the cold o' the moon.

'Thinketh He made it, with the sun to match,
But not the stars; the stars come otherwise;
Only made clouds, winds, meteors, such as that:
Also this isle, what lives and grows thereon,
And snaky sea which rounds and ends the same.

'Thinketh, it came of being ill at ease:
He hated that He cannot change His cold,

Nor cure its ache. 'Hath spied an icy fish
That longed to 'scape the rock-stream where she lived,
And thaw herself within the lukewarm brine
O' the lazy sea her stream thrusts far amid,
A crystal spike 'twixt two warm walls of wave;
Only, she ever sickened, found repulse
At the other kind of water, not her life,
(Green-dense and dim-delicious, bred o' the sun)
Flounced back from bliss she was not born to breathe,
And in her old bounds buried her despair,
Hating and loving warmth alike: so He.

'Thinketh, He made thereat the sun, this isle,
Trees and the fowls here, beast and creeping thing.
Yon otter, sleek-wet, black, lithe as a leech;
Yon auk, one fire-eye in a ball of foam,
That floats and feeds; a certain badger brown
He hath watched hunt with that slant white-wedged eye
By moonlight; and the pie with the long tongue
That pricks deep into oakwarts for a worm,
And says a plain word when she finds her prize,
But will not eat the ants; the ants themselves
That build a wall of seeds and settled stalks
About their hole—He made all these and more,
Made all we see, and us, in spite: how else?
He could not, Himself, make a second self
To be His mate; as well have made Himself:
He would not make what he mislikes or slights,
An eyesore to Him, or not worth His pains:
But did, in envy, listlessness or sport,
Make what Himself would fain, in a manner, be—
Weaker in most points, stronger in a few,
Worthy, and yet mere playthings all the while,
Things He admires and mocks too,—that is it.
Because, so brave, so better though they be,
It nothing skills if He begin to plague.
Look now, I melt a gourd-fruit into mash,
Add honeycomb and pods, I have perceived,
Which bite like finches when they bill and kiss,—

Then, when froth rises bladdery, drink up all,
Quick, quick, till maggots scamper through my brain;
Last, throw me on my back i' the seeded thyme,
And wanton, wishing I were born a bird.
Put case, unable to be what I wish,
I yet could make a live bird out of clay:
Would not I take clay, pinch my Caliban
Able to fly?—for, there, see, he hath wings,
And great comb like the hoopoe's to admire,
And there, a sting to do his foes offence,
There, and I will that he begin to live,
Fly to yon rock-top, nip me off the horns
Of grigs high up that make the merry din,
Saucy through their veined wings, and mind me not.
In which feat, if his leg snapped, brittle clay,
And he lay stupid-like,—why, I should laugh;
And if he, spying me, should fall to weep,
Beseech me to be good, repair his wrong,
Bid his poor leg smart less or grow again,—
Well, as the chance were, this might take or else
Not take my fancy: I might hear his cry,
And give the manikin three sound legs for one,
Or pluck the other off, leave him like an egg,
And lessoned he was mine and merely clay,
Were this no pleasure, lying in the thyme,
Drinking the mash, with brain become alive,
Making and marring clay at will? So He.

'Thinketh, such shows nor right nor wrong in Him,
Nor kind, nor cruel: He is strong and Lord.
'Am strong myself compared to yonder crabs
That march now from the mountain to the sea;
'Let twenty pass, and stone the twenty-first,
Loving not, hating not, just choosing so.
'Say, the first straggler that boasts purple spots
Shall join the file, one pincer twisted off;
'Say, this bruised fellow shall receive a worm,
And two worms he whose nippers end in red;
As it likes me each time, I do: so He.

Well then, 'supposeth He is good i' the main,
Placable if His mind and ways were guessed,
But rougher than His handiwork, be sure!
Oh, He hath made things worthier than Himself,
And envieth that, so helped, such things do more
Than He who made them! What consoles but this?
That they, unless through Him, do nought at all,
And must submit: what other use in things?
'Hath cut a pipe of pithless elder-joint
That, blown through, gives exact the scream o' the jay
When from her wing you twitch the feathers blue:
Sound this, and little birds that hate the jay
Flock within stone's throw, glad their foe is hurt:
Put case such pipe could prattle and boast forsooth
'I catch the birds, I am the crafty thing,
'I make the cry my maker cannot make
'With his great round mouth; he must blow through
          mine!'
Would not I smash it with my foot? So He.

But wherefore rough, why cold and ill at ease?
Aha, that is a question! Ask, for that,
What knows,—the something over Setebos
That made Him, or He, may be, found and fought,
Worsted, drove off and did to nothing, perchance.
There may be something quiet o'er His head,
Out of His reach, that feels nor joy nor grief,
Since both derive from weakness in some way.
I joy because the quails come; would not joy
Could I bring quails here when I have a mind:
This Quiet, all it hath a mind to, doth.
'Esteemeth stars the outposts of its couch,
But never spends much thought nor care that way.
It may look up, work up,—the worse for those
It works on! 'Careth but for Setebos
The many-handed as a cuttle-fish,
Who, making Himself feared through what He does,
Looks up, first, and perceives he cannot soar
To what is quiet and hath happy life;

Next looks down here, and out of very spite
Makes this a bauble-world to ape yon real,
These good things to match those as hips do grapes.
'Tis solace making baubles, ay, and sport.
Himself peeped late, eyed Prosper at his books
Careless and lofty, lord now of the isle:
Vexed, 'stitched a book of broad leaves, arrow-shaped,
Wrote thereon, he knows what, prodigious words;
Has peeled a wand and called it by a name;
Weareth at whiles for an enchanter's robe
The eyed skin of a supple ocelot;
And hath an ounce sleeker than youngling mole,
A four-legged serpent he makes cower and couch,
Now snarl, now hold its breath and mind his eye,
And saith she is Miranda and my wife:
'Keeps for his Ariel a tall pouch-bill crane
He bids go wade for fish and straight disgorge;
Also a sea-beast, lumpish, which he snared,
Blinded the eyes of, and brought somewhat tame,
And split its toe-webs, and now pens the drudge
In a hole o' the rock and calls him Caliban;
A bitter heart that bides its time and bites.
'Plays thus at being Prosper in a way,
Taketh his mirth with make-believes: so He.

His dam held that the Quiet made all things
Which Setebos vexed only: 'holds not so.
Who made them weak, meant weakness He might vex.
Had He meant other, while His Hand was in,
Why not make horny eyes no thorn could prick,
Or plate my scalp with bone against the snow,
Or overscale my flesh 'neath joint and joint,
Like an orc's armour? Ay,—so spoil His sport!
He is the One now: only He doth all.

'Saith, He may like, perchance, what profits Him.
Ay, himself loves what does him good; but why?
'Gets good no otherwise. This blinded beast
Loves whoso places flesh-meat on his nose,

But, had he eyes, would want no help, but hate
Or love, just as it liked him: He hath eyes.
Also it pleaseth Setebos to work,
Use all His hands, and exercise much craft,
By no means for the love of what is worked.
'Tasteth, himself, no finer good i' the world
When all goes right, in this safe summer-time,
And he wants little, hungers, aches not much,
Than trying what to do with wit and strength.
'Falls to make something: 'piled yon pile of turfs,
And squared and stuck there squares of soft white chalk,
And, with a fish-tooth, scratched a moon on each,
And set up endwise certain spikes of tree,
And crowned the whole with a sloth's skull a-top,
Found dead i' the woods, too hard for one to kill.
No use at all i' the work, for work's sole sake;
'Shall some day knock it down again: so He.

'Saith He is terrible: watch His feats in proof!
One hurricane will spoil six good months' hope.
He hath a spite against me, that I know,
Just as He favours Prosper, who knows why?
So it is, all the same, as well I find.
'Wove wattles half the winter, fenced them firm
With stone and stake to stop she-tortoises
Crawling to lay their eggs here: well, one wave,
Feeling the foot of Him upon its neck,
Gaped as a snake does, lolled out its large tongue,
And licked the whole labour flat: so much for spite.
'Saw a ball flame down late (yonder it lies)
Where, half an hour before, I slept i' the shade:
Often they scatter sparkles: there is force!
'Dug up a newt He may have envied once
And turned to stone, shut up inside a stone.
Please Him and hinder this?—What Prosper does?
Aha, if He would tell me how! Not He!
There is the sport: discover how or die!
All need not die, for of the things o' the isle
Some flee afar, some dive, some run up trees;

Those at His mercy,—why, they please Him most
When . . . when . . . well, never try the same way twice!
Repeat what act has pleased, He may grow wroth.
You must not know His ways, and play Him off,
Sure of the issue. 'Doth the like himself:
'Spareth a squirrel that it nothing fears
But steals the nut from underneath my thumb,
And when I threat, bites stoutly in defence:
'Spareth an urchin that contrariwise,
Curls up into a ball, pretending death
For fright at my approach: the two ways please.
But what would move my choler more than this,
That either creature counted on its life
To-morrow and next day and all days to come,
Saying, forsooth, in the inmost of its heart,
'Because he did so yesterday with me,
'And otherwise with such another brute,
'So must he do henceforth and always.'—Ay?
Would teach the reasoning couple what 'must' means!
'Doth as he likes, or wherefore Lord? So He.

'Conceiveth all things will continue thus,
And we shall have to live in fear of Him
So long as He lives, keeps His strength: no change,
If He have done His best, make no new world
To please Him more, so leave off watching this,—
If He surprise not even the Quiet's self
Some strange day,—or, suppose, grow into it
As grubs grow butterflies: else, here are we,
And there is He, and nowhere help at all.

'Believeth with the life, the pain shall stop.
His dam held different, that after death
He both plagued enemies and feasted friends:
Idly! He doth His worst in this our life,
Giving just respite lest we die through pain,
Saving last pain for worst,—with which, an end.
Meanwhile, the best way to escape His ire
Is, not to seem too happy. 'Sees, himself,
Yonder two flies, with purple films and pink,

Bask on the pompion-bell above: kills both.
'Sees two black painful beetles roll their ball
On head and tail as if to save their lives:
Moves them the stick away they strive to clear.

Even so, 'would have Him misconceive, suppose
This Caliban strives hard and ails no less,
And always, above all else, envies Him;
Wherefore he mainly dances on dark nights,
Moans in the sun, gets under holes to laugh,
And never speaks his mind save housed as now:
Outside, 'groans, curses. If He caught me here,
O'erheard this speech, and asked 'What chucklest at?'
'Would, to appease Him, cut a finger off,
Or of my three kid yearlings burn the best,
Or let the toothsome apples rot on tree,
Or push my tame beast for the orc to taste:
While myself lit a fire, and made a song
And sung it, '*What I hate, be consecrate*
'*To celebrate Thee and Thy state, no mate*
'*For Thee; what see for envy in poor me?*'
Hoping the while, since evils sometimes mend,
Warts rub away and sores are cured with slime,
That some strange day, will either the Quiet catch
And conquer Setebos, or likelier He
Decrepit may doze, doze, as good as die.

———————

[What, what? A curtain o'er the world at once!
Crickets stop hissing; not a bird—or, yes,
There scuds His raven that has told Him all!
It was fool's play, this prattling! Ha! The wind
Shoulders the pillared dust, death's house o' the move,
And fast invading fires begin! White blaze—
A tree's head snaps—and there, there, there, there, there,
His thunder follows! Fool to gibe at Him!
Lo! 'Lieth flat and loveth Setebos!
'Maketh his teeth meet through his upper lip,
Will let those quails fly, will not eat this month
One little mess of whelks, so he may 'scape!]

CONFESSIONS

I

WHAT is he buzzing in my ears?
  'Now that I come to die,
'Do I view the world as a vale of tears?'
  Ah, reverend sir, not I!

II

What I viewed there once, what I view again
  Where the physic bottles stand
On the table's edge,—is a suburb lane,
  With a wall to my bedside hand.

III

That lane sloped, much as the bottles do,
  From a house you could descry
O'er the garden-wall: is the curtain blue
  Or green to a healthy eye?

IV

To mine, it serves for the old June weather
  Blue above lane and wall;
And that farthest bottle labelled 'Ether'
  Is the house o'ertopping all.

V

At a terrace, somewhere near the stopper,
  There watched for me, one June,
A girl: I know, sir, it's improper,
  My poor mind's out of tune.

VI

Only, there was a way . . . you crept
  Close by the side, to dodge
Eyes in the house, two eyes except:
  They styled their house 'The Lodge.'

VII

What right had a lounger up their lane?
 But, by creeping very close,
With the good wall's help,—their eyes might strain
 And stretch themselves to Oes,

VIII

Yet never catch her and me together,
 As she left the attic, there,
By the rim of the bottle labelled 'Ether,'
 And stole from stair to stair,

IX

And stood by the rose-wreathed gate. Alas,
 We loved, sir—used to meet:
How sad and bad and mad it was—
 But then, how it was sweet!

MAY AND DEATH

I

I wish that when you died last May,
 Charles, there had died along with you
Three parts of spring's delightful things;
 Ay, and, for me, the fourth part too.

II

A foolish thought, and worse, perhaps!
 There must be many a pair of friends
Who, arm in arm, deserve the warm
 Moon-births and the long evening-ends.

III

So, for their sake, be May still May!
 Let their new time, as mine of old,
Do all it did for me: I bid
 Sweet sights and sounds throng manifold.

IV

Only, one little sight, one plant,
　　Woods have in May, that starts up green
Save a sole streak which, so to speak,
　　Is spring's blood, spilt its leaves between,—

V

That, they might spare; a certain wood
　　Might miss the plant; their loss were small:
But I,—whene'er the leaf grows there,
　　Its drop comes from my heart, that's all.

DEAF AND DUMB

A GROUP BY WOOLNER

ONLY the prism's obstruction shows aright
The secret of a sunbeam, breaks its light
Into the jewelled bow from blankest white;
　　So may a glory from defect arise:
Only by Deafness may the vexed Love wreak
Its insuppressive sense on brow and cheek,
Only by Dumbness adequately speak
　　As favoured mouth could never, through the eyes.

PROSPICE

FEAR death?—to feel the fog in my throat,
　　The mist in my face,
When the snows begin, and the blasts denote
　　I am nearing the place,
The power of the night, the press of the storm,
　　The post of the foe;
Where he stands, the Arch Fear in a visible form,
　　Yet the strong man must go:
For the journey is done and the summit attained,
　　And the barriers fall,
Though a battle's to fight ere the guerdon be gained,
　　The reward of it all.

I was ever a fighter, so—one fight more,
  The best and the last!
I would hate that death bandaged my eyes, and forbore,
  And bade me creep past.
No! let me taste the whole of it, fare like my peers
  The heroes of old,
Bear the brunt, in a minute pay glad life's arrears
  Of pain, darkness and cold.
For sudden the worst turns the best to the brave,
  The black minute's at end,
And the elements' rage, the fiend-voices that rave,
  Shall dwindle, shall blend,
Shall change, shall become first a peace out of pain,
  Then a light, then thy breast,
O thou soul of my soul! I shall clasp thee again,
  And with God be the rest!

EURYDICE TO ORPHEUS

A PICTURE BY LEIGHTON

But give them me, the mouth, the eyes, the brow!
Let them once more absorb me! One look now
  Will lap me round for ever, not to pass
Out of its light, though darkness lie beyond:
Hold me but safe again within the bond
  Of one immortal look! All woe that was,
Forgotten, and all terror that may be,
Defied,—no past is mine, no future: look at me!

YOUTH AND ART

I

It once might have been, once only:
  We lodged in a street together,
You, a sparrow on the housetop lonely,
  I, a lone she-bird of his feather.

II

Your trade was with sticks and clay,
    You thumbed, thrust, patted and polished,
Then laughed 'They will see some day
    'Smith made, and Gibson demolished.'

III

My business was song, song, song;
    I chirped, cheeped, trilled and twittered,
'Kate Brown's on the boards ere long,
    'And Grisi's existence embittered!'

IV

I earned no more by a warble
    Than you by a sketch in plaster;
You wanted a piece of marble,
    I needed a music-master.

V

We studied hard in our styles,
    Chipped each at a crust like Hindoos,
For air looked out on the tiles,
    For fun watched each other's windows.

VI

You lounged, like a boy of the South,
    Cap and blouse—nay, a bit of beard too;
Or you got it, rubbing your mouth
    With fingers the clay adhered to.

VII

And I—soon managed to find
    Weak points in the flower-fence facing,
Was forced to put up a blind
    And be safe in my corset-lacing.

VIII

No harm! It was not my fault
    If you never turned your eye's tail up
As I shook upon E *in alt*,
    Or ran the chromatic scale up:

IX

For spring bade the sparrows pair,
  And the boys and girls gave guesses,
And stalls in our street looked rare
  With bulrush and watercresses.

X

Why did not you pinch a flower
  In a pellet of clay and fling it?
Why did not I put a power
  Of thanks in a look, or sing it?

XI

I did look, sharp as a lynx,
  (And yet the memory rankles)
When models arrived, some minx
  Tripped up-stairs, she and her ankles.

XII

But I think I gave you as good!
  'That foreign fellow,—who can know
'How she pays, in a playful mood,
  'For his tuning her that piano?'

XIII

Could you say so, and never say
  'Suppose we join hands and fortunes,
'And I fetch her from over the way,
  'Her piano, and long tunes and short tunes?'

XIV

No, no: you would not be rash,
  Nor I rasher and something over:
You've to settle yet Gibson's hash,
  And Grisi yet lives in clover.

XV

But you meet the Prince at the Board,
  I'm queen myself at *bals-paré*,
I've married a rich old lord,
  And you're dubbed knight and an R.A.

XVI

Each life unfulfilled, you see;
   It hangs still, patchy and scrappy:
We have not sighed deep, laughed free,
   Starved, feasted, despaired,—been happy.

XVII

And nobody calls you a dunce,
   And people suppose me clever:
This could but have happened once,
   And we missed it, lost it for ever.

A FACE

IF one could have that little head of hers
 Painted upon a background of pale gold,
Such as the Tuscan's early art prefers!
   No shade encroaching on the matchless mould
Of those two lips, which should be opening soft
   In the pure profile; not as when she laughs,
For that spoils all: but rather as if aloft
   Yon hyacinth, she loves so, leaned its staff's
Burthen of honey-coloured buds to kiss
And capture 'twixt the lips apart for this.
Then her lithe neck, three fingers might surround,
How it should waver on the pale gold ground
Up to the fruit-shaped, perfect chin it lifts!
I know, Correggio loves to mass, in rifts
Of heaven, his angel faces, orb on orb
Breaking its outline, burning shades absorb:
But these are only massed there, I should think,
   Waiting to see some wonder momently
   Grow out, stand full, fade slow against the sky
   (That's the pale ground you'd see this sweet face by),
   All heaven, meanwhile, condensed into one eye
Which fears to lose the wonder, should it wink.

A LIKENESS

Some people hang portraits up
In a room where they dine or sup:
　　And the wife clinks tea-things under,
And her cousin, he stirs his cup,
　　Asks, 'Who was the lady, I wonder?'
''Tis a daub John bought at a sale,'
　　Quoth the wife,—looks black as thunder:
'What a shade beneath her nose!
'Snuff-taking, I suppose,—'
Adds the cousin, while John's corns ail.

Or else, there's no wife in the case,
But the portrait's queen of the place,
Alone 'mid the other spoils
Of youth,—masks, gloves and foils,
And pipe-sticks, rose, cherry-tree, jasmine,
　　And the long whip, the tandem-lasher,
And the cast from a fist ('not, alas! mine,
　　'But my master's, the Tipton Slasher'),
And the cards where pistol-balls mark ace,
And a satin shoe used for cigar-case,
And the chamois-horns ('shot in the Chablais')
　　And prints—Rarey drumming on Cruiser,
　　And Sayers, our champion, the bruiser,
And the little edition of Rabelais:
Where a friend, with both hands in his pockets,
　　May saunter up close to examine it,
　　And remark a good deal of Jane Lamb in it,
'But the eyes are half out of their sockets;
'That hair's not so bad, where the gloss is,
'But they've made the girl's nose a proboscis:
'Jane Lamb, that we danced with at Vichy!
'What, is not she Jane? Then, who is she?'

All that I own is a print,
An etching, a mezzotint;
'Tis a study, a fancy, a fiction,
Yet a fact (take my conviction)

Because it has more than a hint
 Of a certain face, I never
Saw elsewhere touch or trace of
In women I've seen the face of:
 Just an etching, and, so far, clever.

I keep my prints, an imbroglio,
Fifty in one portfolio.
When somebody tries my claret,
We turn round chairs to the fire,
Chirp over days in a garret,
 Chuckle o'er increase of salary,
Taste the good fruits of our leisure,
Talk about pencil and lyre,
 And the National Portrait Gallery:
Then I exhibit my treasure.
After we've turned over twenty,
 And the debt of wonder my crony owes
 Is paid to my Marc Antonios,
He stops me—'*Festina lentè!*
'What's that sweet thing there, the etching?'
How my waistcoat-strings want stretching,
 How my cheeks grow red as tomatos,
How my heart leaps! But hearts, after leaps, ache.

'By the by, you must take, for a keepsake,
 'That other, you praised, of Volpato's.'
The fool! would he try a flight further and say—
He never saw, never before to-day,
What was able to take his breath away,
A face to lose youth for, to occupy age
With the dream of, meet death with,—why, I'll not engage
But that, half in a rapture and half in a rage,
I should toss him the thing's self—''Tis only a duplicate,
'A thing of no value! Take it, I supplicate!'

MR. SLUDGE, 'THE MEDIUM'

Now, don't, sir! Don't expose me! Just this once!
This was the first and only time, I'll swear,—
Look at me,—see, I kneel,—the only time,
I swear, I ever cheated,—yes, by the soul
Of Her who hears—(your sainted mother, sir!)
All, except this last accident, was truth—
This little kind of slip!—and even this,
It was your own wine, sir, the good champagne,
(I took it for Catawba, you're so kind)
Which put the folly in my head!

       'Get up?'
You still inflict on me that terrible face?
You show no mercy?—Not for Her dear sake,
The sainted spirit's, whose soft breath even now
Blows on my cheek—(don't you feel something, sir?)
You'll tell?

   Go tell, then! Who the devil cares
What such a rowdy chooses to . . .

        Aie—aie—aie!
Please, sir! your thumbs are through my windpipe, sir!
Ch—ch!

   Well, sir, I hope you've done it now!
Oh Lord! I little thought, sir, yesterday,
When your departed mother spoke those words
Of peace through me, and moved you, sir, so much,
You gave me—(very kind it was of you)
These shirt-studs—(better take them back again,
Please, sir)—yes, little did I think so soon
A trifle of trick, all through a glass too much
Of his own champagne, would change my best of friends
Into an angry gentleman!

       Though, 'twas wrong.
I don't contest the point; your anger's just:
Whatever put such folly in my head,
I know 'twas wicked of me. There's a thick

Dusk undeveloped spirit (I've observed)
Owes me a grudge—a negro's, I should say,
Or else an Irish emigrant's; yourself
Explained the case so well last Sunday, sir,
When we had summoned Franklin to clear up
A point about those shares i' the telegraph:
Ay, and he swore . . . or might it be Tom Paine? . . .
Thumping the table close by where I crouched,
He'd do me soon a mischief: that's come true!
Why, now your face clears! I was sure it would!
Then, this one time . . . don't take your hand away,
Through yours I surely kiss your mother's hand . . .
You'll promise to forgive me?—or, at least,
Tell nobody of this? Consider, sir!
What harm can mercy do? Would but the shade
Of the venerable dead-one just vouchsafe
A rap or tip! What bit of paper 's here?
Suppose we take a pencil, let her write,
Make the least sign, she urges on her child
Forgiveness? There now! Eh? Oh! 'Twas your foot,
And not a natural creak, sir?

                              Answer, then!
Once, twice, thrice . . . see, I'm waiting to say 'thrice!'
All to no use? No sort of hope for me?
It's all to post to Greeley's newspaper?

What? If I told you all about the tricks?
Upon my soul!—the whole truth, and nought else,
And how there's been some falsehood—for your part,
Will you engage to pay my passage out,
And hold your tongue until I'm safe on board?
England's the place, not Boston—no offence!
I see what makes you hesitate: don't fear!
I mean to change my trade and cheat no more,
Yes, this time really it's upon my soul!
Be my salvation!—under Heaven, of course.
I'll tell some queer things. Sixty Vs must do.
A trifle, though, to start with! We'll refer
The question to this table?

How you're changed!
Then split the difference; thirty more, we'll say.
Ay, but you leave my presents! Else I'll swear
'Twas all through those: you wanted yours again,
So, picked a quarrel with me, to get them back!
Tread on a worm, it turns, sir! If I turn,
Your fault! 'Tis you'll have forced me! Who's obliged
To give up life yet try no self defence?
At all events, I'll run the risk. Eh?

Done!
May I sit, sir? This dear old table, now!
Please, sir, a parting egg-nogg and cigar!
I've been so happy with you! Nice stuffed chairs,
And sympathetic sideboards; what an end
To all the instructive evenings! (It's alight.)
Well, nothing lasts, as Bacon came and said.
Here goes,—but keep your temper, or I'll scream!

Fol-lol-the-rido-liddle-iddle-ol!
You see, sir, it's your own fault more than mine;
It's all your fault, you curious gentlefolk!
You're prigs,—excuse me,—like to look so spry,
So clever, while you cling by half a claw
To the perch whereon you puff yourselves at roost,
Such piece of self-conceit as serves for perch
Because you chose it, so it must be safe.
Oh, otherwise you're sharp enough! You spy
Who slips, who slides, who holds by help of wing,
Wanting real foothold,—who can't keep upright
On the other perch, your neighbour chose, not you:
There's no outwitting you respecting him!
For instance, men love money—that, you know
And what men do to gain it: well, suppose
A poor lad, say a help's son in your house,
Listening at keyholes, hears the company
Talk grand of dollars, V-notes, and so forth,
How hard they are to get, how good to hold,
How much they buy,—if, suddenly, in pops he—
'*I*'ve got a V-note!'—what do you say to him?

What's your first word which follows your last kick?
'Where did you steal it, rascal?' That's because
He finds you, fain would fool you, off your perch,
Not on the special piece of nonsense, sir,
Elected your parade-ground: let him try
Lies to the end of the list,—'He picked it up,
'His cousin died and left it him by will,
'The President flung it to him, riding by,
'An actress trucked it for a curl of his hair,
'He dreamed of luck and found his shoe enriched,
'He dug up clay, and out of clay made gold'—
How would you treat such possibilities?
Would not you, prompt, investigate the case
With cow-hide? 'Lies, lies, lies,' you'd shout: and why?
Which of the stories might not prove mere truth?
This last, perhaps, that clay was turned to coin!
Let's see, now, give him me to speak for him!
How many of your rare philosophers,
In plaguy books I've had to dip into,
Believed gold could be made thus, saw it made
And made it? Oh, with such philosophers
You're on your best behaviour! While the lad—
With him, in a trice, you settle likelihoods,
Nor doubt a moment how he got his prize:
In his case, you hear, judge and execute,
All in a breath: so would most men of sense.

But let the same lad hear you talk as grand
At the same keyhole, you and company,
Of signs and wonders, the invisible world;
How wisdom scouts our vulgar unbelief
More than our vulgarest credulity;
How good men have desired to see a ghost,
What Johnson used to say, what Wesley did,
Mother Goose thought, and fiddle-diddle-dee:—
If he break in with, 'Sir, I saw a ghost!'
Ah, the ways change! He finds you perched and prim;
It's a conceit of yours that ghosts may be:
There's no talk now of cow-hide. 'Tell it out!

'Don't fear us! Take your time and recollect!
'Sit down first: try a glass of wine, my boy!
'And, David, (is not that your Christian name?)
'Of all things, should this happen twice—it may—
'Be sure, while fresh in mind, you let us know!'
Does the boy blunder, blurt out this, blab that,
Break down in the other, as beginners will?
All's candour, all's considerateness—'No haste!
'Pause and collect yourself! We understand!
'That's the bad memory, or the natural shock,
'Or the unexplained *phenomena!*'

                              Egad,
The boy takes heart of grace; finds, never fear,
The readiest way to ope your own heart wide,
Show—what I call your peacock-perch, pet post
To strut, and spread the tail, and squawk upon!
'Just as you thought, much as you might expect!
'There be more things in heaven and earth, Horatio,' . . .
And so on. Shall not David take the hint,
Grow bolder, stroke you down at quickened rate?
If he ruffle a feather, it's 'Gently, patiently!
'Manifestations are so weak at first!
'Doubting, moreover, kills them, cuts all short,
'Cures with a vengeance!'

                          There, sir, that's your style!
You and your boy—such pains bestowed on him,
Or any headpiece of the average worth,
To teach, say, Greek, would perfect him apace,
Make him a Person ('Porson'? thank you, sir!)
Much more, proficient in the art of lies.
You never leave the lesson! Fire alight,
Catch you permitting it to die! You've friends;
There's no withholding knowledge,—least from those
Apt to look elsewhere for their souls' supply:
Why should not you parade your lawful prize?
Who finds a picture, digs a medal up,
Hits on a first edition,—he henceforth
Gives it his name, grows notable: how much more,

Who ferrets out a 'medium'? 'David's yours,
'You highly-favoured man? Then, pity souls
'Less privileged! Allow us share your luck!'
So, David holds the circle, rules the roast,
Narrates the vision, peeps in the glass ball,
Sets-to the spirit-writing, hears the raps,
As the case may be.

          Now mark! To be precise—
Though I say, 'lies' all these, at this first stage,
'Tis just for science' sake: I call such grubs
By the name of what they'll turn to, dragonflies.
Strictly, it's what good people style untruth;
But yet, so far, not quite the full-grown thing:
It's fancying, fable-making, nonsense-work—
What never meant to be so very bad—
The knack of story-telling, brightening up
Each dull old bit of fact that drops its shine.
One does see somewhat when one shuts one's eyes,
If only spots and streaks; tables do tip
In the oddest way of themselves: and pens, good Lord,
Who knows if you drive them or they drive you?
'Tis but a foot in the water and out again;
Not that duck-under which decides your dive.
Note this, for it's important: listen why.

I'll prove, you push on David till he dives
And ends the shivering. Here's your circle, now:
Two-thirds of them, with heads like you their host,
Turn up their eyes, and cry, as you expect,
'Lord, who'd have thought it!' But there's always one
Looks wise, compassionately smiles, submits
'Of your veracity no kind of doubt,
'But—do you feel so certain of that boy's?
'Really, I wonder! I confess myself
'More chary of my faith!' That's galling, sir!
What, he the investigator, he the sage,
When all's done? Then, you just have shut your eyes,
Opened your mouth, and gulped down David whole,
You! Terrible were such catastrophe!

So, evidence is redoubled, doubled again,
And doubled besides; once more, 'He heard, we heard,
'You and they heard, your mother and your wife,
'Your children and the stranger in your gates:
'Did they or did they not?' So much for him,
The black sheep, guest without the wedding-garb,
The doubting Thomas! Now's your turn to crow:
'He's kind to think you such a fool: Sludge cheats?
'Leave you alone to take precautions!'
                                        Straight
The rest join chorus. Thomas stands abashed,
Sips silent some such beverage as this,
Considers if it be harder, shutting eyes
And gulping David in good fellowship,
Than going elsewhere, getting, in exchange,
With no egg-nogg to lubricate the food,
Some just as tough a morsel. Over the way,
Holds Captain Sparks his court: is it better there?
Have not you hunting-stories, scalping-scenes,
And Mexican War exploits to swallow plump
If you'd be free o' the stove-side, rocking-chair,
And trio of affable daughters?
                                Doubt succumbs!
Victory! All your circle's yours again!
Out of the clubbing of submissive wits,
David's performance rounds, each chink gets patched,
Every protrusion of a point's filed fine,
All's fit to set a-rolling round the world,
And then return to David finally,
Lies seven-feet thick about his first half-inch.
Here's a choice birth o' the supernatural,
Poor David's pledged to! You've employed no tool
That laws exclaim at, save the devil's own,
Yet screwed him into henceforth gulling you
To the top o' your bent,—all out of one half-lie!

You hold, if there's one half or a hundredth part
Of a lie, that's his fault,—his be the penalty!
I dare say! You'd prove firmer in his place?

You'd find the courage,—that first flurry over,
That mild bit of romancing-work at end,—
To interpose with 'It gets serious, this;
'Must stop here. Sir, I saw no ghost at all.
'Inform your friends I made . . . well, fools of them,
'And found you ready-made. I've lived in clover
'These three weeks: take it out in kicks of me!'
I doubt it. Ask your conscience! Let me know,
Twelve months hence, with how few embellishments
You've told almighty Boston of this passage
Of arms between us, your first taste o' the foil
From Sludge who could not fence, sir! Sludge, your boy!
I lied, sir,—there! I got up from my gorge
On offal in the gutter, and preferred
Your canvas-backs: I took their carver's size,
Measured his modicum of intelligence,
Tickled him on the cockles of his heart
With a raven feather, and next week found myself
Sweet and clean, dining daintily, dizened smart,
Set on a stool buttressed by ladies' knees,
Every soft smiler calling me her pet,
Encouraging my story to uncoil
And creep out from its hole, inch after inch,
'How last night, I no sooner snug in bed,
'Tucked up, just as they left me,—than came raps!
'While a light whisked' . . . 'Shaped somewhat like a
          star?'
'Well, like some sort of stars, ma'am.'—'So we thought!
'And any voice? Not yet? Try hard, next time,
'If you can't hear a voice; we think you may:
'At least, the Pennsylvanian "mediums" did.'
Oh, next time comes the voice! 'Just as we hoped!'
Are not the hopers proud now, pleased, profuse
O' the natural acknowledgment?

                                   Of course!
So, off we push, illy-oh-yo, trim the boat,
On we sweep with a cataract ahead,
We're midway to the Horseshoe: stop, who can,

The dance of bubbles gay about our prow!
Experiences become worth waiting for,
Spirits now speak up, tell their inmost mind,
And compliment the 'medium' properly,
Concern themselves about his Sunday coat,
See rings on his hand with pleasure. Ask yourself
How you'd receive a course of treats like these!
Why, take the quietest hack and stall him up,
Cram him with corn a month, then out with him
Among his mates on a bright April morn,
With the turf to tread; see if you find or no
A caper in him, if he bucks or bolts!
Much more a youth whose fancies sprout as rank
As toadstool-clump from melon-bed. 'Tis soon,
'Sirrah, you spirit, come, go, fetch and carry,
'Read, write, rap, rub-a-dub, and hang yourself!'
I'm spared all further trouble; all's arranged;
Your circle does my business; I may rave
Like an epileptic dervish in the books,
Foam, fling myself flat, rend my clothes to shreds;
No matter: lovers, friends and countrymen
Will lay down spiritual laws, read wrong things right
By the rule o' reverse. If Francis Verulam
Styles himself Bacon, spells the name beside
With a *y* and a *k*, says he drew breath in York,
Gave up the ghost in Wales when Cromwell reigned,
(As, sir, we somewhat fear he was apt to say,
Before I found the useful book that knows)
Why, what harm's done? The circle smiles apace,
'It was not Bacon, after all, you see!
'We understand; the trick's but natural:
'Such spirits' individuality
'Is hard to put in evidence: they incline
'To gibe and jeer, these undeveloped sorts.
'You see, their world's much like a jail broke loose,
'While this of ours remains shut, bolted, barred,
'With a single window to it. Sludge, our friend,
'Serves as this window, whether thin or thick,
'Or stained or stainless; he's the medium-pane

'Through which, to see us and be seen, they peep:
'They crowd each other, hustle for a chance,
'Tread on their neighbour's kibes, play tricks enough!
'Does Bacon, tired of waiting, swerve aside?
'Up in his place jumps Barnum—"I'm your man,
'"I'll answer you for Bacon!" Try once more!'

Or else it's—'What's a "medium"? He's a means,
'Good, bad, indifferent, still the only means
'Spirits can speak by; he may misconceive,
'Stutter and stammer,—he's their Sludge and drudge,
'Take him or leave him; they must hold their peace,
'Or else, put up with having knowledge strained
'To half-expression through his ignorance.
'Suppose, the spirit Beethoven wants to shed
'New music he's brimful of; why, he turns
'The handle of this organ, grinds with Sludge,
'And what he poured in at the mouth o' the mill
'As a Thirty-third Sonata, (fancy now!)
'Comes from the hopper as bran-new Sludge, nought else.
'The Shakers' Hymn in G, with a natural F,
'Or the "Stars and Stripes" set to consecutive fourths.'

Sir, where's the scrape you did not help me through,
You that are wise? And for the fools, the folk
Who came to see,—the guests, (observe that word!)
Pray do you find guests criticize your wine,
Your furniture, your grammar, or your nose?
Then, why your 'medium'? What's the difference?
Prove your madeira red-ink and gamboge,—
Your Sludge, a cheat—then, somebody's a goose
For vaunting both as genuine. 'Guests!' Don't fear!
They'll make a wry face, nor too much of that,
And leave you in your glory.

                              'No, sometimes
'They doubt and say as much!' Ay, doubt they do!
And what's the consequence? 'Of course they doubt'—
(You triumph) 'that explains the hitch at once!

'Doubt posed our "medium," puddled his pure mind;
'He gave them back their rubbish: pitch chaff in,
'Could flour come out o' the honest mill?' So, prompt
Applaud the faithful: cases flock in point,
'How, when a mocker willed a "medium" once
'Should name a spirit James whose name was George,
' "James" cried the "medium,"—'twas the test of truth!'
In short, a hit proves much, a miss proves more.
Does this convince? The better: does it fail?
Time for the double-shotted broadside, then—
The grand means, last resource. Look black and big!
'You style us idiots, therefore—why stop short?
'Accomplices in rascality: this we hear
'In our own house, from our invited guest
'Found brave enough to outrage a poor boy
'Exposed by our good faith! Have you been heard?
'Now, then, hear us; one man's not quite worth twelve.
'You see a cheat? Here's some twelve see an ass
'Excuse me if I calculate: good day!'
Out slinks the sceptic, all the laughs explode.
Sludge waves his hat in triumph!

                                        Or—he don't.
There's something in real truth (explain who can!)
One casts a wistful eye at, like the horse
Who mopes beneath stuffed hay-racks and won't munch
Because he spies a corn-bag: hang that truth,
It spoils all dainties proffered in its place!
I've felt at times when, cockered, cosseted
And coddled by the aforesaid company,
Bidden enjoy their bullying,—never fear,
But o'er their shoulders spit at the flying man,—
I've felt a child; only, a fractious child
That, dandled soft by nurse, aunt, grandmother,
Who keep him from the kennel, sun and wind,
Good fun and wholesome mud,—enjoined be sweet,
And comely and superior,—eyes askance
The ragged sons o' the gutter at their game,
Fain would be down with them i' the thick o' the filth,

Making dirt-pies, laughing free, speaking plain,
And calling granny the grey old cat she is.
I've felt a spite, I say, at you, at them,
Huggings and humbug—gnashed my teeth to mark
A decent dog pass! It's too bad, I say,
Ruining a soul so!

              But what's 'so,' what's fixed,
Where may one stop? Nowhere! The cheating's nursed
Out of the lying, softly and surely spun
To just your length, sir! I'd stop soon enough:
But you're for progress. 'All old, nothing new?
'Only the usual talking through the mouth,
'Or writing by the hand? I own, I thought
'This would develop, grow demonstrable,
'Make doubt absurd, give figures we might see,
'Flowers we might touch. There's no one doubts you,
      Sludge!
'You dream the dreams, you see the spiritual sights,
'The speeches come in your head, beyond dispute.
'Still, for the sceptics' sake, to stop all mouths,
'We want some outward manifestation!—well,
'The Pennsylvanians gained such; why not Sludge?
'He may improve with time!'

               Ay, that he may!
He sees his lot: there's no avoiding fate.
'Tis a trifle at first. 'Eh, David? Did you hear?
'You jogged the table, your foot caused the squeak,
'This time you're . . . joking, are you not, my boy?'
'N-n-no!'—and I'm done for, bought and sold hence-
     forth.
The old good easy jog-trot way, the . . . eh?
The . . . not so very false, as falsehood goes,
The spinning out and drawing fine, you know,—
Really mere novel-writing of a sort,
Acting, or improvising, make-believe,
Surely not downright cheatery,—any how,
'Tis done with and my lot cast; Cheat's my name:
The fatal dash of brandy in your tea

Has settled how you'll have the souchong's smack:
The caddy gives way to the dram-bottle.

Then, it's so cruel easy! Oh, those tricks
That can't be tricks, those feats by sleight of hand,
Clearly no common conjuror's!—no indeed!
A conjuror? Choose me any craft i' the world
A man puts hand to; and with six months' pains
I'll play you twenty tricks miraculous
To people untaught the trade: have you seen glass blown,
Pipes pierced? Why, just this biscuit that I chip,
Did you ever watch a baker toss one flat
To the oven? Try and do it! Take my word,
Practise but half as much, while limbs are lithe,
To turn, shove, tilt a table, crack your joints,
Manage your feet, dispose your hands aright,
Work wires that twitch the curtains, play the glove
At end o' your slipper,—then put out the lights
And . . . there, there, all you want you'll get, I hope!
I found it slip, easy as an old shoe.

Now, lights on table again! I've done my part,
You take my place while I give thanks and rest.
'Well, Judge Humgruffin, what's your verdict, sir?
'You, hardest head in the United States,—
'Did you detect a cheat here? Wait! Let's see!
'Just an experiment first, for candour's sake!
'I'll try and cheat you, Judge! The table tilts:
'Is it I that move it? Write! I'll press your hand:
'Cry when I push, or guide your pencil, Judge!'
Sludge still triumphant! 'That a rap, indeed?
'That, the real writing? Very like a whale!
'Then, if, sir, you—a most distinguished man,
'And, were the Judge not here, I'd say, . . . no matter!
'Well, sir, if you fail, you can't take us in,—
'There's little fear that Sludge will!'

                              Won't he, ma'am?
But what if our distinguished host, like Sludge,
Bade God bear witness that he played no trick,

While you believed that what produced the raps
Was just a certain child who died, you know,
And whose last breath you thought your lips had felt?
Eh? That's a capital point, ma'am: Sludge begins
At your entreaty with your dearest dead,
The little voice set lisping once again,
The tiny hand made feel for yours once more,
The poor lost image brought back, plain as dreams,
Which image, if a word had chanced recall,
The customary cloud would cross your eyes,
Your heart return the old tick, pay its pang!
A right mood for investigation, this!
One's at one's ease with Saul and Jonathan,
Pompey and Cæsar: but one's own lost child . . .
I wonder, when you heard the first clod drop
From the spadeful at the grave-side, felt you free
To investigate who twitched your funeral scarf
Or brushed your flounces? Then, it came of course
You should be stunned and stupid; then, (how else?)
Your breath stopped with your blood, your brain struck
        work.
But now, such causes fail of such effects,
All's changed,—the little voice begins afresh,
Yet you, calm, consequent, can test and try
And touch the truth. 'Tests? Didn't the creature tell
'Its nurse's name, and say it lived six years,
'And rode a rocking-horse? Enough of tests!
'Sludge never could learn that!'

                                He could not, eh?
You compliment him. 'Could not?' Speak for yourself!
I'd like to know the man I ever saw
Once,—never mind where, how, why, when,—once saw,
Of whom I do not keep some matter in mind
He'd swear I 'could not' know, sagacious soul!
What? Do you live in this world's blow of blacks,
Palaver, gossipry, a single hour
Nor find one smut has settled on your nose,
Of a smut's worth, no more, no less?—one fact

Out of the drift of facts, whereby you learn
What someone was, somewhere, somewhen, somewhy?
You don't tell folk—'See what has stuck to me!
'Judge Humgruffin, our most distinguished man,
'Your uncle was a tailor, and your wife
'Thought to have married Miggs, missed him, hit you!'—
Do you, sir, though you see him twice a-week?
'No,' you reply, 'what use retailing it?
'Why should I?' But, you see, one day you *should*,
Because one day there's much use,—when this fact
Brings you the Judge upon both gouty knees
Before the supernatural; proves that Sludge
Knows, as you say, a thing he 'could not' know:
Will not Sludge thenceforth keep an outstretched face
The way the wind drives?

                              'Could not!' Look you now,
I'll tell you a story! There's a whiskered chap,
A foreigner, that teaches music here
And gets his bread,—knowing no better way:
He says, the fellow who informed of him
And made him fly his country and fall West
Was a hunchback cobbler, sat, stitched soles and sang,
In some outlandish place, the city Rome,
In a cellar by their Broadway, all day long;
Never asked questions, stopped to listen or look,
Nor lifted nose from lapstone; let the world
Roll round his three-legged stool, and news run in
The ears he hardly seemed to keep pricked up.
Well, that man went on Sundays, touched his pay,
And took his praise from government, you see;
For something like two dollars every week,
He'd engage tell you some one little thing
Of some one man, which led to many more,
(Because one truth leads right to the world's end)
And make you that man's master—when he dined
And on what dish, where walked to keep his health
And to what street. His trade was, throwing thus
His sense out, like an ant-eater's long tongue,

Soft, innocent, warm, moist, impassible,
And when 'twas crusted o'er with creatures—slick,
Their juice enriched his palate. 'Could not Sludge!'

I'll go yet a step further, and maintain,
Once the imposture plunged its proper depth
I' the rotten of your natures, all of you,—
(If one's not mad nor drunk, and hardly then)
It's impossible to cheat—that's, be found out!
Go tell your brotherhood this first slip of mine,
All to-day's tale, how you detected Sludge,
Behaved unpleasantly, till he was fain confess,
And so has come to grief! You'll find, I think,
Why Sludge still snaps his fingers in your face.
There now, you've told them! What's their prompt
        reply?
'Sir, did that youth confess he had cheated me,
'I'd disbelieve him. He may cheat at times;
'That's in the "medium"-nature, thus they're made,
'Vain and vindictive, cowards, prone to scratch.
'And so all cats are; still, a cat's the beast
'You coax the strange electric sparks from out,
'By rubbing back its fur; not so a dog,
'Nor lion, nor lamb: 'tis the cat's nature, sir!
'Why not the dog's? Ask God, who made them beasts!
'D'ye think the sound, the nicely-balanced man
'(Like me'—aside)—'like you yourself,'—(aloud)
'—He's stuff to make a "medium"? Bless your soul,
''Tis these hysteric, hybrid half-and-halfs,
'Equivocal, worthless vermin yield the fire!
'We take such as we find them, 'ware their tricks,
'Wanting their service. Sir, Sludge took in you—
'How, I can't say, not being there to watch:
'He was tried, was tempted by your easiness,—
'He did not take in me!'

                        Thank you for Sludge!
I'm to be grateful to such patrons, eh,
When what you hear's my best word? 'Tis a challenge

'Snap at all strangers, half-tamed prairie-dog,
'So you cower duly at your keeper's beck!
'Cat, show what claws were made for, muffling them
'Only to me! Cheat others if you can,
'Me, if you dare!' And, my wise sir, I dared—
Did cheat you first, made you cheat others next,
And had the help o' your vaunted manliness
To bully the incredulous. You used me?
Have not I used you, taken full revenge,
Persuaded folk they knew not their own name,
And straight they'd own the error! Who was the fool
When, to an awe-struck wide-eyed open-mouthed
Circle of sages, Sludge would introduce
Milton composing baby-rhymes, and Locke
Reasoning in gibberish, Homer writing Greek
In noughts and crosses, Asaph setting psalms
To crotchet and quaver? I've made a spirit squeak
In sham voice for a minute, then outbroke
Bold in my own, defying the imbeciles—
Have copied some ghost's pothooks, half a page,
Then ended with my own scrawl undisguised.
'All right! The ghost was merely using Sludge,
'Suiting itself from his imperfect stock!'
Don't talk of gratitude to me! For what?
For being treated as a showman's ape,
Encouraged to be wicked and make sport,
Fret or sulk, grin or whimper, any mood
So long as the ape be in it and no man—
Because a nut pays every mood alike.
Curse your superior, superintending sort,
Who, since you hate smoke, send up boys that climb
To cure your chimney, bid a 'medium' lie
To sweep you truth down! Curse your women too,
Your insolent wives and daughters, that fire up
Or faint away if a male hand squeeze theirs,
Yet, to encourage Sludge, may play with Sludge
As only a 'medium,' only the kind of thing
They must humour, fondle . . . oh, to misconceive
Were too preposterous! But I've paid them out!

They've had their wish—called for the naked truth,
And in she tripped, sat down and bade them stare:
They had to blush a little and forgive!
'The fact is, children talk so; in next world
'All our conventions are reversed,—perhaps
'Made light of: something like old prints, my dear!
'The Judge has one, he brought from Italy,
'A metropolis in the background,—o'er a bridge,
'A team of trotting roadsters,—cheerful groups
'Of wayside travellers, peasants at their work,
'And, full in front, quite unconcerned, why not?
'Three nymphs conversing with a cavalier,
'And never a rag among them: "fine," folk cry—
'And heavenly manners seem not much unlike!
'Let Sludge go on; we'll fancy it's in print!'
If such as came for wool, sir, went home shorn,
Where is the wrong I did them? 'Twas their choice;
They tried the adventure, ran the risk, tossed up
And lost, as some one's sure to do in games;
They fancied I was made to lose,—smoked glass
Useful to spy the sun through, spare their eyes:
And had I proved a red-hot iron plate
They thought to pierce, and, for their pains, grew blind,
Whose were the fault but theirs? While, as things go,
Their loss amounts to gain, the more's the shame!
They've had their peep into the spirit-world,
And all this world may know it! They've fed fat
Their self-conceit which else had starved: what chance
Save this, of cackling o'er a golden egg
And compassing distinction from the flock,
Friends of a feather? Well, they paid for it,
And not prodigiously; the price o' the play,
Not counting certain pleasant interludes,
Was scarce a vulgar play's worth. When you buy
The actor's talent, do you dare propose
For his soul beside? Whereas my soul you buy!
Sludge acts Macbeth, obliged to be Macbeth,
Or you'll not hear his first word! Just go through
That slight formality, swear himself's the Thane,

And thenceforth he may strut and fret his hour,
Spout, spawl, or spin his target, no one cares!
Why hadn't I leave to play tricks, Sludge as Sludge?
Enough of it all! I've wiped out scores with you—
Vented your fustian, let myself be streaked
Like tom-fool with your ochre and carmine,
Worn patchwork your respectable fingers sewed
To metamorphose somebody,—yes, I've earned
My wages, swallowed down my bread of shame,
And shake the crumbs off—where but in your face?

As for religion—why, I served it, sir!
I'll stick to that! With my *phenomena*
I laid the atheist sprawling on his back,
Propped up Saint Paul, or, at least, Swedenborg!
In fact, it's just the proper way to baulk
These troublesome fellows—liars, one and all,
Are not these sceptics? Well, to baffle them,
No use in being squeamish: lie yourself!
Erect your buttress just as wide o' the line,
Your side, as they build up the wall on theirs;
Where both meet, midway in a point, is truth
High overhead: so, take your room, pile bricks,
Lie! Oh, there's titillation in all shame!
What snow may lose in white, snow gains in rose!
Miss Stokes turns—Rahab,—nor a bad exchange!
Glory be on her, for the good she wrought,
Breeding belief anew 'neath ribs of death,
Brow-beating now the unabashed before,
Ridding us of their whole life's gathered straws
By a live coal from the altar! Why, of old,
Great men spent years and years in writing books
To prove we've souls, and hardly proved it then:
Miss Stokes with her live coal, for you and me!
Surely, to this good issue, all was fair—
Not only fondling Sludge, but, even suppose
He let escape some spice of knavery,—well,
In wisely being blind to it! Don't you praise
Nelson for setting spy-glass to blind eye

And saying . . . what was it—that he could not see
The signal he was bothered with? Ay, indeed!

I'll go beyond: there's a real love of a lie,
Liars find ready-made for lies they make,
As hand for glove, or tongue for sugar-plum.
At best, 'tis never pure and full belief;
Those furthest in the quagmire,—don't suppose
They strayed there with no warning, got no chance
Of a filth-speck in their face, which they clenched teeth,
Bent brow against! Be sure they had their doubts,
And fears, and fairest challenges to try
The floor o' the seeming solid sand! But no!
Their faith was pledged, acquaintance too apprised,
All but the last step ventured, kerchiefs waved,
And Sludge called 'pet': 'twas easier marching on
To the promised land; join those who, Thursday next,
Meant to meet Shakespeare; better follow Sludge—
Prudent, oh sure!—on the alert, how else?—
But making for the mid-bog, all the same!
To hear your outcries, one would think I caught
Miss Stokes by the scruff o' the neck, and pitched her
    flat,
Foolish-face-foremost! Hear these simpletons,
That's all I beg, before my work's begun,
Before I've touched them with my finger-tip!
Thus they await me (do but listen, now!
It's reasoning, this is,—I can't imitate
The baby voice, though) 'In so many tales
'Must be some truth, truth though a pin-point big,
'Yet, some: a single man's deceived, perhaps—
'Hardly, a thousand: to suppose one cheat
'Can gull all these, were more miraculous far
'Than aught we should confess a miracle'—
And so on. Then the Judge sums up—(it's rare)—
Bids you respect the authorities that leap
To the judgment-seat at once,—why don't you note
The limpid nature, the unblemished life,
The spotless honour, indisputable sense

Of the first upstart with his story? What—
Outrage a boy on whom you ne'er till now
Set eyes, because he finds raps trouble him?

Fools, these are: ay, and how of their opposites
Who never did, at bottom of their hearts,
Believe for a moment?—Men emasculate,
Blank of belief, who played, as eunuchs use,
With superstition safely,—cold of blood,
Who saw what made for them i' the mystery,
Took their occasion, and supported Sludge
—As proselytes? No, thank you, far too shrewd!
—But promisers of fair play, encouragers
O' the claimant; who in candour needs must hoist
Sludge up on Mars' Hill, get speech out of Sludge
To carry off, criticize, and cant about!
Didn't Athens treat Saint Paul so?—at any rate,
It's 'a new thing' philosophy fumbles at.
Then there's the other picker-out of pearl
From dung-heaps,—ay, your literary man,
Who draws on his kid gloves to deal with Sludge
Daintily and discreetly,—shakes a dust
O' the doctrine, flavours thence, he well knows how,
The narrative or the novel,—half-believes,
All for the book's sake, and the public's stare,
And the cash that's God's sole solid in this world!
Look at him! Try to be too bold, too gross
For the master! Not you! He's the man for muck;
Shovel it forth, full-splash, he'll smooth your brown
Into artistic richness, never fear!
Find him the crude stuff; when you recognize
Your lie again, you'll doff your hat to it,
Dressed out for company! 'For company,'
I say, since there's the relish of success:
Let all pay due respect, call the lie truth,
Save the soft silent smirking gentleman
Who ushered in the stranger: you must sigh
'How melancholy, he, the only one
'Fails to perceive the bearing of the truth

'Himself gave birth to!'—There's the triumph's smack!
That man would choose to see the whole world roll
I' the slime o' the slough, so he might touch the tip
Of his brush with what I call the best of browns—
Tint ghost-tales, spirit-stories, past the power
Of the outworn umber and bistre!

                    Yet I think
There's a more hateful form of foolery—
The social sage's, Solomon of saloons
And philosophic diner-out, the fribble
Who wants a doctrine for a chopping-block
To try the edge of his faculty upon,
Prove how much common sense he'll hack and hew
I' the critical minute 'twixt the soup and fish!
These were my patrons: these, and the like of them
Who, rising in my soul now, sicken it,—
These I have injured! Gratitude to these?
The gratitude, forsooth, of a prostitute
To the greenhorn and the bully—friends of hers,
From the wag that wants the queer jokes for his club,
To the snuff-box-decorator, honest man,
Who just was at his wits' end where to find
So genial a Pasiphae! All and each
Pay, compliment, protect from the police:
And how she hates them for their pains, like me!
So much for my remorse at thanklessness
Toward a deserving public!

              But, for God?
Ay, that's a question! Well, sir, since you press—
(How you do tease the whole thing out of me!
I don't mean you, you know, when I say 'them':
Hate you, indeed! But that Miss Stokes, that Judge!
Enough, enough—with sugar: thank you, sir!)
Now for it, then! Will you believe me, though?
You've heard what I confess; I don't unsay
A single word: I cheated when I could,
Rapped with my toe-joints, set sham hands at work,
Wrote down names weak in sympathetic ink,

Rubbed odic lights with ends of phosphor-match,
And all the rest; believe that: believe this,
By the same token, though it seem to set
The crooked straight again, unsay the said,
Stick up what I've knocked down; I can't help that:
It's truth! I somehow vomit truth to-day.
This trade of mine—I don't know, can't be sure
But there was something in it, tricks and all!
Really, I want to light up my own mind.
They were tricks,—true, but what I mean to add
Is also true. First,—don't it strike you, sir?
Go back to the beginning,—the first fact
We're taught is, there's a world beside this world,
With spirits, not mankind, for tenantry;
That much within that world once sojourned here,
That all upon this world will visit there,
And therefore that we, bodily here below,
Must have exactly such an interest
In learning what may be the ways o' the world
Above us, as the disembodied folk
Have (by all analogic likelihood)
In watching how things go in the old home
With us, their sons, successors, and what not.
Oh yes, with added powers probably,
Fit for the novel state,—old loves grown pure,
Old interests understood aright,—they watch!
Eyes to see, ears to hear, and hands to help,
Proportionate to advancement: they're ahead,
That's all—do what we do, but noblier done—
Use plate, whereas we eat our meals off delf,
(To use a figure.)

                Concede that, and I ask
Next what may be the mode of intercourse
Between us men here, and those once-men there?
First comes the Bible's speech; then, history
With the supernatural element,—you know—
All that we sucked in with our mothers' milk,
Grew up with, got inside of us at last,

Till it's found bone of bone and flesh of flesh.
See now, we start with the miraculous,
And know it used to be, at all events:
What's the first step we take, and can't but take,
In arguing from the known to the obscure?
Why this: 'What was before, may be to-day.
'Since Samuel's ghost appeared to Saul, of course
'My brother's spirit may appear to me.'
Go tell your teacher that! What's his reply?
What brings a shade of doubt for the first time
O'er his brow late so luminous with faith?
'Such things have been,' says he, 'and there's no doubt
'Such things may be: but I advise mistrust
'Of eyes, ears, stomach, and, more than all, your brain,
'Unless it be of your great-grandmother,
'Whenever they propose a ghost to you!'
The end is, there's a composition struck;
'Tis settled, we've some way of intercourse
Just as in Saul's time; only, different:
How, when and where, precisely,—find it out!
I want to know, then, what's so natural
As that a person born into this world
And seized on by such teaching, should begin
With firm expectancy and a frank look-out
For his own allotment, his especial share
I' the secret,—his particular ghost, in fine?
I mean, a person born to look that way,
Since natures differ: take the painter-sort.
One man lives fifty years in ignorance
Whether grass be green or red,—'No kind of eye
'For colour,' say you; while another picks
And puts away even pebbles, when a child,
Because of bluish spots and pinky veins—
'Give him forthwith a paint-box!' Just the same
Was I born . . . 'medium,' you won't let me say,—
Well, seer of the supernatural
Everywhen, everyhow and everywhere,—
Will that do?

        I and all such boys of course

Started with the same stock of Bible-truth;
Only,—what in the rest you style their sense,
Instinct, blind reasoning but imperative,
This, betimes, taught them the old world had one law
And ours another: 'New world, new laws,' cried they:
'None but old laws, seen everywhere at work,'
Cried I, and by their help explained my life
The Jews' way, still a working way to me.
Ghosts made the noises, fairies waved the lights,
Or Santa Claus slid down on New Year's Eve
And stuffed with cakes the stocking at my bed,
Changed the worn shoes, rubbed clean the fingered slate
O' the sum that came to grief the day before.

This could not last long: soon enough I found
Who had worked wonders thus, and to what end:
But did I find all easy, like my mates?
Henceforth no supernatural any more?
Not a whit: what projects the billiard-balls?
'A cue,' you answer: 'Yes, a cue,' said I;
'But what hand, off the cushion, moved the cue?
'What unseen agency, outside the world,
'Prompted its puppets to do this and that,
'Put cakes and shoes and slates into their mind,
'These mothers and aunts, nay even schoolmasters?'
Thus high I sprang, and there have settled since.
Just so I reason, in sober earnest still,
About the greater godsends, what you call
The serious gains and losses of my life.
What do I know or care about your world
Which either is or seems to be? This snap
O' my fingers, sir! My care is for myself;
Myself am whole and sole reality
Inside a raree-show and a market-mob
Gathered about it: that's the use of things.
'Tis easy saying they serve vast purposes,
Advantage their grand selves: be it true or false,
Each thing may have two uses. What's a star?
A world, or a world's sun: doesn't it serve

As taper also, time-piece, weather-glass,
And almanac? Are stars not set for signs
When we should shear our sheep, sow corn, prune trees?
The Bible says so.

                    Well, I add one use
To all the acknowledged uses, and declare
If I spy Charles's Wain at twelve to-night,
It warns me, 'Go, nor lose another day,
'And have your hair cut, Sludge!' You laugh: and why?
Were such a sign too hard for God to give?
No: but Sludge seems too little for such grace:
Thank you, sir! So you think, so does not Sludge!
When you and good men gape at Providence,
Go into history and bid us mark
Not merely powder-plots prevented, crowns
Kept on kings' heads by miracle enough,
But private mercies—oh, you've told me, sir,
Of such interpositions! How yourself
Once, missing on a memorable day
Your handkerchief—just setting out, you know,—
You must return to fetch it, lost the train,
And saved your precious self from what befell
The thirty-three whom Providence forgot.
You tell, and ask me what I think of this?
Well, sir, I think then, since you needs must know,
What matter had you and Boston city to boot
Sailed skyward, like burnt onion-peelings? Much
To you, no doubt: for me—undoubtedly
The cutting of my hair concerns me more,
Because, however sad the truth may seem,
Sludge is of all-importance to himself.
You set apart that day in every year
For special thanksgiving, were a heathen else:
Well, I who cannot boast the like escape,
Suppose I said 'I don't thank Providence
'For my part, owing it no gratitude'?
'Nay, but you owe as much'—you'd tutor me,
'You, every man alive, for blessings gained

'In every hour o' the day, could you but know!
'I saw my crowning mercy: all have such,
'Could they but see!' Well, sir, why don't they see?
'Because they won't look,—or perhaps, they can't.'
Then, sir, suppose I can, and will, and do
Look, microscopically as is right,
Into each hour with its infinitude
Of influences at work to profit Sludge?
For that's the case: I've sharpened up my sight
To spy a providence in the fire's going out,
The kettle's boiling, the dime's sticking fast
Despite the hole i' the pocket. Call such facts
Fancies, too petty a work for Providence,
And those same thanks which you exact from me
Prove too prodigious payment: thanks for what,
If nothing guards and guides us little men?
No, no, sir! You must put away your pride,
Resolve to let Sludge into partnership!
I live by signs and omens: look at the roof
Where the pigeons settle—'If the further bird,
'The white, takes wing first, I'll confess when thrashed;
'Not, if the blue does'—so I said to myself
Last week, lest you should take me by surprise:
Off flapped the white,—and I'm confessing, sir!
Perhaps 'tis Providence's whim and way
With only me, i' the world: how can you tell?
'Because unlikely!' Was it likelier, now,
That this our one out of all worlds beside,
The what-d'you-call-'em millions, should be just
Precisely chosen to make Adam for,
And the rest o' the tale? Yet the tale's true, you know:
Such undeserving clod was graced so once;
Why not graced likewise undeserving Sludge?
Are we merit-mongers, flaunt we filthy rags?
All you can bring against my privilege
Is, that another way was taken with you,—
Which I don't question. It's pure grace, my luck:
I'm broken to the way of nods and winks,
And need no formal summoning. You've a help;

Holloa his name or whistle, clap your hands,
Stamp with your foot or pull the bell: all's one,
He understands you want him, here he comes.
Just so, I come at the knocking: you, sir, wait
The tongue o' the bell, nor stir before you catch
Reason's clear tingle, nature's clapper brisk,
Or that traditional peal was wont to cheer
Your mother's face turned heavenward: short of these
There's no authentic intimation, eh?
Well, when you hear, you'll answer them, start up
And stride into the presence, top of toe,
And there find Sludge beforehand, Sludge that sprang
At noise o' the knuckle on the partition-wall!
I think myself the more religious man.
Religion's all or nothing; it's no mere smile
O' contentment, sigh of aspiration, sir—
No quality o' the finelier-tempered clay
Like its whiteness or its lightness; rather, stuff
O' the very stuff, life of life, and self of self.
I tell you, men won't notice; when they do,
They'll understand. I notice nothing else:
I'm eyes, ears, mouth of me, one gaze and gape,
Nothing eludes me, everything's a hint,
Handle and help. It's all absurd, and yet
There's something in it all, I know: how much?
No answer! What does that prove? Man's still man,
Still meant for a poor blundering piece of work
When all's done; but, if somewhat's done, like this,
Or not done, is the case the same? Suppose
I blunder in my guess at the true sense
O' the knuckle-summons, nine times out of ten,—
What if the tenth guess happen to be right?
If the tenth shovel-load of powdered quartz
Yield me the nugget? I gather, crush, sift all,
Pass o'er the failure, pounce on the success.
To give you a notion, now—(let who wins, laugh!)
When first I see a man, what do I first?
Why, count the letters which make up his name,
And as their number chances, even or odd,

Arrive at my conclusion, trim my course:
Hiram H. Horsefall is your honoured name,
And haven't I found a patron, sir, in you?
'Shall I cheat this stranger?' I take apple-pips,
Stick one in either canthus of my eye,
And if the left drops first—(your left, sir, stuck)
I'm warned, I let the trick alone this time.
You, sir, who smile, superior to such trash,
You judge of character by other rules:
Don't your rules sometimes fail you? Pray, what rule
Have you judged Sludge by hitherto?

                        Oh, be sure,
You, everybody blunders, just as I,
In simpler things than these by far! For see:
I knew two farmers,—one, a wiseacre
Who studied seasons, rummaged almanacs,
Quoted the dew-point, registered the frost,
And then declared, for outcome of his pains,
Next summer must be dampish: 'twas a drought.
His neighbour prophesied such drought would fall,
Saved hay and corn, made cent. per cent. thereby,
And proved a sage indeed: how came his lore?
Because one brindled heifer, late in March,
Stiffened her tail of evenings, and somehow
He got into his head that drought was meant!
I don't expect all men can do as much:
Such kissing goes by favour. You must take
A certain turn of mind for this,—a twist
I' the flesh, as well. Be lazily alive,
Open-mouthed, like my friend the ant-eater,
Letting all nature's loosely-guarded motes
Settle and, slick, be swallowed! Think yourself
The one i' the world, the one for whom the world
Was made, expect it tickling at your mouth!
Then will the swarm of busy buzzing flies,
Clouds of coincidence, break egg-shell, thrive,
Breed, multiply, and bring you food enough.

I can't pretend to mind your smiling, sir!

Oh, what you mean is this! Such intimate way,
Close converse, frank exchange of offices,
Strict sympathy of the immeasurably great
With the infinitely small, betokened here
By a course of signs and omens, raps and sparks,—
How does it suit the dread traditional text
O' the 'Great and Terrible Name'? Shall the Heaven of
    Heavens
Stoop to such child's play?

        Please, sir, go with me
A moment, and I'll try to answer you.
The '*Magnum et terribile*' (is that right?)
Well, folk began with this in the early day;
And all the acts they recognized in proof
Were thunders, lightnings, earthquakes, whirlwinds, dealt
Indisputably on men whose death they caused.
There, and there only, folk saw Providence
At work,—and seeing it, 'twas right enough
All heads should tremble, hands wring hands amain,
And knees knock hard together at the breath
O' the Name's first letter; why, the Jews, I'm told,
Won't write it down, no, to this very hour,
Nor speak aloud: you know best if't be so.
Each ague-fit of fear at end, they crept
(Because somehow people once born must live)
Out of the sound, sight, swing and sway o' the Name,
Into a corner, the dark rest of the world,
And safe space where as yet no fear had reached;
'Twas there they looked about them, breathed again,
And felt indeed at home, as we might say.
The current o' common things, the daily life,
This had their due contempt; no Name pursued
Man from the mountain-top where fires abide,
To his particular mouse-hole at its foot
Where he ate, drank, digested, lived in short:
Such was man's vulgar business, far too small
To be worth thunder: 'small,' folk kept on, 'small,'
With much complacency in those great days!

A mote of sand, you know, a blade of grass—
What was so despicable as mere grass,
Except perhaps the life o' the worm or fly
Which fed there? These were 'small' and men were great.
Well, sir, the old way's altered somewhat since,
And the world wears another aspect now:
Somebody turns our spyglass round, or else
Puts a new lens in it: grass, worm, fly grow big:
We find great things are made of little things,
And little things go lessening till at last
Comes God behind them. Talk of mountains now?
We talk of mould that heaps the mountain, mites
That throng the mould, and God that makes the mites.
The Name comes close behind a stomach-cyst,
The simplest of creations, just a sac
That's mouth, heart, legs and belly at once, yet lives
And feels, and could do neither, we conclude,
If simplified still further one degree:
The small becomes the dreadful and immense!
Lightning, forsooth? No word more upon that!
A tin-foil bottle, a strip of greasy silk,
With a bit of wire and knob of brass, and there's
Your dollar's-worth of lightning! But the cyst—
The life of the least of the little things?

                                        No, no!
Preachers and teachers try another tack,
Come near the truth this time: they put aside
Thunder and lightning: 'That's mistake,' they cry,
'Thunderbolts fall for neither fright nor sport,
'But do appreciable good, like tides,
'Changes o' the wind, and other natural facts—
' "Good" meaning good to man, his body or soul.
'Mediate, immediate, all things minister
'To man,—that's settled: be our future text
' "We are His children!" ' So, they now harangue
About the intention, the contrivance, all
That keeps up an incessant play of love,—
See the Bridgewater book.

Amen to it!

Well, sir, I put this question: I'm a child?
I lose no time, but take you at your word:
How shall I act a child's part properly?
Your sainted mother, sir,—used you to live
With such a thought as this a-worrying you?
'She has it in her power to throttle me,
'Or stab or poison: she may turn me out,
'Or lock me in,—nor stop at this, to-day,
'But cut me off to-morrow from the estate
'I look for'—(long may you enjoy it, sir!)
'In brief, she may unchild the child I am.'
You never had such crotchets? Nor have I!
Who, frank confessing childship from the first,
Cannot both fear and take my ease at once,
So, don't fear,—know what might be, well enough,
But know too, child-like, that it will not be,
At least in my case, mine, the son and heir
O' the kingdom, as yourself proclaim my style.
But do you fancy I stop short at this?
Wonder if suit and service, son and heir
Needs must expect, I dare pretend to find?
If, looking for signs proper to such an one,
I straight perceive them irresistible?
Concede that homage is a son's plain right,
And, never mind the nods and raps and winks,
'Tis the pure obvious supernatural
Steps forward, does its duty: why, of course!
I have presentiments; my dreams come true:
I fancy a friend stands whistling all in white
Blithe as a boblink, and he's dead I learn.
I take dislike to a dog my favourite long,
And sell him; he goes mad next week and snaps.
I guess that stranger will turn up to-day
I have not seen these three years; there's his knock.
I wager 'sixty peaches on that tree!'—
That I pick up a dollar in my walk,
That your wife's brother's cousin's name was George—
And win on all points. Oh, you wince at this?

You'd fain distinguish between gift and gift,
Washington's oracle and Sludge's itch
O' the elbow when at whist he ought to trump?
With Sludge it's too absurd? *Fine, draw the line
Somewhere, but, sir, your somewhere is not mine!*

Bless us, I'm turning poet! It's time to end.
How you have drawn me out, sir! All I ask
Is—am I heir or not heir? If I'm he,
Then, sir, remember, that same personage
(To judge by what we read i' the newspaper)
Requires, beside one nobleman in gold
To carry up and down his coronet,
Another servant, probably a duke,
To hold egg-nogg in readiness: why want
Attendance, sir, when helps in his father's house
Abound, I'd like to know?

                              Enough of talk!
My fault is that I tell too plain a truth.
Why, which of those who say they disbelieve,
Your clever people, but has dreamed his dream,
Caught his coincidence, stumbled on his fact
He can't explain, (he'll tell you smilingly)
Which he's too much of a philosopher
To count as supernatural, indeed,
So calls a puzzle and problem, proud of it:
Bidding you still be on your guard, you know,
Because one fact don't make a system stand,
Nor prove this an occasional escape
Of spirit beneath the matter: that's the way!
Just so wild Indians picked up, piece by piece,
The fact in California, the fine gold
That underlay the gravel—hoarded these,
But never made a system stand, nor dug!
So wise men hold out in each hollowed palm
A handful of experience, sparkling fact
They can't explain; and since their rest of life
Is all explainable, what proof in this?
Whereas I take the fact, the grain of gold,

And fling away the dirty rest of life,
And add this grain to the grain each fool has found
O' the million other such philosophers,—
Till I see gold, all gold and only gold,
Truth questionless though unexplainable,
And the miraculous proved the commonplace!
The other fools believed in mud, no doubt—
Failed to know gold they saw: was that so strange?
Are all men born to play Bach's fiddle-fugues,
'Time' with the foil in carte, jump their own height,
Cut the mutton with the broadsword, skate a five,
Make the red hazard with the cue, clip nails
While swimming, in five minutes row a mile,
Pull themselves three feet up with the left arm,
Do sums of fifty figures in their head,
And so on, by the scores of instances?
The Sludge with luck, who sees the spiritual facts
His fellows strive and fail to see, may rank
With these, and share the advantage.

                                        Ay, but share
The drawback! Think it over by yourself;
I have not heart, sir, and the fire's gone grey.
Defect somewhere compensates for success,
Everyone knows that. Oh, we're equals, sir!
The big-legged fellow has a little arm
And a less brain, though big legs win the race:
Do you suppose I 'scape the common lot?
Say, I was born with flesh so sensitive,
Soul so alert, that, practice helping both,
I guess what's going on outside the veil,
Just as a prisoned crane feels pairing-time
In the islands where his kind are, so must fall
To capering by himself some shiny night,
As if your back-yard were a plot of spice—
Thus am I 'ware o' the spirit-world: while you,
Blind as a beetle that way,—for amends,
Why, you can double fist and floor me, sir!
Ride that hot hardmouthed horrid horse of yours,

Laugh while it lightens, play with the great dog,
Speak your mind though it vex some friend to hear,
Never brag, never bluster, never blush,—
In short, you've pluck, when I'm a coward—there!
I know it, I can't help it,—folly or no,
I'm paralyzed, my hand's no more a hand,
Nor my head a head, in danger: you can smile
And change the pipe in your cheek. Your gift's not mine.
Would you swap for mine? No! but you'd add my gift
To yours: I dare say! I too sigh at times,
Wish I were stouter, could tell truth nor flinch,
Kept cool when threatened, did not mind so much
Being dressed gaily, making strangers stare,
Eating nice things; when I'd amuse myself,
I shut my eyes and fancy in my brain
I'm—now the President, now Jenny Lind,
Now Emerson, now the Benicia Boy—
With all the civilized world a-wondering
And worshipping. I know it's folly and worse;
I feel such tricks sap, honeycomb the soul,
But I can't cure myself: despond, despair,
And then, hey, presto, there's a turn o' the wheel,
Under comes uppermost, fate makes full amends;
Sludge knows and sees and hears a hundred things
You all are blind to,—I've my taste of truth,
Likewise my touch of falsehood,—vice no doubt,
But you've your vices also: I'm content.

What, sir? You won't shake hands? 'Because I cheat!
'You've found me out in cheating!' That's enough
To make an apostle swear! Why, when I cheat,
Mean to cheat, do cheat, and am caught in the act,
Are you, or, rather, am I sure o' the fact?
(There's verse again, but I'm inspired somehow.)
Well then I'm not sure! I may be, perhaps,
Free as a babe from cheating: how it began,
My gift,—no matter; what 'tis got to be
In the end now, that's the question; answer that!
Had I seen, perhaps, what hand was holding mine,

Leading me whither, I had died of fright:
So, I was made believe I led myself.
If I should lay a six-inch plank from roof
To roof, you would not cross the street, one step,
Even at your mother's summons: but, being shrewd,
If I paste paper on each side the plank
And swear 'tis solid pavement, why, you'll cross
Humming a tune the while, in ignorance
Beacon Street stretches a hundred feet below:
I walked thus, took the paper-cheat for stone.
Some impulse made me set a thing o' the move
Which, started once, ran really by itself;
Beer flows thus, suck the siphon; toss the kite,
It takes the wind and floats of its own force.
Don't let truth's lump rot stagnant for the lack
Of a timely helpful lie to leaven it!
Put a chalk-egg beneath the clucking hen,
She'll lay a real one, laudably deceived,
Daily for weeks to come. I've told my lie,
And seen truth follow, marvels none of mine;
All was not cheating, sir, I'm positive!
I don't know if I move your hand sometimes
When the spontaneous writing spreads so far,
If my knee lifts the table all that height,
Why the inkstand don't fall off the desk a-tilt,
Why the accordion plays a prettier waltz
Than I can pick out on the piano-forte,
Why I speak so much more than I intend,
Describe so many things I never saw.
I tell you, sir, in one sense, I believe
Nothing at all,—that everybody can,
Will, and does cheat: but in another sense
I'm ready to believe my very self—
That every cheat's inspired, and every lie
Quick with a germ of truth.

                              You ask perhaps
Why I should condescend to trick at all
If I know a way without it? This is why!

There's a strange secret sweet self-sacrifice
In any desecration of one's soul
To a worthy end,—isn't it Herodotus
(I wish I could read Latin!) who describes
The single gift o' the land's virginity,
Demanded in those old Egyptian rites,
(I've but a hazy notion—help me, sir!)
For one purpose in the world, one day in a life,
One hour in a day—thereafter, purity,
And a veil thrown o'er the past for evermore!
Well, now, they understand a many things
Down by Nile city, or wherever it was!
I've always vowed, after the minute's lie,
And the end's gain,—truth should be mine henceforth.
This goes to the root o' the matter, sir,—this plain
Plump fact: accept it and unlock with it
The wards of many a puzzle!

                              Or, finally,
Why should I set so fine a gloss on things?
What need I care? I cheat in self-defence,
And there's my answer to a world of cheats!
Cheat? To be sure, sir! What's the world worth else?
Who takes it as he finds, and thanks his stars?
Don't it want trimming, turning, furbishing up
And polishing over? Your so-styled great men,
Do they accept one truth as truth is found,
Or try their skill at tinkering? What's your world?
Here are you born, who are, I'll say at once,
Of the luckiest kind, whether in head and heart,
Body and soul, or all that helps them both.
Well, now, look back: what faculty of yours
Came to its full, had ample justice done
By growing when rain fell, biding its time,
Solidifying growth when earth was dead,
Spiring up, broadening wide, in seasons due?
Never! You shot up and frost nipped you off,
Settled to sleep when sunshine bade you sprout;
One faculty thwarted its fellow: at the end,

All you boast is 'I had proved a topping tree
'In other climes'—yet this was the right clime
Had you foreknown the seasons. Young, you've force
Wasted like well-streams: old,—oh, then indeed,
Behold a labyrinth of hydraulic pipes
Through which you'd play off wondrous waterwork;
Only, no water's left to feed their play.
Young,—you've a hope, an aim, a love: it's tossed
And crossed and lost: you struggle on, some spark
Shut in your heart against the puffs around,
Through cold and pain; these in due time subside:
Now then for age's triumph, the hoarded light
You mean to loose on the altered face of things,—
Up with it on the tripod! It's extinct.
Spend your life's remnant asking, which was best,
Light smothered up that never peeped forth once,
Or the cold cresset with full leave to shine?
Well, accept this too,—seek the fruit of it
Not in enjoyment, proved a dream on earth,
But knowledge, useful for a second chance,
Another life,—you've lost this world—you've gained
Its knowledge for the next. What knowledge, sir,
Except that you know nothing? Nay, you doubt
Whether 'twere better have made you man or brute,
If aught be true, if good and evil clash.
No foul, no fair, no inside, no outside,
There's your world!

                    Give it me! I slap it brisk
With harlequin's pasteboard sceptre: what's it now?
Changed like a rock-flat, rough with rusty weed,
At first wash-over o' the returning wave!
All the dry dead impracticable stuff
Starts into life and light again; this world
Pervaded by the influx from the next.
I cheat, and what's the happy consequence?
You find full justice straightway dealt you out,
Each want supplied, each ignorance set at ease,
Each folly fooled. No life-long labour now

As the price of worse than nothing! No mere film
Holding you chained in iron, as it seems,
Against the outstretch of your very arms
And legs i' the sunshine moralists forbid!
What would you have? Just speak and, there, you see!
You're supplemented, made a whole at last,
Bacon advises, Shakespeare writes you songs,
And Mary Queen of Scots embraces you.
Thus it goes on, not quite like life perhaps,
But so near, that the very difference piques,
Shows that e'en better than this best will be—
This passing entertainment in a hut
Whose bare walls take your taste since, one stage more,
And you arrive at the palace: all half real,
And you, to suit it, less than real beside,
In a dream, lethargic kind of death in life,
That helps the interchange of natures, flesh
Transfused by souls, and such souls! Oh, 'tis choice!
And if at whiles the bubble, blown too thin,
Seem nigh on bursting,—if you nearly see
The real world through the false,—what *do* you see?
Is the old so ruined? You find you're in a flock
O' the youthful, earnest, passionate—genius, beauty,
Rank and wealth also, if you care for these:
And all depose their natural rights, hail you,
(That's me, sir) as their mate and yoke-fellow,
Participate in Sludgehood—nay, grow mine,
I veritably possess them—banish doubt,
And reticence and modesty alike!
Why, here's the Golden Age, old Paradise
Or new Eutopia! Here's true life indeed,
And the world well won now, mine for the first time!

And all this might be, may be, and with good help
Of a little lying shall be: so, Sludge lies!
Why, he's at worst your poet who sings how Greeks
That never were, in Troy which never was,
Did this or the other impossible great thing!
He's Lowell—it's a world (you smile applause)

Of his own invention—wondrous Longfellow,
Surprising Hawthorne! Sludge does more than they,
And acts the books they write: the more his praise!

But why do I mount to poets? Take plain prose—
Dealers in common sense, set these at work,
What can they do without their helpful lies?
Each states the law and fact and face o' the thing
Just as he'd have them, finds what he thinks fit,
Is blind to what missuits him, just records
What makes his case out, quite ignores the rest.
It's a History of the World, the Lizard Age,
The Early Indians, the Old Country War,
Jerome Napoleon, whatsoever you please,
All as the author wants it. Such a scribe
You pay and praise for putting life in stones,
Fire into fog, making the past your world.
There's plenty of 'How did you contrive to grasp
'The thread which led you through this labyrinth?
'How build such solid fabric out of air?
'How on so slight foundation found this tale,
'Biography, narrative?' or, in other words,
'How many lies did it require to make
'The portly truth you here present us with?'
'Oh,' quoth the penman, purring at your praise,
''Tis fancy all; no particle of fact:
'I was poor and threadbare when I wrote that book
'"Bliss in the Golden City." I, at Thebes?
'We writers paint out of our heads, you see!'
'—Ah, the more wonderful the gift in you,
'The more creativeness and godlike craft!'
But I, do I present you with my piece,
It's 'What, Sludge? When my sainted mother spoke
'The verses Lady Jane Grey last composed
'About the rosy bower in the seventh heaven
'Where she and Queen Elizabeth keep house,—
'You made the raps? 'Twas your invention that?
'Cur, slave and devil!'—eight fingers and two thumbs
Stuck in my throat!

Well, if the marks seem gone,
'Tis because stiffish cock-tail, taken in time,
Is better for a bruise than arnica.
There, sir! I bear no malice: 't is n't in me.
I know I acted wrongly: still, I've tried
What I could say in my excuse,—to show
The devil's not all devil . . . I don't pretend,
He's angel, much less such a gentleman
As you, sir! And I've lost you, lost myself,
Lost all-l-l-l- . . .

No—are you in earnest, sir?
O yours, sir, is an angel's part! I know
What prejudice prompts, and what's the common course
Men take to soothe their ruffled self-conceit:
Only you rise superior to it all!
No, sir, it don't hurt much; it's speaking long
That makes me choke a little: the marks will go!
What? Twenty V-notes more, and outfit too,
And not a word to Greeley? One—one kiss
O' the hand that saves me! You'll not let me speak,
I well know, and I've lost the right, too true!
But I must say, sir, if She hears (she does)
Your sainted . . . Well, sir,—be it so! That's, I think,
My bed-room candle. Good-night! Bl-l-less you, sir!

R-r-r, you brute-beast and blackguard! Cowardly
    scamp!
I only wish I dared burn down the house
And spoil your sniggering! Oh what, you're the man?
You're satisfied at last? You've found out Sludge?
We'll see that presently: my turn, sir, next!
I too can tell my story: brute,—do you hear?—
You throttled your sainted mother, that old hag,
In just such a fit of passion: no, it was . . .
To get this house of hers, and many a note
Like these . . . I'll pocket them, however . . . five,
Ten, fifteen . . . ay, you gave her throat the twist,
Or else you poisoned her! Confound the cuss!

Where was my head? I ought to have prophesied
He'll die in a year and join her: that's the way.

I don't know where my head is: what had I done?
How did it all go? I said he poisoned her,
And hoped he'd have grace given him to repent,
Whereon he picked this quarrel, bullied me
And called me cheat: I thrashed him,—who could help?
He howled for mercy, prayed me on his knees
To cut and run and save him from disgrace:
I do so, and once off, he slanders me.
An end of him! Begin elsewhere anew!
Boston's a hole, the herring-pond is wide,
V-notes are something, liberty still more.
Beside, is he the only fool in the world?

APPARENT FAILURE

'We shall soon lose a celebrated building.' *Paris Newspaper.*

I

No, for I'll save it! Seven years since,
　　I passed through Paris, stopped a day
To see the baptism of your Prince;
　　Saw, made my bow, and went my way:
Walking the heat and headache off,
　　I took the Seine-side, you surmise,
Thought of the Congress, Gortschakoff,
　　Cavour's appeal and Buol's replies,
So sauntered till—what met my eyes?

II

Only the Doric little Morgue!
　　The dead-house where you show your drowned:
Petrarch's Vaucluse makes proud the Sorgue,
　　Your Morgue has made the Seine renowned.
One pays one's debt in such a case;
　　I plucked up heart and entered,—stalked,
Keeping a tolerable face
　　Compared with some whose cheeks were chalked:
Let them! No Briton's to be baulked!

III

First came the silent gazers; next,
    A screen of glass, we're thankful for;
Last, the sight's self, the sermon's text,
    The three men who did most abhor
Their life in Paris yesterday,
    So killed themselves: and now, enthroned
Each on his copper couch, they lay
    Fronting me, waiting to be owned.
I thought, and think, their sin's atoned.

IV

Poor men, God made, and all for that!
    The reverence struck me; o'er each head
Religiously was hung its hat,
    Each coat dripped by the owner's bed,
Sacred from touch: each had his berth,
    His bounds, his proper place of rest,
Who last night tenanted on earth
    Some arch, where twelve such slept abreast,—
Unless the plain asphalte seemed best.

V

How did it happen, my poor boy?
    You wanted to be Buonaparte
And have the Tuileries for toy,
    And could not, so it broke your heart?
You, old one by his side, I judge,
    Were, red as blood, a socialist,
A leveller! Does the Empire grudge
    You've gained what no Republic missed?
Be quiet, and unclench your fist!

VI

And this—why, he was red in vain,
    Or black,—poor fellow that is blue!
What fancy was it turned your brain?
    Oh, women were the prize for you!

Money gets women, cards and dice
　　Get money, and ill-luck gets just
The copper couch and one clear nice
　　Cool squirt of water o'er your bust,
The right thing to extinguish lust!

VII

It's wiser being good than bad;
　　It's safer being meek than fierce:
It's fitter being sane than mad.
　　My own hope is, a sun will pierce
The thickest cloud earth ever stretched;
　　That, after Last, returns the First,
Though a wide compass round be fetched;
　　That what began best, can't end worst,
Nor what God blessed once, prove accurst.

From 'FIFINE AT THE FAIR'

1872

PROLOGUE

AMPHIBIAN

I

THE fancy I had to-day,
  Fancy which turned a fear!
I swam far out in the bay,
  Since waves laughed warm and clear.

II

I lay and looked at the sun,
  The noon-sun looked at me:
Between us two, no one
  Live creature, that I could see.

III

Yes! There came floating by
  Me, who lay floating too,
Such a strange butterfly!
  Creature as dear as new:

IV

Because the membraned wings
  So wonderful, so wide,
So sun-suffused, were things
  Like soul and nought beside.

V

A handbreadth over head!
  All of the sea my own,
It owned the sky instead;
  Both of us were alone.

VI

I never shall join its flight,
    For, nought buoys flesh in air.
If it touch the sea—good night!
    Death sure and swift waits there.

VII

Can the insect feel the better
    For watching the uncouth play
Of limbs that slip the fetter,
    Pretend as they were not clay?

VIII

Undoubtedly I rejoice
    That the air comports so well
With a creature which had the choice
    Of the land once. Who can tell?

IX

What if a certain soul
    Which early slipped its sheath,
And has for its home the whole
    Of heaven, thus look beneath,

X

Thus watch one who, in the world,
    Both lives and likes life's way,
Nor wishes the wings unfurled
    That sleep in the worm, they say?

XI

But sometimes when the weather
    Is blue, and warm waves tempt
To free oneself of tether,
    And try a life exempt

XII

From worldly noise and dust,
    In the sphere which overbrims
With passion and thought,—why, just
    Unable to fly, one swims!

XIII

By passion and thought upborne,
  One smiles to oneself—'They fare
Scarce better, they need not scorn
  Our sea, who live in the air!'

XIV

Emancipate through passion
  And thought, with sea for sky,
We substitute, in a fashion,
  For heaven—poetry:

XV

Which sea, to all intent,
  Gives flesh such noon-disport
As a finer element
  Affords the spirit-sort.

XVI

Whatever they are, we seem:
  Imagine the thing they know;
All deeds they do, we dream;
  Can heaven be else but so?

XVII

And meantime, yonder streak
  Meets the horizon's verge;
That is the land, to seek
  If we tire or dread the surge:

XVIII

Land the solid and safe—
  To welcome again (confess!)
When, high and dry, we chafe
  The body, and don the dress.

XIX

Does she look, pity, wonder
  At one who mimics flight,
Swims—heaven above, sea under,
  Yet always earth in sight?

EPILOGUE

THE HOUSEHOLDER

I

SAVAGE I was sitting in my house, late, lone:
  Dreary, weary with the long day's work:
Head of me, heart of me, stupid as a stone:
  Tongue-tied now, now blaspheming like a Turk;
When, in a moment, just a knock, call, cry,
  Half a pang and all a rapture, there again were we!—
'What, and is it really you again?' quoth I:
  'I again, what else did you expect?' quoth She.

II

'Never mind, hie away from this old house—
  Every crumbling brick embrowned with sin and shame!
Quick, in its corners ere certain shapes arouse!
  Let them—every devil of the night—lay claim,
Make and mend, or rap and rend, for me! Good-bye!
  God be their guard from disturbance at their glee,
Till, crash, comes down the carcass in a heap!' quoth I:
  'Nay, but there's a decency required!' quoth She.

III

'Ah, but if you knew how time has dragged, days,
    nights!
  All the neighbour-talk with man and maid—such
    men!
All the fuss and trouble of street-sounds, window-sights:
  All the worry of flapping door and echoing roof; and
    then,
All the fancies . . . Who were they had leave, dared try
  Darker arts that almost struck despair in me?
If you knew but how I dwelt down here!' quoth I:
  'And was I so better off up there?' quoth She.

IV

'Help and get it over! *Re-united to his wife*
   (How draw up the paper lets the parish-people know?)
Lies M., or N., departed from this life,
   Day the this or that, month and year the so and so.
What i' the way of final flourish? Prose, verse? Try!
   Affliction sore long time he bore, or, what is it to be?
Till God did please to grant him ease. Do end!' quoth I:
   'I end with—Love is all and Death is nought!' quoth
   She.

From 'PACCHIAROTTO, &c.'

1876

PROLOGUE

I

O THE old wall here! How I could pass
    Life in a long Midsummer day,
My feet confined to a plot of grass,
    My eyes from a wall not once away!

II

And lush and lithe do the creepers clothe
    Yon wall I watch, with a wealth of green:
Its bald red bricks draped, nothing loth,
    In lappets of tangle they laugh between.

III

Now, what is it makes pulsate the robe?
    Why tremble the sprays? What life o'er-brims
The body,—the house, no eye can probe,—
    Divined as, beneath a robe, the limbs?

IV

And there again! But my heart may guess
    Who tripped behind; and she sang perhaps:
So, the old wall throbbed, and its life's excess
    Died out and away in the leafy wraps.

V

Wall upon wall are between us: life
    And song should away from heart to heart.
I—prison-bird, with a ruddy strife
    At breast, and a lip whence storm-notes start—

VI

Hold on, hope hard in the subtle thing
    That's spirit: though cloistered fast, soar free;
Account as wood, brick, stone, this ring
    Of the rueful neighbours, and—forth to thee!

AT THE 'MERMAID'

The figure that thou here seest . . . Tut!
Was it for gentle Shakespeare put?
                                    B. Jonson. (*Adapted*.)

I

I—'Next Poet?' No, my hearties,
   I nor am nor fain would be!
Choose your chiefs and pick your parties,
   Not one soul revolt to me!
I, forsooth, sow song-sedition?
   I, a schism in verse provoke?
I, blown up by bard's ambition,
   Burst—your bubble-king? You joke.

II

Come, be grave! The sherris mantling
   Still about each mouth, mayhap,
Breeds you insight—just a scantling—
   Brings me truth out—just a scrap.
Look and tell me! Written, spoken,
   Here's my life-long work: and where
—Where's your warrant or my token
   I'm the dead king's son and heir?

III

Here's my work: does work discover—
   What was rest from work—my life?
Did I live man's hater, lover?
   Leave the world at peace, at strife?
Call earth ugliness or beauty?
   See things there in large or small?
Use to pay its Lord my duty?
   Use to own a lord at all?

IV

Blank of such a record, truly
   Here's the work I hand, this scroll,
Yours to take or leave; as duly,
   Mine remains the unproffered soul.

So much, no whit more, my debtors—
   How should one like me lay claim
To that largess elders, betters
   Sell you cheap their souls for—fame?

V

Which of you did I enable
   Once to slip inside my breast,
There to catalogue and label
   What I like least, what love best,
Hope and fear, believe and doubt of,
   Seek and shun, respect—deride?
Who has right to make a rout of
   Rarities he found inside?

VI

Rarities or, as he'd rather,
   Rubbish such as stocks his own:
Need and greed (O strange) the Father
   Fashioned not for him alone!
Whence—the comfort set a-strutting,
   Whence—the outcry 'Haste, behold!
Bard's breast open wide, past shutting,
   Shows what brass we took for gold!'

VII

Friends, I doubt not he'd display you
   Brass—myself call orichalc,—
Furnish much amusement; pray you
   Therefore, be content I baulk
Him and you, and bar my portal!
   Here's my work outside: opine
What's inside me mean and mortal!
   Take your pleasure, leave me mine!

VIII

Which is—not to buy your laurel
   As last king did, nothing loth.
Tale adorned and pointed moral
   Gained him praise and pity both.

Out rushed sighs and groans by dozens,
　Forth by scores oaths, curses flew:
Proving you were cater-cousins,
　Kith and kindred, king and you!

IX

Whereas do I ne'er so little
　(Thanks to sherris) leave ajar
Bosom's gate—no jot nor tittle
　Grow we nearer than we are.
Sinning, sorrowing, despairing,
　Body-ruined, spirit-wrecked,—
Should I give my woes an airing,—
　Where's one plague that claims respect?

X

Have you found your life distasteful?
　My life did, and does, smack sweet.
Was your youth of pleasure wasteful?
　Mine I saved and hold complete.
Do your joys with age diminish?
　When mine fail me, I'll complain.
Must in death your daylight finish?
　My sun sets to rise again.

XI

What, like you, he proved—your Pilgrim—
　This our world a wilderness,
Earth still grey and heaven still grim,
　Not a hand there his might press,
Not a heart his own might throb to,
　Men all rogues and women—say,
Dolls which boys' heads duck and bob to,
　Grown folk drop or throw away?

XII

My experience being other,
　How should I contribute verse
Worthy of your king and brother?
　Balaam-like I bless, not curse.

I find earth not grey but rosy,
 Heaven not grim but fair of hue.
Do I stoop? I pluck a posy.
 Do I stand and stare? All's blue.

XIII

Doubtless I am pushed and shoved by
 Rogues and fools enough: the more
Good luck mine, I love, am loved by
 Some few honest to the core.
Scan the near high, scout the far low!
 'But the low come close:' what then?
Simpletons? My match is Marlowe;
 Sciolists? My mate is Ben.

XIV

Womankind—'the cat-like nature,
 False and fickle, vain and weak'—
What of this sad nomenclature
 Suits my tongue, if I must speak?
Does the sex invite, repulse so,
 Tempt, betray, by fits and starts?
So becalm but to convulse so,
 Decking heads and breaking hearts?

XV

Well may you blaspheme at fortune!
 I 'threw Venus'[1] (Ben, expound!)
Never did I need importune
 Her, of all the Olympian round.
Blessings on my benefactress!
 Cursings suit—for aught I know—
Those who twitched her by the back tress,
 Tugged and thought to turn her—so!

XVI

Therefore, since no leg to stand on
 Thus I'm left with,—joy or grief
Be the issue,—I abandon
 Hope or care you name me Chief!

' The best cast in dice (three sixes) is called Venus.

Chief and king and Lord's anointed,
  I?—who never once have wished
Death before the day appointed:
  Lived and liked, not poohed and pished!

XVII

'Ah, but so I shall not enter,
  Scroll in hand, the common heart—
Stopped at surface: since at centre
  Song should reach *Welt-schmerz*, world-smart!'
'Enter in the heart'? Its shelly
  Cuirass guard mine, fore and aft!
Such song 'enters in the belly
  And is cast out in the draught.'

XVIII

Back then to our sherris-brewage!
  'Kingship' quotha? I shall wait—
Waive the present time: some new age . . .
  But let fools anticipate!
Meanwhile greet me—'friend, good fellow,
  Gentle Will,' my merry men!
As for making Envy yellow
  With 'Next Poet'—(Manners, Ben!)

HOUSE

SHALL I sonnet-sing you about myself?
  Do I live in a house you would like to see?
Is it scant of gear, has it store of pelf?
  'Unlock my heart with a sonnet-key?'

II

Invite the world, as my betters have done?
  'Take notice: this building remains on view,
Its suites of reception every one,
  Its private apartment and bedroom too;

III

'For a ticket, apply to the Publisher.'
  No: thanking the public, I must decline.
A peep through my window, if folk prefer;
  But, please you, no foot over threshold of mine!

IV

I have mixed with a crowd and heard free talk
  In a foreign land where an earthquake chanced:
And a house stood gaping, nought to balk
  Man's eye wherever he gazed or glanced.

V

The whole of the frontage shaven sheer,
  The inside gaped: exposed to day,
Right and wrong and common and queer,
  Bare, as the palm of your hand, it lay.

VI

The owner? Oh, he had been crushed, no doubt!
  'Odd tables and chairs for a man of wealth!
What a parcel of musty old books about!
  He smoked,—no wonder he lost his health!

VII

'I doubt if he bathed before he dressed.
  A brasier?—the pagan, he burned perfumes!
You see it is proved, what the neighbours guessed:
  His wife and himself had separate rooms.'

VIII

Friends, the goodman of the house at least
  Kept house to himself till an earthquake came:
'Tis the fall of its frontage permits you feast
  On the inside arrangement you praise or blame.

IX

Outside should suffice for evidence:
  And whoso desires to penetrate
Deeper, must dive by the spirit-sense—
  No optics like yours, at any rate!

X

'Hoity toity! A street to explore,
   Your house the exception! "*With this same key
Shakespeare unlocked his heart*," once more!'
   Did Shakespeare? If so, the less Shakespeare he!

SHOP

I

So, friend, your shop was all your house!
   Its front, astonishing the street,
Invited view from man and mouse
      To what diversity of treat
      Behind its glass—the single sheet!

II

What gimcracks, genuine Japanese:
   Gape-jaw and goggle-eye, the frog;
Dragons, owls, monkeys, beetles, geese;
      Some crush-nosed human-hearted dog:
      Queer names, too, such a catalogue!

III

I thought 'And he who owns the wealth
   Which blocks the window's vastitude,
—Ah, could I peep at him by stealth
      Behind his ware, pass shop, intrude
      On house itself, what scenes were viewed!

IV

'If wide and showy thus the shop,
   What must the habitation prove?
The true house with no name a-top—
      The mansion, distant one remove,
      Once get him off his traffic-groove!

V

'Pictures he likes, or books perhaps;
    And as for buying most and best,
Commend me to these City chaps!
    Or else he's social, takes his rest
    On Sundays, with a Lord for guest.

VI

'Some suburb-palace, parked about
    And gated grandly, built last year:
The four-mile walk to keep off gout;
    Or big seat sold by bankrupt peer:
    But then he takes the rail, that's clear.

VII

'Or, stop! I wager, taste selects
    Some out o' the way, some all-unknown
Retreat: the neighbourhood suspects
    Little that he who rambles lone
    Makes Rothschild tremble on his throne!'

VIII

Nowise! Nor Mayfair residence
    Fit to receive and entertain,—
Nor Hampstead villa's kind defence
    From noise and crowd, from dust and drain,—
    Nor country-box was soul's domain!

IX

Nowise! At back of all that spread
    Of merchandize, woe's me, I find
A hole i' the wall where, heels by head,
    The owner couched, his ware behind,
    —In cupboard suited to his mind.

X

For why? He saw no use of life
    But, while he drove a roaring trade,
To chuckle 'Customers are rife!'
    To chafe 'So much hard cash outlaid
    Yet zero in my profits made!

XI

'This novelty costs pains, but—takes?
    Cumbers my counter! Stock no more!
This article, no such great shakes,
    Fizzes like wildfire? Underscore
    The cheap thing—thousands to the fore!'

XII

'Twas lodging best to live most nigh
    (Cramp, coffinlike as crib might be)
Receipt of Custom; ear and eye
    Wanted no outworld: 'Hear and see
    The bustle in the shop!' quoth he.

XIII

My fancy of a merchant-prince
    Was different. Through his wares we groped
Our darkling way to—not to mince
    The matter—no black den where moped
    The master if we interloped!

XIV

Shop was shop only: household-stuff?
    What did he want with comforts there?
'Walls, ceiling, floor, stay blank and rough,
    So goods on sale show rich and rare!
    "*Sell and scud home*" be shop's affair!'

XV

What might he deal in? Gems, suppose!
    Since somehow business must be done
At cost of trouble,—see, he throws
    You choice of jewels, everyone,
    Good, better, best, star, moon and sun!

XVI

Which lies within your power of purse?
    This ruby that would tip aright
Solomon's sceptre? Oh, your nurse
    Wants simply coral, the delight
    Of teething baby,—stuff to bite!

XVII

Howe'er your choice fell, straight you took
    Your purchase, prompt your money rang
On counter,—scarce the man forsook
    His study of the 'Times,' just swang
    Till-ward his hand that stopped the clang,—

XVIII

Then off made buyer with a prize,
    Then seller to his 'Times' returned;
And so did day wear, wear, till eyes
    Brightened apace, for rest was earned:
    He locked door long ere candle burned.

XIX

And whither went he? Ask himself,
    Not me! To change of scene, I think.
Once sold the ware and pursed the pelf,
    Chaffer was scarce his meat and drink,
    Nor all his music—money-chink.

XX

Because a man has shop to mind
    In time and place, since flesh must live,
Needs spirit lack all life behind,
    All stray thoughts, fancies fugitive,
    All loves except what trade can give?

XXI

I want to know a butcher paints,
    A baker rhymes for his pursuit,
Candlestick-maker much acquaints
    His soul with song, or, haply mute,
    Blows out his brains upon the flute!

XXII

But—shop each day and all day long!
    Friend, your good angel slept, your star
Suffered eclipse, fate did you wrong!
    From where these sorts of treasures are,
    There should our hearts be—Christ, how far!

PISGAH-SIGHTS. I

I

OVER the ball of it,
  Peering and prying,
How I see all of it,
  Life there, outlying!
Roughness and smoothness,
  Shine and defilement,
Grace and uncouthness:
  One reconcilement.

II

Orbed as appointed,
  Sister with brother
Joins, ne'er disjointed
  One from the other.
All's lend-and-borrow;
  Good, see, wants evil,
Joy demands sorrow,
  Angel weds devil!

III

'Which things must—*why* be?'
  Vain our endeavour!
So shall things aye be
  As they were ever.
'Such things should *so* be!'
  Sage our desistence!
Rough-smooth let globe be,
  Mixed—man's existence!

IV

Man—wise and foolish,
  Lover and scorner,
Docile and mulish—
  Keep each his corner!

Honey yet gall of it!
   There's the life lying,
And I see all of it,
   Only, I'm dying!

PISGAH-SIGHTS. II

I

COULD I but live again,
   Twice my life over,
Would I once strive again?
   Would not I cover
Quietly all of it—
   Greed and ambition—
So, from the pall of it,
   Pass to fruition?

II

'Soft!' I'd say, 'Soul mine!
   Three-score and ten years,
Let the blind mole mine
   Digging out deniers!
Let the dazed hawk soar,
   Claim the sun's rights too!
Turf 'tis thy walk's o'er,
   Foliage thy flight's to.'

III

Only a learner,
   Quick one or slow one,
Just a discerner,
   I would teach no one.
I am earth's native:
   No rearranging it!
I be creative,
   Chopping and changing it?

IV

March, men, my fellows!
　　Those who, above me,
(Distance so mellows)
　　Fancy you love me:
Those who, below me,
　　(Distance makes great so)
Free to forego me,
　　Fancy you hate so!

V

Praising, reviling,
　　Worst head and best head,
Past me defiling,
　　Never arrested,
Wanters, abounders,
　　March, in gay mixture,
Men, my surrounders!
　　I am the fixture.

VI

So shall I fear thee,
　　Mightiness yonder!
Mock-sun—more near thee,
　　What is to wonder?
So shall I love thee,
　　Down in the dark,—lest
Glowworm I prove thee,
　　Star that now sparklest!

FEARS AND SCRUPLES

I

HERE's my case. Of old I used to love him
　　This same unseen friend, before I knew:
Dream there was none like him, none above him,—
　　Wake to hope and trust my dream was true.

II

Loved I not his letters full of beauty?
  Not his actions famous far and wide?
Absent, he would know I vowed him duty;
  Present, he would find me at his side.

III

Pleasant fancy! for I had but letters,
  Only knew of actions by hearsay:
He himself was busied with my betters;
  What of that? My turn must come some day.

IV

'Some day' proving—no day! Here's the puzzle.
  Passed and passed my turn is. Why complain?
He's so busied! If I could but muzzle
  People's foolish mouths that give me pain!

V

'Letters?' (hear them!) 'You a judge of writing?
  Ask the experts!—How they shake the head
O'er these characters, your friend's inditing—
  Call them forgery from A to Z!

VI

'Actions? Where's your certain proof' (they bother)
  'He, of all you find so great and good,
He, he only, claims this, that, the other
  Action—claimed by men, a multitude?'

VII

I can simply wish I might refute you,
  Wish my friend would,—by a word, a wink,—
Bid me stop that foolish mouth,—you brute you!
  He keeps absent,—why, I cannot think.

VIII

Never mind! Though foolishness may flout me,
  One thing's sure enough: 'tis neither frost,
No, nor fire, shall freeze or burn from out me
  Thanks for truth—though falsehood, gained—though
    lost.

IX

All my days, I'll go the softlier, sadlier,
    For that dream's sake! How forget the thrill
Through and through me as I thought 'The gladlier
    Lives my friend because I love him still!'

X

Ah, but there's a menace someone utters!
    'What and if your friend at home play tricks?
Peep at hide-and-seek behind the shutters?
    Mean your eyes should pierce through solid bricks?

XI

'What and if he, frowning, wake you, dreamy?
    Lay on you the blame that bricks—conceal?
Say "*At least I saw who did not see me,*
    Does see now, and presently shall feel"?'

XII

'Why, that makes your friend a monster!' say you:
    'Had his house no window? At first nod,
Would you not have hailed him?' Hush, I pray you!
    What if this friend happen to be—God?

NATURAL MAGIC

I

ALL I can say is—I saw it!
The room was as bare as your hand.
I locked in the swarth little lady,—I swear,
From the head to the foot of her—well, quite as bare!
'No Nautch shall cheat me,' said I, 'taking my stand
At this bolt which I draw!' And this bolt—I withdraw it,
And there laughs the lady, not bare, but embowered
With—who knows what verdure, o'erfruited, o'er-
    flowered?
      Impossible! Only—I saw it!

II

All I can sing is—I feel it!
This life was as blank as that room;
I let you pass in here. Precaution, indeed?
Walls, ceiling and floor,—not a chance for a weed!
Wide opens the entrance: where's cold now, where's
    gloom?
No May to sow seed here, no June to reveal it,
Behold you enshrined in these blooms of your bringing,
These fruits of your bearing—nay, birds of your winging!
    A fairy-tale! Only—I feel it!

MAGICAL NATURE

I

FLOWER—I never fancied, jewel—I profess you!
    Bright I see and soft I feel the outside of a flower.
Save but glow inside and—jewel, I should guess you,
    Dim to sight and rough to touch: the glory is the dower.

II

You, forsooth, a flower? Nay, my love, a jewel—
    Jewel at no mercy of a moment in your prime!
Time may fray the flower-face: kind be time or cruel,
    Jewel, from each facet, flash your laugh at time!

BIFURCATION

We were two lovers; let me lie by her,
My tomb beside her tomb. On hers inscribe—
'I loved him; but my reason bade prefer
Duty to love, reject the tempter's bribe
Of rose and lily when each path diverged,
And either I must pace to life's far end
As love should lead me, or, as duty urged,
Plod the worn causeway arm-in-arm with friend.

So, truth turned falsehood: "*How I loathe a flower,*
How prize the pavement!" still caressed his ear—
The deafish friend's—through life's day, hour by hour,
As he laughed (coughing) "*Ay, it would appear!*"
But deep within my heart of hearts there hid
Ever the confidence, amends for all,
That heaven repairs what wrong earth's journey did,
When love from life-long exile comes at call.
Duty and love, one broadway, were the best—
Who doubts? But one or other was to choose.
I chose the darkling half, and wait the rest
In that new world where light and darkness fuse.'

Inscribe on mine—'I loved her: love's track lay
O'er sand and pebble, as all travellers know.
Duty led through a smiling country, gay
With greensward where the rose and lily blow.
"*Our roads are diverse: farewell, love!*" said she;
"'*Tis duty I abide by: homely sward*
And not the rock-rough picturesque for me!
Above, where both roads join, I wait reward.
Be you as constant to the path whereon
I leave you planted!" But man needs must move,
Keep moving—whither, when the star is gone
Whereby he steps secure nor strays from love?
No stone but I was tripped by, stumbling-block
But brought me to confusion. Where I fell,
There I lay flat, if moss disguised the rock,
Thence, if flint pierced, I rose and cried "*All 's well!*
Duty be mine to tread in that high sphere
Where love from duty ne'er disparts, I trust,
And two halves make that whole, whereof—since here
One must suffice a man—why, this one must!"'
Inscribe each tomb thus: then, some sage acquaint
The simple—which holds sinner, which holds saint!

APPEARANCES

I

AND so you found that poor room dull,
    Dark, hardly to your taste, my dear?
Its features seemed unbeautiful:
    But this I know—'twas there, not here,
You plighted troth to me, the word
Which—ask that poor room how it heard.

II

And this rich room obtains your praise
    Unqualified,—so bright, so fair,
So all whereat perfection stays?
    Ay, but remember—here, not there,
The other word was spoken! Ask
This rich room how you dropped the mask!

ST. MARTIN'S SUMMER

I

No protesting, dearest!
    Hardly kisses even!
        Don't we both know how it ends?
How the greenest leaf turns serest,
    Bluest outbreak—blankest heaven,
        Lovers—friends?

II

You would build a mansion,
    I would weave a bower
        —Want the heart for enterprise.
Walls admit of no expansion:
    Trellis-work may haply flower
        Twice the size.

III

What makes glad Life's Winter?
  New buds, old blooms after.
    Sad the sighing 'How suspect
Beams would ere mid-Autumn splinter,
  Rooftree scarce support a rafter,
    Walls lie wrecked?'

IV

You are young, my princess!
  I am hardly older:
    Yet—I steal a glance behind.
Dare I tell you what convinces
  Timid me that you, if bolder,
    Bold—are blind?

V

Where we plan our dwelling
  Glooms a graveyard surely!
    Headstone, footstone moss may drape,—
Name, date, violets hide from spelling,—
  But, though corpses rot obscurely,
    Ghosts escape.

VI

Ghosts! O breathing Beauty,
  Give my frank word pardon!
    What if I—somehow, somewhere—
Pledged my soul to endless duty
  Many a time and oft? Be hard on
    Love—laid there?

VII

Nay, blame grief that's fickle,
  Time that proves a traitor,
    Chance, change, all that purpose warps,—
Death who spares to thrust the sickle
  Laid Love low, through flowers which later
    Shroud the corpse!

VIII

And you, my winsome lady,
  Whisper with like frankness!
    Lies nothing buried long ago?
Are yon—which shimmer mid the shady
  Where moss and violet run to rankness—
    Tombs or no?

IX

Who taxes you with murder?
  My hands are clean—or nearly!
    Love being mortal needs must pass.
Repentance? Nothing were absurder.
  Enough: we felt Love's loss severely;
    Though now—alas!

X

Love's corpse lies quiet therefore,
  Only Love's ghost plays truant,
    And warns us have in wholesome awe
Durable mansionry; that's wherefore
  I weave but trellis-work, pursuant
    —Life, to law.

XI

The solid, not the fragile,
  Tempts rain and hail and thunder.
    If bower stand firm at Autumn's close,
Beyond my hope,—why, boughs were agile;
  If bower fall flat, we scarce need wonder
    Wreathing—rose!

XII

So, truce to the protesting,
  So, muffled be the kisses!
    For, would we but avow the truth,
Sober is genuine joy. No jesting!
  Ask else Penelope, Ulysses—
    Old in youth!

XIII

For why should ghosts feel angered?
　　Let all their interference
　　　　Be faint march-music in the air!
'Up! Join the rear of us the vanguard!
　　Up, lovers, dead to all appearance,
　　　　Laggard pair!'

XIV

The while you clasp me closer,
　　The while I press you deeper,
　　　　As safe we chuckle,—under breath,
Yet all the slyer, the jocoser,—
　　'So, life can boast its day, like leap-year,
　　　　Stolen from death!'

XV

Ah me—the sudden terror!
　　Hence quick—avaunt, avoid me,
　　　　You cheat, the ghostly flesh-disguised!
Nay, all the ghosts in one! Strange error!
　　So, 'twas Death's self that clipped and coyed me,
　　　　Loved—and lied!

XVI

Ay, dead loves are the potent!
　　Like any cloud they used you,
　　　　Mere semblance you, but substance they!
Build we no mansion, weave we no tent!
　　Mere flesh—their spirit interfused you!
　　　　Hence, I say!

XVII

All theirs, none yours the glamour!
　　Theirs each low word that won me,
　　　　Soft look that found me Love's, and left
What else but you—the tears and clamour
　　That's all your very own! Undone me—
　　　　Ghost-bereft!

HERVÉ RIEL

I

ON the sea and at the Hogue, sixteen hundred ninety-two,
  Did the English fight the French,—woe to France!
And, the thirty-first of May, helter-skelter through the
  blue,
Like a crowd of frightened porpoises a shoal of sharks
  pursue,
    Came crowding ship on ship to Saint-Malo on the
    Rance,
With the English fleet in view.

II

'Twas the squadron that escaped, with the victor in full
  chase;
  First and foremost of the drove, in his great ship,
  Damfreville;
    Close on him fled, great and small,
    Twenty-two good ships in all;
And they signalled to the place
'Help the winners of a race!
  Get us guidance, give us harbour, take us quick—or,
  quicker still,
  Here's the English can and will!'

III

Then the pilots of the place put out brisk and leapt on
  board;
  'Why, what hope or chance have ships like these to
  pass?' laughed they:
'Rocks to starboard, rocks to port, all the passage scarred
  and scored,—
Shall the "Formidable" here, with her twelve and eighty
  guns,
  Think to make the river-mouth by the single narrow
  way,
Trust to enter—where 'tis ticklish for a craft of twenty
  tons,

And with flow at full beside?
　　Now, 'tis slackest ebb of tide.
Reach the mooring? Rather say,
While rock stands or water runs,
　　Not a ship will leave the bay!'

IV

Then was called a council straight.
Brief and bitter the debate:
'Here's the English at our heels; would you have them
　　take in tow
All that's left us of the fleet, linked together stern and bow,
For a prize to Plymouth Sound?
Better run the ships aground!'
　　(Ended Damfreville his speech.)
'Not a minute more to wait!
　　Let the Captains all and each
Shove ashore, then blow up, burn the vessels on the
　　beach!
France must undergo her fate.

V

Give the word!' But no such word
Was ever spoke or heard;
　　For up stood, for out stepped, for in struck amid all
　　these
—A Captain? A Lieutenant? A Mate—first, second,
　　third?
　　No such man of mark, and meet
　　With his betters to compete!
But a simple Breton sailor pressed by Tourville for the
　　fleet,
A poor coasting-pilot he, Hervé Riel the Croisickese.

VI

And 'What mockery or malice have we here?' cries Hervé
　　Riel:
　　'Are you mad, you Malouins? Are you cowards, fools,
　　or rogues?

Talk to me of rocks and shoals, me who took the sound-
       ings, tell
On my fingers every bank, every shallow, every swell
    'Twixt the offing here and Grève where the river dis-
       embogues?
Are you bought by English gold? Is it love the lying's for?
              Morn and eve, night and day,
              Have I piloted your bay,
Entered free and anchored fast at the foot of Solidor.
    Burn the fleet and ruin France? That were worse than
       fifty Hogues!
       Sirs, they know I speak the truth!
              Sirs, believe me there's a way!
Only let me lead the line,
    Have the biggest ship to steer,
    Get this "Formidable" clear,
Make the others follow mine,
And I lead them, most and least, by a passage I know
       well,
    Right to Solidor past Grève,
       And there lay them safe and sound;
       And if one ship misbehave,—
    —Keel so much as grate the ground,
Why, I've nothing but my life,—here's my head!' cries
    Hervé Riel.

VII

Not a minute more to wait.
'Steer us in, then, small and great!
    Take the helm, lead the line, save the squadron!' cried
       its chief.
Captains, give the sailor place!
    He is Admiral, in brief.
Still the north-wind, by God's grace!
See the noble fellow's face
As the big ship, with a bound,
Clears the entry like a hound,
Keeps the passage, as its inch of way were the wide sea's
       profound!

See, safe thro' shoal and rock,
　How they follow in a flock,
Not a ship that misbehaves, not a keel that grates the
　　　ground,
　Not a spar that comes to grief!
The peril, see, is past.
All are harboured to the last,
And just as Hervé Riel hollas 'Anchor!'—sure as fate,
Up the English come,—too late!

VIII

So, the storm subsides to calm:
　They see the green trees wave
　On the heights o'erlooking Grève.
Hearts that bled are stanched with balm.
'Just our rapture to enhance,
　Let the English rake the bay,
Gnash their teeth and glare askance
　As they cannonade away!
'Neath rampired Solidor pleasant riding on the Rance!'
How hope succeeds despair on each Captain's coun-
　　　tenance!
Out burst all with one accord,
　'This is Paradise for Hell!
　　Let France, let France's King
　　Thank the man that did the thing!'
What a shout, and all one word,
　'Hervé Riel!'
As he stepped in front once more,
　Not a symptom of surprise
　In the frank blue Breton eyes,
Just the same man as before.

IX

Then said Damfreville, 'My friend,
I must speak out at the end,
　Though I find the speaking hard.
Praise is deeper than the lips:
You have saved the King his ships,
　You must name your own reward.

'Faith, our sun was near eclipse!
Demand whate'er you will,
France remains your debtor still.
Ask to heart's content and have! or my name's not
    Damfreville.'

X

Then a beam of fun outbroke
On the bearded mouth that spoke,
As the honest heart laughed through
Those frank eyes of Breton blue:
'Since I needs must say my say,
    Since on board the duty's done,
    And from Malo Roads to Croisic Point, what is it but
        a run?—
Since 'tis ask and have, I may—
    Since the others go ashore—
Come! A good whole holiday!
    Leave to go and see my wife, whom I call the Belle
        Aurore!'
    That he asked and that he got,—nothing more.

XI

Name and deed alike are lost:
Not a pillar nor a post
    In his Croisic keeps alive the feat as it befell;
Not a head in white and black
On a single fishing-smack,
In memory of the man but for whom had gone to wrack
    All that France saved from the fight whence England
        bore the bell.
Go to Paris: rank on rank
    Search the heroes flung pell-mell
On the Louvre, face and flank!
    You shall look long enough ere you come to Hervé Riel.
So, for better and for worse,
Hervé Riel, accept my verse!
In my verse, Hervé Riel, do thou once more
Save the squadron, honour France, love thy wife the
    Belle Aurore!

A FORGIVENESS

I AM indeed the personage you know.
As for my wife,—what happened long ago,—
You have a right to question me, as I
Am bound to answer.

('Son, a fit reply!'
The monk half spoke, half ground through his clenched
teeth,
At the confession-grate I knelt beneath.)

Thus then all happened, Father! Power and place
I had as still I have. I ran life's race,
With the whole world to see, as only strains
His strength some athlete whose prodigious gains
Of good appal him: happy to excess,—
Work freely done should balance happiness
Fully enjoyed; and, since beneath my roof
Housed she who made home heaven, in heaven's behoof
I went forth every day, and all day long
Worked for the world. Look, how the labourer's song
Cheers him! Thus sang my soul, at each sharp throe
Of labouring flesh and blood—'She loves me so!'

One day, perhaps such song so knit the nerve
That work grew play and vanished. 'I deserve
Haply my heaven an hour before the time!'
I laughed, as silverly the clockhouse-chime
Surprised me passing through the postern-gate
—Not the main entry where the menials wait
And wonder why the world's affairs allow
The master sudden leisure. That was how
I took the private garden-way for once.

Forth from the alcove, I saw start, ensconce
Himself behind the porphyry vase, a man
My fancies in the natural order ran:

U

'A spy,—perhaps a foe in ambuscade,—
A thief,—more like, a sweetheart of some maid
Who pitched on the alcove for tryst perhaps.'

'Stand there!' I bid.

                Whereat my man but wraps
His face the closelier with uplifted arm
Whereon the cloak lies, strikes in blind alarm
This and that pedestal as,—stretch and stoop,—
Now in, now out of sight, he thrids the group
Of statues, marble god and goddess ranged
Each side the pathway, till the gate's exchanged
For safety: one step thence, the street, you know!

Thus far I followed with my gaze. Then, slow,
Near on admiringly, I breathed again,
And—back to that last fancy of the train—
'A danger risked for hope of just a word
With—which of all my nest may be the bird
This poacher covets for her plumage, pray?
Carmen? Juana? Carmen seems too gay
For such adventure, while Juana's grave
—Would scorn the folly. I applaud the knave!
He had the eye, could single from my brood
His proper fledgeling!'

               As I turned, there stood
In face of me, my wife stone-still stone-white.
Whether one bound had brought her,—at first sight
Of what she judged the encounter, sure to be
Next moment, of the venturous man and me,—
Brought her to clutch and keep me from my prey:
Whether impelled because her death no day
Could come so absolutely opportune
As now at joy's height, like a year in June
Stayed at the fall of its first ripened rose:
Or whether hungry for my hate—who knows?—
Eager to end an irksome lie, and taste
Our tingling true relation, hate embraced
By hate one naked moment:—anyhow

There stone-still stone-white stood my wife, but now
The woman who made heaven within my house.
Ay, she who faced me was my very spouse
As well as love—you are to recollect!

'Stay!' she said. 'Keep at least one soul unspecked
With crime, that's spotless hitherto—your own!
Kill me who court the blessing, who alone
Was, am, and shall be guilty, first to last!
The man lay helpless in the toils I cast
About him, helpless as the statue there
Against that strangling bell-flower's bondage: tear
Away and tread to dust the parasite,
But do the passive marble no despite.
I love him as I hate you. Kill me! Strike
At one blow both infinitudes alike
Out of existence—hate and love! Whence love?
That's safe inside my heart, nor will remove
For any searching of your steel, I think.
Whence hate? The secret lay on lip, at brink
Of speech, in one fierce tremble to escape,
At every form wherein your love took shape,
At each new provocation of your kiss.
Kill me!'

                We went in.

                        Next day after this,
I felt as if the speech might come. I spoke—
Easily, after all.

                'The lifted cloak
Was screen sufficient: I concern myself
Hardly with laying hands on who for pelf—
Whate'er the ignoble kind—may prowl and brave
Cuffing and kicking proper to a knave
Detected by my household's vigilance.
Enough of such! As for my love-romance—
I, like our good Hidalgo, rub my eyes
And wake and wonder how the film could rise
Which changed for me a barber's basin straight

Into—Mambrino's helm? I hesitate
Nowise to say—God's sacramental cup!
Why should I blame the brass which, burnished up,
Will blaze, to all but me, as good as gold?
To me—a warning I was overbold
In judging metals. The Hidalgo waked
Only to die, if I remember,—staked
His life upon the basin's worth, and lost:
While I confess torpidity at most
In here and there a limb; but, lame and halt,
Still should I work on, still repair my fault
Ere I took rest in death,—no fear at all!
Now, work—no word before the curtain fall!'

The 'curtain'? That of death on life, I meant:
My 'word,' permissible in death's event,
Would be—truth, soul to soul; for, otherwise,
Day by day, three years long, there had to rise
And, night by night, to fall upon our stage—
Ours, doomed to public play by heritage—
Another curtain, when the world, perforce
Our critical assembly, in due course
Came and went, witnessing, gave praise or blame
To art-mimetic. It had spoiled the game
If, suffered to set foot behind our scene,
The world had witnessed how stage-king and queen,
Gallant and lady, but a minute since
Enarming each other, would evince
No sign of recognition as they took
His way and her way to whatever nook
Waited them in the darkness either side
Of that bright stage where lately groom and bride
Had fired the audience to a frenzy-fit
Of sympathetic rapture—every whit
Earned as the curtain fell on her and me,
—Actors. Three whole years, nothing was to see
But calm and concord; where a speech was due
There came the speech: when smiles were wanted too
Smiles were as ready. In a place like mine,

Where foreign and domestic cares combine,
There's audience every day and all day long;
But finally the last of the whole throng
Who linger lets one see his back. For her—
Why, liberty and liking: I aver,
Liking and liberty! For me—I breathed,
Let my face rest from every wrinkle wreathed
Smile-like about the mouth, unlearned my task
Of personation till next day bade mask,
And quietly betook me from that world
To the real world, not pageant: there unfurled
In work, its wings, my soul, the fretted power.
Three years I worked, each minute of each hour
Not claimed by acting:—work I may dispense
With talk about, since work in evidence,
Perhaps in history; who knows or cares?

After three years, this way, all unawares,
Our acting ended. She and I, at close
Of a loud night-feast, led, between two rows
Of bending male and female loyalty,
Our lord the king down staircase, while, held high
At arm's length did the twisted tapers' flare
Herald his passage from our palace, where
Such visiting left glory evermore.
Again the ascent in public, till at door
As we two stood by the saloon—now blank
And disencumbered of its guests—there sank
A whisper in my ear, so low and yet
So unmistakable!

                    'I half forget
The chamber you repair to, and I want
Occasion for one short word—if you grant
That grace—within a certain room you called
Our "Study," for you wrote there while I scrawled
Some paper full of faces for my sport.
That room I can remember. Just one short
Word with you there, for the remembrance' sake!'

'Follow me thither!' I replied.

We break
The gloom a little, as with guiding lamp
I lead the way, leave warmth and cheer, by damp
Blind disused serpentining ways afar
From where the habitable chambers are,—
Ascend, descend stairs tunnelled through the stone,—
Always in silence,—till I reach the lone
Chamber sepulchred for my very own
Out of the palace-quarry. When a boy,
Here was my fortress, stronghold from annoy,
Proof-positive of ownership; in youth
I garnered up my gleanings here—uncouth
But precious relics of vain hopes, vain fears;
Finally, this became in after years
My closet of entrenchment to withstand
Invasion of the foe on every hand—
The multifarious herd in bower and hall,
State-room,—rooms whatsoe'er the style, which call
On masters to be mindful that, before
Men, they must look like men and something more.
Here,—when our lord the king's bestowment ceased
To deck me on the day that, golden-fleeced,
I touched ambition's height,—'twas here, released
From glory (always symbolled by a chain!)
No sooner was I privileged to gain
My secret domicile than glad I flung
That last toy on the table—gazed where hung
On hook my father's gift, the arquebuss—
And asked myself 'Shall I envisage thus
The new prize and the old prize, when I reach
Another year's experience?—own that each
Equalled advantage—sportsman's—statesman's tool?
That brought me down an eagle, this—a fool!'

Into which room on entry, I set down
The lamp, and turning saw whose rustled gown
Had told me my wife followed, pace for pace.
Each of us looked the other in the face.
She spoke. 'Since I could die now . . .'

(To explain
Why that first struck me, know—not once again
Since the adventure at the porphyry's edge
Three years before, which sundered like a wedge
Her soul from mine,—though daily, smile to smile,
We stood before the public,—all the while
Not once had I distinguished, in that face
I paid observance to, the faintest trace
Of feature more than requisite for eyes
To do their duty by and recognize:
So did I force mine to obey my will
And pry no further. There exists such skill,—
Those know who need it. What physician shrinks
From needful contact with a corpse? He drinks
No plague so long as thirst for knowledge—not
An idler impulse—prompts inquiry. What,
And will you disbelieve in power to bid
Our spirit back to bounds, as though we chid
A child from scrutiny that's just and right
In manhood? Sense, not soul, accomplished sight,
Reported daily she it was—not how
Nor why a change had come to cheek and brow.)

'Since I could die now of the truth concealed,
Yet dare not, must not die—so seems revealed
The Virgin's mind to me—for death means peace,
Wherein no lawful part have I, whose lease
Of life and punishment the truth avowed
May haply lengthen,—let me push the shroud
Away, that steals to muffle ere is just
My penance-fire in snow! I dare—I must
Live, by avowal of the truth—this truth—
I loved you! Thanks for the fresh serpent's tooth
That, by a prompt new pang more exquisite
Than all preceding torture, proves me right!
I loved you yet I lost you! May I go
Burn to the ashes, now my shame you know?'

I think there never was such—how express?—
Horror coquetting with voluptuousness,

As in those arms of Eastern workmanship—
Yataghan, kandjar, things that rend and rip,
Gash rough, slash smooth, help hate so many ways,
Yet ever keep a beauty that betrays
Love still at work with the artificer
Throughout his quaint devising. Why prefer,
Except for love's sake, that a blade should writhe
And bicker like a flame?—now play the scythe
As if some broad neck tempted,—now contract
And needle off into a fineness lacked
For just that puncture which the heart demands?
Then, such adornment! Wherefore need our hands
Enclose not ivory alone, nor gold
Roughened for use, but jewels? Nay, behold!
Fancy my favourite—which I seem to grasp
While I describe the luxury. No asp
Is diapered more delicate round throat
Than this below the handle! These denote
—These mazy lines meandering, to end
Only in flesh they open—what intend
They else but water-purlings—pale contrast
With the life-crimson where they blend at last?
And mark the handle's dim pellucid green,
Carved, the hard jadestone, as you pinch a bean,
Into a sort of parrot-bird! He pecks
A grape-bunch; his two eyes are ruby-specks
Pure from the mine: seen this way,—glassy blank,
But turn them,—lo the inmost fire, that shrank
From sparkling, sends a red dart right to aim!
Why did I choose such toys? Perhaps the game
Of peaceful men is warlike, just as men
War-wearied get amusement from that pen
And paper we grow sick of—statesfolk tired
Of merely (when such measures are required)
Dealing out doom to people by three words,
A signature and seal: we play with swords
Suggestive of quick process. That is how
I came to like the toys described you now,
Store of which glittered on the walls and strewed

The table, even, while my wife pursued
Her purpose to its ending. 'Now you know
This shame, my three years' torture, let me go,
Burn to the very ashes! You—I lost,
Yet you—I loved!'

          The thing I pity most
In men is—action prompted by surprise
Of anger: men? nay, bulls—whose onset lies
At instance of the firework and the goad!
Once the foe prostrate,—trampling once bestowed,—
Prompt follows placability, regret,
Atonement. Trust me, blood-warmth never yet
Betokened strong will! As no leap of pulse
Pricked me, that first time, so did none convulse
My veins at this occasion for resolve.
Had that devolved which did not then devolve
Upon me, I had done—what now to do
Was quietly apparent.

          'Tell me who
The man was, crouching by the porphyry vase!'
'No, never! All was folly in his case,
All guilt in mine. I tempted, he complied.'

'And yet you loved me?'

          'Loved you. Double-dyed
In folly and in guilt, I thought you gave
Your heart and soul away from me to slave
At statecraft. Since my right in you seemed lost,
I stung myself to teach you, to your cost,
What you rejected could be prized beyond
Life, heaven, by the first fool I threw a fond
Look on, a fatal word to.'

          'And you still
Love me? Do I conjecture well or ill?'

'Conjecture—well or ill! I had three years
To spend in learning you.'

'We both are peers
In knowledge, therefore: since three years are spent
Ere thus much of yourself I learn—who went
Back to the house, that day, and brought my mind
To bear upon your action, uncombined
Motive from motive, till the dross, deprived
Of every purer particle, survived
At last in native simple hideousness,
Utter contemptibility, nor less
Nor more. Contemptibility—exempt
How could I, from its proper due—contempt?
I have too much despised you to divert
My life from its set course by help or hurt
Of your all-despicable life—perturb
The calm, I work in, by—men's mouths to curb,
Which at such news were clamorous enough—
Men's eyes to shut before my broidered stuff
With the huge hole there, my emblazoned wall
Blank where a scutcheon hung,—by, worse than all,
Each day's procession, my paraded life
Robbed and impoverished through the wanting wife
—Now that my life (which means—my work) was grown
Riches indeed! Once, just this worth alone
Seemed work to have, that profit gained thereby
Of good and praise would—how rewardingly!—
Fall at your feet,—a crown I hoped to cast
Before your love, my love should crown at last.
No love remaining to cast crown before,
My love stopped work now: but contempt the more
Impelled me task as ever head and hand,
Because the very fiends weave ropes of sand
Rather than taste pure hell in idleness.
Therefore I kept my memory down by stress
Of daily work I had no mind to stay
For the world's wonder at the wife away.
Oh, it was easy all of it, believe,
For I despised you! But your words retrieve
Importantly the past. No hate assumed
The mask of love at any time! There gloomed

A moment when love took hate's semblance, urged
By causes you declare; but love's self purged
Away a fancied wrong I did both loves
— Yours and my own: by no hate's help, it proves,
Purgation was attempted. Then, you rise
High by how many a grade! I did despise—
I do but hate you. Let hate's punishment
Replace contempt's! First step to which ascent—
Write down your own words I re-utter you!
"*I loved my husband and I hated—who
He was, I took up as my first chance, mere
Mud-ball to fling and make love foul with!*" Here
Lies paper!'

      'Would my blood for ink suffice!'

'It may: this minion from a land of spice,
Silk, feather—every bird of jewelled breast—
This poignard's beauty, ne'er so lightly prest
Above your heart there . . .'

          'Thus?'

             'It flows, I see.
Dip there the point and write!'

           'Dictate to me!
Nay, I remember.'

        And she wrote the words.
I read them. Then—'Since love, in you, affords
License for hate, in me, to quench (I say)
Contempt—why, hate itself has passed away
In vengeance—foreign to contempt. Depart
Peacefully to that death which Eastern art
Imbued this weapon with, if tales be true!
Love will succeed to hate. I pardon you—
Dead in our chamber!'

          True as truth the tale.
She died ere morning: then, I saw how pale
Her cheek was ere it wore day's paint-disguise,
And what a hollow darkened 'neath her eyes,
Now that I used my own. She sleeps, as erst
Beloved, in this your church: ay, yours!

Immersed
In thought so deeply, Father? Sad, perhaps?
For whose sake, hers or mine or his who wraps
—Still plain I seem to see!—about his head
The idle cloak,—about his heart (instead
Of cuirass) some fond hope he may elude
My vengeance in the cloister's solitude?
Hardly, I think! As little helped his brow
The cloak then, Father—as your grate helps now!

FILIPPO BALDINUCCI ON THE PRIVILEGE OF BURIAL

A REMINISCENCE OF A.D. 1676

I

'No, boy, we must not'—so began
    My Uncle (he's with God long since)
A-petting me, the good old man!
    'We must not'—and he seemed to wince,
And lost that laugh whereto had grown
    His chuckle at my piece of news,
How cleverly I aimed my stone—
    'I fear we must not pelt the Jews!

II

'When I was young indeed,—ah, faith
    Was young and strong in Florence too!
We Christians never dreamed of scathe
    Because we cursed or kicked the crew.
But now—well, well! The olive-crops
    Weighed double then, and Arno's pranks
Would always spare religious shops
    Whenever he o'erflowed his banks!

III

'I'll tell you'—and his eye regained
    Its twinkle—'tell you something choice!
Something may help you keep unstained
    Your honest zeal to stop the voice

Of unbelief with stone-throw—spite
  Of laws, which modern fools enact,
That we must suffer Jews in sight
  Go wholly unmolested! Fact!

IV

'There was, then, in my youth, and yet
  Is, by our San Frediano, just
Below the Blessed Olivet,
  A wayside ground wherein they thrust
Their dead,—these Jews,—the more our shame!
  Except that, so they will but die,
Christians perchance incur no blame
  In giving hogs a hoist to stye.

V

'There, anyhow, Jews stow away
  Their dead; and,—such their insolence,—
Slink at odd times to sing and pray
  As Christians do—all make-pretence!—
Which wickedness they perpetrate
  Because they think no Christians see.
They reckoned here, at any rate,
  Without their host: ha, ha, he, he!

VI

'For, what should join their plot of ground
  But a good Farmer's Christian field?
The Jews had hedged their corner round
  With bramble-bush to keep concealed
Their doings: for the public road
  Ran betwixt this their ground and that
The Farmer's, where he ploughed and sowed,
  Grew corn for barn and grapes for vat.

VII

'So, properly to guard his store
  And gall the unbelievers too,
He builds a shrine and, what is more,
  Procures a painter whom I knew,

One Buti (he's with God) to paint
    A holy picture there—no less
Than Virgin Mary free from taint
    Borne to the sky by angels: yes!

VIII

Which shrine he fixed,—who says him nay?—
    A-facing with its picture-side
Not, as you'd think, the public way,
    But just where sought these hounds to hide
Their carrion from that very truth
    Of Mary's triumph: not a hound
Could act his mummeries uncouth
    But Mary shamed the pack all round!

IX

'Now, if it was amusing, judge!
    —To see the company arrive,
Each Jew intent to end his trudge
    And take his pleasure (though alive)
With all his Jewish kith and kin
    Below ground, have his venom out,
Sharpen his wits for next day's sin,
    Curse Christians, and so home, no doubt!

X

'Whereas, each phyz upturned beholds
    Mary, I warrant, soaring brave!
And in a trice, beneath the folds
    Of filthy garb which gowns each knave,
Down drops it—there to hide grimace,
    Contortion of the mouth and nose
At finding Mary in the place
    They'd keep for Pilate, I suppose!

XI

'At last, they will not brook—not they!—
    Longer such outrage on their tribe:
So, in some hole and corner, lay
    Their heads together—how to bribe

The meritorious Farmer's self
    To straight undo his work, restore
Their chance to meet and muse on pelf—
    Pretending sorrow, as before!

XII

'Forthwith, a posse, if you please,
    Of Rabbi This and Rabbi That
Almost go down upon their knees
    To get him lay the picture flat.
The spokesman, eighty years of age,
    Grey as a badger, with a goat's
Not only beard but bleat, 'gins wage
    War with our Mary. Thus he dotes:—

XIII

'"*Friends, grant a grace! How Hebrews toil*
    Through life in Florence—why relate
To those who lay the burden, spoil
    Our paths of peace? We bear our fate,
But when with life the long toil ends,
    Why must you—the expression craves
Pardon, but truth compels me, friends!—
    Why must you plague us in our graves?

XIV

'"*Thoughtlessly plague, I would believe!*
    For how can you—the lords of ease
By nurture, birthright—e'en conceive
    Our luxury to lie with trees
And turf,—the cricket and the bird
    Left for our last companionship:
No harsh deed, no unkindly word,
    No frowning brow nor scornful lip!

XV

'"*Death's luxury, we now rehearse*
    While, living, through your streets we fare
And take your hatred: nothing worse
    Have we, once dead and safe, to bear!

So we refresh our souls, fulfil
  Our works, our daily tasks; and thus
Gather you grain—earth's harvest—still
  The wheat for you, the straw for us.

XVI

'"'What flouting in a face, what harm,
  In just a lady borne from bier
By boys' heads, wings for leg and arm?'
  You question. Friends, the harm is here—
That just when our last sigh is heaved,
  And we would fain thank God and you
For labour done and peace achieved,
  Back comes the Past in full review!

XVII

'"*At sight of just that simple flag,*
  Starts the foe-feeling serpent-like
From slumber. Leave it lulled, nor drag—
  Though fangless—forth, what needs must strike
When stricken sore, though stroke be vain
  Against the mailed oppressor! Give
Play to our fancy that we gain
  Life's rights when once we cease to live!

XVIII

'"*Thus much to courtesy, to kind,*
  To conscience! Now to Florence folk!
There's core beneath this apple-rind,
  Beneath this white-of-egg there's yolk!
Beneath this prayer to courtesy,
  Kind, conscience—there's a sum to pouch!
How many ducats down will buy
  Our shame's removal, sirs? Avouch!

XIX

'"*Removal, not destruction, sirs!*
  Just turn your picture! Let it front
The public path! Or memory errs,
  Or that same public path is wont

To witness many a chance befall
    Of lust, theft, bloodshed—sins enough,
Wherein our Hebrew part is small.
    Convert yourselves!"—he cut up rough.

xx

'Look you, how soon a service paid
    Religion yields the servant fruit!
A prompt reply our Farmer made
    So following: "*Sirs, to grant your suit*
Involves much danger! How? Transpose
    Our Lady? Stop the chastisement,
All for your good, herself bestows?
    What wonder if I grudge consent?

xxi

'"*—Yet grant it: since, what cash I take*
    Is so much saved from wicked use.
We know you! And, for Mary's sake,
    A hundred ducats shall induce
Concession to your prayer. One day
    Suffices: Master Buti's brush
Turns Mary round the other way,
    And deluges your side with slush.

xxii

'"*Down with the ducats therefore!"* Dump,
    Dump, dump it falls, each counted piece,
Hard gold. Then out of door they stump,
    These dogs, each brisk as with new lease
Of life, I warrant,—glad he'll die
    Henceforward just as he may choose,
Be buried and in clover lie!
    Well said Esaias—"*stiff-necked Jews!*"

xxiii

'Off posts without a minute's loss
    Our Farmer, once the cash in poke,
And summons Buti—ere its gloss
    Have time to fade from off the joke—

To chop and change his work, undo
  The done side, make the side, now blank,
Recipient of our Lady—who,
  Displaced thus, had these dogs to thank!

XXIV

'Now, boy, you're hardly to instruct
  In technicalities of Art!
My nephew's childhood sure has sucked
  Along with mother's-milk some part
Of painter's-practice—learned, at least,
  How expeditiously is plied
A work in fresco—never ceased
  When once begun—a day, each side.

XXV

'So, Buti—(he's with God)—begins:
  First covers up the shrine all round
With hoarding; then, as like as twins,
  Paints, t'other side the burial-ground,
New Mary, every point the same;
  Next, sluices over, as agreed,
The old; and last—but, spoil the game
  By telling you? Not I, indeed!

XXVI

'Well, ere the week was half at end,
  Out came the object of this zeal,
This fine alacrity to spend
  Hard money for mere dead men's weal!
How think you? That old spokesman Jew
  Was High Priest, and he had a wife
As old, and she was dying too,
  And wished to end in peace her life!

XXVII

'And he must humour dying whims,
  And soothe her with the idle hope
They'd say their prayers and sing their hymns
  As if her husband were the Pope!

And she did die—believing just
　This privilege was purchased! Dead
In comfort through her foolish trust!
　"*Stiff-necked ones*," well Esaias said!

XXVIII

'So, Sabbath morning, out of gate
　And on to way, what sees our arch
Good Farmer? Why, they hoist their freight—
　The corpse—on shoulder, and so, march!
"*Now for it, Buti!*" In the nick
　Of time 'tis pully-hauly, hence
With hoarding! O'er the wayside quick
　There's Mary plain in evidence!

XXIX

'And here's the convoy halting: right!
　O they are bent on howling psalms
And growling prayers, when opposite!
　And yet they glance, for all their qualms,
Approve that promptitude of his,
　The Farmer's—duly at his post
To take due thanks from every phyz,
　Sour smirk—nay, surly smile almost!

XXX

'Then earthward drops each brow again;
　The solemn task's resumed; they reach
Their holy field—the unholy train:
　Enter its precinct, all and each,
Wrapt somehow in their godless rites;
　Till, rites at end, up-waking, lo
They lift their faces! What delights
　The mourners as they turn to go?

XXXI

'Ha, ha, he, he! On just the side
　They drew their purse-strings to make quit
Of Mary,—Christ the Crucified
　Fronted them now—these biters bit!

Never was such a hiss and snort,
    Such screwing nose and shooting lip!
Their purchase—honey in report—
    Proved gall and verjuice at first sip!

XXXII

'Out they break, on they bustle, where,
    A-top of wall, the Farmer waits
With Buti: never fun so rare!
    The Farmer has the best: he rates
The rascal, as the old High Priest
    Takes on himself to sermonize—
Nay, sneer " *We Jews supposed, at least,*
    Theft was a crime in Christian eyes!"

XXXIII

' " *Theft?* " cries the Farmer. " *Eat your words!*
    Show me what constitutes a breach
Of faith in aught was said or heard!
    I promised you in plainest speech
I'd take the thing you count disgrace
    And put it here—and here 'tis put!
Did you suppose I'd leave the place
    Blank, therefore, just your rage to glut?

XXXIV

' " *I guess you dared not stipulate*
    For such a damned impertinence!
So, quick, my greybeard, out of gate
    And in at Ghetto! Haste you hence!
As long as I have house and land,
    To spite you irreligious chaps
Here shall the Crucifixion stand—
    Unless you down with cash, perhaps!"

XXXV

'So snickered he and Buti both.
    The Jews said nothing, interchanged
A glance or two, renewed their oath
    To keep ears stopped and hearts estranged

From grace, for all our Church can do;
  Then off they scuttle: sullen jog
Homewards, against our Church to brew
  Fresh mischief in their synagogue.

XXXVI

'But next day—see what happened, boy!
  See why I bid you have a care
How you pelt Jews! The knaves employ
  Such methods of revenge, forbear
No outrage on our faith, when free
  To wreak their malice! Here they took
So base a method—plague o' me
  If I record it in my Book!

XXXVII

'For, next day, while the Farmer sat
  Laughing with Buti, in his shop,
At their successful joke,—rat tat,—
  Door opens, and they're like to drop
Down to the floor as in there stalks
  A six-feet-high herculean-built
Young he-Jew with a beard that baulks
  Description. "*Help ere blood be spilt!*"

XXXVIII

—'Screamed Buti: for he recognized
  Whom but the son, no less no more,
Of that High Priest his work surprised
  So pleasantly the day before!
Son of the mother, then, whereof
  The bier he lent a shoulder to,
And made the moans about, dared scoff
  At sober Christian grief—the Jew!

XXXIX

'"*Sirs, I salute you! Never rise!*
  No apprehension!" (Buti, white
And trembling like a tub of size,
  Had tried to smuggle out of sight

The picture's self—the thing in oils,
    You know, from which a fresco's dashed
Which courage speeds while caution spoils)
    "*Stay and be praised, sir, unabashed!*

XL

'"*Praised,—ay, and paid too: for I come*
    To buy that very work of yours.
My poor abode, which boasts—well, some
    Few specimens of Art, secures
Haply, a masterpiece indeed
    If I should find my humble means
Suffice the outlay. So, proceed!
    Propose—ere prudence intervenes!"

XLI

'On Buti, cowering like a child,
    These words descended from aloft,
In tone so ominously mild,
    With smile terrifically soft
To that degree—could Buti dare
    (Poor fellow) use his brains, think twice?
He asked, thus taken unaware,
    No more than just the proper price!

XLII

'"*Done!*" cries the monster. "*I disburse*
    Forthwith your moderate demand.
Count on my custom—if no worse
    Your future work be, understand,
Than this I carry off! No aid!
    My arm, sir, lacks nor bone nor thews:
The burden's easy, and we're made,
    Easy or hard, to bear—we Jews!"

XLIII

'Crossing himself at such escape,
    Buti by turns the money eyes
And, timidly, the stalwart shape
    Now moving doorwards; but, more wise,

The Farmer,—who, though dumb, this while
   Had watched advantage,—straight conceived
A reason for that tone and smile
   So mild and soft! The Jew—believed!

XLIV

'Mary in triumph borne to deck
   A Hebrew household! Pictured where
No one was used to bend the neck
   In praise or bow the knee in prayer!
Borne to that domicile by whom?
   The son of the High Priest! Through what?
An insult done his mother's tomb!
   Saul changed to Paul—the case came pat!

XLV

'"Stay, dog Jew . . . gentle sir, that is!
   Resolve me! Can it be, she crowned,—
Mary, by miracle, Oh bliss!—
   My present to your burial ground?
Certain, a ray of light has burst
   Your veil of darkness! Had you else,
Only for Mary's sake, unpursed
   So much hard money? Tell—oh, tell 's!"*

XLVI

'Round—like a serpent that we took
   For worm and trod on—turns his bulk
About the Jew. First dreadful look
   Sends Buti in a trice to skulk
Out of sight somewhere, safe—alack!
   But our good Farmer faith made bold:
And firm (with Florence at his back)
   He stood, while gruff the gutturals rolled—

XLVII

'"Ay, sir, a miracle was worked,
   By quite another power, I trow,
Than ever yet in canvas lurked,
   Or you would scarcely face me now!

A certain impulse did suggest
A certain grasp with this right-hand,
Which probably had put to rest
Our quarrel,—thus your throat once spanned

XLVIII

'"*But I remembered me, subdued*
That impulse, and you face me still!
And soon a philosophic mood
Succeeding (hear it, if you will!)
Has altogether changed my views
Concerning Art. Blind prejudice!
Well may you Christians tax us Jews
With scrupulosity too nice!

XLIX

'"*For, don't I see,—let's issue join!—*
Whenever I'm allowed pollute
(*I—and my little bag of coin*)
Some Christian palace of repute,—
Don't I see stuck up everywhere
Abundant proof that cultured taste
Has Beauty for its only care,
And upon Truth no thought to waste?

L

'"'*Jew, since it must be, take in pledge*
Of payment '—*so a Cardinal*
Has sighed to me as if a wedge
Entered his heart—' *this best of all*
My treasures!' *Leda, Ganymede*
Or Antiope: swan, eagle, ape,
(*Or what 's the beast of what 's the breed*)
And Jupiter in every shape!

LI

'"*Whereat if I presume to ask*
'*But, Eminence, though Titian's whisk*
Of brush have well performed its task,
How comes it these false godships frisk

In presence of—what yonder frame
    Pretends to image? Surely, odd
It seems, you let confront The Name
    Each beast the heathen called his god!'

LII

'"*Benignant smiles me pity straight*
    The Cardinal, ' 'Tis Truth, we prize!
Art's the sole question in debate!
    These subjects are so many lies.
We treat them with a proper scorn
    When we turn lies—called gods forsooth—
To lies' fit use, now Christ is born.
    Drawing and colouring are Truth.

LIII

'"'Think you I honour lies so much
    As scruple to parade the charms
Of Leda—Titian, every touch—
    Because the thing within her arms
Means Jupiter who had the praise
    And prayer of a benighted world?
He would have mine too, if, in days
    Of light, I kept the canvas furled!'

LIV

'"*So ending, with some easy gibe.*
    What power has logic! I, at once,
Acknowledged error in our tribe
    So squeamish that, when friends ensconce
A pretty picture in its niche
    To do us honour, deck our graves,
We fret and fume and have an itch
    To strangle folk—ungrateful knaves!

LV

'"*No, sir! Be sure that—what's its style,*
    Your picture?—shall possess ungrudged
A place among my rank and file
    Of Ledas and what not—be judged

Just as a picture! and (because
I fear me much I scarce have bought
A Titian) Master Buti's flaws
Found there, will have the laugh flaws ought!"

LVI

'So, with a scowl, it darkens door—
This bulk—no longer! Buti makes
Prompt glad re-entry; there's a score
Of oaths, as the good Farmer wakes
From what must needs have been a trance,
Or he had struck (he swears) to ground
The bold bad mouth that dared advance
Such doctrine the reverse of sound!

LVII

'Was magic here? Most like! For, since,
Somehow our city's faith grows still
More and more lukewarm, and our Prince
Or loses heart or wants the will
To check increase of cold. 'Tis " *Live*
And let live! Languidly repress
The Dissident! In short,—contrive
Christians must bear with Jews: no less!"

LVIII

'The end seems, any Israelite
Wants any picture,—pishes, poohs,
Purchases, hangs it full in sight
In any chamber he may choose!
In Christ's crown, one more thorn we rue!
In Mary's bosom, one more sword!
No, boy, you must not pelt a Jew!
O Lord, how long? How long, O Lord?'

From 'LA SAISIAZ'

1878

I

GOOD, to forgive;
    Best, to forget!
    Living, we fret;
Dying, we live.
Fretless and free,
    Soul, clap thy pinion!
    Earth have dominion,
Body, o'er thee!

II

Wander at will,
    Day after day,—
    Wander away,
Wandering still—
Soul that canst soar!
    Body may slumber:
    Body shall cumber
Soul-flight no more.

III

Waft of soul's wing!
    What lies above?
    Sunshine and Love,
Skyblue and Spring!
Body hides—where?
    Ferns of all feather,
    Mosses and heather,
Yours be the care!

From 'THE TWO POETS OF CROISIC'

1878

I

SUCH a starved bank of moss
  Till that May-morn,
Blue ran the flash across:
  Violets were born!

II

Sky—what a scowl of cloud
  Till, near and far,
Ray on ray split the shroud:
  Splendid, a star!

III

World—how it walled about
  Life with disgrace
Till God's own smile came out:
  That was thy face!

I

WHAT a pretty tale you told me
  Once upon a time
—Said you found it somewhere (scold me!)
  Was it prose or was it rhyme,
Greek or Latin? Greek, you said,
While your shoulder propped my head.

II

Anyhow there's no forgetting
  This much if no more,
That a poet (pray, no petting!)
  Yes, a bard, sir, famed of yore,
Went where suchlike used to go,
Singing for a prize, you know.

III

Well, he had to sing, nor merely
   Sing but play the lyre;
Playing was important clearly
   Quite as singing: I desire,
Sir, you keep the fact in mind
For a purpose that's behind.

IV

There stood he, while deep attention
   Held the judges round,
—Judges able, I should mention,
   To detect the slightest sound
Sung or played amiss: such ears
Had old judges, it appears!

V

None the less he sang out boldly,
   Played in time and tune,
Till the judges, weighing coldly
   Each note's worth, seemed, late or soon,
Sure to smile 'In vain one tries
Picking faults out: take the prize!'

VI

When, a mischief! Were they seven
   Strings the lyre possessed?
Oh, and afterwards eleven,
   Thank you! Well, sir,—who had guessed
Such ill luck in store?—it happed
One of those same seven strings snapped.

VII

All was lost, then! No! a cricket
   (What 'cicada'? Pooh!)
—Some mad thing that left its thicket
   For mere love of music—flew
With its little heart on fire,
Lighted on the crippled lyre.

VIII

So that when (ah joy!) our singer
    For his truant string
Feels with disconcerted finger,
    What does cricket else but fling
Fiery heart forth, sound the note
Wanted by the throbbing throat?

IX

Ay and, ever to the ending,
    Cricket chirps at need,
Executes the hand's intending,
    Promptly, perfectly,—indeed
Saves the singer from defeat
With her chirrup low and sweet.

X

Till, at ending, all the judges
    Cry with one assent
'Take the prize—a prize who grudges
    Such a voice and instrument?
Why, we took your lyre for harp,
So it shrilled us forth F sharp!'

XI

Did the conqueror spurn the creature,
    Once its service done?
That's no such uncommon feature
    In the case when Music's son
Finds his Lotte's power too spent
For aiding soul-development.

XII

No! This other, on returning
    Homeward, prize in hand,
Satisfied his bosom's yearning:
    (Sir, I hope you understand!)
—Said 'Some record there must be
Of this cricket's help to me!'

XIII

So, he made himself a statue:
  Marble stood, life-size;
On the lyre, he pointed at you,
  Perched his partner in the prize:
Never more apart you found
Her, he throned, from him, she crowned.

XIV

That's the tale: its application?
  Somebody I know
Hopes one day for reputation
  Through his poetry that's—Oh,
All so learned and so wise
And deserving of a prize!

XV

If he gains one, will some ticket,
  When his statue's built,
Tell the gazer ''Twas a cricket
  Helped my crippled lyre, whose lilt
Sweet and low, when strength usurped
Softness' place i' the scale, she chirped?

XVI

'For as victory was nighest,
  While I sang and played,—
With my lyre at lowest, highest,
  Right alike,—one string that made
"Love" sound soft was snapt in twain,
Never to be heard again,—

XVII

'Had not a kind cricket fluttered,
  Perched upon the place
Vacant left, and duly uttered
  "Love, Love, Love," whene'er the bass
Asked the treble to atone
For its somewhat sombre drone.'

XVIII

But you don't know music! Wherefore
    Keep on casting pearls
To a—poet? All I care for
    Is—to tell him that a girl's
'Love' comes aptly in when gruff
Grows his singing. (There, enough!)

From 'DRAMATIC IDYLS'

FIRST SERIES

1879

PHEIDIPPIDES

Χαίρετε, νικῶμεν.

FIRST I salute this soil of the blessed, river and rock!
Gods of my birthplace, dæmons and heroes, honour to all!
Then I name thee, claim thee for our patron, co-equal in
    praise
—Ay, with Zeus the Defender, with Her of the ægis and
    spear!
Also, ye of the bow and the buskin, praised be your peer,
Now, henceforth and forever,—O latest to whom I upraise
Hand and heart and voice! For Athens, leave pasture and
    flock!
Present to help, potent to save, Pan—patron I call!

Archons of Athens, topped by the tettix, see, I return!
See, 'tis myself here standing alive, no spectre that speaks!
Crowned with the myrtle, did you command me, Athens
    and you,
'Run, Pheidippides, run and race, reach Sparta for aid!
Persia has come, we are here, where is She?' Your com-
    mand I obeyed,
Ran and raced: like stubble, some field which a fire runs
    through,
Was the space between city and city: two days, two nights
    did I burn
Over the hills, under the dales, down pits and up peaks.

Into their midst I broke: breath served but for 'Persia has
    come!
Persia bids Athens proffer slaves'-tribute, water and
    earth;

Razed to the ground is Eretria—but Athens, shall Athens
    sink,
Drop into dust and die—the flower of Hellas utterly die,
Die, with the wide world spitting at Sparta, the stupid, the
    stander-by?
Answer me quick, what help, what hand do you stretch
    o'er destruction's brink?
How,—when? No care for my limbs!—there's lightning
    in all and some—
Fresh and fit your message to bear, once lips give it birth!'

O my Athens—Sparta love thee? Did Sparta respond?
Every face of her leered in a furrow of envy, mistrust,
Malice,—each eye of her gave me its glitter of gratified
    hate!
Gravely they turned to take counsel, to cast for excuses.
    I stood
Quivering,—the limbs of me fretting as fire frets, an inch
    from dry wood:
'Persia has come, Athens asks aid, and still they debate?
Thunder, thou Zeus! Athené, are Spartans a quarry
    beyond
Swing of thy spear? Phoibos and Artemis, clang them
    "Ye must"!'

No bolt launched from Olumpos! Lo, their answer at last!
'Has Persia come,—does Athens ask aid,—may Sparta
    befriend?
Nowise precipitate judgment—too weighty the issue at
    stake!
Count we no time lost time which lags through respect to
    the Gods!
Ponder that precept of old, "No warfare, whatever the
    odds
In your favour, so long as the moon, half-orbed, is unable
    to take
Full-circle her state in the sky!" Already she rounds to
    it fast:
Athens must wait, patient as we—who judgment suspend.'

Athens,—except for that sparkle,—thy name, I had
    mouldered to ash!
That sent a blaze through my blood; off, off and away
    was I back,
—Not one word to waste, one look to lose on the false
    and the vile!
Yet 'O Gods of my land!' I cried, as each hillock and
    plain,
Wood and stream, I knew, I named, rushing past them
    again,
'Have ye kept faith, proved mindful of honours we paid
    you erewhile?
Vain was the filleted victim, the fulsome libation! Too
    rash
Love in its choice, paid you so largely service so slack!

'Oak and olive and bay,—I bid you cease to enwreathe
Brows made bold by your leaf! Fade at the Persian's
    foot,
You that, our patrons were pledged, should never adorn
    a slave!
Rather I hail thee, Parnes,—trust to thy wild waste tract!
Treeless, herbless, lifeless mountain! What matter if
    slacked
My speed may hardly be, for homage to crag and to cave
No deity deigns to drape with verdure?—at least I can
    breathe,
Fear in thee no fraud from the blind, no lie from the
    mute!'

Such my cry as, rapid, I ran over Parnes' ridge;
Gully and gap I clambered and cleared till, sudden, a bar
Jutted, a stoppage of stone against me, blocking the way.
Right! for I minded the hollow to traverse, the fissure
    across:
'Where I could enter, there I depart by! Night in the
    fosse?
Athens to aid? Though the dive were through Erebos,
    thus I obey—

Out of the day dive, into the day as bravely arise! No
    bridge
Better!'—when—ha! what was it I came on, of wonders
    that are?

There, in the cool of a cleft, sat he—majestical Pan!
Ivy drooped wanton, kissed his head, moss cushioned his
    hoof:
All the great God was good in the eyes grave-kindly—the
    curl
Carved on the bearded cheek, amused at a mortal's awe,
As, under the human trunk, the goat-thighs grand I saw.
'Halt, Pheidippides!'—halt I did, my brain of a whirl:
'Hither to me! Why pale in my presence?' he gracious
    began:
'How is it,—Athens, only in Hellas, holds me aloof?

'Athens, she only, rears me no fane, makes me no feast!
Wherefore? Than I what godship to Athens more helpful
    of old?
Ay, and still, and forever her friend! Test Pan, trust me!
Go, bid Athens take heart, laugh Persia to scorn, have
    faith
In the temples and tombs! Go, say to Athens, "The
    Goat-God saith:
When Persia—so much as strews not the soil—is cast in
    the sea,
Then praise Pan who fought in the ranks with your most
    and least,
Goat-thigh to greaved-thigh, made one cause with the
    free and the bold!"

'Say Pan saith: "Let this, foreshowing the place, be the
    pledge!"
(Gay, the liberal hand held out this herbage I bear
—Fennel—I grasped it a-tremble with dew—whatever it
    bode)
'While, as for thee . . .' But enough! He was gone. If
    I ran hitherto—

Be sure that, the rest of my journey, I ran no longer, but
    flew.
Parnes to Athens—earth no more, the air was my
    road:
Here am I back. Praise Pan, we stand no more on the
    razor's edge!
Pan for Athens, Pan for me! I too have a guerdon rare!

***

Then spoke Miltiades. 'And thee, best runner of Greece,
Whose limbs did duty indeed,—what gift is promised
    thyself?
Tell it us straightway,—Athens the mother demands of
    her son!'
Rosily blushed the youth: he paused: but, lifting at length
His eyes from the ground, it seemed as he gathered the
    rest of his strength
Into the utterance—'Pan spoke thus: "For what thou
    hast done
Count on a worthy reward! Henceforth be allowed thee
    release
From the racer's toil, no vulgar reward in praise or in
    pelf!"

'I am bold to believe, Pan means reward the most to my
    mind!
Fight I shall, with our foremost, wherever this fennel may
    grow,—
Pound—Pan helping us—Persia to dust, and, under the
    deep,
Whelm her away for ever; and then,—no Athens to
    save,—
Marry a certain maid, I know keeps faith to the brave,—
Hie to my house and home: and, when my children shall
    creep
Close to my knees,—recount how the God was awful yet
    kind,
Promised their sire reward to the full—rewarding him—
    so!'

Unforeseeing one! Yes, he fought on the Marathon day:
So, when Persia was dust, all cried 'To Akropolis!
Run, Pheidippides, one race more! the meed is thy due!
"Athens is saved, thank Pan," go shout!' He flung down
    his shield,
Ran like fire once more: and the space 'twixt the Fennel-
    field
And Athens was stubble again, a field which a fire runs
    through,
Till in he broke: 'Rejoice, we conquer!' Like wine
    through clay,
Joy in his blood bursting his heart, he died—the bliss!

So, to this day, when friend meets friend, the word of
    salute
Is still 'Rejoice!'—his word which brought rejoicing
    indeed.
So is Pheidippides happy for ever,—the noble strong man
Who could race like a God, bear the face of a God, whom
    a God loved so well;
He saw the land saved he had helped to save, and was
    suffered to tell
Such tidings, yet never decline, but, gloriously as he began,
So to end gloriously—once to shout, thereafter be mute:
'Athens is saved!'—Pheidippides dies in the shout for his
    meed.

NED BRATTS

'TWAS Bedford Special Assize, one daft Midsummer's
    Day:
A broiling blasting June,—was never its like, men say.
Corn stood sheaf-ripe already, and trees looked yellow as
    that;
Ponds drained dust-dry, the cattle lay foaming around
    each flat.
Inside town, dogs went mad, and folk kept bibbing beer
While the parsons prayed for rain. 'Twas horrible, yes—
    but queer:

Queer—for the sun laughed gay, yet nobody moved a
    hand
To work one stroke at his trade: as given to understand
That all was come to a stop, work and such worldly ways,
And the world's old self about to end in a merry blaze.
Midsummer's Day moreover was the first of Bedford
    Fair,
With Bedford Town's tag-rag and bobtail a-bowsing
    there.

But the Court House, Quality crammed: through doors
    ope, windows wide,
High on the Bench you saw sit Lordships side by side.
There frowned Chief Justice Jukes, fumed learned Brother
    Small,
And fretted their fellow Judge: like threshers, one and all,
Of a reek with laying down the law in a furnace. Why?
Because their lungs breathed flame—the regular crowd
    forbye
From gentry pouring in—quite a nosegay, to be sure!
How else could they pass the time, six mortal hours
    endure
Till night should extinguish day, when matters might
    haply mend?
Meanwhile no bad resource was—watching begin and end
Some trial for life and death, in a brisk five minutes'
    space,
And betting which knave would 'scape, which hang, from
    his sort of face.

So, their Lordships toiled and moiled, and a deal of work
    was done
(I warrant) to justify the mirth of the crazy sun
As this and t'other lout, struck dumb at the sudden show
Of red robes and white wigs, boggled nor answered 'Boh!'
When asked why he, Tom Styles, should not—because
    Jack Nokes
Had stolen the horse—be hanged: for Judges must have
    their jokes,

And louts must make allowance—let's say, for some blue
 fly
Which punctured a dewy scalp where the frizzles stuck
 awry—
Else Tom had fleered scot-free, so nearly over and done
Was the main of the job. Full-measure, the gentles
 enjoyed their fun,
As a twenty-five were tried, rank puritans caught at prayer
In a cow-house and laid by the heels,—have at 'em, devil
 may care!—
And ten were prescribed the whip, and ten a brand on the
 cheek,
And five a slit of the nose—just leaving enough to tweak.

Well, things at jolly high-tide, amusement steeped in fire,
While noon smote fierce the roof's red tiles to heart's
 desire,
The Court a-simmer with smoke, one ferment of oozy
 flesh,
One spirituous humming musk mount-mounting until its
 mesh
Entoiled all heads in a fluster, and Serjeant Postlethwayte
—Dashing the wig oblique as he mopped his oily pate—
Cried 'Silence, or I grow grease! No loophole lets in air?
Jurymen,—Guilty, Death! Gainsay me if you dare!'
—Things at this pitch, I say,—what hubbub without the
 doors?
What laughs, shrieks, hoots and yells, what rudest of
 uproars?

Bounce through the barrier throng a bulk comes rolling
 vast!
Thumps, kicks,—no manner of use!—spite of them rolls
 at last
Into the midst a ball which, bursting, brings to view
Publican Black Ned Bratts and Tabby his big wife too:
Both in a muck-sweat, both . . . were never such eyes uplift
At the sight of yawning hell, such nostrils—snouts that
 sniffed

Sulphur, such mouths a-gape ready to swallow flame!
Horrified, hideous, frank fiend-faces! yet, all the same,
Mixed with a certain . . . eh? how shall I dare style—
    mirth
The desperate grin of the guess that, could they break
    from earth,
Heaven was above, and hell might rage in impotence
Below the saved, the saved!

                       'Confound you! (no offence!)
Out of our way,—push, wife! Yonder their Worships be!'
Ned Bratts has reached the bar, and 'Hey, my Lords,'
    roars he,
'A Jury of life and death, Judges the prime of the land,
Constables, javelineers,—all met, if I understand,
To decide so knotty a point as whether 'twas Jack or Joan
Robbed the henroost, pinched the pig, hit the King's
    Arms with a stone,
Dropped the baby down the well, left the tithesman in the
    lurch,
Or, three whole Sundays running, not once attended
    church!
What a pother—do these deserve the parish-stocks or
    whip,
More or less brow to brand, much or little nose to snip,—
When, in our Public, plain stand we—that's we stand
    here,
I and my Tab, brass-bold, brick-built of beef and beer,
—Do not we, slut? Step forth and show your beauty, jade!
Wife of my bosom—that's the word now! What a trade
We drove! None said us nay: nobody loved his life
So little as wag a tongue against us,—did they, wife?
Yet they knew us all the while, in their hearts, for what
    we are
—Worst couple, rogue and quean, unhanged—search
    near and far!
Eh, Tab? The pedlar, now—o'er his noggin—who warned
    a mate
To cut and run, nor risk his pack where its loss of weight

Was the least to dread,—aha, how we two laughed a-
          good
As, stealing round the midden, he came on where I stood
With billet poised and raised,—you, ready with the
          rope,—
Ah, but that's past, that's sin repented of, we hope!
Men knew us for that same, yet safe and sound stood we!
The lily-livered knaves knew too (I've baulked a d——)
Our keeping the "Pied Bull" was just a mere pretence:
Too slow the pounds make food, drink, lodging, from
          out the pence!
There's not a stoppage to travel has chanced, this ten
          long year,
No break into hall or grange, no lifting of nag or steer,
Not a single roguery, from the clipping of a purse
To the cutting of a throat, but paid us toll. Od's curse!
When Gipsy Smouch made bold to cheat us of our due,
—Eh, Tab? the Squire's strong-box we helped the rascal
          to—
I think he pulled a face, next Sessions' swinging-time!
He danced the jig that needs no floor,—and, here's the
          prime,
'Twas Scroggs that houghed the mare! Ay, those were
          busy days!

'Well, there we flourished brave, like scripture-trees
          called bays,
Faring high, drinking hard, in money up to head
—Not to say, boots and shoes, when . . . Zounds, I
          nearly said—
Lord, to unlearn one's language! How shall we labour,
          wife?
Have you, fast hold, the Book? Grasp, grip it, for your life!
See, sirs, here's life, salvation! Here's—hold but out my
          breath—
When did I speak so long without once swearing?
          'Sdeath,
No, nor unhelped by ale since man and boy! And yet
All yesterday I had to keep my whistle wet

While reading Tab this Book: book? don't say "book"—
    they're plays,
Songs, ballads and the like: here's no such strawy blaze,
But sky wide ope, sun, moon, and seven stars out full-
    flare!
Tab, help and tell! I'm hoarse. A mug or—no, a prayer!
Dip for one out of the Book! Who wrote it in the Jail
—He plied his pen unhelped by beer, sirs, I'll be bail!

'I've got my second wind. In trundles she—that's Tab.
"Why, Gammer, what's come now, that—bobbing like
    a crab
On Yule-tide bowl—your head's a-work and both your
    eyes
Break loose? Afeard, you fool? As if the dead can rise!
Say—Bagman Dick was found last May with fuddling-
    cap
Stuffed in his mouth: to choke's a natural mishap!"
"Gaffer, be—blessed," cries she, "and Bagman Dick as
    well!
I, you, and he are damned: this Public is our hell:
We live in fire: live coals don't feel!—once quenched,
    they learn—
Cinders do, to what dust they moulder while they burn!"

'"If you don't speak straight out," says I—belike I
    swore—
"A knobstick, well you know the taste of, shall, once
    more,
Teach you to talk, my maid!" She ups with such a face,
Heart sunk inside me. "Well, pad on, my prate-apace!"

'"I've been about those laces we need for ... never mind!
If henceforth they tie hands, 'tis mine they'll have to
    bind.
You know who makes them best—the Tinker in our cage,
Pulled-up for gospelling, twelve years ago: no age
To try another trade,—yet, so he scorned to take
Money he did not earn, he taught himself the make

Of laces, tagged and tough—Dick Bagman found them so!
Good customers were we! Well, last week, you must
    know
His girl,—the blind young chit, who hawks about his
    wares,—
She takes it in her head to come no more—such airs
These hussies have! Yet, since we need a stoutish lace,—
'I'll to the jail-bird father, abuse her to his face!'
So, first I filled a jug to give me heart, and then,
Primed to the proper pitch, I posted to their den—
Patmore—they style their prison! I tip the turnkey, catch
My heart up, fix my face, and fearless lift the latch—
Both arms a-kimbo, in bounce with a good round oath
Ready for rapping out: no 'Lawks' nor 'By my troth!'

"'There sat my man, the father. He looked up: what
    one feels
When heart that leapt to mouth drops down again to
    heels!
He raised his hand . . . Hast seen, when drinking out the
    night,
And in, the day, earth grow another something quite
Under the sun's first stare? I stood a very stone.

"'Woman!' (a fiery tear he put in every tone),
'How should my child frequent your house where lust
    is sport,
Violence—trade? Too true! I trust no vague report.
Her angel's hand, which stops the sight of sin, leaves
    clear
The other gate of sense, lets outrage through the ear.
What has she heard!—which, heard shall never be again.
Better lack food than feast, a Dives in the—wain
Or reign or train—of Charles!' (His language was not
    ours:
'Tis my belief, God spoke: no tinker has such powers.)
'Bread, only bread they bring—my laces: if we broke
Your lump of leavened sin, the loaf's first crumb would
    choke!'

"'Down on my marrow-bones! Then all at once rose he:
His brown hair burst a-spread, his eyes were suns to see:
Up went his hands: 'Through flesh, I reach, I read thy
    soul!
So may some stricken tree look blasted, bough and bole,
Champed by the fire-tooth, charred without, and yet,
    thrice-bound
With dreriment about, within may life be found,
A prisoned power to branch and blossom as before,
Could but the gardener cleave the cloister, reach the core,
Loosen the vital sap: yet where shall help be found?
Who says "How save it?"—nor "Why cumbers it the
    ground?"
Woman, that tree art thou! All sloughed about with
    scurf,
Thy stag-horns fright the sky, thy snake-roots sting the
    turf!
Drunkenness, wantonness, theft, murder gnash and
    gnarl
Thine outward, case thy soul with coating like the marle
Satan stamps flat upon each head beneath his hoof!
And how deliver such? The strong men keep aloof,
Lover and friend stand far, the mocking ones pass by,
Tophet gapes wide for prey: lost soul, despair and die!
What then? "Look unto me and be ye saved!" saith
    God:
"I strike the rock, outstreats the life-stream at my rod!
Be your sins scarlet, wool shall they seem like,—although
As crimson red, yet turn white as the driven snow!"'

"'There, there, there! All I seem to somehow under-
    stand
Is—that, if I reached home, 'twas through the guiding
    hand
Of his blind girl which led and led me through the streets
And out of town and up to door again. What greets
First thing my eye, as limbs recover from their swoon?
A book—this Book she gave at parting. 'Father's
    boon—

The Book he wrote: it reads as if he spoke himself:
He cannot preach in bonds, so,—take it down from shel
When you want counsel,—think you hear his very voice!'

'"Wicked dear Husband, first despair and then rejoice!
Dear wicked Husband, waste no tick of moment more,
Be saved like me, bald trunk! There's greenness yet at
        core,
Sap under slough! Read, read!"

                                    'Let me take breath, my lords!
I'd like to know, are these—hers, mine, or Bunyan's
        words?
I'm 'wildered—scarce with drink,—nowise with drink
        alone!
You'll say, with heat: but heat's no stuff to split a stone
Like this black boulder—this flint heart of mine: the
        Book—
That dealt the crashing blow! Sirs, here's the fist that
        shook
His beard till Wrestler Jem howled like a just-lugged bear!
You had brained me with a feather: at once I grew aware
Christmas was meant for me. A burden at your back,
Good Master Christmas? Nay,—yours was that Joseph's
        sack,
—Or whose it was,—which held the cup,—compared with
        mine!
Robbery loads my loins, perjury cracks my chine,
Adultery . . . nay, Tab, you pitched me as I flung!
One word, I'll up with fist . . . No, sweet spouse, hold
        your tongue!

'I'm hasting to the end. The Book, sirs—take and read!
You have my history in a nutshell,—ay, indeed!
It must off, my burden! See,—slack straps and into pit,
Roll, reach the bottom, rest, rot there—a plague on it!
For a mountain's sure to fall and bury Bedford Town,
"Destruction"—that's the name, and fire shall burn it
        down!

O 'scape the wrath in time! Time's now, if not too late.
How can I pilgrimage up to the wicket-gate?
Next comes Despond the slough: not that I fear to pull
Through mud, and dry my clothes at brave House
    Beautiful—
But it's late in the day, I reckon: had I left years ago
Town, wife, and children dear . . . Well, Christmas did,
    you know!—
Soon I had met in the valley and tried my cudgel's
    strength
On the enemy horned and winged, a-straddle across its
    length!
Have at his horns, thwick—thwack: they snap, see! Hoof
    and hoof—
Bang, break the fetlock-bones! For love's sake, keep
    aloof
Angels! I'm man and match,—this cudgel for my flail,—
To thresh him, hoofs and horns, bat's wing and serpent's
    tail!
A chance gone by! But then, what else does Hopeful
    ding
Into the deafest ear except—hope, hope's the thing?
Too late i' the day for me to thrid the windings: but
There's still a way to win the race by death's short
    cut!
Did Master Faithful need climb the Delightful Mounts?
No, straight to Vanity Fair,—a fair, by all accounts,
Such as is held outside,—lords, ladies, grand and gay,—
Says he in the face of them, just what you hear me say.
And the Judges brought him in guilty, and brought him
    out
To die in the market-place—St. Peter's Green's about
The same thing: there they flogged, flayed, buffeted,
    lanced with knives,
Pricked him with swords,—I'll swear, he'd full a cat's
    nine lives,—
So to his end at last came Faithful,—ha, ha, he!
Who holds the highest card? for there stands hid, you
    see,

Behind the rabble-rout, a chariot, pair and all:

He's in, he's off, he's up, through clouds, at trumpet-call,

Carried the nearest way to Heaven-gate! Odds my life—

Has nobody a sword to spare? not even a knife?

Then hang me, draw and quarter! Tab—do the same by her!

O Master Worldly-Wiseman . . . that's Master Interpreter,

Take the will, not the deed! Our gibbet's handy close:

Forestall Last Judgment-Day! Be kindly, not morose!

There wants no earthly judge-and-jurying: here we stand—

Sentence our guilty selves: so, hang us out of hand!

Make haste for pity's sake! A single moment's loss

Means—Satan's lord once more: his whisper shoots across

All singing in my heart, all praying in my brain,

"It comes of heat and beer!"—hark how he guffaws plain!

"To-morrow you'll wake bright, and, in a safe skin, hug

Your sound selves, Tab and you, over a foaming jug!

You've had such qualms before, time out of mind!"
    He's right!

Did not we kick and cuff and curse away, that night

When home we blindly reeled, and left poor humpback Joe

I' the lurch to pay for what . . . somebody did, you know!

Both of us maundered then "Lame humpback,—never more

Will he come limping, drain his tankard at our door!

He'll swing, while—somebody . . ." Says Tab, "No, for I'll peach!"

"I'm for you, Tab," cries I, "there's rope enough for each!"

So blubbered we, and bussed, and went to bed upon

The grace of Tab's good thought: by morning, all was gone!

We laughed—"What's life to him, a cripple of no
    account?"
Oh, waves increase around—I feel them mount and
    mount!
Hang us! To-morrow brings Tom Bearward with his
    bears:
One new black-muzzled brute beats Sackerson, he swears:
(Sackerson, for my money!) And, baiting o'er, the Brawl
They lead on Turner's Patch,—lads, lasses, up tails all,—
I'm i' the thick o' the throng! That means the Iron Cage,
—Means the Lost Man inside! Where's hope for such
    as wage
War against light? Light's left, light's here, I hold light
    still,
So does Tab—make but haste to hang us both! You
    will?'

I promise, when he stopped you might have heard a
    mouse
Squeak, such a death-like hush sealed up the old Mote
    House.
But when the mass of man sank meek upon his knees,
While Tab, alongside, wheezed a hoarse 'Do hang us,
    please!'
Why, then the waters rose, no eye but ran with tears,
Hearts heaved, heads thumped, until, paying all past
    arrears
Of pity and sorrow, at last a regular scream outbroke
Of triumph, joy and praise.

                  My Lord Chief Justice spoke,
First mopping brow and cheek, where still, for one that
    budged,
Another bead broke fresh: 'What Judge, that ever judged
Since first the world began, judged such a case as this?
Why, Master Bratts, long since, folk smelt you out, I
    wis!
I had my doubts, i' faith, each time you played the fox
Convicting geese of crime in yonder witness-box—

Yea, much did I misdoubt, the thief that stole her eggs
Was hardly goosey's self at Reynard's game, i' feggs!
Yet thus much was to praise—you spoke to point,
    direct—
Swore you heard, saw the theft: no jury could suspect—
Dared to suspect,—I'll say,—a spot in white so clear:
Goosey was throttled, true: but thereof godly fear
Came of example set, much as our laws intend;
And, though a fox confessed, you proved the Judge's
    friend.
What if I had my doubts? Suppose I gave them breath,
Brought you to bar: what work to do, ere "Guilty,
    Death,"—
Had paid our pains! What heaps of witnesses to drag
From holes and corners, paid from out the County's
    bag!
Trial three dog-days long! *Amicus Curiæ*—that's
Your title, no dispute—truth-telling Master Bratts!
Thank you, too, Mistress Tab! Why doubt one word you
    say?
Hanging you both deserve, hanged both shall be this day!
The tinker needs must be a proper man. I've heard
He lies in Jail long since: if Quality's good word
Warrants me letting loose,—some householder, I mean—
Freeholder, better still,—I don't say but—between
Now and next Sessions . . . Well! Consider of his case,
I promise to, at least: we owe him so much grace.
Not that—no, God forbid!—I lean to think, as you,
The grace that such repent is any jail-bird's due:
I rather see the fruit of twelve years' pious reign—
Astræa Redux, Charles restored his rights again!
—Of which, another time! I somehow feel a peace
Stealing across the world. May deeds like this increase!
So, Master Sheriff, stay that sentence I pronounced
On those two dozen odd: deserving to be trounced
Soundly, and yet . . . well, well, at all events despatch
This pair of—shall I say, sinner-saints?—ere we catch
Their jail-distemper too. Stop tears, or I'll indite
All weeping Bedfordshire for turning Bunyanite!'

So, forms were galloped through. If Justice, on the spur,
Proved somewhat expeditious, would Quality demur?
And happily hanged were they,—why lengthen out my
    tale?—
Where Bunyan's Statue stands facing where stood his
    Jail.

NED BRATTS

53 forms were galloped through. If Just . . on the spot,
Proved somewhat sudden . . . . . why, 'tis mercy's flame,
And mercy . . . .
Bunyan's somnolet . . . . stood his

From 'DRAMATIC IDYLS'

SECOND SERIES
1880

PAN AND LUNA

Si credere dignum est.—*Georgic.* iii. 390.

O WORTHY of belief I hold it was,
Virgil, your legend in those strange three lines!
No question, that adventure came to pass
One black night in Arcadia: yes, the pines,
Mountains and valleys mingling made one mass
Of black with void black heaven: the earth's confines,
The sky's embrace,—below, above, around,
All hardened into black without a bound.

Fill up a swart stone chalice to the brim
With fresh-squeezed yet fast-thickening poppy-juice:
See how the sluggish jelly, late a-swim,
Turns marble to the touch of who would loose
The solid smooth, grown jet from rim to rim,
By turning round the bowl! So night can fuse
Earth with her all-comprising sky. No less,
Light, the least spark, shows air and emptiness.

And thus it proved when—diving into space,
Stript of all vapour, from each web of mist
Utterly film-free—entered on her race
The naked Moon, full-orbed antagonist
Of night and dark, night's dowry: peak to base,
Upstarted mountains, and each valley, kissed
To sudden life, lay silver-bright: in air
Flew she revealed, Maid-Moon with limbs all bare.

Still as she fled, each depth—where refuge seemed—
Opening a lone pale chamber, left distinct
Those limbs: mid still-retreating blue, she teemed
Herself with whiteness,—virginal, uncinct

By any halo save what finely gleamed
To outline not disguise her: heaven was linked
In one accord with earth to quaff the joy,
Drain beauty to the dregs without alloy.

Whereof she grew aware. What help? When, lo,
A succourable cloud with sleep lay dense:
Some pine-tree-top had caught it sailing slow,
And tethered for a prize: in evidence
Captive lay fleece on fleece of piled-up snow
Drowsily patient: flake-heaped how or whence,
The structure of that succourable cloud,
What matter? Shamed she plunged into its shroud.

Orbed—so the woman-figure poets call
Because of rounds on rounds—that apple-shaped
Head which its hair binds close into a ball
Each side the curving ears—that pure undraped
Pout of the sister paps—that . . . Once for all,
Say—her consummate circle thus escaped
With its innumerous circlets, sank absorbed,
Safe in the cloud—O naked Moon full-orbed!

But what means this? The downy swathes combine,
Conglobe, the smothery coy-caressing stuff
Curdles about her! Vain each twist and twine
Those lithe limbs try, encroached on by a fluff
Fitting as close as fits the dented spine
Its flexile ivory outside-flesh: enough!
The plumy drifts contract, condense, constringe,
Till she is swallowed by the feathery springe.

As when a pearl slips lost in the thin foam
Churned on a sea-shore, and, o'er-frothed, conceits
Herself safe-housed in Amphitrite's dome,—
If, through the bladdery wave-worked yeast, she meets
What most she loathes and leaps from,—elf from gnome
No gladlier,—finds that safest of retreats
Bubble about a treacherous hand wide ope
To grasp her—(divers who pick pearls so grope)—

So lay this Maid-Moon clasped around and caught
By rough red Pan, the god of all that tract:
He it was schemed the snare thus subtly wrought
With simulated earth-breath,—wool-tufts packed
Into a billowy wrappage. Sheep far-sought
For spotless shearings yield such: take the fact
As learned Virgil gives it,—how the breed
Whitens itself for ever: yes, indeed!

If one forefather ram, though pure as chalk
From tinge on fleece, should still display a tongue
Black 'neath the beast's moist palate, prompt men baulk
The propagating plague: he gets no young:
They rather slay him,—sell his hide to caulk
Ships with, first steeped in pitch,—nor hands are wrung
In sorrow for his fate: protected thus,
The purity we love is gained for us.

So did Girl-moon, by just her attribute
Of unmatched modesty betrayed, lie trapped,
Bruised to the breast of Pan, half-god half-brute,
Raked by his bristly boar-sward while he lapped
—Never say, kissed her! that were to pollute
Love's language—which moreover proves unapt
To tell how she recoiled—as who finds thorns
Where she sought flowers—when, feeling, she touched—
        horns!

Then—does the legend say?—first moon-eclipse
Happened, first swooning-fit which puzzled sore
The early sages? Is that why she dips
Into the dark, a minute and no more,
Only so long as serves her while she rips
The cloud's womb through and, faultless as before,
Pursues her way? No lesson for a maid
Left she, a maid herself thus trapped, betrayed?

Ha, Virgil? Tell the rest, you! 'To the deep
Of his domain the wildwood, Pan forthwith
Called her, and so she followed'—in her sleep,
Surely?—'by no means spurning him.' The myth

Explain who may! Let all else go, I keep
—As of a ruin just a monolith—
Thus much, one verse of five words, each a boon:
Arcadia, night, a cloud, Pan, and the moon.

'TOUCH him ne'er so lightly, into song he broke:
Soil so quick-receptive,—not one feather-seed,
Not one flower-dust fell but straight its fall awoke
Vitalizing virtue: song would song succeed
Sudden as spontaneous—prove a poet-soul!'

                                Indeed?
Rock's the song-soil rather, surface hard and bare:
Sun and dew their mildness, storm and frost their rage
Vainly both expend,—few flowers awaken there:
Quiet in its cleft broods—what the after age
Knows and names a pine, a nation's heritage.

From 'JOCOSERIA'

1883

WANTING is—what?
Summer redundant,
Blueness abundant,
—Where is the blot?
Beamy the world, yet a blank all the same,
—Framework which waits for a picture to frame:
What of the leafage, what of the flower?
Roses embowering with nought they embower!
Come then, complete incompletion, O comer,
Pant through the blueness, perfect the summer!
  Breathe but one breath
  Rose-beauty above,
  And all that was death
  Grows life, grows love,
   Grows love!

CRISTINA AND MONALDESCHI

AH, but how each loved each, Marquis!
 Here's the gallery they trod
 Both together, he her god,
 She his idol,—lend your rod,
Chamberlain!—ay, there they are—'*Quis
 Separabit?*'—plain those two
 Touching words come into view,
 Apposite for me and you:

Since they witness to incessant
 Love like ours: King Francis, he—
 Diane the adored one, she—
 Prototypes of you and me.
Everywhere is carved her Crescent
 With his Salamander-sign—
 Flame-fed creature: flame benign
 To itself or, if malign,

Only to the meddling curious,
 —So, be warned, Sir! Where's my head?
 How it wanders! What I said
 Merely meant—the creature, fed
Thus on flame, was scarce injurious
 Save to fools who woke its ire,
 Thinking fit to play with fire.
 'Tis the Crescent you admire?

Then, be Diane! I'll be Francis.
 Crescents change,—true!—wax and wane,
 Woman-like: male hearts retain
 Heat nor, once warm, cool again.
So, we figure—such our chance is—
 I as man and you as . . . What?
 Take offence? My Love forgot
 He plays woman, I do not?

I—the woman? See my habit,
 Ask my people! Anyhow,
 Be we what we may, one vow
 Binds us, male or female. Now,—
Stand, Sir! Read! '*Quis separabit?*'
 Half a mile of pictured way
 Past these palace-walls to-day
 Traversed, this I came to say.

You must needs begin to love me;
 First I hated, then, at best,
 —Have it so!—I acquiesced;
 Pure compassion did the rest.
From below thus raised above me,
 Would you, step by step, descend,
 Pity me, become my friend,
 Like me, like less, loathe at end?

That's the ladder's round you rose by!
 That—my own foot kicked away,
 Having raised you: let it stay,
 Serve you for retreating? Nay.

Close to me you climbed: as close by,
    Keep your station, though the peak
    Reached proves somewhat bare and bleak!
    Woman 's strong if man is weak.

Keep here, loving me forever!
    Love's look, gesture, speech, I claim;
    Act love, lie love, all the same—
    Play as earnest were our game!
Lonely I stood long: 'twas clever
    When you climbed, before men's eyes,
    Spurned the earth and scaled the skies,
    Gained my peak and grasped your prize.

Here you stood, then, to men's wonder;
    Here you tire of standing? Kneel!
    Cure what giddiness you feel,
    This way! Do your senses reel?
Not unlikely! What rolls under?
    Yawning death in yon abyss
    Where the waters whirl and hiss
    Round more frightful peaks than this.

Should my buffet dash you thither . . .
    But be sage! No watery grave
    Needs await you: seeming brave
    Kneel on safe, dear timid slave!
You surmised, when you climbed hither,
    Just as easy were retreat
    Should you tire, conceive unmeet
    Longer patience at my feet?

Me as standing, you as stooping,—
    Who arranged for each the pose?
    Lest men think us friends turned foes,
    Keep the attitude you chose!
Men are used to this same grouping—
    I and you like statues seen.
    You and I, no third between,
    Kneel and stand! That makes the scene.

Mar it—and one buffet . . . Pardon!
   Needless warmth—wise words in waste!
   'Twas prostration that replaced
   Kneeling, then? A proof of taste.
Crouch, not kneel, while I mount guard on
   Prostrate love—become no waif,
   No estray to waves that chafe
   Disappointed—love's so safe!

Waves that chafe? The idlest fancy!
   Peaks that scare? I think we know
   Walls enclose our sculpture: so
   Grouped, we pose in Fontainebleau.
Up now! Wherefore hesitancy?
   Arm in arm and cheek by cheek,
   Laugh with me at waves and peak!
   Silent still? Why, pictures speak.

See, where Juno strikes Ixion,
   Primatice speaks plainly! Pooh—
   Rather, Florentine Le Roux!
   I've lost head for who is who—
So it swims and wanders! Fie on
   What still proves the female! Here,
   By the staircase!—for we near
   That dark 'Gallery of the Deer.'

Look me in the eyes once! Steady!
   Are you faithful now as erst
   On that eve when we two first
   Vowed at Avon, blessed and cursed
Faith and falsehood? Pale already?
   Forward! Must my hand compel
   Entrance—this way? Exit—well,
   Somehow, somewhere. Who can tell?

What if to the self-same place in
   Rustic Avon, at the door
   Of the village church once more,
   Where a tombstone paves the floor

By that holy-water basin
  You appealed to—'As, below,
  This stone hides its corpse, e'en so
  I your secrets hide'? What ho!

Friends, my four! You, Priest, confess him!
  I have judged the culprit there:
  Execute my sentence! Care
  For no mail such cowards wear!
Done, Priest? Then, absolve and bless him!
  Now—you three, stab thick and fast,
  Deep and deeper! Dead at last?
  Thanks, friends—Father, thanks! Aghast?

What one word of his confession
  Would you tell me, though I lured
  With that royal crown abjured
  Just because its bars immured
Love too much? Love burst compression,
  Fled free, finally confessed
  All its secrets to that breast
  Whence . . . let Avon tell the rest!

MARY WOLLSTONECRAFT AND FUSELI

OH but is it not hard, Dear?
  Mine are the nerves to quake at a mouse:
If a spider drops I shrink with fear:
  I should die outright in a haunted house;
While for you—did the danger dared bring help—
From a lion's den I could steal his whelp,
With a serpent round me, stand stock-still,
Go sleep in a churchyard,—so would will
Give me the power to dare and do
Valiantly—just for you!

Much amiss in the head, Dear,
  I toil at a language, tax my brain
Attempting to draw—the scratches here!
  I play, play, practise and all in vain:

But for you—if my triumph brought you pride,
I would grapple with Greek Plays till I died,
Paint a portrait of you—who can tell?
Work my fingers off for your 'Pretty well:'
Language and painting and music too,
Easily done—for you!

Strong and fierce in the heart, Dear,
  With—more than a will—what seems a power
To pounce on my prey, love outbroke here
  In flame devouring and to devour.
Such love has laboured its best and worst
To win me a lover; yet, last as first,
I have not quickened his pulse one beat,
Fixed a moment's fancy, bitter or sweet:
Yet the strong fierce heart's love's labour's due,
Utterly lost, was—you!

ADAM, LILITH, AND EVE

ONE day it thundered and lightened.
Two women, fairly frightened,
Sank to their knees, transformed, transfixed,
At the feet of the man who sat betwixt;
And 'Mercy!' cried each—'if I tell the truth
Of a passage in my youth!'

Said This: 'Do you mind the morning
I met your love with scorning?
As the worst of the venom left my lips,
I thought "If, despite this lie, he strips
The mask from my soul with a kiss—I crawl
His slave,—soul, body and all!"'

Said That: 'We stood to be married;
The priest, or someone, tarried;
"If Paradise-door prove locked?" smiled you;
I thought, as I nodded, smiling too,
"Did one, that's away, arrive—nor late
Nor soon should unlock Hell's gate!"'

It ceased to lighten and thunder.
Up started both in wonder,
Looked round and saw that the sky was clear,
Then laughed 'Confess you believed us, Dear!'
'I saw through the joke!' the man replied
They re-seated themselves beside.

IXION

HIGH in the dome, suspended, of Hell, sad triumph,
    behold us!
  Here the revenge of a God, there the amends of a
    Man.
Whirling for ever in torment, flesh once mortal, immortal
  Made—for a purpose of hate—able to die and revive,
Pays to the uttermost pang, then, newly for payment
    replenished,
  Doles out—old yet young—agonies ever afresh;
Whence the result above me: torment is bridged by a
    rainbow,—
  Tears, sweat, blood,—each spasm, ghastly once, glori-
    fied now.
Wrung, by the rush of the wheel ordained my place of
    reposing,
  Off in a sparklike spray,—flesh become vapour thro'
    pain,—
Flies the bestowment of Zeus, soul's vaunted bodily
    vesture,
  Made that his feats observed gain the approval of
    Man,—
Flesh that he fashioned with sense of the earth and the
    sky and the ocean,
  Framed should pierce to the star, fitted to pore on the
    plant,—
All, for a purpose of hate, re-framed, re-fashioned, re-
    fitted
  Till, consummate at length,—lo, the employment of
    sense!

Pain's mere minister now to the soul, once pledged to her
    pleasure—
Soul, if untrammelled by flesh, unapprehensive of pain!
Body, professed soul's slave, which serving beguiled and
    betrayed her,
    Made things false seem true, cheated thro' eye and
    thro' ear,
Lured thus heart and brain to believe in the lying re-
    ported,—
Spurn but the traitorous slave, uttermost atom, away,
What should obstruct soul's rush on the real, the only
    apparent?
    Say I have erred,—how else? Was I Ixion or Zeus?
Foiled by my senses I dreamed; I doubtless awaken in
    wonder:
    This proves shine, that—shade? Good was the evil
    that seemed?
Shall I, with sight thus gained, by torture be taught I was
    blind once?
    Sisuphos, teaches thy stone—Tantalos, teaches thy
    thirst
Aught which unaided sense, purged pure, less plainly
    demonstrates?
No, for the past was dream: now that the dreamers
    awake,
Sisuphos scouts low fraud, and to Tantalos treason is
    folly.
    Ask of myself, whose form melts on the murderous
    wheel,
What is the sin which throe and throe prove sin to the
    sinner!
    Say the false charge was true,—thus do I expiate, say,
Arrogant thought, word, deed,—mere man who conceited
    me godlike,
    Sat beside Zeus, my friend—knelt before Heré, my love!
What were the need but of pitying power to touch and
    disperse it,
    Film-work—eye's and ear's—all the distraction of
    sense?

How should the soul not see, not hear,—perceive and as
  plainly
  Render, in thought, word, deed, back again truth—not
  a lie?
'Ay, but the pain is to punish thee!' Zeus, once more,
  for a pastime,
  Play the familiar, the frank! Speak and have speech in
  return!
I was of Thessaly king, there ruled and a people obeyed
  me:
  Mine to establish the law, theirs to obey it or die:
Wherefore? Because of the good to the people, because
  of the honour
  Thence accruing to me, king, the king's law was
  supreme.
What of the weakling, the ignorant criminal? Not who,
  excuseless,
  Breaking my law braved death, knowing his deed and
  its due—
Nay, but the feeble and foolish, the poor transgressor, of
  purpose
  No whit more than a tree, born to erectness of bole,
Palm or plane or pine, we laud if lofty, columnar—
  Loathe if athwart, askew,—leave to the axe and the
  flame!
Where is the vision may penetrate earth and beholding
  acknowledge
  Just one pebble at root ruined the straightness of stem?
Whose fine vigilance follows the sapling, accounts for
  the failure,
  —Here blew wind, so it bent: there the snow lodged,
  so it broke?
Also the tooth of the beast, bird's bill, mere bite of the
  insect
  Gnawed, gnarled, warped their worst: passive it lay to
  offence.
King—I was man, no more: what I recognized faulty I
  punished,
  Laying it prone: be sure, more than a man had I proved,

Watch and ward o'er the sapling at birth-time had saved
 it, nor simply
  Owned the distortion's excuse,—hindered it wholly:
 nay, more—
Even a man, as I sat in my place to do judgment, and
 pallid
  Criminals passing to doom shuddered away at my foot,
Could I have probed thro' the face to the heart, read plain
 a repentance,
  Crime confessed fools' play, virtue ascribed to the wise,
Had I not stayed the consignment to doom, not dealt
 the renewed ones
  Life to retraverse the past, light to retrieve the misdeed?
Thus had I done, and thus to have done much more it
 behoves thee,
  Zeus who madest man—flawless or faulty, thy work!
What if the charge were true, as thou mouthest,—Ixion
 the cherished
  Minion of Zeus grew vain, vied with the godships and
 fell,
Forfeit thro' arrogance? Stranger! I clothed, with the
 grace of our human,
  Inhumanity—gods, natures I likened to ours.
Man among men I had borne me till gods forsooth must
 regard me
  —Nay, must approve, applaud, claim as a comrade at
 last.
Summoned to enter their circle, I sat—their equal, how
 other?
  Love should be absolute love, faith is in fulness or
 nought.
'I am thy friend, be mine!' smiled Zeus: 'If Heré attract
 thee,'
  Blushed the imperial cheek, 'then—as thy heart may
 suggest!'
Faith in me sprang to the faith, my love hailed love as its
 fellow,
  'Zeus, we are friends—how fast! Heré, my heart for
 thy heart!'

Then broke smile into fury of frown, and the thunder of
   'Hence, fool!'
  Then thro' the kiss laughed scorn 'Limbs or a cloud
    was to clasp?'
Then from Olumpus to Erebos, then from the rapture to
   torment,
  Then from the fellow of gods—misery's mate, to the
    man!
—Man henceforth and for ever, who lent from the glow
   of his nature
  Warmth to the cold, with light coloured the black and
    the blank.
So did a man conceive of your passion, you passion-
   protesters!
  So did he trust, so love—being the truth of your lie!
You to aspire to be Man! Man made you who vainly
   would ape him:
  You are the hollowness, he—filling you, falsifies void.
Even as—witness the emblem, Hell's sad triumph sus-
   pended,
  Born of my tears, sweat, blood—bursting to vapour
    above—
Arching my torment, an iris ghostlike startles the darkness,
  Cold white—jewelry quenched—justifies, glorifies pain.
Strive, mankind, though strife endure through endless
   obstruction,
  Stage after stage, each rise marred by as certain a fall!
Baffled for ever—yet never so baffled but, e'en in the
   baffling,
  When Man's strength proves weak, checked in the
    body or soul—
Whatsoever the medium, flesh or essence,—Ixion's
  Made for a purpose of hate,—clothing the entity Thou,
—Medium whence that entity strives for the Not-Thou
   beyond it,
  Fire elemental, free, frame unencumbered, the All,—
Never so baffled but—when, on the verge of an alien
   existence,
  Heartened to press, by pangs burst to the infinite Pure,

Nothing is reached but the ancient weakness still that
 arrests strength,
  Circumambient still, still the poor human array,
Pride and revenge and hate and cruelty—all it has burst
 through,
  Thought to escape,—fresh formed, found in the fashion
  it fled,—
Never so baffled but—when Man pays the price of en-
 deavour,
  Thunderstruck, downthrust, Tartaros-doomed to the
  wheel,—
Then, ay, then, from the tears and sweat and blood of
 his torment,
  E'en from the triumph of Hell, up let him look and
  rejoice!
What is the influence, high o'er Hell, that turns to a
 rapture
  Pain—and despair's murk mists blends in a rainbow of
  hope?
What is beyond the obstruction, stage by stage tho' it
 baffle?
  Back must I fall, confess 'Ever the weakness I fled'?
No, for beyond, far, far is a Purity all-unobstructed!
  Zeus was Zeus—not Man: wrecked by his weakness, I
  whirl.
Out of the wreck I rise—past Zeus to the Potency o'er him!
  I—to have hailed him my friend! I—to have clasped
  her—my love!
Pallid birth of my pain,—where light, where light is,
 aspiring
  Thither I rise, whilst thou—Zeus, keep the godship and
  sink!

NEVER THE TIME AND THE PLACE

NEVER the time and the place
 And the loved one all together!
This path—how soft to pace!
 This May—what magic weather!

Where is the loved one's face?
In a dream that loved one's face meets mine,
But the house is narrow, the place is bleak
Where, outside, rain and wind combine
With a furtive ear, if I strive to speak,
With a hostile eye at my flushing cheek,
With a malice that marks each word, each sign!
O enemy sly and serpentine,
Uncoil thee from the waking man!
Do I hold the Past
Thus firm and fast
Yet doubt if the Future hold I can?
This path so soft to pace shall lead
Thro' the magic of May to herself indeed!
Or narrow if needs the house must be,
Outside are the storms and strangers: we—
Oh, close, safe, warm sleep I and she,
—I and she!

PAMBO

Suppose that we part (work done, comes play)
With a grave tale told in crambo
—As our hearty sires were wont to say—
Whereof the hero is Pambo?

Do you happen to know who Pambo was?
Nor I—but this much have heard of him:
He entered one day a college-class,
And asked—was it so absurd of him?—

'May Pambo learn wisdom ere practise it?
In wisdom I fain would ground me:
Since wisdom is centred in Holy Writ,
Some psalm to the purpose expound me!'

'That psalm,' the Professor smiled, 'shall be
Untroubled by doubt which dirtieth
Pellucid streams when an ass like thee
Would drink there—the Nine-and-thirtieth.

'Verse first: *I said I will look to my ways*
That I with my tongue offend not.
How now? Why stare? Art struck in amaze?
  Stop, stay! The smooth line hath an end knot!

'He's gone!—disgusted my text should prove
  Too easy to need explaining?
Had he waited, the blockhead might find I move
  To matter that pays remaining!'

Long years went by, when—'Ha, who's this?
  Do I come on the restive scholar
I had driven to Wisdom's goal, I wis,
  But that he slipped the collar?

'What? Arms crossed, brow bent, thought-immersed?
  A student indeed! Why scruple
To own that the lesson proposed him first
  Scarce suited so apt a pupil?

'Come back! From the beggarly elements
  To a more recondite issue
We pass till we reach, at all events,
  Some point that may puzzle ... Why "pish" you?'

From the ground looked piteous up the head:
  'Daily and nightly, Master,
Your pupil plods thro' that text you read,
  Yet gets on never the faster.

'At the self-same stand,—now old, then young!
  I will look to my ways—were doing
As easy as saying!—*that I with my tongue*
  Offend not—and 'scape pooh-poohing

'From sage and simple, doctor and dunce?
  Ah, nowise! Still doubts so muddy
The stream I would drink at once,—but once!
  That—thus I resume my study!'

Brother, brother, I share the blame,
Arcades sumus ambo!
Darkling, I keep my sunrise-aim,
Lack not the critic's flambeau,
And *look to my ways*, yet, much the same,
Offend with my tongue—like Pambo!

Lyrics from
'FERISHTAH'S FANCIES'
1884

ROUND us the wild creatures, overhead the trees,
Underfoot the moss-tracks,—life and love with these!
I to wear a fawn-skin, thou to dress in flowers:
All the long lone Summer-day, that greenwood life of
  ours!

Rich-pavilioned, rather,—still the world without,—
Inside—gold-roofed silk-walled silence round about!
Queen it thou on purple,—I, at watch and ward
Couched beneath the columns, gaze, thy slave, love's
  guard!

So, for us no world? Let throngs press thee to me!
Up and down amid men, heart by heart fare we!
Welcome squalid vesture, harsh voice, hateful face!
God is soul, souls I and thou: with souls should souls have
  place.

Wish no word unspoken, want no look away!
What if words were but mistake, and looks—too sudden,
  say!
Be unjust for once, Love! Bear it—well I may!

Do me justice always? Bid my heart—their shrine—
Render back its store of gifts, old looks and words of
  thine
—Oh, so all unjust—the less deserved, the more divine?

You groped your way across my room i' the dear dark
  dead of night;
At each fresh step a stumble was: but, once your lamp
  alight,
Easy and plain you walked again: so soon all wrong grew
  right!

What lay on floor to trip your foot? Each object, late
 awry,
Looked fitly placed, nor proved offence to footing free—
 for why?
The lamp showed all, discordant late, grown simple sym-
 metry.

Be love your light and trust your guide, with these explore
 my heart!
No obstacle to trip you then, strike hands and souls apart!
Since rooms and hearts are furnished so,—light shows
 you,—needs love start?

Man I am and man would be, Love—merest man and
 nothing more.
Bid me seem no other! Eagles boast of pinions—let them
 soar!
I may put forth angel's plumage, once unmanned, but
 not before.

Now on earth, to stand suffices,—nay, if kneeling serves,
 to kneel:
Here you front me, here I find the all of heaven that earth
 can feel:
Sense looks straight,—not over, under,—perfect sees
 beyond appeal.

Good you are and wise, full circle: what to me were more
 outside?
Wiser wisdom, better goodness? Ah, such want the
 angel's wide
Sense to take and hold and keep them! Mine at least has
 never tried.

Fire is in the flint: true, once a spark escapes,
Fire forgets the kinship, soars till fancy shapes
Some befitting cradle where the babe had birth—
Wholly heaven's the product, unallied to earth.
Splendours recognized as perfect in the star!—
In our flint their home was, housed as now they are.

So, the head aches and the limbs are faint!
    Flesh is a burthen—even to you!
Can I force a smile with a fancy quaint?
    Why are my ailments none or few?

In the soul of me sits sluggishness:
    Body so strong and will so weak!
The slave stands fit for the labour—yes,
    But the master's mandate is still to seek.

You, now—what if the outside clay
    Helped, not hindered the inside flame?
My dim to-morrow—your plain to-day,
    Yours the achievement, mine the aim?

So were it rightly, so shall it be!
    Only, while earth we pace together
For the purpose apportioned you and me,
    Closer we tread for a common tether.

You shall sigh 'Wait for his sluggish soul!
    Shame he should lag, not lamed as I!'
May not I smile 'Ungained her goal:
    Body may reach her—by-and-by?'

When I vexed you and you chid me,
    And I owned my fault and turned
My cheek the way you bid me,
    And confessed the blow well earned,—

My comfort all the while was
    —Fault was faulty—near, not quite!
Do you wonder why the smile was?
    O'erpunished wrong grew right.

But faults you ne'er suspected,
    Nay, praised, no faults at all,—
Those would you had detected—
    Crushed eggs whence snakes could crawl!

Once I saw a chemist take a pinch of powder
—Simple dust it seemed—and half-unstop a phial:
—Out dropped harmless dew. 'Mixed nothings make'—
 quoth he—
'Something!' So they did: a thunderclap, but louder—
Lightning-flash, but fiercer—put spectators' nerves to
 trial:
Sure enough, we learned what was, imagined what might
 be.

Had I no experience how a lip's mere tremble,
Look's half hesitation, cheek's just change of colour,
These effect a heartquake,—how should I conceive
What heaven there may be? Let it but resemble
Earth myself have known! No bliss that's finer, fuller,
Only—bliss that lasts, they say, and fain would I believe.

Verse-making was least of my virtues: I viewed with
 despair
Wealth that never yet was but might be—all that verse-
 making were
If the life would but lengthen to wish, let the mind be
 laid bare.
So I said 'To do little is bad, to do nothing is worse'—
  And made verse.

Love-making,—how simple a matter! No depths to
 explore,
No heights in a life to ascend! No disheartening
 Before,
No affrighting Hereafter,—love now will be love ever-
 more.
So I felt 'To keep silence were folly:'—all language above,
  I made love.

Not with my Soul, Love!—bid no Soul like mine
 Lap thee around nor leave the poor Sense room!
Soul,—travel-worn, toil-weary,—would confine
 Along with Soul, Soul's gains from glow and gloom,

Captures from soarings high and divings deep.
Spoil-laden Soul, how should such memories sleep?
Take Sense, too—let me love entire and whole—
    Not with my Soul!

Eyes shall meet eyes and find no eyes between,
  Lips feed on lips, no other lips to fear!
No past, no future—so thine arms but screen
  The present from surprise! not there, 'tis here—
Not then, 'tis now:—back, memories that intrude!
Make, Love, the universe our solitude,
And, over all the rest, oblivion roll—
    Sense quenching Soul!

    Ask not one least word of praise!
      Words declare your eyes are bright?
    What then meant that summer day's
      Silence spent in one long gaze?
      Was my silence wrong or right?

    Words of praise were all to seek!
      Face of you and form of you,
    Did they find the praise so weak
    When my lips just touched your cheek—
      Touch which let my soul come through?

'Why from the world,' Ferishtah smiled, 'should thanks
  Go to this work of mine? If worthy praise,
Praised let it be and welcome: as verse ranks,
  So rate my verse: if good therein outweighs
Aught faulty judged, judge justly! Justice says:
Be just to fact, or blaming or approving:
But—generous? No, nor loving!

'Loving! what claim to love has work of mine?
  Concede my life were emptied of its gains
To furnish forth and fill work's strict confine,
  Who works so for the world's sake—he complains
  With cause when hate, not love, rewards his pains.
I looked beyond the world for truth and beauty:
Sought, found and did my duty.'

EPILOGUE

OH, Love—no, Love! All the noise below, Love,
  Groanings all and moanings—none of Life I lose!
All of Life's a cry just of weariness and woe, Love—
  'Hear at least, thou happy one!' How can I, Love, but
    choose?

Only, when I do hear, sudden circle round me
  —Much as when the moon's might frees a space from
    cloud—
Iridescent splendours: gloom—would else confound me—
  Barriered off and banished far—bright-edged the black-
    est shroud!

Thronging through the cloud-rift, whose are they, the
    faces
  Faint revealed yet sure divined, the famous ones of old?
'What'—they smile—'our names, our deeds so soon
    erases
  Time upon his tablet where Life's glory lies enrolled?

'Was it for mere fool's-play, make-believe and mumming,
  So we battled it like men, not boylike sulked or
    whined?
Each of us heard clang God's "Come!" and each was
    coming:
  Soldiers all, to forward-face, not sneaks to lag behind!

'How of the field's fortune? That concerned our Leader!
  Led, we struck our stroke nor cared for doings left and
    right:
Each as on his sole head, failer or succeeder,
  Lay the blame or lit the praise: no care for cowards:
    fight!'

Then the cloud-rift broadens, spanning earth that's under,
  Wide our world displays its worth, man's strife and
    strife's success:
All the good and beauty, wonder crowning wonder,
  Till my heart and soul applaud perfection, nothing less.

Only, at heart's utmost joy and triumph, terror
   Sudden turns the blood to ice: a chill wind disencharms
All the late enchantment! What if all be error—
   If the halo irised round my head were, Love, thine
     arms?

<small>Palazzo Giustinian-Recanati,</small>
   <small>Venice:</small> *December* 1, 1883.

From 'PARLEYINGS WITH CERTAIN PEOPLE'

1887

DANCE, yellows and whites and reds,—
Lead your gay orgy, leaves, stalks, heads
Astir with the wind in the tulip-beds!

There's sunshine; scarcely a wind at all
Disturbs starved grass and daisies small
On a certain mound by a churchyard wall.

Daisies and grass be my heart's bedfellows
On the mound wind spares and sunshine mellows:
Dance you, reds and whites and yellows!

From 'ASOLANDO'

1889

NOW

OUT of your whole life give but a moment!
All of your life that has gone before,
All to come after it,—so you ignore,
So you make perfect the present,—condense,
In a rapture of rage, for perfection's endowment,
Thought and feeling and soul and sense—
Merged in a moment which gives me at last
You around me for once, you beneath me, above me—
Me—sure that despite of time future, time past,—
This tick of our life-time's one moment you love me!
How long such suspension may linger? Ah, Sweet—
The moment eternal—just that and no more—
When ecstasy's utmost we clutch at the core
While cheeks burn, arms open, eyes shut and lips meet!

HUMILITY

WHAT girl but, having gathered flowers,
Stript the beds and spoilt the bowers,
From the lapful light she carries
Drops a careless bud?—nor tarries
To regain the waif and stray:
'Store enough for home'—she'll say.

So say I too: give your lover
Heaps of loving—under, over,
Whelm him—make the one the wealthy!
Am I all so poor who—stealthy
Work it was!—picked up what fell:
Not the worst bud—who can tell?

SUMMUM BONUM

ALL the breath and the bloom of the year in the bag of
    one bee:
  All the wonder and wealth of the mine in the heart of
    one gem:
In the core of one pearl all the shade and the shine of the
    sea:
  Breath and bloom, shade and shine,—wonder, wealth,
    and—how far above them—
      Truth, that's brighter than gem,
      Trust, that's purer than pearl,—
Brightest truth, purest trust in the universe—all were for
  me
      In the kiss of one girl.

A PEARL, A GIRL

A SIMPLE ring with a single stone
    To the vulgar eye no stone of price:
Whisper the right word, that alone—
    Forth starts a sprite, like fire from ice,
And lo, you are lord (says an Eastern scroll)
Of heaven and earth, lord whole and sole
    Through the power in a pearl.

A woman ('tis I this time that say)
    With little the world counts worthy praise
Utter the true word—out and away
    Escapes her soul: I am wrapt in blaze,
Creation's lord, of heaven and earth
Lord whole and sole—by a minute's birth—
    Through the love in a girl!

SPECULATIVE

OTHERS may need new life in Heaven—
    Man, Nature, Art—made new, assume!
Man with new mind old sense to leaven,
    Nature—new light to clear old gloom,
Art that breaks bounds, gets soaring-room.

I shall pray: 'Fugitive as precious—
  Minutes which passed,—return, remain!
Let earth's old life once more enmesh us,
  You with old pleasure, me—old pain,
So we but meet nor part again!'

BAD DREAMS. I

Last night I saw you in my sleep:
  And how your charm of face was changed!
I asked 'Some love, some faith you keep?'
  You answered 'Faith gone, love estranged.'
Whereat I woke—a twofold bliss:
  Waking was one, but next there came
This other: 'Though I felt, for this,
  My heart break, I loved on the same.'

BAD DREAMS. II

You in the flesh and here—
  Your very self! Now, wait!
One word! May I hope or fear?
  Must I speak in love or hate?
Stay while I ruminate!

The fact and each circumstance
  Dare you disown? Not you!
That vast dome, that huge dance,
  And the gloom which overgrew
A—possibly festive crew!

For why should men dance at all—
  Why women—a crowd of both—
Unless they are gay? Strange ball—
  Hands and feet plighting troth,
Yet partners enforced and loth!

Of who danced there, no shape
  Did I recognize: thwart, perverse,
Each grasped each, past escape
  In a whirl or weary or worse:
Man's sneer met woman's curse,

While he and she toiled as if
    Their guardian set galley-slaves
To supple chained limbs grown stiff:
    Unmanacled trulls and knaves—
The lash for who misbehaves!

And a gloom was, all the while,
    Deeper and deeper yet
O'ergrowing the rank and file
    Of that army of haters—set
To mimic love's fever-fret.

By the wall-side close I crept,
    Avoiding the livid maze,
And, safely so far, outstepped
    On a chamber—a chapel, says
My memory or betrays—

Closet-like, kept aloof
    From unseemly witnessing
What sport made floor and roof
    Of the Devil's palace ring
While his Damned amused their king.

Ay, for a low lamp burned,
    And a silence lay about
What I, in the midst, discerned
    Though dimly till, past doubt,
'Twas a sort of throne stood out—

High seat with steps, at least:
    And the topmost step was filled
By—whom? What vestured priest?
    A stranger to me,—his guild,
His cult, unreconciled

To my knowledge how guild and cult
    Are clothed in this world of ours:
I pondered, but no result
    Came to—unless that Giaours
So worship the Lower Powers.

When suddenly who entered?
  Who knelt—did you guess I saw?
Who—raising that face where centred
  Allegiance to love and law
So lately—off-casting awe,

Down-treading reserve, away
  Thrusting respect . . . but mine
Stands firm—firm still shall stay!
  Ask Satan! for I decline
To tell—what I saw, in fine!

Yet here in the flesh you come—
  Your same self, form and face,—
In the eyes, mirth still at home!
  On the lips, that commonplace
Perfection of honest grace!

Yet your errand is—needs must be
  To palliate—well, explain,
Expurgate in some degree
  Your soul of its ugly stain.
Oh, you—the good in grain—

How was it your white took tinge?
  'A mere dream'—never object!
Sleep leaves a door on hinge
  Whence soul, ere our flesh suspect,
Is off and away: detect

Her vagaries when loose, who can!
  Be she pranksome, be she prude,
Disguise with the day began:
  With the night—ah, what ensued
From draughts of a drink hell-brewed?

Then She: 'What a queer wild dream!
  And perhaps the best fun is—
Myself had its fellow—I seem
  Scarce awake from yet. 'Twas this—
Shall I tell you? First, a kiss!

'For the fault was just your own,—
    'Tis myself expect apology:
You warned me to let alone
    (Since our studies were mere philology)
That ticklish (you said) Anthology.

'So, I dreamed that I passed *exam*
    Till a question posed me sore:
"Who translated this epigram
    By—an author we best ignore?"
And I answered "Hannah More"!'

BAD DREAMS. III

THIS was my dream: I saw a Forest
    Old as the earth, no track nor trace
Of unmade man. Thou, Soul, explorest—
    Though in a trembling rapture—space
Immeasurable! Shrubs, turned trees,
Trees that touch heaven, support its frieze
Studded with sun and moon and star:
While—oh, the enormous growths that bar
Mine eye from penetrating past
    Their tangled twine where lurks—nay, lives
Royally lone, some brute-type cast
    I' the rough, time cancels, man forgives.

On, Soul! I saw a lucid City
    Of architectural device
Every way perfect. Pause for pity,
    Lightning! nor leave a cicatrice
On those bright marbles, dome and spire,
Structures palatial,—streets which mire
Dares not defile, paved all too fine
For human footstep's smirch, not thine—
Proud solitary traverser,
    My Soul, of silent lengths of way—
With what ecstatic dread, aver,
    Lest life start sanctioned by thy stay!

Ah, but the last sight was the hideous!
   A City, yes,—a Forest, true,—
But each devouring each. Perfidious
   Snake-plants had strangled what I knew
Was a pavilion once: each oak
Held on his horns some spoil he broke
By surreptitiously beneath
Upthrusting: pavements, as with teeth,
Griped huge weed widening crack and split
   In squares and circles stone-work erst.
Oh, Nature—good! Oh, Art—no whit
   Less worthy! Both in one—accurst!

BAD DREAMS. IV

It happened thus: my slab, though new,
   Was getting weather-stained,—beside,
Herbage, balm, peppermint o'ergrew
   Letter and letter: till you tried
Somewhat, the Name was scarce descried.

That strong stern man my lover came:
   —Was he my lover? Call him, pray,
My life's cold critic bent on blame
   Of all poor I could do or say
To make me worth his love one day—

One far day when, by diligent
   And dutiful amending faults,
Foibles, all weaknesses which went
   To challenge and excuse assaults
Of culture wronged by taste that halts—

Discrepancies should mar no plan
   Symmetric of the qualities
Claiming respect from—say—a man
   That's strong and stern. 'Once more he pries
Into me with those critic eyes!'

No question! so—'Conclude, condemn
　　Each failure my poor self avows!
Leave to its fate all you contemn!
　　There's Solomon's selected spouse:
Earth needs must hold such maids—choose them!'

Why, he was weeping! Surely gone
　　Sternness and strength: with eyes to ground
And voice a broken monotone—
　　'Only be as you were! Abound
In foibles, faults,—laugh, robed and crowned

'As Folly's veriest queen,—care I
　　One feather-fluff? Look pity, Love,
On prostrate me—your foot shall try
　　This forehead's use—mount thence above,
And reach what Heaven you dignify!'

Now, what could bring such change about?
　　The thought perplexed: till, following
His gaze upon the ground,—why, out
　　Came all the secret! So, a thing
Thus simple has deposed my king!

For, spite of weeds that strove to spoil
　　Plain reading on the lettered slab,
My name was clear enough—no soil
　　Effaced the date when one chance stab
Of scorn . . . if only ghosts might blab!

INAPPREHENSIVENESS

WE two stood simply friend-like side by side,
Viewing a twilight country far and wide,
Till she at length broke silence. 'How it towers
Yonder, the ruin o'er this vale of ours!
The West's faint flare behind it so relieves
Its rugged outline—sight perhaps deceives,

Or I could almost fancy that I see
A branch wave plain—belike some wind-sown tree
Chance-rooted where a missing turret was.
What would I give for the perspective glass
At home, to make out if 'tis really so!
Has Ruskin noticed here at Asolo
That certain weed-growths on the ravaged wall
Seem' . . . something that I could not say at all,
My thought being rather—as absorbed she sent
Look onward after look from eyes distent
With longing to reach Heaven's gate left ajar—
'Oh, fancies that might be, oh, facts that are!'
What of a wilding? By you stands, and may
So stand unnoticed till the Judgment Day,
One who, if once aware that your regard
Claimed what his heart holds,—woke, as from its sward
The flower, the dormant passion, so to speak—
Then what a rush of life would startling wreak
Revenge on your inapprehensive stare
While, from the ruin and the West's faint flare,
You let your eyes meet mine, touch what you term
Quietude—that's an universe in germ—
The dormant passion needing but a look
To burst into immense life!'

      'No, the book
Which noticed how the wall-growths wave' said she
'Was not by Ruskin.'

    I said 'Vernon Lee?'

WHICH?

So, the three Court-ladies began
 Their trial of who judged best
In esteeming the love of a man:
Who preferred with most reason was thereby confessed
Boy-Cupid's exemplary catcher and cager;
An Abbé crossed legs to decide on the wager.

First the Duchesse: 'Mine for me—
   Who were it but God's for Him,
   And the King's for—who but he?
Both faithful and loyal, one grace more shall brim
His cup with perfection: a lady's true lover,
He holds—save his God and his king—none above her.'

'I require'—outspoke the Marquise—
   'Pure thoughts, ay, but also fine deeds:
   Play the paladin must he, to please
My whim, and—to prove my knight's service exceeds
Your saint's and your loyalist's praying and kneeling—
Show wounds, each wide mouth to my mercy appealing.'

Then the Comtesse: 'My choice be a wretch,
   Mere losel in body and soul,
   Thrice accurst! What care I, so he stretch
Arms to me his sole saviour, love's ultimate goal,
Out of earth and men's noise—names of "infidel,"
   "traitor,"
Cast up at him? Crown me, crown's adjudicator!'

And the Abbé uncrossed his legs,
   Took snuff, a reflective pinch,
   Broke silence: 'The question begs
Much pondering ere I pronounce. Shall I flinch?
The love which to one and one only has reference
Seems terribly like what perhaps gains God's preference.'

THE POPE AND THE NET

WHAT, he on whom our voices unanimously ran,
Made Pope at our last Conclave? Full low his life began:
His father earned the daily bread as just a fisherman.

So much the more his boy minds book, gives proof of
   mother-wit,
Becomes first Deacon, and the Priest, then Bishop: see
   him sit
No less than Cardinal ere long, while no one cries 'Unfit!'

But someone smirks, some other smiles, jogs elbow and
  nods head:
Each winks at each: ''I-faith, a rise! Saint Peter's net,
  instead
Of sword and keys, is come in vogue!' You think he
  blushes red?

Not he, of humble holy heart! 'Unworthy me!' he sighs:
'From fisher's drudge to Church's prince—it is indeed a
  rise:
So, here's my way to keep the fact for ever in my eyes!'

And straightway in his palace-hall, where commonly is
  set
Some coat-of-arms, some portraiture ancestral, lo, we met
His mean estate's remainder in his fisher-father's net!

Which step conciliates all and some, stops cavil in a trice:
'The humble holy heart that holds of new-born pride no
  spice!
He's just the saint to choose for Pope!' Each adds ''Tis
  my advice.'

So, Pope he was: and when we flocked—its sacred slipper
  on—
To kiss his foot, we lifted eyes, alack the thing was
  gone—
That guarantee of lowlihead,—eclipsed that star which
  shone!

Each eyed his fellow, one and all kept silence. I cried
  'Pish!
I'll make me spokesman for the rest, express the common
  wish.
Why, Father, is the net removed?' 'Son, it hath caught
  the fish.'

MUCKLE-MOUTH MEG

FROWNED the Laird on the Lord: 'So, red-handed I catch
    thee?
  Death-doomed by our Law of the Border!
We've a gallows outside and a chiel to dispatch thee:
  Who trespass—hangs: all's in order.'

He met frown with smile, did the young English gallant:
  Then the Laird's dame: 'Nay, Husband, I beg!
He's comely: be merciful! Grace for the callant
  —If he marries our Muckle-mouth Meg!'

'No mile-wide-mouthed monster of yours do I marry:
  Grant rather the gallows!' laughed he.
'Foul fare kith and kin of you—why do you tarry?'
  'To tame your fierce temper!' quoth she.

'Shove him quick in the Hole, shut him fast for a week:
  Cold, darkness and hunger work wonders:
Who lion-like roars now, mouse-fashion will squeak,
  And "it rains" soon succeed to "it thunders." '

A week did he bide in the cold and the dark
  —Not hunger: for duly at morning
In flitted a lass, and a voice like a lark
  Chirped 'Muckle-mouth Meg still ye're scorning?

'Go hang, but here's parritch to hearten ye first!'
  'Did Meg's muckle-mouth boast within some
Such music as yours, mine should match it or burst:
  No frog-jaws! So tell folk, my Winsome!'

Soon week came to end, and, from Hole's door set
    wide,
  Out he marched, and there waited the lassie:
'Yon gallows, or Muckle-mouth Meg for a bride!
  Consider! Sky's blue and turf's grassy:

'Life's sweet: shall I say ye wed Muckle-mouth Meg?'
    'Not I' quoth the stout heart: 'too eerie
The mouth that can swallow a bubbly-jock's egg:
    Shall I let it munch mine? Never, Dearie!'

'Not Muckle-mouth Meg? Wow, the obstinate man!
    Perhaps he would rather wed me!'
'Ay, would he—with just for a dowry your can!'
    'I'm Muckle-mouth Meg' chirruped she.

'Then so—so—so—so—' as he kissed her apace—
    'Will I widen thee out till thou turnest
From Margaret Minnikin-mou', by God's grace,
    To Muckle-mouth Meg in good earnest!'

FLUTE-MUSIC, WITH AN ACCOMPANIMENT

He. AH, the bird-like fluting
        Through the ash-tops yonder—
    Bullfinch-bubblings, soft sounds suiting
        What sweet thoughts, I wonder?
    Fine-pearled notes that surely
        Gather, dewdrop-fashion,
    Deep-down in some heart which purely
        Secrets globuled passion—
    Passion insuppressive—
        Such is piped, for certain;
    Love, no doubt, nay, love excessive
        'Tis, your ash-tops curtain.

    Would your ash-tops open
        We might spy the player—
    Seek and find some sense which no pen
        Yet from singer, sayer,
    Ever has extracted:
        Never, to my knowledge,
    Yet has pedantry enacted
        That, in Cupid's College,

Just this variation
    Of the old old yearning
Should by plain speech have salvation,
    Yield new men new learning.

'Love!' but what love, nicely
    New from old disparted,
Would the player teach precisely?
    First of all, he started
In my brain Assurance—
    Trust—entire Contentment—
Passion proved by much endurance;
    Then came—not resentment,
No, but simply Sorrow:
    What was seen had vanished:
Yesterday so blue! To-morrow
    Blank, all sunshine banished.

Hark! 'Tis Hope resurges,
    Struggling through obstruction—
Forces a poor smile which verges
    On Joy's introduction.
Now, perhaps, mere Musing:
    'Holds earth such a wonder?
Fairy-mortal, soul-sense-fusing
    Past thought's power to sunder!'
What? calm Acquiescence?
    'Daisied turf gives room to
Trefoil, plucked once in her presence—
    Growing by her tomb too!'

She. All's your fancy-spinning!
    Here's the fact: a neighbour
Never-ending, still beginning,
    Recreates his labour:
Deep o'er desk he drudges,
    Adds, divides, subtracts and
Multiplies, until he judges
    Noonday-hour's exact sand

Shows the hourglass emptied:
　　Then comes lawful leisure,
Minutes rare from toil exempted,
　　Fit to spend in pleasure.

Out then with—what treatise?
　　Youth's Complete Instructor
How to play the Flute. Quid petis?
　　Follow Youth's conductor
On and on, through *Easy*,
　　Up to *Harder*, *Hardest*
Flute-piece, till thou, flautist wheezy,
　　Possibly discardest
Tootlings hoarse and husky,
　　Mayst expend with courage
Breath—on tunes once bright now dusky—
　　Meant to cool thy porridge.

That's an air of Tulou's
　　He maltreats persistent,
Till as lief I'd hear some Zulu's
　　Bone-piped bag, breath-distent,
Madden native dances.
　　I'm the man's familiar:
Unexpectedness enhances
　　What your ear's auxiliar
—Fancy—finds suggestive.
　　Listen! That's *legato*
Rightly played, his fingers restive
　　Touch as if *staccato*.

He.　Ah, you trick-betrayer!
　　Telling tales, unwise one?
So the secret of the player
　　Was—he could surprise one
Well-nigh into trusting
　　Here was a musician
Skilled consummately, yet lusting
　　Through no vile ambition

After making captive
    All the world,—rewarded
Amply by one stranger's rapture,
    Common praise discarded.

So, without assistance
    Such as music rightly
Needs and claims,—defying distance,
    Overleaping lightly
Obstacles which hinder,—
    He, for my approval,
All the same and all the kinder
    Made mine what might move all
Earth to kneel adoring:
    Took—while he piped Gounod's
Bit of passionate imploring—
    Me for Juliet: who knows?

No! as you explain things,
    All's mere repetition,
Practise-pother: of all vain things
    Why waste pooh or pish on
Toilsome effort—never
    Ending, still beginning—
After what should pay endeavour
    —Right-performance? winning
Weariness from you who,
    Ready to admire some
Owl's fresh hooting—Tu-whit, tu-who—
    Find stale thrush-songs tiresome.

She. Songs, Spring thought perfection,
    Summer criticizes:
What in May escaped detection,
    August, past surprises,
Notes, and names each blunder.
    You, the just-initiate,
Praise to heart's content (what wonder?)
    Tootings I hear vitiate

Romeo's serenading—
    I who, times full twenty,
Turned to ice—no ash-tops aiding
    At his *caldamente*.

So, 'twas distance altered
    Sharps to flats? The missing
Bar when syncopation faltered
    (You thought—paused for kissing!)
Ash-tops too felonious
    Intercepted? Rather
Say—they well-nigh made euphonious
    Discord, helped to gather
Phrase, by phrase, turn patches
    Into simulated
Unity which botching matches,—
    Scraps redintegrated.

He. Sweet, are you suggestive
    Of an old suspicion
Which has always found me restive
    To its admonition
When it ventured whisper
    'Fool, the strifes and struggles
Of your trembler—blusher—lisper
    Were so many juggles,
Tricks tried—oh, so often!—
    Which once more do duty,
Find again a heart to soften,
    Soul to snare with beauty.'

Birth-blush of the briar-rose,
    Mist-bloom of the hedge-sloe,
Someone gains the prize: admire rose
    Would he, when noon's wedge—slow—
Sure, has pushed, expanded
    Rathe pink to raw redness?
Would he covet sloe when sanded
    By road-dust to deadness?

So—restore their value!
  Ply a water-sprinkle!
Then guess sloe is fingered, shall you?
  Find in a rose a wrinkle?

Here what played Aquarius?
  Distance—ash-tops aiding,
Reconciled scraps else contrarious,
  Brightened stuff fast fading.
Distance—call your shyness:
  Was the fair one peevish?
Coyness softened out of slyness.
  Was she cunning, thievish,
All-but-proved impostor?
  Bear but one day's exile,
Ugly traits were wholly lost or
  Screened by fancies flexile—

Ash-tops these, you take me?
  Fancies' interference
Changed . . .
    But since I sleep, don't wake me!
  What if all's appearance?
Is not outside seeming
  Real as substance inside?
Both are facts, so leave me dreaming:
  If who loses wins I'd
Ever lose,—conjecture,
  From one phrase trilled deftly,
All the piece. So, end your lecture,
  Let who lied be left lie!

'IMPERANTE AUGUSTO NATUS EST——'

WHAT it was struck the terror into me?
This, Publius: closer! while we wait our turn
I'll tell you. Water's warm (they ring inside)
At the eighth hour, till when no use to bathe.

Here in the vestibule where now we sit,
One scarce stood yesterday, the throng was such
Of loyal gapers, folk all eye and ear
While Lucius Varius Rufus[1] in their midst
Read out that long-planned late-completed piece,
His Panegyric on the Emperor.
'Nobody like him' little Flaccus[2] laughed
'At leading forth an Epos with due pomp!
Only, when godlike Cæsar swells the theme,
How should mere mortals hope to praise aright?
Tell me, thou offshoot of Etruscan kings!'
Whereat Mæcenas smiling sighed assent.

I paid my quadrans,[3] left the Thermæ's roar
Of rapture as the poet asked 'What place
Among the godships Jove, for Cæsar's sake,
Would bid its actual occupant vacate
In favour of the new divinity?'
And got the expected answer 'Yield thine own!'—
Jove thus dethroned, I somehow wanted air,
And found myself a-pacing street and street,
Letting the sunset, rosy over Rome,
Clear my head dizzy with the hubbub—say
As if thought's dance therein had kicked up dust
By trampling on all else: the world lay prone,
As—poet-propped, in brave hexameters—
Their subject triumphed up from man to God.
Caius Octavius Cæsar the August—
Where was escape from his prepotency?
I judge I may have passed—how many piles
Of structure dropt like doles from his free hand
To Rome on every side? Why, right and left,
For temples you've the Thundering Jupiter,
Avenging Mars, Apollo Palatine:
How count Piazza, Forum—there's a third
All but completed. You've the Theatre
Named of Marcellus—all his work, such work!—

[1] Poet and friend of Virgil.   [2] Horace.
[3] Roman coin of small value.

513

One thought still ending, dominating all—
With warrant Varius sang 'Be Cæsar God!'
By what a hold arrests he Fortune's wheel,
Obtaining and retaining heaven and earth
Through Fortune, if you like, but favour—no!
For the great deeds flashed by me, fast and thick
As stars which storm the sky on autumn nights—
Those conquests! but peace crowned them,—so, of peace!
Count up his titles only—these, in few—
Ten years Triumvir, Consul thirteen times,
Emperor, nay—the glory topping all—
Hailed Father of his Country, last and best
Of titles, by himself accepted so:
And why not? See but feats achieved in Rome—
Not to say, Italy—he planted there
Some thirty colonies—but Rome itself
All new-built, 'marble now, brick once,' he boasts:
This Portico, that Circus. Would you sail?
He has drained Tiber for you: would you walk?
He straightened out the long Flaminian Way.
Poor? Profit by his score of donatives!
Rich—that is, mirthful? Half-a-hundred games
Challenge your choice! There's Rome—for you and me
Only? The centre of the world besides!
For, look the wide world over, where ends Rome?
To sunrise? There's Euphrates—all between!
To sunset? Ocean and immensity:
North,—stare till Danube stops you: South, see Nile,
The Desert and the earth-upholding Mount.
Well may the poet-people each with each
Vie in his praise, our company of swans,
Virgil and Horace, singers—in their way—
Nearly as good as Varius, though less famed:
Well may they cry, 'No mortal, plainly God!'

Thus to myself myself said, while I walked:
Or would have said, could thought attain to speech,
Clean baffled by enormity of bliss
The while I strove to scale its heights and sound

Its depths—this masterdom o'er all the world
Of one who was but born,—like you, like me,
Like all the world he owns,—of flesh and blood.
But he—how grasp, how gauge his own conceit
Of bliss to me near inconceivable?
Or—since such flight too much makes reel the brain—
Let's sink—and so take refuge, as it were,
From life's excessive altitude—to life's
Breathable wayside shelter at its base!
If looms thus large this Cæsar to myself
—Of senatorial rank and somebody—
How must he strike the vulgar nameless crowd,
Innumerous swarm that's nobody at all?
Why,—for an instance,—much as yon gold shape
Crowned, sceptred, on the temple opposite—
Fulgurant Jupiter—must daze the sense
Of—say, yon outcast begging from its step!
What, anti-Cæsar, monarch in the mud,
As he is pinnacled above thy pate?
Ay, beg away! thy lot contrasts full well
With his whose bounty yields thee this support—
Our Holy and Inviolable One,
Cæsar, whose bounty built the fane above!
Dost read my thought? Thy garb, alack, displays
Sore usage truly in each rent and stain—
Faugh! Wash though in Suburra! 'Ware the dogs
Who may not so disdain a meal on thee!
What, stretchest forth a palm to catch my alms?
Aha, why yes: I must appear—who knows?—
I, in my toga, to thy rags and thee—
Quæstor—nay, Ædile, Censor—Pol! perhaps
The very City-Prætor's noble self!
As to me Cæsar, so to thee am I?
Good: nor in vain shall prove thy quest, poor rogue!
Hither—hold palm out—take this quarteras!

And who did take it? As he raised his head,
(My gesture was a trifle—well, abrupt),
Back fell the broad flap of the peasant's-hat,

The homespun cloak that muffled half his cheek
Dropped somewhat, and I had a glimpse—just one!
One was enough. Whose—whose might be the face?
That unkempt careless hair—brown, yellowish—
Those sparkling eyes beneath their eyebrows' ridge
(Each meets each, and the hawk-nose rules between)
—That was enough, no glimpse was needed more!
And terrifyingly into my mind
Came that quick-hushed report was whispered us,
'They do say, once a year in sordid garb
He plays the mendicant, sits all day long,
Asking and taking alms of who may pass,
And so averting, if submission help,
Fate's envy, the dread chance and change of things
When Fortune—for a word, a look, a nought—
Turns spiteful and—the petted lioness—
Strikes with her sudden paw, and prone falls each
Who patted late her neck superiorly,
Or trifled with those claw-tips velvet-sheathed.'
'He's God!' shouts Lucius Varius Rufus: 'Man
And worms'-meat any moment!' mutters low
Some Power, admonishing the mortal-born.

Ay, do you mind? There's meaning in the fact
That whoso conquers, triumphs, enters Rome,
Climbing the Capitolian, soaring thus
To glory's summit,—Publius, do you mark—
Ever the same attendant who, behind,
Above the Conqueror's head supports the crown
All-too-demonstrative for human wear,
—One hand's employment—all the while reserves
Its fellow, backward flung, to point how, close
Appended from the car, beneath the foot
Of the up-borne exulting Conqueror,
Frown—half-descried—the instruments of shame,
The malefactor's due. Crown, now—Cross, when?

Who stands secure? Are even Gods so safe?
Jupiter that just now is dominant—

Are not there ancient dismal tales how once
A predecessor reigned ere Saturn came,
And who can say if Jupiter be last?
Was it for nothing the grey Sibyl wrote
'Cæsar Augustus regnant, shall be born
In blind Judæa'—one to master him,
Him and the universe? An old-wife's tale?

Bath-drudge! Here, slave! No cheating! Our turn next.
No loitering, or be sure you taste the lash!
Two strigils, two oil-drippers, each a sponge!

DEVELOPMENT

My Father was a scholar and knew Greek.
When I was five years old, I asked him once
'What do you read about?'
                'The siege of Troy.'
'What is a siege and what is Troy?'
                     Whereat
He piled up chairs and tables for a town,
Set me a-top for Priam, called our cat
—Helen, enticed away from home (he said)
By wicked Paris, who couched somewhere close
Under the footstool, being cowardly,
But whom—since she was worth the pains, poor puss—
Towzer and Tray,—our dogs, the Atreidai,—sought
By taking Troy to get possession of
—Always when great Achilles ceased to sulk,
(My pony in the stable)—forth would prance
And put to flight Hector—our page-boy's self.
This taught me who was who and what was what:
So far I rightly understood the case
At five years old: a huge delight it proved
And still proves—thanks to that instructor sage
My Father, who knew better than turn straight
Learning's full flare on weak-eyed ignorance,
Or, worse yet, leave weak eyes to grow sand-blind,
Content with darkness and vacuity.

It happened, two or three years afterward,
That—I and playmates playing at Troy's Siege—
My Father came upon our make-believe.
'How would you like to read yourself the tale
Properly told, of which I gave you first
Merely such notion as a boy could bear?
Pope, now, would give you the precise account
Of what, some day, by dint of scholarship,
You'll hear—who knows?—from Homer's very mouth.
Learn Greek by all means, read the "Blind Old Man,
Sweetest of Singers"—*tuphlos* which means "blind,"
Hedistos which means "sweetest." Time enough!
Try, anyhow, to master him some day;
Until when, take what serves for substitute,
Read Pope, by all means!'
              So I ran through Pope,
Enjoyed the tale—what history so true?
Also attacked my Primer, duly drudged,
Grew fitter thus for what was promised next—
The very thing itself, the actual words,
When I could turn—say, Buttmann to account.

Time passed, I ripened somewhat: one fine day,
'Quite ready for the Iliad, nothing less?
There's Heine, where the big books block the shelf:
Don't skip a word, thumb well the Lexicon!'

I thumbed well and skipped nowise till I learned
Who was who, what was what, from Homer's tongue,
And there an end of learning. Had you asked
The all-accomplished scholar, twelve years old,
'Who was it wrote the Iliad?'—what a laugh!
'Why, Homer, all the world knows: of his life
Doubtless some facts exist: it's everywhere:
We have not settled, though, his place of birth:
He begged, for certain, and was blind beside:
Seven cities claimed him—Scio, with best right,
Thinks Byron. What he wrote? Those Hymns we have.
Then there's the "Battle of the Frogs and Mice,"

That's all—unless they dig "Margites" up
(I'd like that) nothing more remains to know.'

Thus did youth spend a comfortable time;
Until—'What's this the Germans say is fact
That Wolf found out first? It's unpleasant work
Their chop and change, unsettling one's belief:
All the same, while we live, we learn, that's sure.'
So, I bent brow o'er *Prolegomena*.
And, after Wolf, a dozen of his like
Proved there was never any Troy at all,
Neither Besiegers nor Besieged,—nay, worse,—
No actual Homer, no authentic text,
No warrant for the fiction I, as fact,
Had treasured in my heart and soul so long—
Ay, mark you? and as fact held still, still hold,
Spite of new knowledge, in my heart of hearts
And soul of souls, fact's essence freed and fixed
From accidental fancy's guardian sheath.
Assuredly thenceforward—thank my stars!—
However it got there, deprive who could—
Wring from the shrine my precious tenantry,
Helen, Ulysses, Hector and his Spouse,
Achilles and his Friend?—though Wolf—ah, Wolf!
Why must he needs come doubting, spoil a dream?

But then 'No dream's worth waking'—Browning says:
And here's the reason why I tell thus much.
I, now mature man, you anticipate,
May blame my Father justifiably
For letting me dream out my nonage thus,
And only by such slow and sure degrees
Permitting me to sift the grain from chaff,
Get truth and falsehood known and named as such.
Why did he ever let me dream at all,
Not bid me taste the story in its strength?
Suppose my childhood was scarce qualified
To rightly understand mythology,
Silence at least was in his power to keep:

I might have—somehow—correspondingly—
Well, who knows by what method, gained my gains,
Been taught, by forthrights not meanderings,
My aim should be to loathe, like Peleus' son,
A lie as Hell's Gate, love my wedded wife,
Like Hector, and so on with all the rest.
Could not I have excogitated this
Without believing such men really were?
That is—he might have put into my hand
The 'Ethics'? In translation, if you please,
Exact, no pretty lying that improves,
To suit the modern taste: no more, no less—
The 'Ethics': 'tis a treatise I find hard
To read aright now that my hair is grey,
And I can manage the original.
At five years old—how ill had fared its leaves!
Now, growing double o'er the Stagirite,
At least I soil no page with bread and milk,
Nor crumple, dogsear and deface—boys' way.

REPHAN[1]

How I lived, ere my human life began
In this world of yours,—like you, made man,—
When my home was the Star of my God Rephan?

Come then around me, close about,
World-weary earth-born ones! Darkest doubt
Or deepest despondency keeps you out?

Nowise! Before a word I speak,
Let my circle embrace your worn, your weak,
Brow-furrowed old age, youth's hollow cheek—

Diseased in the body, sick in soul,
Pinched poverty, satiate wealth,—your whole
Array of despairs! Have I read the roll?

[1] Suggested by a very early recollection of a prose story by the noble woman and imaginative writer, Jane Taylor, of Norwich [actually Ongar.]—R. B. (1889).

All here? Attend, perpend! O Star
Of my God Rephan, what wonders are
In thy brilliance fugitive, faint and far!

Far from me, native to thy realm,
Who shared its perfections which o'erwhelm
Mind to conceive. Let drift the helm,

Let drive the sail, dare unconfined
Embark for the vastitude, O Mind,
Of an absolute bliss! Leave earth behind!

Here, by extremes, at a mean you guess:
There, all's at most—not more, not less:
Nowhere deficiency nor excess.

No want—whatever should be, is now:
No growth—that's change, and change comes—how
To royalty born with crown on brow?

Nothing begins—so needs to end:
Where fell it short at first? Extend
Only the same, no change can mend!

I use your language: mine—no word
Of its wealth would help who spoke, who heard,
To a gleam of intelligence. None preferred,

None felt distaste when better and worse
Were uncontrastable: bless or curse
What—in that uniform universe?

Can your world's phrase, your sense of things
Forth-figure the Star of my God? No springs,
No winters throughout its space. Time brings

No hope, no fear: as to-day, shall be
To-morrow: advance or retreat need we
At our stand-still through eternity?

All happy: needs must we so have been,
Since who could be otherwise? All serene:
What dark was to banish, what light to screen?

Earth's rose is a bud that's checked or grows
As beams may encourage or blasts oppose:
Our lives leapt forth, each a full-orbed rose—

Each rose sole rose in a sphere that spread
Above and below and around—rose-red:
No fellowship, each for itself instead.

One better than I—would prove I lacked
Somewhat: one worse were a jarring fact
Disturbing my faultlessly exact.

How did it come to pass there lurked
Somehow a seed of change that worked
Obscure in my heart till perfection irked?—

Till out of its peace at length grew strife—
Hopes, fears, loves, hates,—obscurely rife,—
My life grown a-tremble to turn your life?

Was it Thou, above all lights that are,
Prime Potency, did Thy hand unbar
The prison-gate of Rephan my Star?

In me did such potency wake a pulse
Could trouble tranquillity that lulls
Not lashes inertion till throes convulse

Soul's quietude into discontent?
As when the completed rose bursts, rent
By ardors till forth from its orb are sent

New petals that mar—unmake the disc—
Spoil rondure: what in it ran brave risk,
Changed apathy's calm to strife, bright, brisk,

Pushed simple to compound, sprang and spread
Till, fresh-formed, facetted, floretted,
The flower that slept woke a star instead?

No mimic of Star Rephan! How long
I stagnated there where weak and strong,
The wise and the foolish, right and wrong,

Are merged alike in a neutral Best,
Can I tell? No more than at whose behest
The passion arose in my passive breast,

And I yearned for no sameness but difference
In thing and thing, that should shock my sense
With a want of worth in them all, and thence

Startle me up, by an Infinite
Discovered above and below me—height
And depth alike to attract my flight,

Repel my descent: by hate taught love.
Oh, gain were indeed to see above
Supremacy ever—to move, remove,

Not reach—aspire yet never attain
To the object aimed at! Scarce in vain,—
As each stage I left nor touched again.

To suffer, did pangs bring the loved one bliss,
Wring knowledge from ignorance,—just for this—
To add one drop to a love-abyss!

Enough: for you doubt, you hope, O men,
You fear, you agonize, die: what then?
Is an end to your life's work out of ken?

Have you no assurance that, earth at end,
Wrong will prove right? Who made shall mend
In the higher sphere to which yearnings tend?

Why should I speak? You divine the test.
When the trouble grew in my pregnant breast
A voice said 'So wouldst thou strive, not rest?

'Burn and not smoulder, win by worth,
Not rest content with a wealth that's dearth?
Thou art past Rephan, thy place be Earth!'

REVERIE

I KNOW there shall dawn a day
    —Is it here on homely earth?
Is it yonder, worlds away,
    Where the strange and new have birth,
That Power comes full in play?

Is it here, with grass about,
    Under befriending trees,
When shy buds venture out,
    And the air by mild degrees
Puts winter's death past doubt?

Is it up amid whirl and roar
    Of the elemental flame
Which star-flecks heaven's dark floor,
    That, new yet still the same,
Full in play comes Power once more?

Somewhere, below, above,
    Shall a day dawn—this I know—
When Power, which vainly strove
    My weakness to o'erthrow,
Shall triumph. I breathe, I move,

I truly am, at last!
    For a veil is rent between
Me and the truth which passed
    Fitful, half-guessed, half-seen,
Grasped at—not gained, held fast.

I for my race and me
    Shall apprehend life's law:
In the legend of man shall see
    Writ large what small I saw
In my life's tale: both agree.

As the record from youth to age
  Of my own, the single soul—
So the world's wide book: one page
  Deciphered explains the whole
Of our common heritage.

How but from near to far
  Should knowledge proceed, increase?
Try the clod ere test the star!
  Bring our inside strife to peace
Ere we wage, on the outside, war!

So, my annals thus begin:
  With body, to life awoke
Soul, the immortal twin
  Of body which bore soul's yoke
Since mortal and not akin.

By means of the flesh, grown fit,
  Mind, in surview of things,
Now soared, anon alit
  To treasure its gatherings
From the ranged expanse—to-wit,

Nature,—earth's, heaven's wide show
  Which taught all hope, all fear:
Acquainted with joy and woe,
  I could say 'Thus much is clear,
Doubt annulled thus much: I know.

'All is effect of cause:
  As it would, has willed and done
Power: and my mind's applause
  Goes, passing laws each one,
To Omnipotence, lord of laws.'

Head praises, but heart refrains
  From loving's acknowledgment.
Whole losses outweigh half-gains:
  Earth's good is with evil blent:
Good struggles but evil reigns.

Yet since Earth's good proved good—
  Incontrovertibly
Worth loving—I understood
  How evil—did mind descry
Power's object to end pursued—

Were haply as cloud across
  Good's orb, no orb itself:
Mere mind—were it found at loss
  Did it play the tricksy elf
And from life's gold purge the dross?

Power is known infinite:
  Good struggles to be—at best
Seems—scanned by the human sight,
  Tried by the senses' test—
Good palpably: but with right

Therefore to mind's award
  Of loving, as power claims praise?
Power—which finds nought too hard,
  Fulfilling itself all ways
Unchecked, unchanged: while barred,

Baffled, what good began
  Ends evil on every side.
To Power submissive man
  Breathes 'E'en as Thou art, abide!'
While to good 'Late-found, long-sought,

'Would Power to a plenitude
  But liberate, but enlarge
Good's strait confine,—renewed
  Were ever the heart's discharge
Of loving!' Else doubts intrude.

For you dominate, stars all!
  For a sense informs you—brute,
Bird, worm, fly, great and small,
  Each with your attribute
Or low or majestical!

Thou earth that embosomest
　　Offspring of land and sea—
How thy hills first sank to rest,
　　How thy vales bred herb and tree
Which dizen thy mother-breast—

Do I ask? 'Be ignorant
　　Ever!' the answer clangs:
Whereas if I plead world's want,
　　Soul's sorrows and body's pangs,
Play the human applicant,—

Is a remedy far to seek?
　　I question and find response:
I—all men, strong or weak,
　　Conceive and declare at once
For each want its cure. 'Power, speak!

'Stop change, avert decay,
　　Fix life fast, banish death,
Eclipse from the star bid stay,
　　Abridge of no moment's breath
One creature! Hence, Night, hail, Day!

What need to confess again
　　No problem this to solve
By impotence? Power, once plain
　　Proved Power,—let on Power devolve
Good's right to co-equal reign!

Past mind's conception—Power!
　　Do I seek how star, earth, beast,
Bird, worm, fly, gained their dower
　　For life's use, most and least?
Back from the search I cower.

Do I seek what heals all harm,
　　Nay, hinders the harm at first,
Saves earth? Speak, Power, the charm!
　　Keep the life there unamerced
By chance, change, death's alarm!

As promptly as mind conceives,
  Let Power in its turn declare
Some law which wrong retrieves,
  Abolishes everywhere
What thwarts, what irks, what grieves!

Never to be! and yet
  How easy it seems—to sense
Like man's—if somehow met
  Power with its match—immense
Love, limitless, unbeset

By hindrance on every side!
  Conjectured, nowise known,
Such may be: could man confide
  Such would match—were Love but shown
Stript of the veils that hide—

Power's self now manifest!
  So reads my record: thine,
O world, how runs it? Guessed
  Were the purport of that prime line,
Prophetic of all the rest!

'In a beginning God
  Made heaven and earth.' Forth flashed
Knowledge: from star to clod
  Man knew things: doubt abashed
Closed its long period.

Knowledge obtained Power praise.
  Had Good been manifest,
Broke out in cloudless blaze,
  Unchequered as unrepressed,
In all things Good at best—

Then praise—all praise, no blame—
  Had hailed the perfection. No!
As Power's display, the same
  Be Good's—praise forth shall flow
Unisonous in acclaim!

Even as the world its life,
　　So have I lived my own—
Power seen with Love at strife,
　　That sure, this dimly shown,
—Good rare and evil rife.

Whereof the effect be—faith
　　That, some far day, were found
Ripeness in things now rathe,
　　Wrong righted, each chain unbound,
Renewal born out of scathe.

Why faith—but to lift the load,
　　To leaven the lump, where lies
Mind prostrate through knowledge owed
　　To the loveless Power it tries
To withstand, how vain! In flowed

Ever resistless fact:
　　No more than the passive clay
Disputes the potter's act,
　　Could the whelmed mind disobey
Knowledge the cataract.

But, perfect in every part,
　　Has the potter's moulded shape,
Leap of man's quickened heart,
　　Throe of his thought's escape,
Stings of his soul which dart

Through the barrier of flesh, till keen
　　She climbs from the calm and clear,
Through turbidity all between,
　　From the known to the unknown here,
Heaven's 'Shall be,' from Earth's 'Has been'?

Then life is—to wake not sleep,
　　Rise and not rest, but press
From earth's level where blindly creep
　　Things perfected, more or less,
To the heaven's height, far and steep.

Where, amid what strifes and storms
    May wait the adventurous quest,
Power is Love—transports, transforms
    Who aspired from worst to best,
Sought the soul's world, spurned the worms'.

I have faith such end shall be:
    From the first, Power was—I knew.
Life has made clear to me
    That, strive but for closer view,
Love were as plain to see.

When see? When there dawns a day,
    If not on the homely earth,
Then yonder, worlds away,
    Where the strange and new have birth,
And Power comes full in play.

EPILOGUE

At the midnight in the silence of the sleep-time,
    When you set your fancies free,
Will they pass to where—by death, fools think, im-
        prisoned—
Low he lies who once so loved you, whom you loved so,
            —Pity me?

Oh to love so, be so loved, yet so mistaken!
    What had I on earth to do
With the slothful, with the mawkish, the unmanly?
Like the aimless, helpless, hopeless, did I drivel
            —Being—who?

One who never turned his back but marched breast
        forward,
    Never doubted clouds would break,
Never dreamed, though right were worsted, wrong would
        triumph,
Held we fall to rise, are baffled to fight better,
            Sleep to wake.

No, at noonday in the bustle of man's work-time
    Greet the unseen with a cheer!
Bid him forward, breast and back as either should be,
'Strive and thrive!' cry 'Speed,—fight on, fare ever
            There as here!'

INDEX OF TITLES

INDEX OF FIRST LINES

OF

SHORTER POEMS AND SONGS

SET IN GREAT BRITAIN AT THE UNIVERSITY PRESS, OXFORD,
AND REPRINTED BY RICHARD CLAY (THE CHAUCER PRESS), LTD.,
BUNGAY, SUFFOLK